INTERNATIONAL ECONOMIC L.
General Editor: John H. Jackson

TRANSATLANTIC ECONOMIC DISPUTES

RENEWALS 458-4574

DATE DUE			
GAYLORD			PRINTED IN U.S.A.

Transatlantic Economic Disputes

The EU, the US, and the WTO

Edited by

ERNST-ULRICH PETERSMANN

and

MARK A. POLLACK

OXFORD

UNIVERSITY PRESS

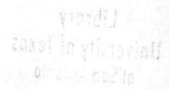

OXFORD
UNIVERSITY PRESS

Great Clarendon Street, Oxford OX2 6DP

Oxford University Press is a department of the University of Oxford.
It furthers the University's objective of excellence in research, scholarship,
and education by publishing worldwide in

Oxford New York

Auckland Bangkok Buenos Aires Cape Town Chennai
Dar es Salaam Delhi Hong Kong Istanbul Karachi Kolkata
Kuala Lumpur Madrid Melbourne Mexico City Mumbai Nairobi
São Paulo Shanghai Singapore Taipei Tokyo Toronto

Oxford is a registered trade mark of Oxford University Press
in the UK and in certain other countries

Published in the United States
by Oxford University Press Inc., New York

British Library Cataloguing in Publication Data
Data available

Library of Congress Cataloging in Publication Data
Data available

ISBN 0-19-926172-5
ISBN 0-19-926173-3 (pbk.)

1 3 5 7 9 10 8 6 4 2

Typeset by Kolam Information Services Pvt. Ltd, Pondicherry, India
Printed in Great Britain
on acid-free paper by
T.J. International, Padstow, Cornwall

Dedication

To the memory of Robert E. Hudec (1934–2003) whose pioneering research on dispute settlement in international trade inspired lawyers, economists, and trade diplomats all over the world.

General Editor's Preface

This impressive volume is part of the Oxford University Press series of books dealing with subjects of the very broad landscape of International Economic Law. The goal of this series is to tackle the risks and dangers inherent in a 'globalized' and interdependent world such as the one in which we now live. Through this series, it is our aim to examine these risks and dangers with sufficient depth and analysis so as to contribute significantly to the urgently required understanding of the landscape of international economic law. As General Editor I am delighted to introduce the latest volume in the International Economic Law Series, a volume of essays edited by Ernst-Ulrich Petersmann and Mark A. Pollack.

Professors Petersmann and Pollack, and their colleagues, have recently undertaken a very ambitious programme at the European University Institute (EUI), in Florence, Italy. This is a programme designed to develop understanding about the transatlantic trade relationship. In the context of that programme, Professors Petersmann and Pollack have sponsored a series of ingenious conferences to probe different aspects of the rather recent trends of this currently 'tender relationship', which we call transatlantic. This volume is a compendium largely of case-studies undertaken by a variety of authors who are outstanding experts and practitioners in the area of dispute settlement under the WTO system. Each of these studies has been selected by the conference organizers to shed light on some of the intricacies of the dispute settlement process and its jurisprudence, as it relates to the relationship between North America and Europe.

There is little doubt that the broader topic of the transatlantic relationship is extraordinarily important for the world today, and furthermore, there is little doubt that the WTO and its dispute settlement mechanisms are having a considerable impact on that relationship and therefore need to be much better understood by practitioners, diplomats, government officials, and scholars. Thus, it is my pleasure to welcome this book as an addition to scholarship that will enhance this needed understanding.

JOHN H. JACKSON*

---

* *University Professor of Law*, Georgetown University Law Center (GULC), Washington, DC; *Director*, Institute of International Economic Law, GULC; *General Editor*, International Economic Law Series, Oxford University Press; *Editor in Chief, Journal of International Economic Law*, Oxford University Press.

Acknowledgements

The editors acknowledge with gratitude the financial support of the BP Chair in Transatlantic Relations which was established, thanks to a generous grant by the Euro-American company BP, in the Robert Schuman Centre for Advanced Studies of the European University Institute at Florence in September 2001, and made possible the preparation of this volume and the organization of the two international conferences out of which this book grew. The editors also express their appreciation to Navraj Ghaleigh for his invaluable editorial assistance in the preparation of this volume and of its index.

Contents

Notes on Contributors

Aaron, D.L. : David L. Aaron is Senior International Advisor, Dorsey & Whitney LLP, and former US Undersecretary of Commerce for International Trade.

Abbott, F.M. : Frederick Abbott is Edward Ball Eminent Scholar Professor of International Law at the Florida State University College of Law. He is Co-Rapporteur of the ILA Committee on International Trade Law, serves as consultant on TRIPS matters for UNCTAD, the World Bank and the WHO, and as arbitrator for the WIPO Arbitration and Mediation Center.

Abbott, K.W. : Kenneth W. Abbott is the Elizabeth Froehling Horner Professor of Law and Commerce at Northwestern University School of Law, and Director of the Northwestern Center for International and Comparative Studies. His research applies approaches from international relations theory to issues of international trade, international organizations and governance, and other fields.

Abbott, R.E. : At the time of these conferences Roderick Abbott was a serving official at the EC Commission (Deputy Director-General, DG Trade). Now retired from the Commission, he has been appointed, since October 2002, to be a Deputy Director-General at the World Trade Organization in Geneva.

Berman, F.D. : Sir Franklin Berman was the Legal Adviser to the British Foreign Office between 1991 and 1999. He now practises in the fields of international law and international commercial arbitration and holds visiting Professorships at Oxford, Cape Town and King's College London. He chairs the Claims Committee of the Austrian General Settlement Fund for the compensation of victims of Nazi persecution and is a Judge *ad hoc* of the International Court of Justice.

Bermann, G.A. : George Bermann is Gellhorn Professor of Law and Jean Monnet Professor of European Union Law at Columbia University School of Law (New York) and Director, European Legal Studies Center and author of books and articles on European Union Law, Transnational Litigation and Arbitration, and International Trade Law.

Busch, M.L. : Marc Busch is Associate Professor at Queen's School of Business, Queen's University, Kingston, Ontario, Canada, and an associate of the Canadian Institute for Advanced Research.

Cottier, T. : Thomas Cottier is Professor of European and International Economic Law and Director of the Department of Economic Law, both at the University of Bern. He is also a Director of the World Trade Institute and has been a member and Chairman of numerous WTO/GATT panels. He has published extensively in the field of trade law and intellectual property, most recently, *Intellectual property: trade, competition, and sustainable development* (Michigan University Press, 2003) with Petros C. Mavroidis.

Esty, D.C. : Daniel C. Esty is Professor of Environmental Studies at Yale University.

Hauser, H. : Heinz Hauser is Professor of International Economics at the University of St Gallen, Director of the Swiss Institute for International Economics and Applied Economic Research, St Gallen, and Managing Editor of the Journal *Aussenwirtschaft*.

Hudec, R.E. : Robert E. Hudec was Research Professor of International Law at the Fletcher School of Law and Diplomacy at Tufts University until his death in March 2003. He began his association with GATT/WTO affairs in 1963, serving as Assistant General Counsel in the Office of the US Trade Representative. He subsequently wrote several books and numerous monographs about international trade law, and served as a member of six dispute settlement panels under GATT, WTO, and NAFTA.

Josling, T. : Tim Josling is Senior Fellow at the Institute for International Studies, Stanford University.

Mavroidis, P.C. : Petros Mavroidis is Professor of Law at the University of Neuchâtel and at Columbia Law School, New York, and CEPR.

Mehta, K. : K. Mehta is Director, Directorate A, DG Competition, European Commission.

Meng, W. : Werner Meng is Professor of Law, Dr.iur., Director of the Institute of European Legal Studies at the University of the Saarland in Germany, Visiting Professor at the World Trade Institute in Bern and at Tulane University in New Orleans, and Visiting Professorial Fellow at the Institute of International Economic Law of Georgetown University School of Law, Washington DC.

Paemen, H. : Hugo Paemen is currently Adjunct Professor at the BMW Center for German and European Studies of the Edmund A. Walsh School of Foreign Service (Georgetown University). He also serves as Senior Advisor to Hogan & Hartson LLP, and to the German Marshall Fund and is Co-Chairman of the European-American Business Council (EABC). Prior to joining Hogan & Hartson, Ambassador Paemen served from 1995–1999 as Head of the European Commission's Washington Delegation.

Palmeter, D. : David Palmeter is a partner in the law firm of Sidley Austin Brown & Wood, Washington, DC.

Petersmann, E.-U. : Dr Ernst-Ulrich Petersmann is joint chair Professor of Public Law and Policy at the European University Institute in Florence and at its Robert Schuman Centre for Advanced Studies where he directs the BP Chair in Transatlantic Relations. He previously taught at the Universities of Geneva, Lausanne, Fribourg, St Gallen (Switzerland), Saarland, Heidelberg, Hamburg (Germany), and was visiting professor in the US, China and South Africa. He was legal adviser in the WTO, GATT and the German Ministry of Economic Affairs, and chairman, member or secretary of numerous GATT and WTO dispute settlement panels.

Pollack, M.A. : Mark A. Pollack is Associate Professor of Political Science at the University of Wisconsin-Madison. He formerly served as Senior Research Fellow in the BP Chair in Transatlantic Relations at the European University Institute in Florence, Italy.

Reinhardt, E. : Eric Reinhardt is Associate Professor of Political Science at Emory University in Atlanta, Georgia, US.

Roitinger, A. : Alexander Roitinger is Research Associate at the Swiss Institute for International Economics and Applied Economic Research, St Gallen.

Schaefer, M. : Matthew Schaefer is an Associate Professor of Law at the University of Nebraska College of Law, a term member of the Council on Foreign Relations (New York), and an editorial board member of the *Journal of International Economic Law*. In 1999, he served as a director in the International Economic Affairs Office of the National Security Council at the White House and in 1993–94 he served as a consultant to state governors on the NAFTA and WTO Uruguay Round Agreements.

Shaffer, G. : Gregory Shaffer is Associate Professor of Law, University of Wisconsin Law School, and Senior Fellow at the UW Center on World Affairs and the Global Economy. Professor Shaffer's publications include the book *Defending Interests: Public-Private Partnerships in W.T.O. Litigation* (Brookings Institution Press, forthcoming 2003), and the edited volume *Transatlantic Governance in the Global Economy* (Rowman & Littlefield, 2001).

Sørensen, F. : Frederik Sørensen retired in 2001 from the European Commission. He was head of the Air Transport Division which included responsibility for air transport relations with third countries including the US. He is now active as a counsellor on aeropolitical and air transport regulatory issues.

Spiwak, L.J. : L.J. Spiwak is President of the Phoenix Center for Advanced Legal & Economic Public Policy Studies, Washington, DC (http://www.phoenix-center.org); Visiting Professor of Law, Institut d'Etudes Internationales – Faculty of Law, University of Toulouse, France.

Tangermann, S. : After having been Professor at the University of Göttingen for 25 years, Stefan Tangermann is now Director for Food, Agriculture and Fisheries at the OECD. He has done extensive research and writing in the field of agriculture and trade.

Trachtman, J.P. : Joel Trachtman is Professor of International Law at The Fletcher School of Law and Diplomacy. His research examines the law and economics of international economic integration. He is on the boards of the *American Journal of International Law*, the *European Journal of International Law* and the *Journal of International Economic Law*.

Weiss, F. : Fredl Weiss is Professor of International Economic Law and International Organisations at the University of Amsterdam and Director of the Amsterdam Law School. He has previously lectured at the London School of Economics and has worked as legal adviser in the EFTA Secretariat and as consultant in the legal affairs division of the GATT Secretariat. He is visiting professor at the Universities of Minnesota and of Wuhan. He has published widely on International and European economic and trade law, including 'Improving WTO Dispute Settlement Procedures: Issues and Lessons from the practice of other International Courts and Tribunals' (ed., 2000, Cameron/May), 'Free Movement of Persons within the European Community' with Frank Wooldridge (Kluwer Law International, 2002) and 'International Law of Sustainable Development: principle and practice' (co-ed with N. Schrijver, Kluwer Law International, forthcoming 2003).

List of Abbreviations

AB	Appellate Body
AFL	American Federation of Labor
ANCA	Airport Noise and Capacity Act
APA	Administrative Procedure Act
ASME	American Society of Mechanical Engineers
CAEP	Committee on Aviation Environmental Protection
CAP	Common Agricultural Policy
CBO	Congressional Budget Office
CIO	Congress of Industrial Organizations
CRS	computerized reservation system
CSJA	civil subsonic jet aircraft
DISC	domestic international sales corporation
DOJ	Department of Justice
DOT	Department of Trade
DS	dispute settlement
DSB	Dispute Settlement Body
DSU	Dispute Settlement Understanding
EC	European Community
ECAC	European Civil Aviation Conference
ECJ	European Court of Justice
EEA	European Economic Area
EFSA	European Food Safety Authority
EPA	Environmental Protection Agency
ETI	extra-territorial income
ETUC	European Trade Union Confederation
EUI	European University Institute
FAA	Federal Aviation Administration
FCC	Federal Communications Commission
FDA	Food and Drug Administration
FDI	foreign direct investment
FSC	Foreign Sales Corporation
FTA	Free Trade Agreement
FTC	Federal Trade Commission
GATS	General Agreement on Trade in Services
GATT	General Agreement on Tariffs and Trade
GMO	genetically modified organism
GMP	good manufacturing practice
GPA	Government Procurement Agreement

ICAO	International Civil Aviation Organization
ICJ	International Court of Justice
IEC	International Electrotechnical Commission
IEEPA	International Economic Emergency Powers Act
ILO	International Labour Organization
IMF	International Monetary Fund
IP	intellectual property
IPR	intellectual property right
IRC	Internal Revenue Code
ISA	International Sugar Agreement
ISO	International Organization for Standardization
JAP	Joint Action Plan
MAI	Multilateral Agreement on Investments
MEA	Multilateral Environmental Agreement
MFN	most favoured nation
MRA	mutual recognition agreement
NAFTA	North American Free Trade Agreement
NCSL	National Conference of State Legislatures
NFTC	National Foreign Trade Council
NLD	National League for Democracy
NRA	national regulatory authority
NTA	New Transatlantic Agenda
NTB	non-tariff barrier
OECD	Organization for Economic Co-operation and Development
OSHA	Occupational Health and Safety Administration
PCIJ	Permanent Court of International Justice
RBT	rational business test
RCSJA	recertificated civil subsonic jet aircraft
SLG	Senior Level Group
SPS	Sanitary and Phytosanitary Standards
TABD	Transatlantic Business Dialogue
TACD	Transatlantic Consumer Dialogue
TAED	Transatlantic Environment Dialogue
TAFTA	Transatlantic Free Trade Area
TALD	Transatlantic Labour Dialogue
TBT	technical barrier to trade
TEP	Transatlantic Economic Partnership
TLD	Transatlantic Legislators' Dialogue
TRIMS	Trade-Related Investment Measures
TRIPS	Trade-Related Aspects of Intellectual Property Rights
UN	United Nations
UNEP	United Nations Environment Programme

USPTO   US Patent and Trademark Office
USTR   US Trade Representative
WIPO   World Intellectual Property Organization
WTO   World Trade Organization

PART I

PREVENTION AND SETTLEMENT OF TRANSATLANTIC ECONOMIC DISPUTES: INTRODUCTORY CHAPTERS

1

Prevention and Settlement of Transatlantic Economic Disputes: Legal Strategies for EU/US Leadership

ERNST-ULRICH PETERSMANN

> Consult before you legislate; negotiate before you litigate; compensate before you
> retaliate; and comply—at any rate.
>
> Pascal Lamy[1]

INTRODUCTION AND SUMMARY: THE EUI/BP DISPUTE PREVENTION AND DISPUTE SETTLEMENT PROJECT

In July 2001 and May 2002, the European University Institute (EUI) at Florence organized two international conferences on *Dispute Prevention and Dispute Settlement in the Transatlantic Partnership*. The EUI/BP dispute prevention and dispute settlement project was inspired by two earlier conferences on *Transatlantic Governance in the Global Economy*[2] at the University of Wisconsin (Madison) and on *Transatlantic Regulatory Co-operation* at Columbia University (New York).[3] In close co-operation with the organizers of these earlier conferences, the EUI dispute prevention and dispute settlement project pursues essentially three objectives:

A *first objective* is to analyze recent transatlantic economic disputes involving the European Community (EC) and the United States (US) and to categorize these disputes from legal, economic and political perspectives, for instance according to their underlying conflicts of interests and 'optimal level' of dispute prevention and settlement. Each of the 14 case-studies discussed at the EUI conferences was prepared by an expert from one side of the Atlantic and

---

[1] Speech at the US Chamber of Commerce at Brussels on 7 March 2001.
[2] M. Pollack & G.C. Shaffer (eds), *Transatlantic Governance in the Global Economy* (2001).
[3] G.A. Bermann, M. Herdegen & P.L. Lindseth (eds), *Transatlantic Regulatory Cooperation* (2001).

commented upon by another expert from the other side of the Atlantic. The focus was on four different kinds of disputes: traditional, discriminatory import restrictions (eg, EC import restrictions on bananas) and export subsidies (eg, US tax treatment of 'Foreign Sales Corporations' (FSCs)); the increasingly diverse 'regulatory disputes' resulting from differences in domestic regulation (eg, of beef hormones, genetically modified foods, ozone depleting chemicals, aircraft engines, air transport regulation, telecommunications, competition policy); 'high policy disputes' over trade sanctions imposed for foreign policy reasons (eg, in response to violations of core labour rights in Myanmar and expropriation of foreign property in Cuba); and intergovernmental disputes over the protection of individual rights (such as protection of personal data, investor rights and intellectual property rights). Each case-study was asked to address, *inter alia*, the following questions:

(1) Why did the dispute arise? What were the essential facts, incentives, conflicts of interests, and political pressures underlying the dispute?
(2) Which national and international, political and legal procedures were used for the settlement of the dispute? Were the applicable domestic procedures (eg, Section 301 of the US Trade Act, the EC's Trade Barriers Regulation) and international dispute settlement procedures (eg, inside and outside the World Trade Organization (WTO)) adequate? Which changes of the procedures would be desirable in order to reduce the risk of similar disputes in the future?
(3) What was the role of private interests in the emergence and settlement of the dispute before, during and after the invocation of WTO dispute settlement procedures?
(4) Which government departments were involved? How did they react to the private complaints? Have they been unduly subservient to industry pressures ('regulatory capture')?
(5) What have been the main impediments to an amicable solution of the dispute? What was the role of third parties (states) intervening or involved in the dispute?
(6) Was the dispute due to the inadequacy of the applicable substantive rules (eg, inadequate guidance of 'result-oriented' trade rules stated in terms of trade effects)?
(7) Which changes in the applicable substantive rules could reduce the risk of future similar disputes? Is there a need for new additional bilateral or multilateral rules?
(8) Could the Transatlantic Partnership institutions contribute to the settlement of this kind of dispute? Who should initiate any such reforms (eg, for additional bilateral agreements and institutional co-operation between the EU and US)?
(9) How could the factors causing this kind of dispute be reduced? Should domestic policy-making processes be changed (eg, stronger involvement of domestic courts, parliaments, regulatory agencies)?

(10) Should the EU and US take joint initiatives in the Transatlantic Partnership and/or in the WTO for the better prevention or settlement of this kind of dispute?

The conference participants included EU and US ambassadors and trade policy officials, former WTO Appellate Body members and dispute settlement panelists, legal advisers in the WTO, in the EU Commission and in the Office of the US Trade Representative, as well as other legal, economic and political experts from both sides of the Atlantic. Our hope was to reach a better understanding not only of the case-studies, but also of the political and legal preconditions for preventing or settling such disputes effectively. The reports on these case-studies, duly revised so as to incorporate the comments and discussions, are published in Part II of this book.

A *second objective* of the EUI dispute prevention and dispute settlement project is to examine the assumptions, relevance and weaknesses of the various legal, political and economic theories on prevention and settlement of international economic disputes. Five 'analytical cross-sectoral studies' on legal, political and economic theories of international dispute prevention and dispute settlement, including case-studies on the 'early warning system' for dispute prevention in the Transatlantic Partnership and on the possibility of 'decentralizing' the settlement of certain transatlantic disputes by strengthening private legal remedies and private access to domestic courts inside the EC and US, are published in Part III of this book. The limitation of all these case-studies to transatlantic *economic* relations is based on the historical experience that citizens have strong self-interests in mutually beneficial economic co-operation. However, the progressive extension of functional economic integration in Europe—from the Coal and Steel Community to a customs union, common market, single market, monetary union and 'area of freedom, security and justice' (Article 61 EC Treaty) towards a political union with a 'common foreign and security policy' (Article 11 EU Treaty)—illustrates the political dimensions of economic integration law. The transatlantic commitment to the multilateral WTO rules and WTO institutions for dispute prevention and dispute settlement has become even more important since the breakdown of the transatlantic security system as a result of the war in Iraq in spring 2003 and the opposition by European NATO allies to its prior authorization by the UN Security Council and by NATO. Will the unilateral 'liberal imperialism' of the US, aimed at changing non-democratic regimes in order to eliminate the causes of international terrorism and protect 'democratic peace' (for example, in the Middle East), adversely affect the continuing 'multilateral Wilsonianism' in transatlantic economic co-operation and challenge—as a nationalist, power-oriented alternative—also the EU's 'international constitutionalism'?[4] While the case-studies

---

[4] On the need for working out a new transatlantic security concept defining the common NATO interests and the needed reforms of the UN security system, see E.U. Petersmann, 'Now is the Time to Devise a New Atlantic Charter', *Financial Times*, 24 April 2003. Again, European economic

take into account the often broader political dimensions and repercussions of economic disputes, a thematic focus on economic disputes has obvious advantages. As F. Berman remarks in his contribution, 'a general dispute settlement mechanism for the Euro-Atlantic relationship would have an enormous burden to bear, a burden so great that it raises the question whether any single institution or mechanism could be robust and powerful enough to sustain it'.[5]

A *third objective* of this project is to offer policy recommendations for improving dispute prevention and dispute settlement in transatlantic relations. The value premises and policy recommendations in Part IV of this book are as diverse as their authors: 'realist' politicians and state-centred international lawyers, for instance, define the 'public interest' more in terms of rights and obligations of governments and emphasize the importance of intergovernmental dispute prevention and dispute settlement in the WTO so as to take into account the 'external effects' of many transatlantic disputes on relations with third countries. Citizen-oriented human rights defenders and constitutional lawyers, by contrast, argue for defining the transatlantic 'public interest' of EU and US citizens by the same 'constitutional principles of justice' that are recognized as part of the 'constitutional contract' inside the EU and the US. For instance, the general citizen interest in open markets, non-discriminatory competition and rule of law should be protected in transatlantic relations among EU and US citizens no less than among EU citizens inside the EC. From such a citizen perspective, the EC Treaty's customs union rules (eg, the prohibitions of tariffs and discriminatory non-tariff trade barriers) should be construed as constituting individual freedoms to be protected by national and EC courts not only in trade relations among EC member states but also in transatlantic trade relations with the US. The numerous transatlantic disputes over welfare-reducing trade restrictions in violation of WTO rules and of the EC's customs union obligations (cf Articles 23–27 EC, Article XXIV of the General Agreement on Tariffs and Trade (GATT)) illustrate that the general citizen interest in open markets, non-discriminatory competition and rule of law is not adequately protected in transatlantic relations.

There was agreement on the currently insufficient political support (eg, in the US Congress and in EU institutions) for concluding a Transatlantic Free Trade Area (TAFTA) or a 'New Transatlantic Marketplace Agreement' as proposed by the EU Commission in 1998 (including a 'free trade area in services' plus elimination of all industrial tariffs on a most-favoured-nation (MFN) basis). The current Doha Development Round on global trade liberalization and trade regulation in the WTO offers more economic gains than bilateral liberalization. Participants disagreed, however, on whether a TAFTA remains a worthwhile regional objective among the world's largest trade and investment partners that can go beyond the imperfect WTO framework (eg, following the recent initia-

integration (such as the European Monetary Union) could serve as a model for the needed reforms of the European Security and Defence Policy.

[5] See the contribution in Part III by F. Berman.

tives for free trade agreements by the EU with Canada and Mexico); or whether EU/US leadership should instead focus on worldwide 'first best policy instruments' (such as non-discriminatory liberalization of tariffs and of non-tariff barriers in the WTO).

Other policy recommendations emphasize a number of common insights such as:

—Many transatlantic economic disputes reflect conflicts of interests *within* the EU or *within* the US (eg, between general consumer interests in open and non-discriminatory market competition and 'rent-seeking' producer interests in import restrictions and export subsidies) rather than conflicts between the national US interest and the 'Community interest' of the EU.

—As transatlantic economic disputes increasingly relate to domestic regulation and to one-sided influence by domestic interest groups on domestic policy-making processes, there is a common interest in promoting 'transatlantic constituencies' supporting non-discriminatory domestic and transatlantic policy-making processes. In order to further enhance domestic and transatlantic policy consensus and dispute prevention strategies, transatlantic co-operation among legislative and regulatory authorities must be extended.[6] Following the example of the successful transatlantic co-operation among competition authorities, new transatlantic constituencies should be promoted, for instance through closer co-operation between the US Food and Drugs Authority and the new European Food Safety Authority. However, notwithstanding the crucial role of courts in realizing economic integration inside the EU and inside the US, there is no transatlantic consensus on establishing a Transatlantic Market Court.

—Dispute prevention and dispute settlement between the EU and the US often serve as precedents for dispute prevention and dispute settlement in relations with third countries. These and other 'external effects' of many transatlantic economic disputes call for joint EU/US leadership and justify the practice of settling many transatlantic disputes through the multilateral WTO system rather than bilaterally outside the WTO.

—Compliance with mutually agreed WTO rules, WTO dispute settlement procedures, and joint EU/US leadership in WTO negotiations on additional world trade rules offer effective dispute prevention and dispute settlement strategies. WTO rules have been ratified by domestic parliaments and serve 'democratic functions' by promoting freedom, non-discrimination and mutually beneficial co-operation among citizens across frontiers. WTO-inconsistent trade restrictions affect less than 2 per cent of transatlantic trade and investments.

---

[6] The Transatlantic Declaration of 1990, the New Transatlantic Agenda (NTA) and Joint Action Plan of 1995, and the Transatlantic Economic Partnership (TEP) of 1998 have already set up a number of regularly meeting institutions such as the biannual EU-US summit meetings, the Senior Level Group and NTA Task Force, the TEP Steering Committee and Working Groups, the Transatlantic Early Warning System, the Transatlantic Legislators' Dialogue, the Transatlantic Business Dialogue, the Transatlantic Consumer Dialogue, the Transatlantic Environmental and Labour Dialogues.

Nevertheless, there remains a need for EU/US leadership to strengthen compliance with WTO law and the democratic legitimacy and social acceptability of WTO decision-making processes.

—Just as intergovernmental disputes over discriminatory trade restrictions have become rare inside the EU and inside the US (eg, among states), there remains scope for 'decentralizing' some of the transatlantic disputes by strengthening legal remedies and private access to domestic courts. Many intergovernmental disputes in the WTO emerge from commercial disputes and are termed colloquially according to the private actors behind the governmental parties (eg, 'Kodak-Fuji case'). The case-study on the EC's complaint in the WTO against US—Section 211 Omnibus Appropriations Act of 1998 ('Havana Club') concluded 'that the dispute between Pernod Ricard, a France-based multinational distiller and distributor, and Bacardi-Martini, a US-based multinational distiller and distributor, should have been resolved as a private commercial dispute and not as a systemic test of world trade system rules'.[7] Reciprocal EU-US agreements on making domestic courts available for deciding on private commercial complaints with due regard to relevant international rules (eg, as foreseen in Article XX of the WTO Agreement on Government Procurement) could prevent and 'de-politicize' intergovernmental disputes by leaving them to domestic courts.

A better understanding, prevention and settlement of transatlantic economic disputes remains a major policy problem. The introductory chapters in Part I of this book give an overview of some of these legal and political problems. The case-studies in Part II, the cross-sectoral analytical studies in Part III, and the policy recommendations in Part IV are written from diverse legal, political and economic perspectives due to the fact that their authors often define the value premises (eg, the 'public interest') and optimal methods for the prevention and settlement of transatlantic disputes in different manners. In order to assist in the needed political consensus-building, the EUI dispute prevention and dispute settlement project will continue—in co-operation with Columbia University and other universities in the US—to promote closer academic review and public scrutiny of the escalating number of transatlantic disputes and mutually welfare-reducing trade sanctions.

I. Alternative Methods of Dispute Prevention and Dispute Settlement in Transatlantic Relations: The Broader Context

Dispute prevention and dispute settlement in transatlantic relations cannot be understood without taking into account the broader legal, political and economic context of transatlantic relations, notably the institution-building and

---

[7] See the case-study below by F.M. Abbott and T. Cottier, 'Dispute Prevention and Dispute Settlement in the Field of Intellectual Property Rights and Electronic Commerce'.

intergovernmental, transgovernmental and transnational links between the EU and the US designed to solve economic and political problems in transatlantic relations. This *internal governance* of the transatlantic relationship, and the interrelationships between transatlantic dispute prevention and dispute settlement and other internal governance processes, are examined by Mark A. Pollack in the second chapter of this introduction. The external effects of transatlantic dispute management on relations with third countries—such as the *global governance* problems in the WTO and the pertinent roles of the EU and US as global actors (eg, in the Doha Development Round of the WTO)—are mentioned in many contributions to this book, and are discussed more thoroughly in separate reports by the BP Chair at the EUI.[8]

Since the international peace conferences in 1899 and 1907 at The Hague, states have concluded an ever increasing number of international treaties regulating the alternative political and legal methods of international dispute settlement, such as negotiations, good offices, inquiries, mediation, conciliation, arbitration and recourse to permanent national and international courts.[9] In accordance with the sovereign freedom of states to decide on their peaceful means of dispute settlement (cf Article 33 of the UN Charter), all these methods are also available for the prevention and settlement of disputes in transatlantic relations. Several case-studies in Part II of this book refer to the fact that many intergovernmental disputes between the EC and the US are preceded or followed by private complaints in domestic courts, for instance private actions by US exporters in the European Court of Justice (ECJ) (eg for the annulment of the EC regulations restricting imports of bananas, or for compensation of the damages caused by these import restrictions following the WTO dispute settlement rulings on their inconsistency with the EC's WTO obligations) and by EC exporters in US courts (eg, challenging the legality of US anti-dumping duties, countervailing duties, safeguard measures, or the politically motivated refusal to extend the protection for the registered trademark 'Havana Club'). This introductory chapter begins with a brief overview of some basic legal and policy problems of dispute prevention and dispute settlement in transatlantic relations

---

[8] See, eg, the reports on the recent BP conferences on *Preparing the Doha Development Round: WTO Negotiators Meet the Academics* which analyze major subjects and EU/US leadership in the Doha Development Round negotiations in the WTO—E.U. Petersmann (ed), *Preparing the Doha Development Round in the WTO: Improvements and Clarifications of the Dispute Settlement Understanding* (2002); E.U. Petersmann (ed), *Challenges to the Legitimacy and Efficiency of the World Trading System: Democratic Governance and Competition Culture in the WTO* (2003).

[9] For surveys of the vast literature on alternative methods of dispute settlement see, eg, J.G. Merrills, *International Dispute Settlement* (1998); J. Collier & V. Lowe, *The Settlement of Disputes in International Law* (1999); P. Sands, R. Mackenzie & Y. Shany, *Manual on International Courts and Tribunals* (1999); E.U. Petersmann, *The GATT/WTO Dispute Settlement System* (1997); E.U. Petersmann (ed), 'Dispute Settlement Procedures of International Organizations at Geneva, Special Issue of the Journal of International Economic Law' (1999) 2 *JIEL*, 185–398; P. Behrens, 'Alternative Methods of Dispute Settlement in International Economic Relations', in E.U. Petersmann & G. Jaenicke (eds), *Adjudication of International Trade Disputes in International and National Economic Law* (1992) 5–13.

(section I); it then discusses the case-studies and different kinds of transatlantic disputes (section II) as well as legal, economic and political theories of dispute prevention and dispute settlement (section III). The policy recommendations are reproduced in Part IV of this book.

A. Definition of 'disputes', 'dispute prevention' and 'dispute settlement'

Disputes are characterized by (1) specific disagreements concerning matters of fact, law or policy between (2) two or more parties so that (3) a claim or assertion by one party is met with refusal, counter-claim or denial by another. In order to distinguish disputes from divergent claims, F. Berman suggests defining the term 'dispute' by the additional criterion (4) that one or more parties require the dispute to be settled by recourse to additional dispute settlement procedures.[10] International dispute settlement procedures tend to be limited to particular kinds of disputes. The Dispute Settlement Understanding (DSU) of the WTO, for instance, applies only to 'disputes brought pursuant to the consultation and dispute settlement provisions of the agreements listed in Appendix 1 to this Understanding' (Article 1). In their dispute settlement practice, WTO members carefully distinguish between 'matters formally raised under the consultation and dispute settlement provisions of the covered agreements' (Article 2:5 DSU) and other matters raised under WTO consultations outside the scope of application of the DSU (eg, under Articles XVI:1, XVIII:A,B GATT).

'Legal disputes' may involve a variety of different claims. The DSU, for instance, permits not only 'violation complaints' but also 'non-violation complaints' about lawful measures if they 'nullify or impair' bona fide expectations about competitive conditions or other treaty benefits and treaty objectives (cf Article 26 DSU). The contested measures, even if lawful, are perceived negatively as potential 'nullification or impairment' of treaty benefits which may entitle the complainant to withdraw WTO commitments in order to restore the agreed 'balance of concessions'. However, 'requests for conciliation and the use of the dispute settlement procedures should not be intended or considered as contentious acts' (Article 3:10 DSU). The WTO dispute settlement system is viewed positively as 'a central element in providing security and predictability to the multilateral trading system' which 'serves to preserve the rights and obligations of Members under the covered agreements, and to clarify the existing provisions of those agreements in accordance with customary rules of interpretation of public international law' (Article 3:2).

The distinction between 'prevention' and 'settlement' of a dispute is fluid and depends on the perceptions of the parties.[11] Many transatlantic policy conflicts (eg, over EC import restrictions on hormone-fed beef and genetically modified

[10] The contribution by F. Berman in Part III of this book defines 'dispute' as 'a disagreement on a defined issue of law or fact, or law and fact combined, which has brought the interests of two or more States into conflict and which they (or at least some amongst them) require to have settled'.
[11] See the contribution by F. Berman in Part III of this book.

organisms) were, for several years, deliberately left 'legally unsettled' in the hope of negotiating an agreed solution. The adoption of dispute settlement findings by the Dispute Settlement Body (DSB) entails 'recommendations' and/or legally binding 'rulings' (cf Article 21 DSU, Article XXIII GATT) that usually settle the legal dispute over the correct interpretation of WTO rules in the concrete dispute. This clarification of the 'primary' legal rights and obligations of the WTO members concerned does, however, not necessarily ensure a definitive 'political settlement' of the dispute by means of compliance with the 'secondary' WTO obligations 'to secure the withdrawal of the measures concerned if these are found to be inconsistent with the provisions of any of the covered agreements' (Article 3:7 DSU). In the transatlantic disputes over the EC import restrictions on bananas and hormone-fed beef, or over the US export subsidies for FSCs, the WTO dispute settlement rulings were not implemented within the 'reasonable period of time' (Article 21 DSU) and led to 'follow-up disputes' over the WTO-consistency of the implementing measures and over the amount of countermeasures pursuant to Article 22 DSU. The DSU rules on 'Surveillance of Implementation of Recommendations and Rulings' (Article 21 DSU), and on 'Compensation and the Suspension of Concessions' (Article 22 DSU), illustrate the successive political and legal phases of disputes until their final 'settlement' by mutual agreement.

B. Is there a shortage of international dispute settlement procedures in transatlantic relations?

The numerous international treaties on alternative dispute settlement procedures tend to focus on ten (among the potentially unlimited number of) different international dispute settlement methods (cf Table 1): (1) bilateral and/or multilateral negotiations; (2) good offices; (3) mediation; (4) inquiries; (5) conciliation; (6) ad hoc or institutionalized arbitration; (7) judicial settlement by permanent national and international courts; (8) 'resort to regional agencies or arrangements', or (9) to 'other peaceful means of their own choice' (Article 33 UN Charter); and (10) dispute settlement by the UN Security Council (eg, pursuant to Articles 34–38 UN Charter) or by other UN organs or other international organizations. Many international treaties, including the UN Charter and also the 1994 WTO Agreement, view these political and legal procedures as complementary options and define different modalities for their use.[12]

There are fundamental legal, political and economic differences between domestic, interstate, and transnational dispute settlement mechanisms.[13] Whereas private complaints in domestic courts depend on private initiative,

---

[12] Cf, E.U. Petersmann, 'Alternative Dispute Resolution—Lessons for the WTO?' in F. Weiss (ed), *Improving WTO Dispute Settlement Procedures: Issues and Lessons from the Practice of other International Courts and Tribunals* (2000) 27–42.

[13] Cf, R.O. Keohane, A. Moravcsik & A.M. Slaughter, 'Legalized Dispute Resolution: Interstate and Transnational' 54 *International Organization* (Summer 2000), 457–488.

interstate disputes are controlled by governments; the latter often assert discretion as to whether they are willing to grant diplomatic protection to their citizens by espousing private citizen claims vis-à-vis foreign governments. Interstate dispute settlement proceedings, like international law, 'operate in the shadow of power'.[14] Transnational disputes—characterized by delegation of jurisdiction to independent courts, acceptance of private access to such courts, and resolution of international disputes through application of general legal principles—tend to limit the political influence of governments: '[c]ompared to interstate dispute resolution, transnational dispute resolution tends to generate more litigation, jurisprudence more autonomous of national interests, and an additional source of pressure for compliance'.[15] The jurisprudence of North American Free Trade Agreement (NAFTA) arbitral tribunals, of the ECJ and of the European Court of Human Rights confirms that, in response to private complaints against governments, international courts often apply general principles of law (eg, on non-contractual state liability to private parties) and assert new legal norms (eg, based on general principles of constitutional law common to the contracting parties) in ways promoting a progressive 'legalization' of politics, better compliance with rule of law, and judicial decisions protecting citizen interests against abuses of government powers.[16]

1. *Intergovernmental dispute settlement mechanisms*

In contrast to the frequent submission of transatlantic disputes to the WTO, few transatlantic disputes have been submitted to other intergovernmental dispute settlement procedures, such as the International Court of Justice (ICJ),[17] the dispute settlement procedures of the International Civil Aviation Organization (invoked by the US in their dispute with the EC over hushkits), or the Law of the Sea Tribunal. Apart from the Transatlantic Early Warning system,[18] the Transatlantic Partnership arrangements do not provide for special dispute settlement procedures. There does not, however, seem to be a shortage of intergovernmental dispute settlement procedures among the EC and the US. The infrequent recourse to such procedures outside the WTO appears to be influenced by the much more reserved attitude of the US vis-à-vis compulsory international adjudication (eg, by the ICJ and the newly established International Criminal Court),

---

[14] Keohane, Moravcsik & Slaughter, supra note 13, at 458.

[15] Ibid, at 458.

[16] See, eg, A. Afilalo, 'Constitutionalization through the back door: a European perspective on NAFTA's investment chapter' (2001) 34 *New York University Journal of International Law and Policy* 1. See also the special issue of the journal *International Organization* in 2000 on 'Legalization and World Politics' whose editors distinguish three dimensions of 'legalization' depending on: (1) the degree to which rules are obligatory; (2) the level of precision of the rules; and (3) the extent to which authority to interpret and make rules is delegated to courts and other 'third parties'. While legalization is not treated as an intrinsic value, its potential contribution to mutually beneficial co-operation and limitation of the anarchical self-help character of international politics is recognized.

[17] See, eg, the ICJ judgments on the ELSI investment dispute between the US and Italy (1989) and on the Lagrand dispute between Germany and the USA (2001).

[18] See the contribution by Meng in Part III of this book.

compared with the more positive attitude of most EU member states. The increasing criticism in the US that WTO dispute settlement jurisprudence has become 'overextended' and is 'politically unsustainable'[19] is rarely heard in Europe.

2. Transnational dispute settlement procedures

In European integration, private access to the EC Court and to the EFTA Court has been of fundamental importance for creating a single European market and a European Economic Area (EEA) beyond the EC. Can a transatlantic market be created without private access to similar legal and judicial dispute settlement and enforcement mechanisms? The US government has promoted transgovernmental dispute settlement procedures under chapter 11 (investor-state arbitration) and chapter 19 of the North American Free Trade Agreement (private access to NAFTA dispute settlement panels) as well as in international investment and intellectual property treaties with developing countries (eg, providing for ICSID and UNCITRAL 'mixed arbitration' between states and private investors). Yet neither the EU nor the US have so far proposed private access to a Transatlantic Market Court so as to decentralize and de-politicize certain categories of transatlantic disputes. What political lesson should be drawn from the increasing criticism that 'mixed international arbitration' (eg, between foreign investors and home states pursuant to chapter 11 of NAFTA) may undermine basic principles of constitutional democracy?[20] Is the EC court model more appropriate for strengthening the rule of law in a transparent manner than the NAFTA model of secretive intergovernmental or 'mixed' arbitration?

3. Domestic courts as guardians of transatlantic market integration?

Inside constitutional democracies like the EU and the US, disputes about discriminatory taxes and non-tariff trade barriers are usually decided by domestic courts at the request of private complainants on the basis of constitutional guarantees of freedom of trade and 'access to justice'.[21] Constitutional theory and economic theory demonstrate that the mutual advantages of freedom of trade, rule of law and access to courts do not depend on the nationality of the

---

[19] Cf, C. Barfield, *Free Trade, Sovereignty, Democracy. The Future of the World Trade Organization* (2001).

[20] See, eg, *Private Rights, Public Problems—A Guide to NAFTA's Controversial Chapter on Investor Rights, International Institute for Sustainable Development and WWF* (2001), and the *New York Times* of 11 March 2001: 'Their meetings are secret. Their members are generally unknown. The decisions they reach need not be fully disclosed. Yet the way a small group of international tribunals handles disputes between investors and foreign governments has led to national laws being revoked, justice systems questioned and environmental regulations challenged. And it is all in the name of protecting the rights of foreign investors under the North American Free Trade Agreement.'

[21] Cf, the contributions to M. Hilf & E.U. Petersmann (eds), *National Constitutions and International Economic Law* (1993); C. Harlow, 'Access to Justice as a Human Right: The European Convention and the European Union', in P. Alston *et al* (eds), *The EU and Human Rights* (1999) 187–214.

TABLE 1.1. Alternative dispute resolution under international law

Political methods (Characteristics: flexibility of procedures, control by the parties, freedom to accept or reject proposed settlements, avoidance of 'winner-loser' situations, political and legal considerations)	Legal methods (Characteristics: rule-oriented legally binding decisions by independent judges based on previously agreed procedures and substantive rules of law that reflect the long-term interests of the parties)
Consultation/negotiation: voluntary or obligatory, ad hoc or institutionalized, bilateral or multilateral principal means of preventing/settling disputes (= conflicting claims) peacefully by agreed solutions among the parties to the dispute (the negotiators retain control over their dispute; success depends on the belief by both parties that the benefits of an agreement outweigh their losses; prior negotiation is not a general prerequisite of adjudication by the ICJ; risk of positional power-oriented rather than principled, rule-oriented bargaining)	**International adjudication:** submission of a dispute to a standing international tribunal for judicial settlement based on the procedures and applicable substantive international law specified in the tribunal's statute
Good offices: intervention by a third party in a dispute so as to encourage and assist the disputants to negotiate (eg, by offering them technical facilities and additional channels of communication)	**Public international arbitration:** submission of a dispute to ad hoc arbitrators appointed by the parties for judicial settlement based on the procedures and applicable substantive international law agreed among the parties to the dispute
Mediation: active non-binding proposals by a third party, with the consent of the disputants which retain control of the dispute	**Mixed international arbitration:** submission of a dispute between a private party (eg, a foreign investor) and a state-party to international arbitration (eg, based on the 1965 Convention on the International Centre for Investment Disputes)
Inquiry: ascertainment of disputed facts by a third party (eg, a fact-finding commission) so as to provide the disputants with an objective assessment (possibly accepted in advance as binding on the disputants)	**Private international arbitration:** submission of a dispute between private parties over their compliance with international treaty rules (eg, in the 1994 WTO Agreement on Preshipment Inspection) to a private international arbitration procedure provided for in the international treaty
Conciliation: ascertainment of facts and examination of the claims by independent third parties on a formal legal and institutionalized basis (usually a conciliation commission) so as to submit non-binding proposals for a settlement	**Judicial settlement by domestic courts:** submission of a dispute between a private party and a government over compliance with international law rules to a standing domestic tribunal

investors, producers, traders and consumers. What prevents the world's most powerful constitutional democracies from establishing a more liberal transatlantic market among themselves? Why are transatlantic relations dominated by so many discriminatory trade restrictions which have been successfully liberalized *inside* Europe and in relations between the EU and associated third states? Is it a normal consequence of the size of transatlantic relations that there are more WTO dispute settlement proceedings between the EU and the US than between any other WTO members?

Adjudication and co-operation among judges are essential parts of any rule of law system. From a rational citizen perspective, rule of law and judicial protection in 'foreign affairs' are no less important than in 'domestic affairs'.[22] In both the EU and the US, the achievement of an internal market was legally and judicially secured by private access to domestic courts and decentralized enforcement of the common market rules by self-interested citizens and domestic judges. Also in transatlantic relations, dispute prevention and dispute settlement depend on stronger legal and judicial remedies against the widespread government failures in transatlantic relations.

The WTO Agreement prescribes private access to *domestic* courts in WTO member states and in the EC (cf Table 1.2). GATT Article XXIV and GATS Article V also permit regional integration agreements to provide that trade disputes among their member states *must* (cf Article 292 EC), or *may* be submitted to special dispute settlement procedures provided in the Treaty concerned (cf chapters 11, 19 and 20 NAFTA). Parallel dispute settlement proceedings (eg, regarding safeguard and anti-dumping measures) in domestic courts and in GATT/WTO dispute settlement proceedings are not rare and illustrate the legal complexity of disputes among governments over the treatment of private economic operators by national courts and administrations.

Enforcement of international rules through domestic courts has many political, economic and legal advantages (eg, in terms of private access to justice, democratic legitimacy of national courts enforcing rules ratified by national parliaments, legal effectiveness of national judgments). The EC and US governments have, however, so far not dared to entrust domestic citizens and domestic courts with the reciprocal, decentralized enforcement of WTO rules in transatlantic relations. Nor is it clear which WTO rules, and what areas of disputes (eg, about trade in goods, services, investments, intellectual property rights, product and production standards), lend themselves to such decentralized judicial enforcement, and how the WTO consistency of such domestic jurisprudence could be promoted.

---

[22] Cf, T.M. Franck, *Political Questions—Judicial Answers. Does the Rule of Law Apply to Foreign Affairs?* (1992), who shows 'that there are no valid reasons—constitutional, prudential, technical or policy-driven—for treating foreign-relations cases differently from any others' (p 7). Franck criticizes 'the conceptual chaos that surrounds judicial treatment of cases with foreign-affairs implications' in the US based on the 'political question doctrine' which, according to Franck, is 'wholly incompatible with American constitutional theory' and not based on 'consistent jurisprudence but only a welter of contradictory cases' (cf, pp 4–9).

TABLE 1.2. The integrated WTO dispute settlement system (Annex 2 to the 1994 Agreement establishing the WTO)

Political methods of dispute settlement	Legal methods of dispute settlement
Consultations (Art 4)	Panel procedure (Arts 6–16, 18, 19)
Good offices (Arts 5, 24)	Appellate review procedure (Arts 17–19)
Conciliation (Arts 5, 24)	Rulings by Dispute Settlement Body on panel and appellate reports (Arts 16, 17)
Mediation (Arts 5, 24)	Arbitration among states (Arts 21, 22, 25)

Recommendations by
  – Panels (Art 19)
  – Appellate Body (Art 19)
  – Dispute Settlement Body (Arts 16, 17)
	Private international arbitration (eg, Art 4 Agreement on Preshipment Inspection)

Surveillance of implementation of recommendations and rulings (Art 21)	Domestic court proceedings (eg, Art X GATT, Art 13 Anti-Dumping Agreement, Art 23 Agreement on
Compensation and suspension of concessions (Art 22)	Subsidies, Arts 32, 41–50 TRIPS Agreement, Art XX Agreement on Government Procurement)

4. Is there a shortage of transatlantic dispute prevention mechanisms?

Dispute prevention is mainly a function of the effectiveness and legitimacy of mutually agreed rules of conduct. The WTO Agreement is the most comprehensive treaty between the EU and the US and the most important legal basis for promoting transatlantic economic integration. The successful launching of a new 'round' of WTO negotiations in November 2001, and the frequent recourse to WTO dispute settlement procedures by both the EU and the US, illustrate the continuing commitment of the EU and the US to compliance with, and progressive improvements of, WTO rules as legal framework for mutually beneficial trade liberalization and trade regulation. Yet, even though WTO rules offer first-best policy instruments for worldwide liberalization, they remain sub-optimal for the regional goal of realizing a common transatlantic market.

Most transatlantic economic disputes are about welfare-reducing trade restrictions and trade distortions which are presented by one side as 'WTO consistent' and challenged by the other side as a 'nullification or impairment' of WTO obligations. The EU-US Action Plan of 1995 for creating a *new transatlantic marketplace* proceeds from the insight that WTO rules are sub-optimal for maximizing economic welfare, equal citizen rights and dispute prevention in transatlantic relations. WTO rules are no obstacle to a TAFTA or to other transatlantic agreements (eg, on mutual recognition of national and EC standards). Why are the EU and US concluding an ever increasing number of free trade agreements with third countries but not among themselves?

From a rational citizen perspective, there is no doubt that—also in transatlantic relations between EU and US citizens—legal guarantees of freedom of trade (*plus* non-discriminatory government regulation of 'market failures' and supply of 'public goods') and judicial protection of individual rights and rule of law would offer the legally most effective, economically most efficient and politically most democratic policy instruments for maximizing equal freedoms of citizens, economic welfare and 'democratic peace'. Commitment to a TAFTA for goods and services could also put pressure on third WTO members to participate in worldwide WTO liberalization so as to avoid trade discrimination and trade diversion resulting from a TAFTA. The 'realist' opponents of a TAFTA tend to exaggerate transitional problems (such as liberalization of agricultural trade) without explaining their opposition convincingly:

—TAFTA would offer the most effective means of overcoming trade protectionism and disputes in transatlantic relations in favour of free trade and rule of law.
—Rather than undermining the WTO world trade and legal system, TAFTA could help the EU-US partnership to serve as a motor for WTO reforms (just as EC and NAFTA states continue to lead WTO reforms).[23]
—European and American history teaches that reciprocal free trade agreements are the only effective political instruments for overcoming welfare-reducing trade protectionism by 'de-politicizing' and 'decentralizing' the settlement of disputes (ie, leaving it to individual producers, investors, traders and consumers concerned to defend their individual rights through recourse to *domestic courts* rather than to 'diplomatic protection', intergovernmental dispute settlement proceedings and welfare-reducing trade sanctions).
—Rule of law in the transatlantic marketplace will hardly ever be possible as long as politicians and judges inside the US and in the EU prevent citizens from invoking and enforcing the agreed international rules in domestic courts.[24]

---

[23] It should not be overlooked that the WTO framework would continue to go far beyond a TAFTA (eg, as regards liberalization of services, harmonization of intellectual property law, coverage of world trade, worldwide rule-making and adjudication). There would be numerous possibilities for countering the fear that 'creation of a single market by countries representing 60% of the world's GDP would be taken as a sure sign that the rich have definitively turned their back on the poor' (A. Taylor, 'Economic Tensions between the European Union and United States: Underlying Causes and Possible Cures', in *Resolving and Preventing US-EU Trade Disputes*, (2001), 3, at 10). On potential disadvantages of a TAFTA for worldwide liberalization see R.J. Langhammer, D. Piazolo & H. Siebert, 'Assessing Proposals for a Transatlantic Free Trade Area' (2002) 57 *Swiss Review of International Economic Relations (Aussenwirtschaft)* 161–185.

[24] Cf, T.M. Franck & G.H. Fox (eds), *International Law Decisions in National Courts* (1996), Introduction at 10: 'the extent to which national courts are willing to give effect to decisions of international tribunals is also influenced by the degree those disputes are seen as having been privatized. When ... the litigation in an international tribunal is perceived by national courts to implicate the national interest, there is likely to be greater reluctance to implement the "foreign" judges' decision, particularly in courts such as those of Great Britain and the U.S., where issues of "foreign affairs" tend to be relegated by the national judiciaries to the experts of the Foreign Office and State Department. It is not surprising, therefore, that U.S. courts have demonstrated considerable willingness to give effect to decisions made by tribunals under the New York and Algiers rules, since

5. Should the EU and US introduce a system of mediating EU-US disputes outside the WTO?

During the preparation of the EU-US summit meeting on 14 June 2001, US proposals for alternative dispute settlement through a system of mediation outside the WTO remained controversial. In the summit declaration, both sides agreed on the need for speedier and more effective resolution of their disputes. The EC expressed, however, political and legal concerns at formal mediation outside the WTO between the two most powerful WTO members, for instance because bilateral deals could subsequently be legally challenged by third WTO members in the WTO dispute settlement framework.

The US's propensity for 'unilateralism' and 'bilateralism' may also be motivated by the fact that unilateral pressures and bilateral negotiations enable the US government to use American political and economic clout more easily so as to accommodate domestic political pressures (eg, from the US Congress and industries funding electoral campaigns) than is possible in rule-based multilateral adjudication. Mediation and bilaterally agreed departures from multilateral WTO rules risk undermining the rule of law (eg, by inviting additional protectionist pressures) and, contrary to certain claims,[25] are not more democratic than transparent, judicial enforcement of WTO rules ratified by domestic parliaments. Multilateral WTO dispute settlement rulings offer legal and political advantages (such as the clarification of WTO rules on a reciprocal and multilateral basis) which cannot be achieved through bilateral consultations and mediation. In view of the unilateral US decisions to probe (in June 2001) and apply (in March 2002) import restrictions on steel without prior consultations with the EU, Trade Commissioner Lamy expressed repeated scepticism vis-à-vis proposals to institutionalize and further develop consultation and mediation mechanisms in the Transatlantic Partnership: '[t]he experience of steel is the case for not putting too much hope in an early warning system'.[26]

C. Lack of constitutional protection of a liberal transatlantic market: limits and divergences of American and European constitutionalism

American constitutionalism has served not only as a model for many postwar democratic constitutions in Europe. American international liberalism has also strongly influenced the provisions in the UN Charter and in the Bretton Woods Agreements on self-determination, sovereign equality of states, international peace based on respect for human rights, and a welfare-increasing international division of labour.[27] The Transatlantic Partnership institutions—eg, the Transat-

---

the interests being adjudicated are perceived as "commercial activity" in the sense established by the Foreign Sovereign Immunities Act of 1976.'

[25] Barfield, supra note 19.
[26] *Inside US Trade*, 8 June 2001.
[27] See, eg, M. Mandelbaum, *The Ideas that Conquered the World* (2002).

lantic Legislators' Dialogue and the Transatlantic Civil Society Dialogues— reflect these common constitutional traditions. The substantive constitutional provisions on protection of freedom of trade are, however, fundamentally different on the two sides of the Atlantic. Inside the US, freedom of trade is constitutionally protected through objective principles (eg, the 'commerce clause' in Art I of the Constitution) rather than through judicial protection of free movements of goods, services, persons, capital and payments as fundamental individual rights (as in EC law). In transatlantic relations, neither US courts nor the ECJ protect freedom of trade as a constitutional individual right.

US courts have long since emphasized that 'no one has a vested right to trade with foreign nations'.[28] The US Congress traditionally excludes 'direct effects' of international trade agreements (like the WTO Agreements) in US courts vis-à-vis federal legislation: '[n]o provision of any of the Uruguay Round Agreements, nor the application of any such provision to any person or circumstances, that is inconsistent with any law of the United States shall have effect';[29] and no person other than the US 'shall have any cause of action or defense under any of the Uruguay Round Agreements', nor may it challenge 'any action or inaction... of the United States, any State, or any political subdivision of a state on the ground that such action or inaction is inconsistent' with one of the WTO agreements.[30] Transatlantic trade lacks constitutional protection and remains subject to numerous legislative and executive restrictions in the US, without judicial review by US courts of whether such restrictions are consistent with the international treaty obligations of the US (eg, under GATT and WTO law).

The progressive evolution of the EC from a customs union towards a supranational legal community has led to a new kind of 'international constitutional law' in Europe that is fundamentally different from national American constitutionalism and from the intergovernmental structures of NAFTA. The basic idea of constitutionalism—ie that commitment to 'higher ranking law' may be the most effective means of protecting general citizen interests against welfare-reducing abuses of regulatory powers—has led all EC member states to commit themselves to supranational EC guarantees of an 'internal market... without internal frontiers' (Article 14) and 'a system ensuring that competition in the internal market is not distorted' (Article 3 (g)). The common market rules are effectively enforced by the EC Commission and by the ECJ as independent, international guardians of the 'Community interest' as well as by national courts

---

[28] In a 1904 decision (*Buttfield v Stranahan*, 192 US, 470, 493), the US Supreme Court decided 'that no one has a vested right to trade with foreign nations, which is so broad in character as to limit and restrict the power of Congress to determine what articles... may be imported into this country and the terms upon which a right to import may be exercised'. While this decision seemed to imply the existence of a 'right to trade with foreign nations' subject to congressional legislation, subsequent court decisions have quoted from the 1904 judgment only 'that no one has a vested right to trade with foreign nations'. For a criticism of this jurisprudence see the contributions by Petersmann to Hilf & Petersmann, supra note 21.

[29] Section 102, Uruguay Round Agreements Act, Pub L No 103–465, 108 Stat 4809 (1994).

[30] Ibid, s 102(c)(1).

at the request of EC citizens invoking the EC Treaty guarantees of free movements of goods, services, persons, capital, payments and freedom of competition
as individual rights. As a result, intergovernmental disputes among EC member
states have become rare.[31] The ECJ construes the EC Treaty as a 'constitutional
charter' and, as regards internal trade inside the EC, has recognized that 'the
principles of free movement of goods and freedom of competition, together with
freedom of trade as a fundamental right, are general principles of Community
law of which the Court ensures observance'.[32] As regards external trade relations, however, the ECJ has concluded from the intergovernmental structures
and reciprocity principles of WTO law that the 'purpose of the WTO agreements
is to govern relations between States or regional organizations for economic
integration and not to protect individuals' who, as a consequence, 'cannot rely
on them before the courts and . . . any infringement of them will not give rise to
non-contractual liability on the part of the Community'.[33] Hence, as in the US,
transatlantic trade relations remain subject to national and EC restrictions
without effective judicial review by the ECJ of whether such trade restrictions
are consistent with the WTO obligations of the EC.[34]

The widespread abuses of trade policy power—also in transatlantic economic
relations, as illustrated by the case-studies on EC import restrictions on bananas
and on US 'contingency protection' safeguards—and the increasing number of
transatlantic conflicts over divergent European and US regulations can be seen as
indications of the need for additional constitutional and judicial restraints on
protectionist abuses of regulatory powers. For instance, transatlantic judicial
mechanisms could help to 'decentralize' and 'de-politicize' the settlement of
certain intergovernmental disputes by granting private actors direct access to a
transatlantic court. Yet, the failure of NAFTA to effectively restrain 'contingency
protection', and the frequent submission of disputes among NAFTA countries to
WTO dispute settlement procedures rather than to NAFTA procedures, illustrate that dispute prevention and dispute settlement may be easier to achieve on

---

[31] See, eg, N. Brown & T. Kennedy, *The Court of Justice of the EC* (1994) 105, 114. Since the entry
into force of the EC Treaty in 1958, only one single infringement proceeding among EC member states
has proceeded to judgment. Case 141/78 *France v UK* [1979] ECR 2923).

[32] Case 240/83 *ADBHU* [1985] ECR 531, para 9.

[33] According to the same judgment, 'it is only where the Community intended to implement a
particular obligation assumed in the context of the WTO, or where the Community measure refers
expressly to the precise provisions in the WTO agreements, that it is for the Community judicature to
review the legality of the Community measure in question in the light of the WTO rules', cf, ECJ, Case
T-210/00 *Etablissements Biret & Cie SA v EU Council* [2002] 2 CMLR 31, paras 71–73. On appeal
by Biret SA, AG S. Alber at the ECJ has, however, concluded that EC law protects a fundamental right
to freedom of economic activity and that the lower court's inaction 'unlawfully restricted the right to
freedom of a citizen'. AG Alber said WTO rules were applicable in this case because the EU had not
met the deadline for implementing the WTO ruling against its beef ban (see *Financial Times*, 21 May
2003).

[34] Even though there have been more than 30 GATT and WTO dispute settlement findings of illegal
EC import restrictions and export subsidies, the ECJ has consistently ignored such GATT and WTO
jurisprudence in the numerous complaints invoking GATT/WTO rules and has never found itself a
violation of GATT/WTO rules by the EC.

the basis of *worldwide* rules and WTO dispute settlement procedures than *bilaterally*.

The EU and US governments prefer to submit most of their transatlantic disputes to intergovernmental dispute settlement procedures in the WTO. EU and US citizens have no direct access to special transatlantic dispute settlement procedures, for example following the model of private access to international dispute settlement panels in the NAFTA (chapters 11 and 19). Private access to domestic courts in the EC and US often offers no effective remedies because EC and US courts do not apply WTO rules and refuse to protect free movement of goods, services, persons and capital in transatlantic relations as individual rights.[35] None of the intergovernmental, transgovernmental and transnational Transatlantic Partnership institutions[36] has so far called for 'higher law' guarantees of a transatlantic market, or for additional constitutional restraints on trade policy discretion in transatlantic relations, for instance through establishment of a TAFTA with an independent Transatlantic Court protecting individual rights of EC and US citizens.

D. WTO law and procedures: an important framework for transatlantic co-operation, dispute prevention and dispute settlement

As the world's largest economies and investment partners, the EU and the US play a central role in the evolution of the world trading system and for the successful conclusion of the Doha Development Round of the WTO. This global responsibility is duly reflected in the four priority areas for EU-US co-operation set forth in the 'New Transatlantic Agenda' of 1995:

(1) promoting peace and stability, democracy and development around the world;

(2) responding to global challenges (such as international crime, environmental and health problems);

(3) contributing to the expansion of world trade and closer economic relations; and

(4) building transatlantic contacts between business people, scientists, educators and others so as to foster co-operation at the grassroots level.

The EU and the US, taken together, account for almost half of world trade. It is therefore not surprising that they are also the most frequent complainants, defendants and third party interveners in WTO dispute settlement proceedings. Out of 273 invocations of the WTO dispute settlement procedures from 1995 till October 2002, 53 concerned disputes between the EU (or individual EU member

---

[35] For comparative constitutional law analyses see Hilf & Petersmann, supra note 21.

[36] On these three levels of transatlantic governance—intergovernmental, transgovernmental and transnational—see M.A. Pollack & G.C. Shaffer, supra note 2, Parts I and V.

states) and the US as complainants/defendants.[37] In numerous additional complaints by third WTO countries against either the EU or the US, the other transatlantic partner intervened in support of the complainant and used the third party complaint as a means for preventing a transatlantic dispute (eg, over the interpretation of rights and obligations under the WTO and the WTO-consistency of certain trade measures). The fact that only 14 WTO disputes between the EU and the US led to panel and Appellate Body reports confirms that most WTO dispute settlement complaints between the EU and the US are settled bilaterally without submitting the dispute to a WTO dispute settlement panel. In cases of US complaints against individual EU member states, the EU always succeeded in persuading the US to pursue the complaint against the EU rather than only against an individual EU member state. In five disputes between the EU and the US (ie, bananas, hormones, FSCs, US Anti-Dumping Act of 1916, Section 110(5) of the US Copyright Act), the complainant had recourse to Article 21.5 and/or Article 22 of the DSU in order to request authorization by the WTO of countermeasures in response to non-implementation of the dispute settlement rulings.

Transatlantic dispute prevention in GATT and the WTO takes also place through negotiations and adoption of new rules. The case-study by Professors Tangermann and Josling confirms, for example, that the WTO Agreement on Agriculture has significantly reduced the number of disputes over agricultural subsidies in transatlantic relations. There seem to be many other areas where joint EU/US initiatives for additional bilateral rules (eg, on mutual recognition of technical and sanitary standards) and multilateral WTO rules (eg, on technical regulations, sanitary standards, international air transport and telecommunications services) have contributed in the past, and can contribute in the future, to the prevention of transatlantic disputes. Just as the dispute settlement procedures in the Canada-US Free Trade Agreement served as a model for certain reforms of GATT dispute settlement procedures (notably the 1989 Mid-Term Uruguay Round Agreement on improvements to the GATT dispute settlement procedures),[38] bilaterally agreed transatlantic dispute settlement arrangements (such as the agreed recourse to bilateral arbitration under Article 25 DSU in the EU-US dispute over Section 110(5) of the US Copyright Act) can serve as precedent for reforms of multilateral WTO dispute settlement procedures. Hence, transatlantic and worldwide trade liberalization, regulation and dispute settlement offer mutually beneficial synergies. For instance:

—Multilateral rule-making in the WTO makes it possible to overcome conflicts among divergent national regulations and discriminatory market access bar-

---

[37] See the chronological list of all DSU invocations in document WT/DSB/W/209/Add.1 of 18 November 2002.

[38] These reforms are published and explained in E.U. Petersmann, 'The Uruguay Round Negotiations 1986–1991', in E.U. Petersmann & M. Hilf (eds), *The New GATT Round of Multilateral Trade Negotiations* (1991) 501, 511 *et seq*, 610 *et seq*.

riers that countries are willing to liberalize only on the basis of reciprocal concessions by trading partners.
—The most-favoured-nation treatment obligations of WTO law require extending bilateral trade liberalization and regulation to third WTO members, and may serve as a model for similar agreements (eg, on mutual recognition of technical standards) with third countries.
—Many transatlantic disputes and their settlement affect the future inter-pretation and application of WTO rules and, by clarifying the contested meaning of rules, may prevent disputes also vis-à-vis third WTO member countries.
—Comprehensive worldwide or regional 'package deals' (eg, on a TAFTA) may enable 'strategic reforms' (eg, limitation of anti-dumping practices, co-operation among competition authorities, harmonization of environmental impact assessment requirements, mutual agreement on direct applicability of certain WTO prohibitions before domestic reforms) that may not be politically feasible unilaterally or in bilateral 'single issue negotiations'.

E. The perspective of EU and US citizens: disadvantages and limits of the WTO system for the settlement of 'multi-level disputes' among citizens

The state-centred assumption underlying the classic international law theory on the peaceful settlement of disputes—ie, a conflict between the national interest of one state and the national interest of another (eg, as in the case of a territorial border dispute)—does not hold for many transatlantic economic disputes. Economists emphasize not only that intergovernmental disputes about discrim-inatory market access barriers are primarily due to conflicts of interests *within* states rather than among states:

In a question of trade policy the interests of the home producers who are in favour of a protective tariff are opposed to the joint interests both of the consumers and of all the other producers of every nation. The alleged international front is thus in reality a home front and every trade concession is not a sacrifice which the entire nation is forced to make in favour of the foreigner, but one which the special group of protection seekers is forced to concede to the rest of the nation. That this actual conflict of interests which cuts through the middle of the nation is disguised as a conflict between home and abroad is only a superficial phenomenon.[39]

Economists also demonstrate that multilateral trade agreements serve not only 'international functions' (such as reciprocal trade liberalization among states) but also important 'domestic policy functions': by offering export industries access to foreign markets, WTO rules increase domestic political support for reciprocal trade liberalization and make it politically easier for governments to overcome the protectionist pressures from import-competing producers so as to

---

[39] W. Röpke, *International Order and Economic Integration* (1959) 15.

promote general consumer welfare through trade liberalization.[40] From the perspective of human rights and democracy, reciprocal international guarantees of freedom, non-discrimination, and rule of law (eg, in WTO law) serve important 'constitutional functions': equal freedoms of citizens at home can be extended and legally protected across frontiers, in conformity with the equal freedoms of their states, through internationally agreed guarantees of freedom, non-discrimination, and rule of law. Ethics (eg, Kant's 'categorical imperative' and normative individualism) and human rights suggest that the intergovernmental rights to market access and to non-discriminatory competition should be construed as corresponding obligations of governments to protect equal individual citizens rights across frontiers.[41]

From such citizen-oriented perspectives, national and international law must focus on equal citizen rights and on the corresponding constitutional obligations of governments to promote general consumer welfare and general citizen welfare through consumer-driven open markets and non-discriminatory regulation (eg, of 'market failures' and 'public goods', including democratically agreed rules for the promotion of 'producer welfare' and 'social justice' such as Articles XIX, XX GATT). Intergovernmental WTO dispute settlement procedures have a number of legal, political and economic disadvantages. For example:

—WTO negotiations and WTO rules are often 'producer-driven' and justify discriminatory trade protectionism that reduces consumer welfare and freedom of citizens.
—This perceived lack of legitimacy is reflected in the 'double standards' that prompt the EU and US governments to enforce WTO rules in intergovernmental relations, but to insist on domestic policy discretion to disregard WTO rules and to prevent domestic citizens and domestic courts from reviewing compliance with WTO obligations by their own governments.
—Legal remedies under WTO law are limited in many respects. For instance, WTO panel and appellate review procedures often last up to 20 months. Even if the dispute settlement ruling finds a measure illegal, the defendant has a 'reasonable period' of usually 15 months for implementing the ruling (cf Article 21 DSU). The focus on termination of the illegal measure, without reparation of injury for past damage, implies that governments may violate WTO rules for up to three years without any risk of effective sanctions.

---

[40] Cf, eg, E.U. Petersmann, 'Trade Policy as a Constitutional Problem. On the "Domestic Policy Functions" of International Trade Rules', (1986) 41 *Swiss Review of International Economic Relations (Aussenwirtschaft)* 405–439.

[41] Cf, E.U. Petersmann, *Constitutional Functions and Constitutional Problems of International Economic Law* (1991) ch VII. For an explanation of the mutual consistency of the citizen-centred value premises of ethics (eg, Kant's 'categorical imperative' and Rawls' 'principles of justice'), 'constitutional economics', human rights and constitutional democracies, see E.U. Petersmann, 'Constitutional Economics, Human Rights and the Future of the WTO' (2003) 58 *Swiss Review of International Economic Relations (Aussenwirtschaft)* 49–91; 'Constitutionalism and International Adjudication: How to Constitutionalize the UN Dispute Settlement System?' (1999) 31 *New York University Journal of International Law and Politics* 753–790.

—The EU and US have repeatedly failed to implement dispute settlement rulings (eg, on bananas, hormones, FSC, protection of the trademark 'Havana Club') even beyond the 'reasonable period of time' (Article 21 DSU).

—As many transatlantic WTO disputes are only 'secondary intergovernmental disputes' that are caused by conflicts among producer and consumer interests inside states, optimal dispute prevention and dispute settlement strategies should intervene directly at the source of the domestic policy problems, for instance by enabling domestic citizens to invoke and enforce the WTO obligations of their own governments in domestic courts. Discretionary negotiations and WTO dispute settlement proceedings among governments which, for domestic policy reasons, often have political self-interests in circumventing their own WTO obligations, are 'second best instruments' that are suboptimal from the point of view of general citizen interests in legal protection of consumer welfare and of equal freedoms across frontiers.

In their comparative political analysis of transatlantic trade conflicts under GATT 1947 and under the WTO, Professors Busch and Reinhardt doubt whether the legal reforms of the DSU have improved the 'outcomes' of US-EU disputes. Their empirical analysis finds that 'the apparent success in resolving US-EC disputes since 1995 is due largely to the expansion of the WTO's scope in new areas, such as intellectual property and trade in services'. When 'GATT-era cases pitting the US and EC against each other have recurred under the WTO, the institution has fared no better than its predecessor'.[42]

Lawyers might perceive the 'outcomes' of WTO dispute settlement proceedings in a more positive manner. The quasi-automatic adoption of panel and appellate reports settles the dispute over the interpretation of rules and enhances legal security. Even if the contested measure (eg, the EC's import restrictions on hormone-fed beef) continue to be maintained for political reasons, and countermeasures further reduce economic welfare, the multilateral surveillance and authorization of countermeasures in the WTO are conducive to promotion of rule of law. Yet, also from a legal perspective, the legal remedies and enforcement measures in the WTO are inadequate in several ways and are less developed than legal remedies in EC law and in domestic legal systems. From a citizen perspective, it is regrettable that the ECJ has denied citizens the right to invoke legally binding WTO dispute settlement rulings in domestic courts and to rely on compliance by EC institutions with their WTO obligations and EC Treaty obligations to act in conformity with international law.[43]

F. Is the large number of EU-US disputes in the WTO cause for concern?

Since the entry into force of the WTO Agreement in 1995, more than 50 disputes under the DSU involved the EU and the US on different sides of the dispute (as

---

[42] See the contribution by Busch & Reinhardt below.   [43] See supra note 33 and related text.

complainants or defendants), without including WTO disputes in which the EU
and US intervened as third parties on different sides.[44] Even though the number
of current bilateral disputes is much smaller and concerns less than 2 per cent of
transatlantic trade and investments, some of these disputes caused political and
economic concerns far beyond the particular dispute. US Trade Representative
R. Zoellick warned European Parliamentarians on 15 May 2001 that the EC's
complaint against the US tax treatment for FSCs had represented an excessive
recourse to WTO dispute settlement procedures: 'any attempt by Europe to
impose $4 billion in sanctions against the United States would be like using a
nuclear weapon on the global trading system . . . We must be more creative in
settling bilateral disputes . . . we must look for more opportunities for engagement short of formal WTO resolution. Litigation is not always the solution for
solving every problem.'[45]

A bilateral compromise, a few weeks earlier, between the EU and US to end
their nine years of GATT and WTO disputes over the discriminatory EC import
restrictions for bananas offered an example for such 'creative dispute settlement'
and was celebrated as a result of the personal friendship between US Trade
Representative Zoellick and EU Trade Commissioner Lamy and of their
common sense 'that we're anchored in a relationship that's bigger than any
one issue'.[46] Yet, is it not a sign of weakness of constitutional democracies if
freedom of trade and compliance with international law depend on the friendship among trade politicians? The EC's recourse to WTO dispute settlement
procedures in response to the US import restrictions on steel in March 2002, and
the EC's threat of introducing unilateral trade sanctions in June 2002, illustrated
once again that the WTO dispute settlement system—even though imperfect and
sub-optimal from a citizen perspective—remains essential for containing protectionist abuses of government powers. As indicated in Article 3 DSU, recourse to
WTO dispute settlement proceedings is a positive sign of a functioning legal
system. The contested trade restrictions and trade distortions, rather than recourse to WTO dispute settlement procedures, are the primary legal, economic
and political problems.

If inadequate respect for international law (such as existing WTO rules) and
inadequate legal disciplines on discriminatory foreign policy measures are major
sources of transatlantic disputes, is the transatlantic partnership the 'wrong
forum' for addressing the apparent political problem that 'the U.S. system is so
much less sensitive to international law than comparable European systems', and
'the United States *corpus juris* has been among the least permeable of national
systems, despite early judicial deference to international law as part of the law

---

[44] See supra note 37 and the monthly lists of WTO Disputes on the website of the WTO. WTO
disputes involving the EU and the US are also listed in the Annexes to the WTO's Trade Policy Review
Reports on the US and the EU (see, eg, WT/TPR/S/72 of 14 June 2000, 167–173).
[45] *International Trade Daily*, BNA Monitoring Service, 16 May 2001.
[46] Cf, *Financial Times*, 12 and 27 April 2001. Personal relations between former USTR Barshefsky
and EU Trade Commissioner Lord Brittan had apparently been tense.

of the United States'?[47] The 'European Union's unsavory reputation as a serial violator of multilateral trade rules'[48] can hardly serve as a model for strengthening the rule of law in transatlantic relations. What political lesson can be drawn from the experience inside the EC and also inside the US that rule of law among states (eg, compliance with the customs union rules of the EC) could be secured only if both state and federal courts (including the ECJ) co-operated in joint judicial enforcement of the rules? Since EU and US politicians may have no self-interest in limiting their policy discretion by additional judicial restraints, how can EU and US citizens defend their constitutional interests in judicial protection of maximum freedom and other human rights across frontiers? What can academics do to promote rule of law, judicial dialogue, and co-operation between national and international courts in transatlantic relations?

G. 'Positive disputes', 'negative disputes', and criteria for their evaluation

In a world of limited resources and unlimited demand by self-interested individuals and antagonistic groups, conflicts of interests and disputes are inevitable facts of life in every society. In today's globally integrated world economy where some 200 states insist on their 'sovereign equality' in regulating interdependent transnational issues, competition for scarce resources (eg, mobile international capital, environmental resources) and disputes over the 'external effects' of national regulations have become inevitable facts also in international relations. Ethics, economics and other social sciences emphasize the positive social functions of many social struggles (eg, competition among producers and consumers in economic markets, competition among citizens and politicians in political markets). Human rights and constitutional democracy proceed from 'normative individualism' (ie, that values can be derived only from the individual and from respect for his human dignity) and value legal disputes positively if they enable an ever more precise definition, delimitation and protection of equal human rights, equal sovereign rights of states and of constitutional restraints on abuses of powers.

The basic function of law, economics and politics is to prevent and settle disputes by agreed rules, procedures and incentives for reconciling conflicting self-interests of individuals and groups with their common long-term interests (ie, the *public interest*, eg, in economic consumer welfare and in democratic citizen welfare). All national and international legal systems aim at dispute prevention and dispute settlement on the basis of agreed rules, government interventions, judicial clarification and enforcement of rules, and alternative

---

[47] Quotations from T.M. Franck & G.H. Fox (eds), 'Introduction', in Franck & Fox (eds), *International Law Decisions in National Courts* (1996) 5–6, who emphasize 'the importance of fostering synergy between the national and international judiciaries' (at 5), and regret that 'United States judges, in particular, are less familiar with the procedures and jurisdictions of international tribunals' (at 9).

[48] *Financial Times* editorial on 'Banana deal', 12 April 2001.

political and legal methods of dispute settlement. Courts are important parts of
national and international governance mechanisms in view of their judicial rule-
enforcement functions, dispute settlement and dispute prevention functions (eg,
by clarifying the contested meaning of rules of conduct so as to avoid similar
future disputes).[49]

Due to the power-oriented character of international relations and the diversity of individual and democratic preferences, the legal criteria for distinguishing
'positive' from 'negative conflicts' remain controversial. The paradigm of the
classical international law theory on the peaceful settlement of disputes—ie,
sovereign equality of states, non-intervention into their domestic affairs, and
consent as the basis for the agreed settlement of disputes (cf Articles 2, 33 UN
Charter)—has become increasingly challenged, for instance vis-à-vis 'failed
states' and the power-oriented UN security system. In constitutional democracies, parliaments (eg, the US Congress) and human rights groups insist that the
democratic legitimacy of intergovernmental agreements is limited by their parliamentary ratification and by their respect for human rights. The US Trade Act
2002, for instance, explicitly requests a report from the US administration on
whether WTO dispute settlement bodies have complied with their legal obligation that '[r]ecommendations and rulings of the DSB cannot add to or diminish
the rights and obligations provided in the covered agreements' (Article 3:2 DSU).
UN human rights bodies advocate a 'human rights approach to international
trade' which 'sets the promotion and protection of human rights as objectives of
trade liberalization, not exceptions', and 'promotes international co-operation
for the realization of human rights and freedoms in the context of trade liberalization'.[50] From an EC perspective, it is hardly satisfactory that the EC—even in
areas of EC treaty-making powers—has not yet been admitted into various state-
centred UN bodies (like the International Monetary Fund (IMF) and the International Labour Organization (ILO)) and has no direct access to their dispute
settlement systems.

The 'public interest' to be protected through intergovernmental dispute settlement proceedings may be defined very differently depending on the relevant
perspective (eg, a citizen-oriented human rights approach, a state-centred
international law approach, or an EC perspective focusing on 'Community
interests'). The private and governmental self-interests may be closely intertwined if, pursuant to Section 301 of the US Trade Act and the corresponding
EC Trade Barriers Regulation, citizens can request their respective governments
to initiate intergovernmental dispute settlement proceedings over illegal market
access barriers abroad and other 'unreasonable' trade distortions that impede

[49] Cf, A. Stone Sweet, *Governing with Judges: Constitutional Politics in Europe* (2000).
[50] Report of the High Commissioner for Human Rights on *Liberalization of Trade in Services and Human Rights*, document E/CN.4/Sub.2/2002/9, p2. Cf, E.U. Petersmann, 'Human Rights and the WTO', in *The Kluwer Compendium of the WTO* (2003).

their private economic transactions.[51] The 'analytical papers' in Part III of this book, written by lawyers, economists, political scientists and practitioners, illustrate these different perceptions of transatlantic disputes:

- *Lawyers* tend to value legal remedies and judicial decisions as positive contributions to the rule of law. They usually welcome the DSU requirement that 'all solutions to matters formally raised under the consultation and dispute settlement provisions of the covered agreements, including arbitration awards, shall be consistent with those agreements and shall not nullify or impair benefits accruing to any Member under those agreements, nor impede the attainment of any objective of those agreements' (Article 3:5). Since classic international law focuses on the freedom of states rather than on the freedom of their citizens, both US and EC institutions often refuse to grant their domestic citizens individual rights to invoke GATT/WTO rules in domestic courts. The artificial legal dichotomies (eg, between the customs union rules in GATT/WTO law and the corresponding customs union rules in the EC Treaty) blur the fact that the WTO rules on non-discriminatory conditions of competition are designed to protect freedom, non-discrimination and consumer welfare of private economic operators and other domestic citizens.

- *Economists* emphasize the lower costs of dispute prevention compared with dispute settlement, especially in the WTO which does not provide for reparation of injury caused by violations of WTO rules and countermeasures. Dispute settlement jurisprudence is viewed positively by economists if the jurisprudence contributes to the development of efficient rules which increase legal security and reduce transaction costs. Economic theories of 'efficient breaches of legal rules' are applied in the contribution by Hauser & Roitinger who attribute positive value to certain rule violations: 'violation of WTO Agreements and non-compliance with Dispute Settlement Body rulings should be considered as an instrument for renegotiation ... providing indispensable flexibility to the world trading system'.[52] Such economic cost-benefit analyses depend on individual circumstances.

- *Political scientists* are concerned with political behaviour. They may define 'dispute settlement' neither in legal terms (eg, legally binding dispute settlement rulings, legal compliance with such rulings) nor in terms of economic efficiency, but rather in terms of 'early settlement' avoiding a 'cult of offensive litigation'.[53] Lawyers and economists have often criticized such mutually

---

[51] Cf, C.T. Garcia Molyneux, *Domestic Structures and International Trade. The Unfair Trade Instruments of the United States and the EU* (2001). Out of 19 private complaints submitted under the EC Trade Barriers Regulation (until summer 2002), eight led to the initiation of WTO dispute settlement proceedings by the EC.

[52] See the contribution by Hauser & Roitinger in Part III.

[53] See the contribution by Busch & Reinhardt who define 'successful outcomes' as the 'policy result of a dispute, rather than the nature of a ruling *per se*'. The case-study by F. Abbott & T. Cottier criticizes the 'politicization' of the EU/US dispute over the trademark 'Havana Club' which

agreed conflict-prevention (eg, by means of a bilateral 'voluntary export restraint') if it violates GATT rules and reduces consumer welfare. The fact that most invocations of GATT and WTO dispute settlement procedures do not lead to adversarial panel procedures confirms the importance of mutual co-operation for 'win-win situations' and for the necessary political support at home. The study by Spiwak on the 'telecoms war' concludes: 'both sides on the transatlantic partnership must first take more aggressive steps to create a "constituency for competition" in their own respective domestic markets before they continue to throw stones at each other'.[54] Sørensen's study of the settlement of transatlantic air transport disputes explains the settlement of the dispute on 'hushkits' by the fact that, in parallel to the dispute settlement proceeding in the Council of the International Civil Aviation Organization (ICAO), both sides continued to participate in the elaboration and final adoption by the ICAO of new aircraft noise standards.[55]

- *Trade diplomats* enjoy listing their victories in the Machiavellian WTO arena, and admit their 'greatest difficulty in keeping the political level or elected representatives in line'. They recognize that 'there are quite a large number of WTO cases dealing with US application of their trade remedy laws (safeguard actions, both anti-dumping and anti-subsidy cases) which quite simply would not be necessary if US statutes and the rules of application in practice had been brought fully into line with the WTO agreements'. Even though they admit the political importance of 'the "being condemned in public" factor which would not have resulted from simple bilateral dialogue',[56] trade warriors are sometimes agnostic or even hostile toward the 'methodological individualism' of citizen-centred reform proposals aimed at limiting abuses of trade policy powers.

H. Optimal dispute prevention and dispute settlement strategies must target the source of the conflict of interests: need for 'multi-level analyses'

International negotiations, rule-making and dispute settlement among governments are preceded, influenced and followed by *domestic* negotiations between government representatives, parliamentarians and domestic constituencies. The complex interrelationships between 'multi-level', international and domestic rule-making, rule-application and adjudication need to be better understood so as to design more effective dispute prevention and dispute settlement mechanisms. There is a need for 'multi-level analyses' and 'multi-level solutions', for

---

'transformed a fairly ordinary commercial trademark dispute between two well-financed private enterprises into a matter of high politics'.

[54] See the contribution by Spiwak.

[55] See the contribution by Sørensen.

[56] The quotations are from the written comment (28 April 2002) by former ambassador R. Abbott which, like other written comments on the conference papers, could not be included in this book.

instance by empowering not only governments but also their citizens to enforce international guarantees of freedom and non-discrimination through courts.

If dispute prevention fails, private and public complainants can choose among a large variety of national and international dispute settlement mechanisms, such as intergovernmental adjudication (eg, in the International Court of Justice, WTO dispute settlement panels), transgovernmental adjudication (eg, in the ECJ), or adjudication in domestic courts.[57] The Transatlantic Partnership institutions and 'civil society dialogues' offer additional procedures and institutions for transnational co-operation and dispute prevention among representatives of governments, business, labour, consumers and environmental interests.[58] The preceding analysis leads to three important policy conclusions:

(1) Optimal dispute prevention and dispute settlement strategies should intervene directly at the source of the conflict of interests. Many transatlantic disputes among governments have their origin in domestic conflicts of interests inside states and can be prevented and settled more efficiently at the domestic policy level and in domestic courts. Identification of the domestic origin of transatlantic economic disputes may sometimes be difficult, as illustrated by the US complaint against the EC's import restrictions on bananas (the US agreed to a GATT waiver in favour of the EC's tariff preferences for ACP bananas but challenged the EC's discriminatory import licensing scheme).

(2) Optimal dispute prevention and dispute settlement strategies vary according to the different kinds and different legal contexts of transatlantic disputes. For example, the law of the UN, the IMF, the ILO, the WTO and the World Intellectual Property Organization (WIPO) provide for very different membership rules (eg, EC membership in the FAO, WTO and Law of the Sea Agreement but *not* in the UN, IMF, ILO and WIPO) and for diverse procedures for the settlement of transatlantic and other disputes. Some of the recent transatlantic policy differences—eg, among the European Central Bank and the US Federal Reserve regarding monetary policies and interest rates,[59] or among EU and US foreign policy-makers on how to respond to the risk of aggression by Iraq, or whether economic sanctions in response to the violation of core labour rights by the military rulers in Myanmar should be internationally co-ordinated in the ILO or in the WTO—have led to intense policy co-ordination on very different policy levels (eg, among central bankers, UN Security Council representatives) that have—until the war in Iraq—prevented major transatlantic conflicts.

(3) The evaluation of optimal dispute prevention and dispute settlement strategies depends on the value premises: the state-centred paradigm of

---

[57] Cf, eg, R.O. Keohane, A. Moravcsik & A.M. Slaughter, supra note 13.

[58] On the multi-level 'transatlantic dialogues' and on multi-level negotiations see the introduction by Pollack & Shaffer, supra note 2, at 4–7, 20 *et seq.*

[59] See, eg, 'A New Policy Divide Across the Atlantic—Monetary policy has rarely been so different', *Financial Times*, 8 November 2002, 12.

interpreting international agreements as creating exclusive rights and obligations of governments, to be enforced through intergovernmental dispute settlement procedures and sanctions, is inappropriate for the transatlantic market relations among the world's leading democracies. From the point of view of 'normative individualism' and human rights, economic markets must serve general consumer welfare, just as political markets and constitutional democracy must serve general citizen welfare, subject to democratic legislation balancing diverse human rights and citizen rights.[60] International guarantees of freedom and non-discrimination, like domestic democratic legislation, should be construed as empowering individuals to pursue their equal rights across frontiers and as creating obligations of governments not only in intergovernmental relations, but first and foremost vis-à-vis their citizens. Not only inside the US and inside the EU, but also in transatlantic market relations can and should disputes among producers, traders and consumers be decided by domestic courts with due regard to the applicable national and international rules ratified by domestic parliaments.

II. THE DIFFICULT CATEGORIZATION OF TRANSATLANTIC ECONOMIC DISPUTES: OVERVIEW AND LEGAL PERSPECTIVES OF THE CASE-STUDIES

Part II of this book reproduces the following case-studies which were discussed at the conferences in July 2001 and May 2002:

(1) Manifestly Illegal Import Restrictions and Non-Compliance with WTO Dispute Settlement Rulings: Lessons from the *Banana Dispute* (Professors Weiss & Davey).

(2) Safeguard Measures, Anti-Dumping and Countervailing Disputes in the Transatlantic Partnership: How to Control 'Contingency Protection' More Effectively? (D. Palmeter & Professor Bourgeois).

(3) Production Subsidies, Export Subsidies and Tax Treatment of 'Foreign Sales Corporations': Lessons from Past GATT and WTO Disputes (Professors Hudec, Bronckers, Tangermann & Josling).

(4) Non-Discriminatory Sanitary and Phyto-Sanitary Standards: Lessons from the Disputes over *Hormones* and *Genetically Modified Organisms* (Professors Mavroidis & Bermann).

---

[60] This premise is consistent with the 'human rights approach to international trade' advocated by the UN High Commissioner for Human Rights and by other UN human rights bodies and is explained in detail in E.U. Petersmann, supra note 50. Whereas a 'human rights approach' emphasizes that the rights of governments under WTO law (eg Article XX GATT) may be obligations under human rights law (eg to protect human health), a 'constitutional approach' emphasizes that the WTO guarantees of freedom, non-discrimination and rule of law serve 'constitutional functions' not only among states but also for the legal and judicial protection of freedom, non-discrimination and rule of law among private participants in international trade.

(5) Disputes over Technical Barriers to Trade: Are WTO and EC Rules Adequate? (Professors Abbott & Demaret).

(6) Conflict Avoidance in the Context of the Bilateral EC-US Agreements on the Co-ordination of Competition Policies (K.Mehta & Professor Janow).

(7) Conflict Avoidance in the Context of Mutual Recognition of Technical, Data Protection and Health Standards (Professors Shaffer & Nicolaidis).

(8) Government Procurement Disputes: Lessons from the Dispute over Massachusetts' 1996 Act Regulating State Contracts with Companies Doing Business with Burma (Professor Schaefer & A. Haagsma).

(9) Avoidance and Settlement of 'High Policy Disputes': Lessons from the Dispute over 'The Cuban Liberty and Democratic Solidarity Act' (H. Paemen & D. Aaron).

(10) EU-US Trade-Related Environmental Disputes: Are WTO Dispute Settlement Mechanisms and Multilateral Environmental Agreements Sufficient? (Professor Esty & C. Bail).

(11) Dispute Prevention and Dispute Settlement in International Services Trade: The Example of Telecommunications and the 'Cultural Exception' (Professors Spiwak & Footer).

(12) International Air Transport Liberalization and Regulation (F. Sørensen & R. Loughlin).

(13) Dispute Prevention and Dispute Settlement in the Field of Intellectual Property Rights and Electronic Commerce (Professors Abbott & Cottier).

(14) The case-study by Professors Malanczuk & Howse on Investment Disputes in the Transatlantic Partnership: Choices among Alternative Dispute Settlement Fora was discussed, but not submitted for publication.

The case-studies show an enormous variety of contested measures: national legislation at federal or state levels; EC regulations, EC directives, EC decisions or inaction by EC bodies (eg, non-approval of new genetically modified organisms); administrative actions (eg, on government procurement, merger control, economic sanctions) at international, national or sub-national levels; judicial decisions; and private business practices subject to review by national or EC authorities. They also illustrate the numerous legal and political interdependencies between 'multi-level' rule-making, policy-making and settlement of related disputes at national and international levels. The case-studies cover transatlantic trade in goods, services, investments and intellectual property rights. According to their underlying conflicts of interests, one can distinguish four major categories of disputes: disputes over discriminatory and economically harmful border measures (section A below); disputes over non-discriminatory internal regulations (section B below); 'high policy disputes' (section C below); and disputes over private rights (section D below).

In line with the diversity of theories of international relations and international law, the legal and political analyses of the case-studies often remain controversial depending on the value premises and methods applied (eg, economic analysis of law). For instance, should the 'public interest' be defined from a national or international 'realist perspective' (eg, focusing on freedom and power of states) or from a citizen perspective (eg, focusing on constitutional citizen rights and corresponding government obligations)? Should violations of WTO rules (eg, in the case of EC import restrictions on hormone-fed beef) be viewed negatively (eg, in view of their economic costs and illegality) or positively in transatlantic relations (eg, as political instruments for renegotiating 'incomplete contracts', as claimed in the contribution by the economists Hauser & Roitinger)? Participants recognized not only the importance of intergovernmental WTO procedures for the prevention and settlement of transatlantic disputes; they emphasized also the many inadequacies of intergovernmental WTO procedures and the limited scope of remedies under WTO law. The conference contributions offer 'building blocks' for elaborating more realistic, interdisciplinary theories of dispute prevention and dispute settlement. Additional empirical and theoretical analyses are needed in order to clarify how dispute prevention can be further improved in transatlantic and domestic decision-making processes.

A. Disputes over trade discrimination: need for making WTO rules more policy-relevant in domestic decision-making processes

Most transatlantic disputes (eg, on EC import restrictions on bananas, US 'contingency protection' measures, EC export subsidies for pasta, US export subsidies for 'FSC') fall into the category of traditional GATT disputes about welfare-reducing *trade discrimination* in violation of WTO rules ratified by parliaments in both the EU and the US. In most cases, the measures had been introduced in response to protectionist pressures by import-competing producers (eg, steel producers in the US), domestic traders (eg, banana importers in the EC), or export industries (eg, US industries using FSCs as a means of benefiting from export subsidies). Political election cycles and domestic rules for election campaign financing clearly influenced the adoption of some of the contested measures (such as US import restrictions on steel), as well as the procedures for the settlement of disputes (eg, on the EC's import restrictions on bananas). The case-study by Palmeter attributes the fact that, eg, WTO safeguard clauses, and WTO anti-dumping and countervailing duty rules, are so much more frequently used (and abused) in the US than in the EC, to the divergent domestic legislation implementing WTO rules.[61] In a minority of cases, trade restrictions had been motivated by non-economic concerns in importing countries (eg, about health and environmental risks of imported goods).

Economics teaches that discriminatory market access restrictions and market distortions are likely to reduce consumer welfare. The WTO prohibitions of discriminatory trade measures have been ratified by domestic parliaments and,

---

[61] See the case-study by D. Palmeter.

due to their higher legal rank in EU law (cf, Article 300(7) EC Treaty) and in US law (subject to the 'later in time rule'),[62] are legally binding on all government institutions inside the EU and the US. The case-studies show ample evidence, however, that:

- the EC and US governments often violate the WTO prohibitions in response to protectionist pressures at home;
- in both the EC and the US, governments prevent their own citizens and their domestic judges from invoking the WTO obligations of their governments in domestic courts;
- at the intergovernmental level, however, the EC and US governments remain eager to protect their respective export industries by enforcing WTO rules in the WTO against foreign governments, eg, through EC challenges of US 'contingency protection' measures [63] and US challenges of the EC's import restrictions on bananas and other products in the WTO.[64]

Experience with European integration (eg, the EC Treaty provisions on re-placement of discriminatory anti-dumping measures by non-discriminatory competition rules) suggests that such disputes (eg, about anti-dumping measures) can be prevented most effectively through free trade agreements commit-ting governments to the use of 'first best policy instruments' (eg, non-discriminatory competition rules) rather than welfare-reducing trade restric-tions. In the negotiations on NAFTA, however, Canada's proposals for replacing anti-dumping rules by non-discriminatory competition rules were not accepted by the US government. It remains doubtful whether a TAFTA would be more successful than NAFTA in limiting protectionist abuses of discretionary trade policy powers. The acceptance, in NAFTA chapter 19, of private access to international dispute settlement panels reviewing national anti-dumping and countervailing duty determinations indicates that the US recognizes the inad-equate judicial remedies available under US law. The case-study by Palmeter concludes, however, that 'reform through the judiciary... is not likely to be a realistic option for any transatlantic institutions in the foreseeable future... The key... is not in institutional reform but in policy reform.'[65]

In *domestic* decision-making processes leading to the adoption of discrimin-atory trade restrictions and trade distortions, international legal obligations (eg, under GATT and WTO rules) often play a much lesser role than in the ensuing *intergovernmental* discussions about the prevention and settlement of disputes. In both the EU and the US, the domestic legislation on the implementation of WTO rules prevents citizens from invoking the rules before domestic courts.[66]

---

[62] On the legal status of WTO law in EC law and in US law see the contributions to J. Jackson & A. Sykes (eds), *Implementing the Uruguay Round* (1997).
[63] See the case-study by Palmeter in Part II.
[64] See the case-study by Weiss in Part II.
[65] See the contribution by Palmeter in Part II.
[66] For details see the comparative studies in J. Jackson & A. Sykes, supra note 62.

As a consequence, GATT/WTO legal rules are often discredited ('WTO blah-blah'[67]) and ignored in domestic decision-making processes so as to accommodate political pressures from domestic interest groups. At the intergovernmental level of WTO consultations and WTO dispute settlement proceedings, however, the same governments are keen to enforce WTO rules as legally binding and justiciable restraints on discretionary government powers. Similar 'double standards' and political 'prisoner dilemmas' of domestic trade policy-making are reflected in the asymmetrical recognition of individual *rights to protection* (eg, under US anti-dumping laws), and individual rights to petition WTO dispute settlement proceedings against foreign governments (eg, under Section 301 of the US Trade Act and the corresponding EC Trade Barriers Regulation), without recognition of individual *rights to import*, or rights to challenge WTO violations by one's own government.[68]

The large number of transatlantic disputes about welfare-reducing, discriminatory trade restrictions are signs of 'government failures' and 'constitutional failures' in transatlantic relations. From the point of view of the general citizen interest in a non-discriminatory transatlantic market and in legal and judicial protection of citizen rights and rule of law across frontiers, the current dispute prevention and dispute settlement mechanisms in transatlantic relations are inadequate. Neither in the EU nor in the US have citizens effective judicial remedies against protectionist abuses of trade policy powers in violation of WTO rules, for instance if the US Congress uses its constitutional power to adopt legislation in violation of prior treaty obligations of the US, or if EC and US trade diplomats negotiate WTO rules protecting protectionist producer interests rather than consumer welfare. Even though—according to Palmeter— 'rational negotiators, operating behind a veil of ignorance, would reject virtually all of the WTO's substantive anti-dumping regime', elected politicians are often not willing to defend Rawlsian 'principles of justice' (eg, that 'a free competitive market trading scheme is to everyone's mutual advantage').[69]

The EC Treaty does not confer powers on the EC Council to violate international treaty obligations ratified by parliaments in all EC member states (cf, Article 300(7) EC Treaty). The large number of GATT/WTO dispute settlement findings of illegal EC restrictions suggests a lack of effective constitutional 'checks and balances' limiting abuses of the EC's trade policy powers. The EC Treaty does not provide for parliamentary control of the EC's common commercial policy powers by the European Parliament (cf, Art 133 EC). The case-study by Weiss shows that—even though exporters and importers challenged the EC import restrictions on bananas in the ECJ as well as in national administrative, tax and constitutional courts—judicial remedies in the ECJ often remain inef-

[67] See the case-study by M. Schaefer.
[68] Cf, eg, the case-study by Palmeter and, more generally, E.U. Petersmann, 'Strengthening the Domestic Legal Framework of the GATT Multilateral Trade System', in E.U. Petersmann & M. Hilf, supra note 38, at 33 *et seq.*
[69] J. Rawls, *The Law of Peoples* (1999) 42.

fective in the trade policy area as long as the ECJ takes into account neither the relevant WTO obligations of governments nor WTO dispute settlement findings of the illegality of the EC's import restrictions on bananas.

A reciprocal EU-US agreement to allow EU and US citizens to invoke certain precise and unconditional WTO obligations in domestic courts would offer more effective and more democratic dispute prevention and dispute settlement strategies in transatlantic relations and could serve as a model for multilateral WTO reforms. Empowering private exporters and importers involved in the dispute, and requiring EU and US courts to decide the dispute on the basis of all relevant agreed rules (including WTO rules), could prevent many intergovernmental disputes, without excluding subsequent recourse to WTO dispute settlement procedures if the domestic court's interpretation of WTO rules should remain controversial. The EU and US governments prefer, however, the current lack of effective domestic judicial review of their trade policies. EU and US judges might likewise find it easier to exercise judicial self-restraint vis-à-vis the trade policy discretion of governments rather than to apply the complex WTO rules for the benefit of investors, producers, traders and consumers who rely on respect for international law in transatlantic relations. The case-studies (eg., by Josling & Tangermann, and Hudec) confirm that, given this lack of effective judicial remedies in domestic courts, international WTO negotiations (eg, on additional WTO legal disciplines for agricultural subsidies and sanitary standards) and WTO dispute settlement proceedings offer 'second best instruments' for preventing and settling transatlantic economic disputes.

B. Disputes over non-discriminatory internal regulations: need to expand transatlantic constituencies and transatlantic regulatory co-operation

Transatlantic disputes about prima facie *non-discriminatory internal regulations* (eg, for health, environmental and consumer protection) raise different legal and procedural problems, for instance regarding the 'scientific justifiability', 'necessity', proportionality or *de facto* discrimination of *de jure* non-discriminatory product regulations that are often elaborated in close collaboration with national producer interests by national and intergovernmental expert bodies (like the FAO Codex Alimentarius Commission) or by private standardizing bodies. Several case-studies demonstrate that mutual trust, common standards and international co-operation among regulatory agencies (eg, for competition policies) have enabled successful prevention and settlement of international disputes.[70] Lack of confidence (eg, in the risk assessments by domestic health and environmental regulators) and divergent domestic standards (eg, in merger control investigations, treatment of genetically modified organisms) contributed to conflicting regulations and disputes.[71] The case-studies suggest that more transatlantic regulatory co-operation (eg, in fields such as competition policy,

[70] See the case-study by K. Mehta.   [71] See, eg, the case-study by G. Shaffer.

mutual recognition agreements, data privacy, common risk assessments of the new European Food Safety Authority and the US Food and Drugs Authority) are needed for promoting bilateral dispute prevention in this second category of 'behind the border' regulatory disputes.

The WTO Agreements on Technical Barriers to Trade, Sanitary and Phyto-Sanitary Standards, GATS, TRIPS and Government Procurement were all initiated by the EU and US in order to further liberalize and regulate international trade and make the WTO dispute settlement system available for prevention and settlement of disputes in these areas. The initiatives for new international rules (eg, on trade-related competition and investments) to be negotiated in the Doha Development Round can further reinforce dispute prevention and dispute settlement in transatlantic relations.

The need to promote transatlantic regulatory co-operation and transatlantic political constituencies for mutually beneficial policy-making raises numerous policy questions. For instance:

- What changes in the domestic legal and political infrastructures for policy-making could contribute to this objective in Europe (eg, establishment of new European regulatory authorities like the new European Food Safety Authority) and in the US (eg, election campaign finance reforms as incentives for 'less parochial' legislative processes)?
- Could additional joint transatlantic institutions and constituencies, as suggested by Ambassador Aaron, improve transatlantic dispute prevention and facilitate joint EU-US leadership for reforms of worldwide rules so as to strengthen rule of law, liberal trade and democratic international governance?
- Given the inevitable focus of legislators and regulators on domestic interests and the frequent *de jure* non-discriminatory taxes and regulations with *de facto* discriminatory impact on competing imports (eg, of European automobiles), transatlantic disputes challenging violations of the WTO prohibitions of *de facto* discrimination should be seen as 'positive disputes' that can often be settled more easily *ex post* through WTO dispute settlement proceedings than *ex ante* through prior intergovernmental dispute prevention.

C. 'Wrong disputes': bilateral dispute prevention 'in the shadow of the law'

The transatlantic disputes over US tax rebates (or tax exemptions) for 'domestic international sales corporations' (DISC) and, following the US implementation of the 'DISC dispute settlement ruling' under GATT 1947, for FSCs has continued for almost three decades. Underlying this dispute are systemic divergences of EU and US income tax systems. The case-study by Hudec finds that 'the FSC case was the wrong kind of case to bring before the WTO dispute settlement procedure.... To file a legal complaint against FSC was to invite a legal deadlock that would damage the credibility of the WTO dispute settlement system, and that would become a large irritant in US-EC trade relations.'[72] The WTO practice of settling most disputes through consultations, without request for the establishment of a dispute settlement panel, confirms that WTO members are aware of the legal and political limits of international adjudication and of the advantages of preventing 'wrong disputes' which might 'overload' the GATT/ WTO dispute settlement system if there is no political majority for the 'system change' needed for the implementation of a dispute settlement ruling.

Negotiation theories recommend 'principled bargaining' rather than 'positional bargaining' (regardless of whether the latter is based on 'hard' or 'soft' procedures): both parties are likely to gain from focusing on their common interests by inventing options for mutual gain based on objective standards.[73] Several case-studies (eg, by Mehta, Paemen, K. Abbott)—notably on conflict avoidance in the context of the bilateral EC-US agreements on co-ordination of competition policies, on mutual recognition of technical and health standards, data protection, and on the settlement of the dispute over the 'Cuban Liberty and Democratic Solidarity Act' through the bilateral 'Understanding with Respect to Disciplines for the Strengthening of Investment Protection' of May 1998— identify certain categories of disputes (eg, 'high policy disputes' over politically motivated trade sanctions, unilateral application of EU or US competition law to transatlantic mergers involving companies on the other side of the Atlantic) that lend themselves more to settlement through bilateral negotiations and mutual agreement than to multilateral adjudication in worldwide organizations such as the WTO or the ICAO (see, eg, the US request for arbitration in the ICAO regarding the EC restrictions on 'hushkits' for airplanes).

Such bilateral negotiations often take place 'in the shadow of the law'[74] after invocation of the WTO dispute settlement procedures. The case-study by former EU Ambassador Paemen, and the comments on his case analysis by his political counterpart US Ambassador Aaron, on the bilateral resolution of the transatlantic dispute over the US trade sanctions against Cuba, illustrate the importance of using negotiation methods that 'don't bargain over positions', 'separate the people from the problem', 'focus on interests, not positions', 'invent options for mutual gain', and 'insist on using objective criteria'.[75] As the US Congress was the politically more powerful partner in this dispute over the application of US trade sanctions against Cuba to exports and persons from the EC, the EC

---

[72] See the case-study by Hudec.

[73] See, eg, R. Fisher & W. Ury, *Getting to Yes. Negotiating Agreement Without Giving In* (1991). On the distinction between 'distributive bargaining' (where the parties adopt a zero-sum mentality because they believe that there are limited resources to divide) and 'integrative bargaining' (usually on multiple issues so as to facilitate mutually beneficial solutions) see eg, J.M. Nolan-Haley, *Alternative Dispute Resolution* (2001).

[74] On the influence of law and legal values on the incentives for mediation and conciliation see eg, Y. Dezalay & B.G. Garth, *Dealing in Virtue. International Commercial Arbitration and the Construction of a Transnational Legal Order* (1996).

[75] The citations are the four central recommendations of the Harvard Negotiations Method as described in R. Fisher & W. Ury, supra note 73, Part II.

successfully changed its 'Best Alternative to a Negotiated Agreement'.[76] The EC's invocation of the WTO dispute settlement procedures, the EC's subsequent request to establish a WTO dispute settlement panel, the EC's convincing demonstration of the violation of WTO rules by the US application of the US sanctions vis-à-vis exports and citizens of the EC, and the EC's continuation and broadening of the bilateral negotiations in order to elaborate a comprehensive 'package deal' that respected the US interests and elaborated mutually beneficial objective criteria for investment protection to be incorporated into the Multilateral Agreement on Investments (MAI)—all these successive steps gradually changed the power relationship in the negotiations, invented options for jointly influencing the MAI negotiations on multilateral investment rules in the OECD, and finally enabled a mutually agreed settlement of the dispute that was welcomed by both parties as fair and enabled the suspension of the WTO panel proceedings.

The case-studies by Esty and by K. Abbott on the increasing conflicts between EU and US environmental and health protection policies shows that such bilateral negotiations on the merits may also be influenced by simultaneous negotiations on multilateral rules (eg, on the provisions in the Cartagena Protocol to the UN Convention on Biodiversity relating to genetically modified organisms) that could prejudge the outcome of the transatlantic dispute (eg, about the WTO consistency of EC prohibitions or labelling requirements for imports of genetically modified agricultural products). The International Competition Network among more than 50 national competition authorities, launched in November 2001 at the joint initiative of the EU and US competition authorities, is another example for multilateral regulatory co-operation outside the WTO in order to prevent future competition and trade disputes (eg, in the area of merger control).

By contrast, the GATT procedures for good offices, conciliation and mediation were resorted to only once by the EC and the US in 1982, and without success, regarding their transatlantic dispute over EC tariff treatment of citrus products. In July 2001, the WTO Director-General took the initiative of elaborating and circulating new procedures for requesting good offices, conciliation or mediation pursuant to Article 5 DSU;[77] these new procedures have been invoked for the first time by the Philippines, Thailand and the EC in a joint request for mediation in October 2002.[78] The rare use, often with little success, of the GATT/WTO provisions on conciliation and mediation by third parties seems to be due not only to the weak political influence of the GATT/WTO Directors-General on domestic interest group politics, but also to the multilateral legal nature of most disputes about the interpretation and application of GATT/WTO rules. For example, the WTO requirements to extend bilateral trade concessions to all other WTO members entail that cumulative compensation claims may cause more adjustment problems than compliance with WTO dispute settlement

---

[76] Cf, Fisher & Ury, ibid, Part III.   [77] Cf, WTO document WT/DSB/25, 17 July 2001.
[78] Cf, WTO document WT/GC/66, 16 October 2002.

rulings by termination of illegal restrictions. Even if the disputing parties bilaterally agree on a dispute settlement, such bilateral settlement does not prevent complaints from third WTO members challenging violations of WTO rules. Moreover, if a WTO member loses a panel or appellate proceeding, the prevailing interpretation of WTO rules will become available also for the defeated member for future complaints against other WTO members acting in violation of the agreed interpretations.[79] Even though dispute settlement rulings by the DSB are only legally binding on the parties to the concrete dispute, WTO jurisprudence leads to progressive clarifications of WTO rules that must be respected by all WTO members—a legal and political result that cannot be achieved through bilateral ad hoc mediation or other bilateral dispute settlement.

D. Disputes over investments and intellectual property rights: 'decentralization' and 'de-politicization' of intergovernmental disputes

The investment dispute between the US and Italy concerning the requisitioning of an Italian subsidiary (Elettronica Sicula SPA (ELSI)) of a US corporation in violation of Italian law illustrates how transatlantic investment disputes—even if covered by a bilateral Treaty of Friendship, Commerce and Navigation between an EC member state (Italy) and the US—may continue for decades. The dispute arose in 1968 when the mayor of Palermo (Sicily) requisitioned the plant. The company subsequently filed a petition for bankruptcy. The administrative appeal and judicial remedies initiated by ELSI led to a series of judgments by the Italian Court of First Instance, the Court of Appeal and the Italian Corte di Cassazione which, in 1975, confirmed that the requisition had violated Italian law. The claim for damages was espoused by the US government in 1974 and formally rejected by Italy in 1978. Only in 1987 did the US institute judicial proceedings against Italy in the ICJ. By judgment of July 1989, the ICJ rejected the US complaint and found that Italy was not guilty of any international illegality, tort or wrong.[80]

The six years of national and 15 years of intergovernmental dispute settlement proceedings in the ELSI case illustrate that, from the citizen perspective (eg, the point of view of the investor), the traditional international law methods of diplomatic protection offer inadequate legal and judicial remedies. Trade-related investment disputes may also be brought to the WTO pursuant to the dispute settlement procedures of the Subsidies Agreement, the Agreement on

---

[79] In the transatlantic dispute over US 'customs user fees', for instance, the US agreed to the adoption of the GATT dispute settlement findings on the GATT-inconsistency of the 'customs user fees' and, after adapting its customs user fees accordingly, enforced the newly agreed GATT interpretations vis-à-vis all other GATT contracting parties.

[80] Case concerning ELSI, International Court of Justice, 1989 Reports 15. For critical comments on 'the Court's lack of appreciation of the very specific facts of the case, the narrow reasoning and the almost complete adherence to conceptualism as opposed to equity' see F.A. Mann, 'Foreign Investment in the International Court of Justice: The ELSI Case' (1992) *AJIL* 92–102.

Trade-Related Investment Measures (TRIMS), the GATS and the TRIPS Agreement. In the transatlantic dispute over the EC's Regime for the Importation, Sale and Distribution of Bananas,[81] for instance, the US and the other complainants (Ecuador, Guatemala, Honduras, Mexico) alleged that the EC's allocation of import quotas and of import licences was inconsistent with a number of WTO provisions, including Article 2 of the TRIMS Agreement.[82] Yet, WTO law and WTO dispute settlement procedures offer no reparation of injury and financial compensation; the private action for damages by the US company involved (United Brands) in the ECJ appears unlikely to succeed as long as the ECJ continues to ignore WTO law and WTO dispute settlement rulings and explicitly holds that individuals cannot rely on WTO rules before the court and 'any infringement of them will not give rise to non-contractual liability on the part of the Community'.[83]

Inside the EC, freedom of establishment, free movement of capital (including foreign direct investments (FDI) and other private property rights), and private access to national courts and to the EC courts are protected by comprehensive constitutional guarantees of fundamental individual rights (cf, eg, Articles 43 and 56 EC Treaty). As regards capital movements and FDI in relation to third states, the EC's recent proposal for consultation and dispute settlement provisions to be included in a new WTO agreement on liberalization and protection of FDI suggests only intergovernmental dispute settlement procedures: 'any possible dispute concerning a future multilateral framework on FDI to be negotiated and agreed in the WTO should also be fully covered by the WTO Dispute Settlement mechanism'.[84] NAFTA chapter 11, by contrast, protects investor rights and FDI not only through international guarantees similar to those in the bilateral investment treaties of the US; it also provides for direct private access to international investor-state arbitration. Why is it that, in transatlantic investment relations, the EU and US governments are not willing to go beyond inter-governmental dispute settlement methods? Does the controversial and incoherent jurisprudence (eg, on 'regulatory takings' and 'annulment' of arbitration awards) under chapter 11 of NAFTA[85] prove that secretive, international investor-state arbitration offers hardly a model for prevention and settlement of disputes over private rights in transatlantic relations? Could domestic courts protect citizen rights more effectively if governments would not prevent domestic judges from applying relevant WTO rules?

---

[81] WTO document WT/DS27/R (1997).

[82] Having found that the EC's import licensing regime violated Article III:4 GATT, the Panel did not, however, consider it necessary to rule on its consistency with Article 2 of the TRIMS Agreement. On the three other WTO disputes in which the complainant invoked the TRIMS Agreement, see, eg, M. Lara, 'The Agreement on Trade-Related Investment Measures', in *The Kluwer Compendium of the WTO* (2003).

[83] ECJ, supra note 33.

[84] 'Concept Paper on Consultation and the Settlement of Disputes between Members', WT/WGTI/W/141, para 13, 11 September 2002.

[85] See, eg, the literature referred to in notes 16 and 20 supra.

The case-study by Abbott & Cottier on the EC's WTO complaint against the US treatment of the trademark 'Havana Club' concludes, 'that the dispute between Pernod Ricard, a France-based multinational distiller and distributor, and Bacardi-Martini, a U.S.-based multinational distiller and distributor, should have been resolved as a private commercial dispute and not as a systemic test of world trade system rules... By politicizing the dispute, both the EU and U.S. found themselves arguing legal positions that are most likely contrary to their longer term commercial interests.'[86] The fact that—out of 24 complaints filed under the TRIPS Agreement to the end of April 2002—one half concerned transatlantic relations between the EC, Canada and the US, bears witness to the political influence of pharmaceutical, chemical and other industrial holders of intellectual property rights on both sides of the Atlantic. According to Abbott & Cottier, many of these intergovernmental disputes about private commercial interests could be prevented or de-politicized by empowering the private actors involved to invoke and enforce the relevant TRIPS provisions in domestic courts whose remedial powers are more appropriate for the relevant private holders of intellectual property rights. In the WIPO, the treaty provisions on intergovernmental dispute settlement proceedings in the ICJ have never been used so far. Private recourse to the WIPO's newly established international arbitration centre is, however, rapidly increasing (notably as regards disputes over 'domain names').

III. Legal, economic and political theories of dispute prevention and dispute settlement

Part III of this book reproduces five 'cross-sectoral' studies by lawyers, economists and political scientists on dispute prevention and dispute settlement in transatlantic relations. The first contribution on 'Legal Theories on International Dispute Prevention and Dispute Settlement' by F. Berman, the former legal adviser in the UK Foreign Office, concludes that 'an analysis which admits individuals and private entities as objects of law, but retains States or governments as its sole subjects, is no longer remotely adequate to cater for the current complexities of the international legal system or for the ways in which international law and national legal systems interweave themselves into one another'. According to Berman, it is the 'conception of a public interest..., far more than any question of the standing of a private interest in the diplomatic field, that legitimately conditions the policy approach of governments in deciding whether or not to construct dispute settlement procedures in such a way as to open them up to direct access by private interests'.[87]

For the economists Hauser and Roitinger, as well as for the political scientists Busch and Reinhardt, dispute prevention and dispute settlement in transatlantic

---

[86] See the contribution by Abbott & Cottier in Part II.   [87] See the contribution by Berman.

relations depend on agreement among the governments concerned, even if a bilateral agreement deviates from multilaterally agreed rules (eg, WTO law) and reduces general citizen welfare and consumer welfare in both the EU and US. The analysis by Meng of the 'Transatlantic Early Warning System', which was set up by the EU and US in order to identify sources of future conflicts and intergovernmental means of preventing and 'managing' such conflicts, goes beyond the perception of states as unitary actors and discusses conflicts of interests inside the EU and inside the US, eg, conflicts between the legislative, executive or judicial branches of government if legislation or a court judgment require the introduction of trade restrictions that are criticized by the executive as a violation of international WTO obligations. The contribution by Trachtman analyzes transatlantic disputes from the perspective of citizen interests and citizen rights and asks, whose right is it anyhow?

A. How to define the 'public interest' in transatlantic relations? Discriminatory market distortions and foreign policy discretion as sources of transatlantic disputes

As noted by F. Berman, the diversity of legal, economic and political theories of dispute prevention and dispute settlement is largely due to the diverse concepts of the 'public interest' in national and international law and policy. Mainstream legal, political and economic theories perceive international relations as being dominated by 'sovereign states' which operate as rational, unitary actors in their pursuit of exogenous, fixed 'state interests' and—due to the anarchic structure, uncertainty and risks of international relations—rely primarily on power.[88] There are also other 'public choice reasons' why international lawyers, diplomats and trade politicians tend to favour the traditional international law assumption that, in matters of foreign policy, governments must enjoy broad discretion to define the 'public interest' and to protect it through intergovernmental dispute settlement procedures. For example, foreign policy discretion to tax and restrict the trade transactions of domestic citizens (eg, by means of anti-dumping duties) entails the power to distribute 'protection rents' in exchange for political support by domestic voters and interest groups (eg, the powerful textiles and steel lobbies in the US Congress). Trade politicians may have strong self-interests in foreign policy discretion and intergovernmental dispute settlement procedures controlled by government representatives.

US congressmen, non-governmental organizations and citizens in Europe and North America increasingly criticize state-centred international law (eg, the power-oriented collective security system of the UN Charter) and non-transparent, intergovernmental dispute settlement procedures (eg, in the WTO) from the perspective of parliamentary democracy.[89] For obvious reasons, the

---

[88] For an overview of theories of the state in international relations see J.M. Hobson, *The State and International Relations* (2000).
[89] See, eg, C. Barfield, supra note 19.

elected representatives of US citizens and of the 50 states in the US Congress, and the constitutional 'checks and balances' among the legislative, executive and judicial branches of the US government, enjoy a degree of democratic legitimacy which government representatives and bureaucracies in worldwide organizations cannot assert. The 'later-in-time rule' justifying the power of the US Congress to override the 'domestic law effects' of international treaties by subsequent US legislation,[90] and the explicit limitation (eg, in the Uruguay Round Agreement Act of 1994) of judicial review by US courts of compliance by the US with international treaty obligations, illustrate this widespread democratic distrust vis-à-vis power-oriented international law. The lack of constitutional protection of freedom of trade in transatlantic relations, described above (section I.C), further illustrates that constitutional democracy in the US operates—in the trade policy area—more in the sense of parliamentary democracy than as a constitutional safeguard of equal freedoms and consumer welfare of US citizens against congressional abuses of powers.

The 'prisoners' dilemma of parliamentary democracy' is reflected in various contributions to this book. The case-study by Palmeter on the widespread protectionist abuses of the 'contingency protection regime' in the EU and US concludes:

Rawlsian analysis makes clear that most of the current regime would be rejected by rational representatives of economically aware, just peoples, operating from the original position, because 'a free competitive market trading scheme is to everyone's mutual advantage.' But that is not the situation in which the trading system currently finds itself. The people, no doubt, are motivated by justice, but they are not, by and large, economically aware. Reduction in the confrontational nature of the contingency regime requires that this be changed.[91]

Palmeter is, however, sceptical as to whether the needed legal reforms can be achieved through the judiciary or through the legislature: in view of the 'rational ignorance' of voters and the short-term perspectives of self-interested politicians, there is neither popular demand nor legislative support for unilateral legislative or judicial reforms in favour of an open transatlantic market. This policy-conclusion is consistent with the historical experience in Europe and North America: free trade areas (like EFTA and NAFTA) and common markets (eg, inside federal states and the EC) could be realized only through reciprocal international agreements among states that limited trade policy discretion to discriminate against imports and protected private access to courts and judicial review of discriminatory or unnecessary trade restrictions inside federal states, NAFTA and the EC.

The study by Trachtman on the role of private parties in EC-US dispute settlement likewise emphasizes the need for better informed democratic politics

---

[90] Cf, the contributions by J. Jackson and by Hudec & Morrison, to Hilf & Petersmann, supra note 21.

[91] See the contribution by Palmeter.

and for more effective judicial safeguards. Trachtman recognizes that 'trade policy *within* existing rules' is likely to be dominated by producer interests and by short-term political interests in discretionary trade protection.[92] Trachtman accepts that 'political markets' (democracy) and the EC's 'common market' are constructed by means of constitutional law based on democratic citizen rights and inalienable human rights. Like most other US lawyers, Trachtman refuses, however, to consider a similar constitutional approach[93] for protecting the general citizen interest in an open transatlantic market: 'broader natural law or economic principles of free trade provide little basis for determining the scope and character of private participation'; 'private participation in WTO dispute settlement should not be determined by natural law assertions, for the market is constructed, and the property, contract and trading rights allocated to individuals are determined not by natural law, but by politics, hopefully informed by comparative institutional analysis.'[94]

Inside North America and also inside Europe, the constitutional protection of non-discriminatory freedom of trade and of 'democratic peace' among US citizens, Canadian citizens and among EU citizens continues to be celebrated as the hallmark of constitutional democracies. Inside federal states, it is recognized long since that power-oriented theories of international law and of discriminatory majority politics have persistently failed (eg, during the time of the US, German and Swiss confederations in the eighteenth and nineteenth centuries) to protect the general citizen interest in maximizing equal freedoms, consumer welfare and rule of law across frontiers. How can EU and US citizens protect themselves against the widespread protectionist abuses of trade policy powers by their own governments? How can transatlantic disputes over mutually welfare-reducing trade discrimination be prevented and settled in a way respecting the common 'public interests' of EU and US citizens?

B. Constitutional theory and market theory as conflict prevention theories: need for reciprocal restraints on discriminatory abuses of foreign policy powers

Human rights and constitutional democracies, like the EU and the US, proceed from the premise of 'normative individualism', ie, that values can be derived only from the individual whose personal autonomy (human dignity) and diverse preferences must be legally respected. In a world of scarcity and individual diversity, different persons' interests inevitably come into conflict (eg, the seller's interest in a high price and the buyer's interest in a low price). Moral theory (eg, the 'categorical imperative' as formulated by Immanuel Kant) and constitutional

---

[92] Cf, Petersmann, supra note 41, chs V and VI.

[93] On the important distinction, in constitutional theory, between 'choices within rules' and 'choices among rules' see J. Buchanan & G. Brennan, *The Reason of Rules* (1985).

[94] Cf, the contribution by Trachtman in Part III.

theory claim that the basic social function of rules and of democratic governments must be to prevent such conflicts by enabling each individual to pursue his or her private ends as a matter of individual right, not only as a matter of government benevolence.[95] The rulers cannot know the 'public good' (eg, consumer welfare) independently from constitutional rules and markets protecting and revealing individuals' evaluations, private demand and supply. Just as human rights theory and economic market theory perceive citizens and individual market participants as rational maximizers of their self-interests, constitutional theory conceptualizes politicians and government officials as self-interested utility maximizers who, in political markets no less than in economic markets, also pursue rational self-interests (eg, in political re-election).

In order to prevent conflicts and limit abuses of public and private power, constitutional theory posits that equal citizen rights and human rights must be protected through a 'limiting constitution' as well as an 'enabling constitution' providing for non-discriminatory democratic legislation, its administrative implementation, and for judicial remedies against abuses of power not only in political markets (democracy) but also in economic markets.[96] From a rational citizen perspective, the 'public interest' must be defined in a manner reconciling general citizen interests (eg, in maximum equal freedom and other 'Rawlsian principles of justice'), legitimate group interests (eg, of democratic majorities), 'state interests' and international 'Community interests' (eg, of the EC).[97] Without constitutional rules ensuring the overall coherence of national and international law and policies, conflicts between national and international rules and policies cannot be prevented or settled effectively. The main function of human rights and constitutional citizen rights—including the transnational 'market freedoms' protected by the EC Treaty—is to protect fundamental individual interests through 'higher law' so that they no longer depend on democratic majorities.

The modern 'liberal theory of international law'[98] likewise defines the 'public interest' in terms of equal citizen rights and contests the democratic legitimacy of the 'realist' perception of international relations as a 'billiard ball system' composed of states acting as indistinguishable 'black boxes'. From a citizen perspective, state preferences and foreign policies must respect the preferences of individuals and of groups inside states and their constitutionally agreed rights, including their 'inalienable human rights' that are today universally recognized

---

[95] Cf, E.U. Petersmann, *Time for Integrating Human Rights into the Law of Worldwide Organizations*, Jean Monnet Working Paper Harvard University (2001).

[96] Cf, eg, E.U. Petersmann, *Constitutional Economics, Human Rights and the Future of the WTO*, supra note 41; V.J. Vanberg, *The Constitution of Markets* (2001).

[97] Cf, E.U. Petersmann, 'From "State Sovereignty" toward "Popular Sovereignty" and "Individual Sovereignty" in the International Relations Law of the EU?' in N. Walker (ed), *Sovereignty in Transition* (2003).

[98] Cf, A.M. Slaughter, 'International Law in a World of Liberal States' (1995) 6 *EJIL* 503. For a criticism, see J.E. Alvarez, 'Do Liberal States Behave Better? A Critique of Slaughter's Liberal Theory' (2001) 12 *EJIL* 183.

by all UN member states in numerous international treaties and UN resolutions.[99] The fact that constitutional democracies protect 'democratic peace'
not only among domestic citizens but have hardly ever started a war against
another democracy,[100] is seen as empirical evidence for the need to 'constitutionalize' not only *domestic policy powers* but also *foreign policy powers*.[101]
European integration law is seen as an example for the possibility of limiting the
Hobbesian war of each against all by means of international guarantees of
individual freedom, non-discriminatory competition, rule of law and 'constitutional checks and balances' across frontiers. The strong reliance of European
integration on international judicial protection of rule of law and of individual
rights illustrates the importance of transnational co-operation among national
and international judges for creating a 'transnational community of law' based
on legal and judicial protection of citizen rights.[102]

Inside the EU and inside the US, the public interest in a common market is
protected by means of constitutional rules designed to protect the liberty and
non-discriminatory competition of domestic citizens against discriminatory
abuses of regulatory powers.[103] Freedom of trade inside the EU and inside the
US no longer depend on democratic majorities in individual member states.
Constitutional theory explains that personal self-development (human dignity)
and human rights require not only a constitutionally limited democracy but also
an 'economic constitution' protecting the general citizen interest ('public interest') in open and non-discriminatory division of labour among free citizens:
'government failures' and 'market failures' must be constitutionally constrained
not only in *political markets* but no less in *economic markets* so as to protect
human dignity, freedom and equal citizen rights against abuses of public power
as well as of private power.[104]

State governments in the EU and in the US are no longer granted powers to
distort competition and redistribute income among domestic citizens by means
of discriminatory trade restrictions inside federal states and inside the EC.
Foreign policy powers to tax domestic citizens by means of discriminatory tariffs
and restrictions of transnational trade transactions call for similar constitutional
limitations and safeguards of the public interest. Constitutional theory suggests

---

[99] Cf, E.U. Petersmann, 'Constitutional Primacy and Indivisibility of Human Rights? The Unfin-
ished "Human Rights Revolution" and the Emerging Global Integration Law', in S. Griller (ed),
International Economic Governance and Non-Economic Issues (2003) 211–266.

[100] For empirical evidence supporting this 'democratic peace hypothesis' see P.K. Huth & T.L.
Allee, *The Democratic Peace and Territorial Conflict in the Twentieth Century* (2002).

[101] On the need for a 'foreign policy constitution' see E.U. Petersmann, 'The Foreign Policy
Constitution of the EC: A Kantian Perspective', in U. Immenga, W. Möschel & D. Reuter (eds),
Festschrift für E.Mestmäcker (1996) 433–448.

[102] Cf, A.M. Slaughter, 'The Real New World Order' (1997) 76 *Foreign Affairs* 183.

[103] For a comparative study of constitutional and judicial protection of liberal trade in federal
states (eg, US, Switzerland, Germany) and in the EC see Petersmann, supra note 41.

[104] On this common constitutional dilemma ('paradox of freedom') of market economies and
democracies see eg, G. Amato, *Antitrust and the Bounds of Power* (1997); D. Gerber, *Law and
Competition in Twentieth Century Europe* (1998); Petersmann, supra note 41, ch III.

various techniques and incentives for negotiating long-term constraints 'behind a veil of uncertainty' so that negotiators focus on their common long-term interests rather than on their conflicting short-term interests. Inside Europe and inside NAFTA—albeit not yet in transatlantic relations—citizens have succeeded in 'decentralizing' and 'de-politicizing' international disputes by defining the 'public interest' in terms of equal citizen rights, including private rights of access to domestic and international courts mandated to protect individual rights against abuses of powers at home and abroad.[105]

If transatlantic economic and political relations are examined from such a constitutional citizen perspective for their capacity to protect equal freedoms and non-discriminatory competition among citizens as welfare-increasing con-flict-prevention strategies, the absence of constitutional safeguards of a liberal and non-discriminatory transatlantic market, and the lack of effective parliamentary and judicial control of the EC's common commercial policy (cf, Article 133 EC Treaty), are signs of 'constitutional failures': the frequent transatlantic economic disputes and violations of the WTO's legal constraints on discretionary trade policy powers are primarily due to 'policy failures' by governments that pursue their political self-interests rather than the general citizen interest in open markets and rule of law. As EU citizens have not agreed to the frequent discriminatory market restrictions in violation of WTO rules, such restrictions of the freedom and consumer welfare of EU citizens lack democratic legitimacy.

Can the Transatlantic Partnership institutions contribute to the demo-cratic consensus-building for constitutional reforms protecting an open, non-discriminatory transatlantic market maximizing equal freedom and consumer welfare of EU and US citizens? Palmeter's analysis of the 'contingency protection regime' recognizes that, for domestic policy reasons, the needed reforms may be politically acceptable only through reciprocal agreements rather than unilat-erally: 'should the EC and the US both favour liberalization of the regime, it is doubtful that they would meet serious opposition in the WTO'.[106]

US Presidents have often emphasized the moral underpinnings of free trade: '[o]pen trade is not just an economic opportunity, it is a moral impera-tive'.[107] Yet, there is a widespread misconception in the US that transnational guarantees of individual rights and private access to international adjudication—as they have become accepted by all EC states—are inconsistent with na-tional sovereignty and parliamentary democracy in the US.[108] The *internal* EU

---

[105] Cf, A.M. Slaughter & L. Helfer, 'Toward a Theory of Effective Supranational Adjudication' (1997) 107 *Yale Law Journal* 273.

[106] See the case-study by Palmeter.

[107] US President Bush, who continued, '[t]rade creates jobs for the unemployed. When we negotiate for open markets, we are providing new hope for the world's poor. And when we promote open trade, we are promoting political freedom. Societies that open to commerce across their borders will open to democracy within their borders, not always immediately, and not always smoothly, but in good time' (*Wall Street Journal*, 15 May 2001).

[108] Cf, Barfield, supra note 19. On the EU's move to a new concept of pooled and limited sovereignty, and the US's new insistence on 'external sovereignty' and hegemonic freedom from

experience—that rule of law *among* nations is no less important than *within* nations, and international adjudication can limit abuses of foreign policy powers—underlies some of the bold EU proposals for further *legalization* of the WTO dispute settlement system, for instance by moving from ad hoc to more permanent WTO panellists, by converting the mandate of WTO Appellate Body members into full-time appointments, introducing a new remand authority for the Appellate Body, and strengthening WTO rules on implementation of dispute settlement rulings.[109] The EU and US governments emphasize, nonetheless, that the only rights for private parties under the WTO dispute settlement system can be rights to transparency and to presentation of 'amicus curiae' briefs.

Human rights revolutions and constitutional democracies have usually emerged through bottom-up struggles by citizens and by courageous judges rather than through top-down reforms by benevolent rulers. Since World War II, transatlantic co-operation among citizens across the Atlantic continues to expand into ever broader fields. Citizens increasingly criticize the state-centred paradigms of classical international law, and the exclusion of the European Parliament from the common commercial policy powers of the EC (cf, Article 133 EC), as anachronistic for transatlantic division of labour among free citizens in constitutional democracies. Just as all 25 governments in the EC and accession countries have recognized that national and international government powers must be constitutionally limited by 'inalienable human rights' and by free movements of goods, services, persons and capital as fundamental rights of EU citizens, the rational self-interests of EU and US citizens in open and non-discriminatory co-operation across the Atlantic, and in more effective constitutional restraints on abuses of public and private power in transatlantic relations, are likely to lead to increasing democratic challenges of the frequent trade restrictions introduced by EU and US governments in violation of WTO rules ratified by domestic parliaments. Protecting constitutional rights of EU and US citizens to non-discriminatory market competition and rule of law across the Atlantic offers the most effective and most democratic dispute prevention strategy. Without stronger constitutional safeguards, protectionist producer interests will continue to prevail in many areas of transatlantic relations.

C. Dispute-prevention through respect for non-discriminatory policy instruments

Ethics, economics, human rights and constitutional law teach that *non-discriminatory* national rules may legitimately differ from country to country depending on the value preferences and 'social contract' of their citizens. As the mutual advantages of voluntary co-operation among free citizens do not depend

international legal constraints, see R.O. Keohane, 'Ironies of Sovereignty: The EU and the United States' (2002) 40 *Journal of Common Market Studies* 743–765.

109 See, Contribution of the European Communities and its Member States to the Improvement of the WTO Dispute Settlement Understanding, Communication from the EC, WTO Doc. TN/DS/W/1, 13 March 2002.

on the nationality of the producers, investors, traders and consumers involved, government powers to adopt *discriminatory* market access restrictions and other welfare-reducing market distortions need to be constitutionally restrained not only inside states but also across frontiers. Domestic policy discretion regarding *non-discriminatory* policy instruments, however, needs to be constitutionally protected.[110]

WTO dispute resolution is often facilitated by the economic insight that WTO requirements to remove discriminatory trade restrictions are mutually beneficial; the country 'losing' a WTO dispute settlement proceeding retains its policy discretion protected by WTO law to pursue its policy objectives through more efficient, non-discriminatory policy instruments. For instance, GATT's border adjustment rules (in Articles II, III and VI) leave every country four options regarding non-discriminatory product taxes and product regulations:[111] (1) to apply internal product taxes and other product regulations to domestic and imported products alike (eg, so as to prevent or internalize 'consumption externalities', such as health risks and environmental harm, pursuant to the 'destination principle'); (2) to exempt exported products from domestic taxes and regulations on the assumption that they will be subject to the taxes and product regulations in the importing country; (3) to subject traded products to 'double taxation' and 'double regulation' in both the exporting and importing country; or (4) to exempt traded products from taxes and regulations in both the exporting and importing country. The GATS and TRIPS agreements likewise set out minimum standards that leave each WTO member large discretion in many policy areas (such as competition, investment, environmental and social policies).

GATT rules only exceptionally permit subjecting imported products to domestic *process and production methods*. 'Production externalities' can usually be addressed more efficiently in the country of production whose regulatory sovereignty over domestic production should prevail unless there are 'externalities' adversely affecting the importing country. GATT's border adjustment rules, and GATT's safeguard clauses for the supply of non-economic national and international public goods, are widely considered to be consistent with economic theory.[112] 'Regulatory disputes' may be avoided more efficiently by 'regulatory competition' than by 'regulatory harmonization'.[113]

---

[110] On the protection of domestic policy autonomy in GATT/WTO law (eg Articles III, XVI, XX, XXVIII GATT, Articles VI and XIX GATS, Articles 8, 30, 31, 40 of the TRIPS Agreement, see Petersmann, *Constitutional Economics, Human Rights and the Future of the WTO*, supra note 41, chapter VII.

[111] Cf, F. Roessler, 'Diverging Domestic Policies and Multilateral Trade Integration', in J.N. Bhagwati & R.E. Hudec (eds), *Fair Trade and Harmonization: Prerequisites for Free Trade?*, Vol 2 (1996) 21 *et seq.*

[112] Cf, E.U. Petersmann, *The Need for Integrating Trade and Competition Rules in the WTO World Trade and Legal System* (1996) 17–19; 'International Trade Law and International Environmental Law: Environmental Taxes and Border Tax Adjustments in WTO Law and EC Law', in R.L. Revesz, P. Sands & R.B. Stewart (eds), *Environmental Law, the Economy and Sustainable Development* (2000) 127–155.

[113] Cf, D.C. Esty & D. Gerardin (eds), *Regulatory Competition and Economic Integration* (2001), who conclude, '[t]here is no simple answer to the question of whether regulatory competition or

Transatlantic relations will remain characterized by competition among individuals, among companies and governments. The WTO remains the most important forum for negotiating transatlantic rules on liberalization of market access barriers, on minimum standards for the harmonization of domestic laws, and for the multilateral settlement of international economic disputes. Just as many disputes among NAFTA countries are submitted to WTO dispute settlement procedures rather than to NAFTA dispute settlement mechanisms, the 'external effects' of many transatlantic disputes can be avoided better through multilateral rather than bilateral dispute prevention and dispute settlement mechanisms.

The evolving WTO case-law (eg, on unilateral uses of Article XX GATT in cases of 'inter-jurisdictional externalities') reflects the need for 'dynamic jurisprudence' that can help to adapt national and international law to the changing environment in which private actors and governments compete. For instance, in response to the justified criticism of the 1991 GATT panel finding that US import restrictions on tuna were not 'necessary' for the protection of dolphins in the High Seas, the WTO jurisprudence on Article XX GATT has considerably evolved and now admits unilateral import restrictions (eg, by the US on shrimps) if they are part of a non-discriminatory safeguard system (eg, for the protection of highly migratory sea turtles) even before negotiations on a multilateral agreement have succeeded.[114] Unilateral import restrictions as a means of enabling importing countries to influence production methods in exporting countries are also used by the EC (see, eg, the EC ban on furs caught with cruel animal traps, EC restrictions on genetically modified organisms). Apart from settling disputes, WTO jurisprudence contributes to prevention of future disputes through new interpretations of WTO rules that can deal more effectively with 'prisoner dilemma situations' endangering collective interests (eg, in protection of the environment, non-discriminatory conditions of competition, rule of law).

D. 'Negative comity', 'positive comity' and 'mutual recognition' as conflict-prevention strategies for co-ordinating 'legitimate regulatory differences'

There remain fundamental differences between constitutional traditions in the EU and in the US (eg, as regards economic and social human rights), their legal and federal structures and policy-making processes (eg, in the EU as an international organization with much more limited powers, without effective parliamentary control in the foreign policy area, and without EU membership in most worldwide organizations). The powers and policy approaches of EU and US regulatory agencies also diverge in many respects (eg, vis-à-vis science-based

---

regulatory cooperation promotes efficiency and enhances welfare. Instead, a particularized inquiry into the specific regulatory domain is required' (p xxxi).

[114] See the Panel report of June 2001 (WT/DS58/RW) and Appellate Body report of October 2001 (WT/DS58/AB/RW) on United States—Import Prohibition of Certain Shrimp and Shrimp Products—Recourse to Article 21.5 by Malaysia.

health and agricultural policies, the *precautionary principle* in environmental law and policy). The hegemonic power of the US, and the effective democratic control of foreign policy-making by the US Congress, entail an often sceptical attitude of the US vis-à-vis international organizations (eg, on international standardization) where US representatives tend to be outnumbered by representatives from EC member states. Different democratic value-preferences (eg, greater reliance on individual responsibility, market mechanisms and science-based standards in the US) and different policy-making processes make 'legitimate regulatory differences' and 'regulatory competition' in transatlantic relations inevitable.

Respect for 'sovereign equality' and for legitimate regulatory differences must therefore remain the '*Grundnorm*' for international governance in transatlantic relations.[115] The resulting 'regulatory competition' requires 'negative' and 'positive comity' and 'mutual recognition'—by legislators, regulators, administrators and judges—of different but equivalent rules and standards in separate jurisdictions. The case-study by Mehta illustrates how 'negative comity' and 'positive comity' obligations in the EU-US Agreements on Co-operation in the Field of Competition Policy have enhanced 'transgovernmental dispute prevention' among EU and US competition authorities in more than 300 cases.[116] The 1997 EU-US agreements on mutual recognition of divergent but equivalent regulatory standards (eg, for telecommunications, medical devices, pharmaceuticals, electronic equipment, recreational crafts, veterinary examinations) reflect the same insight that mutual recognition of different procedures on the two sides of the Atlantic (eg, for standard-setting) may offer a more democratic, and more decentralized method of transatlantic regulatory co-ordination and avoidance of regulatory conflicts than common standards adopted by majority decisions in international standard-setting bodies that are not subject to effective democratic and judicial scrutiny.[117]

E. Need to distinguish 'primary conflicts' over non-discriminatory measures from 'secondary international conflicts' over discriminatory restrictions or distortions

International lawyers tend to distinguish international disputes according to the international legal rules concerned (eg, 'GATT disputes', 'GATS disputes', 'TRIPS disputes', investment disputes). A more relevant distinction relates to whether international disputes involve legal conflicts of national 'public

---

[115] Cf, A.M. Slaughter, 'Agencies on the loose? Holding government networks accountable', in Berman, Herdegen & Lindseth, supra note 3, 521, 536 *et seq*.
[116] See, in addition to the case-study by Mehta, Y. Devuyst, 'Transatlantic Competition Relations', in Pollack & Shaffer, supra note 2, 127–152.
[117] See the case-study by K. Abbott in Part II of this book as well as M. Egan, 'Mutual Recognition and Standard Setting: Public and Private Strategies for Governing Markets', in Pollack & Shaffer, supra note 2, 179–210.

interests' *between states* to be decided on the basis of international law ('primary conflicts'), or legal conflicts of interests *within states* (eg, protectionist producer interests vs national consumer interests in liberal trade) that could be settled in domestic courts but, for domestic policy reasons, 'spill over' to the intergovernmental level ('secondary disputes'). 'Primary conflicts' usually relate to legitimate *non-discriminatory* legislative or other measures (eg, on food security, environmental resources) that are consistent with the domestic constitution and laws of the country concerned (eg, the EC complaint against Section 110(5) of the US Copyright Act; the various US complaints against alleged failures of Denmark, Greece, Ireland and Portugal to adequately protect intellectual property rights). The non-discriminatory nature, domestic legality and democratic legitimacy of such legislative measures may call for judicial deference at the international level and may make the implementation of a negative WTO dispute settlement ruling politically more difficult.

'Secondary disputes' are typically about discriminatory policy measures that are often inconsistent with international law (eg, WTO rules) and reduce the economic welfare of the country concerned. They may either be lawful under domestic laws (eg, in the case of the WTO panel and appellate proceedings against the US Anti-dumping Act of 1916[118] and against the US tax legislation establishing special tax treatment for FSCs[119]). Or the discriminatory measures may be inconsistent not only with international law but also with domestic law (especially if international law forms an 'integral part' of domestic law as in the EC) in view of their discriminatory and welfare-reducing effects (eg, in case of the EC import restrictions on bananas). Since the contested measures discriminate in favour of domestic groups (eg, producer interests) at the expense of other domestic groups (eg, consumer interests), such disputes may be more effectively resolved in domestic courts directly among the affected citizens concerned—provided domestic judges are not prevented from applying the relevant international rules ratified by domestic parliaments as legal constraints for domestic policy-making.

The case-studies identify some 'secondary' transatlantic disputes that could be settled through recourse to *domestic courts*. For example, the EC complaint in the WTO against the discriminatory trade effects of the 1996 Act Regulating State Contracts with Companies Doing Business with or in Burma (Myanmar), adopted by the Commonwealth of Massachusetts, was withdrawn after the US District Court[120] and the US Supreme Court[121] decided that the Massachusetts Burma law was an unconstitutional infringement of the federal government's power over foreign affairs.[122] Recourse to international procedures may no longer be necessary if the domestic courts declare the contested measure illegal. This is particularly so if domestic courts are required to apply not only domestic

---

[118] See the Appellate Body report in document WT/DS136/AB/R, 28 August 2000.
[119] See the Appellate Body report in document WT/DS108/AB/R, 24 February 2000.
[120] See (1999) *International Legal Materials* (ILM) 665.   [121] See (2000) *ILM* 1235.
[122] See the case-study by Professor Schaefer.

law but also international law (as in the case of domestic *challenge proceedings* pursuant to Article XX of the WTO Agreement on Government Procurement). Yet, as long as EC and US courts are prevented from applying WTO rules, most 'secondary' transatlantic disputes (eg, about the EC import restrictions on bananas, US import restrictions on steel) spill over into intergovernmental transatlantic disputes.

F. Decentralization and prevention of 'secondary international disputes' through access to domestic courts

Many trade policy measures (such as tariffs, anti-dumping measures, counter-vailing duties, safeguard measures) can be challenged simultaneously by private operators in domestic courts and by their home state in WTO dispute settlement proceedings. WTO rules do not require prior exhaustion of local remedies before initiation of an intergovernmental WTO dispute settlement proceeding.[123]

1. *Access to domestic courts as conflict-prevention strategy?*

In view of the strict deadlines for WTO dispute settlement proceedings, recourse to WTO procedures may enable a speedier and—if domestic courts refuse to review the consistency of the contested measure with international law—a more comprehensive settlement of disputes. In the US, Section 102 of the 1994 Uruguay Round Agreements Act of the US Congress requires that '[n]o provision of any of the Uruguay Round Agreements, nor the application of any such provision to any person or circumstances, that is inconsistent with any law of the United States shall have effect'. Moreover, no person other than the US government 'shall have any cause of action or defense under any of the Uruguay Round Agreements' or challenge 'any action or inaction . . . of the United States, any State, or any political subdivision of a state on the ground that such action or inaction is inconsistent' with one of the Uruguay Round Agreements.[124] WTO law is thus unlikely to be directly applied by US courts in any proceeding other than a proceeding brought by the US government for the purpose of enforcing obligations under these agreements. To the extent that the Uruguay Round Agreements Act does not specifically implement the international obligations, Section 102(a)(2) requires prior US legislation and US regulatory powers to prevail.

In the EU, the ECJ has many times confirmed that 'the EEC is a Community based on the rule of law, inasmuch as neither its Member States nor its institutions can avoid a review of the question whether the measures adopted by them are in conformity with the basic constitutional charter, the Treaty'. According to the ECJ, the EC Treaty 'established a complete system of legal

---

[123] On the non-application of the 'prior exhaustion of local remedies' rule in GATT and WTO law see, E.U. Petersmann, supra note 9, at 240–244.

[124] Section 102, Uruguay Round Agreements Act, Pub.L.No 103–465, 108 Stat. 4809 (1994).

remedies and procedures designed to permit the Court of Justice to review the legality of measures adopted by the institutions'.[125] The ECJ has also consistently held that international treaties and general international law binding on the EC form an integral part of the Community legal system with legal primacy over secondary EC law.[126] When the EC Commission initiated an infringement proceeding under Article 226 EC Treaty against Germany for the latter's failure to comply with the International Dairy Agreement negotiated in the context of GATT 1947, the ECJ applied these GATT obligations without any comment. The ECJ concluded that Community law had to be construed in conformity with international treaty obligations, and Germany had failed to comply with the GATT and EC obligations concerned.[127] Hence, as in the US, WTO obligations can be enforced through domestic courts by the federal government (EC) vis-à-vis member states. This recourse to domestic courts can obviate WTO dispute settlement proceedings by third WTO members.

2. Can 'judicial protectionism' be overcome through reciprocal agreements?

The ECJ has recognized the judicial applicability of GATT and WTO rules in cases concerning member states.[128] Yet, whenever EC member states and EC citizens complained over the violation of GATT and WTO rules by the EC, none of the more than 35 GATT and WTO dispute settlement findings against the EC was ever taken into account by the ECJ. GATT and WTO rules were recognized by the ECJ as relevant criteria for the interpretation of Community rules only if EC regulations explicitly referred to the implementation of such GATT and WTO obligations.[129]

Even though many GATT and WTO guarantees of freedom and non-discrimination are unconditional and more precise than the vague and incomplete customs union rules of the EC Treaty (eg, Articles 25 and 28), the ECJ denied the right of EU member states as well as of EU citizens to invoke these rules directly before the courts.[130] The legal arguments advanced by the ECJ (such as the safeguard clauses in GATT/WTO law, the 'flexibility' of certain GATT/WTO commitments, the possibility of avoiding countermeasures by agreed compensation pursuant to Article 22 DSU) are in apparent contradiction with other judgments by the same court (eg, in the *Kupferberg* case) and with the

[125] Case 294/83 *Partie Ecologiste Les Verts v European Parliament* [1986] ECR 1339, consideration 23.

[126] See Case C-162/96 *Racke GmbH & Co v Hauptzollant Mainz* [1998] ECR I-3655; Case C-61/94 *Commission v Germany (International Dairy Agreement)* [1996] ECR I-3989.

[127] Case C-61/94, ibid eg para 52.

[128] See supra note 127 and the more recent Case C-53/96 *Hermès International v FHT Marketing Choice BV* [1998] ECR I-3603 and Case C-300/98 *Parfums Christian Dior SA v Tuk Consultancy BV* [2000] ECR I-11307.

[129] See notably Case 70/87 *Fediol v Commission* [1989] ECR 1781; Case C-69/89 *Nakajima v Council* [1991] ECR I-2069.

[130] See notably Case C-280/93 *Germany v Council (Banana Case)* [1994] ECR I-4973; Case C-149/96 *Portugal v Council* [1999] ECR I-8395.

precise and unconditional nature of many GATT/WTO rules.[131] The ECJ's true reasons appear to be *judicial self-restraint* in view of the lack of reciprocal 'direct applicability' of WTO rules in other WTO countries and the judicial deference of the court vis-à-vis the foreign policy powers of the EC.

Thus, when Germany requested the ECJ to declare the EC's 'framework agreement on bananas' of 1994 to be in violation of EC law and GATT law, the ECJ annulled the EC's approval of this agreement on the ground of inconsistency of the discriminatory import restrictions with the non-discrimination requirements of EC law. The more precise non-discrimination requirements of GATT law were, however, not mentioned by the court notwithstanding their legal status as an 'integral part of the Community legal system'.[132] It was only through subsequent WTO dispute settlement proceedings that the US could achieve a WTO ruling that the EC's import restrictions were also inconsistent with Articles I, III, X and XI:1 GATT, as well as with Article 1 of the WTO Licensing Agreement and Articles II and XVII GATS.[133] Yet, such intergovernmental WTO disputes, and the high economic costs of illegal trade restrictions and countermeasures, could have been prevented by enabling EU and US citizens to do what they do inside the EC, inside the US and also in NAFTA chapter 11 investment disputes, ie, to invoke and enforce precise and unconditional guarantees of freedom and non-discrimination in domestic courts.

3. *Prevention of intergovernmental disputes by private access to a Transatlantic Market Court?*

In view of the often very long procedures and inadequate international legal expertise in domestic courts, another possibility of preventing intergovernmental dispute settlement procedures and mutually welfare-reducing trade sanctions could be to conclude a reciprocal EU-US agreement on the application and enforcement of certain precise and unconditional WTO rules through a joint Transatlantic Market Court. Private access to such a transatlantic court, composed of highly respected EU and US judges (eg, former Supreme Court judges), could offer a 'win-win-situation' for all governments and private actors involved:

(1) Private complaints and domestic judges could prevent the emergence of intergovernmental disputes by clarifying, applying and enforcing mutually agreed WTO rules vis-à-vis contested domestic policy measures.

(2) Rather than petitioning their home governments (eg, pursuant to Section 301 of the US Trade Act and the corresponding EC Trade Barriers

---

[131] This was rightly criticized by Advocate-General Tesauro in Case *C-53/96 Hermès*, supra note 128.

[132] See Case C-122/95 *Germany v Council (Banana Framework Agreement)* [1998] ECR I-973, and Case C-364/95 *T Port GmbH v Hauptzollamt Hamburg-Jonas* [1998] ECR I-1023.

[133] On the 12 GATT and WTO panel, appellate and arbitration reports on the inconsistency of the EC's import restrictions on bananas with GATT and WTO law see E.U. Petersmann, 'The WTO Panel and Arbitration Reports on the EC Banana Regime' 3 *Bridges Between Trade and Sustainable Development* (April 1999) 3–4.

Regulation) to initiate WTO dispute settlement proceedings, private operators would themselves fully control judicial proceedings and would have to
act more responsibly.

(3) Private actors and domestic judges could act as guardians of the rule of law
in transatlantic relations, thereby promoting transgovernmental and transnational integration.

(4) In the EU, such an agreement would contribute to strengthening the rule of
law and democratic legitimacy also *inside* the EC in view of the legal status
of WTO law as an integral part of the Community legal system with legal
primacy vis-à-vis secondary EC law. Even in the US, such an agreement
would correspond well to the requirement of the US Constitution that 'all
treaties made . . . under the authority of the United States shall be the supreme law of the land' (Article VI, clause 2).

(5) By opening such a reciprocal EU-US agreement to other WTO members
(notably in Europe and North America), decentralized dispute prevention
and dispute settlement could be promoted also in relations with third countries and thereby strengthen and 'de-politicize' the intergovernmental, multilateral WTO dispute settlement system.

(6) By promoting co-operation between national and international judges, the
agreement could help to overcome the introverted disregard of international
law by judges and policy-makers in the US, in the EU and in most other
WTO member states. The EC experience suggests that co-operation between
national and EC judges can render dispute settlement on both national and
international levels more effective. As in European integration, such judicial
co-operation could evolve into a powerful motor for promoting human rights
and rule of law in transatlantic relations and beyond.

G. Criteria for distinguishing 'positive conflicts' from 'negative conflicts'[134]

In both the EU and the US, individual access to courts is recognized as a human
right and essential condition of rule of law and constitutional democracy.[135]
Legal conflicts and their judicial settlement are viewed positively as a means of
peaceful change and as indispensable engines for legal and judicial clarification,
application and enforcement of rules. In international relations among democratic and non-democratic states, conflicts are often perceived negatively in
view of the risks of power politics and military escalation. In transatlantic
relations among democracies, however, the historical reality of 'democratic
peace' calls for a positive and differentiated view of transatlantic conflicts of
interests.

---

[134] The term 'positive conflict' is used by Slaughter, supra note 115, at 542.
[135] See, eg, C. Harlow, 'Access to Justice as a Human Right', in P. Alston *et al* (eds), *The EU and
Human Rights* (1999) 187–213; J. Hart Ely, *Democracy and Distrust: A Theory of Judicial Review*
(1980).

1. *'Positive conflicts' as indispensable part of constitutional democracies: substantive and due process functions of judicial review*

In transatlantic relations among constitutional democracies, international guarantees (eg, in WTO law) of individual freedom across frontiers and domestic constitutional guarantees of equal individual freedoms serve complementary functions. Just as human rights law requires that, 'in the exercise of his rights and freedoms, everyone shall be subject only to such limitations as are determined by law solely for the purpose of securing due recognition and respect for the rights and freedoms of others and of meeting the just requirements of morality, public order and the general welfare in a democratic society',[136] the 'general exceptions' in WTO law and EC law require governmental trade restrictions to comply with principles of non-discrimination, necessity and proportionality (cf, eg, Article XX GATT and Article XIV GATS) subject to judicial review.[137] In both domestic and international law, guarantees of access to courts are indispensable safeguards against abuses of regulatory powers. By enabling citizens and courts to review whether individual rights have been properly respected and balanced in legislative and administrative decision-making processes, human rights and access to courts promote an ever more precise clarification, application and enforcement of human rights and of legislative and administrative rules, notwithstanding the need for judicial deference vis-à-vis legislative and administrative 'margins of regulatory discretion'.[138] Apart from their 'substantive function' to promote the coherent interpretation and legal protection of equal freedoms of individuals and of states across frontiers, judicial settlement of disputes also serves 'procedural functions' to enhance 'due process of law' and 'access to justice'.[139] Transatlantic governance should serve as a model for the rest of the world in promoting judicial protection of equal freedoms and of non-discriminatory competition among free citizens across frontiers.

---

[136] Article 29:2 of the Universal Declaration of Human Rights of 1948 which, today, is widely recognized in state practice as reflecting 'general principles' of international law. Also in the field of economic and social human rights, there is worldwide recognition (eg, in Article 4 of the 1966 UN Covenant on Economic, Social and Cultural Human Rights which has been ratified today by some 140 states) that 'the State may subject such rights only to such limitations as are determined by law only in so far as this may be compatible with the nature of these rights and solely for the purpose of promoting the general welfare in a democratic society'.

[137] On these parallels between human rights law, WTO law and EC law see Petersmann, supra note 50.

[138] See, eg, H.C. Yourow, *The Margin of Appreciation Doctrine in the Dynamics of European Human Rights Jurisprudence* (1996). See also the criticism by Franck (supra note 21) that the 'political question doctrine' used by US courts goes far beyond what is required by human rights and constitutional law.

[139] Cf, R.E. Hudec, 'The Role of Judicial Review in Preserving Liberal Foreign Trade Policies', in Hilf & Petersmann, supra note 21, at 503–518; E.U. Petersmann, *The GATT/WTO Dispute Settlement System*, supra note 9, at 237–240.

60 Ernst-Ulrich Petersmann

2. 'Negative conflicts' and 'wrong' dispute settlement cases

'Primary international disputes'—for example, over non-discriminatory labelling requirements for genetically modified food—reflect conflicting values and regulatory *conflicts among countries* that may be prevented and settled best through *international* policy co-ordination, regulatory co-operation or *international* negotiations on new international rules (eg, for the treatment of genetically modified organisms).

'Secondary international disputes'—for example, about discriminatory government measures that are inconsistent with international and domestic law (including international law as 'supreme law of the land')—reflect *conflicts of interests within countries* that may be prevented or settled more efficiently by domestic law and domestic courts. Several case-studies have identified transatlantic disputes where recourse to intergovernmental dispute settlement proceedings could have been avoided through judicial recognition by domestic courts of the WTO-inconsistency of the measures concerned (eg, the EC import restrictions on bananas challenged by US companies in the ECJ). The possible interactions between national and international dispute settlement proceedings are illustrated by the EC's 1987 complaint against Section 337 of the US Tariff Act of 1930. The Dutch exporter had first challenged the 'exclusion order' by the US International Trade Commission in the Court of Appeals for the Federal Circuit; following the court's adverse judgment and disregard of the relevant GATT rules, the EC initiated dispute settlement proceedings under the GATT before the US Supreme Court decided on the complainant's application for review of the exclusion order.[140]

Some case-studies have identified disputes which, because of their far-reaching political implications, lent themselves better to political rather than to judicial dispute settlement methods (eg, the dispute over the 'Helms-Burton legislation' of the US Congress). The fact that, since the entry into force of the EC Treaty in 1958, only one dispute among EC member states led to a judgment by the ECJ[141] offers ample evidence for the possibility of preventing or 'decentralizing' disputes among states through constitutional rules. If an EC member state does not comply with EC rules, other governments usually leave it to EC citizens or to the European Commission to enforce EC rules through the courts. Similarly, chapter 11 of NAFTA leaves it to private complainants to enforce NAFTA's investment rules through international investor-state arbitration. Notwithstanding the shortcomings of secretive arbitration focusing on investors' rights under chapter 11 of NAFTA, espousal of citizen rights by way of 'diplomatic protection', and the resulting transformation of private disputes into intergovernmental disputes, remain second-best policy instruments.

The case-study by Hudec on the 'FSC dispute' concludes that submission of 'wrong cases' to adjudication may lead to 'negative conflicts' whose 'political

---

[140] See Basic Instruments and Selected Documents 36th Supplement, GATT 1990, at 345, 354.
[141] See supra note 31.

costs' may be higher than the gains from 'legal victories', for instance if they endanger democratic acceptance of international adjudication. The case-studies by Ambassadors Paemen and Aaron on the Helms-Burton dispute emphasize the advantages of political compromises based on 'joint problem-solving' rather than 'the bid and ask format of typical trade negotiations'.[142] Yet, 'when a regulatory issue involves powerful private interests, governments often cannot resolve them unless they are recognized early or time is left to calm things down'.[143] Political constraints and consumer attitudes may limit the utility of WTO dispute settlement rulings. In the dispute over the EC's import restrictions on genetically modified organisms, for example, the US has for many years 'refrained from going to the WTO because even a victory there would not induce the European consumer to ingest more GMO foods'.[144] Governments may also prefer to avoid judicial proceedings if 'regulators and trade officials know that rules are passed that are senseless, merely to respond to public concern no matter how unfounded'.[145]

US trade politicians have occasionally complained that some WTO complaints by the EC were not 'producer-driven' but 'revenge cases' motivated by bureaucratic self-interests in balancing the scores of 'WTO victories' and in countering US pressures for 'carousel sanctions'. Yet, it is far from obvious why 'producer-driven complaints' are more legitimate than 'public interest complaints' and 'rule-enforcement complaints'. Rule of law requires a legal culture and 'judicial culture' that recognizes public as well as private complaints and adversarial judicial procedures as legitimate.

Yet, certain rules may unduly discourage negotiations and induce 'too many disputes' leading to a 'litigious society' with unnecessarily high transaction costs. Economics explains, for instance, that 'external effects' (eg, in case of restraints of competition, environmental pollution, medical mistreatment) can be prevented ('internalized') most effectively through private rights of action, legal liability rules, judicial remedies and constitutional limitations of policy discretion. Yet, views about 'optimal litigation rules' and 'negative conflicts' differ. For instance, Europeans often criticize private rights to 'treble damages', 'class actions' and 'contingency fees' in US antitrust laws and consumer protection laws as 'excessive'. Americans, by contrast, attribute the inadequate private competition law enforcement in Europe to inadequate legal and judicial protection of private rights to damages, to restitution (eg, recovery of payments made in violation of EC law), interim relief and collective claims.[146]

---

[142] Quotation from the conference paper by Ambassador Aaron, at 4 (not published in this book).
[143] Aaron, ibid, 2.
[144] Aaron, ibid, 2. In December 2002, following an EC Council decision to impose labelling requirements on imports of genetically modified organisms, US congressmen publicly requested the US Trade Representative to challenge the EC's labelling requirements in WTO dispute settlement proceedings. In May 2003, the US and several other WTO members requested consultations under the WTO Dispute Settlement Understanding on the EC's import restrictions on GMOs.
[145] Aaron, ibid, 3.
[146] Cf, eg, C.A. Jones, *Private Enforcement of Antitrust Law in the EU, UK and USA* (1999).

3. Legal criteria for defining 'negative conflicts': the example of domestic court proceedings without effective legal remedies

The effectiveness of judicial remedies depends, *inter alia*, on the application of all relevant legal rules by the courts. Transatlantic disputes caused by violations of WTO rules cannot be effectively settled by domestic courts if the judges do not interpret and apply domestic law in conformity with higher-ranking international law or, in case of conflict, ignore WTO obligations that are binding on all government institutions.

The ECJ emphasizes that Article 300(7) EC Treaty requires all EC institutions and EC member states to interpret and apply their powers in conformity with international treaties and general international law rules binding on the EC.[147] Unlike the US Congress, the EC Council has not been granted constitutional power to adopt regulations in clear violation of previously agreed international treaties. Nor does the EC Treaty exempt trade policy measures from the constitutional task assigned to the ECJ to 'ensure that in the interpretation and application of this Treaty the law is observed' (Article 220). Yet, ECJ judgments have never taken into account the more than 30 GATT and WTO dispute settlement findings against the EC; nor has the ECJ ever found an inconsistency of an EC act with GATT or WTO law. In the dispute over the EC import restrictions on bananas, the obvious disregard, by all EC institutions, of precise and unconditional GATT guarantees of freedom and non-discrimination prompted German tax courts and administrative courts to refuse to implement certain EC regulations.[148]

Should the more than 40 complaints by private economic operators and EC member states to the ECJ against the EC's manifestly illegal import restrictions on bananas be viewed as 'negative conflicts' and 'wrong cases' because they involved high economic, political and 'legal costs' without offering effective legal and judicial remedies against obvious violations of WTO rules and of EC law (eg, Article 300(7))? Even if the illegal EC regulations involved high social costs and the ECJ offered no effective judicial remedies, the adversely affected complainants cannot be blamed for seeking judicial redress from the ECJ. It was not the private access to domestic courts which caused these conflicts and 'wrong cases'; it was rather the fact that the EU governments, like the US government, do not offer effective legal and judicial remedies to domestic citizens adversely affected by WTO violations of their own governments.

4. Political criteria for defining 'negative conflicts'

Is recourse to adjudication and WTO dispute settlement proceedings 'politically wrong' if governments cannot comply with adverse dispute settlement rulings

---

[147] For a discussion of this ECJ jurisprudence see E.U. Petersmann, 'International Activities of the EU and Sovereignty of Member States', in E. Cannizzaro (ed), *The European Union as an Actor in International Relations* (2002) 321–345.

[148] For a discussion of these cases see E.U. Petersmann, 'Darf die EG das Völkerrecht ignorieren?' [1997] *European Journal of Business Law (EuZW)* 325–331.

due to strong domestic political opposition? The EC's complaint against the US Helms-Burton Act imposing sanctions on investments in Cuba, and the US complaints against the EC import restrictions on hormone-fed beef and genetically modified organisms, have been occasionally criticized as endangering the WTO dispute settlement system because the defending governments lacked political support for 'delivering' regulatory reforms. The past history of GATT and WTO dispute settlement proceedings offers, however, little guidance for identifying disputes where 'political dispute management' has been made more difficult by WTO rulings clarifying the legal obligations.

IV. Conclusion

This introductory chapter explained the EUI dispute prevention and dispute settlement project and its main policy conclusions. The overview of alternative methods of dispute prevention and dispute settlement in transatlantic relations (section I) showed not only the diversity of *intergovernmental* dispute prevention and dispute settlement mechanisms, but also an obvious lack of effective legal and judicial remedies of EU and US citizens against violations of WTO obligations by their own governments. The 14 case-studies of recent transatlantic disputes were classified into four different categories depending on the policy measures concerned and on their underlying conflicts of interests (section II). The survey of different legal, economic and political theories of dispute prevention and dispute settlement (section III) explained their different value premises (eg, focus on 'state interests', 'citizen interests' or 'Community interests') and the need for constitutional rules that (1) limit discriminatory abuses of foreign policy discretion; (2) protect domestic policy autonomy for non-discriminatory market regulations; (3) promote 'negative comity', 'positive comity' and 'mutual recognition' as conflict prevention strategies; and (4) 'decentralize' and 'de-politicize' intergovernmental disputes by empowering EU and US citizens to invoke and enforce precise and unconditional WTO guarantees of freedom and non-discrimination in domestic courts so as to promote rule of law, non-discriminatory conditions of competition and 'participatory democracy' in transatlantic relations.

The need for such constitutional rules protecting general consumer welfare and general citizen welfare is recognized for the prevention and settlement of disputes *inside* the EU and *inside* the US. Yet, transatlantic relations among EU citizens and US citizens are *not* governed by such constitutional principles of justice. Both the EU and US governments prefer to treat their citizens as objects rather than legal subjects of the international rules governing the transatlantic division of labour (notably WTO law). The EU's evolution into an 'international constitutional democracy' based on 'multi-level constitutionalism' limiting the widespread previous 'government failures' and 'constitutional failures' in Europe, and the US' evolution into the most powerful international hegemon insisting on its 'sovereign right' of 'international unilateralism' as determined by national constitutional democracy, lead to 'system frictions' that continue to prevent citizen-oriented international dispute prevention and dispute settlement methods (eg, based on a TAFTA and on direct citizen access to a Transatlantic Market Court). The policy recommendations for preventing or settling 'primary', 'secondary' and 'wrong' disputes more effectively in transatlantic relations, and for promoting 'positive disputes' and avoiding 'negative disputes', are summarized and discussed in more detail in Part IV of this book.

2

The Political Economy of
Transatlantic Trade Disputes

MARK A. POLLACK[1]

The European Union and the United States are the largest economies and the largest trade and investment partners on earth, and the interdependence of these two economies has grown rapidly in the course of the past decade. During the 1990s the volume of transatlantic trade more than doubled, making the EU and the US each other's most important trading partner. Foreign direct investment between the US and the EU has grown even more rapidly, doubling in value during the last three years of the 1990s alone; indeed, it is estimated that some 3.5 million American jobs rely on foreign investment from the EU, with a similar number of Europeans employed by US firms.

These developments have created a *de facto* transatlantic marketplace, yet they have also led to new strains on the transatlantic partnership and to a new and challenging economic agenda for EU/US co-operation. Prior to the 1990s, much of the transatlantic economic relationship was dominated by traditional trade questions such as tariffs, quotas, and other direct barriers to trade typically imposed at US and EU borders, and several of the chapters in this book examine the continuing importance of these cases in the transatlantic relationship.[2] With the decline in tariffs and quotas in most areas of transatlantic trade, however, non-tariff barriers to trade—most notably, 'behind-the-border' domestic

---

[1] This chapter draws substantially on a report prepared by the BP Chair in Transatlantic Relations (2002) for Her Majesty's Treasury (United Kingdom) and for the Ministry of Finance, Government of the Kingdom of the Netherlands. The author is grateful to the various contributors to that report, including Gregory C. Shaffer (University of Wisconsin), Rebecca Steffenson (European University Institute), and especially Alasdair Young (University of Glasgow), who prepared the original versions of Tables 4 and 5 and Appendices 1–3 for the BP Chair Report, and significantly influenced my thinking about the nature of traditional and new-style trade disputes. Thanks also to Helen Wallace, Ernst-Ulrich Petersmann, Claus-Dieter Ehlermann, Roderick Abbott, Alasdair Young, and the participants in the BP Chair Conference on 'Preventing and Settling Transatlantic Economic Disputes' (European University Institute, Florence, 4–5 May 2002) for constructive comments on earlier drafts; and to the many officials of the European Commission and the US Mission to the EU who agreed to be interviewed (most on condition of anonymity) for this research. Despite these many debts, responsibility for this chapter, including its omissions or errors, remains my own.

[2] See, inter alia, Friedl Weiss's chapter on the bananas case; David Palmeter's chapter on safeguard measures, anti-dumping, and countervailing duties; Robert Hudec's discussion of Foreign Sales Corporations (essentially, an export subsidy); and Tim Josling and Stefan Tangermann's chapter on agricultural disputes.

regulations adopted in response to legitimate public concerns about the environment, consumer protection, food safety and data privacy—have emerged alongside traditional trade barriers as the primary challenges to a mutually beneficial EU/US trade and investment relationship. Such regulatory disputes, indeed, make up the majority of the case-study chapters that follow in Part II of this book.

The transatlantic relationship has come under repeated strain during the past decade as a result of both traditional and new-style regulatory disputes, a representative sample of which are examined in detail in this volume. Such disputes, the European Commission has pointed out, concern only an estimated 1–2 per cent of the total value of transatlantic trade and investment, yet these disputes could potentially spread to other areas of the transatlantic relationship; it is therefore in the interests of both sides to ensure that such disputes are prevented from arising through timely consultations where possible, and settled efficiently and amicably in other cases. Many of these disputes—especially traditional tariff, quota, anti-dumping and subsidies disputes—can be and are dealt with effectively through the dispute settlement procedure of the World Trade Organization (WTO) to which the EU and the US are both parties. New-style regulatory disputes, however, often involve domestic laws adopted for legitimate purposes following democratic deliberation, and these disputes can place considerable strain on the WTO system, particularly in cases where the losing party would have difficulty complying with an adverse WTO ruling.

This chapter traces the emergence of new-style regulatory disputes as an increasingly common and important occurrence in the transatlantic economic partnership, and examines the variously successful efforts of the US and the EU to co-operate in preventing and settling such disputes. The chapter is not intended as a summary of the case-studies that follow—although it does draw extensively from those case-studies as well as from other primary and secondary source materials—nor does it attempt to synthesize the various analytical chapters and policy statements at the end of this volume. What this chapter *does* do, however, is to set the stage for the case-studies and other chapters in the book, by presenting briefly: the political economy of the transatlantic economic relationship (Section I); the universe of transatlantic economic disputes, including traditional and regulatory disputes (Section II); the US/EU diplomatic architecture established largely to prevent and settle such disputes (Section III); and the recent experience of transatlantic regulatory co-operation, which many authors (including this one) believe to be the most promising method of preventing new-style regulatory disputes from occurring (Section IV).

I. THE TRANSATLANTIC MARKETPLACE AND THE CHANGING EU/US ECONOMIC AGENDA

The EU and the US are the largest economies and the largest trade and investment partners on earth, and the interdependence of these two economies has grown rapidly over the course of the past decade. Taken together, the US and the EU account for roughly one half of both world GDP and global trade.

The EU and the US are also each other's most important trading partner. As Table 2.1 illustrates, the volume of EU/US trade more than doubled during the 1990s, and the two countries are currently each other's largest trading partners. Indeed, recent data on trade in services, summarized in Table 2.2, demonstrates even more clearly the importance of the transatlantic trade relationship, with the US accounting for some 40 per cent of the EU's total imports and exports of services, which in turn account for between one-third and one-half of total transatlantic trade. Furthermore, EU/US trade has been largely balanced over the decade of the 1990s.

Notwithstanding the impressive growth of EU/US trade, it is the investment relationship that most clearly distinguishes the contemporary transatlantic marketplace. As Table 2.3 makes clear, the EU in 2000 was far and away the largest investor in the US, its $794 billion in foreign direct investment (FDI) constituting 65 per cent of total FDI in the US.[3] The US is similarly the largest source of FDI in the EU, with some $561 billion invested in 2000. These high levels of EU investment are estimated to provide roughly 3.5 million jobs in the US, with a similar number of European jobs relying on US investment in the EU.[4] The large and growing investment relationship also explains a considerable portion of the recent growth in bilateral US/EU trade, since an estimated 20–30 per cent of all bilateral trade takes the form of intrafirm trade within firms operating on both sides of the Atlantic.

With the simultaneous growth of transatlantic trade and investment and the gradual decline in EU and US tariffs and quotas following successive waves of

TABLE 2.1. Transatlantic trade, 1980–2000, in millions of euros (share of EU total)

	1980	1990	2000
EU imports from US	50,733 (18.1%)	88,957 (20.5%)	197,992 (19.3%)
EU exports to US	29,543 (14.0%)	82,004 (20.0%)	232,037 (24.7%)

Source: DG Trade, http://europa.eu.int/comm/trade/pdf/bilstat/econo_usa.xls

TABLE 2.2. Transatlantic trade in services, in millions of euros (share of EU total)

	1998	1999	2000
EU imports from US	79,874 (36.0%)	99,042 (40.9%)	116,474 (40.7%)
EU exports to US	77,039 (33.4%)	92,199 (37.3%)	117,403 (40.3%)

Source: DG Trade, http://europa.eu.int/comm/trade/pdf/bilstat/econo_usa.xls

[3] *The EU and the 50 US States*, website of the EU Mission to the US, http://www.eurunion.org/partner/usstates/usstates.htm. Consulted on 21 January 2003.
[4] *The EU and the 50 US States*, op cit.

TABLE 2.3. Transatlantic foreign direct investment, in millions of euros (share of EU total)

	1998	1999	2000
US FDI flows into EU	60,697 (57.1%)	83,798 (75.4%)	121,271 (68.8%)
EU FDI flows to US	133,416 (60.2%)	196,794 (63.2%)	172,027 (47.5%)
US FDI stocks in EU	366,462 (60%)	439,928 (60.9%)	561,199 (62.5%)
EU FDI stocks in US	398,190 (48.3%)	622,496 (52.4%)	794,523 (51.3%)

Source: DG Trade, http://europa.eu.int/comm/trade/pdf/bilstat/econo_usa.xls

trade liberalization, the transatlantic economic agenda has been transformed. Prior to the 1990s, much of the EU/US economic relationship was dominated by trade questions, and specifically by co-operation and conflict over tariffs, quotas, and other direct barriers to trade typically imposed at US and EU borders. With the decline in tariffs and quotas in most areas of transatlantic trade, however, non-tariff barriers to trade have increased in importance as potential sources of international trade tension. Such non-tariff barriers have been addressed in the EU for decades, through the use of regulatory harmonization and more recently through the mutual recognition of national standards. Similarly, the GATT system began as early as the Tokyo Round (1973–1979) to address non-tariff barriers to trade, most notably through the Technical Barriers to Trade (TBT) Agreement and more recently through the 1994 Sanitary and Phytosanitary Standards (SPS) Agreement, both of which apply international law disciplines to trade-distorting national regulations.

Notwithstanding these new rules, however, 'behind-the-border' US and EU regulations on a diverse array of topics—ranging from the environment and food safety to consumer protection and data privacy—have emerged during the past decade as significant obstacles to transatlantic and global trade and investment.[5] In some cases, such domestic regulations have led to trade disputes between the US and the EU, and to increasing demands from businesses on both sides of the Atlantic for co-operation among US and European regulatory authorities to prevent and settle such disputes and facilitate access to the European and American markets.

II. TRADE AND REGULATORY DISPUTES IN THE TRANSATLANTIC ECONOMIC PARTNERSHIP

Despite the obvious importance of the EU/US trade and investment relationship—or indeed because of it—economic disputes have been and remain an important feature of the transatlantic partnership. Indeed, the settlement and,

[5] As Miles Kahler wrote in 1995: 'Increasingly the points of conflict among the industrialized countries are not the familiar ones of barriers to exchange at the border, but an entire array of

where possible, prevention of such disputes was a large part of the motivation behind the establishment of the New Transatlantic Agenda agreement of 1995, and retains an important place in bilateral economic relations.

A. Classifying disputes: traditional trade issues vs 'behind-the-border' regulatory disputes

Transatlantic economic disputes arise from various sources, and can be settled—or left unsettled—by a similar variety of means. In terms of their sources, we can distinguish between two broad categories of transatlantic trade disputes: (1) 'traditional' trade disputes regarding discriminatory national measures such as tariffs and quotas imposed at the border, as well as subsidies, anti-dumping actions and safeguard measures which discriminate explicitly between domestic and foreign producers; and (2) 'new-style' disputes about the trade-distorting effects of 'behind-the-border' regulations that act as non-tariff barriers to international trade in goods, services, and intellectual property.[6]

With the gradual decline of tariffs and quotas as direct barriers to investment, and the simultaneous increase in domestic economic regulation on both sides of the Atlantic in response to concerns about the environment, consumer protection, public health and the like, the frequency of these new-style disputes has increased drastically during the course of the 1990s and early 2000s. Some of these disputes, like the ongoing conflicts over the regulation and marketing of hormone-treated beef and genetically modified organisms (GMOs), have generated considerable controversy on both sides of the Atlantic and placed strains on the transatlantic economic partnership.

The rise of such transatlantic regulatory disputes, in turn, has prompted questions about what Miles Kahler and others have termed 'system friction' between the respective regulatory systems of the EU and the US. In a survey of transatlantic economic relations conducted in 1995, Kahler concluded that there existed at best partial evidence of system friction between the US and the EU, noting that some issues (eg, agriculture and audiovisual services) did indeed divide the US and EU systems fundamentally, while on other 'new' issues like

---

"domestic" policies that produce conflict by appearing to restrict market access or alter the terms of competition. The agenda of behind-the-border issues that has become more prominent in the 1990s will only grow as economic integration continues and groups mobilize to seek new benchmarks for an international "level playing field".' See M. Kahler, *Regional Futures and Transatlantic Relations* (1995) 5.

[6] As used here, the category of 'new-style' regulatory disputes includes not only regulatory disputes arising from classic product regulations, but also disputes arising from regulations for the protection of individual rights as well as those resulting from the non-discriminatory but extrajurisdictional use of market regulations to achieve foreign policy aims, most notably through the use of economic sanctions. Put differently, the term 'new-style' disputes can be understood as a short-hand reference to the final three categories in Ernst-Ulrich Petersmann's four-part typology of cases; see p 32 above. Furthermore, it is worth noting that, while the frequency of regulatory disputes has increased in recent years, the existence of such disputes is not entirely new, but in fact dates back to the founding of the GATT in 1947; see E.-U. Petersmann, *The GATT/WTO Dispute Settlement System* (1997) 248.

labour standards and the environment the EU and the US generally shared common views.[7]

Surveying the landscape of transatlantic economic relations eight years later, it remains true that the EU and the US are united by many common values and common interests. Nevertheless, in a growing number of issue-areas including food safety, data privacy, copyright protection, taxation, accountancy standards and others, the US and the EU have arguably experienced 'system friction', in the form of a large number of simmering regulatory disputes, summarized in Appendix 1 at the end of this chapter.

As Table 2.4 makes clear, the contemporary transatlantic relationship is characterized by *both* traditional trade conflicts and new-style regulatory disputes. Indeed, traditional disputes about tariffs and quotas (eg, bananas), subsidies (eg, Foreign Sales Corporations), anti-dumping measures and safeguard actions (eg, steel) constitute some of the most high-profile disputes between the US and the EU. With a few exceptions, however, these disputes primarily concern traditional trade measures that are within the 'core business' of the multilateral trading system, which has well established rules and an effective, functioning dispute settlement procedure within the WTO. Put simply, the WTO Dispute Settlement Understanding provides a body of multilateral rules governing the

TABLE 2.4. Classifying US-EU trade disputes

		Agriculture	*Industrial goods*	*Services*
Traditional	Border-measures	Bananas Belgian rice duties Tariff-rate quota corn gluten feed	Harbour tax Anti-dumping (steel, uranium) CVD (steel) Safeguard actions (steel)	
	Subsidies	Export subsidies	Airbus FSC	
New-style	Regulatory barriers	Beef hormones GMOs	Hushkits Public procurement	Audio-visual Professional services Telecommunications Data privacy
	IPR		Havana Club	Irish Music/copyright Greek protection of movies

[7] Kahler, *Regional Futures and Transatlantic Relations*. For good discussions of regulatory barriers in US/EU trade relations, see also D. Vogel, *Barriers or Benefits? Regulation in Transatlantic Trade* (1997); and A.R. Young, 'Risk, Positive Integration and System Friction: The Single European Market and World Trade,' paper presented at the Council of European Studies Conference, 14–16 March 2002.

permissible use of tariffs, quotas, and other trade-restrictive practices; a forum for consultation and, if necessary, litigation among the parties to a dispute before WTO panels and the Appellate Body; a binding requirement for member states to comply with DSU panel and Appellate Body decisions; and authorized retaliation in the event of prolonged non-compliance with those decisions.[8]

By contrast, regulatory disputes implicate national laws and regulations that are often adopted for legitimate reasons of consumer and environmental protection or public health, and after extensive democratic or administrative processes. Furthermore, as Petersmann points out in chapter 1 of this volume, many regulatory disputes arise from national (or EU) regulations that do not discriminate (at least directly) between domestic and imported goods and services, although they may have the secondary effect of distorting transatlantic and international trade and investment. For this reason, transatlantic regulatory disputes can be more bitter and intractable than traditional trade disputes, in so far as both sides believe that they are 'doing the right thing', and in so far as domestic political actors resist subordinating domestic regulations to the exigencies of international trade. Such regulatory disputes also create particularly difficult questions for the WTO dispute settlement procedure, in so far as they call for a politically sensitive balance between the economic imperative of liberalized international trade on the one hand, and the economic and non-economic motivations behind domestic regulations on the other hand.

Largely for this reason, both the US and the EU have generally avoided bringing such regulatory conflicts before the WTO, preferring in most instances to manage their regulatory differences through bilateral consultation and cooperation. Table 2.5, which summarizes EU/US WTO disputes by subject matter, demonstrates clearly the continuing dominance of traditional trade issues (tariffs, subsidies, countervailing duties, and anti-dumping) and the effort by both sides to keep politically sensitive regulatory issues away from the WTO. (For more information about the subjects and status of all EU/US trade disputes before the WTO, see Appendices 2 and 3 at the end of this chapter.)

Simplifying slightly, existing regulatory as well as traditional trade disputes can be addressed in any one of three ways (summarized in Table 2.6 below). First, the EU and the US may engage in direct consultations about regulatory barriers to trade and resolve the dispute without resorting to WTO dispute resolution; examples include the dispute over airplane 'hushkits', resolved through a negotiated settlement between the EU and the US, and the public procurement case involving a Massachusetts state law imposing sanctions against firms doing

---

[8] For excellent overviews of the WTO dispute resolution procedure and its predecessor within the GATT, see inter alia: E.-U. Petersmann (ed), *The GATT/WTO Dispute Settlement System: International Law, International Organizations and Dispute Settlement* (1997); R.E. Hudec, 'The New WTO Dispute Settlement Procedure: An Overview of the First Three Years' (1999) 8 *Minnesota Journal of Global Trade* 1–53; Busch and Reinhardt in Part III of this volume; and BP Chair in Transatlantic Relations 2001. For a provocative challenge to the DSU, see C.E. Barfield, *Free Trade, Sovereignty and Democracy: The Future of the World Trade Organization* (2001).

TABLE 2.5. Transatlantic trade disputes in the WTO: overview and context

	Tariffs, quotas, customs duties, rules of origin, retaliatory measures	Trade defence instruments (a-d, CVD, subsidies)	Technical TBTs (classification, labelling, testing)	Substantive TBTs (process & product requirements)	Subsidies	GATS	TRIPS	TRIMS	GPA	Other
EU-US (EU as third party)	6	9 (11)		1 (1)	1		3		1	2
EU-Rest of World (RoW)	14	6			1	1	3	4	3	4
RoW—EU	12	3	4	2			1		1	
US-EU (US as third party)	8	(1)	(1)	1 (1)	8	1	8			
US—RoW	10	7	3	2	7	2	6	3	1	
RoW—US	7	21		5			1		1	1
RoW—RoW	17	30	1	6	10			3		

Sources: Adapted from DG Trade 'WTO-Dispute Settlement' (updated 15 January 2002), http://europa.eu.int/comm/trade/pdf/cases.xls, accessed 15 February 2002; and the WTO's dispute database (http://www.wto.org/english/tratop_e/dispu_e/dispu_status_e.htm), accessed 15 February 2002.

TABLE 2.6. Methods of dispute resolution, with examples

Negotiated agreement or unilateral action	WTO dispute settlement	Simmering disputes
Hushkits	Beef hormones (EU not in compliance)	GMOs
Massachusetts/Myanmar		
Public procurement	Irish Music/Copyright (EU/US compensation agreement)	

business in Myanmar, which was resolved unilaterally through the application of US federal law. Second, one party may challenge the legality of the other's regulations before the WTO, as in the case of the US challenge to the EU ban on hormone-treated beef, or the EU challenge to a provision of US copyright law; in cases where the disputed regulation is ruled to be in violation of WTO requirements, however, compliance has proven difficult. Third and finally, given the difficulties of resolving such disputes through either bilateral negotiations or WTO litigation, most regulatory disputes are allowed to simmer indefinitely, with periodic consultations and exchange of information among the two sides, but no resolution of the resulting trade tensions. As Appendix 1 makes clear, the overwhelming majority of current transatlantic regulatory disputes fall into this third category.

The sources of such regulatory disputes, and the difficulties they pose for traditional dispute settlement procedures, are illustrated below in four brief case-studies focusing on: (1) the US challenge to EU legislation prohibiting the use of airplane 'hushkits'; (2) the US challenge to the EU's ban on hormone-treated beef and the related dispute over the EU's moratorium on the approval of genetically modified foods and crops; (3) the EU's challenge to the aforementioned Massachusetts public procurement law; and (4) the EU's challenge to a provision of the US Copyright Act. Although not a thorough review of the entire universe of EU/US regulatory disputes, these four cases do illustrate the types of regulations adopted and challenged by both the EU and the US, as well as the various methods of dispute resolution mentioned above. The policy implications of these cases are discussed at the end of this section.

B. Airplane 'hushkits'

Many EU/US disputes concern the technical barriers to trade (TBTs) caused by divergent national regulations setting technical standards in areas ranging from the specifications for industrial machinery and emissions standards for motor vehicles to nutritional labelling requirements for packaged foods. As Kenneth W. Abbott points out in his contribution to this volume, many such national regulations are identified by business or governments as TBTs within the trans-atlantic relationship, and a far smaller percentage of these have emerged as high-profile trade disputes.[9] To date, no disputes have been litigated between the EU and the US under the TBT Agreement, although one particularly prominent case did create significant tensions in the transatlantic relationship, namely the US challenge to the EU's ban on airplane 'hushkits'.

Hushkits are equipment packages designed to reduce the noise emissions of aircraft through the use of sound-absorbing materials, with the aim of bringing older planes into compliance with the so-called 'Chapter 3' noise pollution standards adopted within the International Civil Aviation Organization (ICAO). In 1999, the EU, which had long pressed unsuccessfully for the adoption of stricter standards within the ICAO, adopted a Regulation establishing a ban on the registration of older aircraft fitted with hushkits, on the grounds that such aircraft only barely complied with Chapter 3 standards, and were substan-tially more polluting than newer planes. The ban on new registrations was to enter into force in May 2000; from April 2002, moreover, hushkitted aircraft registered in third countries would not be allowed to operate within EU territory.

Although nominally intended to decrease noise pollution around airports in heavily populated regions of Europe, the EU's Hushkits Regulation met with howls of protest in the US, where the use of hushkits had been encouraged by US authorities as a cost-effective way of meeting Chapter 3 standards. A ban on the registration of hushkitted aircraft, the US argued, would therefore impose a disproportionate burden on US airlines, which estimated that the Regulation cost them some $2 billion by depressing the value of their existing fleets while benefiting European carriers that had relied more extensively on the purchase of new aircraft designed specifically to meet Chapter 3 specifications. In legal terms, moreover, the US argued that the Regulation violated the terms of the ICAO agreement, which simply set a performance standard for planes and did not authorize parties to set more demanding standards or to mandate a specific design standard (eg, a ban on the use of hushkits). The US accordingly lodged a formal ICAO complaint against the 15 EU member states in March 2000.

After extensive bilateral discussion as well as multilateral negotiations within the ICAO, in October 2001 the US and the EU reached a settlement of the case. The first step in this settlement was the multilateral resolution adopted on 4 October in the ICAO assembly urging states to pursue a 'balanced approach' to noise reduction, adopting local operating restrictions only where supported by an assessment of the costs and benefits, and only after fully assessing alternative

---

[9] This section draws largely on Abbott's case-study, in Part II of this volume, of transatlantic disputes over TBTs in general, and the hushkits case in particular. For other accounts of the hushkits dispute, see also B.A. Claes, 'Comment: Aircraft Noise Regulation in the European Union: The Hushkit Problem' 65 *Southern Methodist University School of Law Journal of Air Law and Commerce* 329–382; and J. Peterson, 'Get Away from Me Closer, You're Near Me Too Far: Europe and America after the Uruguay Round,' in M.A. Pollack and G. Shaffer (eds), *Transatlantic Governance in the Global Economy* (2001) 45–72 at 58–59.

measures to reduce noise. At the same time, the ICAO agreed to a new and stricter set of 'Chapter 4' standards, to take effect beginning in 2006.

Consistent with the provisions of the ICAO agreements, the EU agreed on 25 October to withdraw the original Hushkits Regulation by April 2002 (the date when it would have applied to third-country aircraft), in return for which the US agreed to withdraw its complaint before the ICAO. In place of the original Regulation, the Union agreed to adopt a new Directive replacing the general ban on hushkitted planes with a less trade-distorting provision allowing noise-sensitive airports in congested urban areas to limit the use of planes that are 'marginally' compliant with Chapter 3 standards.

Despite the initial acrimony between the US and the EU, the hushkits case represents a successful effort at bilateral dispute resolution in a broader multilateral setting. In this case, the EU agreed, after receiving assurance and guidance from the ICAO, to adopt a more discriminating and less trade-distorting regulatory approach which satisfies the trade concerns of the US while allowing the EU to address the problems of noise pollution around the Union's most congested urban airports. As we shall see presently, however, not all such regulatory conflicts have proven so amenable to negotiated agreement.

C. Hormone-treated beef and genetically modified organisms

EU and US food-safety regulations constitute some of the most important regulatory barriers to international trade, and have been the source of some of the most politically difficult and intractable transatlantic regulatory disputes, pitting each side's sovereign right to regulate the safety of its food against its international obligations under WTO law.[10] Within the US, regulation of food safety was among the earliest and most politically sensitive tasks of the federal government, which has delegated much of the power for domestic regulation to agencies like the Food and Drug Administration (FDA), which has jealously guarded its reputation as an independent and impartial regulator, making decisions on the basis of scientific tests rather than political pressures. In the EU, by contrast, food safety regulation is carried out in part by national regulators, and in part by the EU's political bodies, including the Council of Ministers, the European Parliament, and the Commission. The deficiencies of this patchwork regulatory process were painfully revealed, however, by a series of food safety crises during the latter half of the 1990s, including most notably the BSE crisis of 1996, and the Union has responded forcefully with the creation of a European

---

[10] For a detailed analysis of transatlantic disputes over food safety and GMOs, see the case-study by Petros Mavroidis in Part II of this volume; M.A. Pollack and G.C. Shaffer, 'The Challenge of Reconciling Regulatory Differences: Food Safety and GMOs in the Transatlantic Relationship' in M.A. Pollack and G. Shaffer (eds), *Transatlantic Governance in the Global Economy* (2001) 153–178; D. Vogel, 'Ships Passing in the Night: The Changing Politics of Risk Regulation in the United States and the European Union,' European University Institute, RSCAS Working Paper No 2001/16; and A.R. Young, 'Trading Up or Trading Blows? US Politics and Transatlantic Trade in Genetically Modified Food,' RSCAS Working Paper No 2001/30.

Food Safety Authority, and with an insistence on the application of the so-called 'precautionary principle', justifying regulatory action in the absence of clear scientific evidence and on the basis of consumer concerns and social and economic criteria.

Precisely because food safety regulations can act as non-tariff barriers to trade in agricultural products, the EU and the US have agreed to subject their domestic regulations to the discipline of international guidelines such as the UN Codex Alimentarius Commission which establishes international standards for food safety, and more recently the 1994 WTO Agreement on the Application of Sanitary and Phytosanitary Measures (the SPS Agreement). The SPS Agreement does not establish binding international standards for food safety, nor does it automatically pre-empt the adoption of domestic standards that might constitute non-tariff barriers to trade. The agreement does, however, incorporate and promote the adoption of international standards as well as establish trade rules that limit the ability of states to adopt food safety regulations that are not scientifically grounded. The terms of the SPS Agreement are, moreover, enforceable under the WTO dispute settlement procedure.

The consequences of the divergent EU and US regulatory processes, and the difficulties of resolving disputes through the WTO dispute settlement procedure, can be illustrated most clearly by the long-standing EU/US dispute over the issue of hormone-treated beef. The conflict began in 1989, when the EU announced a ban on the sale and marketing of beef treated with any one of six growth-promoting hormones that had been tested and certified as safe by the FDA. In 1995, following the entry into force of the SPS Agreement, the US took legal action before the WTO, alleging that the EU ban was inconsistent with the terms of the SPS Agreement since it was not based on scientific evidence, risk assessment, or international standards. After a protracted legal battle involving the issuing of a panel report and a subsequent appeal, the WTO Dispute Settlement Body held with the US that the EU had failed to base its ban on a scientific risk assessment, and ordered the EU to bring its domestic regulations into compliance with WTO law.

Despite the clear ruling against it, the EU, faced with opposition from public opinion and hopeful of producing scientific findings that would eventually justify the maintenance of the ban, failed to comply with the Appellate Body's decision. The US therefore retaliated against the EU in May 1999, imposing tariffs of $116.8 million against EU agricultural products such as *foie gras*, Roquefort cheese, and Dijon mustard. These US tariffs in turn sparked protests among French and European farmers, who seized on the beef hormones case as a symbol of the threat posed by Americanization and globalization to European regulations and traditions. Since 1999, the US and the EU have continued to consult regularly about this case, but the Union remains firm in its refusal to alter its domestic law, and the US persists in the application of retaliatory sanctions against the EU.

The transatlantic dispute over the regulation of GMOs—or more precisely, genetically modified foods and crops—is analytically similar to the beef hormones case, although the potential economic stakes in this area of GMOs are potentially far greater. Here again, the US Food and Drug Administration decided in the early 1990s that genetically modified foods were not substantially different from conventional foods, and therefore required no special procedures for approval or marketing, and on that basis US farmers and seed producers have quickly embraced the use of genetically modified foods and crops. By contrast, the EU has taken a more cautious approach in a series of directives and regulations, requiring specific approval procedures for genetically modified crops as well as labelling of foods from genetically modified varieties. Since 1998, moreover, the Council has maintained a *de facto* moratorium on the approval of new GM varieties, even though the EU's scientific committees have continued formally to approve a number of varieties as posing no health risks to consumers.

The GMO issue has been the subject of intense consultation between the US and the EU in recent years, including the creation of an EU-US Biotechnology Forum which issued a joint report on the subject in December 2000[11] as well as a Biotech Working Group within the Transatlantic Economic Partnership. Such fora have provided for a useful exchange of information among regulators as well as trade officials, yet the positions of the two sides remain far apart, with at best modest signs of convergence in the EU and US approaches.

For several years, the US refrained from bringing a case against the EU before the WTO, partly for fear that the EU, facing a potential backlash against both GMOs and the WTO, would be unable to comply. Nevertheless, faced with the potential spread of the EU approach to third countries, the United States in May 2003 officially challenged the EU's de facto ban on approvals of new GM varieties, calling for the creation of a WTO panel to decide the legality of the EU position.[12] Although the outcome of the US challenge is unlikely to be known for several years, its immediate result has been to further inflame and politicize an already sensitive issue in transatlantic relations.[13]

D. Public procurement and the Massachusetts/Myanmar case

The previous two cases involved US challenges to EU regulations setting requirements for the marketing and use of industrial or agricultural products. Regulatory disputes can, however, be directed at US as well as EU regulations, and they

[11] The EU/US Biotechnology Consultative Forum, 'Final Report', available at http://europa.eu.int/comm/external_relations/us/biotech/biotech.htm.

[12] E. Alden and T. Buck, 'Crop Ban Opponents Launch Case Against EU', *Financial Times*, 14 May 2003, p 13.

[13] D. Victor and F. Runge, 'A Trade Battle that Will Cost America Dear', *Financial Times*, 15 May 2003.

can concern regulations governing questions other than product standards. An excellent example is the EU/US dispute over the 1996 Act adopted by the state of Massachusetts regulating state contracts with companies doing business in Myanmar (formerly Burma), examined and analysed in depth by Matthew Schaefer in his contribution to this volume. The law in question was adopted in June 1996 by the Massachusetts State Legislature, with the avowed aim of securing human rights and democratic elections in Myanmar, which was then under military rule and subject to sanctions from the US federal government as well as the EU. Specifically, the Massachusetts law imposed sanctions on foreign as well as domestic firms doing business in Myanmar, with the aim of motivating such firms to withdraw from activities in that country.

As Schaefer points out, the Massachusetts/Myanmar dispute illustrates two recurrent tensions in EU/US trade relations.[14] First, the case illustrates the problems encountered when individual US states like Massachusetts, which are not directly party to the WTO, adopt laws and regulations in possible contravention of WTO law. Anticipating such problems during the negotiation of the 1994 Government Procurement Agreement (GPA), the EU had emphasized the importance for the US of binding the states, and the US federal government responded by asking each of the states to submit a voluntary 'letter of commitment' agreeing to be bound; 37 states, including Massachusetts, submitted such letters, resulting in a substantial, but incomplete, mechanism to ensure state-level compliance with the GPA.

Second, the Massachusetts law in question also represents the extraterritorial application of US (state or federal) laws which employ trade and other economic provisions to secure a foreign policy aim (in this case, the cause of democracy and human rights in Myanmar). Specifically, the Massachusetts law attempted to penalize not only American firms but also foreign firms for investing in Myanmar, even if such investments were legal in those firms' home countries. In this latter sense, the Massachusetts/Myanmar case bears a striking similarity to the extraterritorial sanctions applied by the US in the well-known Helms-Burton and Iran-Libya Sanctions Acts, in which the US federal government adopted extraterritorial sanctions against corporations doing business in Cuba, Iran and Libya.[15]

In the Massachusetts case, the law was challenged before the WTO by the EU (joined by Japan), which sought to have the law ruled incompatible with US obligations under the GPA. Before the WTO panel could rule, however, the law was successfully challenged and overruled *under US federal law* when the US Supreme Court held that federal action in this area (ie, the federal sanctions law

---

[14] See case-study by Schaefer in Part II of this volume. See also J. Hellweg, 'The Retreat of the State? The Massachusetts Burma Law and Local Empowerment in the Context of Globalization(s)' (2000) 18 *Wisconsin International Law Journal* 477–510.

[15] The latter cases were resolved, at least temporarily, when President Clinton agreed in 1998 to waive such sanctions in a bilateral agreement with the EU leaders; see case-study by Hugo Paemen in Part II of this volume.

against Burma) had pre-empted such sanctions by the state of Massachusetts, whose law was therefore held to be unconstitutional.

The successful resolution of the Massachusetts/Myanmar dispute suggests several lessons for the prevention and settlement of similar cases in the future, according to Schaefer. In terms of dispute prevention, he argues, this case points to the importance of informing state governors and legislators about the constitutional limitations on the extraterritorial use of economic sanctions, as well as their obligations under WTO agreements (at least in so far as the states themselves agree to be bound by them). In terms of dispute settlement, finally, the Massachusetts case suggests that litigation in domestic courts under US law may in some cases be a more effective and comprehensive constraint on state sanctions than WTO law, which should therefore be employed with restraint in such cases.

E. Intellectual property rights and the Irish Music case

In addition to trade in goods and services and public procurement, national laws and regulations regarding intellectual property rights can also have international trade repercussions, even when those regulations apply without discrimination to domestic as well as foreign producers. Indeed, protection of intellectual property has been the subject of no fewer than 11 WTO disputes between the US and the EU since 1995. The challenges posed by intellectual property disputes are illustrated by several cases, including the 'Havana Club' case reviewed in this volume by Frederick Abbott, and by the so-called 'Irish music case', in which the EU challenged provisions of US copyright law before the WTO.[16] In the former case, Abbott correctly points out, a private dispute over ownership of a trademark was effectively exported to the international level through a WTO legal case; in the latter, by contrast, non-discriminatory aspects of US copyright law were challenged for lack of compliance with WTO obligations, creating substantial legal and political challenges for both the US and the EU. Let us therefore consider the Irish music case briefly here.[17]

The US law in question was the 1976 Copyright Act, as amended by the 1998 Fairness in Music Licensing Act. Specifically, Article 110(5) of the amended Act included a 'business exemption' according to which establishments such as bars, shops and restaurants below a certain size (ie, 2,000–3,750 square feet) were allowed to play radio and television music without paying fees to royalty-collecting bodies. The relevant provisions of the Act had been adopted only

---

[16] See case-study by Frederick Abbott in Part II of this volume.

[17] For useful background on the case, filed before the WTO as DS160, see L.R. Helfer, 'World Music on a U.S. Stage: A Berne/TRIPS and Economic Analysis of the Fairness in Music Licensing Act' (2000) 80 *Boston University Law Review* 93–204; M. LaFrance, 'Congress Trips Over International Law: WTO Finds Unfairness in Music Licensing Act' (2001) 11 *Journal of Art and Entertainment Law* 397–424; and L. Sindelar, 'Not So Fair After All—International Aspects of the Fairness in Music Licensing Act' (2001) 14 *The Transnational Lawyer* 435–471.

after long and difficult negotiations between the representatives of US performing rights organizations on the one side, and the National Licensed Beverage Association on the other, and sought (however successfully) to balance the rights of copyright holders with the interests of small restaurant and bar owners.

Although the US law applied equally to domestic as well as foreign copyright holders, in 1997 the Irish Music Rights Organization (IMRO), a collective music management company representing Irish musicians such as the rock group U2, filed a complaint about the law before the European Commission. IMRO claimed that the derogation in the law was in violation of US commitments under both the International Agreement on Trade Related Aspects of International Property Rights (TRIPS) as well as the Berne Convention for the Protection of Literary and Artistic Works, since it failed to protect authors' rights, resulting in an estimated loss of $1.21 million annually for IMRO's members. The Commission, having investigated the case, agreed with IMRO that the law violated US obligations under the TRIPS agreement, and initiated a formal complaint before the WTO in 1998.

In June 2000, a WTO panel issued a decision in favour of the EU, calling on the US to bring Section 110(5)(B) of the Copyright Act (the aforementioned business exemption) into conformity with the TRIPS agreement. In response to the panel's report, the US announced that it would not appeal the panel decision, but also that it would require time to amend its existing copyright legislation. In the interim, the US and the EU agreed to establish a WTO arbitration panel, which would decide on the level of compensation to be granted by the US to the EU pending modification of the Act. In November 2001, the arbitrators accordingly assessed the annual losses suffered by EU copyright owners, and hence the level of compensation to be paid by the US, at some $1.08 million. In light of this finding, EU Trade Commissioner Pascal Lamy and US Trade Representative (USTR) Robert Zoellick agreed the following month to a temporary solution, whereby the USTR would seek authorization from Congress to establish a special fund worth $3.3 million over three years to finance projects and activities for the benefit of EU music creators, pending revision of the US law.

The December 2001 agreement between the US and the EU was presented by EU Trade Commissioner Pascal Lamy as 'a good example of how we can manage our problems in a cooperative manner, while keeping in mind our international commitments'.[18] However, while the US and the EU have indeed reached an amicable three-year agreement on this issue, the Irish music case also serves as an additional example of the difficulties encountered by both sides in amending domestic regulations in response to trade concerns and WTO rulings. Although the EU side insisted on the US obligation to amend its law, and explicitly retained its right to return to the WTO in the event of non-compliance, at the time of writing there is no sign of any imminent US effort to bring its domestic law into

---

[18] Commission of the European Communities, 'EU and US Agree on Temporary Compensation in Copyright Dispute,' Press Release; IP: 01/1860.

compliance, and an extended US agreement to compensation remains a probable alternative for the foreseeable future.

F. Settling—and preventing—transatlantic regulatory conflicts

This review of four transatlantic regulatory conflicts, although selective and incomplete, nevertheless points to the particular difficulties of regulatory disputes, which raise different substantive and political challenges when compared with traditional trade disputes. As we have seen, such disputes often involve domestic laws adopted for legitimate purposes after democratic deliberation, sometimes (although not always) without any intent to discriminate against imported goods and services. As we have also seen, litigation of regulatory disputes can place severe strain on the WTO system, particularly in cases like beef-hormones, copyright, and potentially GMOs, where the losing party would have difficulty complying with an adverse WTO ruling. Largely for this reason, both the US and the EU have generally resisted taking regulatory disputes before the WTO, preferring to settle—and, if possible, prevent—such disputes through bilateral co-operation. The architecture of this transatlantic economic co-operation, and the first attempts at regulatory co-operation between the two politics, are examined in the following sections.

III. TRANSATLANTIC ECONOMIC GOVERNANCE

One of the most striking features of the transatlantic economic relationship over the past decade has been the dramatic increase in both formal and informal co-operation among the authorities of the US and the EU, in the framework of agreements such as the 1995 New Transatlantic Agenda (NTA) and the 1998 Transatlantic Economic Partnership (TEP). Perhaps most interestingly for our purposes here, much of this co-operation has been driven, not by security concerns (which are dealt with largely in the context of the NATO alliance) but by a mutual concern to manage the increasingly interdependent economic relationship between the US and the EU, and to manage the increasing number of trade disputes that have arisen in that relationship. The following sections, therefore, examine the overall architecture of transatlantic economic co-operation created by these agreements, before turning in Section IV to the motives for, and the empirical record of, transatlantic regulatory co-operation in recent years.

A. From the NTA to the TEP: institutions for economic governance

Transatlantic relations between the US and the countries of Western Europe have long been based on common values and interests in terms of both security and economic interdependence. Throughout the Cold War, transatlantic co-operation took place largely though the North Atlantic Treaty Organization (NATO) in the area of security, and through common US and European participation in various multilateral economic forums including the Organization for Economic Co-operation and Development (OECD), the G-7 (now G-8) group of highly industrialized economies, and the General Agreement on Tariffs and Trade (GATT).

Co-operation between the US and its European partners is therefore not new, but the *character* of the relationship changed substantially during the 1990s, with an ever-greater emphasis on economic as well as security co-operation, and a greater recognition by the US of the EU (in addition to its member states) as an important interlocutor. Three transatlantic agreements signed in the 1990s underpin this new transatlantic partnership and the increasingly liberalized EU/US economic relationship. The Transatlantic Declaration (1990), the NTA (1995) and the TEP (1998) have each played an important role in creating a transatlantic framework for economic co-operation and introducing formal transatlantic institutions to manage the relationship. This upgrading of the EU/ US relationship, in turn, can be traced to several interrelated developments during that decade, including the end of the Cold War, the maturation of the EU as an economic and political actor, and the relentless expansion of transatlantic economic exchange which created pressures for joint management of the emerging transatlantic marketplace.[19]

The end of the Cold War was clearly a precipitating cause for the upgrading of the transatlantic relationship. As early as 1990, the US presidential administration of George H.W. Bush proposed a Transatlantic Declaration to reaffirm US/European solidarity following the fall of the Iron Curtain and the collapse of the Soviet Union. While that Transatlantic Declaration itself focused largely on security issues rather than economic co-operation, the diminution of the security threat from post-Soviet Russia facilitated an increasing emphasis on economic issues by the Clinton administration, reflected in both the 1995 NTA and the 1998 TEP.[20]

This economic focus has in turn been reinforced by the maturation of the EU, which emerged during the late 1980s and early 1990s as the world's largest internal market and the most important trading partner of the US. Simultaneously with the development of the EU's internal market came the increasing influence of EU political institutions, including the European Commission (which plays a vital role in the EU legislative process as well as serving as trade negotiator and economic regulator in fields such as competition policy) and the Council of Ministers and European Parliament (which collectively adopt an

[19] This section draws on the analysis presented in M.A. Pollack and G.C. Shaffer, 'Transatlantic Governance in Historical and Theoretical Perspective' in M.A. Pollack and G. Shaffer (eds), *Transatlantic Governance in the Global Economy* (2001) 3–42.

[20] For good discussions, see A. Gardner, *A New Era in US-EU Relations? The Clinton Administration and the New Transatlantic Agenda* (1997); and J. Peterson and M. Green Cowles, 'Clinton, Europe, and Economic Diplomacy: What Makes the EU Different?' (1998) 11 *Governance* 251–271.

increasingly large portion of European economic legislation). Although the powers of the respective EU institutions still varies considerably across sectors, the Commission has clearly emerged as the Union's primary interlocutor with the US on economic issues, while the legislative activities of the Council and the Parliament have the potential to influence economic interests in the US. The institutions of the NTA have therefore attempted to incorporate the Commission and the Council presidency through biannual summits and other high-level meetings, as well as members of the European Parliament through the Transatlantic Legislators' Dialogue (see below).

Beyond the end of the Cold War and the maturation of the EU, finally, lies the relentless increase of transatlantic economic exchange. Increased transatlantic trade and investment have created new demands for market access and economic co-operation from producer groups such as the Transatlantic Business Dialogue, while other consumer, labour, and environmental groups have sought to ensure that transatlantic co-operation takes into account their diverse interests. Indeed, as we shall see below, the increasingly close economic relationship between the EU and the US has created new prospects for both trade conflicts and regulatory co-operation, and has resulted in what might be termed 'scuttle diplomacy'—the scurrying of EU and US government authorities to cope with the incessant conflicts which, although they compose only a small fraction of EU/US economic exchange, threaten to poison a mutually advantageous economic relationship.[21] Largely for this reason, the US and the EU have established an increasingly complex institutional structure designed to facilitate economic and security co-operation, resolve and prevent disputes, and integrate civil-society groups into the process of transatlantic economic governance.

1. The Transatlantic Declaration

The process of institutionalizing the EU/US relationship began simultaneously with the end of the Cold War in 1989, when US President Bush and EU Commission President Jacques Delors agreed to work to ensure regular meetings between high-level EU and US officials. On 27 February 1990, this agreement bore fruit in the shape of a 'Transatlantic Declaration', pursuant to which the US and EC agreed to establish an institutional framework 'for regular and intensive consultation'. Specifically, the Declaration called for biannual EU/US summit meetings between the presidents of the US, the European Commission, and the European Council, as well as regular meetings between the US Secretary of State, the EC Commission and the US Cabinet. These meetings, it was hoped, would open lines of communication, create networks, facilitate information sharing, and reduce the impact of disputes in transatlantic relations.

In substantive terms, the Transatlantic Declaration identified three major goals:

---

[21] M.A. Pollack and G. Shaffer, 'Who Governs?' in M.A. Pollack and G. Shaffer (eds), *Transatlantic Governance in the Global Economy* (2001) 287–305 at 291.

- economic liberalization;
- educational, scientific and cultural co-operation; and
- co-operation in fighting international crime, terrorism and environmental degradation.[22]

While these policy areas were identified as priorities, the agreement failed to provide a more detailed agenda for meeting its goals. The content of the agreement has been described as cosmetic, minimalist and lacking in substantive innovations, and would soon be supplemented by other, more detailed economic agreements.[23]

2. The New Transatlantic Agenda

The next stage in developing the transatlantic economic relationship came with the NTA, which was signed at the EU/US Summit in Madrid in 1995, and established four priority areas for closer co-operation:

- promoting peace and stability, democracy and development around the world (in particular, in Central and Eastern Europe, Russia, and the Middle East);
- responding to global challenges (with a focus on international crime, drug trafficking, terrorism, migration, and health and environmental issues);
- 'contributing to the expansion of world trade and promoting closer economic relations' (including both bilateral and multilateral liberalization of trade and investment); and
- building bridges across the Atlantic (specifically, direct contacts among 'business people, scientists, educators and others').[24]

In addition to the six-page NTA itself, the two partners also adopted a much more detailed Joint Action Plan (JAP) which outlined specific policy areas where deeper co-operation could be pursued. The economic chapter of the JAP was arguably the most ambitious of the four, calling for both the strengthening of the multilateral trading system and the creation of a liberalized 'transatlantic marketplace', with a special focus on bilateral regulatory co-operation.[25] The NTA itself also acknowledged the role of the Transatlantic Business Dialogue, which would later prove to be influential in setting the agenda for transatlantic economic co-operation.

In institutional terms, the NTA established new transatlantic governance mechanisms and a more established policy process. First, it created a Senior Level Group of EU and US officials, together with a lower-level NTA Task Force to help drive, co-ordinate, monitor and implement the agenda of transatlantic relations between the continuing EU/US summits. Although this framework has

---

[22] 'Transatlantic Declaration', available at http://www.eurunion.org/partner/transatldec.htm.
[23] See, eg, K. Featherstone and R. Ginsberg, *The United States and the European Union in the 1990s: Partners in Transition* (1996); and J. Peterson, *Europe and America: Prospects for Partnership* (1996).
[24] 'The New Transatlantic Agenda', available at http://www.eurunion.org/partner/agenda.htm.
[25] 'Joint US-EU Action Plan', available at http://www.eurunion.org/partner/actplan.htm.

since been criticized as excessively bureaucratic and focused on summit-driven 'deliverables' (see below), the NTA framework has proven useful in co-ordinating EU and US responses to both economic and security issues, and remains the overarching framework for transatlantic relations today.

3. The Transatlantic Economic Partnership

The drive for an ever-closer transatlantic economic relationship was revived in 1998 amidst revelations that co-operation in many policy areas had fallen short of initial expectations.[26] Despite the NTA and its institutions, high-profile trade disputes over bananas, beef and extraterritorial sanctions continued, highlighting the need for further transatlantic commitment to facilitate economic exchange and contain conflict. In that context, the European Commission took the initiative in April 1998, calling for negotiations on a 'single comprehensive agreement' to implement a 'New Transatlantic Marketplace'. The Commission's proposal had four central objectives:

- the 'removal of technical barriers to trade in goods through an extensive process of mutual recognition and/or harmonization';
- the elimination 'by 2010 of all industrial tariffs on an MFN basis';
- the formation of a 'free trade area in services'; and
- further liberalization in the areas of government procurement, intellectual property rights, and investment.[27]

The US had little time to respond, however, as the initiative failed to secure the support of the Council of Ministers. In its place, the US and the EU agreed in May 1998 to the somewhat less ambitious TEP, which aimed to tackle bilateral regulatory barriers to trade and to identify common positions within multilateral trade negotiations. In substantive terms, the TEP and its accompanying Action Plan focused more directly than the NTA on regulatory co-operation and on the possible harmonization of standards as a means of removing technical barriers to trade, and it committed both sides to negotiations in specific issue-areas including services, intellectual property, food safety and biotechnology.[28]

In addition, the TEP created a new set of institutions to manage the economic aspects of the relationship, including a 'TEP Steering Group', charged with monitoring, implementing and reviewing TEP objectives, as well as expert-level working groups. The TEP also emphasized the importance of early warning of potential trade and regulatory disputes, and fostered the creation of an institutionalized 'early warning system' following the Bonn EU/US summit in

[26] Gardner, *A New Era in US/EU Relations?*, op cit.

[27] European Commission, *The New Transatlantic Marketplace*: Draft Communication from the Commission to the Council, the European Parliament and the Economic and Social Committee (1998), available at http://europa.eu.int/comm.dg01/sectiona.htm.

[28] 'Transatlantic Economic Partnership: Action Plan', available at http://europa.eu.int/comm/trade/bilateral/usa/1109tep.htm. For a useful review of the TEP, see European Commission, *The Transatlantic Economic Partnership Overview and Assessment*, Coordination: DG TRADE.E.3, October.

TABLE 2.7. Transatlantic co-operation agreements at a glance

Transatlantic agreement	Year	Impact on the economic relationship
Transatlantic Declaration	1990	Contains a broad commitment to economic liberalization.
New Transatlantic Agenda (NTA) and Joint Action Plan (JAP)	1995	Includes a chapter on contributing to the expansion of world trade and promoting closer economic relations; JAP discusses building a 'new transatlantic marketplace' through increased regulatory co-operation.
Transatlantic Economic Partnership (TEP)	1998	Outlines three main goals for the transatlantic economic relationship: (1) market access gains for goods, services, and agricultural products; (2) multilateral and bilateral trade liberalization of goods, services and capital; (3) deepening dialogue between non-governmental organizations, parliamentarians, and government.

June 1999. Finally, the TEP explicitly encouraged the participation of not only business but other civil society groups, which would lead in time to the creation of the transatlantic consumer, environment, and labour dialogues.

Today's transatlantic economic relationship is managed largely by a set of institutions that were created in stages by the Transatlantic Declaration, the NTA and the TEP. Combined, these institutions constitute a framework for long-term as well as day-to-day economic co-operation and dispute resolution.

4. EU/US summits

The biannual EU/US summit is the primary forum for intergovernmental exchange in the NTA process, consisting of the highest level of contact between the Presidents of the US, the EU Commission and the Council Presidency. The transatlantic policy cycle begins and ends with these biannual summits, where decisions are 'made' about the general scope for co-operation and where 'deliverables'—in the form of new bilateral agreements about regulatory co-operation or the resolution of specific disputes—are announced. The summits encourage policy co-ordination because they create deadlines for progress chapters and exert pressure on lower-level officials to produce results.

5. Senior Level Group and the NTA Task Force

The Senior Level Group (SLG) serves as a contact point between the EU/US summit and the working level of the transatlantic dialogue. It has roughly six formal members including the US Undersecretary of State for Economic Affairs, Commission delegates from the Directorates-General for external relations and trade, Council Presidency representatives, and representatives of the 'Article 133 committee' dealing with international trade matters. The primary tasks of the SLG are to prepare the agenda of the biannual summits, 'shopping for deliverables' to be announced on those occasions, and to monitor the implementation of the NTA and the TEP.

Logistically, the SLG typically meets twice during each Council Presidency, with the first meeting used to assess potential areas of co-operation and conflict, and the second meeting finalizing the agenda for the EU/US summit and confirming the contents of its progress chapter, which is presented to summit leaders. Below the SLG, an 'NTA Task Force' meets somewhat more frequently (often through videoconferencing) to follow specific dossiers in both the security and economic realms.

6. TEP Steering Group and working groups

The TEP institutions, including the Steering Group and working groups, bring together policy experts to deal with economic issues in greater detail. The Steering Group consists of the US Deputy Assistant Secretary of State for Economic Affairs, Commission officials at the Head-of-Unit level, and a Council Presidency representative. Originally designed to co-ordinate negotiating approaches within the WTO and to act as an 'early warning system' to identify possible trade disputes, the TEP Steering Group has evolved into the primary co-ordinating body for transatlantic economic relations, including negotiations about regulatory co-operation in specific areas.

The Steering Group is assisted by the TEP working groups which are sector-specific and thus mirror the sectors laid out by the TEP including agriculture, biotechnology, trade, services, and global electronic commerce. Their main task is to find areas where the EU and the US can work together under the TEP framework and to chapter any progress or problems to the Steering Group.

7. The transatlantic early warning system

The 1998 TEP declaration highlighted the need to identify potential trade disputes before they emerge. Thus, as W. Meng describes, the two sides agreed in June of 1999 to formalize an early warning system for this purpose.[29] Essentially the transatlantic early warning system sparks an inter-agency process to identify potential economic disputes at an early stage, most notably with regard to domestic EU or US legislation that might act as a barrier to transatlantic trade and investment. The task of spotting such potential disputes is delegated to the

---

[29] See the contribution by W. Meng in Part III of this volume. See also the 'Joint U.S.-EU Statement on "Early Warning" Mechanism,' 21 June 1999, available at http://europa.eu.int/comm/trade/pdf/early_warning.pdf.

TEP Steering Group, which reports early warning items to the Senior Level Group, which in turn may take them into account when preparing the EU/US summit agenda. The TEP Steering Group also assigns contact points, facilitating consultations and agreeing on timelines for reporting back on items highlighted as potential transatlantic policy frictions. Unlike similar early warning systems within the EU, however, the transatlantic early warning system does *not* require that either side pause or reconsider its proposed legislation or regulations. The result is a system that, while respecting the regulatory sovereignty of both sides, does not guarantee prevention or resolution of potential conflicts.

8. The Transatlantic Legislators' Dialogue

An underlying feature of the early warning concept is the desire to get both EU and US domestic policy makers to consider the external implications of internal policies. However, the early warning system is a bureaucratic tool. The important task of raising awareness between EU and US legislators lies with the Transatlantic Legislators' Dialogue (TLD), a product of the NTA's 'building bridges' chapter. The TLD brings together members of the US Congress and the European Parliament so as to create awareness on each side of the transatlantic trade impact of EU and US legislative acts.

Thus far, however, the TLD has not lived up to initial expectations, for three reasons. First, TLD participation is largely limited to members of the US House of Representatives and the European Parliament with a particular interest in transatlantic relations, and may not include members of committees drafting legislation with transatlantic repercussions; the US Senate, moreover, is thus far excluded from the TLD. Second, there is insufficient contact between the TLD and other parts of the transatlantic dialogue, for example the SLG. Third, meetings of the TLD have been held only rarely, and typically with weak attendance on the US side, and the Dialogue has yet to engage in or settle any serious economic disputes between the US and the EU.

9. The transatlantic civil society dialogues

The fourth and final chapter of the NTA encourages the establishment of 'people to people' links as a way of building bridges across the Atlantic and bringing a civil-society component to transatlantic co-operation. In addition to supporting ad hoc exchange between educators and scientists, the EU and the US have encouraged and in some cases subsidized the establishment of formal dialogues among European and American business, consumer and environmental groups, and labour unions. The 1995 NTA made specific mention of the Transatlantic Business Dialogue (TABD), while the 1998 TEP invited civil society input 'on issues relevant to international trade as a constructive contribution to policy making'. In practice, however, not all dialogues have been created or function as equals.

The TABD is the oldest, best organized, and most influential dialogue in the transatlantic economic relationship. Launched in 1995 at the initiative of the US

Commerce Department and the EU Commission, the TABD brings together some 200 European and American CEOs for annual meetings which make joint recommendations on transatlantic policy issues.[30] From the beginning, the TABD focused the attention of US and European legislators and regulators on the importance of non-tariff barriers to trade, calling explicitly for EU/US regulatory co-operation and mutual recognition of standards—an approach it has labelled 'approved once, accepted everywhere'.[31] In keeping with this approach, the TABD has been active in pressing for the adoption and implementation of specific agreements, including the 1997 Mutual Recognition Agreements and the 2000 Safe Harbour Agreement on data privacy (examined below). In addition, the TABD participates actively in the transatlantic early warning system, identifying in its annual reports those domestic laws and regulations that might create obstacles to transatlantic trade and investment.[32]

One result of this process is that the TABD has become a valuable source of information for EU and US policy makers. Sixty per cent of the TABD's original recommendations resurfaced in the NTA and the JAP.[33] Some members estimate that one-third of its recommendations have been taken on board by transatlantic policy makers.[34] Nevertheless, there is an increasing perception within the TABD that much of the 'low-hanging fruit' has been picked, in terms of transatlantic trade liberalization and regulatory co-operation, and a fear that governments 'can't deliver' regulatory reforms demanded by business.[35] In addition, the TABD faces the challenge of interacting with the other officially recognized dialogues, with which it may not always agree.

The decision to include consumers, environmentalists and workers in the transatlantic dialogue was the result of pressure from NGOs, the European Commission and eventually the US State Department. The success of the TABD sparked criticism from the NGO community, which argued that the influence of the TABD was unbalanced by an absence of civil society input. In response to these concerns, the State Department and the European Commission both agreed to provide funds to establish a new Transatlantic Consumer Dialogue. There was some objection to government sponsorship of the groups,

---

[30] For good discussions of the TABD, see M. Green Cowles, 'The New Transatlantic Dialogue: Transforming the New Transatlantic Dialogue' in M.A. Pollack and G. Shaffer (eds), *Transatlantic Governance in the Global Economy* (2001) 213–233; and the website of the TABD at http://www.tabd.org.

[31] 'Cincinnati Recommendations: Transatlantic Business Dialogue', 16–18 November 2000, 4, available at http://www.tabd.org/recommendations/Cincinnati00.pdf.

[32] Ibid, 5.

[33] M. Green Cowles, 'Transatlantic Cooperation and Discord in the New Economy: A Case-Study of the Global Business Dialogue on e-Commerce,' paper delivered at the Biennial Conference of the European Community Studies Association, Madison, Wisconsin, 31 May 2001.

[34] B.J. Steffenson, 'The Institutionalization of EU–US Relations: Decision Making, Institution Building, and the New Transatlantic Agenda', unpublished PhD dissertation, University of Glasgow, Department of Politics, 2001.

[35] M.A. Pollack (ed), *The New Transatlantic Agenda at Five: A Critical Assessment* (San Domenico di Fiesole: BP Chair in Transatlantic Relations, Robert Schuman Centre for Advanced Studies, European University Institute, 2001) 12.

particularly in the US, where it was feared that the consumer dialogue was a way to 'greenwash' the TEP. There was also a divide among its members over the issue of trade liberalization, most notably at the first meeting of the TACD, which was overshadowed by a dispute between groups such as Public Citizen which generally oppose trade liberalization, and other groups such as Consumer Union which support trade liberalization as a means of increasing consumer choice.[36]

Despite this rocky start, the TACD has become an efficient organization, with a secretariat in London and a steering committee that has organized its roughly 60 members into working groups on food, electronic commerce and trade. In its working groups, annual meetings, and recommendations, the TACD has focused largely on transatlantic regulatory issues—in areas such as data privacy, food safety, and the application of the 'precautionary principle' in risk regulation—because many consumer groups feared a downward spiral of regulatory standards as a result of increasing trade liberalization. Nevertheless, despite its high level of activity, some members of the TACD feel that they have not had a sufficient impact on the NTA process, which they regard as being dominated by a free-trade agenda.

Attempts to forge a functioning dialogue between the European and American environmental and labour movements have been the least successful. Despite initial attempts to create an environmental dialogue, the Transatlantic Environment Dialogue (TAED) suspended its activities in 2000, citing a lack of funding from the US side.[37] The TAED had, until this point, held three meetings and established a steering committee as well as working groups on climate protection, bio-diversity and forest conservation, food and agriculture, and industry. The TAED also offered a number of official recommendations on safe energy sources, biotechnology, waste management and emissions standards, although TAED members, like their TACD counterparts, argued that the TABD continued to enjoy privileged access to EU and US policy makers.

Finally, while the Transatlantic Labour Dialogue is officially still a functioning forum, it is the least developed of the transatlantic civil-society dialogues. The TALD is little more than a modest exchange between the European Trade Union Confederation (ETUC) and the American Federation of Labour and the Congress of Industrial Organizations (AFL-CIO), with no organizational structure,

---

[36] For an excellent discussion of the TACD and its activities, see F. Bignami and S. Charnovitz, 'Transatlantic Civil Society Dialogues' in M.A. Pollack and G.C. Shaffer (eds), *Transatlantic Governance in the Global Economy* (2001) 255–284; see also the TACD website at: http://www.tacd.org.

[37] The USIA funding for the TAED ($100,000) was subject to approval from the Senate Finance Committee. In January 2000 the objection of Senator Jesse Helms to TAED funding blocked the approval of funds, and stopped the State Department from issuing the grant. The TAED argued that this demonstrated the US government's lack of dedication to the project. See 'Transatlantic Environment Dialogue suspends its activities due to the failure of US government to stick to its commitments,' accessed on 12 March 2002 on the TAED website: http://www.tiesweb.org/taed/index.html. For a good general discussion of the TAED, see Bignami and Charnovitz, 'Transatlantic Civil Society Dialogues,' op cit.

secretariat or formal objectives. The TALD did hold several meetings in 1998 and 1999 and 2000, but produced only six recommendations from those meetings. Simplifying only slightly, the ETUC and AFL-CIO have chosen to emphasize their shared interests in a global labour dialogue, and have demonstrated little commitment to a specifically transatlantic agenda within the framework of the NTA or the TEP.[38]

In sum, the transatlantic civil-society dialogues have arguably served a useful purpose in fostering transatlantic discussion among businesses and nongovernmental organizations (most notably in the business and consumer sectors), and in producing concrete recommendations for transatlantic economic co-operation. However, the relative weight of these organizations remains highly uneven, and the current arrangement is highly segmented and marked by a lack of any 'dialogue among the dialogues', which might lead to the creation of a genuine transatlantic public sphere.

B. An effective framework for economic co-operation?

In recent years, both official reviews and academic studies have focused on the institutions of the NTA and the TEP, asking whether these institutions are an adequate framework for transatlantic economic as well as security co-operation. In its 2001 review of the NTA, for example, the European Commission argued that institutions such as the TEP Steering Group, the NTA Task Force and the Senior Level Group serve useful purposes in fostering dialogue and co-operation between EU officials and their US counterparts, but also noted a number of weaknesses in the current structure, including the summit-driven demand for often artificial 'deliverables' at six-month intervals, and the difficulty in focusing on medium- to long-term priorities given the inevitable demands of pressing short-term issues. The Commission therefore proposed a number of reforms to the current institutions, including the establishment of explicit medium-term priorities and the possible reduction of the number of EU/US summits to one per year.[39]

By and large, the Commission's recommendations were welcomed by the US government, which agreed to the establishment of a set of medium-term priorities in the context of the June 2001 Göteborg summit. By contrast, no progress has been made on the suggestion of reducing the number of transatlantic summits, largely because of the difficulties posed by the rotating six-month presidency on the EU side. In addition, as we have seen, a number of calls have been made in recent years for a more transparent and accountable process of

---

[38] For an excellent discussion of the TALD, see J. Knauss and D. Trubek, 'The Transatlantic Labor Dialogue: Minimal Action in a Weak Structure' in M.A. Pollack and G. Shaffer (eds), *Transatlantic Governance in the Global Economy* (2001) 235–254.

[39] Commission of the European Communities, *Reinforcing the Transatlantic Relationship: Focusing on Strategy and Delivering Results*, COM(2001)154 of 20 March 2001, available at, http://www.eurunion.org/partner/TransatlAgenda.pdf.

transatlantic economic governance, with more balanced input from civil society and with a greater role for democratically elected legislators. Thus far, however, these calls have met with no systematic response from either the US or the EU.

Moving from institutions to 'deliverables', a recent study by Eric Philippart and Pascaline Winand has attempted to measure the policy outputs of the NTA, by examining the joint reports of the Senior Level Group since 1995 in order to determine to what extent, and in which areas, the goals of the JAP had been missed, met, or exceeded. Summarizing a complex analysis, Philippart and Winand find that the extent and level of co-operation varies both across and within the four chapters of the NTA, with genuine joint action in some areas and lower levels of co-operation (such as the exchange of information) or inactivity in others. In the area of foreign policy co-operation, for example, the authors find that EU/US co-operation has been most successful and resulted in the most extensive joint action within Europe itself, while yielding fewer and less binding outcomes in other regions. In the area of economic co-operation, the authors find that the NTA has been most active in the establishment of a 'transatlantic marketplace', with relatively extensive trade and regulatory co-operation, but far less active and successful in co-ordinating economic policies in the WTO and other multilateral fora.[40] In the following sections, therefore, we turn from a discussion of institutions and process to a more explicit analysis of bilateral efforts to prevent transatlantic economic disputes through regulatory co-operation.

IV. TRANSATLANTIC REGULATORY CO-OPERATION

In the past six years alone, the US and the EU have signed nine formal regulatory co-operation agreements in areas as diverse as competition policy, data privacy, customs procedures, veterinary standards, and the mutual recognition of testing and certification procedures (Table 2.8). These formal regulatory agreements, moreover, represent only a fraction of the contacts that occur among US and EU regulators both bilaterally and in various multilateral fora.

A. Why co-operate?

The incentives for US and EU regulators to engage in formal and informal co-operation vary across different issue-areas, but can generally be classed into two broad categories.[41] First, regulators may co-operate because they view such co-

---

[40] E. Philippart and P. Winand, 'Deeds Not Words? Evaluating and Explaining the US-EU Policy Output' in Philippart and Winand (eds), *Ever Closer Partnership: Policymaking in US-EU Relations* (2001) 431–463.

[41] G. Bermann, 'Regulatory Cooperation between the European Commission and U.S. Administrative Agencies' (1996) 9 *Administrative Law Journal of the American University* 933–983 at 961. For an excellent set of essays on various aspects of transatlantic regulatory co-operation, see also G. Bermann, M. Herdegen and P. Lindstreth (eds), *Transatlantic Regulatory Co-Operation: Legal Problems and Political Prospects* (2001).

TABLE 2.8. Transatlantic regulatory co-operation agreements

Agreement	Targeted Regulations	Year
Competition Policy Agreement	Competition regulations	1991
EC/US Agreement on Drug Precursors	Illicit drug regulations	1997
EC/US Customs and Co-operation Agreement	Customs certifications	1997
EU/US General Mutual Recognition Agreements	Conformity assessment testing in six sectors: telecommunications equipment, electromagnetic compatibility, electrical safety, recreational craft, medical devices, and pharmaceutical good manufacturing practices	1997
EU/US Positive Comity Agreement	Competition relations	1998
EU/US Agreement Concerning the Establishment of Global Technical Regulations for Wheeled Vehicles, Equipment and Parts	Technical regulations	1999
EU/US Veterinary Equivalence Agreement	Animal export certifications	1999
EU/US Safe Harbour Agreement	Data protection regulations	2000
Joint Declaration on US/EU Co-operation in the Field of Metrology and Measurement Standards	Measurement equivalence in product certification	2000
EU/US Agreement on Mutual Recognition of Certificates of Conformity for Marine Equipment	Mutual recognition of marine equipment regulations	2001
EU/US Guidelines on Regulatory Co-operation and Transparency	Non-binding guidelines for co-operation among EU and US regulators regarding technical barriers to trade	2002

Source: European Commission, DG TRADE, http://europa.eu.int/comm/trade/bilateral/usa/usa.htm

operation as useful in carrying out their essential rulemaking responsibilities in an increasingly integrated transatlantic and global marketplace. Such co-operation need not, and typically does not, involve joint rulemaking activities, but focuses instead on exchanges of information, identification of best practice, and early notification of new regulations being considered within either polity. In the area of food safety, for example, the European Commission and the US FDA have not identified or implemented common standards, for the reasons discussed above, yet the two regulators do engage in an ongoing dialogue both bilaterally and within the Codex Alimentarius (the global body for the establishment of food safety standards), and the Commission consulted extensively with its US counterparts in the design of the European Food Safety Authority. Similar bilateral exchanges occur regularly in other issue-areas, as well as within multi-lateral standard-setting bodies such as the International Standards Organization (for industrial standards) and the International Conference on Harmonization (for registration of pharmaceuticals).

A second and partially overlapping motivation for regulatory co-operation—most germane to the themes of this volume—is of course to avoid, or resolve, bilateral disputes about the potential trade-distorting effects of national regula-tions. As we have seen, domestic economic regulations can become a source of transatlantic economic tension, in two distinct ways. First, domestic regulations in areas such as consumer or environmental protection, food safety, or copyright protection can create non-tariff barriers to international trade and investment; examples include the recent disputes over the EU's Data Privacy Directive and its ban on hormone-treated beef, as well as over the disputed provisions of the US Copyright Act. Second, US and EU domestic regulators may apply their domestic regulations in an extrajurisdictional fashion, as for example when EU and US competition authorities insist on the right to review mergers among firms in the other constituency in so far as the proposed merger creates effects in the regula-tor's domestic jurisdiction, or when the US (or its constituent states) employs trade and economic sanctions as an instrument of foreign policy. In such cases, George Bermann has pointed out, 'the line between simple regulatory [co-operation] . . . and the settlement of trade disputes can become highly blurred'.[42] Indeed, as we have already seen, the prevention and settlement of transatlantic trade disputes has been a major motivation for the NTA and for specific efforts at US/EU regulatory co-operation.

B. The empirical record

The full range of regulatory co-operation agreements and practices between the US and the EU is beyond the scope of this chapter. Interviews with practitioners from the US and the EU reveal that considerable informal co-operation takes place across virtually every conceivable area of US and EU regulation, with little attention from the press, scholars, or political actors. Fortunately, the contribu-tions to this volume feature extensive analyses of three important cases of bilateral regulatory co-operation, in the fields of competition policy, the negoti-ation of EU/US Mutual Recognition Agreements, and the Safe Harbour Agree-ment on data privacy regulation. Taken together, these three cases, reviewed all too briefly here, illustrate the range of incentives for regulatory co-operation, as well as the various means for such co-operation and the significant obstacles that often stand in its way.

---

[42] Bermann, 'Regulatory Cooperation', op cit, 966.

1. Transatlantic competition policy co-operation

One of the earliest regulatory co-operation agreements signed between EU and US authorities, and one of the most successful, concerns co-operation in the enforcement of each side's respective competition policy laws, including most notably the examination of proposed mergers and acquisitions, reviewed by K. Mehta in his contribution to this volume.[43]

The incentives for co-operation in this area are substantial. First, as in other areas of regulation, EU and US regulators confront similar problems, and are increasingly called upon to rule upon the same cases, placing a premium on the sharing of information. Second, both US and EU courts have ruled that their respective regulators—namely, the Department of Justice and the Federal Trade Commission (FTC) on the US side, and the Directorate-General for Competition on the EU side—may enforce domestic competition laws extraterritorially against firms based outside their domestic jurisdiction, if and in so far as the behaviour in question (eg, a proposed merger) produces effects on competition in the domestic market. Such extraterritorial application of both EU and US competition law raises serious issues about the duplication of effort by the two sets of regulators, not to mention the adverse economic and political impact of inconsistent or conflicting decisions on the same case by EU and US regulators.

These concerns increased substantially in the early 1990s, moreover, with the rapid rise in cross-border mergers and acquisitions that accompanied the completion of the Union's '1992' internal market initiative. At approximately the same time, moreover, the EU adopted the 1990 Merger Control Regulation, which gave the Commission regulatory authority to review mergers above certain size thresholds and made the Commission an important interlocutor for the EU in this area. It was in this context of increasing cross-border mergers and increasing EU authority over such mergers that Competition Commissioner Leon Brittan proposed in 1990 to expand EU competition policy co-operation with third countries, beginning with a formal agreement with the US. US regulators responded positively to Brittan's proposal, and US and EU regulators agreed in 1991 to adopt an agreement committing them to co-operation in the area of competition policy, including the sharing of non-confidential information and co-ordination of enforcement activities. This agreement was later supplemented by two secondary agreements: the 1998 Positive Comity Agreement (which seeks to restrict the extraterritorial application of antitrust laws in non-merger cases, but has been formally invoked only once) and the 1999 Administrative

---

[43] This section draws on the analysis offered by K. Mehta in Part II of this volume. For excellent analyses of US/EU competition-policy co-operation, see also S.J. Evenett, A. Lehmann and B. Steil, *Antitrust Goes Global: What Future for Transatlantic Co-operation?* (2000); Y. Devuyst, 'Transatlantic Competition Policy Cooperation' in M.A. Pollack and G. Shaffer (eds), *Transatlantic Governance in the Global Economy* (2001) 127–151; and C. Damro, 'Building an International Identity: The EU and Extraterritorial Competition Policy' (2001) 8 *Journal of European Public Policy* 208–226.

Arrangements on Attendance in Hearings (which provide guidelines for the participation of EU and US regulators in each other's hearings).

In the decade since the signature of the first competition policy agreement, EU/US competition policy co-operation has generally operated smoothly and successfully, with regulators from the Commission, the Justice Department and the FTC sharing information and co-ordinating enforcement activities on a daily basis and co-operating successfully on over 600 cases during the course of the 1990s, including almost 500 merger decisions. The general success of EU/US competition policy co-operation in the area of merger control can be attributed to the broad transatlantic agreement among EU and US regulators about the basic scope and tools of policy, which has facilitated the task of co-ordinating enforcement actions and generating mutual trust among regulators.

Nevertheless, successful co-operation and conflict prevention between US and EU regulators can be hampered by persistent differences in the scope and focus of US and EU competition law, the procedures employed by both sides, and the exigencies of confidentiality which limit the sharing of information by US and EU agencies. These limitations can be illustrated in the atypical but well-known Boeing/McDonnell Douglas merger (both American firms), which was approved by the FTC in July 1997 only to be held up by Commission insistence that the companies agree to formal undertakings to satisfy its competition concerns. Although the case caused substantial strains in the transatlantic relationship, the companies concerned eventually agreed to the Commission's proposed remedies, allowing the merger to proceed.[44]

An even more dramatic difference of opinion occurred with regard to the proposed merger of two other US firms, GE and Honeywell, in 2001. Here again, US regulators approved the proposed merger, only to see the European Commission reject it in July 2001 after announcing that the firms' proposed remedies had failed to satisfy the Commission's concerns. Perhaps most strikingly, and unlike the previous case of EU/US disagreement in the Boeing/McDonnell Douglas merger, a number of analysts claimed that the disagreement between US and EU regulators reflected an underlying and fundamental difference in the criteria for assessing proposed mergers.[45] Although the resulting predictions of other imminent US/EU conflicts are almost certainly overstated, it is worthwhile noting that the Commission, in its December 2001 Green Paper on the review of the Merger Control Regulation, proposed to launch a debate on whether the Union should abandon its traditional 'dominance test' (ie, assessing whether a proposed merger would create a dominant position for the merged firm in the relevant market) in favour of a 'substantial lessening of competition' test (similar

---

[44] Devuyst, 'Transatlantic Competition Policy Cooperation', op cit, 142–145.

[45] See, eg, W.J. Kolasky and L.B. Greenfield, 'A View to a Kill: The Lost GE /Honeywell Deal Reveals a Trans-Atlantic Clash of Essentials,' *Legal Times*, 30 July 2001, 28; and D.S. Evans, 'The New Trustbusters: Brussels and Washington Part Ways,' *Foreign Affairs*, January/February 2002, 14–21.

to that already used in the US, Canada, and Australia).[46] Whether the Union will move in this direction remains unclear. If so, however, it would represent a striking example of regulatory convergence among regulators already notable for their similar (if not identical) regulatory philosophies and procedures.

2. *The US/EU mutual recognition agreements*

With the gradual decline of transatlantic tariff barriers, non-tariff barriers—including most notably national regulations relating to the safety, environmental impact and other characteristics of products—have increased in importance as irritants in the transatlantic trade relationship. Largely for this reason, the TABD and other producer groups on both sides of the Atlantic have pressed for transatlantic regulatory agreements to reduce the costs of complying with multiple regulatory standards in European and American markets. During the late 1990s, this push for transatlantic regulatory co-operation took its most promising and highest-profile form in the negotiation of the 1997 EU/US Mutual Recognition Agreement (MRA), which provides for mutual recognition of testing and certification requirements in six sectors.

The use of mutual recognition agreements had been an important component of the EU's internal market programme of the late 1980s and early 1990s, and was presented as an alternative to time-consuming and politically controversial harmonization of the national regulations of the various EU member states. In place of such harmonization, the concept of mutual recognition would allow a continuing diversity of national regulations (subject only to EU guidelines setting down 'essential requirements' for those regulations), together with a commitment by each member state to allow the importation and marketing of any product legally marketed in other member states.

By contrast with the EU model, the 1997 transatlantic MRA is less ambitious, since it does not provide for the mutual recognition of US and EU product standards as such, but only the mutual recognition of testing and certification procedures used to establish compliance with the respective US and European standards. Nevertheless, as Gregory Shaffer points out in his detailed case-study in this volume, the negotiation and especially the implementation of transatlantic MRAs has proven difficult, due to the substantial differences in regulatory procedure and philosophy across the two sides of the Atlantic.[47] In the EU, Shaffer points out, EU and national regulators interact regularly with the dual mandate of ensuring public safety and facilitating free trade within the internal market. By contrast, independent American regulators such as the FDA and the Occupational Safety and Health Administration (OSHA), operate under mandates and organizational cultures that emphasize US public health and safety and are silent on relations with foreign regulators. As *independent* regulators,

---

[46] European Commission, *Green Paper on the Review of Council Regulation (EEC) No. 4064/89*, COM(2001)745/6 final of 11 December 2001, 38–40.

[47] See the case-study by Shaffer in Part II of this volume.

moreover, these agencies are anxious to defend their autonomy against US trade policymakers as well as foreign regulators, and enjoy the legal and informational resources to resist what they perceive to be any compromise of their primary regulatory missions.

EU and US negotiators initially discussed negotiating mutual recognition arrangements in 11 sectors, but ultimately whittled this down to six, reflecting the respective priorities of the US (which sought agreement in areas such as telecommunications) and the EU (which insisted on agreements in pharmaceuticals and medical devices, where European firms had encountered high costs in complying with US standards). In consequence, the 1997 MRA consists of a framework agreement and six annexes respectively covering telecommunications equipment, electromagnetic compatibility, electrical safety, recreational craft, medical devices, and pharmaceutical good manufacturing practices.

Implementation of the MRAs takes place through a joint committee of US and EU trade officials who meet semi-annually, and through joint sectoral committees which oversee the implementation of the six individual annexes. Nevertheless, as Shaffer demonstrates in painstaking detail, implementation of the 1997 MRA remains uneven. Although three of the annexes (regarding telecommunications, recreational craft, and electromagnetic compatibility) have been implemented as required, the implementation of the other three annexes (on electrical safety, medical devices and pharmaceuticals) remains behind schedule, largely because of slowness by the FDA and OSHA in recognizing the equivalency of certification by European government regulators and private laboratories. Given the independence of these US regulatory agencies, both the USTR and its European counterparts have been limited in their ability to force the pace of US compliance.[48]

In sum, while MRAs have been promoted as a means of reconciling transatlantic regulatory differences and facilitating international trade without regulatory harmonization, in practice the negotiation and implementation of these agreements has proven more difficult than expected due to the very different sectoral interests and regulatory procedures and philosophies of the US and the EU. Successful MRAs, Shaffer points out, cannot be accomplished 'on the cheap', but require significant additional resources to finance the effective implementation of agreements by regulators with limited funds, and to promote the creation of transatlantic regulatory networks to build mutual trust among reluctant regulators.

3. *Data privacy and the Safe Harbour Agreement*

Both the US and the EU have adopted extensive regulation regarding the protection of personal data privacy. As in other areas, however, the US and the EU have

---

[48] In addition to the 1997 MRA, on 12 June 2001, the US and the EU initialled an Agreement on Mutual Recognition of Certificates of Conformity for Marine Equipment, which goes beyond the earlier agreements by recognizing not only testing and certification procedures but also basic regula-

taken different approaches to the problem of data privacy, giving rise to potential disputes regarding the transfer of personal data across jurisdictions with differing regulatory approaches. More specifically, the problem of differing approaches to data privacy protection led to a major transatlantic dispute following the adoption of the EU's 1998 Data Privacy Directive, and to an innovative attempt at co-operation through the US/EU Safe Harbour Agreement, which has attempted to provide a negotiated interface between persistently different US and EU approaches to data privacy regulation.

The transatlantic dispute over data privacy is reviewed in detail by Shaffer in his contribution to this book, and dates effectively from 24 October 1998, when Directive (EC) 95/46 on the Protection of Individuals with Regard to the Processing of Personal Data and the Free Movement of Such Data became effective.[49] By contrast with the US approach to data privacy, which is based largely on self-regulation within guidelines set down by sector-specific federal laws, the EU's Data Privacy Directive establishes a cross-sectoral set of regulations governing the use of personal data by the public and private sectors. Specifically, the Directive prohibits data controllers from processing information unless the individual 'unambiguously' consents to such processing, and it requires member states to enforce European standards at the national level and to provide judicial remedies for infringement of data privacy rights. Most importantly for our purposes here, Article 25 of the Directive provides that member states shall prohibit all data transfers to a third country if the Commission finds that the country does not ensure 'an adequate level of protection' of data privacy. Since it appeared that the US might not provide for 'adequate' data privacy protection under the Directive's criteria, US and EU authorities engaged in intensive negotiations to avoid a ban on data flows to the US, culminating in their agreement on Safe Harbour Principles in March 2000.

Under the agreement, EU member states must recognize that US firms' adherence to these Principles is sufficient to protect them from member state challenge. The guidelines set forth seven core data privacy principles for industry to follow, which respectively cover the following issues: Notice, Choice, Onward Transfer, Security, Data Integrity, Access and Enforcement. US firms join the Safe Harbour programme by annually certifying to the US Department of Commerce that they will comply with the Principles. The Department of Commerce then places the company's name on its website list of certifying firms, while the FTC may take

---

tory standards and procedures. This more ambitious approach, however, has been possible primarily because of pre-existing harmonization of international standards through the International Maritime Organization. See case-study by Shaffer in Part II of this volume.

[49] This section draws extensively from the case-study by Gregory C. Shaffer in Part II of this volume. For other useful analyses of the data privacy case, see, eg, G.C. Shaffer, 'Globalization and Social Protection: The Impact of EU and International Rules in Ratcheting Up of US Privacy Standards' (2000) 25 *Yale Journal of International Law* 1–88; C. Kuner, 'Beyond Safe Harbour: European Data Protection Law and Electronic Commerce' (2001) 31 *International Lawyer* 79–88; and J. Reidenberg, 'E-Commerce and Trans-Atlantic Privacy' (2001) 8 *Houston Law Review* 717–749.

enforcement actions against firms that falsely claim to be in compliance with the Principles.

The Safe Harbour Agreement is an innovative approach to transatlantic regulatory co-operation, allowing each polity to retain its distinct regulatory approach while providing individual US firms with the option of complying with the Principles as a means of gaining access to the European market. Implementation of the agreement, however, remains in its infancy, and analysts differ in their views of its success. Critics point in particular to the relatively small number of US companies that have certified their adherence to the Principles, and the voluntary nature of the process for US firms.[50] Nevertheless, as Shaffer demonstrates, companies engaged in transatlantic business operate in the shadow of the EU Directive's potential enforcement, and the adoption of the Principles has spurred greater attention to data privacy protection within the US, including the development of US privacy programmes such as TRUSTe, which rates the privacy protection of internet sites, and the privacy seal of the Better Business Bureau OnLine. In the longer term, the success or failure of the Safe Harbour Agreement will ultimately depend on its widespread adoption by US firms; on the effective enforcement of the Principles by regulatory authorities and courts on both sides of the Atlantic; and on continuing co-operation among US and EU regulators in responding to the inevitable technological changes in this area.

C. Obstacles to transatlantic regulatory co-operation

Although brief and selective, this review of co-operation across three sectors suggests several tentative conclusions about both the benefits and the potential obstacles to transatlantic regulatory co-operation.

With regard to the potential benefits of transatlantic regulatory co-operation, we have identified two. First, as we have seen, regulatory co-operation has the potential to enhance the efficiency of regulation, through the exchange of information and best practice, the provision of early warning of potential disputes, the avoidance or management of conflicting regulatory decisions, and the gradual building of mutual trust among regulators. Second, regulatory co-operation can facilitate transatlantic trade and investment by removing duplicative regulatory requirements and other non-tariff barriers within the transatlantic marketplace. Such co-operation, moreover, need not involve the complete harmonization or convergence of EU and US regulations, although there is some preliminary evidence of convergence in specific issue-areas, including the acceptance by the US of a mutual recognition scheme similar to that long practised

---

[50] As of 24 February 2003, there were 302 firms certifying their compliance with the Principles. See the US Department of Commerce website for safe harbour, http://www.export.gov/safeHarbour/, accessed on 24 February 2003.

in the EU, and the EU's active discussion of moving from its current 'dominance test' to a possible new standard for regulatory mergers closer to that employed by competition authorities in the US.

Yet, despite the obvious promise of transatlantic regulatory co-operation, a broad survey of EU/US co-operation in various areas, including the three case-studies analyzed above, points to a number of potential obstacles to successful transatlantic regulatory co-operation:

- **Regulatory independence.** In a number of areas, US regulators enjoy greater regulatory independence than their European counterparts, and may resist what they perceive to be an effort to compromise domestic regulatory stand-ards and processes in the interests of international trade. The result in some cases is that the USTR and other central agencies of the federal government encounter difficulty guaranteeing compliance with regulatory agreements by specific regulatory agencies, such as the FDA and OSHA, if and in so far as these agencies believe that implementation of those agreements would com-promise established US regulatory standards and procedures.

- **Transparency and administrative law requirements.** Across a wide range of issue-areas, US regulators express concern about the different administrative law requirements for regulators in the US and the EU, most notably in the area of transparency. In the US, regulators are required to adhere to the 'notice-and-comment' rulemaking procedures of the Administrative Procedure Act, which requires agencies to provide public notice of proposed regulations in the *Federal Register*, allow individuals to submit comments prior to the final adoption of new rules, and keep a public record of the regulatory process. The EU rulemaking procedure, although typically characterized by wide-spread consultation of interested parties, does not incorporate these features.

- **Confidential information.** The need to protect confidential information of firms and other private parties also places limits on the ability of both sides to co-operate in the adoption and implementation of regulations, particularly in the enforcement of US and EU competition laws regarding cartels and concentrations, where firms have been more reluctant to agree to the sharing of confidential information than in the area of merger control reviewed above.

- **Multi-level governance.** The US and the EU are both federal or quasi-federal governance systems, with regulatory powers divided in most sectors between the federal /EU level on the one hand, and individual states/member states or even local governments on the other. In terms of regulatory co-operation, this division of regulatory powers means that US executive-branch negotiators and EU Commission officials are frequently charged with negotiating regulatory agreements in areas where the states retain at least partial regulatory compe-tence, and to charges from both sides that their counterparts are unable to 'deliver the states'. Examples of such state regulatory powers on the US side include the regulation of insurance and other services as well as public procurement, where the EU has insisted that the participation of individual US states is vital to the enforcement of regulatory agreements.[51] Similar problems afflict the EU side, where Commission efforts to engage in regulatory co-operation may be frustrated by resistance among individual member states, as in the case of GMOs, or by the slow adoption of EU-level regulations, as in the case of financial services.

- **Regulatory sovereignty.** Ultimately, the adoption of the broad regulatory frameworks for economic activity, consumer and environmental protection, and other areas is entrusted, on both sides of the Atlantic, to democratically accountable bodies such as the Congress and President in the US and the Council of Ministers and European Parliament in the EU. Within the EU, the harmonization and mutual recognition of national regulations has been accomplished in large part through a deliberate transfer of regulatory sovereignty to the European level (as in EU merger control); through the pooling of regulatory sovereignty in the Council of Ministers and the European Parliament (as in data privacy and food safety); and through the mutual recognition of standards as enforced by the European Court of Justice. To date, however, the EU and the US have proven unwilling to compromise their regulatory sovereignty in the various agreements reviewed above; indeed, even the most successful experiment in transatlantic regulatory co-operation, that in competition policy, is predicated explicitly on each side's ability to co-operate without any substantial change to its domestic regulatory objectives and procedures.

The existence of these various obstacles does not, of course, mean that transatlantic regulatory co-operation is doomed to failure. Some areas, like competition policy, are subject to relatively few obstacles to successful co-operation, while others, such as food safety, encounter multiple obstacles. Even in difficult areas like food safety, moreover, regular exchange of information has proven useful in allowing regulators on each side to understand each other's regulatory philosophies and procedures, and gradually to build up the trust among regulators that will be required for the successful operation of future efforts at mutual recognition or harmonization of regulations.

As a first step in this direction, the EU and the US agreed in April 2002 to the adoption of a set of non-binding 'EU/US Guidelines on Regulatory Co-operation and Transparency'. Although this joint statement of principles does not bind either the US or the EU to any specific regulatory measures, and explicitly excludes the sensitive area of agriculture, the agreement does call for regularized exchange of information between EU and US regulators, and for consideration of harmonization or mutual recognition of standards 'as may be appropriate, in specific cases', to minimize unnecessary technical barriers to trade. In addition,

---

[51] For a good discussion of the obstacles posed by US federalism in regulatory co-operation, see European Commission, *The Transatlantic Economic Partnership: Overview and Assessment*, Coordination: DG TRADE.E.3, October 2000.

the document suggests that both EU and US regulators should apply potentially far-reaching principles of transparency in rule-making, including public notification of, and comment on, proposed regulations. The implementation of the guidelines is to be reviewed on an ongoing basis by the TEP/TBT Working Group.[52]

The significance of the new EU/US Guidelines will depend on their implementation in practice across an array of issue-areas in the months and years to come. Regardless of the success of this specific endeavour, however, regulatory cooperation remains an important priority for the EU and the US in achieving their respective regulatory aims while also preventing and resolving potential trade disputes.

CONCLUSIONS: THE NEW TRANSATLANTIC ECONOMIC AGENDA

The US and the EU have an extraordinarily close and important economic relationship, the health of which is vital to both sides; yet the successive liberalization of transatlantic trade and investment has raised—and will continue to raise—disputes between the two partners, including traditional disputes as well as the behind-the-border regulatory disputes emphasized in this chapter. To be clear, it is not argued in this chapter that traditional trade disputes are disappearing: witness the case-studies on bananas, safeguard measures, anti-dumping, countervailing duties, and export subsidies, all examined at length in this volume. Furthermore, despite the generally low level of tariffs between the EU and US, tariff peaks and quotas remain for both sides in a number of sensitive areas, which can and should be subject to further reductions in the Doha Round of trade liberalization talks within the WTO. Nevertheless, while the persistence and seriousness of traditional trade disputes should not be underestimated, the multilateral rules-based trading system of the WTO is generally well equipped to address such issues, for which the multilateral Dispute Settlement Understanding was primarily designed.

Perhaps the greatest challenge to the transatlantic economic relationship, therefore, is the expansion of the transatlantic economic agenda to encompass domestic regulations that are adopted for legitimate purposes but act in practice as non-tariff barriers to trade, fragmenting the transatlantic market and in some cases leading to bitter and intractable trade disputes. As we have seen, these types of disputes also create enormous legal and political challenges to the dispute settlement procedure of the WTO, where judgments in areas such as the beef hormones and Irish music disputes have created political controversy

---

[52] 'EU-US Guidelines on Regulatory Cooperation and Transparency,' available at http://europa.eu.int/comm/enterprise/enterprise_policy/gov_relations/regulcooptransat.htm. See also 'Transatlantic Bid to Cut Red Tape,' *European Report*, 10 April 2002; and Michael Mann, 'Drive to Head Off Trade Rifts,' *Financial Times*, 13 April 2002.

without (at the time of writing) securing full compliance from the states concerned.

For these reasons, any attempt to deepen transatlantic economic integration between the US and the EU must address not only tariffs, quotas, and similar disputes about subsidies, anti-dumping actions and safeguard measures, but also the new-style regulatory disputes that are likely to become the most important barriers in the transatlantic marketplace, and place the greatest strains on the EU/US relationship and the multilateral WTO system, in the medium to long-term future. I attempt in Part IV of this volume to draw some policy implications of transatlantic regulatory disputes for possible multilateral, bilateral, and unilateral reforms. Any such reforms, however, should be based on a careful understanding of the varied nature of transatlantic trade disputes, including their causes as well as the effectiveness (or ineffectiveness) of various mechanisms for the prevention and settlement of those disputes, which are examined in detail in Part II of this volume.

APPENDIX 1: EU-US BARRIERS TO TRADE IN GOODS, SERVICES AND FOREIGN INVESTMENT

Type of measure	EU concerns about US rules	US concerns about EU rules
Tariffs	Tariff peaks: Food products; Textiles; Footwear; Leather goods; Jewellery; Ceramics and glass; Trucks; Railway cars; Optical fibres; Tubes for computer monitors. SANCTIONS IN RETALIATION FOR THE EU BAN ON HORMONE-TREATED BEEF Tariff quotas: dairy products, tobacco	BANANAS (tariff quota + discriminatory licensing) (settled) CUMULATIVE RECOVERY SYSTEM (brown rice) ADMINISTRATION OF CUSTOMS DUTIES FOR RICE (B) (agreement 11/01)
Trade defence instruments	1916 ANTIDUMPING ACT SAFEGUARD MEASURES ON STEEL WIRE ROD (3/2000) SAFEGUARD MEASURES ON WELDED STEEL PIPE (3/2000) BYRD AMENDMENT (anti-dumping duties go to injured industry) FAILURE TO LIFT COUNTERVAILING DUTIES AFTER SUNSET REVIEWS	

APPENDIX 1: (*Continued*)

Type of measure	EU concerns about US rules	US concerns about EU rules
	QUOTA ON THE IMPORT OF WHEAT GLUTEN (withdrawn 6/2001) METHODOLOGY OF COUNTERVAILING DUTIES WITH RESPECT TO BRITISH STEEL ANTI-DUMPING DUTIES ON SEAMLESS PIPE	
Other customs barriers	Excessive invoicing requirements EU not recognized as a country of origin TEXTILES & LEATHER: CUSTOMS FORMALITIES & RULES OF ORIGIN Tuna (certification of origin)	
Other levies and charges	Customs fees (eg Merchandise Processing Fee) HARBOUR MAINTENANCE TAX and Harbour Services Fee 50% tax on imported equipment for boats Taxes that fall disproportionately on European automakers • Luxury tax (70%) • Gas Guzzler tax (85%) • CAFÉ penalties (~100%)	
Regulatory barriers to trade	SHRIMP-TURTLE – to import shrimp countries must be certified as matching US efforts to protect sea turtles (EU third party) Tuna-dolphin – to import tuna countries must be approved by the National Marine Fisheries Service General prohibition on the importation of dairy products made from unpasteurized milk Effective prohibition on the importation of yogurt Milk protein for yogurt must come from approved dairies Divergence from international standards	HORMONE-TREATED BEEF Lack of national treatment with respect to GEOGRAPHICAL INDICATIONS for agricultural products and food Poultry treated with chlorinated water Effective moratorium on approval of GM products since 4/98 Mandatory labelling of all foods containing more than 1% GM ingredients Stringent certification of non-hormone-treated beef (new US programme seems adequate)

(Continued)

APPENDIX 1: (*Continued*)

Type of measure	EU concerns about US rules	US concerns about EU rules
	Reliance on third-party conformity assessment (eg, re: electrical equipment and domestic appliances)	Food, feed and fertilizer containing specified risk materials (narrower product range than previous rule)
	US and Canadian content labelling of cars	Treatment and traceability of raw materials for production of gelatine for human consumption (agreement near on health certificate that would enable US exports to resume)
	Approval slower than for US-produced drugs	
	Over-the-counter drug approval requires US market history	
	Extensive product description (textiles and leather)	EU approval of third country establishments exporting animal products (esp. dairy)
	Citrus fruits must be landed at North Atlantic ports	
	Rules on all imports of ruminant animals and animal products from all EU countries because of BSE	Derogation from EU standards required for US wine (ongoing negotiations to try to resolve)
	Ban on some uncooked meat products	Heat or pressure treatment of softwood packing material (new EU rule similar to draft international standard)
	Strict condition on imports of egg products (continuous inspection of production process)	
	Low acid canned food (eg fish and dairy products) subject to detailed prior approval system	Metric-only labelling (implementation delayed to 2009)
	Pre-clearance inspection of apples and pears from some member states for pests	Slow and arbitrary new aircraft certification
	Prohibition on imports of all animals and products from a member state where a disease exists (not just region where found)	Hushkits (dispute brought to ICAO, work on an ICAO standard)
		Labelling of TSP (fertilizer) disadvantages US exports
	Exporters of meat or meat products to the US may not process meat from countries that are not recognized as free from diseases of concern to the US	Restrictive limits on low frequency emissions from electrical and electronic equipment
Regulatory barriers to trade (US state and EU member state level)	Duplicate approval of wine labels State-level safety certification and environmental protection requirements (especially of agricultural and food products) Ban on fuel additive MTBE (CA)	Bans on some approved GM products (A, I & L) No approvals for planting certain GM products (G, P) Unresponsive to requests for field trials of GM crops (Gr)

APPENDIX 1: (*Continued*)

Type of measure	EU concerns about US rules	US concerns about EU rules
		Ban on GM in animal feed adopted (It)—not in force. HCFC bans by Sw & Fn Additional navigation light requirements (Fn) – suspended Testing of wheat leading to virtual ban on imports (transshipment recently permitted) (Gr) Harsh interpretation of EU SPS requirements caused or threatened to cause problems for: processed meat products, poultry products, game meat, seafood, animal feed, wood products (It) Qualitative imports standards and high testing and registration fees for bull semen (It)
Services barriers	50% tax on all non-emergency repairs to US-owned ships carried out outside the US Barriers in mobile communications (investment restrictions, lengthy procedures) De facto reciprocity requirements regarding satellite-based communications services Exclusive digital terrestrial television standard (ATSC) different from EU (DVB-T) Impractical for foreign securities firms to establish branches in order to engage in broker-dealer activities Foreign mutual funds unable to make public offerings because of registration conditions Foreign investment is restricted in coastal and domestic shipping Partnership with US entity required for granting of licences for landing submarine cables	European content requirements for TV broadcasts Access to the single aviation market restricted to firms majority-owned and controlled by EU nationals Banking, insurance and investment services rules require reciprocal treatment by home country (no US firms adversely affected)

(*Continued*)

APPENDIX 1: (*Continued*)

Type of measure	EU concerns about US rules	US concerns about EU rules
	Only US citizens or corporations organized under US law can operate or maintain power facilities on federal land Foreign stake in airlines capped at 49% (25% of voting stock) Foreign-built vessels prohibited from engaging in coastwise trade either directly between or via a foreign port and cannot be registered for dredging, towing or salvage.	
	State-level measures: Prohibitions on EU exporters distributing, rebottling or retailing their own wine Some states require insurance companies to already be established in another state Some states require insurers to buy reinsurance from state-licensed insurance companies	*Member state measures*: Content requirements for radio broadcasts (Fr) Requirements that cinemas show European films (It, Sp) Nationality requirements affecting to varying degrees the provision of legal services (A, Dk, Fn, Fr, G, It) Strict restrictions on advertising by foreign legal consultants (Dk) Nationality requirements affecting to varying degrees the provision of accounting services (A, Dk, Fr)
Foreign investment barriers	National security vetting (Exon-Florio Amendment) US subsidiary required to exploit deep-water ports or to fish in US Exclusive Economic Zone Fishing-vessel-owning entities must be 75% owned and controlled by US citizens Foreign individuals or foreign-controlled corporations cannot acquire licences for using nuclear materials	'Mirror-image' reciprocity applies to investments in the extraction of hydrocarbons (no US firms adversely affected)

APPENDIX 1: (*Continued*)

Type of measure	EU concerns about US rules	US concerns about EU rules
	Conditional national treatment governs participation in government research programmes (subsidiaries in US allowed to participate, but eligibility process more cumbersome)	

Notes: Includes measures in effect + those for which implementation has been suspended as a result of agreement.

Does not include non-discriminatory measures, systemic barriers (such as the presence of monopolies; the pricing of pharmaceuticals; or delays and lack of transparency in standard setting), government procurement, intellectual property protection; subsidies (including FSC) or issues being prosecuted under EU rules.

Barriers in SMALL CAPS are the subject of WTO proceedings (consultations have been requested)
Sources: Commission, *Chapter on United States Barriers to Trade and Investment 2001*; USTR, *National Trade Estimate Chapter: Foreign Trade Barriers 2001*.

APPENDIX 2: WTO CASES BY THE EU AGAINST THE US
(EXCLUDES CASES AS THIRD PARTY)

Title and reference number	Short description of the measures	Relevant WTO provisions	Consultation	Panel	Status
WT/DS38 Cuban Liberty and Democratic Solidarity Act	Extraterritorial application of the US embargo of trade with Cuba in so far as it restricts trade between the EU and Cuba or between the EU and the US. The creation of a right of action in favour of US citizens to sue EU persons and companies in US courts in order to obtain compensation for Cuban properties. The denial of visas and exclusion from the US of persons involved in confiscating or 'trafficking' in confiscated property.	GATT (V, XI, XIII) GATS (II, III, VI, XI, XVI, XVII, Annex on Movement of Natural Persons)	5/96	10/96	Understanding reached (4/97)

(*Continued*)

APPENDIX 2: (*Continued*)

Title and reference number	Short description of the measures	Relevant WTO provisions	Consul- tation	Panel	Status
WT/DS39 Tariff increases on products from the EU	The measures were taken in response to the adoption of EU legislation on the use of hormones in livestock farming, and seek unilaterally to settle the issue without resorting to the mechanisms of the WTO.	GATT (I, II, XXIII) DSU (3, 22, 23)	4/96	9/96	[No report]
WT/DS63 Anti-dumping measures on imports of solid urea from the former German Democratic Republic	By maintaining the order against the five states of the former GDR the US has ignored de jure and de facto their full integration into the reunified Federal Republic of Germany, and thus the economic integration of their companies into the German market economy	Anti-Dumping (9.2, 11)	12/96	—	
WT/DS85 Measures affecting textiles and apparel products	Changes to rules of origin of textile and apparel products, which entered into force on 1 July 1996, adversely affect exports of EU fabrics, scarves and other flat textile products, which are no longer recognized as being of EU origin and lose the free access to the US that they enjoyed before	Textiles (2.4, 4.2, 4.4) Rules of origin (2) GATT (III) TBT (2)	6/97	—	Negotiated solution (9/97)
WT/DS88 Measure affecting government procurement	Massachusetts law regulating state contracts with companies doing business with or in Burma (Myanmar)	GPA (VIIIb, X, XIII)	6/97	9/98	Law overturned under US law
WT/DS100 Measures affecting imports of poultry products	Ban on imports of poultry and poultry products produced in the EU until the United States is able to obtain additional assurances of product safety. No grounds given.	GATT (I, III, X, XI) SPS (2, 3, 4, 5, 8, Annex C) TBT (2, 5)	8/97	—	
WT/DS108 Tax treatment for 'Foreign Sales Corporations'	The FSC scheme provides for an exemption to the general rules established in the US Internal Revenue Code which results in substantial tax savings for US companies exporting through FSCs	Subsidies (3) Agriculture (8, 9, 10)	11/97	7/98	Panel found in favour of the EU

APPENDIX 2: *(Continued)*

Title and reference number	Short description of the measures	Relevant WTO provisions	Consul-tation	Panel	Status
					EU did not consider 'FSC Replacement Act' adequate Panel found in favour of the EU Appellate Body upheld Panel
WT/DS118 Harbour Maintenance Tax	Ad valorem tax (0.125%) on all waterborne imports entering US ports	GATT (I, II, III, VIII, X)	2/98	—	Reform proposed (Harbour Services Fee), but EU still views as problematic
WT/DS136 Anti-dumping Act of 1916	The Act imposes penal sanctions against the importation of goods and their sale in the US when the price is lower than in the country of production or in other foreign countries where the goods are exported	GATT (III:4, VI:1 and VI:2) WTO (XVI:4) Anti-Dumping (1, 2, 3, 4 & 5)	6/98	11/98	Appellate Body found in favour of the EU Implementation pending
WT/DS138 Imposition of counter-vailing duties on certain hot-rolled lead and bismuth carbon steel products originating in the UK	Methodology relied on the presumption (based mostly on pre-WTO legislation and practice) that benefits from prior subsidies pass through without the need to show that a benefit continues to be conferred	Subsidies (1.1b, 10, 14, 19.4)	6/98	1/99	Appellate Body upheld Panel report favouring EU (5/00)
WT/DS151 Measures affecting textiles and apparel products (II)	Same as WT/DS85	Same as WT/DS85	11/98	—	Negotiated solution (9/97)

(Continued)

Mark A. Pollack

APPENDIX 2: (*Continued*)

Title and reference number	Short description of the measures	Relevant WTO provisions	Consul- tation	Panel	Status
WT/DS152 Trade Act of 1974, ss 301–310	Imposes specific, strict time limits within which unilateral determinations must be made that other WTO members have failed to comply with their WTO obligations and trade sanctions must be taken against such WTO members	DSU (3, 21, 22, 23) WTO (XVI.4) GATT (I, II, III, VIII, XI)	11/98	1/99	US through a Statement of Admini- strative Action undertaken to act consistent with WTO obligations Panel ruled that so long as respected compatible (11/ 99)
WT/DS160 US Copyright Act, s 110(5)	US Copyright Act, s 110(5) permits, under certain conditions, the playing of radio and television music in public places without the payment of a royalty fee	TRIPS (9(1), 13)	1/99	4/99	Panel found in favour of the EU (7/00) EU and US have negotiated an arrangement Implementation pending
WT/DS165 Import measures on certain products from the EU	100% tariffs on certain products in retaliation for the EU's failure to bring its banana trade regime into compliance with WTO ruling	GATT (I, II, VIII) DSU (3, 21, 22, 23)	3/99	5/99	Appellate Body found in favour of the EU (12/ 00) US brought sanctions into agreement Sanctions suspended as result of 4/01 agreement
WT/DS166 Safeguard measures on imports of wheat gluten from the EU	Methodology not ensure that all injury due to imports. Imports from Canada were excluded from the investigation	GATT (I, XIX) Agriculture (4.2) Safeguard (2.1, 4, 5, 8, 12)	3/99	6/99	Appellate Body found in favour of the EU (12/ 00)
WT/DS176 Omnibus Appro- priations Act, s 211	Section 211 provides that the registration or renewal in the US of a trademark previously abandoned by a trademark owner whose business and assets have been confiscated under Cuban law is no longer permitted without consent of the previous owner. No US court shall recognize or enforce such rights	TRIPS (2, 15, 16, 41, 42, 62)	7/99	6/00	Appellate Body found in favour of the EU (1/02)

APPENDIX 2: (*Continued*)

Title and reference number	Short description of the measures	Relevant WTO provisions	Consul-tation	Panel	Status
WT/DS186 Tariff Act of 1930, s 337 and amendments thereto	Under s 337, the US can investigate whether imported goods infringe US intellectual property rights and can exclude them from entry into the US. Despite amendment, the EU considers that the procedures and remedies are substantially different from procedures concerning domestic goods and discriminate against European industries and goods	GATT (III) TRIPS (2, 3, 9, 27, 41, 42, 49, 50, 51)	1/00	—	
WT/DS200 Trade Act of 1974, s 306 and amendments thereto ('carousel')	Section 306 provides for a mandatory modification (every six months) of the products subject to sanctions imposed against a WTO member which has not complied with a WTO panel ruling	DSU (3, 21, 22, 23) GATT (I, II, XI, XXIII)	6/00	—	
WT/DS212 Counter vailing measures concerning certain products from the EU (14 cases)	US application of countervailing duties based on an irrefutable presumption that non-recurring subsidies granted to a producer, prior to a change of ownership, 'pass through' to the current producer following the change of ownership	SCM (10, 19, 21)	11/00	8/01	Panel established
WT/DS213 Countervailing duties on certain corrosion-resistant carbon steel flat products from Germany	Results of a full sunset review which maintains CV duties. The original duty was imposed prior to entry into force of WTO agreements. EU considers that it would not have been possible to impose this duty (less than 1%) if the investigation had been governed by the SCM agreement	SCM (10, 11.9, 21)	11/00	8/01	Panel established
WT/DS214 Definitive safeguard measures on imports of steel wire rod and circular welded carbon quality line pipe	EU considers that ss 201 and 202 of the Trade Act of 1974 and s 311 of the NAFTA Implementation Act contain provisions which prevent the US from respecting Safeguards Agreement	Safeguards (2, 3, 4, 5, 8, 12) GATT (I, XIX)	11/00	8/01	Panel established

(*Continued*)

APPENDIX 2: (*Continued*)

Title and reference number	Short description of the measures	Relevant WTO provisions	Consul-tation	Panel	Status
WT/DS217 Continued dumping and subsidy Offset Act of 2000 (Byrd Amendment)	The Act mandates the distribution of the proceeds of duties levied pursuant to a CVD, an AD order or a finding under the Anti-dumping Act of 1921 to the affected domestic producers	AD (5, 8, 18) SCM (11, 18, 32) GATT (X) WTO (XVI)	12/00	7/01	Panel established and joined with panel established by Canada and Mexico (WT/DS234)
WT/DS225 Anti-dumping duties on seamless pipe from Italy	Results of a sunset review which found that anti-dumping duties on imports of seamless line and pressure pipe from Italy, will continue at a rate of 1.27%. EU considers this finding is in breach of AD Agreement (duties not lower than 2%)	AD (5.8, 11.1, 11.3, 17) GATT (XXII:1)	2/01	—	

Note: Columns 'Consultation' and 'Panel' chapter date requested.
Source: Adapted from DG Trade 'WTO—Dispute Settlement' (updated 15 January 2002), http://europa.eu.int/comm/trade/pdf/cases.xls, accessed 15 February 2002; and the WTO's dispute database (http://www.wto.org/english/tratop_e/dispu_e/dispu_status_e.htm), accessed 15 February 2002.

APPENDIX 3: WTO CASES BY THE US AGAINST THE EU AND ITS MEMBER STATES (EXCLUDES CASES AS A THIRD PARTY)

Title and reference number	Short description of the measures	Relevant WTO provisions	Consul-tation	Panel	Status
WT/DS13 Duties on imported grains	Reference price system used to determine the duties applicable to imports of grains appear to result in the application of higher rates of duties to shipments of US grains than is permitted under the EU WTO tariff schedule and to discriminate against US exports of grains	GATT (I, II, VII, X) Agreement on Imple-menting GATT Article VII (10, 11, 22, Annex I)	7/95	3/97	Negotiated agreement (11/95) Request for panel withdrawn following imple-mentation (4/97)
WT/DS26 Measures affecting meat and meat products (hormones)	EU measures prohibiting the importation of meat and meat products that have been treated with growth hormones	GATT (III or XI) SPS (2, 3, 5) TBT (2) Agriculture (4)	1/96	4/96	Appellate Body found in favour of US (2/98) Sanctions in place

APPENDIX 3: *(Continued)*

Title and reference number	Short description of the measures	Relevant WTO provisions	Consul- tation	Panel	Status
WT/DS27 Import regime for bananas	EU regime for the importation, sale and distribution of bananas established by Council Regulation No 404/93 and subsequent legislation, regulations and administrative measures, including those reflecting the provisions of the Framework Agreement on Bananas, which implement, supplement and amend that regime	GATT (I, II, III, X, XI, XIII) Licensing (1, 3) Agriculture TRIMs (2) GATS (II, XVI, XVII)	2/96	4/96	Appellate Body found in favour of the US and Ecuador (9/97) Compliance panel found revised EU regime still incompatible (4/99) US, Ecuador and EU negotiated settlement (4/01)
WT/DS37 Portugal— patent protection under the Industrial Property Act	The term granted existing patents under the Portuguese Industrial Property Act appears to be inconsistent with Portugal's obligations under the TRIPS Agreement	(GATS (33, 65, 70)	4/96		Negotiated solution (5/96)
WT/DS62 Customs classification of some computer equipment	Reclassification of certain LAN adapter cards, automatic data processing machines and units thereof as telecommunications apparatus raised the tariff applied to them	GATT (II)	11/96	2/97	Appellate Body overturned Panel report favouring US (6/98)
WT/DS67 UK—customs classification of some computer equipment	Same as WT/DS62	Same as WT/ DS62	Same as WT/ DS62	Same as WT/ DS62	Same as WT/DS62
WT/DS68 Ireland— customs classification of some computer equipment	Same as WT/DS62	Same as WT/ DS62	Same as WT/ DS62	Same as WT/ DS62	Same as WT/DS62
WT/DS80 Belgium— measures affecting commercial telephone directory services	Conditions for obtaining a licence to publish commercial directories in Belgium	GATS (II, VI, VIII, XVII)	5/97	—	

(Continued)

APPENDIX 3: *(Continued)*

Title and reference number	Short description of the measures	Relevant WTO provisions	Consul- tation	Panel	Status
WT/DS82 Ireland— measures affecting the grant of copyright and neighbouring rights	Ireland appears not to grant copyright and neighbouring rights in accordance with the TRIPS Agreement	TRIPS (9–14, 63, 65)	5/97	1/98	
WT/DS83 Denmark— measures affecting the enforcement of intellectual property rights	Denmark does not appear to make available provisional measures in the context of civil proceedings involving intellectual property rights	TRIPS (50, 63, 65)	5/97	—	Negotiated solution (3/01)
WT/DS86 Sweden— measures affecting the enforcement of intellectual property rights	Sweden does not appear to make available provisional measures in the context of civil proceedings involving intellectual property rights	TRIPS (50, 63, 65)	6/97	—	Negotiated solution (6/97)
WT/DS104 Export subsidies— processed cheese	Export subsidies, including under an inward processing arrangement, in favour of processed cheese distort markets for dairy products and adversely affect US sales of dairy products	Agriculture (8, 9, 10, 11) Subsidies (3)	10/97	—	
WT/DS115 Ireland— measures affecting the grant of copyright and neighbouring rights	Ireland appears not to grant copyright and neighbouring rights in accordance with the TRIPs Agreement	TRIPS (9–14, 63, 65, 70)	1/98	1/98	
WT/DS124 Enforcement of intellectual property rights for motion pictures and television programmes	TV stations in Greece regularly broadcast copyrighted motion pictures and TV programmes without the authorization of copyright owners. Effective remedies against copyright infringement do not appear to be provided or enforced	TRIPS (41, 61)	5/98	—	Negotiated solution (3/01)

APPENDIX 3: (*Continued*)

Title and reference number	Short description of the measures	Relevant WTO provisions	Consul-tation	Panel	Status
WT/DS125 Greece—enforcement of intellectual property rights for motion pictures and television programmes	Same as WT/DS124	Same as WT/DS124	Same as WT/DS124	Same as WT/DS124	Same as WT/DS124
WT/DS127 Belgium—certain income tax measures constituting subsidies	Belgian corporate taxpayers receive a special tax exemption for recruiting a departmental head for exports.	Subsidies (3)	5/98	—	
WT/DS128 Netherlands—certain income tax measures constituting subsidies	Dutch income tax law permits exporters to establish a special 'export reserve' for income derived from export sales	Subsidies (3)	5/98	—	
WT/DS129 Greece—certain income tax measures constituting subsidies	Greek exporters are entitled to a special annual tax deduction calculated as a percentage of export income	Subsidies (3)	5/98	—	
WT/DS130 Ireland—certain income tax measures constituting subsidies	Under Irish income tax law, 'special trading houses' qualify for a special tax rate in respect of trading income from the export sale of Irish-manufactured goods	Subsidies (3)	5/98	—	
WT/DS131 France—certain income tax measures constituting subsidies	French companies may deduct, temporarily, certain start-up expenses of foreign operations through a tax deductible reserve account	Subsidies (3)	5/98	—	
WT/DS158 Import regime for bananas II	Failure to implement the Dispute Settlement Body's recommendations and rulings in WT/DS27 within a reasonable period		1/99		See WT/DS27

(*Continued*)

Mark A. Pollack

APPENDIX 3: (*Continued*)

Title and reference number	Short description of the measures	Relevant WTO provisions	Consul- tation	Panel	Status
WT/DS172 Measures relating to the development of a flight management system	French government has agreed to grant, and the Commission has approved, a loan, on preferential and non-commercial terms to develop a FMS for Airbus aircraft.	Subsidies (5, 6) GATT (XXIII1b)	5/99	—	
WT/DS173 France— measures relating to the development of a flight management system	See WT/DS172	See WT/DS172	See WT/ DS172	See WT/ DS172	See WT/DS172
WT/DS174 Protection of trademarks and geographical indications for agricultural products and foodstuffs	EU rule does not provide national treatment with respect to geographical indications, nor sufficient protection to pre-existing trademarks that are similar or identical to a geographical indication	TRIPS (3, 16, 24, 63, 65)	6/99	—	
WT/DS210 Belgium— administra-tion of measures establishing customs duties for rice	Belgian customs values and duties for rice would lead to a denial of duty rebates for US rice and to duties in excess of the bound rate	GATT (I, II, VII, VIII, X, XI) CVA (1) TBT (2, 3, 5, 6, 7, 9) Agriculture (4)	10/00	1/01	Negotiated solution (11/01)
WT/DS223 Tariff-rate quota on corn gluten feed from the US	TRQ triggered by DSB ruling against the US in WT/DS166.	Safeguards (8.1, 8.2, 8.3) GATT (I, II, XIX)	1/01	—	

Note: Columns 'Consultation' and 'Panel' report date requested.
Source: Adapted from DG Trade 'WTO—Dispute Settlement' (updated 15 January 2002), http://europa.eu.int/ comm/trade/pdf/cases.xls, accessed 15 February 2002; and the WTO's dispute database (http://www.wto.org/english/tratop_e/dispu_e/dispu_status_e.htm), accessed 15 February 2002.

PART II

CASE-STUDIES ON TRANSATLANTIC ECONOMIC DISPUTES

3

Manifestly Illegal Import Restrictions and Non-compliance with WTO Dispute Settlement Rulings: Lessons from the Banana Dispute

F. WEISS

I. PRELIMINARY REMARKS

In many recent scientific and popular writings lawyers, political scientists, economists, journalists and businessmen have presented different perspectives on the apparent erosion of state authority in the global market place.[1] In the sphere of international trade, this loss or erosion of state authority is the result of the emergence of an international legal regime for the conduct of world trade based on the central principle of non-discrimination,[2] a regime which consists of legal rules of conduct as well as of institutional and procedural constraints imposed upon states by international law. Thus, an emerging strengthened rule of international trade law has come to replace unilateral trade policy making, as a traditional attribute of state sovereignty.

The operation of that mechanism as well as of its occasional failure, can best be exemplified on the basis of a summary study of the trade dispute concerning the European Communities' regime on bananas, arguably the most important and protracted trade dispute under the General Agreement on Tariffs and Trade (GATT) and the World Trade Organization (WTO) to date, involving all means of dispute settlement provided under the GATT/WTO dispute settlement mechanism.

---

[1] See, eg, O. Schachter, 'The Erosion of State Authority and its Implications for Equitable Development' in F. Weiss, E. Denters and P. de Waart (eds), *International Economic Law with a Human Face* (1998) 31.
[2] See W. McKean, *Equality and Discrimination under International Law* (1985).

II. Factual background of the dispute on bananas

In order to understand *why the dispute arose* at all and *what essential facts, conflicts of interests and political pressures* were involved, it is appropriate first to summarize briefly the origin and evolution of the EC's banana regime.

A. Origin of EC trade preferences

Originally, the EC's development co-operation was based on an association with those non-European overseas countries and territories having special relations with several EC member states.[3] Despite their disagreement about the nature and design of the EC's future development co-operation,[4] they successfully defended the association as a free-trade area constituted in conformity with Article XXIV GATT.[5] After decolonization and the achievement of independence by the non-European overseas countries and territories, treaties between these and the EC replaced the unilateral decision of the Six embodied in Part IV of the Treaty of Rome. These comprised two 'Yaoundé Conventions' of Association,[6] a plethora of similar agreements,[7] and four Lomé Conventions.[8] In 1996 the EC Commis-

---

[3] See Articles 3(s)(ex 3(k)), 182–188 (ex 131–136(a)), Part IV of the EEC Treaty. On the roots of association in European colonialism, see E. Djamsson, *The Dynamics of Euro-African Co-operation, Being and Analysis and Exposition of Institutional, Legal and Socio-Economic Aspects of Association/Co-operation with the EEC* (1976), 250–1; on the history and evolution of EC development co-operation policy see K. Arts, *Integrating Human Rights into Development Cooperation: the Case of the Lomé Convention* (2000) ch 3.

[4] France preferred associate status to protect economic and cultural ties with its colonies as well as investment, preferential status for French exports and a sphere of influence for the French franc; J. Moss, *The Lomé Conventions and their Implications for the United States* (1982) 1; H. Noor-Abdi, *The Lomé IV Convention: The Legal and Socio-Economic Aspects of African, Caribbean and Pacific States (ACP) and European Community (EC) Cooperation* (1997) 35. Germany and the Netherlands advocated development co-operation based on humanitarian and foreign policy objectives which was not restricted to preferential treatment of a chosen few, but eventually accepted the French association design with minor modifications as a 'side payment' to France for its accession to the Community; I. W. Zartman, *The Politics of Trade Negotiations between Africa and EEC* (1971) 197.

[5] Although challenged, *inter alia*, by Commonwealth countries and the UK, the GATT tolerated the association and took no decision against it; see *Basic Instruments and Selected Documents (BISD), Sixth Supplement* (1958) 89–109.

[6] The first and second Yaundé Conventions, signed on 20 July 1963 and on 29 July 1969 respectively, were each concluded for five year periods (I: 1964–69; II: 1970–75) and differed only slightly from the previous EC Treaty regime. After the UK's accession to the EC, association was offered to all former UK colonies in Africa, the Caribbean and the Pacific Ocean (ACP countries), either by joining the Yaoundé Convention or by means of special association agreements based on Art 310 EC (ex Art 238), or by simple trade agreements; on 6 June 1975 the ACP Group concluded the Georgetown Agreement, the institutional framework necessary to ensure the realization of the objectives of the Lomé Convention.

[7] Association Agreement with Nigeria; Arusha Accord with Uganda, Kenya and Tanzania based on Article 310 EC (ex Article 238).

[8] OJ 1976 L 25 'Lomé I', a 'mixed' agreement like the antecedent Yaoundé agreements, committed both the Community and its member states, but was much more comprehensive in scope than the Yaoundé agreements; see R.H. Green, 'The Child of Lomé: Messiah, Monster or Mouse?' in F. Long

sion initiated a wide-ranging review of future EU-ACP (African, Caribbean and Pacific) relations in anticipation of the expiry of the fourth Lomé Convention in February 2000.[9] Lastly, the Cotonou Partnership Agreement of 2000 came to replace the Lomé regime, substituting genuine economic partnership (going beyond trade) for the previous preferential arrangements.

B. Evolution of the EC's trade regime for bananas

1. *The ancién regime*

In 1991, two thirds of the EC's total import volume of fresh bananas of 3.7 million tonnes originated in Latin American countries, the so-called dollar banana countries;[10] 16 per cent were supplied by ACP countries.[11] Since 1963 a consolidated common external tariff of 20 per cent ad valorem was applied to third country bananas, except to ACP bananas which entered duty free.[12] In the absence of a common EC policy on the import of bananas, different national protectionist import systems for bananas existed in EC member states.[13] Preference was preserved by virtue of Articles 168 and 183 of the fourth Lomé Convention as well as by Article 1 of Protocol 5 to that Convention (the Banana Protocol), which states that 'no ACP State shall be placed, as regards access to its traditional markets and its advantages on these markets, in a less favourable

---

(ed), *The Political Economy of EEC Relations with African, Caribbean and Pacific States, Contribution to the Understanding of the Lomé Conventions on North-South Relations* (1980) 4–27. 'Lomé I' (1975–80), also embodied certain evolving principles of the New International Economic Order, which were then vigorously advocated by UN bodies; 'Lomé IV'(1990–95) and the revised 'Lomé IV' Convention (1996–2000) reflect new trends in international relations, eg, environmental protection, the role of women in development, structural adjustment (cf, UNGA Res. initiating the International Development Strategy for the 4th UN Development Decade, A/RES/45/199, 21 December 1990); see 4th ACP-EEC Convention, signed in Lomé on 15 December 1989 with 69 ACP countries (1990) 29 ILM 783.

[9] See the EC Commission's Green Paper on relations between the EU and the ACP countries on the eve of the 21st century—challenges and options for a new partnership, COM(96)570 final of 20 November 1996; Guidelines for the negotiation of new co-operation agreements with the (ACP) countries, COM(97)537 final of 29 October 1997.

[10] Ecuador, Costa Rica, Colombia, Panama and Honduras.

[11] Mainly Cameroon, Côte d'Ivoire, St Lucia, Jamaica, St Vincent and Dominica; all EC member states except Spain imported Latin American bananas, Germany, Belgium, Denmark, Ireland, Luxembourg and the Netherlands nearly exclusively; France, Greece and Portugal also consumed domestically produced bananas; the production of dollar bananas is generally considered economically more efficient than that of EC and ACP countries, the latter being available in the EU only because of the protectionist practices of several EC member states.

[12] See Council Regulation 2658/87, OJ 1987 L 256/1 as amended by Council Regulation 2913/92, OJ 1992 L 301/1.

[13] National quantitative restrictions applied by EC member states on imports of dollar bananas, notified to the GATT, were due to expire on 30 June 1993. These were placed on a list of residual restrictions of member states and annexed to Council Regulation (EEC) 288/82 of 5 February 1982 relating to the common system applicable to imports which concerned trade measures applied by the member states prior to the creation of the EEC, and maintained thereafter due to the lack of a common policy in respect of banana imports.

situation than in the past or at present'.[14] The completion of the EC's single
market on 1 January 1993, prompted the adoption of EC Council Regulation
(EEC) 404/93, title IV of which established a common market organization for
the banana sector.[15]

2. The trade mechanism of Regulation 404/93

Regulation 404/93 sought to reconcile conflicting goals, internally by harmonizing different bilateral trade agreements involving bananas and, externally, by
balancing GATT obligations with those under the Lomé Convention. The import
licensing mechanism established by Regulation 404/93, together with more than
100 implementing and modifying EC regulations,[16] was of extraordinary complexity, and lacked transparency. It was based on a system of quotas differentiated by source,[17] category,[18] and by group of economic activity.[19] Moreover, it
established four categories of suppliers (traditional,[20] non-traditional,[21] third
country,[22] and EU production[23]) and three categories of trading licences.[24] But

[14] Article 2 of that Protocol provided that all means of the Convention—financial, technical,
industrial and regional co-operation—shall be used with a view to improving the production, and
marketing of ACP bananas.

[15] Council Regulation (EEC) 404/93 of 13 February 1993, OJ 1993 L 47/1.

[16] See E.-U. Petersmann, 'Alternative Dispute Resolution—Lessons from the WTO?' in F. Weiss
(ed), *Improving WTO Dispute Settlement Procedures: Issues & Lessons from the Practice of Other
International Courts & Tribunals* (2001) 27 at 36; see also the list of EC Regulations on the EC's
common market organization for bananas until 1 April 1998 in J.C. Cascante and G.G. Sander, *Der
Streit um die Bananenmarktordnung* (1999) 188 *et seq.*

[17] Community, ACP, third country/dollar area.

[18] 'Traditional' or 'non-traditional' suppliers.

[19] Importers, distributors and ripeners.

[20] Traditional imports are those from 12 ACP countries which enter duty-free up to a maximum of
875,700 tonnes per annum; this general non-tariff quota comprises specific country quotas for
traditional ACP bananas calculated on the basis of the best year for each ACP country prior to
1991; specific ACP country quota licences were allocated on a quarterly basis to an approved
traditional ACP banana supplier for the quantity applied for up to the specific country quota ceiling.

[21] Non-traditional imports from ACP countries are defined as both any quantities in excess of
traditional quantities supplied by traditional ACP countries (ie, above the ceiling of 857,700 tonnes)
and any quantities supplied by ACP countries which are not traditional suppliers of the EC (eg,
Dominican Republic) and from traditional ACP countries share a tariff quota of 2 million tonnes
with third country imports, duty-free for non-traditional ACP imports, and at a 100 ECU/tonne tariff
for third country imports; quantities above 2 million tonnes subject to a tariff of 750 ECU/t for ACP
and 850 ECU/t for third country (dollar banana) imports.

[22] Imports from third (dollar banana) countries, mainly Mexico, Guatemala, Honduras,
Nicaragua, Costa Rica, Venezuela, Colombia and Ecuador are subject to tariff quotas as well as to
tariff-quota-related import licences ('dollar licences') to be applied for and allocated on a quarterly
basis to an approved dollar banana supplier for up to a maximum of 2 million tonnes, and subject to a
security deposit of 15 ECU/t, which the operator forfeits if the licence is not used within three months
of allocation.

[23] Mainly from Canary Islands, Martinique and Guadeloupe covered by common market organization, guaranteeing deficiency payments, or compensation, of up to a maximum quantity of 854,000
tonnes/per annum at pre-single market price levels.

[24] 'A' licences, 66.5%, reserved for traditional traders in dollar bananas, such as Chiquita, Dole,
Del Monte; 'B' licences, 30%, established operators trading in Community and/or ACP bananas, such
as Geest, Fyffes, Iberga and others; and 3.5% for 'C' operators and newcomers. Categories 'A' and 'B'
were sub-divided into groups a, b, and c of economic activity, subject to a weighting coefficient of 57%
for transporters (a), 15% for distributors (b) and 28% for ripeners (c).

that regime was deemed inconsistent with the GATT. This fact was conceded by the EC Commission,[25] as well as by several Central and Latin American countries.[26]

C. Reasons for the conflict: when vested interests rule

Since the beneficiaries of welfare creation through trade are individuals, traders and consumers, it is also appropriate to consider the *role of private interests in the emergence of the dispute* as well as the impact of *unduly great subservience to industry pressures* (so-called 'regulatory capture') upon the dispute settlement process. Panels deal with a particular dispute as framed by the terms of reference given to them. Thus, panels will not and cannot dwell on the reasons why a particular dispute has arisen. Still, an understanding of the broader political, socio-economic, even cultural background of a dispute may provide insights which might assist in achieving improvements in conflict avoidance and conflict management. Dispute analysis by panels necessarily encompasses the elucidation of the background to a dispute. As legal disputes involve disagreement on points of fact and law, it is imperative for panels to obtain an understanding of the factors which shaped the dispute. To be sure, lawyers, especially seasoned litigators, will probably consider applying social science methods and discourse and analysis as nothing other than an unwarranted distraction. After all, their skills consist of identifying and marshalling legally relevant facts. However, although it has to be recognized that legal developments are influenced by factors such as interests, motivations, and objectives, these matters cannot always be taken fully into account by lawyers who have to place more emphasis on the formal requirements of the legal process.

The policy making processes underlying both the original adoption by the EC of the controversial banana regulation and the instigation of panel proceedings by a coalition of WTO members led by the US were based on narrow, antagonistic and politically influential producer and trading interests.[27] The direct and sometimes seemingly irresistible influence of particular companies or sectoral interests on US foreign policy, including trade policy, has been well documented. Nonetheless, the brazenly evident causal link between Chiquita's election campaign donations and the US banana policy appears to have reached an

---

[25] The EC Commission recognized this when it proposed a Community application for a waiver under Article XXV(5) GATT, see Part IV, points 45–46 of the Explanatory Memorandum on the proposal on a Common Organization of the Market in the Banana Sector, COM(92)359 final, 7 August 1992; see also the reply of Commissioner MacSharry to a parliamentary question wherein he admits that a 'waiver' would be required, OJ 1993 C127/18.

[26] See the 'Santa Fee Declaration' of 18 August 1992 by Colombia, Costa Rica, Ecuador, Guatemala, Honduras, Nicaragua, Panama and Venezuela, cited in M. Delal Baer and S. Weintraub (eds), *The NAFTA Debate, Grappling with Unconventional Trade Issues* (1994) 187.

[27] For this assessment see O. Cadot & D. Webber, *Banana Splits and Slipping over Banana Skins: the European and Transatlantic Politics of Bananas*, EUI Working Paper RSC 2001/3 (2001) 2–11; see also I. Weustenfeld, *Die Bananenmarktordnung der EG und der Handel mit Drittstaaten* (1997) 3–21.

unprecedented level of immediacy.[28] In particular, the ACP third parties involved in this case[29] pointed out that both Dole Foods and Del Monte, after Chiquita the largest importers of Latin American bananas into the EC, accepted that some protection is required to support the interests of EU and ACP banana producers. They also expressed surprise about the US decision to commit significant resources to this WTO action at the request of only one of three US companies involved, and against the apparent wishes of other US interests. The EC, for its part, failed with its challenge to the *locus standi* of the US. Regardless of the uncontested prevalence of the interest of companies, the Panel accepted a systemic, US legal interest as sufficient. However, when, as in the banana case, one claimant clearly acts on behalf of private interests, the important distinction between parties whose rights were violated from parties who have only an interest in the outcome gets blurred.[30] Regarding the issue of procedural rules on 'standing', even of American doctrines of standing,[31] it would seem desirable, in the absence of any DSU rules on *locus standi*, to adopt appropriate rules or standards in the near future, or at least to effect an allocation of some screening function to either the DSB or dispute settlement panels.

On the other hand, vested interests in the defence of the EC's preferential banana import regimes were both more diffuse and disguised: disguised as a noble, morally and legally compelling commitment to development assistance for the benefit of needy ACP developing countries. Undeniably, so-called 'regulatory capture', in this case almost amounting to 'privatization' of intergovernmental dispute resolution, and excessive subservience to it, is problematic in several respects. To begin with, it was clearly not contemplated by the drafters of the GATT which, of course, emphasized particularly diplomatic means of dispute settlement. Moreover, executive action at the behest of individual market operators without due consideration given to other interests undermines the conflict screening function of the multilateral system which should enable governments to settle conflicts of interest primarily 'at home'. Lastly, non-transparent dealings between the executive and individual market operators inevitably has a whiff of impropriety, influence peddling, and favouritism, if not corruption, contrary to the principle of transparency, which is one of the central postulates of the multilateral system as a whole.

There is a significant difference between the 'vigilance' of market operators alerting competent national bodies to possible breaches of covered agreements

---

[28] Cadot & Webber, ibid, 19, 27, 32; these authors also cite from an interview of an US government official that 'for a small amount of money [sic], Chiquita has been making US trade policy on this issue', ibid, 31.

[29] Belize, Cameroon, Ivory Coast, Dominica, the Dominican Republic, Ghana, Grenada, Jamaica, St Lucia, St Vincent and the Grenadines, Senegal and Suriname; other third parties were Canada, Colombia, Costa Rica, Nicaragua, Venezuela, India, Japan, the Philippines.

[30] On this see R. Bustamante, 'The Need for a GATT Doctrine of *Locus Standi*: Why the United States Cannot *Stand* the European Community's Banana Import Regime' (1997) 6 *Minn J Global Trade* 533.

[31] Bustamante, ibid, 582.

by other WTO members, and their considerable domination of an intergovern-mental dispute settlement process arising from them.[32] When complainants appear to be beholden and possibly deferential to private interests, the nature of the dispute settlement process is bound to change, and compromise is likely to become more elusive. In order to prevent 'regulatory capture' from preventing or delaying intergovernmental dispute resolution, it might be desirable to set up domestic bodies mandated to scrutinize and report on policy options based on a wider spectrum of, conflicting, interests, if any.

III. BANANA DISPUTE SETTLEMENT: APPROACHES AND TECHNIQUES

A. Some general considerations on GATT/WTO dispute settlement

In view of the sheer duration and complexity of this dispute, it is important to consider *which international* (see B below) *and national* (see C below), *political and legal procedures* were used for its settlement. Generally speaking, states have a positive duty to settle disputes in good faith, and by peaceful means freely chosen by them. Although the selection of a particular method or technique for dispute settlement may depend on a state's perception of a dispute being more 'legal' or 'political' in character, states do not use that classification.[33]

From its inception, the chief characteristic of GATT dispute settlement was adaptability, rather than legal consistency, predictability, and certainty. Its dom-inant aspect was that of 'settlement', of accommodation of interests rather than of a vindication of rights in a 'victory versus defeat' pattern. Because of their dual nature—semi-administrative, semi-judicial—both the GATT substantive and dispute settlement provisions were found 'puzzling', difficult to understand, respect and comply with.[34] This policy option for flexibility in settlement rather than certainty in rule application is reflected in the wide choice of means offered to contracting parties for the settling of their disputes.[35] The substantive trade

---

[32] In the leading case of *Van Gend en Loos*, the ECJ similarly distinguished between the purely 'intergovernmental' (Commission v EC member state) nature of the procedure under Article 226 EC (ex 169), which individuals might trigger by alerting the Commission to some breach of Community law by a member state, and their independent right pursuant to the preliminary reference procedure under Article 234 EC (ex 177) to invoke certain directly applicable provisions of EC Treaty law in domestic courts.

[33] See F. Weiss, 'Dispute Settlement in GATT: The current debate' in W. E. Butler (ed), *The non-use of force in International Law* (1989) 221–239 at 226.

[34] R.E. Hudec, 'The GATT Legal System: A Diplomats' Jurisprudence' (1970) 14 *Journal of World Trade Law* 615–665; E.U. Petersmann, 'Strengthening GATT Procedures for Settling Trade Disputes' (1985) VIII *The World Economy* 339.

[35] Means available comprise: bilateral and multilateral consultations, good offices, conciliation, working parties, panels of experts, advisory opinions of panels, cf, BISD, 12S/65 (1964); friendly advice of the chairman of the contracting parties, cf, BISD, II/12, 35; see also E.U. Petersmann, note 16 above, at 27, and 'Dispute Prevention and Dispute Settlement in the EU-US Transatlantic Partner-ship' in M.A. Pollack & G.C. Shaffer (eds), *Transatlantic Governance in the Global Economy* (2001) 73 *et seq*.

rules merely impose constraints on members as to their choice of trade policy instruments, so that these rules also pursue 'domestic policy objectives'. Thus, substantive trade rules may best be perceived as instruments available to members to resolve conflicts of interest within their jurisdiction, rather than between members. Seen in this way, they may be regarded as instruments enabling governments to resist partisan pressures from domestic traders, importers, consumers, environmentalists, trade unions, administrators, and politicians, all seeking to influence the public choice between protection and open markets. Trade disputes, therefore, have also a national dimension, and are primarily 'domestic' disputes between various interest groups.

B. The international dimension

1. *Three rounds of banana panels*

(a) First banana panel

The first of three basic panel proceedings involved a successful challenge brought by some Central and Latin American countries against certain discriminatory aspects of the import regimes of individual EC member states. Thus, the *First Banana Panel*, a GATT panel, found the quantitative restrictions maintained by France, Italy, Portugal, Spain and the United Kingdom to be inconsistent with Article XI:1 GATT. It also found the EC's tariff preference in the form of duty-free access accorded to ACP bananas, compared to a 20 per cent tariff charged on the like product supplied from Latin American countries, to be inconsistent with Article I GATT.[36]

(b) Second banana panel

The already mentioned complex import licensing regime established by Regulation 404/93 was attacked before another GATT panel, requested by Colombia, Costa Rica, Guatemala, Nicaragua and Venezuela.[37] The panel duly condemned that regime as being in part inconsistent with Articles I,[38] II,[39] and III[40] GATT. The panel also reminded the EC and the other signatories of the Lomé Convention that nothing in its report would prevent them seeking to achieve their treaty objectives, including the promotion of the production and commercialization of bananas from ACP countries, by using GATT consistent policy

---

[36] Panel report on 'EEC—Member States' Import Regimes for Bananas', DS32/R, 3 June 1993, paras 364 *et seq*, 374–375.

[37] Panel report on 'EEC—Import Regime for Bananas', DS38/R, 11 February 1994, (1995) 34 ILM 180 (not adopted).

[38] The preferential tariff rates on bananas accorded by the EEC to ACP countries were found inconsistent with Article I and neither justified by Article XXIV nor by Article XX(h), ibid, paras 170(b), 230.

[39] The specific duties levied by the EEC on imports of bananas were inconsistent with Article II, ibid, paras 170(a), 230.

[40] The allocation of import licences granting access to imports under the tariff quota was inconsistent with Articles III and I and not justified by Article XXIV nor by Article XX(h), ibid, paras 170(c), 230.

instruments.[41] The contracting parties of the Lomé Convention heeded such advice since they applied for a waiver for the fourth ACP-EEC Convention of Lomé with the aim 'to improve legal certainty for the trade of ACP countries'.[42] While resolutely resisting the adoption of both panel reports, the Community concluded a 'Framework Agreement on Banana Imports' (BFA) with four of the five disputants, by which it secured a partial *status quo* which was incorporated into the Community's Uruguay Round schedule.[43]

(c) Third banana panels

On 11 April 1996 Ecuador, Guatemala, Honduras, Mexico and the US requested yet another panel to examine the EC regime which they still deemed inconsistent with several WTO agreements.[44] On 27 May 1997 that panel found substantially in their favour[45] when it held aspects of the EC's import regime for bananas to be inconsistent with its obligations under certain provisions of the GATT,[46] the Licensing Agreement[47] and the GATS.[48] These findings were largely upheld by the Appellate Body.[49] All of the above mentioned Banana Panel reports were unequivocal in their condemnation of various discriminatory EC banana import

---

[41] Ibid, paras 168, 229; this remark may have been a sympathetic gesture towards the EC in view of the 'wide sympathy' for the purpose and objectives of the Lomé Conventions expressed by previous working parties which examined the Lomé Conventions and their predecessor agreements, despite certain 'doubts' as to whether they were fully justified under Article XXIV GATT, ibid, paras 47, 193, 194; see also the rejection by the panel report on 'Norway—Restrictions on Imports of Certain Textile Products' of the notion that any interweaving of Article XXIV and Part IV would allow a developed country to discriminate—non-reciprocally, regarding selective products—against one set of developing contracting parties and in favour of another, in violation of the most fundamental obligations of the General Agreement, BISD 27S/119, para 15 (adopted on 18 June 1980).

[42] Doc L/7604, 19 December 1994; a further extension until 29 February 2000 was granted by Decision of the General Council of the WTO on 14 October 1996, Doc WT/L/186 of 18 October 1996; see also the Report to the General Council of the Parties to the Convention under the Decision of 14 October, Doc WT/L/286 of 19 November 1998.

[43] Framework Agreement on Bananas of 29 March 1994 (Costa Rica, Colombia, Nicaragua, Venezuela, Dominican Republic, EC) (1995) 34 ILM 1: in return for an increase of the tariff quota and a reduction of the in-quota duty on the full tariff quota, these countries agreed to a settlement of their dispute with the Community regarding the banana regime, in particular not to pursue further the adoption of the Second Banana Panel Report by the GATT Council and not to initiate any dispute settlement proceedings against the banana regime until 31 December 2002; see also Germany's unsuccessful challenge of the compatibility of the Framework Agreement with the Treaty of Rome under Article 300(6) EC (ex 228(6)), Opinion 3/94 GATT-WTO-Framework Agreement on Bananas (1995) ECR 4577.

[44] The GATT, the Agreement on Import Licensing Procedures, the Agreement on Agriculture, the General Agreement on Trade in Services (GATS) and the Agreement on Trade-Related Investment Measures (TRIMS).

[45] Panel report on European Communities—Regime for the Importation, Sale and Distribution of Bananas, WT/DS27/R/USA, 22 May 1997; similar reports were simultaneously issued for Ecuador (WT/DS27/R/ECU), Guatemala (WT/DS27/R/GTM), Honduras (WT/DS27/R/HND), and Mexico (WT/DS27/R/MEX).

[46] Articles I:1, III:4, X:3 and XIII:1 GATT.

[47] Article 1.3.

[48] Articles II and XVII GATS.

[49] Report of the Appellate Body, WT/DS27/AB/R, 9 September 1997, adopted by the Dispute Settlement Body (DSB) on 25 September 1997, (1997) 37 ILM 243.

regimes. The non-adoption of the first two of these reports simply confirmed one of the chief shortcomings of the old, pre-WTO dispute settlement system—the ability of the losing party to prevent the adoption of adverse panel reports. However, EC prevarication regarding the implementation of the adopted third Banana Panel and Appellate Body reports unexpectedly exposed a different flaw in the newly codified Understanding on Rules and Procedures Governing the Settlement of Disputes (DSU), which the drafters had inadvertently overlooked: the so-called 'sequencing' problem arising from the interplay of Articles 21 and 22 DSU.

2. Quest for compliance: arbitration, unilateralism, compliance panels

During the compliance phase different interpretations of relevant DSU provisions gave rise to mounting tensions and barely concealed frustrations which soured the transatlantic partnership.

(a) Arbitral awards

(i) Reasonable period of implementation

After the US had ruled out accepting compensation from the EC, the latter stated that it would comply with the decision of the Appellate Body by modifying its banana regime. Disagreement between the US and its co-complainants and the EC as to what constituted a 'reasonable period' of implementation,[50] was settled through a binding arbitration award of 23 December 1997 which allowed the EC until 1 January 1999 to comply.[51]

(ii) Temptation of unilateral action

Upon publication in January 1998 of the EC's proposed banana 'regime change', the US immediately proceeded to a unilateral determination of non-compliance by the EC and even took certain unilateral preparatory steps to retaliate. This move further exacerbated an already acrimonious transatlantic row as well as EC charges of illegal unilateralism. Despite this somewhat rash attempt to pursue self-help through national remedies, the US, nonetheless, requested the DSB on 14 January 1999, pursuant to Article 22.2 DSU, to authorize suspension of the application to the EC and its member states of tariff concessions and related obligations under GATT 1994 covering trade worth US$520 million.[52]

(iii) Level of suspension of concessions or other obligations

The EC disputed the alleged level of nullification or impairments of benefits suffered by the US and requested, pursuant to Article 22.6 DSU, that the original

[50] Article 21(3)(c) DSU; the US sought compliance by July 1998, the EC claimed 15 months as a 'reasonable period'.
[51] WT/DS27/15, Arbitration Award under Article 21.3(c) DSU, by Arbitrator Said El-Naggar, 7 January 1998.
[52] WT/DS27/43; the Wall Street Journal dubbed them the 'Smoot-Banana Tariffs', for details see R. Bhala, International Trade Law: Theory and Practice (2001) 1507.

panel arbitrate on this matter.[53] The DSB, accordingly, decided on 29 January 1999 to submit the issue to arbitration of the original panel.[54] Since by early March that panel had not yet completed its work, the US contrived to aggravate the situation further by imposing on EC products earmarked for retaliation the posting of a security deposit of bonds of 100 per cent of the value of the duties to be charged in the event of a favourable panel ruling.[55] The EC regarded the security deposit regime to be in flagrant breach of the GATT 1994 and of the DSU and urgently requested consultations with the US under Article 4.8 DSU.[56] This time, an interim panel report condemned the US taking action on 3 March, before obtaining DSB authorization, as inconsistent with the DSU. Eventually, on 9 April 1999, the arbitral panel ruled that the level of nullification or impairments consistent with Article 22.4 DSU would be a maximum of US$191.4 million.[57] After adjusting its previously published list of targeted products to the arbitral ruling, the US formally obtained DSB authorization for retaliation on 9 April 1999, the first ever authorization of 'sanctions' since the establishment of the WTO. Ecuador too won a favourable 'compliance' panel ruling under Article 21.5 DSU on 12 April 1999 (see below), and, on 8 November 1999, also requested DSB authorization for the suspension of concessions or other obligations under the TRIPS, GATS and GATT 1994 Agreements in an amount of US$450 million.[58]

(b) Compliance panels: recourse to Article 21.5 DSU

(i) Preliminary procedural skirmishes: self-help or systemic relief?

During internal EC discussions of various reform options,[59] the US, Ecuador and other co-complainants repeatedly expressed the view, directly to the European Commission and at successive DSB meetings, that the proposed amendments were still inconsistent with WTO law. Nonetheless, these were brushed aside, and in July 1998 the EC adopted Regulation 1637/98 amending Regulation (EEC) 404/93,[60] whereupon the US and its co-complainants requested consult-

---

[53] WT/DS27/46.   [54] WT/DSB/M/54.

[55] As a result, the EC products in question were effectively stopped from entering the US as from 3 March 1999.

[56] WT/DS165/1, 5 March 1999.

[57] WT/DS27/ARB, 9 April 1999, para 8.1.

[58] WT/DS27/52, 9 November 1999; Ecuador intended to apply the suspension of concessions or other obligations to 13 of the EC member states, exempting the Netherlands and Denmark. The EC challenged both the level of nullification or impairments of benefits Ecuador had suffered as excessive, and its failure to adopt the correct methodology for 'cross-retaliation' as laid down in Article 22.3 DSU for the suspension of concessions or other obligations across sectors and agreements; on 19 November 1999, and under Article 22.7 DSU, the EC requested arbitration pursuant to Article 22.6 DSU; in their award of 24 March 2000, the arbitrators, members of the original panel, concluded that Ecuador's requested level of suspension was indeed excessive and that it had also, albeit to a limited extent, failed to comply with the principles and procedures set out in Article 22.3 DSU, WT/DS27/ARB/ECU, 24 March 1999, para 171.

[59] For details see R. Bhala, *International Trade Law: Theory and Practice* (2001) 1502 *et seq.*

[60] Regulation (EC) 1637/98 on the common organization of the market in bananas, of 20 July 1998, OJ 1998 L 210; Commission Regulation (EC) 2362/98 of 28 October 1998 laying down

ations with the EC under Article 21.5 DSU.[61] After the failure of these consultations, Ecuador requested the re-establishment of the original panel to resolve the conflict with the EC concerning the consistency of its measures to implement the recommendations and rulings of the DSB of 25 September 1997.[62]

As already mentioned, the US, for its part, had already in March 1998 announced its intention to make a unilateral determination that the EC implementing measures fail to implement DSB recommendations and rulings and threatened to impose retaliatory tariffs from 1 February 1999, despite the absence of any such multilateral determination. This threatened unilateral approach increased tensions further and was rejected by the EC as being contrary to Article 23, para 2(a) of the DSU.[63] The EC also rejected the view of the US that, as the winning litigant party, it could demand authority from the DSB for retaliation under Article 22.5 DSU without it being necessary to re-submit the dispute about compliance to the original panel. On the contrary, argued the EC, Article 22.2 could not be read in isolation from the mandatory provisions of Article 21.5 and 21.6 DSU which require a dispute about compliance to be submitted to a panel. The US then appeared to grasp a 'multilateral olive branch' as it were, expressing its readiness to submit to the original panel the question of whether the EC's proposals complied with the recommendations and rulings of the DSB. At the same time, however, the US insisted that a panel ruling be made by mid-January 1999, a few days before it would become entitled to request authority to retaliate at the next DSB meeting, while maintaining that it was entitled to retaliate without such a ruling.[64] The EC, consequently, at first refused to participate in Article 21.5 DSU proceedings unless the US suspended its threat of retaliation and, on 25 November 1998, requested in turn consultations with the US regarding the Section 301 procedure of the 1974 Trade Act.[65] The EC then changed its approach and on 14 December 1998 requested the establishment of a panel under Article 21.5 DSU with the mandate to find that the implementing measures of the EC must be presumed to conform to WTO rules unless their conformity had been duly challenged under the appropriate DSU procedures.[66]

detailed rules for the implementation of Council Regulation (EEC) 404/93 regarding imports of bananas into the Community, OJ 1998 L 293.

[61] WT/DS27/18 of 18 August 1998; consultations were held on 17 September 1998, and resumed with Ecuador on 23 November; additional meetings were held on 6 August and 21 September under the auspices of the Chairman of the DSB.

[62] WT/DS27/41 of 18 December 1998.

[63] See WTO Doc WT/DS27/40 of 15 December 1998, on the EC request for the establishment of a panel in accordance with Article 21.5 DSU.

[64] The US had in fact published three notices in the US Federal Register of proposed imposition of prohibitive 100 per cent ad valorem duties on selected products from the EC to take effect on 1 February 1999 after its unilateral determination that 'the measures the EC has undertaken to apply as of January 1999 fail to implement WTO recommendations concerning the EC banana regime'.

[65] See the panel report on US—Sections 301–310 of the Trade Act of 1974, WT/DS152/R, 12 December 1999.

[66] WT/DS27/40.

Thus, the battle lines were drawn for the proper procedure to be followed to challenge the implementation of an adopted panel and Appellate Body report. The critical issue due to the inconsistency between Articles 21.5-6 and 22.5 became known as that of 'sequencing'. It concerned the question as to whether it was open to the US immediately after the expiry of the reasonable period allowed for implementation to request DSB authorization to retaliate pursuant to Article 22.5 DSU, or whether it was necessary, as the EC claimed, first to re-submit the question of compliance to the original panel pursuant to Article 21.5, potentially leading to the spectre of an endless loop without retaliation?

(ii) Recourse to Article 21.5 DSU by the EC and Ecuador

At its meeting of 12 January 1999 the DSB decided to refer the matter raised by the EC on 14 December 1998 to the original panel, in accordance with Article 21.5 DSU. That panel was requested to accept a presumption of conformity of the new EC regime for the importation, sale and distribution of bananas with the recommendations and rulings of the DSB, in the absence of a challenge thereto by the parties to the original dispute under the appropriate DSU procedures. But the panel declined to make such a finding as requested by the EC.[67] It also declined to resolve the matter of the interpretation of the apparently irreconcilable provisions of Articles 21.5-6 and 22.2 DSU, considering their relationship to be a matter best resolved by members of the WTO in the context of the ongoing DSU review rather than in panel proceedings where only one party is present.[68]

At the same meeting on 12 January 1999 the DSB also decided to establish a panel in accordance with Article 21.5 DSU, as had been requested by Ecuador on 18 December 1998.[69] That panel too concluded that the EC had failed to comply with the original recommendations and rulings of the DSB adopted on 25 September 1997.[70] Exceptionally, as requested by Ecuador, it also made specific recommendations to the EC on how it might implement its findings pursuant to Article 19.1 DSU.[71] Following the correction by arbitrators of the level of suspension of concessions it had originally requested, Ecuador made a fresh request for authorization of suspension to the DSB, taking into account the conclusions and suggestions of the arbitrators.[72]

3. *Virtuous multilateralism vs petulant unilateralism*

Trade disputes, especially extended ones such as the banana dispute, are damaging in several ways. In the first place, they are destructive of economic welfare to be derived from the undisturbed functioning of the system. Secondly, pending

---

[67] WT/DS27/RW/EEC, 12 April 1999, para 5.1.
[68] Ibid, para 4.17.   [69] WT/DS27/41.
[70] Panel report by the Reconvened Panel on European Communities—Regime for the Importation, Sale and Distribution of Bananas, WT/DS27/RW/ECU, of 12 April 1999, paras 7.1–7.2, adopted by the DSB on 6 May 1999.
[71] Ibid, paras 6.154–6.159.
[72] Recourse to Article 22.7 DSU by Ecuador, WT/DS27/54 of 8 May 2000.

settlement, they undermine the predictability of the rules, one of the chief systemic values of the multilateral rule-based trade system. Thirdly, inevitable frictions between members tend to cause 'collateral damage', for instance by frustrating the reaching of compromise or delaying progress in ongoing negotiations, between them or with third members, concerning other trade issues. Fourthly, 'good faith' may be another casualty of certain tactics deployed by litigant parties in the course of GATT/WTO dispute settlement procedures. Thus, the use of or threat of concurrent unilateral self-help approaches under domestic legislation, as practised by the US, or the EC's stubborn defence of legally doubtful, if not untenable positions through exploiting every conceivable procedural device under the DSU, is also likely to call in question their legal obligation to proceed in good faith.[73]

4. The national dimension: unilateralist violations of law

It is of course a truism to recall that violations of international law are nearly always 'unilateral'. However, in the banana cases, neither side emerged untainted in this respect. Thus, by defending a discriminatory banana import regime, in GATT/WTO dispute settlement proceedings as well as in proceedings in the European Court of Justice (ECJ) brought by EC market citizens and by EC member states,[74] the EC had repeatedly flouted substantive rules of the multilateral trade system. On the other hand, the US, resorted unilaterally to, *inter alia*, coercive means under domestic legislation, in breach of the multilateral procedural rules for the settlement of disputes laid down in the DSU. In order to apply retaliation effectively, the US enacted the so-called 'carousel' legislation which requires the office of the US Trade Representative (USTR) to review retaliatory actions taken under Section 301 of the Trade Act of 1974 and to revise them, wholly or in part, by rotating the list of products chosen for retaliation, 120 days after their initial effective date, and every 180 days thereafter.[75] Although the first revision date set down for 19 June passed without any revision of the list, the EC requested and held consultations with the US on the carousel provision in July 2000 considering it unlawful under WTO law.[76] However, even by

---

[73] The 'good faith' obligation is both central to the customary rules of interpretation of public international law (Art 31(1) Vienna Convention on the Law of Treaties) and, by reference in Article 3.2 DSU, to the very functioning of the dispute settlement system, as well as generally required conduct under the DSU, see, eg, Articles 3.10, 4.3 DSU.

[74] See, eg, cases C-276/93, *Chiquita Banana Company BV and others v Council of the EC* [1993] ECR I-3345; CT-70/94, *Comafrica SpA and Dole Fresh Fruit Europea Ltd, & Co v Commission of the EC* [1996] ECR II-1741; C-122/95, *Germany v Council of the EC* [1998] ECR I-973, involving annulment by the ECJ of a provision of Council Decision (EC) 94/800 of 22 December 1994 as against category B operators; see also the conclusions of Advocate General G. Tesauro in the case *Hermès International v FHT Marketing Choice BV* [1998] ECR I-3603.

[75] The so-called Combest-Stenholm carousel legislation does not, however, oblige the USTR to rotate the carousel when (1) there is a determination of imminent compliance, or (2) the affected industry agrees not to rotate the sanctions; the provision is also contained in s 407 of the Trade and Development Act of 2000 of 18 May 2000.

[76] Section 306 US Trade Act 1974 and amendments thereto, WT/DS200.

mid-November, 180 days after the entry into force of the law, no rotation occurred. This inaction by the US was probably due to two reasons. The first is that the US needed to preserve some EC goodwill in resolving another WTO dispute, that on Foreign Sales Corporation Tax which a panel of February 2000 had determined constituted an illegal export subsidy, allowing the US until 1 October to revise the legislation. The second reason for inaction may have been linked to the publication by the European Commission of a plan for a new tariff-only banana regime carefully devised to comply with WTO requirements.[77]

The banana interests were fought over in domestic arenas,[78] as well as in regional and international adjudicative bodies, with some degree of interaction between them at all levels. Thus, shortly after the decision by the ECJ of 5 October 1994 dismissing Germany's action for the annulment of the EC's Banana Regulation 404/93,[79] the Office of the USTR promptly embarked on an examination of that regulation under Section 301 of the US Trade Act of 1974 and of the Framework Agreement under Section 302(a) of the same Act.[80] However, before abandoning such unilateral trade action in early 1996, the US and other Latin American countries initiated formal consultations with the Community on this matter (Article 4 DSU). Once the threat of unilateral action had subsided, a moderating influence associated with the objective examination of complex claims, arguments and issues through the WTO dispute settlement process manifested itself.

Naturally, unilateral action, whether legally mandated or discretionary, is based on domestic policy considerations, dependent on the vagaries of domestic politics, on the influence of lobbies or particular interests and thus scarcely conducive to settlement. Its deployment, or threat of it, is the very antithesis of the WTO's multilateral dispute settlement system which, of course, constitutes 'a central element in providing security and predictability to the multilateral trading system' (Article 3(2) DSU). Action prior to the commencement of consultations in accordance with the DSU should be confined to constructive diplomatic dialogue with a view to securing 'a positive solution to the dispute' (Article 3(7) DSU). The nature of the current WTO dispute settlement system demands nothing less.

---

[77] Commission proposal of November 1999, COM(1999) 582 final.

[78] For references to court actions before German domestic courts, see Albrecht Weber, 'Die Bananenmarktordnung unter Aufsicht des BVerfG?', Heft 6/1997 *Europäische Zeitschrift für Wirtschaftsrecht (EuZW)*, 165; Eckhard Pache, 'Das Ende der Bananenmarktordnung?', Heft 1/2, *Europarecht (EuR)* 1995, 95.

[79] Case C-280/93 *Germany v Council* [1994] ECR I-4973.

[80] See 'Proposed Determinations and Action Pursuant to Section 301: European Community Banana Import Regime; United States Request for Public Comment' (1995) 34 ILM 350; 'Initiation of Section 302 Investigation Regarding Policies and Practices of the Governments of Colombia and Costa Rica Concerning the Exportation of Bananas to the European Union; United States Requests for Public Comments', ibid; that investigation was abandoned in 1996 after two of the signatories of the Framework Agreement, Colombia and Costa Rica, had changed their quota systems in favour of Chiquita and Dole; Cadot & Webber, note 27 above, at 27.

IV. Settlement

A. End of a bitter transatlantic trade dispute

At long last, on 11 April 2001, the US and the EC reached an understanding which was followed, on 1 May 2001, by an agreement between the EC and Ecuador to resolve their long-standing banana dispute. Both were hailed as a satisfactory outcome representing a fair balance between competing interests, the main supplier of bananas to the EU, the producers of bananas in the EU, the ACP countries—and of course the European consumers.[81] Finally, on 1 July 2001, the US terminated its retaliatory action under Section 301 of the Trade Act 1974, bringing the increased 100 per cent ad valorem duties down to the level of ordinary customs duties on imports of EU products.

B. Can the 'bananas settlement' bear other fruit?

1. Role of third parties

The settlement of the banana dispute, the longest in the history of WTO dispute settlement, was certainly not 'prompt'.[82] This gives rise to the question as to the *main impediments to an amicable solution of the dispute, particularly the role of third parties intervening.* As has been mentioned above (3.A.), history, spirit and, above all, the procedural rules of the GATT/WTO system of dispute settlement, all favour 'settlement' as the preferred outcome. Before even bringing a case, members are admonished to consider whether it 'would be fruitful' to bring an action, bearing in mind the aim of the dispute settlement mechanism which is to secure 'a positive solution'. Preliminary diplomatic contacts that may take place even prior to consultations offer litigant parties a first opportunity to settle. In any event, a solution mutually acceptable to the parties 'is clearly to be preferred'.[83] Against this background of an emphatic 'systemic' preference for mutually agreed solutions, it might at first appear puzzling that the banana disputes eluded settlement for so long.

Part of the explanation might be found in the fact that WTO dispute settlement cases are rarely 'purely bilateral' in nature, as a great many other WTO members have an interest in the interpretation of WTO provisions as well as in the adjudicative determinations by panels. This has been particularly the case in the 1996/1997 banana dispute which involved 'multiple complaints' of five complainants, eight WTO members intervening to support them as third parties,

---

[81] The understanding provides for phased implementation steps: by 1 July 2001, the EC is to adopt a new licensing system for bananas based on historic reference periods; by 1 January 2002, the EC must shift an additional 100,000 tonnes of bananas into a tariff quota to be open to bananas of Latin American origin (and with respect to which US distributors have a substantial historic share); by 1 January 2006, the EC is committed to the introduction of a tariff-only regime for banana imports.

[82] Article 3.3 DSU.

[83] Article 3.7 DSU.

and 12 other WTO members, all ACP countries, intervening to support the defendant EC.[84] Normally, such third party participation in consultations, panel and Appellate Body proceedings has a beneficial impact which obviates the need for additional dispute settlement proceedings. However, that beneficial contribution to dispute avoidance comes into play only when, as is only the case in about 20 per cent of all complaints brought under the DSU, disputes are settled before being submitted to a panel.[85] Once a dispute has entered the panel phase, the interests of third parties, that is of those with a substantial interest in the matter before a panel,[86] become more closely linked to those of the litigants. Furthermore, although panels should 'consult regularly with the parties to the dispute . . . to develop a mutually satisfactory solution',[87] disputes are only rarely settled during panel proceedings, including at the interim review stage. Moreover, in the banana dispute, ACP third parties even obtained 'enhanced' third party procedural rights, in a sense, almost 'low-cost' litigant status.[88] Seen in this light, it would appear that the vigorous defence of the *status quo* by ACP members intervening as third parties may in fact have constituted an impediment to finding an amicable solution.

2. Enter ADR methods or re-enter diplomatic approaches?

Generally speaking, lawyers love a good argument, including those in governmental service conducting international litigation. But their clients want something different, a quick and cheap solution of their problem. In the WTO context, nearly everyone qualifies as 'client', based on either national economic, private commercial, principled legal or institutionally systemic interest. And what about the much famed short duration of WTO dispute settlement proceedings and their low cost? Surely, the banana dispute prompts some questioning of such assumptions. Was its extended 'run' merely a systemic aberration due to special circumstances which merely confirms the rule of the traditional virtues, or are there structural flaws in need of repair?

Two empirically established factors need to be considered. The first is that trade disputes are rarely settled, suspended or terminated by an agreement on a mutually satisfactory solution after panel proceedings have begun.[89] Once governmental legal machineries are locked into panel proceedings, comprehending let alone accommodating an opponent's interests and supporting argumentation in the pursuit of an amicable solution becomes, apparently, nearly impossible. The second is that the voluntary alternative dispute resolution (ADR) procedures

---

[84] See E.-U. Petersmann, note 16 above, at 34.

[85] Ibid, 35; see also essays in *European University Institute, Resolving and Preventing US-EU Trade Disputes, Six Prize-Winning Essays* (2001).

[86] Article 10.2 DSU.

[87] Article 11 DSU.

[88] WT/DS27/R/ECU, paras 7.4–7.8; see also F. Weiss, 'Third Parties in GATT/WTO Dispute Settlement Proceedings', in E. Denters & N. Schrijver (eds), *Reflections on International Law from the Low Countries in Honour of Paul de Waart* (1998) 458–472.

[89] See Petersmann, note 16 above, at 35.

provided by the DSU, in particular good offices, conciliation and mediation are hardly ever used.[90] Greater use of these flexible methods, which would in any case be without prejudice to either party's rights to panel proceedings, might indeed go a long way towards resolving litigious gridlock such as the one which delayed a timely settlement of the banana dispute. Mediation, for instance, involves an expert outsider nudging the parties to reach agreement. Although under the DSU the expert outsider of choice in this regard is the Director-General, it may well be desirable to establish some kind of independent mediation service. Such a system could draw on the mediation expertise of accredited mediators from a roster set up by the DSB.

V. CONCLUDING REMARKS

The EU and the US are linked to each other by extensive trade and investment relations.[91] Therefore, a transatlantic market place already exists. However, despite the scope and depth of the partnership built on trade agreements and rules, it is paradoxically and inextricably linked to the occurrence of conflicts which tend to be exacerbated in the multilateral system, endangering both the operation and credibility of the WTO. Thus, the ever deepening EU-US partnership is one of coexistence of co-operation and conflict.

Some conflicts, such as those triggered by the Helms-Burton and D'Amato acts of the US Congress which are both extraterritorial in nature, implicated Congress, poisoned transatlantic relations, but were essentially of a transient nature, that is subject to the idiosyncrasies of particular Congressional majorities and of the administration.

A different, less transient type of conflict is one which is more deeply rooted in a strong domestic interest base, involving a high level of political mobilization. To the extent that the resolution of that type of conflict would require changing course or policy, it carries greater political risk. The banana dispute is a reflection of this set of circumstances, involving essentially a 'clash of trading philosophies' between multilateral rules and the preferential trade relations. Indeed, the banana dispute, a product-specific dispute, has proved to be one of the most politically and legally testing and protracted disputes in EU-US transatlantic relations. Its longevity and intensity appears all the more astounding as neither of the main protagonists, the EU and the US, had a substantial producer interest to defend. Nonetheless, it involved acrimonious diplomatic exchanges between them and absorbed a great deal of human and institutional resources, of civil servants, adjudicators, courts and panels.

As the above analysis of the banana dispute has shown, panels will not condone discriminatory treatment of imports. Since substantive rights of non-

---

[90] Article 5 DSU.
[91] EU-US trade accounts for approximately 20% of world trade in goods and 35% of world trade in services.

discriminatory market access have been vindicated, the dispute could scarcely be characterized as one which was due to *the inadequacy of the applicable substantive rules*. Could the panel of its own volition have introduced an element of 'ADR' by means of equitable considerations for the anticipated economic plight of small banana producing APC mono-cultures, taking inspiration from other international tribunals?[92] Or is the rigorous application of the law—*summum ius*, the 'winner takes all'—approach to settlement preferable, both in terms of legal certainty and because, systemically, all are winners anyway?

The most important 'constitutional' function of the WTO system is in fact, its dispute avoidance function. WTO members are encouraged to settle conflicts of interest between different domestic interest groups, such as for instance between producers and consumers, in accordance with their treaty obligations as members of the WTO and by means provided within their own domestic legal order. It is only when WTO members favour or uphold interests of particular domestic pressure groups or even individuals, in breach of their international treaty obligations, that the WTO dispute settlement system may come into play. Therefore, under this system members are enabled to choose domestic conflict resolution in compliance with their treaty obligations and, consequently, avoidance of resort to the system of international dispute settlement and resolution provided by the WTO.

The new institutional framework of such trade, the WTO and, most importantly, the system for the settlement of trade disputes which it administers, have ushered in an era of greater certainty and predictability in the application of trade rules. This is a welcome development which will further strengthen the rule of law in international trade relations. At the same time, and as a corollary to the emergence of a fast growing body of panel and Appellate Body practice, it will in the future become imperative for panels to free themselves from some traditionally restrictive approaches to the interpretation of relevant law and practice. Greater readiness to consider relevant practice of other international tribunals might go a long way towards strengthening the multilateral trading system as an integral part of the global rule of international law.

---

[92] Accepting the US *locus standi*, the panel observed 'that this result is consistent with decisions of international tribunals', see note 45 above, para 7.50; see also note 30 above; greater openness to international law was confirmed by the Appellate Body (AB) report on 'United States—Standards for Reformulated and Conventional Gasoline' in which the AB observed that the 'GATT is not to be read in clinical isolation from public international law', citing decisions of the International Court of Justice, the European Court of Human Rights and the Inter-American Court of Human Rights.

4

Safeguard, Anti-dumping, and Countervailing Duty Disputes in the Transatlantic Partnership: How to Control 'Contingency Protection' More Effectively

D. PALMETER*

> I mean to inquire if, in the civil order, there can be any sure and legitimate rule of administration, men being taken as they are and laws as they might be.
>
> Jean-Jacques Rousseau[1]

The 'contingency protection' regime that applies to transatlantic trade is rooted in the World Trade Organization (WTO). Articles VI and XIX of the General Agreement on Tariffs and Trade 1994 (GATT), and the WTO Agreements on Anti-Dumping, Subsidies and Countervailing Duties, and Safeguards, together with the WTO Dispute Settlement Understanding, provide the legal and institutional framework in which disputes are discussed, litigated, and settled or otherwise concluded.[2] That regime has manifest shortcomings.

Use of this regime in transatlantic trade appears to be decidedly one-sided. In the 24 months from 1 July 1999 through 30 July 2001, the United States imposed definitive anti-dumping duties on European Community exporters on

---

* I would like to thank Niall P. Meagher and Todd J. Friedbacher for comments on an earlier draft. In Europe, 'anti-dumping' is generally used as opposed to 'antidumping', without the hyphen, which prevails in the US. This paper follows the European usage except for direct quotations, and for the titles of articles, books, and laws. Since the European Union operates as the 'European Communities' in the WTO, the abbreviation 'EC' has been used except for direct quotations and titles.

[1] 'The Social Contract (Book I)', in *The Social Contract and the Discourses* (1973) Book I at 181.
[2] GATT 1994 Article VI applies to 'Anti-Dumping and Countervailing Duties,' while Article XIX applies to 'Emergency Action on Imports of Particular Products'. The relevant substantive WTO agreements are known formally as the *Agreement on Implementation of Article VI of the General Agreement on Tariffs and Trade 1994* ('*Anti-Dumping Agreement*'); *Agreement on Subsidies and Countervailing Measures* ('*Subsidies Agreement*'); and *Agreement on Safeguards* ('*Safeguards Agreement*'). The Dispute Settlement Understanding (DSU) is the *Understanding on Rules and Procedures Governing the Settlement of Disputes*.

six occasions; the EC imposed none on US exporters.[3] During the same period, the US imposed definitive countervailing duty orders against EC exporters five times; the EC imposed none against US exporters.[4] The story is similar with safeguard measures, which are generally imposed on a most-favoured-nation basis, and not against the trade of specific countries.[5] Between 1 January 1995 through October 2001, the US initiated 10 safeguard investigations, and imposed definitive measures (tariffs or quotas) on five occasions; during the same period, the EC initiated no safeguard proceedings and imposed no safeguard measures.[6]

The more frequent use by the US of the WTO's contingency protection regime no doubt reflects the fact that the US is primarily responsible for the very existence and structure of that regime. The US included in its proposals for a Charter of the International Trade Organization (ITO) a draft article that became the framework for GATT Article VI dealing with anti-dumping and countervailing duties.[7] Similarly, Article XIX was patterned on provisions of earlier bilateral agreements of the US.[8] The strength of US support for the WTO contingency protection regime, particularly anti-dumping, is reflected by its last-minute insistence in the Uruguay Round that failure to include a special standard of review for anti-dumping cases would be a deal breaker,[9] and by its insistence that anti-dumping should not even be on the table for discussion in any new round of negotiations.[10]

---

[3] WTO, *Report (2000) of the Committee on Anti-Dumping Practices*, G/L 404, Annex C (8 November 2000); *Report (2001) of the Committee on Anti-Dumping Practices*, G/L 495, Annex C (31 October 2001).

[4] WTO, *Report (2000) of the Committee on Subsidies and Countervailing Measures*, G/L 408, Annex F (10 November 2000). The first 12 months of the period accounted for all of the cases. There were no new cases in the following year, but during that time the US had 43 definitive countervailing measures in force worldwide. *Report (2001) of the Committee on Subsidies and Countervailing Measures*, G/L 496 Annex F (1 November 2001). The EC did prevail in a major dispute with the US involving subsidies, but this concerned the prohibited export provisions of the *Subsidies Agreement*, not countervailing duties. *United States—Tax Treatment for 'Foreign Sales Corporation*,' WT/DS108/R (8 October 1999) (Adopted as *modified* by the Appellate Body 20 March 2000).

[5] The *Agreement on Safeguards* allows for departure from MFN principles in limited circumstances. Article 5(b), dealing with the application of measures, would allow departure from MFN, in the case of actual (but not threatened) serious injury under the auspices of the Committee on Safeguards. Article 9 limits application of safeguard measures to products originating in developing countries.

[6] WTO, *Report (2000) of the Committee on Safeguards*, G/L409, Annex 2, (23 November 2000); *Report (2001) of the Committee on Safeguards*, G/L 494, Annex 2 (31 October 2001).

[7] J.H. Jackson, *World Trade and the Law of GATT* (1969) at 403, §16.2.

[8] ibid at 553–4, §23.1. For further background on the US proposals, see C. Wilcox, *A Charter for World Trade* (1949) at 21–23.

[9] E.-U. Petersmann, *The Dispute Settlement System of the World Trade Organization and the Evolution of the GATT Dispute Settlement System Since 1948* (1994) 31 CMLR 1157, at 1204, 1224. See also, J. Croome, *Reshaping the World Trading System* (1995), at 374.

[10] See, eg, 'At Doha, U.S. Aims to Postpone Decision on Dumping, Weighs EU Plan,' *Inside US Trade*, 9 November 2001; 'U.S. Wrestles with Scope, Direction for Talks on Trade Rules,' *Inside US Trade*, 13 November 2001; 'Zoellick Stance on Trade Remedy in WTO Provokes Criticism,' ibid; 'Rockefeller Attacks Zoellick for Doha, Failure to Appear at Markup,' *Inside US Trade*, 14 December 2001.

In the WTO, the EC has successfully challenged anti-dumping, countervailing duty and safeguard protection by the US, while the US, through the first seven years of the WTO's existence (1995 through 2001), never even had occasion to challenge EC use of contingency protection instruments.[11] Indeed, in the WTO's first seven years, there was only one challenge—that by India—to the EC's use of contingency protection, while the US was challenged by non-EC members of the WTO no fewer than nine times. The single challenge to the EC, and all of the challenges to the US, have been, at least in part, successful.[12]

On this record, it seems to fair to say that the US is primarily responsible for the existence of the WTO contingency protection regime that applies to transatlantic trade; that the US is the primary user (and abuser) of that regime; and that, accordingly, the search for problems with the regime, and the solutions to those problems, must begin with the US.[13]

This paper will describe and criticize the WTO contingency protection regime that applies to the transatlantic trade. Part I will consider anti-dumping; Part II, countervailing duties; Part III, safeguards. Part IV will examine the regime in light of the social contract ideas of John Rawls, offering an argument that only increased public awareness of the benefits of liberal trade can effectively control or reduce the confrontational nature of the present regime. Part V will consider whether a change from a multilateral to a bilateral institution could facilitate the process of reducing the level of confrontation. Part VI will conclude.

---

[11] Among the successful challenges were *United States—Anti-Dumping Act of 1916*, WT/DS136/R (31 March 2000) adopted as *affirmed* by the Appellate Body (26 September 2000); *United States—Imposition of Countervailing Duties on Certain Hot-Rolled Lead and Bismuth Carbon Steel Products Originating in the United Kingdom*, WT/DS138/R (23 December 1999) adopted as *affirmed* by the Appellate Body (19 June 2000); and *United States—Definitive Safeguard Measures on Imports of Wheat Gluten from the European Communities*, WT/DS166/R (31 July 2000) adopted as *modified* by the Appellate Body (19 January 2001).

[12] The single EC case was *European Communities—Anti-Dumping Duties on Imports of Cotton-Type Bed Linen from India*, WT/DS141/R (4 September 2000) adopted as *modified* by the Appellate Body (12 March 2001). The challenges to the US from members other than the EC were *United States—Anti-Dumping Duty on Dynamic Random Access Memory Semiconductors (DRAMS) of One Megabit or Above from Korea*, WT/DS99/R (adopted 19 March 1999); *United States—Anti-Dumping Act of 1916 (Challenge by Japan)*, WT/DS162/R (adopted as *affirmed* by the Appellate Body 26 September 2000); *United States—Anti-Dumping Measures on Stainless Steel Plate in Coils and Stainless Steel Sheet and Strip from Korea*, WT/DS179/R (adopted 1 February 2001); *United States—Anti-Dumping Measures on Certain Hot-Rolled Steel Products from Japan*, WT/DS184/R (adopted as *modified* by the Appellate Body 23 August 2001); *United States—Safeguard Measures on Imports of Fresh, Chilled or Frozen lamb Meat from New Zealand and Australia*, WT/DS177/R, WT/DS178/R (adopted as *modified* by the Appellate Body 16 May 2001); *United States—Definitive Safeguard Measures on Imports of Circular Welded Carbon Quality Line Pipe from Korea*, WT/DS202/R (notice of appeal filed 19 November 1999); and *United States—Measures Treating Exports Restraints as Subsidies*, WT/DS194/R (adopted 23 August 2001).

[13] The situation was largely the same under GATT. 'In the case of anti-dumping, the United States, European Community, Canada and Australia account for the vast majority of actions taken. In the anti-subsidy area, the United States is by far the most regular user, accounting for over 90 percent of all cases.' P. Low, *Trading Free* (1995), at 80.

I. Anti-dumping

A. The current regime

Anti-dumping is the most widely-used of the WTO's contingency protection instruments, not only in the transatlantic trade, but also by the EC and the US in their trade with other WTO members, and by many of those other members. As of 30 June 2000, the US led the entire WTO with 300 anti-dumping measures in force, while the EC, with 190, was second. India was next, with 91, followed by Canada with 88, Mexico with 80, Australia with 48, Argentina 45, and Brazil 42.[14] Clearly, anti-dumping is the protectionist instrument of choice. Its use has spread from the traditional users (the US, EC, Australia and Canada) to other WTO members, particularly developing countries whose ability to justify restrictions on market access by use of the balance of payments provisions of GATT was curtailed by an agreement reached in the Uruguay Round.[15]

Dumping, according to the *Anti-Dumping Agreement*, occurs 'if the export price of the product exported from one country to another is less than the comparable price, in the ordinary course of trade, for the like product when destined for consumption in the exporting country'.[16] This definition leads to the shorthand statement that dumping consists of the price discrimination that occurs when an exporter sells for less in a foreign market than in its home market. The definition of dumping certainly encompasses this practice, but the term 'in the ordinary course of trade' encompasses much more, and causes much mischief.

If there are no home market sales of a like product 'in the ordinary course of trade', then the export price may be compared to the price when exported to a third country.[17] Sales in both the domestic market of the exporting country, as well as sales to third countries, may be treated as 'not being in the ordinary course of trade' if their price is lower than their total (fixed and variable) cost of production.[18] Thus, if there are no comparable domestic market or third country sales—if they do not occur at all, or if those that take place are 'below cost'— 'normal value' is 'constructed' based on 'the cost of production in the country of

---

[14] WTO, *Report (2000) of the Committee on Anti-Dumping Practices*, supra note 3.

[15] The *Understanding on Balance of Payments Provisions of the General Agreement on Tariffs and Trade 1994* imposes disciplines on members wishing to avoid WTO commitments for balance-of-payments purposes, and makes invocation of the key GATT 1994 Articles, XII and XVIII:B, subject to challenge under Articles XXII and XIII and the DSU.

[16] *Anti-Dumping Agreement*, Article 2.1.

[17] Ibid, Article 2.2.

[18] 'Sales of the like product in the domestic market of the exporting country or sales to a third country at prices below per unit (fixed and variable) costs of production plus administrative, selling and general costs may be treated as not being in the ordinary course of trade by reason of price and may be disregarded in determining normal value only if the authorities determine that such sales are made within an extended period of time in substantial quantities and are at prices which do not provide for the recovery of all costs within a reasonable period of time.' Article 2.2.1 (footnotes, which are omitted, provide that the 'extended period of time' normally shall be one year, and may not be less than six months, and provide a methodology for calculating 'substantial quantities').

origin plus a reasonable amount for administrative, selling and general costs and for profits'.[19]

Article VI of GATT 1994 permits the imposition of duties to offset dumping if the imports in question cause or threaten material injury.[20] This requirement is implemented by Article 3 of the *Anti-Dumping Agreement*, which provides that a determination of injury shall be based, *inter alia*, on an analysis of 'the consequent impact of these [dumped] imports on domestic producers of such products'.[21]

B. The roots of anti-dumping

The use of the word 'dumping' to describe the practice of selling in a foreign market at prices lower than those charged at home first entered the academic economic literature in the early years of the twentieth century.[22] In the US, this was a time of great concern over the economic power of large corporations and combinations of those corporations, which led to the passage of the Sherman Act, the first US antitrust law, in 1890, and the Wilson Tariff Act of 1894. Both contained provisions that covered predatory price discrimination.[23] To Canada, however, belongs the dubious honour of enacting the world's first, explicit, anti-dumping law—a 1904 measure aimed at dumping by the US Steel Corporation.[24] In 1916, the US enacted its first, explicit anti-dumping law—a law that has been successfully challenged by both the EC and Japan in the WTO.[25] Five years later, the US enacted the Anti-dumping Act of 1921, the statute applicable when GATT was launched in 1948, and which provided the basis of the current US anti-dumping regime.[26]

C. Anti-dumping in GATT and the WTO

John Jackson reports that international attention to dumping dates back to the early 1920s in the League of Nations.[27] He notes also that the ITO-GATT

---

[19] *Anti-Dumping Agreement*, Article 2.2.
[20] Duties may also be imposed, pursuant to Article VI, if dumping materially retards the establishment of an industry.
[21] *Anti-Dumping Agreement*, Article 3.1(b).
[22] J. Viner, *Dumping: A Problem in International Trade* (1991), at 1.
[23] 15 USC §1. The Wilson Tariff Act (28 Stat. 570 (1894), 15 USC §§ 8–11) prohibits agreements between two or more persons or firms, either of which is engaged in importing, where the agreement is intended to restrain trade or increase the market price in the US for the imported article. An agreement to price predatorily could be an agreement intended (ultimately) to increase the market price in the US for the imported article.
[24] Viner, supra note 22, at 86, 192.
[25] *United States—Anti-Dumping Act of 1916*, WT/DS136/R (31 March 2000) and WT/DS/162/R (29 May 2000) (adopted as *affirmed* by the Appellate Body 26 September 2000).
[26] Title VII of the Tariff Act of 1930, as amended, 19 USC §§ 1673–1677k. The 1916 Act is more of an antitrust law, and requires proof in court beyond the elements of dumping. The 1921 Act and its successors are the 'administrative' anti-dumping law used by the government.
[27] Jackson, supra note 7, at 403, § 16.2. Jackson, contrary to Viner, gives 1903, rather than 1904, as the date of Canada's anti-dumping legislation; ibid. Cf, Viner, supra note 22.

preparatory work on anti-dumping also refers to the World Economic Conference of 1933.[28] He further reports that the US did not consider that inclusion of
the ITO's anti-dumping article was 'essential' to GATT, since GATT was viewed
as a temporary measure pending establishment of the ITO.[29] Given the ultimate
failure of the ITO, it is interesting to speculate on what might have happened to
the world trading system if anti-dumping had not been included in GATT.
Unfortunately, anti-dumping was included. In fact, as Kenneth Dam observes,
the provisions of Article VI themselves were designed to accommodate the
existing US Anti-dumping Act of 1921.[30]

The provisions of Article VI, Professor Dam notes with considerable under-
statement, 'frequently lack precision and specificity'.[31] An attempt to remedy
this failing was made in the Kennedy Round, with the adoption of the 1967
*Agreement on Implementation of Article VI of the General Agreement on Tariffs
and Trade*, the 'Kennedy Round Anti-Dumping Code'. The US Congress greeted
this accomplishment with decided hostility, however, expressing the view that, in
agreeing to the Code, the US negotiators had exceeded their authority.[32] Congress immediately adopted legislation directing that the Kennedy Round Code
not be followed by US authorities if it conflicted with pre-existing domestic
law.[33]

The rejection of a negotiated trade agreement by the US Congress led to
demands from the EC and other US trading partners that something be done to
prevent similar occurrences in the future. They saw little benefit to negotiating
agreements twice, first with the US negotiators and second with the Congress.
The answer was 'fast-track' authority, which was first included in the Trade Act
of 1974 authorizing US participation in the Tokyo Round.[34] A new anti-
dumping agreement was negotiated in the Tokyo Round, to which the US
adhered.[35] Like the Kennedy Round Code, however, the Tokyo Round Code
was a plurilateral agreement, applying only to those GATT contracting parties

[28] Jackson, supra note 7, at 403, § 16.2.
[29] Jackson, supra note 7, at 405, § 16.2.
[30] K.W. Dam, *The GATT: Law and International Economic Organization* (1970), at 172. In an
argument made to a GATT Panel in the late 1980s, the EC saw Article VI differently. 'The intention of
the drafters of the Article had not been to condemn dumping itself, but to limit the possibility of taking
measures to counteract dumping and subsidization.' *Japan—Trade in Semi-Conductors*, BISD 35S/
116, 128, para 43 (adopted 4 May 1988).
[31] Ibid.
[32] See R. Long, 'United States Law and the International Anti-dumping Code' (1969) 3 *International Lawyer* 464. Senator Long was then Chair of the Senate Committee on Finance, the
committee in the US Senate with jurisdiction over trade.
[33] Renegotiations Amendments Act of 1968, Pub L No 90–634, § 20, 82 Stat 1345 (1968).
[34] Trade Act of 1974, § 102, Pub L No. 93–618, 88 Stat 1978, 1982–83. 'Fast-track' authority
provides for a greatly enhanced role for Congress in the negotiating process, in exchange for a
straight up or down vote, without amendment, on legislation proposing to implement a trade
agreement.
[35] *Agreement on Implementation of Article VI of the General Agreement on Tariffs and Trade*,
BISD 26S/171.

that adhered to it.[36] This situation ended in 1995 when the WTO *Anti-Dumping Agreement* became effective as to all WTO Members.

D. An abbreviated critique

Anti-dumping has been widely criticized, and deservedly so.[37] It began as a form of competition law—or, to use the term more generally used in the US—antitrust law. It uses substantive antitrust terminology and concepts. Public justifications for it are usually stated in terms of combating predatory pricing, a serious, if rare, antitrust violation. But as the respected and politically independent Congressional Budget Office (CBO) has observed, anti-dumping law is 'a tangled and confusing subject' which:

was once a reasonably close approximation of a prohibition on predatory pricing of imports, and served as a complement to antitrust law, which prohibited predatory pricing by domestic firms. Over the years, however, anti-dumping law and antitrust law have evolved in different directions, so that now the United States treats similar pricing practices differently depending on whether the product being sold is domestically produced or imported.[38]

The CBO, of course, was describing US law, but that law is largely reflective of the WTO *Anti-Dumping Agreement*, which is an instrument designed to reflect and protect the anti-dumping regimes of the transatlantic partners.[39] Anti-dumping generally, not just anti-dumping in the US, 'is simply a packaging of protectionism to make it look like something different'.[40]

The use of antitrust terminology and concepts in anti-dumping leads many economists and competition lawyers to believe—erroneously—that the two sets of laws are similar. They are not. This can be seen from a comparison of some of the terms and concepts of the *Anti-Dumping Agreement* with the US antitrust

[36] This 'GATT *à la carte*', as it came to be called, applied to all of the Tokyo Round Codes and raised serious Article I most-favoured-nation treatment questions—if the provisions of a Code were applied to a signatory but not to a GATT contracting party not a signatory to the Code, was the latter being denied MFN treatment? GATT managed to avoid confrontation on this issue for some 15 years until the adoption of the multilateral WTO agreements.

[37] See, eg, B. Hindley and P.A. Messerlin, *Antidumping Industrial Policy: Legalized Protectionism in the WTO and What to Do About It* (1996); J.M. Finger (ed), *Antidumping: How it Works and Who Gets Hurt* (1993); P.S. Nivola, *Regulating Unfair Trade* (1993); R. Boltuck and R.E. Litan (eds), *Down in the Dumps: Administration of the Unfair Trade Laws* (1991); J. Bovard, *The Fair Trade Fraud* (1991); J. Bhagwati, *Protectionism* (1988).

[38] Congress of the United States, Congressional Budget Office, *How the GATT Affects U.S. Antidumping and Countervailing Duty Policy* iv (September 1994) ('CBO Study').

[39] The *Anti-Dumping Agreement* 'required the EU to adopt only limited changes in its legislation. . . . From the EU perspective, the new Code must be seen as a success: it forces other countries to make considerable changes in their anti-dumping legislations which will favour, *inter alia*, European exporters to those countries. The EU, on the other hand, had to make only slight changes in its legislation and practice.' F. Montag and A. Fiebig, 'The European Union' in K. Steel (ed), *Anti-Dumping under the WTO: A Comparative Review* (1996), at 97, 119–20.

[40] B. Hoekman and M. Kostecki, *The Political Economy of the World Trading System* (1995), at 177.

law most similar to anti-dumping in concept—'primary line' price discrimination cases under the Robinson-Patman Act.[41]

1. Determination of price discrimination

Price discrimination is central both to dumping and to primary line antitrust cases under Robinson-Patman. However, the determination as to whether price discrimination in fact has occurred is made in very different ways under the two sets of laws. As the CBO observed, how pricing practices are treated depends on whether the product being sold is domestically produced or imported.[42]

In antitrust, under Robinson-Patman, the existence of price discrimination typically is determined simply by examination of at least two reasonably contemporaneous sales.[43] While Article 2.4.2 of the *Anti-Dumping Agreement* permits this methodology, it also permits a comparison of annual weighted-average prices, a methodology that can result in distortion depending upon volumes, even if prices are identical.[44] This is the methodology used most of the time by both the EC and the US.

Indeed, the distortion is worse if some domestic market sales are disregarded for being below the cost of production. Thus, if cost of production is 100, and sales in equal volumes are made, over time, in the domestic and the export markets at 90 and 110, the weighted average price in each market would be 100—no discrimination, and equal to cost. But Article 2.2.1 allows the sales below cost in the home market to be disregarded in certain circumstances. In this example, the price of the remaining domestic market sales above cost—those at 110—would be compared to weighted average export prices of 100, resulting in a dumping margin of 10 per cent.[45]

Traditionally, both the EC and the US carried the distortion further by a practice known as 'zeroing', under which transactions with 'negative' dumping margins are disregarded in reaching a weighted average dumping margin. 'Negative' dumping occurs when export price is higher than normal value. For example, assume that normal value is 100, and individual export sales of single units occur at 90 and 110. In this case, there is a 'positive' dumping margin of 10 on the sale made at 90, and a 'negative' margin of 10 on the sale made at 110.

---

[41] 15 USC § 13. The Robinson-Patman Act is sometimes referred to as the 'anti' antitrust law, since many believe it penalizes legitimate price competition. The fact that substitution of Robinson-Patman's provisions for the WTO *Anti-Dumping Agreement* would be a liberalizing move should give competition lawyers and economists some idea of how market restrictive anti-dumping truly is.

[42] CBO Study, supra note 38.

[43] Von Kalinowski, *Antitrust Laws and Regulations* (1988), Vol 4, § 24.03.

[44] For example, assume that on three separate days, a producer sells for the same price in both domestic and export markets. On the first day, 10 units are sold in each market for a price of 100 each; on the second day, 10 units are sold in each market for a price of 200; and on the third day 10 units are sold domestically, but only 5 for export, for a price of 300 each. The result is a sale of 30 units domestically for a total value of 6,000, which yields an average price of 200; for export, however, 25 units are sold for a total value of 4,500, which yields an average price of 180. The dumping margin would be 200–180 = 20/180 = 11.1%.

[45] 110–100 = 10/100.

Instead of averaging these two prices, offsetting the 'positive' margin of dumping on the sale at 90 with the 'negative' margin on the sale at 110, both the EC and the US would determine that the sale at 90 yields a dumping amount of 10, while the sale at 110 yields no margin—therefore, zero. The margin of 10 would then become the numerator in determining the dumping margin.[46] The EC's use of this practice was challenged successfully by India.[47] Accordingly, the EC has announced that it no longer will use 'zeroing' in calculating dumping margins.[48] The US, however, has declined to change its identical practice.[49]

2. Sales in two markets

In Robinson-Patman cases, a showing of price discrimination is exactly that—discrimination in price between two markets. For this to occur, a minimum of two sales is needed, one in each market. This is not the case in anti-dumping.

The *Anti-Dumping Agreement* specifically provides for situations in which 'there are no sales of the like product in the ordinary course of trade in the domestic market of the exporting country' or to a third country. In these circumstances, a comparison is made 'with the cost of production in the country of origin plus a reasonable amount for administrative, selling and general costs and for profits'.[50] Thus, under the *Anti-Dumping Agreement*, it is possible that a single sale of a unique item could be sold below 'normal' value. In the absence of a comparison sale, the authorities simply 'construct' normal value, including what they believe is a 'reasonable' profit, and compare the export price to that amount. There are no short cuts like this for complainants in antitrust law.

3. Adjustments for physical differences

Under Robinson-Patman, the merchandise which is the subject of the alleged price discrimination must be of 'like grade and quality'.[51] The *Anti-Dumping Agreement*, in contrast, permits '[d]ue allowance' for differences in, *inter alia*, 'physical differences'.[52] In anti-dumping, therefore, unlike antitrust, important physical differences do not disqualify use of a particular sale for purposes of comparison.

---

[46] 2 units at 90 and 100 (after the 110 price is 'zeroed') = 2/190 = 95; 95/100 = 5%.

[47] *European Communities—Anti-Dumping Duties on Imports of Cotton-Type Bed Linen from India*, WT/DS141/R (adopted as *modified* by the Appellate Body 12 March 2001).

[48] See, 'EU Offers to Review Anti-dumping Duties in Light of WTO Decision Against "Zeroing"', 49 *International Trade Reporter (BNA)* A-5 (March 13, 2001).

[49] See, 'Commerce Nominee Says WTO Bedlinen Case Will Not Change US Law,' *Inside US Trade*, 6 April 2001: 'Absent a decision directed at an action of the U.S. government and our antidumping laws, nothing in the WTO compels a revision of the Commerce Dept.'s current practices.' Such a decision may be on the way. See, 'Brazil, U.S. to Consult on Potential Challenge to AD Practices,' *Inside US Trade*, 30 November 2001.

[50] Article 2.2.

[51] 15 USC §13(a).

[52] Article 2.4. 'Due allowance' is also made for differences in conditions and terms of sale, levels of trade, 'and any other differences which are also demonstrated to affect price comparability'.

4. Predatory pricing and sales below cost

Perhaps no other issue illustrates the differences in the use of the same economic terminology between anti-dumping and antitrust law than does the term 'below cost'. In antitrust law, sales below variable cost may be used as evidence of predatory intent.[53] The use of cost evidence in anti-dumping law is very different.

There are two crucial differences between the role of below-cost sales in anti-dumping investigations and the common assumption, growing out of widely-known and accepted competition law principles, of what the term 'below cost' means. First, in anti-dumping law, the term does not refer to variable costs, but to *total* costs, a very different measure.[54] While sales below variable cost may well be evidence of predatory intent, a comparable point cannot be made about sales below total cost.

Nevertheless, the variable cost *versus* total cost issue is not the most important difference in the treatment of cost in anti-dumping and competition law. Indeed, it is the second aspect of the treatment of sales below cost in anti-dumping investigations that strikes economists and competition law practitioners as truly bizarre: the cost of production provision of the *Anti-Dumping Agreement* is not at all concerned with below cost sales in the *export* market; to the contrary, the cost of producing the exported merchandise is irrelevant in an anti-dumping proceeding, and need not even be determined. Rather, the *Anti-Dumping Agreement* is concerned only with below cost sales in the exporter's *home* market.[55]

This is precisely the opposite of what competition law theory would expect. In competition law, the question is whether the sales that are at the lower price are below cost. If so, the authorities might infer predatory intent. Thus, competition law officials examining an alleged dumping transaction would look to see (1) whether the export sale is below variable cost and (2) whether it is being supported by supra-competitive home market sales. In anti-dumping law, the question is just the opposite. The anti-dumping question is whether the foreign market prices used to determine whether export prices are too low, are themselves below total cost. If the foreign market sales (usually home market sales) are found to be below total cost, they may be disregarded and not used as the measure of price discrimination. Instead, normal value is 'constructed'.

How confusing all of this can be to those not steeped in the arcana of anti-dumping terminology is revealed in the remarks of former US Commerce Department Undersecretary Jeffery Garten concerning the alleged 'pernicious effects of anti-competitive' dumping practices by Japanese semiconductor producers. 'A combination of a protected home market', Garten said, 'a cartel-

---

[53] P. Areeda and D.F. Turner, *Antitrust Law: An Analysis of Antitrust Principles and their Application* (1978), 710–722; Case C-62/86, *AKZO Chemie v Commission* [1991] ECR I-3359, discussed in American Bar Association, *Competition Laws Outside the United States* (2001), at EU-49 and D.G. Goyder, *EC Competition Law* (1998), at 341–2.

[54] *Anti-Dumping Agreement*, Article 2.2.1 encompasses sales at 'prices below per unit (fixed and variable) costs of production plus administrative, selling and general costs'.

[55] Ibid.

ized home market, substantial resources and aggressive dumping, including below the cost of production, allowed Japanese companies to nearly decimate the US semiconductor industry.'[56] But Garten did not explain why the 'cartelized' Japanese industry with 'substantial resources' was selling below its cost of production *in Japan*. Predatory pricing theory would predict just the opposite.[57] Indeed, it seems fair to suggest that Mr Garten's audience, if it were not versed in anti-dumping law, would interpret his remarks to mean that the Japanese producers were charging high prices in their 'protected' and 'cartelized home market' and were engaged in 'aggressive dumping, including below cost of production' sales, in the *export* market. Few are likely to have suspected that the anti-dumping question was whether the Japanese producers were selling below the cost of production in their protected, cartelized *home* market.

The *Anti-Dumping Agreement's* treatment of sales below total cost is particularly protectionist because it departs radically from common business practices. The CBO observed that 'selling below cost is common and seldom has anything to do with predatory pricing'.[58] Five legitimate reasons for below cost sales are given by the CBO: (1) recessions and mispredicted demand; (2) introduction of new products; (3) loss leaders; (4) life-cycle pricing; and (5) legal constraints, such as laws restricting the layoff of workers.[59] There is no room in the *Anti-Dumping Agreement* for these legitimate practices.

5. Injury

A determination of injury under the *Anti-Dumping Agreement* is concerned with 'the impact of these [dumped] imports on domestic producers of such products'.[60] Competition law standards, by contrast, are not concerned with injury to producers *qua* producers, but with injury to competition itself. Vigorous competition normally is injurious to the least competitive producers in an industry; indeed, competition may be said to be 'injured' if it is not allowed to injure individual competitors. Simply put, the focus of the injury inquiry under the *Anti-Dumping Agreement* is very different from the focus of the inquiry in competition law.

---

[56] 'New Challenges in the World Economy: The Antidumping Law and U.S. Trade Policy,' Remarks by Jeffrey E. Garten, Under Secretary of Commerce for International Trade before the US Chamber of Commerce, Washington, DC, 7 April 1994, at 14 (copy on file with the author).

[57] While Garten's remarks could be interpreted as referring to export sales in the US as below cost, the point is that anti-dumping law makes a determination of the cost of exports irrelevant, and in fact they are never even determined in an anti-dumping investigation. It is only the cost in the comparison market that is relevant. In the vast majority of cases, this is the home market of the exporter, although in limited circumstances, third country sales may be used. *Anti-Dumping Agreement*, Article 2.2.

[58] CBO Study, supra note 38, at 8. This explanation no doubt lies behind the opinion of Judge (now Justice) Stephen Breyer in *Barry Wright Corp v ITT Grinnell Corp*, 724 F2d 227, 236 (1984): 'we conclude that the Sherman Act does not make unlawful prices that exceed both incremental and average costs...'.

[59] CBO Study, supra note 38, at 8.

[60] *Anti-Dumping Agreement*, Article 3.1.

<h2 style="text-align:center">II. Countervailing duties</h2>

A. The current regime

Article VI of GATT 1994, which authorizes the imposition of anti-dumping duties, also provides, *mutatis mutandis*, for the imposition of countervailing duties to offset subsidies on the manufacture, production or export of a product.[61] The *Subsidies Agreement* defines a subsidy as (1) a financial contribution by a government that (2) confers a benefit.[62] A subsidy may transgress WTO norms if it is (3) 'specific to an enterprise or industry or group of enterprises or industries'.[63]

A financial contribution can take many forms—a direct transfer of funds, such as a grant, loan or equity infusion; a potential direct transfer, such as a loan guarantee; tax credits or other fiscal incentives; government provision of goods and services other than general infrastructure; or government support of a non-government entity that does any of these.[64] The injury provisions of Article VI apply, of course, to countervailing duties as well as to anti-dumping. The *Subsidies Agreement* elaborates on this requirement in provisions that parallel those of the *Anti-Dumping Agreement*.[65]

Countervailing duties are not a WTO member's only option when another member subsidizes. The WTO dispute settlement process also is available. If the subsidy at issue is contingent upon export or upon the use of domestic over imported goods, it is prohibited by the *Subsidies Agreement*, and thus may be contested in WTO dispute settlement proceedings.[66] Even if not prohibited, it may be 'actionable' at the WTO if it causes adverse effects to the interest of other members.[67] Members maintaining a prohibited subsidy are required to 'withdraw' it, while members maintaining an actionable subsidy are required either to withdraw the subsidy or remove its adverse effects.[68]

Among the grounds for finding adverse effects is a determination that a subsidy causes injury to the domestic industry of another member within the meaning of the countervailing duty provisions of the *Subsidies Agreement*.[69] Thus, a member whose industry is experiencing material injury as a result of another member's subsidy has the option of proceeding against the measure itself—seeking its withdrawal or the removal of adverse effects—under the WTO's dispute settlement procedures, or of imposing countervailing duties.[70]

---

[61] Article VI:3.   [62] *Subsidies Agreement*, Article 1.1(a)(1) and (a)(2).
[63] Ibid, Article 2.1.   [64] Ibid, Article 1.1(a)(1)(i)–(iv).   [65] Ibid, Article 15.
[66] Ibid, Article 3.   [67] Ibid, Article 5.
[68] Ibid, Articles 4.7 and 7.8, respectively. Another category of subsidies was labelled 'non-actionable'. These included certain subsidies for research, for regional development, and for environmental improvements. See *Subsidies Agreement*, Article 8. This 'non-actionable' designation has expired, and subsidies for these activities now may be proceeded against to the extent that they cause adverse effects to the interests of other members. *Subsidies Agreement*, Article 31.
[69] Article 5(a).
[70] Just what it takes to 'remove the adverse effects' of a subsidy is not explained in the *Subsidies Agreement*. One possibility might be to reduce the subsidy rather than withdraw it entirely. Thus, if a 10% subsidy is causing adverse effects, it is possible that a 5% subsidy would not do so.

One reason countervailing duties might be preferred is that they serve to protect the industry experiencing the injury caused by the subsidy, and serve to provide a more immediate remedy controlled by the affected member. If a subsidy is successfully challenged at the WTO, and the subsidizing member declines to withdraw it or remove its adverse effects, a successful complaining member may obtain compensation or take countermeasures, but neither of these is likely to inure to the benefit of the injured industry.[71]

B. The roots of countervailing duties

Countervailing duties date back to the same late nineteenth to early twentieth century concern over monopolies and predatory practices that produced anti-dumping laws. Indeed, the two were seen as much the same thing. In Jacob Viner's words, '[d]umping is as likely to result from an official or government export bounty as from a private bounty'.[72] The world's first broadly-based countervailing duty law seems to have been the US Tariff Act of 1897, which authorized the Secretary of the Treasury to impose countervailing duties equal to the amount of a direct or indirect subsidy ('bounty or grant') on otherwise dutiable merchandise.[73] During this period, most of the subsidies of concern involved European bounties on the production or export of beet sugar.[74] The 1897 law was 'strictly, perhaps even harshly, enforced'.[75] Eventually, it evolved into section 303 of the Tariff Act of 1930—the infamous 'Smoot-Hawley Tariff'—and was in force when GATT became effective in 1948.

C. Countervailing duties in the GATT and WTO

Countervailing duties are inextricably tied to subsidies, and, as Professor Dam has observed, '[t]he General Agreement is hostile to subsidies'.[76] The same is true of the WTO, where many of the problems that plagued the GATT subsidy regime—particularly the lack of a definition of 'subsidy'—have been resolved by the *Subsidies Agreement*.

Article VI:3 of GATT, largely reflecting the language of US law, permits the imposition of countervailing duties to offset a 'bounty or subsidy determined to have been granted, directly or indirectly, on the manufacture, production or

---

[71] Of course, this would apply only when the injury occurs in the complaining member's home market. If loss of exports in third countries is the basis of the adverse effects, countervailing duties would not be available. It is interesting to note that Article 14 of the *Anti-Dumping Agreement* permits anti-dumping action on behalf of a third country; there is no comparable provision in the *Subsidies Agreement*.

[72] Viner, supra note 22, at 90.

[73] Ibid, at 169. The theory behind not countervailing duty-free merchandise was that there was no domestic interest in its production, only its consumption. The *Subsidies Agreement* makes no such distinction.

[74] Ibid, at 168 ff.

[75] Ibid, at 173.

[76] Dam, supra note 30, at 132.

export of [a] product...'.[77] A more detailed Subsidies Code was negotiated in the Tokyo Round, but there, too, agreement on a definition of the term 'subsidy' could not be reached. Instead, an Annex to the Code set forth an 'Illustrative List' of prohibited export subsidies.[78] That list was carried over in the Uruguay Round to the *Subsidies Agreement*, where its presence, together with the definition of the term 'subsidy', creates some incoherence.[79]

D. An abbreviated critique

While anti-dumping and countervailing duties bear a resemblance to each other, and are included in the same GATT Article, they deal with very different phenomena. Anti-dumping duties deal with the pricing behaviour of private entities, not governments.[80] The WTO imposes no obligations on members with regard to dumping, other than those obligations that deal with the efforts of members to offset it. Countervailing duties, in contrast, deal with the activities of governments *qua* governments in providing subsidies. WTO obligations go both to what members may and may not do in providing subsidies, as well as to what they might do to offset them. For this reason, Professor Dam has noted, 'the arguments for permitting countervailing duties are somewhat more forceful, from a free-trade perspective, than the arguments for anti-dumping duties'.[81] Bernard Hoekman and Michel Kostecki agree that countervailing duties are 'superior' to anti-dumping duties 'in that at least the instrument is better targeted at the source of the perceived externality: government intervention. In contrast to the case of dumping by firms, in the subsidy context it is at least possible to build a case for 'unfair competition'.[82]

Subsidies—and countervailing duties to offset them—present a more fundamental problem to the WTO than do anti-dumping duties, however, because subsidies go to the core of what many view as the legitimate activities of government. 'It is extremely difficult to define subsidies without a common

---

[77] The US countervailing duty law in effect at the time, which is still applicable for non-WTO members and is codified at 19 USC 1303, provides, in relevant part, for the imposition of countervailing duties to offset 'any bounty or grant upon the manufacture or production or export of any article...'.

[78] *Agreement on Interpretation and Application of Article VI, XVI and XXIII of the General Agreement on Tariffs and Trade*, BISD 26S/56, 80.

[79] *Subsidies Agreement*, Annex I. Difficulties arise when a measure encompassed by the definition of subsidy in Article 1 of the *Agreement* would appear to be excluded by an *a contrario* interpretation of an item on the Illustrative List, eg, item (j) which gives, as an example of a prohibited subsidy, '[t]he provision by governments...of export credit guarantee or insurance programmes...at premium rates which are inadequate to cover the long-term operating costs and losses of the programmes'. Government guarantees at premium rates that are adequate to 'break-even' could still be below market, thereby conferring a 'benefit' which fits the Article 1 definition of a subsidy. Thus, without an *a contrario* interpretation, a loan guarantee programme that met the requirements of item (j) would nonetheless be vulnerable—which raises the issue of why, then, have item (j) (or similar items) been included in the Annex at all?

[80] Of course, this could include government-owned corporations that participate in the market.

[81] Dam, supra note 30, at 178.

[82] Hoekman & Kostecki, supra note 40, at 185.

concept about the role of the state.'[83] This follows because 'a major part of government actions consist in the reallocation of resources from one segment of society to another'.[84] The definition of subsidy reached in the Uruguay Round, and set out in the *Subsidies Agreement*, does much to contain these problems, particularly Article 2 dealing with 'specificity'. It is this concept that helps distinguish those activities few would condemn—free public education, for example—from those that may legitimately be called a 'subsidy'. Still, the line may not always be easy to draw. When is a new highway a non-specific item of general infrastructure, and when is it an effective subsidy to a new factory?

Apart from definitional problems of this kind, the *Subsidies Agreement* is riddled with exceptions for favoured economic sectors, such as agriculture. Many of these exceptions can be traced to the US, which 'was forced to accommodate its free trade ideology to the domestic political realities of a farm program that relied on the case of certain important products on a two-price system'.[85] Further, despite their oft-pledged concern for developing countries, the transatlantic partners were key to exceptions in the *Subsidies Agreement* for government-supported export credits, such as loan guarantees, that are not, as a practical matter, available to developing countries.[86] Permitted guarantees operate as a kind of reverse preference.[87] As Jacques Bourgeois has observed, '[g]overnments often do not practice at home what they preach abroad'.[88]

The process of calculating the amount of a subsidy—and, accordingly, the amount of a countervailing duty—is not as blatantly irrational as the process for calculating an anti-dumping duty. Accordingly, countervailing duty methodology has not attracted—nor has it deserved—the wide condemnation that has been visited upon anti-dumping methodology. However, not surprisingly, some rather questionable methodologies have emerged. One of the more noteworthy, which is still an issue in the transatlantic trade, concerns subsidies to government-owned corporations that subsequently are privatized. A formerly government-owned and subsidized steel facility in the United Kingdom was sold to private buyers in an arm's length transaction. The US, nevertheless, imposed countervailing duties on imports from the privatized facility on the ground that the exports continued to benefit from subsidies given to the corporation before it

---

[83] J. Steenbergen, 'Regulation of Subsidies in International Trade' in J.H.J. Bourgeois (ed), *Subsidies and International Trade: A European Lawyers' Perspective* (1991) 21.

[84] G. Depayre & R. Petriccione, 'Definition of Subsidy' in Bourgeois, supra note 83, at 67.

[85] Dam, supra note 30, at 132. It is reliably reported that there are those in the US agricultural community who, contemplating the Common Agricultural Policy of the EC, have come to regret the fact that the US used its disproportionate power, in the early days of GATT, to 'kick agriculture effectively out' of the General Agreement.

[86] The value of a loan guarantee depends on the credit rating of the guarantor. Therefore, guarantees from developed countries, that have high ratings, are worth more than those from poorer countries with lower ratings.

[87] WTO, *Statement by H.E. Celso Lafer, Minister of Foreign Relations (Brazil), Ministerial Conference, Fourth Session, Doha, 9–13 November 2001* 3, WT/MIN(01)/ST/12, 10 November 2001.

[88] 'Introduction: Law and Policy—Cripple Helping Blind?' in Bourgeois, supra note 83, at 2.

was privatized. A WTO panel disagreed, holding that since fair market value was paid for the productive assets, the buyers—those who paid fair market value—received no benefit.[89] Despite this ruling, the US, following the practice adopted in response to the 'zeroing' decision in anti-dumping, has declined to apply the rule to any other cases, until successfully challenged case-by-case.[90]

The transatlantic partners also differ regarding subsidies by member states. In the EC, tight restrictions are imposed on state aids.[91] The situation is very different in the US, where the states are free to subsidize as they please, and frequently do so by granting tax holidays and similar benefits to lure investment. The federal government has no constitutional authority even to regulate, let alone to prohibit, this practice. Since these subsidies rarely if ever would be contingent upon export or on the use of domestic over imported goods, they are not prohibited by the *Subsidies Agreement*. They would, however, be both actionable and countervailable. As a practical matter, however, state taxes in the US are relatively low compared to federal taxes. Consequently, the net amount of any of these subsidies usually is quite small, possibly even *de minimis* within the meaning of the *Subsidies Agreement*.[92]

III. SAFEGUARDS

A. The current regime

The WTO safeguard regime is based on Article XIX of GATT and the WTO *Agreement on Safeguards*. Together they authorize members to suspend tariff or other obligations when increased imports cause or threaten serious injury to a domestic industry—provided that the increased imports are a result of both 'unforeseen developments' and 'the effect of [WTO] obligations'. The *Safeguards Agreement* is intended to 'clarify and reinforce' the disciplines of Article XIX, and 'to re-establish multilateral control over safeguards and eliminate measures that escape such control'.[93] The reference to re-establishing control is concerned with the proliferation of 'gray area' measures—usually 'voluntary' export restraints—which took place in the years before the adoption of the *Agreement*.[94]

---

[89] *United States—Imposition of Countervailing Duties on Certain Hot-Rolled Lead and Bismuth Carbon Steel Products Originating in the United Kingdom*, WT/DS138/R (23 December 1999) (adopted as *Upheld* by the Appellate Body 19 June 2000).

[90] This has led Brazil to request consultations with the US regarding, *inter alia*, its zeroing methodology. *United States—Anti-Dumping Duties on Silicon Metal from Brazil—Request for Consultations from Brazil—Revision*, WT/DS239/1/Rev.1 (7 November 2001).

[91] See Council Regulation 659/1999, OJ 1999 L 083/1, laying down detailed rules for the application of Article 93 of the EC Treaty.

[92] *Subsidies Agreement*, Article 11.9 establishes 1% ad valorem as the de minimis threshold, and requires that when the subsidy is at or below this amount the proceeding be terminated.

[93] *Safeguards Agreement*, Chapeau, cl 2.

[94] See, eg, Croome, *supra* note 9, at 65–70.

Unlike anti-dumping and countervailing duties, safeguard measures (which can include both tariffs and quotas) require no finding of any particular action on the part of the exporter or the government of the exporting country. Safeguards are acknowledged protectionist measures, designed to provide a temporary safety valve for the overall good of the system. Safeguard measures may be imposed initially for a maximum of four years, and may be extended for another four years.[95] In a major change from the prior regime, the *Safeguards Agreement* provides that no compensation is due from the member taking safeguard action for the first three years that a safeguard measure is in effect, if the measure is based on an absolute (as opposed to a relative) increase in imports.[96] Under Article XIX, compensation was required and retaliation could be authorized if a compensation package could not be negotiated.[97] The requirement that a member enacting a safeguard measure compensate or face retaliation was widely believed to be the cause of the post-Kennedy Round rise of anti-dumping actions, beginning in the 1970s, and for the development of 'gray area' measures.

B. The roots of safeguard provisions

'Article XIX', John Jackson writes, 'was a result of United States desires'.[98] It was based on an 'escape clause' (a term sometimes used in place of 'safeguard') in a 1942 bilateral trade agreement between Mexico and the US.[99] The US delegate to the 1946 London Preparatory Conference for the ITO expressed the view that:

Some provision of this kind seems necessary in order that countries will not find themselves in such a rigid position that they could not deal with situations of an emergency character. Therefore, the Article would provide for a modification of commitments to meet such temporary situation.[100]

In the words of former GATT Director-General Olivier Long, Article XIX was '[c]onceived as a safety-valve'.[101] 'Its justification', Professor Dam observes, 'is that the presence of such a clause encourages cautious countries to enter into a greater number of tariff bindings than would otherwise be the case'.[102]

---

[95] *Safeguards Agreement*, Articles 7.1, 7.2.
[96] Ibid, Article 8.3.
[97] Article XIX:2, 3.
[98] Jackson, supra note 7, at 553, § 23.1.
[99] Ibid. The term 'escape clause' may also be reserved for Article XIX, with the term 'safeguard' being used in a broader context to include other provisions that authorize departure from GATT/WTO obligations, such as Article XII (balance of payments) or Article XXVIII (renegotiation of concessions). In practice, however, 'safeguard' frequently seems to be displacing 'escape clause' even when reference to Article XIX alone is intended. Indeed, the chapeau of the *Safeguards Agreement* refers specifically only to Article XIX.
[100] Ibid at 554–555, quoting UN Doc EPCT/C.II/PV.7 at 3 (1946).
[101] O. Long, *Law and Its Limitations in the GATT Multilateral Trade System* (1985), at 57.
[102] Dam, supra note 30, at 99.

C. Safeguards in the GATT and WTO

While Article XIX was used in the first few decades of GATT, Professor Dam suggests that, at least as of 1970, it was not 'invoked so frequently and so abusively that reliance on it by contracting parties more than offsets its favorable effect'.[103] Nevertheless, Olivier Long suggests that by the recession of 1974, 'disenchantment' with Article XIX was increasing.[104] Contracting parties viewed Article XIX as 'too complicated and difficult' to deal with a substantial increase in imports from newly industrialized countries, and grey area measures began to proliferate.[105]

The 1973 Declaration that launched the Tokyo Round stated that the negotiations should examine Article XIX and the safeguard system, and a negotiating group was established. However, the Tokyo Round negotiators were not able to reach agreement.[106] Throughout the 1980s, while safeguards remained very much on the GATT agenda, no progress was made. The 1986 Declaration that launched the Uruguay Round again sought a comprehensive agreement on safeguards.[107] These eventually led to the WTO's *Agreement on Safeguards*.

In the only WTO safeguard dispute to date between the EC and the US, the EC successfully challenged the imposition by the US of safeguard relief on imports of wheat gluten.[108] The case turned on details of the *Safeguards Agreement*, while a potentially troublesome Article XIX issue was avoided by the Panel. Article XIX requires that safeguard action be based on a finding of 'unforeseen developments'. Since 1974, however, US law has had no such requirement.[109] The EC raised the issue, but the panel, for reasons of judicial economy, did not reach it.[110] The US likely will lose on the issue eventually, however, as in a previous case the EC successfully challenged a safeguard measure by Korea on that basis.[111]

D. An abbreviated critique

For a critique of safeguards, Olivier Long has said it best. These clauses, he writes, 'have to achieve a compromise difficult to bring about: to be sufficiently strict so that their exceptional character is obvious, but with a degree

---

[103] Ibid.   [104] Long, supra note 101, at 58.   [105] Ibid.

[106] WTO, *Analytical Index: Guide to GATT Law and Practice* (1995), Vol 1 at 535.

[107] Ibid at 537.

[108] *United States—Definitive Safeguard Measures on Imports of Wheat Gluten from the European Communities*—WT/DS166/R (31 July 2000) (adopted as *modified* by the Appellate Body 22 December 2000) ('*Wheat Gluten Panel*').

[109] Prior to 1974, the US safeguard law directed the authorities 'to determine whether, *as a result in major part of concessions granted under trade agreements*, an article is being imported into the United States in such increased quantities as to cause . . . serious injury'. Trade Expansion Act of 1962 § 301(b)(1), Pub L 87–974, 76 Stat 872 (emphasis added); section 201 of the Trade Act of 1974 eliminated the italicized language. Pub L 93–618, 88 Stat 618, 2012.

[110] *Wheat Gluten Panel*, supra note 108, at para 8.220. The Appellate Body affirmed. AB-2000–10, para 183 (22 December 2000).

[111] The panel in that case sided with Korea, holding that the phrase 'unforeseen developments' in Article XIX merely served as an explanation as to why a measure may be needed. The Appellate Body

of flexibility enough to reassure governments, to induce them to assume maximum commitments, and to facilitate their task of securing ratification of such commitments'.[112]

For many years there was wide agreement that Article XIX, with its compensation requirement, was too strict. With the *Safeguards Agreement*, that burden has been lifted—at the risk of giving members a free chance at protectionism. Yet with anti-dumping laws, members essentially have the same thing—a free chance at protectionism—with more elaborate camouflage in the form of complex accounting calculations that display a false precision. From a liberal trade perspective, the apparent choice between safeguards and anti-dumping is not a particularly attractive one. Olivier Long is resigned to ambiguity. 'It can reasonably be asked', he says, 'whether perfection in this area is attainable, given the strength of economic and political interests at play.'[113] This certainly seems true of the contingency protection regime presently. The challenge is to find a way to make a change.

IV. A RAWLSIAN EXAMINATION OF THE CONTINGENCY PROTECTION REGIME

This study began with a statement by Rousseau, expressing the need, in establishing a civil order, for 'men [to be] taken as they are and laws as they might be'. Following Rousseau, but using more contemporary language, John Rawls has said that a liberal conception of justice 'takes people as they are (by the laws of nature) and constitutional and civil laws as they might be, that is as they would be in a reasonably just and well-ordered democratic society'.[114] A programme to prevent and settle disputes in the transatlantic partnership is, in a meaningful sense, an attempt to establish a form of Rousseau's 'civil order' that, because democracies are involved, should be based on the kind of fair conception of justice that is central to Rawls. The attempt to strengthen that order by controlling or reducing the confrontational nature of the current contingency protection regime must begin with the constraint of people as they are. This constraint limits laws as they might be. It is instructive however to consider why people are as they are with regard to the question of trade protection, and to consider further what the laws as they might be would be—if people were as they could be concerning the question of trade protection generally, and contingency protection specifically.

---

reversed, holding that the phrase does constitute an affirmative obligation. See, *Korea—Definitive Safeguard Measure on Imports of Dairy Products*, WT/DS98/R para 7.42 (21 June 1999) and AB-1999–8, paras 77, 84 (14 December 1999) (adopted 12 January 2000).

[112] Long, supra note 101, at 57.
[113] Ibid.
[114] J. Rawls, *The Law of Peoples* (1999), at 13.

A. People as they are

Rousseau's view of people as they are in a state of nature was decidedly rosy. '[I]n a state of nature', he contended, 'every one is there his own master, and the law of the strongest is of no effect.'[115] Once people left the state of nature, however, everything changed: '[m]an is born free; and everywhere he is in chains'.[116] Rawls moves the discussion forward considerably. He uses the term 'peoples' to distinguish the subject of his concern from states, as traditionally conceived.[117] 'What distinguishes peoples from states', he writes, 'is that just peoples are fully prepared to grant the very same proper respect and recognition to other peoples as equals'.[118] He describes 'liberal democratic peoples' as having 'a certain moral character'.[119] Just as reasonable citizens within a society co-operate on fair terms with other citizens, so liberal peoples 'offer fair terms of cooperation to other peoples'.[120]

Most citizens—most 'peoples'—of nations in the transatlantic partnership would accept Rawls' description of a liberal democratic peoples as applying to themselves and to the others in the partnership. And, indeed, Rawls would agree. Liberal peoples, in his view, live under a constitutional democratic government that 'is effectively under their political and electoral control'.[121] That government 'answers to and protects their fundamental interests'.[122] Those statements fairly apply to the EC and its member states, as well as to the US.

There is a difficulty, however. 'No people', Rawls argues, 'will be willing to count the losses to itself as outweighed by gains to other peoples; and therefore the principle of utility, and other moral principles discussed in moral philosophy, are not even candidates for the Law of Peoples.'[123] This limitation on 'people as they are' must be taken into account in discussing 'laws as they might be'.

B. Laws as they might be

The transatlantic partnership consists of two sets of Rawlsian 'peoples'—one on each side of the ocean. Each of these peoples, through its democratically-established institutions, has adopted its own laws to provide contingency protection against imports. Together with other peoples, they also have established the WTO norms with which their individual regimes are required to comply. As we have seen, however, these individual regimes in fact do not always comply with international norms, something that results from (1) disagreement as to what a

---

[115] 'The Origin of Inequality' in Rousseau, supra note 1, at 81.
[116] 'The Social Contract' in Rousseau, supra note 1, Book I, chapter 1, at 181.
[117] Rawls, supra note 114, at 27.
[118] Ibid., at 35.
[119] Ibid., at 25.
[120] Ibid.
[121] Ibid., at 24.
[122] Ibid.
[123] Ibid., at 60.

particular norm requires; (2) a decision to ignore a norm as long as possible; or (3) a decision to absorb the cost of continued violation of the norm.[124]

Virtually all of the conflict generated by the application of contingency protection measures occurs at the international level, between peoples, and not at the domestic level, within a people—although, to be sure, on each side of the Atlantic there are numerous critics of each contingency protection regime. But *within* each of the partners, most people tend to see the action from an internal perspective, one that was generated by and applies to 'us', not 'them'. It is 'our' political system that established the rule; it is 'our' administrative system that applies it; it is 'our' judicial system that reviews the administrative decision.[125] We tend primarily to justify the action in terms of domestic laws and institutions, and only secondarily, if at all, in terms of the international laws and institutions. Conversely, when 'they' impose contingency protection on 'us', we are indifferent to 'their' laws and institutions, and look to the international laws and institutions as justification for condemnation of the action.

Neither the WTO 'political' system through which the international norms were established, nor the WTO legal system, is seen by the 'peoples' of the transatlantic partnership as 'theirs' in the sense that the EC and US domestic political and legal systems are 'theirs'.[126] In particular, the weak 'political' system that is characteristic of international law generally—the noted absence of an effective and accepted legislature—can strain any attempts to strengthen and institutionalize international legal systems.[127] As Friedrich Kratochwil explains, '[t]he separation of the legal process from the political process in the domestic arena is possible because *both* processes are well institutionalized. However, since the world political process lacks institutionalization, a more effective utilization of the international legal process is considerably hampered.'[128]

What this would seem to mean for the judicial institutions applicable to the transatlantic partners is that they will never benefit from the acceptance that the internal point of view provides, so long as the two 'peoples' view themselves as separate from one another. These institutions do not and will not possess the social 'glue' that permits, for example, judicial review of legislation for constitutionality to be an accepted part of the legal system in the US, despite the extremely controversial nature of some of those decisions.[129] Reform through the judiciary,

---

[124] The first two of these seem a fair characterization of the US position with regard both to 'zeroing' and subsidies granted prior to privatization. See supra, notes 46–49 and 89–90 and accompanying text.

[125] The 'internal point of view' is crucial to the existence of a legal system. See H.L.A. Hart, *The Concept of Law* (1994), at 26. Hart's views are elaborated in some detail in N. MacCormick, *Legal Reasoning and Legal Theory* (1978), at 275–292.

[126] For an examination of the WTO in terms of Hart's criteria for a modern legal system, see D. Palmeter, 'The WTO as a Legal System,' 24 *Fordham Int'l LJ* (November-December 2000) 444.

[127] See Hart, supra note 125, at 214.

[128] F.V. Kratochwil, *Rules, Norms, and Decisions: On the Conditions of Practical and Legal Reasoning in International Relations and Domestic Affairs* (1989) 252.

[129] It is ironic that a democracy refers some of its most political issues to the judiciary in the guise of a lawsuit, but the practice is well established. See A. de Toqueville, *Democracy in America* (1945),

a practice widely accepted in the US—albeit with some grumbling—is not likely
to be a realistic option for any transatlantic institutions in the foreseeable future.
In particular, it would be foolish to expect contingency protection to develop,
through WTO dispute settlement, in the way that antitrust law has developed in
the US through litigation. A reform of the magnitude of that which took place in
the US, when the judiciary largely accepted the economic analysis of antitrust law
proposed by the Chicago School, seems out of the question.[130]

If this analysis is correct, there is little that new institutions, as such, can do to
control contingency protection more effectively. The difficulty is not with the
institutions, but with the rules themselves. These rules were made by the democratic peoples of the transatlantic partnership, through their diplomatic representatives, in a way intended to shield their domestic rules from international
interference. 'In a democracy', Amartya Sen observes, 'people tend to get what
they demand.'[131] The people of the transatlantic partnership have demanded the
contingency protection system that presently prevails. That system reflects the
preferences of 'people as they are'. The key, then, is not in institutional reform
but in policy reform. In democracies, this means convincing 'people as they are'
to adopt different policies. To do that, it is necessary to understand why the
present contingency protection rules prevail.

C. People as they are—and trade protection

GATT from the start was based on the theory of mercantilism, the theory that
exports are good and imports are bad. That theory continues to undergird the
WTO. Imports are the regrettable price of exports.[132] The preamble to GATT
refers to 'reciprocal' trading arrangements, ie, 'I will open my market if you will
open yours'. Reciprocity is 'inevitable', Jagdish Bhagwati writes, 'when governments work on the twin assumptions that trade is good but imports are bad'.[133]
Governments work on these assumptions because of political pressures that, as
Patrick Low observes, 'cannot be wished away'.[134]

These pressures are generated by domestic protectionist groups, those that
stand to lose by trade liberalization. But these pressures are greatly augmented
by those who believe that they—and their entire country—lose by trade liberal-

Vol 1 at 280: '[s]carcely any political question arises in the United States that is not resolved sooner or
later, into a judicial question'. The controversial issues that have been decided by the US Supreme
Court include: racial segregation in the public schools, *Brown v Board of Education*, 347 US 483
(1954); the size and shape of legislative districts, *Baker v Carr*, 369 US 186 (1962); abortion, *Roe
v Wade*, 410 US 113 (1973); prison conditions, *Hutto v Finney*, 437 US 678 (1978); and capital
punishment, *Furman v Georgia*, 408 US 238 (1972).

130 One of the works that led the way was R. Bork, *The Antitrust Paradox: A Policy at War with
Itself* (1978).
131 A. Sen, *Development As Freedom* (1999), at 156.
132 See Hoekman & Kostecki, supra note 40, at 67.
133 'An Unhealthy Obsession with Reciprocity' in J. Bhagwati, *A Stream of Windows* (1998), at 134.
134 Low, supra note 13, at 23.

ization. Protectionism does not appeal just to those with something to protect; it intuitively appeals to most people most of the time, unless they are members of the decided minority who have had the benefit of being taken, step by step, through the reasoning of the counter-intuitive case for free trade. That is why most people believe that we import in order to export, rather than *vice versa*.[135]

A startling example of the intuitive appeal of protectionism is Abraham Lincoln, whom many Americans would consider their greatest president. In February 1861, Lincoln, who had been elected President the previous November, was travelling by train across the country from his home in Springfield, Illinois to Washington for his 4 March inauguration.[136] On 15 February, he stopped in Pittsburgh, Pennsylvania, even then the centre of the US steel industry. In a speech to the citizens of the city, Lincoln made remarks that might fairly be characterized not only as protectionist in sentiment, but as an early justification for anti-dumping measures:

[L]abor being the true standard of value, is it not plain, that if equal labor get a bar of railroad iron out of a mine in England, and another out of a mine in Pennsylvania, each can be laid down in a track at home, cheaper than they could exchange countries, at least by the cost of carriage. If there be a present cause why one can be both made and carried, cheaper, in *money price*, than the other can be made without carrying, that cause is an unnatural, and injurious one, and ought, gradually, if not rapidly to be removed.[137]

Lincoln was a largely self-educated genius, but clearly his education did not include exposure to the writings of Adam Smith or David Ricardo, which probably were not even available on the Illinois frontier of Lincoln's youth. The point, however, is not to berate Lincoln. The point is that, if someone of his genius finds protectionist arguments appealing, it is hardly surprising that most people find them appealing. In democracies, this means that government officials frequently face pressures from protectionist forces that cannot be answered effectively by those who know better.

The usual explanation for this phenomenon is that the forces of protection are organized and concentrated while the consumer voice is fragmented. This is true, but there is more. The protectionists can rely on considerable support from those not directly affected, but who believe the protectionists are right. The average

---

[135] Few seem to consider that when they shop for food, medicine or other essentials, they do not try to maximize their exports of money and minimize their imports of food and medicine.

[136] D.D. Herbert, *Lincoln* (1995), at 273–277. It was not until adoption of the XXth Amendment to the Constitution in 1933 that the date of the President's term was moved up from March to January 20.

[137] 'Speech at Pittsburgh, Pennsylvania, February 15, 1861', *The Collected Works of Abraham Lincoln* (1953), Vol IV at 210. Lincoln's use of the word 'unnatural' to describe a price, which is reminiscent of the medieval notion of a 'just' price, is a 'natural' for defenders of the anti-dumping regime. The obvious economic fallacies in his reasoning include the assumptions that labour is the only contributor to value, that a bar of iron from England and from Pennsylvania are likely to be produced with the same amount of labour, and that the labour will (or should) cost the same in both England and Pennsylvania. Lincoln's geography was somewhat mixed up as well. The iron and steel industry began near Pittsburgh because of plentiful coal. There was little or no iron in the ground. That arrived, for the most part, via the Great Lakes.

person, who has more important things to do in life than to worry about the details of international trade, learns of the subject only through the popular media, and applies an intuitive intelligence that is unlikely to match Lincoln's. To the extent the media covers the subject, it frequently does so in terms of 'injury' to a domestic industry, perhaps showing footage of a closed mill or interviews with those whose jobs have been lost to imports. Words like 'dumping' and 'unfair' and 'subsidized' are used, all of them in context that renders them pejorative—as descriptions of what 'they' are doing to 'us'. Those who do not fear that the same could happen to them are, at the very least, sympathetic to the victims, and usually can see nothing wrong with seeking a 'level playing field' and keeping the 'foreigners' out of 'our' market when 'they' are hurting some of 'us'.

The fact that those with a direct interest in protectionism can rely on a high degree of support from many of those who do not have that direct interest is largely, if not entirely, the result of a lack of appreciation of the benefits of international trade among most people. The very existence of a formal or informal reciprocity requirement supports the view that most people believe that imports are what a country must accept, with reluctance, in order to export. They believe if we are to open our market, we should do so only and to the extent that others open their markets. They would find bizarre the argument that the only reason a country trades is to import, and that exports are the price a country must pay to do so. They have never heard of David Ricardo and wine from Portugal and cloth from England.[138] Few, if any, secondary or post-secondary schools anywhere require this basic knowledge of their graduates.

Yet in no other area of public policy do those with no particular training feel free to pronounce upon it than in economics—whether the question be one of fiscal policy, monetary policy or trade policy. This is true not only of the average person, but of the average person in the media as well. On a day-to-day basis, business and economic reporters, who usually are familiar with basic economic theory, report on developments in the business and economic sections of publications, where they tend to be read by those who share that familiarity. But when the issue becomes 'political' and moves to the front pages—as it does in the US when trade legislation is pending in Congress—the political reporters tend to take over. Too frequently their reports betray a profound ignorance of economics, reflecting the belief that we must accept imports in order to export.

Clearly there is a need to educate the public and the journalists in the fundamental teachings of economics. In democracies, economic policy, including trade policy, ultimately is decided by the voters. If voters are ill informed, how can trade policy be otherwise? The work of educating and informing the public must begin with the economics profession, but this raises a further problem: economists are not particularly enthused about teaching the basics of their science to the public. Economists have an odd bias against those in their ranks who speak to the public, at the level of the basics, in understandable prose. It is not so much

[138] D. Ricardo, *The Principles of Political Economy and Taxation* (1973), ch 10 at 77–93.

that this activity does not merit the accolades that accompany original research. It is, rather, that such activity seems actually to detract from an economist's professional reputation. Paul Samuelson, in the introduction to a recent edition of his classic textbook, gives an example:

Back in those days, a promising scholar was not supposed to write textbooks—certainly not basic texts for beginning sophomores and freshmen. Only hacks were supposed to do that. But because I had already published so many research articles, it seemed that my reputation and prospects for lifetime tenure could afford me the elbow room to respond positively to MIT's request for a new textbook.[139]

In other words, with the work that would secure his Nobel Prize behind him, Samuelson believed his professional reputation could sustain the inevitable hit that would follow from writing for the uninitiated. And this hit would follow, it should be noted, from writing for university students. Never mind that economic literacy also is needed for those who do not study at universities. If this unusual professional attitude is not changed, prospects are not good for educating the public—the ultimate policy makers in democracies—the basics of trade economics.

When basic trade economics are explained to the public, the results can be salutary. During Peter Sutherland's tenure as its last Director-General, GATT issued a report on the impact of trade restraints on consumers. In rather striking language for a document produced by international civil servants, the report explained such things as, '[h]ow governments buy votes on trade with the consumer's money'.[140] Nothing in the report was path breaking; nothing surprised any economist or trade policy official. Yet the public—at least as reflected by the journalistic response to the report—was astounded. Front-page articles and leading segments on television's nightly news informed the public that they were paying significantly higher prices because of tariffs and quotas. Many reporters seemed honestly amazed to learn that governments bought votes with the consumer's money. GATT's report on the cost of trade to consumers, regrettably, has not been repeated.

The GATT report dealt with the costs of protectionism generally, not with the contingency protection system itself. But its reception provides compelling evidence that a public that understands the costs of protectionism most likely would conclude that the current contingency protection system has serious shortcomings, and that it should be overhauled drastically. The question, then, is what kind of contingency protection system would an informed public adopt?

D. Laws as they might be—if people were as they could be

One way to view contingency protection laws as they might be, if people were more familiar with economic theory than they presently are, is to adopt Rawls'

---

[139] P.A. Samuelson & W.D. Nordhaus, *Economics* (1992), at ix–x.
[140] GATT, *Trade, the Uruguay Round and the Consumer—The Sting: How Governments Buy Votes on Trade with the Consumer's Money* (August 1993).

creative addition to social contract theory, the 'original position' with its 'veil of ignorance'.[141] The 'original position' is one of equality among free and rational persons in establishing the fundamental terms of their association. 'Among the essential features of this situation is that no one knows his place in society, his class position or social status, nor does any know his fortune in the distribution of natural assets or abilities, his intelligence, strength and the like.'[142] In *The Law of Peoples*, Rawls extended this idea to international society. He visualized a group of rational representatives of just peoples, behind a 'veil of ignorance', attempting to establish rules to govern their relationship. They 'do not know, for example, the size of the territory, or the population, or the relative strength of the people whose fundamental interests they represent . . . [T]hey do not know the extent of their natural resources, or the level of their economic development, other such information.'[143] Rawls concludes that parties in these circumstances 'will formulate guidelines for setting up cooperative organizations and agree to standards of fairness for trade'.[144] One of these organizations would be 'analo-gous to GATT'.[145] This acceptance of GATT (and by extension the WTO), however, is quite general and certainly is not an endorsement of all of its details, including those that apply to contingency protection.

Of course, there never was, and never could be, a trade negotiation in which the representatives of real parties operated behind a Rawlsian veil of ignorance. Certainly trade negotiators, like all humans, lack clairvoyance and make mis-takes—but they most certainly do know the size of the territory, and the popula-tion, and the relative strength of the people whose fundamental interests they represent. They know the extent of their natural resources, and the level of their economic development. Most importantly, they know the interests of the major players in their economies. Still, it is instructive to hypothesize a veil of ignorance and ask what kind of regime likely would emerge from such a process?

1. Anti-dumping

Negotiators operating under a veil of ignorance might find two possible justifi-cations for having special provisions—provisions other than domestic competi-tion law—to deal with some instances of international price discrimination. One is the market power that the trading system itself might encourage or permit. In a freely operating market, arbitrage usually can be expected to discourage, if not eliminate, most price discrimination. Apart from transaction costs, someone buying at the lower price could immediately turn around and sell the product at a profit where the higher price prevails. This possibility greatly reduces, if it does not eliminate, most incentives to discriminate in price. But tariffs interfere with this process, and the WTO explicitly permits tariffs. To some extent, therefore, a seller in a protected market is also protected from arbitrage. Of

---

[141] J. Rawls, *A Theory of Justice* (1971).   [142] Ibid at 11.
[143] *The Law of Peoples*, supra note 114, at 32–33.   [144] Ibid at 42.
[145] Ibid., footnote 51. The other international organization mentioned by name by Rawls is the World Bank.

course, as tariffs are reduced, this protection is reduced. Still, rational negotiators, dealing with the issue of price discrimination behind a veil of ignorance, likely would take the reduced possibility of market correction through arbitrage when tariffs are present into account in establishing their rules.[146] At the very least, tariffs and quotas are capable of conferring market power on their beneficiaries.

The second justification goes to jurisdictional difficulties. When the alleged price discriminator is outside the territory where the ostensible injury occurs, special procedures might be required that would not be needed when the alleged price discriminator is within the territory. These procedures might differ from those that apply to alleged domestic violators, and therefore could constitute a denial of the national treatment required by GATT Article III. However, GATT already envisions this possibility. Article XX(d) provides an exception from GATT obligations for measures 'necessary to secure compliance with laws or regulations which are not inconsistent with the provisions of this Agreement'.[147]

Apart from possibly dealing with the ability of permitted tariffs to interrupt arbitrage, however, negotiators in a Rawlsian original position, behind a veil of ignorance, are not likely to adopt substantive rules to deal with alleged 'dumping' that differ in any way from the rules they adopt to deal with alleged domestic price discrimination. They would not adopt two rules for determining whether, in fact, price discrimination is occurring, depending on whether the goods were imported or domestically-produced; they would not require sales in two markets for one law, and allow sales to be 'constructed' in the other; they would not require sales of like merchandise in one market and allow adjustments for product differences in the other; they would not use variable cost of production as the indicator of predatory pricing in one market and total cost in the other; they would not examine cost of production in the allegedly protected market in one case, and in the alleged target market in the other; they would not require a showing of injury to competition in one case, and a showing of injury only to competitors in the other. In short, rational negotiators, operating behind a veil of ignorance, would reject virtually all of the WTO's substantive anti-dumping regime.[148]

2. Countervailing duties

The question of subsidies and countervailing duties is likely to present negotiators operating behind a veil of ignorance with more difficult choices than would the question of anti-dumping. They could approach the matter from a purely economic viewpoint and accept the subsidies of other members as a gift. Yet negotiators whose task it is to establish rules based on fairness would not likely

---

[146] The same would apply, *a fortiori*, if quotas were present.

[147] See also, *United States—Section 337 of the Tariff Act of 1930*, BISD 36S/345, 393–396 (adopted 7 November 1989).

[148] They might also reject much of the current procedural regime, even while recognizing that international trade might require special procedural rules.

accept a situation in which some of their own 'peoples' could be the economic victims of subsidies granted by other governments.[149]

Negotiators also would be faced with the fact that redistribution of resources is a legitimate function of government.[150] In the end, they probably would adopt a system very similar to the current WTO subsidies and countervailing duty regime. They would define a subsidy as a 'financial contribution' and a 'benefit', as does Article 1 of the *Subsidies Agreement*. They would provide further that it must be 'specific', as does Article 2. They would agree to prohibit subsidies contingent upon export or on the use of domestic over imported goods, as does Article 3. They would agree that a 'benefit' is conferred when a financial contribution provides something better than the recipient could obtain in the market, even if it did not result in a cost to government.[151]

The definitional and line drawing problems they face could lead negotiators in the original position to make some exceptions to their general rules. However, these exceptions—drawn by rational negotiators, behind a veil of ignorance, on behalf of just peoples—would differ markedly from some of the exceptions in the current *Subsidies Agreement*. For example, the current exceptions for agriculture and for export credits can be viewed as skewed in favour of developed countries, to the detriment of developing countries and their producers and exporters.[152] They would not be part of a subsidies agreement drawn to Rawlsian standards.

An interesting issue is presented by the question of injury. The 1897 US countervailing duty law, which applied until the adoption of the Tokyo Round Subsidies Code, had no injury requirement.[153] A frequently expressed justification for the absence of an injury requirement was that subsidies were 'unfair' practices by governments, and therefore deserved to be countervailed irrespective of injury, in contrast to dumping, which involved the pricing practices of private entities. This position has since been superseded, of course, but it does raise the question, assuming the anti-dumping criterion for injury is changed from injury to competitors to injury to competition, does it follow that the countervailing duty criterion should be changed as well?

---

[149] Rawls' theories are based on his notion of 'justice as fairness'. See *A Theory of Justice*, supra note 141, at 11–17; *The Law of Peoples*, supra note 114, at 3–4; E. Kelly (ed), *John Rawls, Justice as Fairness: A Restatement* (2001).

[150] See, supra note 84 and accompanying text.

[151] A government can confer a benefit in many 'costless' ways, eg, with a guarantee that results in a lower rate of interest to a borrower. The lower rate itself might contribute to the borrower's ability to repay, and thereby obviate any cost to the guaranteeing government.

[152] See, supra notes 85–88 and accompanying text.

[153] Although GATT Article VI requires a showing of material injury, the inconsistent US legislation was 'grandfathered' under the Protocol of Provisional Application under which GATT was implemented. See Jackson, supra note 7, at §3.2, 60–63, §16.5, 424–426. The *Agreement on Implementation of Article VI, XVI and XXIII of the General Agreement on Tariffs and Trade* (the Tokyo Round Code), BISD 26S/56, 65, provided for a finding of material injury at Article 6. The US applied the injury requirement only to GATT contracting parties who were parties to the Code ('countries under the Agreement'). Trade Agreements Act of 1979, 93 Stat 144, adding § 701 to the Tariff Act of 1930, 93 Stat 151.

Not necessarily. If anti-dumping is changed to parallel competition law more closely, its justification will be the well-being of the overall economy generally through the promotion of competition—competition that can be both fair by any reasonable standard and also very injurious to individual competitors. Price discrimination, in this analysis, is no longer demonized. It is viewed simply as price competition, and the very purpose of promoting competition in the economy is to promote consumer welfare through efficiency, a process that of necessity is injurious to the inefficient. Only if price competition is predatory is it anti-competitive, from the viewpoint of competition law.

Negotiators behind a veil of ignorance could take a very different view of subsidies. While subsidies may well be the result of well-intended, even laudable, government efforts to redistribute resources, subsidies are an interference in the market that could adversely affect individual competitors no matter how efficient those competitors might be. Consequently, as noted above, the arguments for countervailing duties, from a free trade perspective, are stronger than the arguments for anti-dumping duties.[154] An agreement on subsidies that permitted duties to offset the injurious effects of subsidies on individual competitors would not, therefore, necessarily be protectionist in any pejorative sense. Negotiators in the original position might well decide that requiring enterprises to meet vigorous price competition, even competition that involves price discrimination, is one thing; requiring them to compete with the resources of public treasuries is another.

3. Safeguards

Part of the motivation behind the negotiating of the *Safeguards Agreement* was to make Article XIX more 'workable'.[155] The difficulty of obtaining safeguard relief in the US in the years immediately following the Kennedy Round was seen by many as one of the reasons for the growth in anti-dumping investigations in the 1970s. There was some thought that a 'workable' safeguard could put the anti-dumping genie back in the bottle. Safeguard relief in the US is legally flexible, and allows policy considerations to play a role they do not play in anti-dumping. It is not without irony, therefore, that negotiators in the original position, operating behind a veil of ignorance, on behalf of just peoples, would not include the possibility of safeguard relief in their agreement.

The rationale for both Article XIX and the *Safeguards Agreement* is the mercantilist theory that underlies GATT and the WTO. That rationale is connected to the idea of reciprocity, and shares with reciprocity the flaws that result 'when governments work on the twin assumptions that trade is good but imports are bad'.[156] Safeguards are grounded in the assumption that a member unwittingly 'paid too much' for a concession from another member and should have some time to permit the injured parties in its territory to adjust.

---

[154] See, supra notes 81–82 and accompanying text.

[155] To be sure, the desire to discourage grey area measures was an extremely important factor as well.

[156] See, supra note 133 and accompanying text.

As a reflection of present political reality, there is much to be said for this assumption. But it is a flawed assumption that would not be accepted by rational negotiators, in a Rawlsian original position. Safeguards may indeed provide a benefit (intended to be temporary) to those in the affected industry, but they do so at the expense of consumers and those in the exporting industry. Safeguards are avowedly protectionist. In addition to their realpolitik justification, however, they are defended as reasonable, humane measures designed to give a brief respite to those injured by imports.

But why, it might be asked, should those injured by imports be any more deserving of assistance than those hurt by other factors in the economy beyond their control? Technological and fashion changes are facts of everyday life in modern societies in general, and among the countries of the transatlantic partnership in particular. These inevitably cause the same kind of job-loss injury that occurs when an industry loses its international competitiveness. Consider, for example, the newspaper industry, an industry (heretofore at least) little affected by international trade. For most of the twentieth century and a good part of the nineteenth, afternoon newspapers were common in many US and European cities. No more. Television news has all but eliminated the afternoon newspaper, costing countless editorial, production and circulation workers their jobs. That's not all. Until a few decades ago, all of those newspapers were produced with 'hot type' made from molten lead on linotype machines. Computers have ended that, at a cost of thousands of composing room jobs. These newspaper people have been just as injured by economic change beyond their control as those who are injured by import competition. Why is their plight any less deserving than the plight of those impacted by imports? Rawls, in fact, has expressly addressed the question of imports and the injury they may cause:

[P]ersons engaged in a particular industry often find that free trade is contrary to their interests. Perhaps the industry cannot remain prosperous without tariffs or other restrictions. But if free trade is desirable from the point of view of equal citizens or of the least advantaged, it is justified even though more specific interests suffer.[157]

Indeed, under Rawls' 'difference principle', free trade, which generally favours the least advantaged in society, is to be encouraged.[158] But Rawls would not leave those injured by imports strictly to their own devices, any more than he would have left the newspaper workers to theirs. 'This does not mean', he explains, 'that the rigors of free trade should be allowed to go unchecked. But the arrangements for softening them are to be considered from an appropriately *general* perspective.'[159] Thus, while Rawls clearly rejects mercantilism, he envisions a generally available social safety net for those who are disadvantaged from whatever cause. Negotiators acting on his principles, supported by a just and economically aware people, would not, therefore, adopt a safeguard mechanism. Instead, they would adopt a broadly-based social safety net.

---

[157] *A Theory of Justice*, supra note 141, at 99.   [158] Ibid at 75–83.
[159] Ibid at 100 (emphasis added).

V. INSTITUTIONAL ASPECTS

The confrontations over contingency protection that take place in the transatlantic partnership result from the rules themselves and not from the WTO, the institution of which they are a part. Nevertheless, the question remains whether an institutional change from the multilateral WTO to a bilateral arrangement could serve to facilitate a reduction in the level of confrontation. A bilateral arrangement could take the form of something as simple as the 1992 bilateral Large Civil Aircraft Agreement[160] or as complex as a free trade area or customs union that qualified under Article XXIV GATT. So long as the people of the transatlantic partnership are as they are, however, any meaningful change in the contingency protection regime is a virtual political impossibility. More important, even if change were politically possible, confining that change to the transatlantic partnership would have undesirable—indeed, unacceptable— consequences of its own.

The political impossibility is demonstrated by the treatment of contingency protection in the 1989 *Canada—United States Free Trade Agreement* (FTA), and the subsequent *North American Free Trade Agreement* (NAFTA). These agreements offer a perspective on the adamancy with which people as they are, in the US, adhere to the present contingency protection regime. The primary aim of Canada in negotiating the FTA was to obtain relief from contingency protection in the US.[161] Canada did not succeed. As a last minute 'fig leaf' to cover Canada's naked failure to achieve its goal, the FTA negotiators hit upon a system of binational panels to replace each party's national judiciary in reviewing its antidumping and countervailing duty decisions.[162] But no change was effected in the laws; no change was effected in the regulations; no change was effected in the administration of the laws. In fact, the judiciary is the only element of the US anti-dumping and countervailing duty system that has not been the subject of significant complaints.[163] The panels simply do the task of the judiciary and apply the existing law and regulations, the law and regulations that are the core of the problem. If the panels do their jobs properly, they should reach the same result a court would have reached. This system was carried over into NAFTA.[164]

---

[160] *Agreement Between the Government of the United States of America and the European Economic Community Concerning the Application of the GATT Agreement on Trade in Civil Aircraft on Trade in Large Civil Aircraft.*

[161] See generally, M. Hart, *Fifty Years of Canadian Trade craft: Canada at the GATT 1947–1997* (1998), at 149–171.

[162] *Canada—United States Free Trade Agreement*, chapter 19.

[163] Obviously, individual decisions may be criticized, but there has been no claim of unfairness or bias in the system of judicial review.

[164] NAFTA, chapter 19. NAFTA Article 802 also continued a regional exception to the contingency protection regime, contained in Article 1102 of the Canada-US FTA, which requires parties to exclude imports from other parties from safeguard measures under certain circumstances. Not surprisingly, this has run afoul of the WTO where a panel found that Articles 2.1 and 4.2 of the *Safeguards Agreement* require symmetry between the scope of the imported products investigated and the scope of the imported products subject to the measure. *United States—Definitive Safeguard Measures on*

That there has been no change in the attitude of people as they are was recently noted in a Comment by the *Financial Times*:

What most Latin American trade partners want from the US is easier access to its market for textiles and agricultural products...and *freedom from arbitrary anti-dumping actions*. Yet, as the fast-track debate has shown, these are all areas where US trade policies are most restrictive and are fiercely defended by domestic producer lobbies.[165]

Clearly, until the attitudes of people as they are change, democratic policy cannot change. It is true, of course, that protectionist lobbies, like most lobbies, are aided by the familiar fact that they are focused on the single issue in which they have a large interest, while the consumer interest is diffused. But the strength of protectionist lobbies is also greatly aided by the degree to which democratic opinion tends to agree with them on the merits. When and if democratic opinion changes, and sees the contingency protection regime as undesirable, a rejection of that system on a multilateral basis seems as likely as a rejection of it bilaterally.

Even if contingency protection could be eliminated bilaterally before it could be eliminated multilaterally, however, the consequences of doing so could be severe. The EC and the US are the two largest trading entities in the WTO. As important as their bilateral relationship is, both have extensive interests and important trading partners elsewhere in the world. For them to exclude each other from the strictures of the highly criticized—and, for the most part, justifiably criticized—contingency protection regime of the WTO, while continuing to apply that regime to other members, would have grave consequences for the EC, the US, those other members, and the WTO itself. On the other hand, should the EC and the US both favour liberalization of the regime, it is doubtful that they would meet serious opposition in the WTO.

VI. CONCLUSION

The mercantilism of GATT and the WTO is explained by the necessity of 'political economy', with the emphasis on 'political'. In order to obtain the necessary political support for trade liberalization, the argument goes, it is necessary to obtain the support of industries (lobbies) with an export interest so that the influence of protectionist lobbies can be overcome. Thus it is that a member lowering its trade barriers, to the benefit of its consumers and its overall economy, is said to be making a 'concession'.

Imports of Wheat Gluten from the European Communities, paras 8.167, 8.182, WT/DS166/R (adopted as *modified* by the Appellate Body 19 January 2001). NAFTA, chapter 11 also provides for arbitration of disputes between the national parties and an investor of another party. While this system might well be adaptable to the transatlantic partnership as an investment measure, it is not structured to deal with the issues presented by the contingency protection regime, which concerns imports, not investments.

[165] 'Latin Trade', 18 January 2002 (emphasis added).

The strategy worked quite well for the first half century of the GATT/WTO system, but for most of that time the system was obscure and, to most people in the transatlantic partnership, unimportant. Economic integration was a much larger topic in Europe, and international trade was a comparatively small part of the US economy. GATT was the domain of specialists, and if it made the newspapers at all, it did so with small items on the inside pages, not with large articles on the front pages. Those who were responsible for the system usually were quite aware of its mercantile fallacy, and ignored it as much as possible as they forged ahead with liberalization, using the contingency protection system as an occasional safety valve.

But the system is no longer obscure, and the control of the elites who understand the fallacies of mercantilism is diminishing in comparison with large numbers who intuitively agree with mercantilism and the protectionist policies it fosters. The ability of the elites to do what is best, because few understand—or even care—what they are doing, has been greatly reduced. The increased use of the contingency protection regime is one consequence.

If that confrontational and corrosive regime is to be reformed, therefore, a larger public is going to have to agree that reform is desirable, even necessary. Rawlsian analysis makes clear that most of the current regime would be rejected by rational representatives of economically aware, just peoples, operating from the original position, because 'a free competitive-market trading scheme is to everyone's mutual advantage'.[166] But that is not the situation in which the trading system currently finds itself. The people, no doubt, are motivated by justice, but they are not, by and large, economically aware. Reduction in the confrontational nature of the contingency protection regime requires that this be changed.

[166] *The Law of Peoples*, supra note 114, at 42.

5

Industrial Subsidies: Tax Treatment of 'Foreign Sales Corporations'

ROBERT E. HUDEC

INTRODUCTION

During its first five years, the WTO dispute settlement procedure has experienced only one significant US-EC dispute over industrial subsidies—the celebrated EU complaint charging that the US income tax exemption for Foreign Sales Corporations (FSCs) constituted an export subsidy in violation of Article 3.1(a) of the Agreement on Subsidies and Countervailing Measures (SCM Agreement).[1]

In the *FSC* case, a panel ruled that the FSC tax exemption did constitute an export subsidy in violation of the SCM Agreement. The Appellate Body (AB) affirmed. The US then passed legislation abolishing the FSC and replacing it with a new tax exemption for a class of foreign-source income known as 'Extra-Territorial Income' (ETI).[2] The EC challenged the ETI legislation under Article 21.5 of the Dispute Settlement Understanding (DSU) as not being in compliance with the FSC ruling. In the 21.5 proceedings, both the Panel and the AB ruled that new ETI legislation was also an export subsidy in violation of the SCM Agreement. They also ruled that the ETI statute's value-added requirement violated GATT Article III:4, and that it did not qualify as a measure to avoid double taxation of foreign income.

Following the 21.5 rulings, the EC requested authority to withdraw concessions on US trade worth $4.04 billion, and published a list of the US products that would be affected by such a withdrawal. The US disputed the amount of the retaliation, and requested that the issue be submitted to arbitration. In August 2002, the arbitration panel ruled that the EC was authorized to withdraw concessions on $4.043 billion of US trade. At the time of writing, no further action had been taken by the parties.

---

[1] WTO documents pertaining to the *FSC* case are issued under the document number WT/DS108. The key documents are the Panel Report in the *FSC* case, WT/DS108/R (8 October 1999); the Appellate Body Report in the *FSC* case, WT/DS108/AB/R (24 February 2000); the Panel 21.5 Report, WT/DS108/RW (20 August 2001); the Appellate Body 21.5 Report, WT/DS108/AB/RW (14 January 2002).

[2] FSC Repeal and Extraterritorial Income Exclusion Act of 2000, Public Law 106–519, 114 Stat 2423.

From the beginning, the EC threat to retaliate on $4 billion worth of US trade has made the *FSC* case a major concern to US-EC trade relations. The speed with which the US Congress replaced FSC with new legislation testifies to the seriousness with which that threat has been viewed. At the same time, however, the US government seems to have been unwilling, or at least unable, to make any economically meaningful changes in the tax benefits formerly granted by FSC, raising the possibility that the US will simply fail to comply and end up in impasse with the EC, and with the entire WTO legal system.

This paper examines the *FSC* case and its aftermath up to the time of publication. Part I examines the origins of the dispute in the 1972 *DISC* cases, and the legal situation resulting from those cases. Part II then examines the *FSC* case itself, looking into the reasons for bringing the case, the legal outcome of the case, the analysis that produced this outcome, and questions left unanswered after that initial ruling. Part III examines the outcome of the 21.5 review of the ETI statute—concentrating on the evolution of the legal definition of 'subsidy', and the contribution this phase of the case did or did not make to answering the questions left after the first decision. Part IV considers the lessons taught by *DISC-FSC-ETI* cases for the functioning of US-EC dispute settlement.

I. The *DISC* cases

A. The origins of the *DISC* cases

1. *The purpose of the DISC*

The DISC tax exemption was enacted in 1971 as part of a package of measures intended to deal with a balance of payments crisis that had forced the US to break its pledge to redeem dollars in gold. The DISC was meant to encourage exports by reducing the income tax payable on export income. The core idea behind the design of the DISC exemption was a desire by the US Treasury Department to emulate the income tax advantages given to many European exporters under the 'territorial' tax systems in several EC countries. Because territorial tax systems usually do not tax income earned outside the country's territory, EC exporters were able to escape income tax on part of their export income by selling their exports to foreign branches or subsidiaries located in tax haven countries, and then having the foreign branches or subsidiaries resell the goods to the ultimate export buyer. The Treasury view was that these initial 'sales' to foreign branches and subsidiaries were largely sham transactions that served no real economic purpose, and that they further distorted the true economic situation by using artificial transfer prices that shifted an excessive amount of income to the foreign branch or subsidiary. DISC was meant to offset these tax advantages by allowing US exporters to escape taxation on a similar portion of their export income. To achieve the maximum balance of payments effect, the DISC tax exemption did not require the exempt income to be earned abroad. Instead, export transactions would be run through a DISC, a domestic subsidiary of the exporting corporation, with the DISC's share of export income to be determined by arbitrary 'administered pricing' rules. The administered pricing rules allocated 50 per cent of export income to the DISC, of which half (ie, 25 per cent of total export income) would be exempt from payment of taxes.[3]

2. *The purpose of the DISC complaint*

The EC's decision to file a GATT legal complaint against DISC was viewed with some surprise at the time. Since its entry into GATT affairs in the late 1950s, the EC had been a firm opponent of a strong dispute settlement process, having taken the view throughout most of the 1960s that 'legalistic' procedures were inappropriate for solving most trade problems. This 'anti-legalist' view happened to be congruent with the EC's need to shelter several questionable elements of the Rome Treaty from GATT legal attack.

In the early 1970s, the US adopted a different legal policy seeking to revive the moribund GATT dispute settlement procedure for use in removing non-tariff barriers. The US began searching out legal violations by trading partners and filed several legal complaints. Two of the complaints were against the EC, both involving agricultural trade.[4] In one of the cases, the US had seemed intent on forcing an immediate ruling that would allow it to use trade retaliation. The new US legal policy brought back recollections of the 1963 'Chicken War' in which US had imposed trade retaliation in an effort to curb the expansion of the EC's Common Agricultural Policy.

At the time the DISC complaint was filed, many observers suspected that the primary purpose of the EC's legal complaint was not the removal of DISC but rather to dissuade the US from overly aggressive use of the dispute settlement process. The DISC was a good target for this purpose. The fact that DISC was created by an act of Congress meant that a ruling of violation would generate a good deal of political attention. The fact that Congress was likely to resist repealing DISC was all the better, because the embarrassment of US inability to comply would be the best source of restraint against further US legal claims.

B. The US claim of legal equivalence

Inside the US government, the response to the DISC complaint was directed by the US Treasury Department—the department with responsibility for tax policy, and with Cabinet rank senior to the US Trade Representative. Treasury's first response was to deny that GATT had any jurisdiction over tax matters, and the US maintained this position for several GATT meetings. Eventually, Treasury

---

[3] Technically, the tax was merely 'deferred' rather than exempted, but, as expected, when DISCs were eliminated in 1985, the deferred taxes were forgiven. By 1982, the exemption had been reduced to 17–18% of export income. See GATT Doc C/M/159 (meeting of 29–30 June 1982).

[4] The development of the new US legal policy is described in R.E. Hudec, *Enforcing International Trade Law* (1991), at 35–40.

agreed to adjudicate the matter in GATT, but only on certain conditions. First, the US filed three counter-complaints against France, Belgium and the Netherlands charging that tax exemptions for foreign-source export income granted under the 'territorial' tax laws of those three countries were equivalent to the tax exemptions granted by DISC. The US claim of GATT violation in these three counter-complaints was stated in conditional form: *if* DISC were in violation of the GATT Article XVI:4 prohibition against export subsidies, *then* so were these three European territorial tax exemptions. The Treasury Department insisted that the three counter-complaints be adjudicated at the same time as the DISC complaint, by the same panel. To make sure its claim of equivalence was understood, it also insisted that the panel contain at least two experts on international taxation. The US conditions were met.[5] (It must be remembered that at this time the GATT dispute settlement procedure moved forward only by consensus, so that the case could not move forward without US agreement to proceed.)

During the proceedings, the EC was unyielding in its insistence that the GATT Article XVI:4 prohibition of export subsidies was never meant to prohibit the subsidy-like effects of the territorial tax system. The territorial system had been well known at the time GATT's developed-country members had agreed to the GATT prohibition on export subsidies in 1955, as well as a similar Organization for European Economic Cooperation (OEEC) prohibition adopted at the same time. None of the European governments in question would have agreed to this prohibition, the EC said, if there had been the slightest indication that Article XVI:4 outlawed this very basic element of the territorial tax system.

As expected, the Panel found DISC to be an export subsidy in violation of Article XVI:4. But the Panel also sustained the US claim of economic equivalence, and on that basis ruled that the tax exemptions in the three European tax systems were also export subsidies in violation of XVI:4. Speaking of the three territorial tax systems, the Panel said

... the particular application of the [territoriality principle by the defendant governments] allowed some part of the export activities belonging to an economic process originating in the country, to be outside the scope of [its] taxes. In this way [the defendant government] had foregone revenue from this source and created a possibility of a pecuniary benefit to exports in those cases where income and corporation tax provisions were significantly more liberal in foreign countries.[6]

For the US, this conclusion validates its position that, if territorial tax exemptions were to be permitted, non-territorial countries must be permitted to grant an equivalent tax subsidy to their own exporters. Thus, the US was quite willing to reverse the Panel ruling against the three European tax systems, but only if

---

[5] For a detailed account of the *DISC* case, see R.E. Hudec, *Enforcing International Trade Law* (1991), at 59–100. An earlier version is R.E. Hudec, 'Reforming GATT Adjudication Procedures: The Lessons of the *DISC* Case' (1988) 72 *Minnesota Law Review* 1443.

[6] BISD 23rd Supp 125, ¶47 (France); ibid at 135, ¶ 34 (Belgium); ibid at 145, ¶ 34 (Netherlands).

DISC were also allowed as a matching subsidy. The EC refused to accept DISC, and so the case plunged into an impasse that lasted for the next five years.

C. The settlement: the 1981 Understanding

The negotiations over the 1979 Tokyo Round Subsidies Code would have been a logical place to resolve the impasse over the *DISC* cases, because the new Code was already making several additions to the law of export subsidies. But the settlement could not be wrapped up in time. In the end, the US and EC inserted a footnote 2 to the 1979 Code's provision on tax subsidies in the Illustrative List of Export Subsidies preserving their positions in the *DISC* case by stating that nothing in the Code 'prejudges the disposition of' that case.

Interestingly, however, the governments were willing to add to the same footnote 2 a provision calling for tax rules that required arm's length pricing in export sales to foreign branches or controlled foreign subsidiaries, a provision which made sense only on the assumption that the foreign-source income of a foreign branch or subsidiary (as properly calculated by arm's length pricing) could properly be exempted from taxation. A settlement was finally adopted in December 1981. At the request of the parties, the GATT Council 'adopted' all four panel reports together with an 'Understanding' which affirmed that the reports were being adopted:

on the understanding that with respect to these cases, and in general, economic processes (including transactions involving exported goods) located outside the territorial limits of the exporting country need not be subject to taxation by the exporting country and should not be regarded as export activities in terms of Article XVI:4 of the General Agreement.[7]

Read in its context, the text of the 1981 Understanding was clearly meant to reverse the panel rulings that the territorial tax exemptions of the three European defendants were export subsidies. But the unqualified nature of the statements—statements that foreign-source export income 'need not be subject to taxation' and 'should not be regarded as export activities'—was not limited to tax exemptions made under territorial tax systems. By its terms it also permitted the sort of matching tax exemptions the US wanted to grant. But the matching tax exemptions would have to meet two primary conditions. First, as the text quoted above makes clear, the exemption was limited to income generated by 'foreign economic processes'—sales activity taking place outside the government's territory. Second, to make sure that such tax exemptions were in fact limited to such foreign-source income, the Understanding contained an additional proviso, taken from footnote 2 of the 1979 Code, requiring that the amount of tax-exempt income be calculated on the basis of arm's length pricing.

[7] BISD, 28th Supp 114 (meeting of 7–8 December 1981). The Council's action was later affirmed by the GATT Contracting Parties at their 38th Session, GATT Doc SR 38/1 (meeting of 15 December 1982).

D. US 'compliance' with the 1981 Understanding: the FSC

After a brief period in which the US argued that DISC itself met these conditions, the US replaced DISC with the FSC tax exemption. The FSC exemption, enacted in 1984, required taxpayers seeking to retain their DISC-type exemption to create an FSC. In turn, the FSC was required to conduct a certain percentage of its export sales activity abroad. After meeting the certain other requirements carried over from the DISC legislation, the FSC was granted roughly the same tax exemption on export income as had been granted to DISCs.

In the view of most observers, the FSC exemption did not meet the requirements of the 1981 Understanding.[8] The 'foreign economic processes' requirements of the FSC were a sham, because very little genuine foreign economic activity was required. In addition, the 'administered pricing rules', which permitted FSCs to allocate about 15 per cent of export income to themselves were viewed as being well in excess of the percentages that would have been yielded by compliance with the arm's length pricing requirement. The FSC scheme had an additional problem of GATT consistency—a condition inherited from the original DISC legislation—limiting the tax exemption to income from the sale of export goods with not less than 50 per cent US value-added. This value-added provision, designed to prevent the exemption from inducing producers to move production overseas, appeared to violate GATT Article III.

The FSC was subjected to considerable criticism in GATT in the years 1983–1985. The main target of this criticism, however, was the US decision to forgive the $10 billion in tax liability that had been accrued under DISC—the DISC having merely 'deferred' tax liability rather than forgiving it. The FSC's other GATT legal flaws were mentioned, but were not pursued. From 1985 to 1997, nothing further was heard about FSC.

II. THE *FSC* CASE

A. The origins of the *FSC* case

1. *The purpose of the FSC legal complaint*

The EC complaint came as a surprise to many WTO observers. Since the EC had not complained about FSC's GATT legal problems since 1985, the common understanding was that the EC had decided to live with FSC. Acceptance of FSC seemed prudent, given the general assumption that it would be politically impossible for the US to terminate the FSC subsidy, due to the large number of important US industries that were benefiting from it. Even if the EC could win, a legal ruling would be a waste of time.

---

[8] For one account of these failings, see Hudec, supra note 5 at 95–98 and 1500–06 respectively.

The first explanation that occurred to many WTO observers was that the EC was using the FSC complaint in the same way that it had used the DISC complaint 25 years before—to discourage what it perceived to be the overly aggressive use of the dispute settlement system by the US. The complaint was initiated in November 1997, just one month after the DSB had adopted the AB ruling against the EC in the *Bananas* case, and during the appeal of the adverse panel ruling in the *Hormones* case. The EC had considered the US complaints in both cases to be unjustified—*Bananas* as inappropriate interference in a dispute between the EC and the Latin American countries producing bananas, *Hormones* as a litigious attack on a non-protectionist health measure based on very strong public health concerns. More irritating still, both complaints appeared to have been dictated by politically influential US industries, raising the spectre that the US government was no longer in control of its WTO litigation policy. And of even greater concern was what seemed to be a public commitment by US authorities to employ trade retaliation whenever WTO legal rulings were not obeyed in a timely manner.

Observers also speculated that the EC might also have been seeking some bargaining leverage to help settle the *Bananas* and *Hormones* cases in a reasonable manner, and so remove the US trade retaliation in those cases. Bargaining leverage would also have been useful to deter US legal complaints against other EC violations. Airbus Industries was mentioned as one firm supporting the complaint, both because it had frequently been the target of complaints about its own extensive subsidies, and because its principal competitor, Boeing, was one of the largest recipients of FSC subsidies.

In sum, the EC had much to gain from a legal victory, even an unenforceable one. Such a victory could help to curb aggressive US litigation policy, and it would not hurt to have some trade-offs to balance against the EC's own WTO legal problems.

2. The role of US litigation policy in WTO legal reform

For the US, a more effective dispute settlement system emerged as a major goal of the Uruguay Round. Due to waning political support from traditional goods exporters, the US Administration was seeking additional support from industries interested in exporting services (banking, insurance, other financial services), and intellectual property goods (pharmaceuticals, high technology goods, music, cinema). These industries were attracted to the WTO by the promise of binding market access rules and intellectual property rules backed by effective dispute settlement sanctions.

Effective dispute settlement also became the key to Congressional acceptance of a deal between the US and other WTO governments in which the US had agreed to undertake certain limitations on the use of its unilateral section 301 enforcement procedures in exchange for a more powerful and effective WTO dispute settlement procedure.

In order to 'sell' the effectiveness of the new WTO dispute settlement procedure to the Congress and to the relevant US industries, the US Administration had
to cater to the rather simplistic idea that enforcement of legal obligations was a
matter of coercion through trade retaliation. Consequently, the Administration
stressed the fact that, under the new WTO dispute settlement procedure, legal
rulings would become binding automatically, and that retaliation would be
automatically available in the case of non-compliance. And it promised to
both private industrial supporters and to the Congress that the Administration
would use these dispute settlement tools aggressively, especially the retaliation
instrument.

The Administration's 'selling' of the WTO dispute settlement system presented
a false picture in two respects. First, the GATT legal system upon which the new
WTO system had been built had never depended on coercion for its success. It
had depended on community diplomatic pressures, and on the members' long-
term interest in having a rule-based trading system. And second, in practice the
rigorousness of the GATT legal system had been tempered by a universal recognition that each country can be a defendant as well as a plaintiff, and by an
appreciation of the political difficulties that governments often faced in complying with the rules. In short, when the US Administration promised a rigorous and
coercive legal policy, it had promised a legal policy that had never worked in the
past, and that the US itself would likely not be able to live up to.

In retrospect, however, the overselling of WTO dispute settlement remedies
was probably a necessary part of obtaining government approval of this major
WTO legal reform. Democratic governments do not make international commitments on the basis of subtle calculations of long term advantage. They have
to be presented with visions of large and essentially costless victories.[9] Even
though Administration officials probably knew the picture they painted was not
wholly accurate, they also had good reason to believe such a picture was the only
way to move their government forward toward a more effective WTO. That
meant, of course, that the promises would have to be broken eventually. But the
art of achieving democratic consensus often works this way, hoping that time
and good excuses will wear down the unrealistic expectations created by overselling.

After the Uruguay Round, therefore, the US Administration was left with the
obligation to carry out its promises about aggressive rule enforcement. The
Administration had to respond to demands for bringing WTO legal complaints,
and, at least the first few times, to use retaliation just as soon as possible.
Moreover, when the first two retaliation measures, in *Bananas* and *Hormones*,
failed to produce immediate compliance, the US Administration was forced to go
along with new 'carousel' legislation that called for expanding the economic

---

[9] A leading example of this phenomenon is the statistical 'proof' of victory in tariff negotiations
submitted by virtually every GATT government. If the trade surpluses projected by each government
were added up, it would take another world economy to absorb the projected trade deficit.

pain of retaliation by periodically rotating the list of products being retaliated against.[10]

The EC reaction to this aggressive US litigation policy was probably the only way to alert the US political audience to the fact that WTO dispute settlement was, alas, a two-sided game, and that the rigorous and coercive legal policy they had been promised would not produce the costless legal victories they were expecting. So far, the didactic function of the *FSC* case seems to have succeeded quite well. Both the Congress and a large cross section of the US business community immediately responded by demanding that the case be settled on a pragmatic basis, including in some cases a call to consider a package deal that would trade off the retaliation in the *Bananas* and *Hormones* cases. When settlement negotiations failed, the Congress was motivated to rush enactment of the FSC replacement legislation in record time. Although Congress has a notoriously short memory and an embarrassingly one-sided perspective on international trade rule enforcement, it can be predicted that the Washington attitude toward trade retaliation will never be quite the same (at least for a while, anyway). The 'carousel' approach to retaliation seems to be in hibernation for the moment.

B. The ruling on the merits

The new SCM Agreement seemed to yield a rather clear answer that the FSC tax exemption was an export-contingent subsidy in violation of SCM Article 3.1(a).[11] Under SCM Article 1.1, the FSC would be a 'subsidy' if the tax exemption involved a 'financial contribution' by the US government to the FSC exporters. Under Article 1.1(a)(1)(ii), tax exemptions are considered financial contributions if they represent the foregoing of tax revenue that is 'otherwise due'. According to the Panel, the foregone tax revenue can be found to be 'otherwise due' if, 'but for' the contested tax exemption, the foregone revenue would have been due and collectible under the prevailing tax laws of the defendant member. Since the US countervailing duty law used exactly this 'but for' definition of 'subsidy' in its regulations, the US was forced to agree to the 'but for' test 'as a general proposition'. In the case of FSC, the Panel found that, but for the FSC exemption, the foreign-source income of FSC corporations would have been taxed under the prevailing 'worldwide' tax rules of section 61 of the US Internal Revenue Code (IRC).

Similarly, there was not really any debate that the FSC 'subsidy' was contingent on exports within the meaning of SCM Article 3.1(a). The FSC law applied

---

[10] Section 407, Trade and Development Act of 2000, 114 Stat 251. To be sure, the carousel proposal was not enacted until 18 May 2000, three years after the *FSC* complaint, but the attitudes toward trade retaliation on which it rests were already visible in 1997.

[11] The EC complaint had also charged that the 50% US value-added requirement violated SCM Article 3.1(b), and GATT Article III, but the Panel decided that it was not necessary to rule on this additional theory of violation.

only to export income, and the acknowledged purpose of the law was to give the kind of matching export subsidy the US believed was authorized by the 1981 Understanding.

Consequently, the primary US defence had to be based on the assertion that the 'subsidy' definition of the SCM Agreement was subject to a special exception for FSC-type tax exemptions. The most powerful case for such an exception was the words of the 1981 Understanding, which said just that. Unfortunately for this US defence, the text of the 1981 Understanding had not been included in the text of the 1994 SCM agreement. The parties agreed that the omission of the 1981 Understanding had not been deliberate; the 1981 Understanding had simply not been discussed at all. Footnote 59 to the SCM Agreement contained an arm's length pricing requirement that made sense only on the assumption that governments may properly grant tax exemptions for foreign-source export income. But the inference from footnote 59 proved to be too slim a reed upon which to build an exception from the explicit text of the SCM Agreement.

The best way to give legal effect to the 1981 Understanding was to argue that the 1981 GATT Council decision adopting the Understanding was a legally binding interpretation of GATT 1947. Under Annex IA of the WTO Agreement, which incorporates 'GATT 1947' into the WTO agreement as 'GATT 1994', GATT 1994 includes not only the official text of GATT 1947 but also 'decisions of the CONTRACTING PARTIES to GATT 1947' that can be regarded as 'legal instruments . . . that . . . entered into force under the GATT 1947 before the entry into force of the WTO agreement'.[12] If the 1981 Understanding could be characterized as such a binding legal instrument, it would have to treated as a legally binding part of the new GATT 1994.[13]

The 1981 Understanding was an interesting example of the ambiguous, 'diplomatic' manner in which the GATT often dealt with contested legal issues. The text of the Understanding was accompanied by a 'chairman's statement' which minimized the effect of what the Understanding itself had said, producing a kind of middle ground between binding and non-binding.[14] The task of interpreting this deliberately ambiguous legal document presented an interesting test of how the new and more rigorous WTO dispute settlement system would approach the 'diplomatic' legal practices of the early GATT.

Both the Panel and the AB took a rather rigorous approach to the ambiguities in the text of the 1981 Understanding and concluded that the Understanding was not a legally binding decision. With that conclusion, the strongest pillar in the US

---

[12] This text is found in para 1(b)(iv) of Annex IA.

[13] There would have been further questions about the exact relationship between GATT 1994 and Uruguay Round agreements such as the SCM agreement, but these were never reached.

[14] The relevant text of the Chairman's statement was as follows: 'Following the adoption of these [DISC] reports, the Chairman noted . . . that the decision does not modify the existing GATT rules in Article XVI:4 as they relate to the taxation of exported goods. He noted also that this decision does not affect and is not affected by the [1979 Tokyo Round Subsidies Code]. Finally, he noted that the adoption of these reports together with the understanding does not affect the rights and obligations of contracting parties under the General Agreement.'

defence collapsed. There would be no exception to the rules of the SCM Agreement, and under those rules the FSC tax exemption was a 'subsidy', contingent on exports in violation of SCM Article 3.1(a).

C. The unanswered questions in the FSC decision

1. The legal definition of a tax subsidy

Despite the fact that the AB affirmed the Panel's ruling that FSC was a tax subsidy, neither the Panel nor the AB decisions in the *FSC* case produced a satisfactory legal definition of a tax subsidy. Neither of the parties considered the Panel's 'but for' test an adequate standard of decision. The EC wanted a different test altogether. The US, while finding the 'but for' test acceptable as a general matter, argued that application of the rule to international tax practices would lead to classification of several 'territorial' tax exemptions as subsidies.[15] And the AB itself reserved judgment on the eventual utility of the 'but for' standard. The inadequacy of the Panel's 'but for' test was soon to be demonstrated in the follow-up compliance proceeding under DSU Article 21.5, in which neither the Panel nor the AB would use the 'but for' test in deciding whether the substitute ETI statute was a tax subsidy.

In order to understand the underlying problems with the 'but for' test, it will be necessary to make a detour here to explain what seems to be the prevailing concept of 'subsidy' and how it appears to be employed in the case of tax subsidies.

The concept of subsidy itself does not have a very solid intellectual base. The GATT and its member countries applied the concept for almost half a century without any multilaterally agreed definition. The definition of 'subsidy' in SCM Article 1.1 was the first such definition. It is an attempt to articulate the conceptual basis of what government had been doing all these years. If the constituent elements of the definition sometimes appear vague, it is because the basis of these intuitive government practices was never entirely clear to begin with. The elements of the definition of tax subsidies suffer from a particular vagueness in this regard.

In ordinary parlance, the term 'subsidy' connotes a transfer of value from a government, or on behalf of a government, to a private recipient. The words of SCM Article 1.1 reflect this core idea when they require a 'financial contribution by a government'. The perception that a particular tax exemption can be a

---

[15] For example, the baseline rule for France is the territorial principle that does not tax foreign-source income. But this baseline rule is set aside by a French version of the US Subpart F that does tax the income of foreign branches and subsidiaries when they are located in a jurisdiction where the tax rate is less than two-thirds of the French tax rate. But the French Subpart F provision is in turn set aside if there is a tax treaty with the low-tax country and the tax treaty removes taxation of foreign-source income. Under the 'but for' rule, it would appear that the present exemption—the tax treaty rule—is to be set aside, and one must then determine whether, in the absence of the tax treaty exemption, the income would be taxed under whatever French tax rules would apply. Assuming the French Subpart F rule would apply, the tax treaty exemption would be a subsidy.

'subsidy' likewise involves a perception that the recipients of certain exemptions are receiving a transfer of value from the government. The key element in this perception of a value transfer is the idea that the taxpayer is being relieved from a tax obligation that would otherwise have been imposed. This is the sense of the 'otherwise due' requirement in Article 1.1(a)(1)(ii). But not every tax measure reducing or eliminating previous tax liability is viewed as a subsidy. It seems to depend on the breadth of the exemption, or on what kind of previous tax liability is being avoided.

Under the framework of analysis employed by the participants in the *FSC* case, national tax laws are perceived as being organized on the basis of certain general principles (referred to by the Panel or AB at different times as 'prevailing standards' or 'general rules').[16] These general principles provide for certain kinds of tax treatment for certain general categories of income that can be grouped together according to common characteristics. For example, a tax system might have a general principle, or general rule, prescribing the tax treatment to be accorded to the category of foreign-source income. Due to the general applicability of such principles, tax liability that rests on those principles seems to be regarded as a more compelling kind of tax liability than the liability imposed by other, *ad hoc* tax rules. And because such tax liability is somehow more compelling, a tax exemption that eliminates that kind of tax liability tends more easily to be viewed as a transfer of tangible value to the taxpayer.

Why are the general principles of a national tax system given this special status in defining tax subsidies? It may be that rules based on general principles tend to involve a stronger policy commitment, so that avoidance of such rules represents a sharper departure from existing tax policy, and thus a more tangible sense of gain to a taxpayer. Or, it may be that departures from the general principles of national tax laws indicate most clearly a purpose of benefiting the particular taxpayers. Absent further guidance from WTO tribunals, this attention to general rules must remain a problematic element.

A key element of all the ideas at work here is the fact that, since the origin of GATT subsidy rules, it has been clearly understood that governments are free to adopt whatever national tax system they like, and thus are also free to change the general principles on which their tax system is constructed. A threshold question in every tax subsidy case, therefore, is whether a particular tax exemption being challenged is a selective exception from an existing general principle, or involves something else—a case where there is no general principle governing the category of income in question, or a case where the exemption itself may involve the creation of a new general principle. In order to respect this often-proclaimed national autonomy in tax policy, it is up to WTO tribunals to make these initial characterizations of the tax rules in question.

The core problem with the 'but for' test is that it does not capture the variations of the subsidy concept just described. In applying the criterion of

---

[16] The AB's term 'normative benchmark' appears not to be limited to general rules.

SCM Article 1.1(a)(1)(ii)—whether the tax revenue foregone by a tax exemption would be 'otherwise due'—the 'but for' test asks whether the tax exempt income would be subject to taxation *absent* the tax exemption itself. This requires looking at the tax legislation that would apply to the tax exempt income in the absence of the tax exemption. In the normal case, this would focus the inquiry on the general principles that govern the tax-exempt income in question, most likely the tax legislation that applied to the tax-exempt income *before* the tax exemption was enacted. In the case where the tax exemption is in fact an exception from a previously applied general rule, the 'but for' test would be looking at the right legislation, and would correctly find a 'subsidy' in those cases where the previously applicable general rule had made the income taxable. But if the previously applicable rule was *not* a general rule, or if the previously applicable rule was no longer the general rule, the 'but for' test would not focus the analysis on the right law, or the right issues.

Both the 'but for' test and 'otherwise due' requirement of SCM Article 1.1(a)(1)(ii) seem to call for a wrong kind of analysis in one special case. If the new tax exemption happens to involve the adoption of a new general principle that changes the basic structure of the nation's tax system, both the 'but for' test and the 'otherwise due' requirement seem to preclude looking at the new measure itself and deciding the subsidy issue on the basis of the general applicability of the new exemption itself. The structure of these two tests seems to require looking at something other than the characteristics of the new measure itself.

Neither the Panel nor the AB decisions in the *FSC* case did anything to address the seeming gap between the 'but for' test and the general concept of tax subsidy just discussed, or in the SCM Agreement itself. The AB's reservations about the 'but for' test involved a concern that governments might be able to circumvent the mechanics of the 'but for' test by designing exemptions in a way that no other tax would apply absent the challenged measure.[17] This problem involved the mechanics rather than the substance of the test. As for the substance, the AB expressed the view that the 'but for' rule had come up with the right answer in the *FSC* case, but having said that, the AB never explained *why* that answer was a correct characterization of the relevant US laws.

The EC asked the Panel not to employ the 'but for' test, but instead offered a different approach based on the distinction, discussed above, between tax measures based on general principle and those that are 'exceptions' to the general principle. The EC proposed that the WTO recognize a distinction between two different types of tax exemption—on the one hand, exemptions that are 'not based on neutral or objective criteria, i.e., the exemption is special or programmatic', and, on the other hand, exemptions which *are* 'neutral and objective' and are 'defined in broad, neutral and objective terms' and '[do] not serve any special programmatic function'.[18] The EC definition seems to be concerned with the

---

[17] AB Report, para 91.
[18] For the Panel's description of the EC arguments, see Panel Report, paras 4.1057–59.

purpose of the measure. Measures that are 'neutral and objective' are measures
that tend to have an independent tax policy purpose. In contrast, 'special or
programmatic' measures tend to be intended to create economic advantages for
certain producer interests—in international terms, a form of trade distortion.[19]

In further elaboration of this principle, the EC acknowledged that its distinction between 'neutral-and-objective' tax exemptions and 'special-and-program-
matic' exemptions resembled the 'specificity' test of SCM Article 2. The
normative linkage here is interesting. The specificity test would appear to be
making a similar distinction between general measures, such as broad infrastructure improvements that serve broader, social policy purposes, and more targeted
resource transfers that are intended to increase the competitiveness of particular
industries. The EC explained that it would prefer not to employ the specificity
test itself, however, having a preference for a less formalistic test. But the policy
basis of the EC's proposed distinction between broad and narrow tax exemptions appeared to be virtually identical in terms of purpose.

The main problem with the EC's more sophisticated test, of course, is that it is
hard to derive such a test from the legal text of SCM Article 1.1(a)(1)(ii) that
speaks in terms of examining whether governments are or are not foregoing
revenue that is 'otherwise due'. A direct analysis of whether tax exemptions are
general or specific would not present any occasion to analyze counter-factual
'otherwise' situations. Based on this textual problem, the Panel rejected the EC's
proposed general-specific test, and held to its simpler 'but for' test as a definition
of 'otherwise due' in SCM Article 1.[20] As noted above, the AB simply held that
the application of the 'but for' test gave a correct answer in the *FSC* case, without
explaining why.

As things stood after the *FSC* case, the WTO did not have an interpretation of
'otherwise due' that offered a coherent framework for answering the many
unanswered questions that remained about the definition of a tax subsidy. One
might have expected further development of the opaque 'otherwise due' standard
in the subsequent panel and AB proceedings under DSU Article 21.5. As we shall
see, that did not happen.

2. The US demand for equal treatment

In the *DISC* case, the US had centred its legal defence on the claim that the tax
exemptions of European territorial tax systems were equivalent in economic
effect to DISC subsidies, and had filed three counter-complaints to prove the
point. The panel reports in the *DISC* case had supported that claim, ruling that
the European tax exemptions were, indeed, export subsidies. The US had never
given up that idea. It held on to DISC for 12 years, and then claimed the right to
replace DISC with FSC for another 15 years. Although there had been some

---

[19] Applying the general-specific distinction suggested by the EC, the French tax treaty exemption
described in note 15 *supra* would not be a subsidy, because the tax treaty provision presumably
exempts all types of foreign-source income from both countries.

[20] Panel Report, para 7.46.

changes in European taxes since the DISC decisions, US officials held to the view
that the European tax systems in 1997 were fundamentally the same, and that
their territorial tax exemptions had fundamentally the same economic effects,
as they had had in 1976.

In the *FSC* case, the US returned to the claim of economic identity, but not as
forcefully as in the *DISC* cases. The US did not file counter-complaints against
territorial tax exemptions this time.[21] The author does not know the reasons for
this decision.[22] It is probable that the legal case against European territorial
systems was simply not as good, because of (1) the subsequent adoption of the
1981 Understanding (which the US was defending) and (2) the subsequent adoption of the exception for measures to avoid double taxation.[23] The US complaint
was now a point about identity of economic effects, not parallel violations.

The US provided the *FSC* Panel with a great deal of information about
European tax exemptions for export income, and detailed tax calculations to
illustrate their comparative economic effects.[24] The US stressed the inequity of
the advantage that would be enjoyed by European exporters if the European
exemptions were permitted and FSC exemptions were not.[25] The EC's primary
response was not to contest the claim of economic disadvantage, but rather to
place the blame for the disadvantage on the shoulders of the US itself. The US
was responsible, said the EC, for having chosen a tax system that placed its
exporters at a disadvantage. The Panel clearly subscribed to this view, stating its
position as follows.

Thus, the United States is free to maintain a world wide tax system, a territorial tax system
or any other type of system it sees fit. This is not the business of the WTO. What it is not
free to do is to establish a regime of direct taxation, provide an exemption from direct
taxes specifically related to exports, and then claim that it is entitled to provide such an
export subsidy because it is necessary to eliminate a disadvantage to exporters created by
the US tax system itself. In our view, this is no different from imposing a corporate income
tax of, say, 75 percent, and then arguing that a special tax rate of 25 percent for exporters
is necessary because the generally applicable corporate tax rate in other members is only
25 percent.[26]

---

[21] The US did file five legal complaints against alleged export subsidies in the tax laws of Belgium,
the Netherlands, Greece, Ireland and France, WT/DS127–131 (5 May 1998), but these involved
smaller tax advantages for exports, with minuscule economic importance compared to FSC. The
complaints were never followed up.
[22] In contrast to the *DISC* case, the *FSC* case was managed by the Office of the US Trade
Representative (USTR) rather than by the Treasury Department. The Treasury and Commerce
Departments participated extensively in the formation of the US legal defence. So did a group of
private sector lawyers representing FSC beneficiaries. A senior USTR lawyer argued the first three
stages of the case. The appeal of the Panel's 21.5 ruling was handled by the office of the US Solicitor
General, with an introductory presentation by the Under-Secretary of the Treasury.
[23] The double-taxation exception was part of the 1981 Understanding, and now appears in the fifth
sentence of footnote 59 of the 1994 SCM Agreement.
[24] eg, Panel Report, paras 4.808–4.815.
[25] Ibid.
[26] Panel Report, para 7.122.

(The AB avoided comment on US claims of inequity by stressing that it was ruling on FSC alone, and was saying nothing about any other tax measure at all.)

The Panel's 'your own fault' response to the US claim for equal treatment both distorted the issue and ultimately begged the question. The analogy distorted the issue by postulating that all European producers, in domestic as well as exporter markets, were paying the same low tax. This was *not* the European tax practice the US was complaining about. The US was complaining about a special tax exemption for the foreign-source income earned by exporters. Both the US and EC were making a special exception to their corporate tax rates. The only difference between the European tax exemption and the US tax exemption was that the European exemption was granted on all kinds of foreign-source income, whereas the US exemption was granted to just the foreign-source income of exporters.

Second, the Panel's 'your own fault' accusation begged the question. The question was whether a rule permitting 'broadly available' tax exemptions but forbidding 'exporter only' exemptions creates an unfair advantage. The Panel's answer simply takes the correctness of the rule as a given. That being so, the Panel reasoned, the US must be at fault because it adopted a tax structure whose competitive disadvantages could not be corrected. The competitive disadvantages could not be corrected because the US had adopted an eccentric tax rule. By that logic, no rule can ever be unfair so long as there is an opportunity to comply with it by changing the rest of one's behaviour. The Panel never even tries to justify the rule's distinction between broad and narrow tax exemptions.

When one looks for a justification of this rule's distinction, the justification is not easy to discern. Why should one government be allowed to create subsidy-like effects in one case but not the other? Why should the WTO reach a different result about a subsidy-like tax exemption for exporters depending on whether the country also taxes, or does not tax, the foreign-source income of its resident opera singers, accountants, and currency speculators?

No plausible economic distinction comes to mind. A subsidy that distorts price relationships between one kind of domestic goods and another can distort comparative advantage, a fact which is often used to explain the specificity requirement in subsidy/countervailing duty law.[27] But, to the author's knowledge, no one has ever suggested that a tax exemption on foreign-source export income is more or less trade-distortive depending on whether tax exemptions are given on non-trade foreign income.

A different justification is implied by the EC's suggested distinction between 'general, objective and neutral' tax exemptions and 'specific, programmatic' tax exemptions mentioned in the previous section. As we noted there, the EC distinction seems to be looking to the purpose of the tax exemption. It seems to want to distinguish between trade distortion that is being caused by deliberate

---

[27] The 'specificity' requirement for actionable subsidies is in SCM Article 2.

trade policy measures, and distortion that is incidental to regulation for another, independent tax-policy purpose.

This deliberate-incidental distinction is a fairly common argument in trade policy discourse of late. It rests in part on a simple normative distinction between incidental harms and deliberate harms. The normative appeal of such a distinction would be rather minimal in the tax subsidy area, however. Whatever innocence of purpose there may have been in the origin of the territorial system, or any other similar exemption of general applicability, that innocence was long ago lost as every export business has nurtured and polished the general exemption until it yields maximum tax savings. Moreover, as time goes on, the continued existence of such innocent exemptions becomes increasingly dependent on the not-so-innocent political weight of exporters who benefit from it.

A different reason for distinguishing between deliberate and incidental harms is a view that governments need a certain freedom to regulate, and cannot be restrained by responsibility for incidental trade-distorting effects of their normal regulatory activity. In the situation presented by the *FSC* case, however, this regulatory sovereignty concern is not really applicable, either. The regulatory sovereignty concern usually makes sense as an argument *against* a WTO prohibition of incidentally trade-distorting measures—a WTO prohibition that would interfere with the government's regulatory mission. In the case of FSC-type measures, however, the incidental-deliberate distinction would be used *in favour of* a WTO prohibition of a subsidy intended to *compensate* for the effects of the incidentally trade-distorting measures. The EC's freedom to regulate is not in issue here.

In the end, a third justification is probably needed to explain the normative appeal of the deliberate-incidental dichotomy as an answer to the US-EC dispute over tax exemptions. The answer probably lies in a general policy objection against allowing governments to adjust for trade advantages and disadvantages caused by differences in the national tax and regulatory policies of other governments. Even though the incidental trade effects of national tax or regulatory measures may produce the same degree of competitive advantage as more deliberate measures, a policy of allowing governments to make compensating adjustments for them would be an invitation to an unending parade of unilateral departures from WTO legal commitments. Moreover, the way things normally work, the power to make unilateral adjustments will most likely be employed by the more powerful WTO members, in whose hands such adjustment measures will have a tendency to swell beyond their original justifications. The actual shape of DISC and FSC, and their evident lack of attention to the legal conditions attached to the permission to use them, stand as monuments to this expectation of abuse.

To the extent that this third justification is the real reason for disallowing the US claim to equal treatment, it means that one answer to the US claim is that it is simply too disruptive to allow affected governments to fix it. In consolation, one might offer the not wholly unfounded speculations that the advantages and disadvantages of differences in national regulatory policy probably balance over time. This may not seem like much consolation, but if the truth were known, a very large part of the present trading system depends on that excuse for not disturbing the many other sleeping dogs of national economic policy. This is just another one.

In sum, the equity claims of the US have not yet been satisfactorily answered, and may never be. It may never be possible, of course, to give a satisfactory explanation to those who benefit from FSC, because they will not want to hear it. But to the extent that objective policy discourse has some effect on outcomes, one must recognize that the discourse on the issue of equal treatment is not yet complete, and that the absence of better answers is likely to contribute to a continued dissatisfaction, of a principled kind, with WTO law in this area.

III. THE 21.5 RULING: THE ETI STATUTE

A. An overview of the ruling

In answer to the ruling in the *FSC* case, the US enacted legislation that was put forward as compliance with the FSC ruling. The legislation was enacted in remarkable time, taking just nine months from the AB decision on 24 February 2000 to the President's signature on 15 November 2000.[28] The new legislation repealed FSC for the most part. In its place, the new legislation created a tax exemption for a new category of income called 'Extra-Territorial Income' (ETI). The new ETI statute replicated the size and shape of the tax exemptions of the former FSC statute. However, it contained several new features designed to circumvent the legal rules that had caused FSC to be ruled WTO-illegal. First, instead of being a tax 'exemption', the ETI law provided that qualifying ETI income was 'excluded from gross income'. This change, the US claimed, placed qualifying ETI income outside tax jurisdiction of the US government, making that income immune from any sort of 'otherwise due' tax liability and thus not a 'subsidy' at all. In addition, the US claimed, the new legislation represented the adoption of a new general principle of US taxation similar to the 'territorial' principle found in many European tax systems—a general principle that could not be treated as a subsidy. Second, the ETI exclusion was made available to any US producer, including producers located abroad, whose goods were consumed outside the US—a change which, the US argued, meant that the subsidy, if any, was no longer 'contingent' on exports. Third, the legislative history of the ETI legislation affirmed that its purpose was to avoid double taxation of foreign-source income. Under footnote 59 of the SCM Agreement, measures to avoid double taxation are not subject to the subsidy prohibitions of the SCM Agreement.

---

[28] FSC Repeal and Extraterritorial Income Exclusion Act of 2000, Public Law 106–519, 114 Stat 2423.

On 7 December 2000, the EC requested the appointment of a panel under DSU Article 21.5 to determine whether the ETI statute was in compliance with the FSC ruling and recommendation. On 20 August 2001, the Panel ruled that the ETI statute was not in compliance with the FSC ruling. It held that notwithstanding its new 'exclusion from gross income' structure, the ETI statute was still a 'subsidy' under Article 1.1 of the SCM Agreement. It held further that, despite provisions making the ETI tax exemption available to some US taxpayers that did not export, it was still an export subsidy under Article 3.1(a) of the SCM Agreement, because the tax exemption was still contingent on exports for all taxpayers who produced goods within the US. The Panel also rejected the new US defence that the ETI tax exemption was a measure to avoid double taxation. In addition to finding that the ETI statute was still an export subsidy in violation of the SCM Agreement, the Panel also found in favour of the EC's additional claim that the ETI statute also violated GATT Article III:4 because, like DISC and FSC before it, it limited the subsidy to income from sale of goods with at least 50 per cent US value-added. On 14 January 2002, the AB affirmed the Panel's key rulings, albeit in some cases on different grounds.

Following adoption of the AB's 21.5 decision, the EC renewed its claim under DSU Article 22.6 for authority to withdraw concessions valued at $4.04 billion. The US contested the claimed amount, and requested arbitration of the disagreement. The arbitration claim was submitted to the original Panel. On 30 August 2002, the Panel ruled that the EC was entitled to withdraw concessions valued at $4.043 billion. At the time of writing, no further steps had been taken.

B. The 'subsidy' issue

The US claim that the new ETI statute had removed the legal flaws that made FSC a 'subsidy' under SCM Article 1.1 was greeted with a great deal of scepticism in the WTO community. To the naked eye, it appeared that the US had simply repackaged the FSC subsidy in some different words—same type of income, same conditions, same quantitative measure of the tax benefit. For the Panel and the AB, a decision in favour of the US on the 'subsidy' issue would have amounted to a confession that the criteria of SCM Article 1.1 were subject to manipulation by means of purely formal changes. No one (except possibly some US government lawyers) expected the US to prevail in its effort to reverse the 'subsidy' characterization. If the result was predictable, however, the process of reaching that conclusion proved to be anything but simple.

1. The Panel's 21.5 ruling

The new US defence against a finding of 'subsidy' created an obstacle to application of the simple 'but for' test. The problem was not that the mechanics of the test would not work on the ETI statute. The 'but for' test could have produced an answer in the following manner: the Panel would have to ask, 'but for the ETI statute—ie, assuming the non-existence of the ETI statute—would the so-called "extraterritorial income" covered by the ETI statute have been subject to taxation under the US laws that would prevail in that situation?' The answer would have been clear. 'Extraterritorial income' would have been subject to full taxation (with appropriate tax credits for foreign taxes). The ETI statute itself so provided. The ETI statute allowed taxpayers *to elect not to use* the exclusion it created. For taxpayers electing not to claim the ETI tax exemption, their 'extraterritorial income' would have been subject to the same tax regime that applied to all foreign-source income—the 'worldwide' rule of US tax law (IRC, section 61) that had been the basis of the 'otherwise due' ruling in the *FSC* case. So analyzed, the revenue foregone by the ETI statute would be found to be 'otherwise due', and thus a 'subsidy' under SCM Article 1.1(a)(1)(ii).

The 'but for' test cannot be applied, however, when the contested tax measure itself is one of the general principles of the national tax system. In the 21.5 proceeding before the Panel, the US explicitly claimed that the ETI statute was just such a fundamental change in US tax law. Because the IRC taxed only earnings that were classified as 'gross income', the government had no jurisdiction to tax earnings that were not classified as 'gross income'. Since ETI classified all 'extraterritorial income' as being outside the 'gross income' category, it had completely removed this category of income from the US tax system. The US carried this argument to the point of claiming that enactment of the ETI law was a fundamental change in the principles of US tax law, 'analogous' to adoption of a territorial tax system similar to the European tax system.[29]

The Panel recognized that the US claim of fundamental change needed to be evaluated before any further issues could be addressed. The Panel undertook its own independent analysis of that claim, and ultimately rejected it. The criteria on which this independent evaluation was based can be discerned rather vaguely, but the Panel's report never quite managed to give a clear explanation of what those criteria were and where they came from.

The one criterion that seemed to emerge from almost every argument about the US claim was the rather simple idea that 'general' or 'fundamental' rules were those that were generally applicable to broad categories of income, such as foreign-source income. The EC continued to advocate the adoption of such a general-specific test, arguing that the AB had implicitly adopted this test in its FSC decision when it had repeatedly referred approvingly to the right of governments to enact tax measures distinguishing 'categories' of income.[30] Even the US seemed to adopt this general-specific distinction in its arguments. The US had presented the concept of 'extraterritorial income' as a very broad category of income that appeared to apply to all income from foreign-based[31] sales of goods. Although the ETI statute's small print reduced the amount of 'extraterritorial

---

[29] First US Submission to 21.5 Panel (7 February 2001), para 78.

[30] The AB references to 'categories' of income appear principally in paras 90 and 98–99 of its FSC report.

[31] The ETI statute retained the FSC statute's requirement that a minuscule percentage of sales activity be conducted abroad.

income' that was actually tax-exempt to a considerably smaller category, not much larger than the former FSC exemption,[32] the US insisted that the principle of excluding all 'extraterritorial income' from gross income was really the 'general rule' of US tax law. According to the US, the small-print provisions that narrowed the actual tax-exempt category were merely the 'exception' to the new general rule dictated by revenue needs.[33]

The Panel's analysis seemed to follow this general-specific distinction. It emphasized the narrowness of the category of income exempted by the ETI statute, stressing the detailed conditions that had to be met to qualify for tax exclusion/exemption.[34] The Panel used the narrowness of these qualifying criteria to emphasize the lack of theoretical coherence to the ETI tax exemption. Thus:

8.28 [The ETI] Act manifestly does not represent a coherent approach to corporate earnings derived from offshore activities only. The conditionality is such that the eligibility [for a tax exclusion] is, in fact, circumscribed carefully to render it only effective, for example, with respect to goods, only with respect to *certain* goods—i.e., *certain* 'qualifying foreign trade property'—produced within or outside the United States, where those goods are for 'use outside the United States' and where those goods fulfill the [50 per cent value-added requirement] included in the definition of qualifying foreign trade property. In short, one is left with the perspective simply of certain carve-outs being provided for in relation to what would otherwise be the prevailing regime of revenue liability in respect of the income concerned.[35]

The implication was new tax measures could not be characterized as general rules or fundamental changes unless they had a certain generality of scope evidencing a coherent tax policy rationale.

Later on, the Panel explained the analysis it had used to determine whether the ETI statute had been a general rule or an exception. Instead of clearly explaining the general-specific distinction, it presented the following rather confusing claim for latitude of judgment.

---

[32] 'Extraterritorial income' was defined as gross income attributable to 'foreign trading gross receipts'; which were in turn defined as receipts from the sale or lease of 'qualifying foreign trade property'; which was in turn defined to *exclude* property destined for use inside the US, property with less than 50% US value-added, and assorted classes of property such as oil and gas, unprocessed softwood lumber, and any other products designated by the President as in short supply. Moreover, the statute limited the amount of the tax exclusion to not more than a certain percentage of extraterritorial income, called 'qualifying foreign trade income', defined by the same three alternative 'rule of thumb' formulas used in FSC.

[33] First US Submission to the 21.5 Panel (7 February 2001), para 81.

[34] Panel 21.5 report, para 8.21. For a summary description of the ETI statute's restrictive conditions, see supra note 32.

[35] The same conclusion is stated in paras 8.26, 8.27 and 8.40 of the Panel Report. The 'prevailing regime' referred to in the quotation was, of course, the 'worldwide' liability rule of IRC, section 61. The Panel nowhere explains why it characterized this law as the prevailing regime, but by this point in the proceedings everyone knew that section 61 applied to all foreign-source income, including ETI-type income, except for exceptions.

8.29 . . . Indeed, discerning what might be described as 'the prevailing domestic standard' for a particular tax regime may be a particularly exacting exercise. In more common usage, it might be rather difficult to discern what is the exception, as it were, and what is the [general] rule. . . . [W]e are not, in this dispute, presented with a situation of such complexity. The dispute does not involve a debatable call as to whether the glass is half-full or half-empty. As outlined above, we have looked at the essential shape and the rationale that is exhibited. In examining that, we have weighed such considerations as the degree of conditionality [general-specific?], the range of limitations [general-specific?] and the manner in which the measure at issue relates to the overall regime [general-specific?]. Taken together, they enable us to assess the nature of the relationship of the measure at issue and the overall regime [general-specific?]. That is precisely [?] how one is in a position to arrive at the judgment required by the terms of the *SCM Agreement*.

Having characterized the ETI statute as an exception ('carve out') to the 'prevailing regime of revenue liability in respect of the income concerned', it remained for the Panel to apply the 'otherwise due' standard of SCM Article 1.1(a)(1)(ii). Instead of applying the 'but for' test, the Panel presented a series of conclusory statements simply asserting that the revenue foregone by the ETI statute was 'otherwise due'. At one point, the Panel says the ETI exclusion can only be 'rationally understood' by comparison with the 'other situation . . . that prevails where the [ETI] Act's conditions for obtaining the "exclusion" are *not* fulfilled'. Without saying what that comparison reveals, or why it matters, the next sentence simply says, '[t]hat leads us to the conclusion that this is to be rightly characterized as the foregoing of revenue otherwise due'.

In sum, the Panel says it did undertake the task of discerning the difference between general tax rules, on the one hand, and, on the other hand, tax rules that are mere exceptions to normal rules. Its conclusion, which surprised no one, was that the ETI statute was merely a narrow exception to the general rule stated in IRC, section 61. The criteria underlying that conclusion seem to have been the intuitive perception that general rules are rules that have a general scope, reflecting coherent tax policy. The conclusion did not, however, articulate these criteria clearly, nor did it give a coherent explanation of how those criteria fit the terms of SCM Article 1.1.

The puzzle is why the Panel avoided giving a more coherent explanation of its decision. Two reasons suggest themselves. First, the intuitively satisfying general-specific distinction was not written into the text of SCM Article 1.1. The Panel itself had said so in the course of rejecting the EC's general/specific argument in the *FSC* case,[36] and may have felt cornered by this statement.

Second, no matter how vehemently the WTO tribunals said they were not litigating the WTO consistency of the tax rules employed by other governments, everything they said would have some bearing on the legal status of those other tax systems as well. The problem was that, without those laws before them, there was no way of knowing what kind of statements would have what kind of

---

[36] See Panel Report, para 7.46.

effects. The safest course in this situation was to say as little as possible, even to the point of not presenting a coherent theory of decision at all.

2. *The Appellate Body's 21.5 ruling*

At the beginning of the appeal proceedings, it appeared that the AB was also inclined to pursue the 'subsidy' issue in terms of the distinction between general rules and specific exceptions. As restated by the US in its written answer, the AB's first question to the US was:

Paragraph 90 of the FSC Appellate Body report, dealing with SCM Article 1.1(a)(1)(ii), said that 'revenue foregone' requires a normative benchmark for comparison on the basis of the tax law of the WTO Member. In determining whether revenue foregone is otherwise due, should panels seek to identify a general rule and an exception to a general rule? If yes, on what criteria should the existence and shape of a general rule and exception to it be based?[37]

In the end, however, the AB never reviewed the Panel's rather cloudy answer to this question. The AB explained that its failure to review the Panel's reasoning was 'partly' due to the fact that the US had changed the main thrust of its defence during the appeal. Instead of continuing to press its argument that the ETI statute was a new general rule that made a fundamental change in the principles of US tax law, the US took the quite different position that the purpose of the ETI statute was to refine a long-standing principle of US tax law regarding foreign-source income.[38] The long-standing principle, said the US, was that foreign-source income could be shielded from US tax liability by creating foreign subsidiary corporations, whose income would be outside the reach of US tax laws until repatriated. (The US explained that Subpart F, which taxed the income of foreign subsidiaries in 'tax haven' situations, was merely an exception to that long-standing principle, for the purpose of curbing abuse.) The purpose of the ETI statute, said the US, had been to simplify this basic non-taxation principle by removing the need to create a foreign subsidiary corporation.

The new US defence relieved the AB from responding to the US claim that the ETI statute was a new general principle in US tax law. Instead, the AB's task was now (1) to determine whether the favourable tax treatment of foreign subsidiaries was in fact the central principle of US taxation of foreign-source income, and (2) if not, to identify the governing principle (or 'prevailing standard') for the tax treatment of such income.

The AB started its analysis by abandoning the search for general rules raised in its first question to the US.

[I]t will usually be difficult to isolate a 'general' rule of taxation and 'exceptions' to that general rule. Instead, we believe that panels should seek to compare the fiscal treatment of

---

[37] Supplemental US Submission to the Appellate Body, 21.5 proceeding (28 November 2001), at 1.
[38] The change in the US argument created enough uncertainty about the US position that the AB asked the US to submit a written version of its answer to certain questions in the oral argument.

legitimately comparable income to determine whether the contested measure involves the foregoing of revenue with is 'otherwise due' in relation to the income in question.[39]

The AB's new position involved two stunning changes of direction. First, of course, it pushed aside the 'general rule' inquiry that had been the focus of the Panel's entire 21.5 analysis, and that had been implicit in much of what had been said in the FSC decision. In doing so, it cut the inquiry adrift from the common sense idea of 'subsidy' implicit in the attention to general rules.

Second, the comparative analysis that replaced the search for general rules offered a literal reading of the word 'otherwise' that seemed to have no connection with any other concept of 'subsidy'. The term 'otherwise due', said the AB, required a comparison between the revenue foregone under the challenged tax exemption and the revenue that would be due in 'some other situation'. That other situation would be 'other rules of taxation of the Member in question'. But instead of following the 'but for' test, in which panels examine the other tax rules that would apply to the *tax-exempt income* in the absence of the contested tax exemption, the AB was telling panels to compare the challenged tax exemption with the tax rules that would apply to *other, comparable income*. The 'but for' test's focus on other tax rules applicable to the tax-exempt income did at least fit the common-sense notion of subsidy, by asking whether the government was handing over revenue that would 'normally' have been collected. The tax treatment of *comparable* income, on the other hand, had no visible connection to the question of whether that revenue would normally have been collected.

The AB offered no further explanation of how this focus on the taxation of comparable income related to the concept of subsidy. Neither did the EC, which seems to have been the source of this idea.[40] The most likely logical relationship would be an unstated assumption that a tax law governing a 'legitimately comparable' kind of income gives some indication of how the exempt income itself would have been treated, especially if that tax law happened to be a general rule or 'prevailing standard'.[41] In other words, looking at the treatment of comparable income could have been a back-door way of looking at how the tax-exempt income itself would have been treated under the general principles of the defendant's tax law. In effect, this would be a back-door version of the 'but for' test, one that could not be blocked by tax laws that try to sever all formal links between the subsidy and the applicable general principles of the defendant's tax system.[42]

[39] AB 21.5 Report, para 91. Emphasis added.

[40] See EC Second Written Submission (27 February 2001), paras 61–64.

[41] Some support for the existence of such an underlying assumption appears in the EC's restatement of the kind of comparison it was urging: ' . . . that is, that the comparison must be between the revenue due under the [contested tax exemption] and the revenue that would be due "in some other situation" under the *prevailing* domestic standard of the Member in question'. EC Second Submission to the 21.5 Panel (27 February 2001), para 72.

[42] In para 91 of its *FSC* report, the AB had expressed concern that the mechanics of the 'but for' test could be blocked by legislation that would somehow eliminate the applicability of any other tax laws to the income covered by a contested subsidy.

In the AB's written report, however, the only criterion for identifying such 'other' tax legislation was the comparability of the 'other' income with the tax-exempt income. The AB explained the idea of comparability with two quite simple illustrations, saying that 'it might not be appropriate' to compare taxation of sales income with taxation of employment income, or taxation of income in the hands of a domestic corporation with taxation of income in the hands of a foreign corporation.[43] The only complexity addressed was the question of what to do when comparable income was subject to different rules. The footnote 'answering' this question gave no real guidance at all, except to plead for wide latitude in judgment ('flexibility'). It said:

For instance, one portion of a domestic corporation's foreign-source income may not be subject to tax in any circumstances; another portion of such income may always be subject to tax; while a third portion may be subject to tax in some circumstances. In such a situation, the outcome of the dispute would depend on which aspect of the rules of taxation was challenged and on a detailed examination of the relationship between the different rules of taxation. The examination under Article 1.1(a)(1)(ii) of the SCM Agreement must be sufficiently flexible to adjust to the complexities of a Member's domestic rules of taxation.[44]

Applying these general directions, the AB began by recalling the US claim that the purpose of the ETI statute had been to refine the treatment of foreign-source income. The AB accepted that purpose arguendo and set out to look for the laws governing the tax treatment of foreign-source income of US corporations and residents. Thus far, the US would have agreed. But the US wanted to argue that the central principle of US tax law on foreign-source income was the US tax rules pertaining to non-taxation of foreign subsidiaries. Without even mentioning this US argument on this point, the AB simply ruled that the 'comparable' tax rules were those governing the taxation of foreign source income in the hands of US citizens and residents.[45]

The 'other' rules found by the AB were, of course, the 'worldwide' rules of IRC, section 61. The AB proclaimed these rules be the 'normative benchmark' to be used in deciding whether the revenue foregone under the ETI statute was 'otherwise due'. The AB then went on to 'compare' the tax treatment provided by the US 'worldwide' rule and the tax treatment provided by the ETI statute. The AB noted the 'marked contrast' between the ETI statute's non-taxation of ETI income, and the taxation of other foreign-source income under the US 'worldwide' tax rule.[46] Without explaining the steps, the AB seems to conclude that this comparison somehow shows that the revenue foregone by the ETI statute was 'otherwise due'.

[43] AB 21.5 Report, paras 90 and 92. The second illustration seems to have been an unexplained rejection of the US claim that the taxation of foreign-source income was in reality governed by rules pertaining to the taxation of foreign subsidiaries.

[44] AB 21.5 Report, footnote 66 to para 91.

[45] AB 21.5 Report, para 98.

[46] AB 21.5 Report, para 102.

At this point, the AB's analysis started slipping in some other factors. First, the AB noted that the 'worldwide' tax rule taxed '*all*' foreign-source income of US citizens and residents—an observation looking suspiciously like a claim of generality.[47] Then, the AB noted that the 'election' feature of the ETI statute meant that the 'worldwide' tax rule would also apply to qualifying ETI income itself, in those cases where the taxpayer elected not to take advantage of the ETI exclusion.[48] And this observation, in turn, led to the conclusion that the 'worldwide' tax rule satisfied the 'but for' test used in the initial FSC decision.

We see this as a confirmation that, *absent the ETI measure*, the United States would tax the [ETI] income under the 'otherwise' applicable rules of taxation we have used as our benchmark.[49]

And finally, the AB pointed out that, with a choice between claiming the ETI exclusion and submitting to the 'worldwide' tax (plus credits for foreign taxes), the taxpayer choosing ETI would naturally do so whenever the tax liability under ETI would be the lower. The AB seemed to think that this option could be classified as a foregoing of 'otherwise due' revenue.[50]

Curiously, the AB's final summary of its grounds of decision did not mention the 'but for' conclusion it had just reached, nor the generality of the 'worldwide liability' rule of IRC, section 61.

In our view, the definitive exclusion from tax of [ETI income], compared with the taxation of other foreign-source income, and coupled with the right of election for taxpayers to use the rules of taxation most favorable to them, means that, under the contested measure [the ETI statute], the United States foregoes revenue on [ETI income] which is otherwise due.[51]

In sum, like the Panel ruling, the AB ruling seems intuitively correct, given the general perception of the ETI statute as another narrow exception to the general principles of US tax law. By the same token, however, the explanation of the result is neither clear nor satisfying. The AB's reliance on an unexplained 'comparability' analysis is particularly disturbing.

The reasons for issuing such a cautious and uninformative opinion were probably those suggested with regard to the opaque Panel Report. First, the text of the 'otherwise due' requirement does not give much textual support to any theory seeking to explain why tax measures are subsidies. And second, the prospect that one's ruling might be establishing rules for countless other tax systems that were not part of the case was enough to induce most tribunals to try to get away with saying as little as possible.

The most likely meaning of the AB's ruling is that the AB was trying to create an interpretation of SCM Article 1.1 that gives WTO tribunals a great degree of

---

[47] AB 21.5 Report, para 102.   [48] AB 21.5 Report, para 103.
[49] AB 21.5 Report, para 103. Emphasis added.
[50] Taken at face value, this last point seems to characterize as a subsidy any tax law that gives the taxpayer the option of choosing the more/most favourable of several options. This point is likely to be controversial.
[51] AB 21.5 Report, para 105.

'flexibility' in deciding whether tax exemptions are subsidies. This would seem to be a response to an unclear legal text, resting on top of a still unclear concept of subsidy. The possibility that a flexible 'comparability' analysis will give WTO tribunals a back-door way to examine what seems to have been the prevailing concept of subsidy in this area—whether tax-exempt income would otherwise have been taxed under the defendant's general rules of taxation—gives some reason to hope that a clearer and more persuasive concept of tax subsidy may eventually emerge in this area.

C. The way forward

Although the rulings of the Panel and the AB on the 'subsidy' issue were far from clear, they probably did put an end to US efforts to re-package the DISC-FSC-ETI type of tax subsidies in a way that would avoid their legal characterization as export subsidies.

At the end of the *ETI* case, attention turned to the possibility of defending such subsidies as 'measures to avoid double taxation' under the fifth sentence of footnote 59 of the Illustrative List of Export Subsidies in Annex I of the SCM Agreement. The fifth sentence of footnote 59 states that Item (e) of the Illustrative List 'is not intended to limit a Member from taking measures to avoid the double taxation of foreign source income earned by its enterprises or the enterprises of another Member'. The AB interpreted this footnote sentence as 'an affirmative defense that justifies a prohibited export subsidy when the measure in question is taken to avoid the double taxation of foreign-source income'.[52] The territorial system of taxation is often associated with avoiding double taxation, and the EC has long taken the position that the territorial tax exemptions found in European tax systems would be covered by footnote 59. The US had not raised this 'double taxation' defence in a timely fashion in the *FSC* case, but had raised it, for the first time, as a defence of the ETI statute in the 21.5 proceeding.

The Panel rejected the defence. It interpreted the fifth sentence as a requirement that the *purpose* of the measure must be avoidance of double taxation. It then examined the structure of the ETI statute to determine whether such a purpose was 'discernible' in the structure of the ETI statute. The Panel found three elements of the statute which persuaded it that such a purpose was not discernible, even though none of the three would have been enough to support a negative conclusion by itself. (1) The statute exempted a great deal of income that was unlikely to be taxed by another state. (2) The statute failed to exempt a great deal of income that would likely have been taxed. (3) The statute overlapped with an extensive network of US bilateral tax treaties, but was not designed to cover those cases where no bilateral treaty existed.[53]

---

[52] AB 21.5 Report, para 133.   [53] Panel 21.5 Report, paras 8.76–8.108.

The AB eschewed such a purpose analysis. Instead, it adopted a rather mechanical test, with what seemed to be a rather generous standard. The AB said that a tax exemption could be viewed as a measure to avoid double taxation to the extent that it exempted income that had been earned by means of virtually any foreign activities that might conceivably be treated as a basis for taxation by a foreign state.[54] But, the AB added, the exemption must be limited to the income actually earned by that foreign activity. The AB then examined the 'rules of thumb' by which the ETI statute determined the amount of income that was to be exempt from taxation. (These were exactly the same 'rules of thumb' that had been used to calculate the amount of the tax exemption under the FSC statute.) The AB found that two of the three calculation formulae provided for exemption of significant amounts of domestic-source income that presented no threat of double taxation, as did special rules waiving the requirement of foreign activity for taxpayers with foreign trading gross receipts of less than $5 million and for sale of associated services in conjunction with sales of goods.[55]

From the very first days of the FSC statute in 1984, the 'rules of thumb' used to calculate the amount of income that would benefit from the tax exemption had been criticized as a violation of the arm's-length pricing requirement of the 1981 Understanding. These rules, it was claimed, granted far greater tax exemptions than were justified by the Understanding's permission to grant tax exemptions to foreign-source income. The EC had made this claim a central part of its case against FSC. This EC claim had been rendered moot by the Panel's ruling that the 1981 Understanding was of no legal effect, and was never ruled on. The AB's ruling on the double taxation issue vindicates these long-standing criticisms of the FSC and ETI subsidies.

Is it possible that DISC-FSC-ETI can be saved after all by meeting the conditions of the double taxation defence of footnote 59? The AB's final conclusion on footnote 59 seemed to leave a generous opening. 'Certainly', the AB said, 'if the ETI measure were confined to those aspects which grant a tax exemption for [properly attributed] "foreign-source income", it would fall within footnote 59'.[56] But a tax exemption limited to the actual amount of foreign-source income attributable to the minuscule foreign activities required by the FSC and ETI statutes would not come close to satisfying the demands of the present beneficiaries. Perhaps more important, such a change would do nothing to eliminate the Article III:4 violation caused by the 50 per cent valued-added requirement. If past experience is a reliable guide, the US Congress will never agree to create a subsidy without such a value-added requirement, for fear of stimulating a greater movement of US production to foreign locations.

The US President has given his assurance that the US will comply with the legal rulings in this case.[57] No time deadline was expressed. [To be continued.]

---

[54] AB 21.5 Report, paras 146–147, 153.
[55] The analysis appears at paras 154–186 of the AB's 21.5 Report.
[56] AB 21.5 Report, para 185.
[57] 'Bush Promises FSC Compliance Without Time Commitment', *Inside US Trade*, 3 May 2002.

IV. The lessons of the *FSC* case

In almost every respect, the *FSC* case was the wrong kind of case to bring before the WTO dispute settlement procedure. The FSC subsidy enjoyed massive support from the US business community, due to the large amounts of money it was putting into the pockets of US exporters. In the view of most informed observers, it would have been impossible for the US government to remove, or substantially reduce, FSC subsidies for the sake of a WTO legal ruling. To file a legal complaint against FSC was to invite a legal deadlock that would damage the credibility of the WTO dispute settlement system, and that would become a large irritant in US-EC trade relations.

In addition, the subject matter of the complaint was manifestly inappropriate for resolution in a single lawsuit before WTO tribunals. The dispute involved a central US defence that its tax practices were no different than, and were justified by, the tax practices of other governments. The fact that the Panel could not consider those other practices challenged, and that its ruling might nonetheless have some impact on them, had to exert a chilling effect on the tribunal's willingness to develop a principled basis of decision.

And finally, both the text and the substantive content of the GATT/WTO rules on tax subsidies were so poorly developed that WTO tribunals had relatively little legal basis for resolving the dispute. The Panel and AB were clearly unsure of what the 'otherwise due' standard meant. A large part of the problem was that there was simply no intellectually rigorous definition of what governments are accustomed to call a 'subsidy'.

Given the total context in which the *FSC* case was brought, however, it is not clear to this author that the EC had any better alternative. As suggested in Part 2(A)(1) above, the author finds it hard to believe that the EC's primary purpose in bringing the *FSC* complaint was to remove FSC itself. In the author's view, the *FSC* complaint was meant to serve the same purposes, *mutatis mutandis,* as the EC's *DISC* complaint 25 years earlier. Just as the *DISC* complaint had been an effort to deter the US from pursuing a too-aggressive litigation policy (by 1972 standards), so its *FSC* complaint was primarily intended to discourage the US from its too-aggressive use of the new WTO dispute settlement procedure, and in particular its retaliation remedy. For that didactic purpose, many of the characteristics that made FSC a 'wrong case' for purposes of effective adjudication were actually pluses. The more difficult it was for the US to comply with the legal ruling, the greater its embarrassment and thus the more effective the message of the complaint—that the US could not itself live by the litigation policy it was seeking to apply to others. Likewise, the failure to reach an amicable settlement early in the case was not necessarily a minus, given that the didactic purpose of the case would not have been served by an early settlement. Although the case itself has yet to be resolved, it can be said with some assurance that Washington has already received the message the *FSC* complaint was trying to send.

As indicated in Part 2(A)(2) above, the author views the EC's *FSC* complaint as a necessary part of a more or less inevitable process that attended US efforts to obtain political consent to the Uruguay Round reforms in WTO dispute settlement. Given the excessive promises of strong enforcement that were needed to obtain that consent, I do not believe it would have been possible to temper the excessive expectations caused by those promises without the powerful message of the FSC lawsuit. That is, the *FSC* case forces the US to face the actual consequences of its very aggressive retaliation policy. The only way to avoid the need to bring such very troublesome retaliatory cases would be to invent a form of democracy that does not require excessive promises to obtain political approval of important international commitments.

The underlying problem illustrated by the *FSC* case is that the WTO now has a legal system whose legal rigour sometimes often exceeds both the clarity and/or the soundness of its legal rules, and also exceeds the political commitment of its members to comply with those rules. There are numerous lacunae in GATT/WTO rules like the inadequate definition of tax subsidies in the SCM Agreement. Likewise, there are also numerous 'untouchable' laws and policies like FSC whose support seems to be greater than national commitments to GATT/WTO law. There is no easy way to work around these potentially fatal problems. The first line of defence obviously has to be a certain restraint in government litigation policy, both in thinking twice before even bringing certain potentially 'wrong' cases, and in allowing plenty of time and flexibility to work out those cases that end in impasse. If the *FSC* case has succeeded in introducing a greater degree of such restraint in US litigation policy (and by 'restraint' I mean restraint on the part of the political interests who demand more aggressive legal enforcement), the *FSC* case has made an important contribution to dealing with this underlying weakness of the WTO legal system.

There is no way, of course, to stop all 'wrong' cases. Indeed, there will be cases where there is no other way to induce the other side even to talk about a problem, and where 'wrong case' litigation is the least bad solution. I believe the *FSC* case was probably one such case. When this happens, it is up to the participants—the Panel, the AB and the parties—to manage the impasse with calm and patience—particularly patience—in the hope that a solution, or at least a face-saving exit, will eventually emerge. The considerably weaker GATT legal system did manage to resolve most of its failures by such patient temporizing. The GATT sat on the *DISC* case for 12 years, end-to-end, before it found a way out through a flimsy settlement. Although the more rigorous legal structure of the new WTO legal system seems not to have room for such temporizing, the behaviour of WTO members to date has shown that they are still able, and still inclined, to take more time when the right answers are not yet in sight. The glacial pace of the EC's prosecution of the *FSC* case is the best example so far of the survival of these old tendencies in the new WTO.

Even though improved legal discipline over tax subsidies may not have been the primary purpose of the *FSC* case, it is still relevant to note that the legal outcome of the case is still unsatisfying with regard to future relations in this area. Perhaps wisely, the final 21.5 rulings by both the Panel and the AB did not produce any clear ground rules for future government conduct in this area. And, as noted in Part 2(C)(2) above, there is still no fully satisfying answer to the US claim of unequal treatment in this area. And finally, the irritation of losing the case seems to have induced a few members of the US Congress to suggest retaliatory legislation involving the less favourable tax treatment of foreign exporters. This unsettled legal situation presents a serious risk of further policy conflict. It would be wise to try to head off such conflict by attempting to negotiate some agreed ground rules in this area. The obvious locale for such negotiations would be OECD, the international institution with the greatest expertise in tax policy. The US business community was deeply involved in preparing the legal defence of FSC before the WTO. Business communities on both sides of the Atlantic would seem to have a common interest in promoting such negotiations.

6

Production and Export Subsidies in Agriculture: Lessons from GATT and WTO Disputes Involving the US and the EC

T. JOSLING and S. TANGERMANN

I. INTRODUCTION

The United States and the European Community have sparred over agricultural subsidies for the past 20 years.[1] Conflicts over domestic farm programmes have spilled over into a number of international trade disputes, in particular in the 1980s. Two complaints against the EC were brought by the US before the General Agreement on Tariffs and Trade (GATT) in 1981, protesting export subsidies paid on wheat flour and pasta; the next year saw another three complaints initiated by the US, on EC export and domestic subsidies on sugar, poultry and canned fruit. This was followed in 1983 by a complaint by the EC about US export subsidies on wheat flour exports, and in 1983 the US complained about EC production subsidies on oilseeds. The oilseed dispute dragged on until finally settled during the negotiations in the Uruguay Round. The Uruguay Round Agreement on Agriculture changed radically the treatment of farm subsidies in international trade rules. Since that time, relative peace has prevailed, though a 1997 complaint to the WTO by the US challenged the operation of EC export subsidies on cheese.

In this paper we attempt to draw some lessons from the history of trade disputes between the US and the EU over agricultural subsidies.[2] The history of the disputes has to be seen, of course, in the broader context of transatlantic disagreements over agricultural policy and of the intense commercial rivalry in the markets for temperate zone farm products.[3] Agriculture is widely (and

---

[1] For convenience the term European Community will be used even for the period since 1995 when the more inclusive term European Union would be more usual.

[2] Research assistance by Rachel Anderson is gratefully acknowledged.

[3] For a fuller discussion of the transatlantic tensions over agriculture see S. Tangermann, 'The Common and Uncommon Agricultural Policies—An Eternal Issue?' in O.G. Mayer & H.-E. Scharrer (eds), *Transatlantic Relations in a Global Economy* (1999).

correctly) considered the epitome of a protected and subsidized sector, with widespread use of export subsidies by several countries to move high cost produce on to world markets. Smaller exporters continually complain about the export subsidies of the EC and about the corresponding programmes operated by the US. Agriculture has certainly caused its share of trade tensions, but the nature of these disputes is of interest both in agricultural terms and as indications of how the GATT/WTO rules have been interpreted in practice. More particularly, the agricultural disputes indicate some interesting features of US-EU trade relationships and the pressures on trade diplomacy from domestic political actors on both sides of the Atlantic.

Surprisingly few of these tensions over agricultural trade have actually reached the stage of the adoption of the report of a panel. Many were settled bilaterally, some reached the panel report stage but the report was never adopted, and others were subsumed in broader ongoing trade negotiations. In a few cases, a subsidy war replaced diplomacy and resulted in an ad hoc accommodation. Therefore one question that must be considered is whether one might have expected more use of trade dispute mechanisms over the past 20 years to resolve transatlantic agricultural trade tensions? Have there been factors that limited the frequency of trade conflicts in the GATT? And has the emergence of the WTO, with its improved dispute settlement disciplines, provided the opportunity for more use of international processes for resolving transatlantic agricultural disputes? Or is the scope for such multilateral processes so limited that the transatlantic partners should be devising and using other channels of dispute resolution?

II. FREQUENCY AND OUTCOME OF AGRICULTURAL SUBSIDY DISPUTES

The multilateral dispute settlement system has proved only marginally useful in settling the transatlantic disputes that have periodically arisen in the area of agricultural subsidies. To illustrate this proposition it is necessary to distinguish between disputes that were brought under GATT rules and those that have been brought under the more clearly defined WTO disciplines. The GATT dispute settlement process was tested to its limits in the 1980s by a succession of acrimonious agricultural subsidy disputes. Though some policies were indeed modified as a result of panel decisions, the record is not impressive. By contrast, the improved WTO dispute settlement mechanism has yet to be faced with a challenge to a major agricultural subsidy programme. The Uruguay Round Agreement on Agriculture both clarified the rules regarding agricultural subsidies and strengthened the procedure for settling disputes involving those rules. One might therefore have expected even more activity in this area since 1995. But the explanation of the outbreak of relative calm has largely to do with the inclusion of Article 13 in the Agreement on Agriculture, commonly known as the Peace Clause, which obliges countries to show 'due restraint' in bringing such actions. Other factors, such as the binding in schedules of levels of permissible subsidies, and the notification of subsidy levels to the Committee on Agriculture, have also had a significant effect.

A. US-EC GATT conflicts over agricultural subsidies

Though adjudicated under the 'old' rules and with weaker dispute settlement procedures, the GATT disputes still have significance in two respects: they illustrate well the frustrations that led up to the adoption of the WTO disciplines, and they give some clue as to what could happen if the Peace Clause is allowed to expire. In a classic discussion of trade disputes brought before the GATT, Hudec lists 207 such complaints over the period 1948–1990.[4] The list includes 20 agricultural trade disputes between the US and the EC. Many of these, however, were about market access rather than about subsidies.[5] Only seven such conflicts centred on agricultural subsidies, all of which occurred during the 1980s.[6] Of these seven, five related to export subsidies and two to domestic subsidy programmes. The two domestic subsidy conflicts proved to be the most 'successful'. In both cases, the US challenged an aspect of the domestic policy of the EU. In each case the panel decided in favour of the US, and the EC subsequently altered its domestic policy. The same cannot be said for the five export subsidy cases, four of which were challenges by the US to the EC export subsidy programmes and one was a challenge by the EC against the US export programmes. In three of these five cases a panel was never established. In the remaining two cases the panel was unable to find violation of the 'equitable share' rule embodied in Article XVI of the GATT, and in any case the panel reports were not adopted. Thus the key question is why the GATT articles proved so ineffectual in resolving the 'trade wars' that have been a feature of the agricultural trade landscape over the past two decades. A brief account of the significance and outcome of each of these cases is necessary before drawing lessons about the success or lack of success of the dispute settlement process in easing tensions between the US and the EC in the area of agriculture.

1. *Domestic subsidy cases*

Before the Uruguay Round, domestic agricultural subsidies were not accorded any special treatment. Article III:8(b) explicitly stated that 'national treatment'

---

[4] R.E. Hudec, *Enforcing International Trade Law: The Evolution of the Modern GATT Legal System* (1993).

[5] Though the market access conflicts are not directly relevant for the present paper, their importance should not be overlooked. The Chicken War of 1963 represented the first major challenge to the nascent EC from its main sponsor, the US. This highly visible trade conflict brought home the potential of the transatlantic partnership for discord as well as harmony. Twenty years later, the issue of tariff preferences for citrus imports from the Mediterranean countries again caused a major political rift at a time when support for EU policy toward its southerly neighbours was broadly in the strategic interest of the US.

[6] The Annex to this chapter contains a listing and brief description of these seven cases, along with a related subsidy case (wine) and the sole WTO case between the EC and the US that addresses agricultural subsidies.

should not prevent 'the payment of subsidies exclusively to domestic producers'. However, subsidizing countries had to observe certain precautions.[7] If the subsidy resulted in increased exports (or reduced imports) it should have been notified to the GATT, and if it had resulted in 'serious prejudice' to the interests of other countries there was an obligation on the subsidizing country to 'discuss the possibility of limiting the subsidization' (Article XVI:1). Moreover, a country negatively affected by another country's subsidy could have taken the matter to the GATT if it felt that it had suffered 'nullification and impairment' of the benefits expected from the agreement. Even if the subsidy itself was not illegal, 'non-violation' nullification and impairment (under Article XXIII:1(b)) could be cause for the subsidizing country to be required to remove the offending instrument.[8] Though GATT cases against domestic agricultural subsidies have not been common, they do have a special place in the legal history of transatlantic challenges to domestic farm policy.

The two domestic subsidy cases that were brought under GATT rules between the EC and the US in the area of agricultural trade demonstrated, at the least, that not all domestic agricultural policies are immune from challenge by outside suppliers. Though both disputes dragged on over several years, they did in the end lead to policy changes. In the case of EC subsidies to the canned fruit sector, subsidies were reduced under a bilateral agreement, and in the case of the EC subsidies paid to oilseed crushers for using domestic seeds a radical change in the Common Agricultural Policy (CAP) was instituted that eventually led to more widespread reforms for the cereal sector.

(a) Canned fruit (1981–85)

The conflict over the EC's subsidies to processors of fruit simmered for much of the 1980s. The US had complained in 1979 about the minimum import price for tomato concentrate, as well as the licence and surety deposits that were used to regulate imports into the EC. Other processed fruits competed with products from the US in third markets. The EC fruit and vegetable system supported prices of the raw product and then compensated processors for the higher cost of the raw materials. Though not one of the more familiar of the regimes of the CAP, the fruit and vegetable programme was well known in California and Florida to those that considered that the EC was unfairly favouring its own southern producers.

In March 1982, the US requested that a GATT panel be set up to investigate the EC subsidies.[9] The case was brought under the GATT Subsidies Code. The panel reported in November 1984, finding that the EC was in violation of their

---

[7] T. Josling, S. Tangermann & T.K. Warley, *Agriculture in the GATT* (1996) at 125.

[8] In addition, the country suffering from the effect of the subsidy could under certain conditions levy a countervailing duty on imports from the subsidizing country. Countervailing duties have been used in agricultural trade somewhat sparingly, with the exception of trade between the US and Canada, and will not be discussed further in this paper.

[9] Hudec, supra note 4, Case No 107.

GATT obligations in respect of subsidies to processors of peaches, pears and fruit cocktails (though not of dried grapes). The subsidy to processors was found to be larger than necessary to compensate for the extra cost of the domestic fruit. Accordingly, the EC's subsidy constituted 'non-violation nullification and impairment'. The panel suggested that the EC avoid action that distorted competition between the domestic and the imported canned fruit. But the panel did not find sufficient evidence of subsidies to growers of these products. The panel report was never adopted, as the EC blocked its consideration by the GATT Subsidies Committee. But, after protracted negotiations, a bilateral settlement was reached between the US and the EC (US-EC Canned Fruit Agreement, 1985) that reduced the scope and level of the subsidies to canners. The EC agreed to cut its aid to peach canners by 25 per cent in 1986–87 and to phase out processing aid to canned peaches in subsequent years.[10] With respect to canned pears, the US accepted the subsidy reductions already announced by the EC.

The bilateral accord was not, however, the end of the story. In August 1988, the US claimed that the EC had violated the terms of the US-EC Canned Fruit Agreement, and domestic pressure began to mount to retaliate against the EC if their subsidies on canned peaches and pears were not reduced.[11] The complaint was both that the US suppliers were being undercut in the EC market, by subsidized local production, and that EC canners were making inroads into foreign markets (specifically in Japan and Canada) traditionally supplied from the US. The US launched an investigation (under section 301) of the EC subsidies, and drew up a list of targeted products for retaliation.[12] The EC once again reduced its subsidies and the US action was suspended.[13] However, the canned fruit saga remained an issue just below the surface. A 1997 US State Department list of worrisome trade practices by the EU included the following observation:

The United States and five other producing countries (Argentina, Australia, Brazil, Chile and South Africa) are continuing to exchange letters with the European Commission regarding the EU's internal support regime for canned fruit. These governments believe that the operation of the EU support regime for fresh peaches and pears has allowed EU fruit processors to unfairly undercut the domestic and export prices for canned fruit of the EU's trading partners. Despite the EU's claims of adherence to the letter of the 1985 U.S.-EC Canned Fruit Agreement, oversupply of the fresh fruit under the support regime may allow processors in certain Member States to ignore the minimum price requirements of the agreement. The industries in all five countries have been hurt by EU exports of cheap

---

[10] K. Featherstone & R.H. Ginsberg, *The United States and the European Union in the 1990s: Partners in Transition* (1996) at 177.

[11] Ibid at 178.

[12] Ibid. Under section 301, 'firms can complain about a foreign country's trade policies or practices that are harmful to U.S. commerce. The section empowers the USTR to investigate the allegations and to negotiate the removal of any trade barriers. USTR may also self-initiate investigations. Specific timeframes for conducting the investigations are specified by law. Section 301 requires that GATT's dispute resolution process be invoked where applicable and, if negotiations fail, to retaliate within 180 days from the date that discovery of a trade agreement violation took place.'

[13] The EU amended its regulation (Council Regulation 1277/84, OJ 1984 L 123/25) to limit the amount of aid.

canned fruit. Modifications in the overall fruit and vegetable production scheme may improve the situation, but it is too early to tell.

The fact that no dispute has come before the WTO suggests that both sides have had an incentive to keep this venerable dispute out of the headlines in recent years.

(b) Oilseeds (1988–93)

The oilseed case is in many ways the archetypal EC/US conflict over agricultural subsidies within the GATT. The US has held a dominant position as an exporter of vegetable oilseeds, particularly soybeans, in the post-war period, in many ways developing the international market for both the oilseeds themselves and the vegetable oil and high protein meal that result from the crushing of the seeds and beans. The market has generally expanded, with rather less domestic protection in the exporting countries than for cereals and considerably freer market access into the importing countries such as the EC and Japan. The EC had from the 1950s been an importer of soybeans, though the oils from such seeds competed with the tree oils (such as olive oil) from southern Europe and imported tropical oils from former colonies. The rapid growth in the importation of the seeds and beans led to the development of a major oilseed crushing industry around the major EC ports.

The import market growth was always a point of contention for European agricultural interests, who pressed continuously for a 'completion' of the CAP, to include protection for oilseeds and the exclusion of imported products.[14] But the GATT effectively precluded such a move. In the Dillon Round the EC had agreed to a zero binding for a number of oilseed products that were of limited interest to domestic producers.[15] For US export interests the preservation of the open access for soybeans became an over-riding priority for any trade talks.[16] For the EC, moving resources into oilseed production was a popular domestic option to counter the increased surplus of grains. Subsidies given to processors of domestic oilseeds seemed a convenient way of stimulating domestic production without having to 'unbind' the oilseed tariff, and such subsidies were initiated in 1966. This trade tension was exacerbated by the rapid development in the animal feed industry of lower-cost poultry and pig rations based on a mix of protein-rich soybean meal and starchy manioc chips, a perfect substitute for corn and barley whose price was kept artificially high by the CAP.[17]

[14] Later, the argument became transformed into a call for 'rebalancing' the CAP. See, U. Koester *et al, Disharmonies in EC and US Agricultural Policies: A Summary of Results and Major Conclusions*, Report for the Commission of the European Communities by the EC/US Study Group, Commission of the European Communities (1988).

[15] This binding was one of the more significant achievements of the Dillon Round, which in other respects provided little in the way of trade liberalization. See Josling, supra note 7, ch 3.

[16] US exports of oilseeds had reached $8 billion a year. The industry claimed that the EC subsidies were costing them around $1.5–2 billion each year. See Hudec, supra note 4, at 559.

[17] Later, corn gluten, citrus pulp and other 'junk' feeds began to enter the mix. These did nothing to help the trade conflict as they also were largely exported from the US. The trade conflict over corn gluten is not discussed here, as it relates to market access rather than subsidies.

The overt trade dispute began in 1988 when the American Soybean Association filed a section 301 petition with the US Trade Representative (USTR).[18] The complaint was brought to the GATT in 1988, when the US alleged that the EC had both violated Article III:4, by encouraging the use of domestic rather than imported oilseeds, and impaired the benefits that the US had expected from the duty-free bindings negotiated in the Dillon Round.[19] The EU argued that the US had been losing market share in part because of new competitive suppliers from Latin America. It resented the direct attack on a component part of the CAP. It resisted the establishment of the panel for two months and delayed the naming of the panellists for a further year. Finally, the panel met and reported in December 1989.

The panel found in favour of the US, that the EC subsidy to oilseed crushers was not a protected subsidy under Article III:8(b), and violated national treatment by favouring the use of domestic oilseeds over imports. Aid to the processors, even if given in a GATT-legal form, would have also constituted non-violation nullification and impairment, as it reduced the size of the market for imports.[20] The EC noted its reservations to the report but did not block it, and the report was adopted by the GATT General Council in January 1990.[21]

Subsequent to the oilseed ruling, the EC changed its agricultural policy instrument. In place of subsidies to processors based on the use of domestic oilseeds, it paid a hectarage subsidy to growers.[22] But this was not enough to satisfy the oilseed interests in the US. The panel was reconvened to consider the new EC policies, and found that though the EC had removed the violation of Article III:4, the effect was still to nullify and impair the benefits that the US might reasonably have hoped to get out of the Dillon Round bindings. The EC attempted to renegotiate the tariff bindings themselves, under Article XXVIII:4, but talks with the US did not reach a conclusion. In turn the US suggested binding arbitration, but the EC refused. The US requested authority to retaliate, under Article XXIII:2, but was rebuffed by the EC.[23] Instead, the US prepared for unilateral retaliation, and set a deadline for the introduction of prohibitive tariffs on $300 million worth of imports from the EC.

The oilseed dispute was working its way through the dispute settlement process at the same time that negotiators were trying to find a new set of rules to apply to agriculture in the Uruguay Round. This coincidence of timing led eventually to a resolution of the oilseed conflict. The bilateral discussions culminating at the Blair House meeting in November 1992 laid the groundwork for a solution. The EC agreed to limit oilseed production and the amount of subsidy afforded to domestic producers. But the significance of the conclusion to the

---

[18] Featherstone & Ginsberg, supra note 10, at 195.

[19] Hudec, supra note 4, Case No 179.   [20] Ibid at 245.

[21] Even in this case, the panel did not actually address the issue of what an acceptable level of subsidy or method of providing such subsidy would be. This task would be left to the Uruguay Round Agreement on Agriculture.

[22] See Council Regulation 3766/91, OJ 1991 L 356/17.

[23] Hudec, supra note 4, at 560.

oilseed conflict was that its resolution cleared the way for an agreement on the framework for the Uruguay Round Agreement on Agriculture. The existence of the talks had facilitated the conclusion of the GATT dispute, but the need to resolve the dispute had provided an opportunity for a 'package' deal that might not have been possible if each element would have been considered in isolation.

(c) Wine (1985–86)

A third subsidy case should be mentioned in passing, though its relevance to the other agricultural subsidy cases is somewhat remote. In 1985 the EC requested a panel to examine certain provisions of the US Wine Equity Act.[24] The contention was that in broadening (albeit temporarily) the definition of the wine industry to include growers, the US was opening the way for an increase in requests for anti-dumping or countervailing duty action under US trade law. EC imports had begun to penetrate the US market and domestic growers were known to be supporting this legislation as a way of countering what they perceived as subsidized trade from the EC.[25] A GATT panel reported that the new definition was indeed contrary to the GATT rules, that define the 'industry' from the point of view of anti-dumping and countervailing duties action as the producers of the product, not of an input to that product.[26] However, the adoption of the report by the Committee on Subsidies was blocked by the US, on the grounds that the expanded definition of the industry was in any case about to expire under the terms of the Act.[27] Thus the wine dispute petered out with little gained by either side.

2. *Export subsidy cases*

If some success can be found in the dispute settlement process in the case of domestic agricultural subsidies, the same cannot be said for export subsidies. The record is of almost total failure to apply any judicial restraint or discipline to the export subsidies in use for farm products. The issue of what constituted a subsidy was not seriously in doubt. But the permissive treatment of primary product export subsidies in Article XVI undermined any attempt to rein in these disruptive trade policies. And even the improved disciplines on subsidies carefully negotiated in the Tokyo Round Subsidy Code proved impossible to deal with in the reality of widespread subsidies to agricultural exports.

Export subsidies for primary products, in contrast to those employed in other sectors, were not prohibited in the GATT.[28] Such subsidies were legal as long as

[24] Ibid, Case No 137.

[25] Most of the wine being imported from the EC did not benefit directly from the CAP regime for wine, and certainly received no explicit export subsidies. But the support for the price of the lower quality bulk wines could have been argued indirectly to have helped EC growers to target the US market for quality and branded wines.

[26] Featherstone & Ginsberg, supra note 10, at 177.

[27] In addition, the action of blocking the adoption of the report was apparently to put pressure on the EC to settle two other cases of contested subsidies (pasta and wheat flour, as discussed below).

[28] Josling, Tangermann & Warley, supra note 7, at 118.

they were not used to gain 'more than an equitable share of world trade' in the product concerned (Article XVI:3).[29] This exception proved to be the Achilles heel of the GATT as far as imposing constraints on the farm programmes of the major exporting countries. In spite of several GATT cases testing the interpretation of the exception, subsidizing countries were rarely found to be in violation of their GATT obligations.[30] The root of the problem was the difficulty that panels had in imparting meaning to the phrase 'equitable share of world trade'. Though an early GATT panel, in 1958, had found that France had exceeded its 'equitable share' of world wheat trade when its exports doubled in a short period of time, displacing the exports of the complaining country, Australia, this was the only successful resort to Article XVI:3.

In an attempt to improve the precision of Article XVI, the Tokyo Round Subsidies Code elaborated on the definition of 'equitable share'. Four problems had bedevilled panels in their interpretation: the assessment of the relevant market in which to measure the share; the relevant quantities of exports to consider; the appropriate reference period to use; and the causality between the export subsidy and the market share.[31] The Subsidies Code was unsuccessful in resolving these problems.

The choice of the relevant market in which to assess an equitable share was never satisfactorily clarified. In the case of French wheat exports, the panel looked at the total world market, though it considered individual markets in assessing the 'damage' incurred by the plaintiff. But when panels considered EC sugar exports (further discussed below), they rejected the evidence that the EC had nearly doubled its overall market share and looked for cases where sales from individual exporting countries had been displaced by the EC subsidies. They found few such markets and took this as a reason to conclude that displacement could not clearly be established.[32] And even when such evidence of displacement seemed overwhelming, as in the case of wheat flour discussed below, the panel found that the market 'had changed considerably in size and nature over the period, and that the changes in market shares were such that cases of displacement . . . [were] not evident'.[33]

Defining the scope of the world market and the reference period also proved problematic for panels. Was food aid under concessional terms part of the world market? What about sales under bilateral agreements or even trade within regional trade agreements? And how might one define a representative period in cases where the subsidies had been in place for years? Or what period should

---

[29] The rules on export subsidies were added to the GATT in 1955, including the primary product exception.

[30] Josling, Tangermann & Warley, supra note 7, at 119.

[31] See Hartwig, 'Die GATT-Regeln fuer die Landwirtschaft: Eine Oekonomische Analyse ihrer Wirksamkeit vor dem Hintergrund der Streitbeilegung' (1992) 134 *Argrarwirtschaft, Sonderheft* 179–88 and Jestaedt, 'Europäisch-amerikanischer Streit um die Subventionierung von Agrarexporten', *RIW-Recht der Internationalen Wirtschaft*, October 1986/Heft 10, at 805–812.

[32] Josling, Tangermann & Warley, supra note 7, at 120.

[33] Ibid at 121.

be used when instability in markets and market shares made any concept of 'normal' conditions a matter of contention. The Subsidies Code made a valiant attempt to define a previous representative period as normally 'the three most recent calendar years in which normal market conditions existed'. However, that merely focused attention on what constituted 'normal' market conditions. But perhaps the greatest difficulty faced by panels in adjudicating export subsidy cases was to establish causality between the subsidy and the change in market shares. After the confidence of the French wheat case, panels appeared overwhelmed by the multiplicity of 'special factors' at work in the markets concerned.[34] As a result, definitive rulings in this area are scarce. The history of US-EC conflicts over export subsidies illustrates the difficulties faced by panels in interpreting the somewhat vague concept of equitable market share.

(a) Wheat flour (1981–86)

If the oilseeds case was prototypical of the conflict over the domestic subsidies paid under the CAP, the wheat flour case was the most significant and persistent trade conflict that focused on export subsidies.[35] The US and the EU (mainly France) had important positions in the market for wheat flour. The EC market share had increased from 29 per cent of world commercial exports in 1959–62 to 75 per cent in 1979–81, while the US share dropped from 25 per cent to 9 per cent over the same period.[36] EC export subsidies reached as high as 50 per cent of the world price in some years. The US milling industry filed a section 301 complaint in December 1975. Consultations under GATT Article XXII were begun in 1977 but adjourned for the duration of the Tokyo Round trade negotiations. The wheat flour complaint thus was waiting in the wings to test the newly-minted Subsidies Code that emerged from the Tokyo Round.[37]

The US initiated its complaint before the GATT under the Subsidies Code in December 1981.[38] The US claimed that subsidies had resulted in EC exports gaining more than an equitable share of world trade, in violation of Article 10:1 of the Subsidies Code. In addition, the US argued that these subsidies had displaced US exports and undercut prices (in violation of Article 10:3) and had 'nullified and impaired' benefits that the US could reasonably expect from the GATT and caused 'serious prejudice' to US exports, in violation of Article 8 of the Code.[39]

[34] Ibid at 122.
[35] It is not clear why the exception for primary products was implicitly extended to include wheat flour, which undergoes some processing (milling) before reaching the market. An interpretive note to Article XVI, section B explicitly defined the nature of commodities falling under the exception as a product 'in its natural form or which has undergone such processing as is customarily required to prepare it for marketing in substantial volume in international trade'. It is certainly not necessary to mill wheat in order to market it in international trade. See ibid at 123, and Jestaedt, supra note 31.
[36] Hudec, supra note 4, at 491.
[37] Ibid.
[38] Ibid, Case No 103.
[39] Ibid at 491.

A panel was formed but could not find any violation of the Subsidies Code. Citing the difficulty of defining 'equitable share' in a complex market situation, the panel was unable to reach any conclusion. They also were unable to find evidence of displacement or price undercutting. In addition, the panel was unable to rule on the nullification and serious injury charges as those concepts were difficult to interpret when third-country trade effects were involved.[40] The report was blocked by the US (after an attempt to have the Subsidies Committee over-rule the panel was rejected by the EC) and not adopted. But the failure of the GATT to resolve this dispute led not to a bilateral deal, as with canned fruit or pasta, but to a trade war, as the US and the EU contested a number of markets for wheat flour, particularly in North Africa and the Middle East.

The use of the GATT to resolve the wheat flour dispute took a different twist a few months later. In April 1983 the EC initiated a GATT complaint against the US.[41] The object of the complaint was the use of subsidies in the Egyptian market, deliberately designed to offset the export subsidies of the EC that were the subject of the US GATT complaint. The subsidy was granted shortly before the panel ruling was known. Sales to Egypt constituted about 50 per cent of EC wheat flour sales, and there was no doubt that the explicit purpose of the subsidy was to challenge the EC in that specific market. The EC complaint was that the US-subsidized sale to Egypt violated Article 10:2 of the Subsidies Code by displacing the traditional supplier (the EC), and Article 10:3 by undercutting the price.[42] A panel was established but never constituted. Apparently, the US withdrew its subsidized exports to the Egyptian market the next year. But the EC had at the least shown that it was prepared to use the GATT mechanism in an attempt to preserve its own markets, rather than merely defend itself against the almost constant attack from other countries.

(b) Pasta (1982–87)

The tensions between the US and the EC in the wheat sector went beyond the sale of wheat flour to the Middle East. US pasta producers had filed a section 301 complaint in October 1981.[43] The US filed a complaint in April 1982 under the GATT Subsidies Code, claiming that the EC was unduly subsidizing pasta exports into the US market.[44] US producers considered that the subsidy that the EC paid to its domestic producers was more than enough to offset the higher cost of durum wheat (the main ingredient for pasta) supported under the CAP.

The case was brought under Article 9 of the Subsidies Code, that prohibited export subsidies on 'non-primary' products. The US argued that the pasta subsidy was illegal as it was paid on a processed product. Only primary products were sheltered from the blanket prohibition on export subsidies. The EC argued

[40] Ibid.   [41] Ibid, Case No 123.   [42] Ibid at 511.

[43] Hudec reports that the producers chose not to request a countervailing duty investigation as the quantity of imports was not large enough to make a case for material injury to the domestic industry. Ibid, at 493.

[44] Ibid, Case No 105.

that Article 9 was adopted amid widespread use of subsidies that compensated for the additional cost of raw materials and that the subsidy was paid solely on the durum wheat component of the processing cost and thus was covered by the GATT exception for primary products. The panel was convened and delivered a split report in May 1983, with three of the four panellists arguing that pasta was indeed an industrial product, and hence that subsidies on its export were therefore illegal. The dissenting panellist agreed with the EC that the use of an export subsidy on the raw material content of processed food exports was widespread and by implication GATT-legal.[45] The report was never adopted by the Subsidies Code Committee, as the EC chose to block its adoption.[46]

The pasta conflict was not finally settled until 1987. Indeed it became tied up in another trade dispute, over citrus preferences to the Mediterranean countries. The US threatened retaliation against EC pasta exports as a part of its strategy to persuade the EC to remove its preferential access for southern Europe and the North African littoral. In August 1986 the citrus case was settled, and this agreement included a decision to wrap up the pasta case. Some months of acrimonious negotiations followed before the US and the EU signed a Pasta Agreement on 5 August 1987. The EC accepted conditions on the level of export subsidy for pasta that limited it to the extra cost of the durum wheat used. And the EC ensured that its position on the legality of raw-material cost subsidies was enshrined in the WTO. Article 11 of the Agreement on Agriculture explicitly allows subsidies that compensate for the higher cost of raw materials.[47]

(c) Poultry (1982–86)

A third export subsidy conflict arose in 1982 over the EC's use of both domestic and export subsidies in the poultry market.[48] The US and the EU had locked horns on poultry trade before, in the infamous 'Chicken War' of 1963, when the US had taken a complaint to the GATT over the increase in import levies for poultry that were introduced at the time of the establishment of the CAP.[49] By the end of the 1970s the main thrust of the world poultry market had switched away from the sales of whole chicken and turkeys into Europe and toward frozen chicken parts into new markets in other regions of the world. The EC became an exporter of many of these products. The US was also concerned about competition from Brazil, a rapidly emerging player in the poultry trade, and about the impact that

---

[45] Further details of the pasta decision are found in Hudec, ibid, who describes this case as one that might have been invented by law professors for the purposes of an examination question. The legal intricacies of the case were more evident than its minimal effect on agricultural trade policy.

[46] Featherstone & Ginsberg, supra note 10, at 182, point out that this was the first time that the EC had blocked the adoption of a GATT panel report, and put this down to a growing sense of confidence in the EC in international commercial relations.

[47] The text of Article 11 states that 'in no case may the per-unit subsidy paid on an incorporated agricultural product exceed the per-unit export subsidy that would be payable on exports of the primary product as such'. WTO, *The Results of the Uruguay Round of Trade Negotiations: The Legal Texts* (1994) at 50.

[48] Hudec, supra note 4, Case No 106.

[49] See Josling, Tangermann & Warley, supra note 7, ch 4 for a full discussion of the Chicken War.

low Brazilian prices were having on the EC export prices. The US, as the market leader in the frozen chicken trade, felt obliged to counter the aggressive trade actions of both the EC and Brazil. The US poultry exporters initiated a section 301 complaint that led to the US requesting consultations within the GATT.

The complaint was brought under the Subsidies Code, Article 10:1, charging that the EC had acquired a more-than-equitable share of the poultry market as a result of its export subsidies, and that certain domestic subsidies were inconsistent with Article 8 of the Code which required countries to avoid adverse trade impacts.[50] Conciliation proceeded simultaneously with the parallel complaint against Brazil. No panel was established, though the trilateral discussions continued for some months until suspended in December 1984. In the end, the parties agreed mutually to restrain their export subsidies. The poultry conflict added little to the definition of equitable shares or to the resolution of subsidy cases, but it indicated that in a growing world market consultations can be a useful way of protracting a dispute until the economic and political climate changes.

(d) Sugar (1982)

In contrast to the growing world market for poultry, continued surpluses and high protection in the sugar market have perpetuated trade problems over the past 30 years. The EC world market share had climbed from about 8 per cent in 1971–76 to 18 per cent in 1981.[51] US sugar producers filed a section 301 complaint on the basis that the EC sugar subsidies were depressing world sugar prices and thus hurting their own revenues. The US brought a case against the EC on sugar export policies in April 1982.[52] The case was brought under GATT Article XVI and the Subsidies Code Article 10, claiming that the EU system of export refunds, financed by a levy on domestic sugar, constituted an export subsidy over and above that which would be legal as a price stabilization instrument (as defined in Article XVI:3(2)). In addition, the subsidies had led to the EC gaining more than an equitable market share, in violation of Article 10:1, which constituted price undercutting, as covered by Article 10:3, and caused injury contrary to the obligation contained in Article 8:3.

The US-EC sugar case never went far. Bilateral consultations were adjourned (for reflection) and were never resumed. No panel was ever established. The EC joined the talks about renewing the International Sugar Agreement, though those talks failed to agree on economically meaningful trade restraints. Moreover, the US sugar policy came under increasing scrutiny, and several requests were made for consultations.[53] In 1988, the EC itself chose to challenge the US import regime, specifically the provisions under section 22 of the Agricultural Adjustment Act (as amended) that allowed the US to impose quantitative restrictions on imports.[54]

---

[50] Hudec, supra note 4, at 495.   [51] Ibid at 500.   [52] Ibid, Case No 109.
[53] These additional cases are listed as Nos 140, 186 and 187 by Hudec.
[54] As this case was primarily about market access rather than subsidies, it will not be discussed here.

The EC's sugar policy had caused problems to other countries. Australia had challenged the EC in the GATT in 1979, and Brazil followed suit in 1980.[55] Both these countries had become low-cost sugar producers and their search for markets was being hampered by the use of subsidies by the EC. One complication in the interpretation of the GATT in the case of sugar was that an international commodity agreement (the International Sugar Agreement, ISA) had been negotiated to which some but not all producers had become signatories. In particular the EC was not a member of the 1977 ISA and therefore was not obliged to restrict exports under that agreement. Clearly the other exporters resented the 'free ride' that this gave the EC, nominally a champion of commodity agreements and market management. In some respects the GATT cases were designed to put pressure on the EC to join the ISA, and indeed they had limited success in this endeavour.

The sugar disputes did not end with the GATT conflicts over subsidies. Both the US and the EC were conscious of the significance of the sugar conflicts for the ongoing Uruguay Round negotiations, and 'each side accused the other of misusing dispute settlement procedures to jockey for advantage' in the negotiations.[56] But over time the tensions over sugar became more apparent between the EC and low-cost exporters such as Australia and Brazil.

B. WTO Disputes

Since the establishment of the WTO, and the setting up of the Dispute Settlement Body, trade dispute activity has increased. But the share of agricultural cases did not keep up with the general increase. Of the 231 consultations recorded by the WTO Secretariat between 1995 and May 2001, only seven involved agricultural disputes between the US and the EC.[57] In fact, there have been very few cases that have arisen over the agricultural subsidies of any country in the period since the Uruguay Round (not counting AD and CVD cases): only one case has related to domestic subsidies, and three cases have been complaints about export subsidies.

Of these cases only one involved a conflict between the US and the EC. The one case related to export subsidies was initiated in October 1997 by the US against EC export subsidies to processed cheese.[58] The US charged that the EC was providing export subsidies, including under an inward processing arrangement, without regard to the export subsidy reduction commitments of the EC

---

[55] The US had supported these two cases, but in a rather low-key way. Hudec suggests that the US had already decided, by signing off on a somewhat weak Tokyo Round Subsidies Code, that it would not fight the EC subsidies through the GATT process. A 'secret' letter from the US to the EU authorities undertook to avoid the use of the Subsidies Code to attack the CAP: Hudec, supra note 4, at 131.

[56] Ibid at 567.

[57] About 50 of the consultations involved the US and the EC.

[58] Details are in WTO document WT/DS104/1.

with respect to processed cheese. These export subsidies, it was claimed, distorted markets for dairy products and adversely affected US sales of dairy products. The subsidies were claimed to be inconsistent with the obligations of the EC under the Agreement on Agriculture and the Agreement on Subsidies and Countervailing Measures.[59] No panel was established, and a bilateral settlement was reached relatively quickly.

The reasons for the relative lack of agricultural export and domestic subsidy cases brought under WTO rules are not hard to find. The Agreement on Agriculture includes, in Article 13, an injunction for members to exercise 'due restraint' in bringing certain cases before the WTO. In addition, the binding of subsidy levels in each member's WTO schedule is a major contribution to the transparency of such instruments. Members have to notify the WTO periodically about their subsidy levels, and these can be challenged by cross-notification. And if a country were to appear to exceed its allowed export subsidy levels, specified both in expenditure and quantity of product, or its limit for trade-distorting domestic subsidy, then a discussion in the Committee on Agriculture (set up as a part of the Uruguay Round) would act as a first avenue for multilateral pressure on that country.[60]

But institutional changes are not the only reason why subsidy disputes have proved rare under the WTO. Reform of the agricultural policies of many countries has led to a lesser reliance on export subsidies by countries that have reformed and less need for those that have not undergone such reform to continue such subsidies.[61] The US has reduced considerably its use of export subsidies for cereals, and the EC has also cut subsidy payments, though to a lesser extent. Domestic policies no longer rely on the ability to clear surpluses off the domestic market (at least, not in the grains market). This has also made it easier to live within the constraints of the WTO on domestic support. In particular, a large part of both the EC and US domestic subsidies are sheltered in the 'blue' and 'green' boxes as a result of broadly decoupling the payments from current output and price.

---

[59] The provisions of these agreements with which these measures were claimed to be inconsistent included the Agreement on Agriculture, Articles 8, 9, 10 and 11; and the Agreement on Subsidies and Countervailing Measures, Article 3.

[60] Whether as a result of the greater transparency or out of respect for the stronger dispute settlement process, countries have been remarkably careful not to exceed their allowable subsidy limits contained in the schedules. Of course, it helps that the domestic support constraints have been less than onerous as a result of aggregation across products, and that export subsidy expenditures in the first two years of the Agreement on Agriculture were sharply down as a result of a period of high world prices. See S. Tangermann, 'Agriculture on the Way to Firm International Trading Rules' in D.L.M. Kennedy & J.D. Southwick (eds), *The Political Economy of International Trade Law. Essays in Honor of Robert E. Hudec* (2002), for a fuller discussion of the implementation of the Agricultural Agreement.

[61] For a full account of the reforms in the 1990s of agricultural policies in the EC and the US see H.W. Moyer & T. Josling, *Agricultural Policy Reform: Politics and Process in the EU and US in the 1990s* (2002).

III. Lessons from past disputes

Whether to take a conflict to the GATT or WTO and make use of the dispute settlement process is ultimately a matter of trade policy. Domestic pressures will often attempt to push governments to that stage, as there is relatively little cost to the industry. (Action through domestic channels, such as anti-dumping requests, by contrast may involve financial and organizational costs.) Clearly, the economic significance of the subsidy being challenged will also be a factor, as will the extent to which the offending policy abroad causes policy problems at home. But the overuse of international panels clearly has a diplomatic cost. Considerations of which cases to take to the GATT/WTO will therefore have to include the likelihood of a favourable ruling from a panel, as well as the prospect of rapid action by the country that is found in violation and the likelihood of counter-challenges by the other party involved. The lesson from past agricultural disputes is that several of these factors have to point in the direction of taking action in the GATT/WTO before the trade irritant warrants the full weight of trade diplomacy. In many other cases the alternatives, including bilateral and other channels, may seem more attractive.

The agricultural disputes described above illustrate these lessons. Only a few cases seemed to meet the criteria for serious attempts at solution within the GATT. Pressure from domestic interests was usually the starting point for each trade conflict, in most cases resulting in a section 301 investigation as a precursor to the GATT consultations. But the US administration clearly uses a filter to ensure that the cases are both economically important and winnable. The importance of the oilseed and wheat flour cases reflect their economic as well as political significance. By contrast, the US is not a sugar exporter and has much less at stake in preventing low prices on world markets.

It is also interesting that all of the US-EC agricultural subsidy cases reviewed above (pasta, flour, wine, poultry, canned fruits, sugar, and oilseeds) had to do with processed foods or the processing sector. There are probably two main reasons for this. One is that the competition among exporters in the area of processed foods is sometimes more intense. Lucrative markets arise and exporters jostle for competitive advantage. Governments help as a way of generating revenue for primary producers and reducing pressures on farm policy. Undifferentiated raw commodities, such as wheat and corn, are sold in bulk through a network of private and public traders. It is not so clear that subsidies in one supplier country have such a negative impact on the profitability of the companies involved. And the farm interests are often cushioned by price support systems from the effect of subsidies abroad. The second reason is that the GATT rules on subsidies are less well defined and more subject to interpretation in the case of processed foods. Indeed much of the legal dispute in these cases has revolved around the scope of the 'primary product' exemption and the extent to which raw material costs can be offset by subsidies.

Under the GATT, it was fair to say that agricultural policies were decided domestically and that trade implications were usually only second-order concerns. Though the subsidy rules in the Subsidies Code did have some impact on the formulation of domestic policy, as was the case with oilseeds in the EC, the export subsidies proved impossible to constrain under the GATT.[62] Countries often did not consider the rules on export subsidies for primary products as binding constraints. In effect, countries took the view that there was not much point in pursuing export subsidies under the GATT once panels had shied away from bold interpretations under Article XVI:3, and thus no firm rulings were made.

The main lesson that many drew from the weakness of Article XVI:3 was that bilateral negotiations offered a more direct and reliable way to prevail upon a subsidizing competitor than a GATT complaint. And when the bilateral process broke down, resort to competitive subsidization was always possible. The 'subsidy wars' of the 1980s arguably had an impact on trade policy in both the US and the EC. Changes in attitudes toward the GATT were noticeable in both the EC and the US over the period. The US changed its policy from passive to aggressive in its use of the dispute settlement mechanism in the period after the Tokyo Round. About the same time the EC also decided that it should be more assertive, and formulated a defensive plan to avoid being forced to change the CAP at the directive of GATT panels.[63] The conflicts during the 1980s should therefore be seen as an aspect of domestic and trade strategy as much as a reflection of the adequacy of the GATT to resolve agricultural subsidy disputes.

IV. PROSPECTS FOR THE FUTURE

The impact of the introduction of new trade rules for agriculture under the WTO has very sharply changed the relationship between domestic and trade policy. The significance of the Uruguay Round in changing the legal basis for trade disputes cannot be too strongly emphasized. After the Uruguay Round Agreement on Agriculture, the rules and commitments became much clearer. The EU and the US have broadly honoured their commitments, including exhibiting 'due restraint'. Scope for conflict has indeed been constrained, or perhaps redirected into areas not so clearly covered by the Agreement on Agriculture.[64]

[62] The success of the two actions against domestic subsidies should not be underestimated. In both cases the EC changed its domestic policy. The oilseeds case had a particularly important role in the development of the CAP.

[63] P.W.B. Phillips, *Wheat, Europe and the GATT: A Political Economy Analysis* (1990).

[64] The most intractable transatlantic agricultural disputes since the establishment of the WTO have been the beef hormone and banana disputes. The beef hormone dispute was about whether the EC had used risk analysis as required by the SPS Agreement in banning the use of six hormones in beef production—see T. Josling, D. Roberts & A. Hassan, *The Beef-Hormone Dispute and its Implications for Trade Policy*, European Forum Working Paper, Stanford University, September 1999. The banana

Are we in for more agricultural trade disputes in the future? Will they clog up the dispute settlement system? Traditional conflicts over subsidies may not be so important in the future. The use of export subsidies in agriculture is on the retreat. The US makes little use of export subsidies and the EC would be happy to be able to give up its dependence on a policy instrument that costs money and benefits foreign consumers (who rarely appreciate the largesse). The EC Commission has signalled in the context of the current agricultural negotiations that it is prepared for further reductions in export subsidies. One would therefore be surprised if conflicts over export subsidies ever became as contentious as in the 1980s.

Conflicts over domestic subsidies to agriculture are likely, by contrast, to continue. They may, however, change in nature, with tensions moving from subsidies to processing to environmental and rural amenity payments, compensation for the costs of animal welfare regulations, and structural assistance to rural areas. And it is probable that there will be trade tensions between the EC and the US over the definitions of subsidies falling into the various categories of the Agreement on Agriculture.[65]

Perhaps the most controversial issue at present is the status of 'counter-cyclical' payments. For the past three years the US has supplemented the 'green' box payments authorized under the 1996 Federal Agricultural Improvement Reform Act with large emergency payments ('Market Loss Assistance') to counter the effect of weak commodity prices on farm incomes. Versions of the next Farm Bill that are being discussed in Congress at the time of writing (May 2003) include a continuation of these counter-cyclical payments. The question is how will they be notified to the WTO? As green box payments, even though they are clearly not divorced from price levels? Or as amber box payments, in which case the limit on such payments (currently $19 billion) would be breached?

Underlying all these issues is the significance of the Peace Clause, ie, Article 13 of the Agreement on Agriculture, that expires in 2003. The question is will there be an explosion of subsidy disputes when the Peace Clause is no longer in place to shelter agricultural subsidies? The Peace Clause has a significance in direct

---

conflict involved violations of GATT Article XIII and the GATS in its allocation of licences for banana imports from Latin America—T. Josling & T. Taylor (eds), *Banana Wars: A Multifaceted Story of Policies in Conflict* (2002). Neither involved any aspect of EC subsidies for agriculture. Similarly, the long-simmering 'non-dispute' about the slow pace of licensing transgenic crops for use on the European market does not relate to agricultural subsidies or farm programmes—I. Sheldon & T. Josling, *Biotech Regulations and the WTO*, paper presented at the IATRC Conference, Tucson, December 2001.

[65] The Agreement on Agriculture specifies three types of domestic support policies: 'amber' box policies that operate directly as price support or are tied to the price of inputs; 'blue' box policies that constitute subsidies conditional on restrictions on output, land use or animal numbers; and 'green' box policies that are not related to current output or prices. Support under 'amber' box policies is calculated (the Aggregate Measure of Support, or AMS) and the allowable expenditures on such policies are agreed in the WTO schedules. Thus disagreements over the definition of a subsidy are most likely to arise when a country is accused by another WTO member of avoiding the bound constraints on amber box policies by labelling (notifying) them as green.

proportion to the likelihood (or the perception of the likelihood) of the success of subsidy challenges under the WTO. The story of the GATT cases discussed in this paper is relevant to this issue. The Peace Clause effectively protects export subsidies (and green box domestic subsidies as well) from the disciplines of Article XVI:3.[66] Experience does not suggest that resort to Article XVI:3 is a sure remedy for aggrieved exporters attempting to restrain export subsidies. 'Open season' on farm subsidies may depend on panels being much more definitive in considering the meaning of 'equitable share of world trade'.

If the WTO dispute settlement mechanism will not necessarily be the locus of the resolution to the trade disputes over subsidies to farm products, between the US and the EC as between other countries, where will the action be? Experience in the Kennedy, Tokyo and Uruguay Rounds suggests that subsidy disputes can be used as a lever in GATT/WTO negotiations. Clearly the current round of trade negotiations will be pivotal in regard to agricultural subsidies. The outcome will determine the future of the special treatment of domestic agricultural subsidies as well as the fate of export subsidies for primary products. One might therefore expect to see some activity aimed at 'clarifying' the interpretation of the WTO agreements as a way of encouraging the negotiation of further reductions in agricultural support and subsidy levels.

With hindsight, the period 1995–2001 may prove to have been the lull before the storm for domestic subsidy disputes between the EU and the US.

---

[66] In addition, export subsidies are protected from challenge under countervailing duty not supported by evidence of injury or threat of injury and from action under the Subsidies Agreement Articles 3, 5 and 6. See R. Steinberg & T. Josling, 'Vulnerability of EU and US Agricultural Subsidies to WTO Challenge with the Expiry of the Peace Clause', *Journal of International Economic Law*, Spring 2003, for a detailed examination of the significance of relaxing the Peace Clause.

Our ref.	Title / Complainant / Defendant/Case Type	Date / Start/ End	Panel	Outcome	301 case / Date Initiated / Initiator	301 actions	Comments	Reinhardt case no	Hudec case no
1	Subsidies of Malt Exports US / EC /				301-5 / 13-Nov-75 / Great Western Malt Company	EC reduced subsidy in 1976; with petitioner's agreement, USTR terminated investigation (19 Jun 1980)			
2	Subsidies on Wheat Flour US / EEC / SCM case	10/8/81 / 1981 / 1983	Panel could not find violation; report not adopted in SCM	Subsidy war	301-6 / 1-Dec-75 / Millers' National Association	Consultations held under GATT in 1977 and 1980; President directed USTR to pursue dispute settlement (1 Aug 1980)	301: US retaliated with subsidy on US wheat flour exports to Egypt (resulted in Hudec case 123) shortly before GATT issues inconclusive panel report	119	103
					301-16 / 2-Nov-78 / Great Plains Wheat, Inc.	After public hearings and consultations, parties agreed to monitor development and consult further, USTR terminated investigation (1 Aug 1980)			

| 3 | Subsidies on Pasta Products US / EEC / SCM case | 2/24/82 / 1982 / 1986 | Panel split: 3:1, majority found EU subsidy illegal, report non-adopted in SCM | Tariff war; 1986 tentative bilateral settlement of pasta and citrus cases—EU reduced subsidies | 301–11 / 12-Nov-76 / Florida Citrus Commission et al | Formal GATT consultations held under Art XXIII (20 Apr 1982), full GATT panel report submitted (14 Dec 1984); after earlier agreement fell through, US and EC reached agreement to concede tariffs and retaliatory duties (10 Aug 1986); further agreements increased EC cheese quota and lowered US tariffs under authority of the Omnibus Trade and Competitiveness Act of 1988 (21 Dec 1988); settlement also led to pasta agreement (see case 301–25) | GATT: US responded with increased tariff on EU pasta, in retaliation for EU citrus tariff preferences for Mediterranean; EU retaliated with higher tariffs on US lemon and walnuts. 301: President determined that EC practices constitute an unfair burden, imposed duties on pasta products (6 Jul 1985); EC imposed retaliatory tariffs on US lemons and walnuts (8 Jul 1985) |

(Continued)

ANNEX: (Continued)

Our ref.	Title / Complainant / Defendant/Case Type	Date / Start/ End	Panel	Outcome	301 case / Date Initiated / Initiator	301 actions	Comments	Reinhardt case no	Hudec case no
					301–25 / 16-Oct-81 / National Pasta Association	After several US-EC consultations, US requested dispute settlement panel from Subsidies Code Committee (7 Apr 1982); panel report favouring US submitted to the Committee (19 May 1983); US raised tariffs on pasta imports in retaliation against EC discriminatory citrus tariffs in 1985 and 1986, US reached agreement with EC to negotiate pasta dispute in connection with citrus settlement, see case 301–11 (10 Aug 1986); agreement reached to reduce EC pasta export subsidies by 27.5 per cent (15 Sep 1987)			

| 4 | Subsidies on Poultry US / EEC / SCM case | 2/24/82 / 1982 / 1984 | No panel established | Trilateral consultations; mutual restraint on X-sub agreed | 301–23 / 17-Sep-81 / National Broiler Council | US-EC consultations held under Art. 12:3 of the Subsidies Code (16 Feb 1982); President directed expeditious examination of Brazilian subsidies, in response to EC claims that their subsidies were necessary to compete against subsidized Brazilian poultry exports (12 Jul 1982); US conducted several informal and formal consultations with Brazil and the EC (30 Aug 1982–23 Jun 1983); US requested 'conciliation', Subsidies Code Committee held five conciliation meetings with no resolution (16 Oct 1984); no action reported in 1990 | GATT: US also involved Brazil | 122 | 106 |

(Continued)

Our ref.	Title / Complainant / Defendant/Case Type	Date / Start/ End	Panel	Outcome	301 case / Date Initiated / Initiator	301 actions	Comments	Reinhardt case no	Hudec case no
5	Production Aids— Canned Fruit US / EEC / GATT case	3/19/82 / 1982 / 1986	Panel found violation for subsidies to processors of peaches and pears, but not for growers, and not for dried grapes; adoption of report blocked by EU	Bilateral settlement with EU reducing subsidies and limiting amount	301–26 / 23-Oct-81 / California Cling Peach Advisory Board et al 301–71 / 8-May-89 / USTR	US consulted with EC under GATT Art XXIII (25 Feb 1982); final dispute panel report issued (20 Jul 1985); President directed USTR to recommend retaliation unless case resolved by 1 Dec 1985 (7 Sep 1985); after threat of retaliation, US and EC reached settlement to phase out processing subsidies (Dec 1985); following consultations over EC failure to fully implement agreement, new investigation (301–71) initiated, and this investigation terminated (1 Oct 1989) EC agreed to reduce its canned fruit subsidies, US and EC clarified interpretation of 1985 Canned Fruit Agreement (see case 301–26) (Jun 1989); USTR terminated investigation (1 Oct 1989)		123	107

6	Export Subsidies on Sugar US / EEC / SCM case	4/7/82 / 1982 / 1983	No panel established; related to failed negotiations on ISA	301–22 / 20-Aug-81 / Great Western Sugar Company	Bilateral consultations adjourned and never resumed	US–EC consultations held under Art. 12:3 of the Subsidies Code (16 Feb 1982); President directed USTR to continue international efforts to eliminate or reduce EC subsidies (28 Jun 1984); USTR denied request of petitioner to reactivate investigation, citing agricultural export subsidies negotiations underway in Uruguay Round (29 Jul 1987); no action reported in 1990	GATT: later, EU (and others) raised complaints about US sugar import restrictions (Hudec 140, 186, 187)	125	109
7	Export Subsidy—Flour to Egypt EEC / US / SCM case	4/7/83/ 1983 / 1983	Panel established but never constituted	According to US sources, US did not offer subsidized low price to Egypt in following year		GATT: explicit purpose of US subs. was to retaliate against EU subsidies (Hudec case 103)	149	123

(Continued)

ANNEX: (Continued)

Our ref.	Title / Complainant / Defendant/Case Type	Date / Start/ End	Panel	Outcome	301 case / Date Initiated / Initiator	301 actions	Comments	Reinhardt case no	Hudec case no
8	Oilseeds Subsidy US / EEC / GATT case	4/22/88/ 1988 / 1992	Panel finds violation of Art III.4 and nullification or impairment, report adopted; reconvened panel finds Art III.4 violation removed by not nullification or impairment	Bilateral settlement at Blair House I	301-63 / 16-Dec-87 / American Soybean Association	US consulted with EC several times both informally and under GATT Art XXIII, EC acquiesced to forming a dispute panel (27 Jun 1989), after favourable panel decision, USTR concluded that US rights were being denied, decided to conclude the investigation and monitor EC compliance with the panel report (31 Jan 1990)	GATT: after adoption of first report, EU changes regime; after second panel, EU tries unsuccessfully to renegotiate tariff binding; US prepares for retaliation	208	179
9	301 Retaliation Threat-Oilseed EEC / US /	7/18/89/ 1989 / 1989						228	200
10	Measures Affecting the Exportation of Processed Cheese US / EC / WTO complaint	1997					WTO document WT/DS104/1		
11	Definition of Wine Industry for CVD EC / US / SMC case	1984					US grape growers (but not wine producers) complained about EU export subsidies for wine; WTO document: WT/DS137/1		

7

The Trade Disputes Concerning Health Policy Between the EC and the US

P.C. MAVROIDIS*

I. NOT WORLDS APART WHEN IT COMES TO HEALTH REGULATION

For a number of reasons that lie beyond my mandate for this paper, transatlantic disputes stemming from divergent health regulation have been quite limited so far. In fact, the only such dispute in this field has been the one over the prohibition to import into the European Community (EC) hormone-treated beef—the notorious Hormones dispute. There is speculation that the evolving regulatory strategy of the EC with respect to genetically modified organisms (GMOs) might lead to one additional dispute; such speculation has however, so far, failed to materialize. As time passes by, the possibility for a new dispute becomes a probability, a remote probability and so on.

The WTO is a negative integration-type of contract when it comes to health policies and, as a result, health policies are unilaterally defined. The disciplines imposed by the WTO contract could be summarized as the obligation to observe non-discrimination (GATT, GATS, TBT, SPS), to ensure that the legislative intervention is necessary to reach the unilaterally defined goals (GATT, GATS, TBT, SPS) and to use, in principle, scientific evidence when regulating (SPS). Hence, depending on whether a particular measure comes under the GATT or another WTO covered agreement, the obligations imposed on the WTO membership might differ.

On both occasions (that is, Hormones and GMOs), the EC regulatory interventions have affected trade interests in the United States. The US private sector alerted the US government to the negative impact that EC policy had on them and persuaded the US Trade Representative (USTR) to submit the disputes to the

* Henrik Horn, Rob Howse, Patrick Low and Joost Pauwelyn kindly discussed with me all issues treated in this paper. Professor George Bermann (Columbia Law School, New York) offered comments on this case-study. Ernst-Ulrich Petersmann read and re-read the manuscript and, without implicating him as to the final result, helped me address a series of inadequacies that appeared in previous drafts.

World Trade Organization (WTO). Only the Hormones dispute, however, followed the normal channel for adjudication of trade disputes before the WTO (consultations, panel proceedings, Appellate Body report).

The dispute linked to the disagreement between the US and the EC as to the latter's strategy with respect to GMOs has not so far reached the panel stage in the WTO. The US, the original complainant in the dispute, has so far decided against moving beyond bilateral consultations, the precise content of which has not been made public. It is not unthinkable that they have settled their dispute; at the time of writing, however, no settlement has been notified to the WTO in accordance with Article 3.6 of the Dispute Settlement Understanding (DSU).

It seems more plausible that the US assessment of the situation now is that a potential complaint against the EC in this context will not yield the expected returns. For Community action is most likely in conformity with the WTO Agreement on Sanitary and Phytosanitary Standards (SPS) whereas EC member states' actions can find legal refuge in the Appellate Body's interpretation of the term 'like products' in the very recent *Asbestos* dispute, where the Appellate Body, albeit in a rather cryptic manner, opted for an interpretation of the term which internalizes risk factors independently of market analysis.[1]

Howse and Mavroidis resume this point in the following manner:

...the thrust of EU-level regulation as it is evolving from the original 1990 Directive through the amended directive is to base decisions about the placing on the market of GMO products within the Union on a case-by-case scientific assessment of the risk to human health and the environment. This is subject to the possibility of precautionary action, where there is not sufficient scientific knowledge available to evaluate risk in the case of some particular GMO. This approach is consonant with evolving international standards, as reflected in the FAO Statement on Biotechnology and the *Cartagena Protocol on Biosafety*. The basic structure of EU regulation as reflected in the amended directive raises few serious risks of violating the SPS Agreement. However, where individual member states choose to act on the basis, in whole or in part, of ethical concerns or considerations (which the amended directive allows them to 'take into account'), and where the measure could not also be wholly justified based on a scientific assessment of the risk, a situation could arise where the appropriate WTO framework be Article III of the GATT and, depending upon whether ethical concerns would be found on a basis for distinguishing modified and unmodified products as 'unlike' products, Article XX(a) of the GATT, the 'public morals' provision might also be justified. However, one of the most promising features of the *amended directive* is the emphasis on public consultation, and

---

[1] By this I do not mean that I subscribe to each and every aspect of the Appellate Body's interpretation of the term. To my mind, a market analysis (that is, a definition of the term 'like/directly substitutable products' using cross-price elasticity as the instrument for analysis instead of the opinion of the bench), would probably end up with a similar outcome: it could very well be the case that European consumers, for reasons that have to do both with information (awareness of risks stemming from the consumption of asbestos-containing products) but also with influence of their consumption pattern by regulation (the fact that they have been living—most of them, at least—within regulatory states), are quite risk averse. See the Appellate Body report on *European Communities—Measures Affecting Asbestos And Asbestos-Containing Products*, WTO Doc WT/DS135/AB/R of 12 March 2001, especially at §122.

publicity and transparency of reasons for decisions with respect to GMOs. Public dissemination of risk assessments and assessment reports, and consultation procedures prior to each decision, as well as in the course of EU-level review of such decisions, may well lead to a more focused and informed public discourse about what is at stake in the GMOs debate. At the same time, such transparency and publicity provides trading partners with additional assurances against the possibility that hidden protection is embedded in case-by-case regulatory decision-making.[2]

Hence, the dispute, at least for the time being, seems to have been set aside. Although in the rest of the paper I deal only with the Hormones dispute, my remarks on dispute-prevention are, however, relevant for a discussion on the EC regulatory strategy with respect to GMOs. In Section 2, I discuss the Hormones dispute and in Section 3, I discuss whether the particular dispute could have been prevented. In Section 4, I move to a more general discussion on dispute prevention.

II. THE HORMONES DISPUTE

A. The factual aspects of the dispute in a nutshell

The facts of the Hormones dispute could be summarized as follows: the EC enacted a Directive which prohibited the sale of hormone-treated beef throughout the EC market. Beef-producers (domestic and foreign) had to incur adjustment costs as a result. The EC market being a lucrative market for US producers and in light of the fact that they were not willing to assume adjustment costs,[3] they asked their government (USTR) to consult and eventually bring a complaint against the EC before the WTO adjudicating bodies.[4]

Consultations led nowhere and a complaint was subsequently lodged. The case was adjudicated under the SPS Agreement which requests that WTO members base, in principle, their regulatory interventions on scientific evidence, but, exceptionally, and respecting the conditions laid down in Article 5.7 SPS, they will be allowed to go ahead with interventions unsupported by science to the extent that they have invoked the *precautionary principle*.

The EC, in the Appellate Body's view, did not possess (neither at the time when the Directive was enacted, nor when the panel was established) any scientific evidence to back up its measures, and neither had it invoked the precautionary principle (Article 5.7 SPS). Under the circumstances, and although the Appellate Body extended the relevance of the precautionary principle beyond the limits of

---

[2] R. Howse & P.C. Mavroidis, 'Europe's Evolving Regulatory Strategy For GMOs—The Issue Of Consistency With WTO Law: Of Kine And Brine' (2000) 24 *Fordham International Law Journal* 317 at 370.

[3] There was evidence in the record that some US beef producers did adjust their production along the lines of the EC Directive.

[4] Canada brought its own complaint as well. In light of the quasi identity of the two complaints, in the remaining part of this paper I focus only on the US complaint.

Article 5.7 SPS, the EC practices were found to be contrary to its obligations under the WTO.[5] As happens under the WTO contract, the EC was granted a reasonable period of time during which it was called to bring its measures into compliance. Its failure to do so provoked a request by the US to adopt counter-measures against it up to the amount of the damage suffered by US producers as a result of the EC Directive.

The two parties disagreed as to the amount of countermeasures (suspension of concessions, in WTO parlance) and the WTO arbitrators were requested to determine their level. They estimated that the US was justified to adopt counter-measures worth $191 million which have been in place ever since.[6] The EC has unilaterally claimed that it now has evidence which justifies the continuing application of the EC Directive.[7] It has not, however, at the time of writing taken a formal *demarche* before the WTO competent authorities to this effect (either by submitting the case as a new dispute before a panel, or, eventually, by requesting the establishment of a 'compliance panel' under Article 21.5 DSU). Consequently, the US countermeasures are still in place.

B. Why a dispute about hormones?

As stated above, WTO members are free to choose the health policies they want to enact at the domestic level. At one extreme (although, arguably, a mere theoretical possibility which probably does not occur in practice), one could imagine WTO members without any health policy. Were WTO members to enact health policies, they would have to apply them in a way that conforms to their WTO obligations. As a result, regulatory diversity among WTO members with respect to health policies can peacefully co-exist with WTO membership. Societies differ: some are risk averse, some not, some more and some less so; some can afford elaborate health policies (because they can generate or simply buy scientific knowledge) and some cannot. Knowledge of the risk is the first step towards design of health policies and it should not be presumed to be available everywhere.

Of course, health policies can be used (and indeed have been sometimes in the past) as a cover for protectionist purposes. The WTO standards to adjudicate health-based trade-obstructing measures serve this objective in principle: to distinguish the wheat from the chaff. In light of the present level of integration among WTO members, the overarching standard of compatibility (to check the necessity but not the proportionality *stricto sensu* of the measure) seems a reasonable one. Only in a constitutional context will the judge move to a *stricto sensu* proportionality, that is he/she will refuse the right to regulatory intervention even when the least restrictive option is used if the negative externalities outweigh the benefits.

---

[5] See the Appellate Body report on *European Communities—Import Restrictions on Meat And Meat Products (Hormones)*, WTO Doc WT/DS26/AB/R.

[6] See the Report By the Arbitrators in WTO Doc WT/DS26/ARB.

[7] See *Financial Times*, 12 May 2000.

Assuming that hormone-treated beef can present a risk to human health (something which was not established during the proceedings at least through recourse to scientific evidence), the EC represents, in this respect, a model of a relatively more risk averse society than the US. Affected US beef-producers lost a lucrative market as a result of the EC intervention and the US agreed to represent their interests before the WTO.

It is the unilateral setting of policies in this respect which is at the origin of the dispute. By this I do not mean that harmonization of health policies (or indeed, any policies) is necessary to avoid trade disputes. There are substantial gains from regulatory competition and the EC itself provides an excellent empirically-tested example showing how regulatory competition can go hand in hand with integration.

All I aim to state here is that the unilateral setting of policies affecting trade carries a risk: WTO members might have the incentive to pursue 'beggar thy neighbour' policies. Since the WTO contract does not provide its members with the carrot to 'internalize' externalities imposed on third parties from the pursuance of national policies, the remaining question is to what extent the WTO contract contains the stick to do so. The stick is, of course, the multilaterally authorized US countermeasures. They have been in place for over three years now and the EC has yet to amend its policies. If the objective function of countermeasures is to persuade recalcitrant WTO members to adopt policies that conform to WTO standards, on this occasion, at least, they have failed. Does this mean that there were no gains at all from submitting this dispute to the WTO? I will argue in what follows, that such a conclusion is quite erroneous.

C. What has been achieved by submitting instead of settling?

As stated above, the US and the EC could not arrive at a bilateral settlement of their dispute and hence the US submitted their complaint to a WTO panel. Was this an unwarranted outcome? The Hormones dispute was the first dispute in the SPS context. The SPS Agreement is one of the 'new generation' WTO agreements where, before Hormones, no practice at all existed. The Hormones report paved the way for two more disputes in the same area. The gains from submitting the dispute to the WTO are, to my mind, substantial.

1. Transparency

As already stated, the only truly transparent aspect of WTO dispute settlement procedures is the multilateral phase. The by-product of the decision to move the dispute to the panel phase was transparency with respect to the EC hormones policy.[8]

---

[8] A purist would respond that this is not a first-best. True. The first-best would be that the WTO membership takes some time to discuss what is wrong with the WTO contract when it comes to requesting notification of bilateral deals. Until that happens, however, only panel processes can guarantee transparency.

2. *Jurisprudence has clarified some aspects of the SPS Agreement*

The panel and the Appellate Body that dealt with this dispute have provided us with some important clarifications of the SPS Agreement:

- we now know that the obligation to have recourse to scientific evidence means that regulatory interventions that are enacted following minority opinions can be in conformity with WTO law;
- we also know, albeit in a rather cryptic manner, that for evidence to be judged scientific, it will have to respect the standards/methodology of the relevant scientific field;
- we further know that the Appellate Body is prepared to show a certain degree of deference towards the intervening authority when adjudicating health-related disputes (a good example is that scientific expertise supporting a regulatory intervention can be submitted for the first time at the panel stage; or that the precautionary principle is not exhausted in Article 5.7 SPS);
- we know that the WTO adjudicating bodies welcome the use of expert witnesses in such disputes and are prepared to appoint experts beyond those appointed by the parties.

All of the above findings helped streamline the WTO case-law in the field of SPS and undoubtedly will continue to be of relevance in the disputes to come.

3. *Institutional gains*

Most importantly, as the SPS disputes submitted to the WTO post-Hormones show, WTO members show their confidence in the WTO institutions by entrusting them with disputes concerning one of the most sensitive fields of domestic regulation. In a way, the Hormones dispute paved the way for more disputes in the field of SPS to be submitted for adjudication to the WTO.

This observation should not be taken lightheartedly: it is one thing for an adjudicating body to discuss an anti-dumping case where protection is afforded in order to protect domestic producers' welfare; it is a different thing to discuss a health-based trade-obstructing measure where, *prima facie* at least, this is not the case. The motive of the regulatory intervention is not relevant when imposing anti-dumping duties; unearthing the true motive of the regulatory intervention in the health example is probably what the dispute will be all about.

The quality of the judicial review and the ensuing quantity of intrusion into the sphere of domestic policy is hence different in the two cases. The WTO membership has to be persuaded that the multilateral adjudicating bodies will treat cases relating to deviations from WTO obligations for non-economic motives with the extra care needed.[9] Through the deferential stance that the

---

[9] The argument, of course, could be advanced that by moving to negative consensus when it comes to establishing panels, much of this discussion is now obsolete. I do not share this view. Practice in the SPS so far suggests that WTO members have submitted only disputes where there was a pre-perceived quasi certainty as to the outcome.

Appellate Body adopted in Hormones, it did signal its resolve to take this extra care. As already stated, two cases in the same field followed shortly thereafter.

III. So, should we be preventing disputes among the transatlantic partners?

It follows from the above that, by submitting the dispute to the WTO, there were some important institutional gains: transparency as to what was in dispute and the ensuing outcome; a jurisprudential evolution in the field of SPS (an agreement most of the provisions of which are far from being self-interpreting); and increased confidence in the WTO membership regarding the use of the WTO dispute settlement procedures even for sensitive cases such as the Hormones dispute.

Is there a downside? For a start, administrative resources (national and international) were committed to resolving the dispute. The opportunity cost is probably not too high (at least as far as the international, WTO, resources are concerned). I think the major downside stems from the EC unwillingness to bring its measures into compliance with the WTO. As a result, the US requested and was authorized to adopt countermeasures. The Hormones dispute thus turned to a mechanism for the EC to re-distribute income internally: those hit by US countermeasures saw their income shrink whereas the income of EC (non-hormone-treated) beef producers flourished. If this outcome is inefficient, then the dispute should probably have been avoided. But any study of the inefficiency of the outcome must reflect the willingness of EC consumers[10] to purchase only hormone-free beef. I assume for the rest of the paper that the two objectives (EC consumers purchase hormone-free beef and there is no need to re-distribute income inside the EC as a result of this consumer preference) can live happily together and I move on to examine how the dispute could have been prevented.

I propose to examine this issue under two hypotheses:

(A) Would consultations *before* adoption of the EC Directive have helped 'smooth out' the divergent points of view expressed on the two sides of the Atlantic?
(B) What kind of settlement could/should have been reached following the adoption of the EC Directive (that is, during the WTO-mandated consultations) that would help avoid the submission of the dispute to a WTO panel?

A. Consultations before the adoption of the EC Directive

It is of course an awkward exercise to construct such a counter-argument. This is why I propose a minimalist approach here so as to avoid far-reaching

[10] I assume that the EC regulatory intervention was not a 'top down' postulate, but the result of a fruitful democratic dialogue.

conclusions. For the purposes of this hypothesis, I assume that the EC invites all interested affected parties (domestic and foreign) to express their point of view prior to the adoption of the Directive. The EC policy will eventually be decided by weighing at least the following factors (not necessarily in this order):

- public anxieties;
- domestic producers' interests;
- domestic consumers' interests; and, since the process is open to foreign interests as well,
- foreign producers' interests; and
- the costs associated with the possibility that the regulatory intervention, if challenged, might be found to be illegal.

There is of course a substantial overlap between the anxieties of the public and the interests of consumers: although consumers (the wider public) would rather pay less than more for the same item, they are (normally) prepared to pay a mark-up to ensure that they will suffer no health problems from the consumption of the item at hand.

Domestic producers' concerns arguably go in the opposite direction. To the extent that they, or at least some of them, incur adjustments costs, they would be opposed to any such measure. It is difficult, however, to mount a serious challenge against an intellectually-coherent health policy. The problem lies in the fact that the EC was not in possession of unambiguous clear-cut scientific evidence that hormone-treated beef is dangerous to human health. At any rate, the interests of those having to incur adjustment costs could be taken care of through subsidies. Payment of such subsidies would guarantee that consumers (as opposed to taxpayers) would not have to internalize the cost of the new health policy (although one should, given the anxieties of the public, assume that a willingness to at least partially cover the ensuing cost should be present).

Foreign producers' interests would constitute the other argument against adoption of the EC Directive. But then again, depending on the importance of adjustment costs, some foreign producers (and indeed, there is empirical evidence that this had been the case in Hormones) would be willing to unilaterally adjust their production patterns along the lines of the EC regulation. The representatives of those foreign producers who refuse to adjust (and who, unlike their EC counterparts, do not benefit from EC subsidies) will make all the noise against adoption of the EC Directive. The discussion will hence move swiftly to a preliminary assessment of the legality of the future regulation.

As is clear from a plain reading of the SPS Agreement, the anxieties of the public can be legitimately protected, at least on a short to medium-term basis, not only in cases where scientific evidence backs up those anxieties but also in cases where there is merely a fear that they might be realized.[11] If the status of

---

[11] This is essentially what the precautionary principle amounts to. When invoked, however, it will have to respect the conditions laid down in the Appellate Body report on *Varietals*, see WTO Doc WT/DS76/AB/R.

scientific evolution is such that it is expected that missing evidence will be acquired within a specified time-horizon, then invoking the precautionary principle is a safe path. Hence, from day one, the EC policy makers know that it is relatively easy to meet the standard of legality expressed in the WTO contract provided that their measure qualifies as an SPS measure and that the SPS Agreement takes precedence over the GATT.

There should be relative certainty among EC legal circles that both these conditions could have been easily met: the EC Directive could relatively easily incorporate the substantive content of an SPS measure as explained in the Annex to the SPS Agreement; moreover, because the SPS Agreement contains a more stringent standard for compliance than Article XX GATT (the need for scientific evidence and the so-called *consistency* requirement expressed in Article 5.5 SPS), the EC authorities could legitimately expect that potential complaining parties would choose the SPS Agreement as the appropriate forum to adjudicate this dispute.

On the other hand, in the presence of the institutional acknowledgement that WTO members can block trade even without support from science, foreign interests would have an Everest to climb in their efforts to persuade the EC not to regulate: they would have to make a persuasive affirmative case that science today insists that no risks can ever stem from the consumption of hormone-treated beef.

But let us assume that the opinion that the EC measure is in violation of the WTO obligations prevails. How much does the EC risk? The EC risks counter-measures the level of which is measured by using a trade effects test: they cannot be higher than the amount of trade diverted from the EC market as a result of the enactment of the EC Directive. The EC has good reasons to assume that not all affected producers will have automatic recourse to countermeasures, for countermeasures are costly.[12] At the end of the day, in the worst case scenario, the EC will have to answer one question: can we afford $191 million worth of counter-measures to protect a health objective of dubious consistency with our WTO obligations? The response will be eased by the fact that there is already over-whelming support among EC citizens to go ahead with the measure.

Therefore, in principle, it seems that the EC authorities would, in the presence of domestic anxieties about hormone-treated beef, most likely end up with enacting the Directive anyway, that is, independently of the degree of involve-ment of foreign interests in the preparatory stages of the Directive.

B. Alternative (successful) consultations after the adoption of the EC Directive

Before discussing whether the picture would have been any different if consult-ations (in the sense of Article 4 DSU) had followed a different pattern, I would like to point out that one cannot rule out a bilateral deal being agreed which would

[12] On this issue, see P.C. Mavroidis, 'Remedies in the WTO Legal System: Between a Rock and a Hard Place' (2000) 11 *European Journal of International Law* 763.

either not have been notified at all or would have been notified in an inadequate/ unsatisfactory manner to the WTO. Indeed, as time and again we have heard from official lips, notification (or, better, absence) of bilateral deals, according to Article 3.6 DSU, is one of the 'black holes' of the system. In the absence of notifications, we are in a difficult, if not impossible, situation to judge whether a bilateral deal respects, as it should in light of Article 3.5 DSU, the WTO contract.

At the current state of affairs, the only fully transparent (as to the ambit of the dispute, the outcome, the implementation process) part of the WTO process is that before the WTO adjudicating bodies (the multilateral part, as opposed to the bilateral consultations). Since the WTO is a multilateral contract and since the cornerstone of the system is the principle of non-discrimination, recourse to non-transparent bilateralism should be viewed with scepticism: for even if no trade interests of third parties are involved, the legal interest to see the contract observed could be affected.

Now I turn to the question I originally asked in this sub-section, namely whether consultations could have followed a different pattern? Now we are in the presence of a markedly different situation: legislation is in place, it is not based on science and the EC has not invoked the precautionary principle either. The EC further knows that any settlement must respect the principle of non-discrimination and, I assume, continues to hold the view that hormone-treated beef should not enter the EC market.

In light of these factors (and the knowledge that countermeasures, in light of the trade involved and a series of other relevant factors,[13] cannot be that harmful), it seems improbable that the EC would be willing to modify its position at this stage.

C. What happened then on the way to heaven?

My analysis so far might seem absurd since I have argued above that the EC could feel reasonably secure about its position, and yet the EC lost before the WTO. How did that happen? To my mind, this happened because the EC did not have the scientific evidence to justify the ban *and* took the political decision not to invoke the precautionary principle. Beyond scientific evidence and the precautionary principle there is no other basis in the SPS Agreement on which regulatory interventions can be based.

It is difficult, if not occasionally presumptuous, to be sure about what might have happened. In light of the *Varietals* case-law, however, I think that had the EC invoked the precautionary principle, it would have left the WTO dispute settlement process on a winning note. And this is what, to my mind, justifies the inflexibility that I describe in sub-sections 3.A and 3.B above.

---

[13] Such as, for example, the possibility of diverting lost export trade, the likelihood that some foreign producers will find the EC market too attractive to avoid adjustment costs, etc.

IV. Is DISPUTE PREVENTION A VALUE IN ITSELF?

Disputes arise of course from differences of opinion. Not all differences of opinion however lead to disputes. Some form of regulatory co-operation between the two transatlantic partners does already take place and is probably intended to serve the purpose of having fewer disputes. The US and the EC have already enacted mutual recognition agreements (MRAs) which substantially reduce the possibility for disputes.[14] To the extent that there are gains from co-operation, such agreements will proliferate. Once again, however, as a series of papers edited by Bermann *et al* point out, the challenge will be to ensure that bilateral gains will not be outweighed by costs at the multilateral level.[15]

In the meantime, that is until regulatory co-operation significantly reduces the risk of seeing transatlantic disputes being brought before the WTO adjudicating bodies, when talking of trade-related disputes, probably the most important aspect of the discussion is the multilateral character of the WTO contract. To discuss and agree behind closed doors and eventually shift costs to non-participants does more damage than the actual costs inflicted: it reduces confidence in the system to administer regulatory policies with impact beyond national borders.

Therefore, the issue of prevention viewed from this angle must be subordinated to the legal obligation and indeed the systemic need to preserve the multilateral character of the WTO contract: a reinvigorated Article 3.6 DSU which would ensure that settlements are notified in detail and discussed *in extenso* by the WTO membership is the necessary pre-condition for any discussion on dispute prevention. In other words, dispute prevention should always respect the balance of rights and obligations struck during the Uruguay Round and expressed in the WTO contract. Now, more than ever, the EC and the US should not only declare but behave as (important) parts of a larger construction.

By this I mean that dispute prevention is not a value in itself: it all depends on *how* it is practised. Yes, it is true that from a probabilistic analysis point of view, the more cases we submit to the WTO, the higher the risk of ending up with a wrong outcome. And this pattern of thinking would suggest that it is probably better to under rather than over-submit. The danger of wrong outcomes can, however, be reduced by providing sufficient normative guidance to adjudicators, by selecting the right people to act as such, and by providing them with adequate institutional guarantees.

The existing WTO framework does not, as empirical evidence now amply suggests, safeguard the system against the risk of WTO-inconsistent dispute prevention. To my mind, however, by observing the WTO disciplines (as the

---

[14] See K. Nicolaidis, 'Non-Discriminatory Mutual Recognition: An Oxymoron In The New WTO Lexicon?' in T. Cottier & P.C. Mavroidis (eds), *Regulatory Barriers And The Principle Of Non-Discrimination In World Trade Law* (2000), 267 and the comments by A. Beviglia-Zampetti, 'Mutual Recognition In The Transatlantic Context: Some Reflections On Future Negotiations', in ibid., 303.

[15] G. Bermann, M. Herdegen and P.L. Lindseth, *Transatlantic Regulatory Cooperation* (2000).

multilateral contract currently stands) and/or by amending the WTO contract so as to introduce a credible threat against potential violators, dispute prevention will be greatly served.

A. Disputes can be prevented if the WTO contract is observed, but there is probably room for Advisory Opinions

It is difficult to imagine how observance of the WTO contract can lead to disputes. True, the WTO contract is, in substantial parts, not self-interpreting. One can easily point to *bona fide* divergent interpretations of the same provisions. The vast majority of disputes, however, stem from largely undisputed violations of the contract: it is not by accident that complaining parties usually prevail.

While both the EC and the US are among the founding fathers of the initial GATT contract, the penetration of WTO law into the domestic legal order is far from complete. To avoid any misunderstandings, I am not arguing in favour of direct effect of WTO law in the EC legal order (or that the WTO be recognized as a self-executing agreement inside the US legal order). But I do argue in favour of an extension of the *Hermes* jurisprudence of the European Court of Justice which requests the national administration to construe domestic law in light of the relevant WTO law. The more relevant to domestic policy that the WTO law becomes in the EC and US legal orders, the smaller the risk of seeing disputes between the two.

As stated, though, there could be cases where the two administrations might legitimately end with divergent interpretations of the same legal obligation. In such cases it is probably useful to introduce some form of Advisory Opinion *à la* the International Court of Justice into the WTO legal order. A more ambitious proposal would be to introduce a 'positive comity' type of obligation whereby the regulating member could be requested by the other party to submit its measures for multilateral review in the context of an Advisory Opinion.[16]

B. Disputes can also be prevented if the cost of non-compliance outweighs the benefits of non-compliance

The current system of WTO remedies, as practice so far shows, is a rather weak means to ensure that WTO obligations will be enforced. This is true especially when it is the EC or the US measures that are found to be inconsistent with the WTO. The EC regime on bananas stayed in place for a number of years following three condemnations by the GATT/WTO, the presence of US

---

[16] In order to avoid violations of the non-discrimination principle, it would be useful to make sure that the requested member retains its discretion as to the final submission of its measures to multilateral review.

countermeasures notwithstanding;[17] the same is true for the EC ban on hormone-treated beef.

Generally, the prospective nature of countermeasures (past damages are not compensated for), and their limitation to the damage caused (which means that any time the profit made from the illegality outweighs the damage caused, the violator has no incentive to comply) are the basic reasons why WTO remedies, as they now stand, cannot *ex ante* guarantee that the contract will be respected by all at all times.

Voices of discontent as to the current state of affairs are heard only in non-governmental circles. In the ongoing DSU review, there was no formal proposal to re-discuss remedies in the WTO legal system.

Unless, however, some bite is added to existing (at least on occasions) demonstrably ineffective remedies, some WTO members will have less of an incentive to comply with the contract. This possibility is for the time being quite remote, since the US and the EC, in their relations with the rest of the WTO membership, can only profit from the current state of affairs.

---

[17] It is quite telling that in the same case, Mexico, although affected by the EC regime, did not request authorization to take countermeasures and Ecuador, although granted authorization, did not adopt countermeasures at the end of the day.

8

US–EU Disputes over Technical Barriers to Trade and the 'Hushkits' Dispute

KENNETH W. ABBOTT

INTRODUCTION

Product standards, conformity assessment procedures and other technical barriers to trade (TBT) are prototypical examples of 'low politics'. Indeed it is difficult to imagine an area of international politics 'lower' than product standards for gas connector hoses, to cite one long-running US-EU dispute.[1] As one might predict in a field where the economic stakes in individual cases are relatively low, TBT represents a notable success story in terms of dispute prevention and management.[2] There have been no formal WTO dispute settlement proceedings between the US and the EU involving TBT issues, although the US did intervene in the Asbestos case brought by Canada.[3]

Beneath this calm surface, however, the situation is stormy. Recent years have witnessed numerous transatlantic disagreements over technical regulations,

---

[1] This paper focuses on disputes between the US and the EU. It does not address disputes between the US and individual EU member states, although in many areas the latter are the relevant regulatory authorities. The US government estimates that EU legislation covering regulated products will eventually be applicable to half of all US exports to Europe. European-level standardization is also significant. See US Trade Representative, 2002 National Trade Estimate Report on Foreign Trade Barriers 110 [hereinafter US Trade Barriers Report], available at http://www.ustr.gov/reports/index.shtml, last visited 12 January 2003.

[2] In addition to the dispute management techniques discussed here, the US and the EU have entered into agreements providing mutual recognition for conformity assessment procedures and related measures in several product areas (MRAs). These agreements should further reduce disputes. MRAs are discussed in detail in Gregory Shaffer's case study in this volume.

[3] The US argued against the EU that the WTO Agreement on Technical Barriers to Trade [hereinafter TBT Agreement] applied to the French regulation in question, as the Appellate Body ultimately held. But the US also argued that the asbestos ban complied with the Agreement. Because the panel held the TBT Agreement did not apply, the dispute was decided on other grounds. Although the Appellate Body reversed the panel on this point, no further proceedings took place because Canada chose not to renew its complaint.

standards[4] and associated procedures adopted by both the US and the EU and affecting a wide range of products. While the economic impact of many of these regulations taken individually is small, their cumulative impact is significant. Disagreements over standards have been addressed in multiple forums, private and public, from the Transatlantic Business Dialogue (TABD) and the Transatlantic Economic Partnership (TEP) to the WTO Committee on TBT and even US-EU summit meetings. Many issues have been satisfactorily resolved, but others linger and may yet develop into full-blown disputes.

Disagreements over standards for products like gas connector hoses have become politically significant not only because of their economic impact, but also because they reflect deeper governance issues. The US and the EU have very different systems for adopting technical regulations and standards; each sees the other's system as creating impediments to trade and hampering transparency, participation and harmonization, the hallmarks of TBT law. Some problems stem from even more basic differences in government structure and regulatory philosophy. These issues are serious enough that in April 2002, after years of negotiation, the two governments agreed to address them directly in voluntary 'Guidelines on Regulatory Co-operation and Transparency'.

Only one disagreement in the general category of TBT regulation has led to a formal US-EU dispute proceeding. That is the 'hushkits' case, in which the US challenged EU restrictions on the registration and operation of certain aircraft retrofitted to comply with noise limitations set by the International Civil Aviation Organization (ICAO). The case is atypical in other respects as well. For one thing, the dispute arose against the backdrop of stalemated multilateral negotiations within ICAO to update its global standard on aircraft noise emissions. The US also took its legal challenge to ICAO, where it was addressed through mediation while multilateral negotiations on noise standards proceeded. The case was settled in 2002 as part of an overall agreement on new ICAO standards and policies.

Section I of this paper discusses US-EU conflicts over technical regulations and standards for ordinary commercial products, typified by the disagreement over gas connector hoses. Because none of these cases has led to a formal dispute proceeding, this section necessarily proceeds somewhat differently from the standard chapter outline established by the editors of this volume. Section II of the paper discusses the hushkits case. Here too, because the dispute arose in the context of ICAO negotiations (rather than trade law) and was submitted to ICAO (rather than the WTO), it has been necessary to modify somewhat the questions addressed. The final section is a brief conclusion.

---

[4] In the WTO TBT Agreement, a 'technical regulation' is defined as a mandatory prescription of product or process characteristics, a 'standard' as a non-mandatory prescription. Agreement on Technical Barriers to Trade, Annex 1, 'Terms and Their Definitions for the Purpose of This Agreement,' paras 1–2, available at http://www.wto.org/english/docs_e /legal_e/17–tbt.doc, last visited 12 January 2003. This paper sometimes uses the term 'standards' to refer to both kinds of prescriptions.

I. Dispute management on TBT

A. Why do disagreements over TBT issues arise?

Although there have been no formal US-EU legal disputes on product standards (except for the hushkits case), a steady stream of disagreements appears in reports of the TABD, the minutes of the WTO TBT Committee, the annual US and EU reports on foreign trade barriers,[5] and similar documents. The range of regulations at issue is extremely broad: in addition to gas connector hoses, it includes motorcycle licensing requirements, rules on disposal of electronic waste, emissions standards for river boats, risk assessment procedures for chemicals, rules on heavy equipment vibrations, standards for on-off switches, certification requirements for industrial fasteners, cosmetics testing procedures, nutrition labelling requirements, and many more.[6]

In each case, conflict arises because the regulation imposes additional costs on foreign suppliers, often seemingly disproportionate to those borne by domestic competitors, making it more difficult to sell profitably into the regulated market. The economic stakes in each individual case are generally small.[7] Taken together, however, TBT issues have become a significant irritant in US-EU relations.

Some current disagreements may yet develop into higher-profile disputes. The most likely candidates appear to be the EU 'end-of-life' directives that, when implemented, will require producers to provide for taking back for reuse or recycling certain waste electrical and electronic equipment (WEEE Directive) and a range of other products at the end of their useful lives—clearly a costly proposition for firms based abroad. The US and other governments have repeatedly voiced concerns over these requirements in multiple forums, including the TBT Committee.

Conflict also arises because of continuing disagreements over the legitimacy of TBT rule-making itself. The US Trade Barriers Report for 2001, for example, raises a number of concerns with the 'evolving EU-wide legislative environment'. These include 'lags in the development of EU standards; delays in the drafting of harmonized legislation for regulated areas; inconsistent application and interpretation by EU Member States ...; overlap and inconsistencies among Directives ...; grey areas between the scope of various Directives; and a frequent tendency to rely on design-based, rather than performance-based, standards'.[8]

---

[5] See, eg, US Trade Barriers Report, note 1 supra, at 110–120; Commission of the EU, 2001 Report on US Barriers to Trade and Investment 18–26 [hereinafter EU Trade Barriers Report], available at http://europa.eu.int/comm/trade/pdf /usrbt2001.pdf, last visited 12 January 2003.

[6] Numerous disagreements have also arisen over regulations on food and other products subject to the WTO Agreement on Sanitary and Phytosanitary Measures (SPS Agreement). SPS disputes are discussed in detail in Petros Mavroidis' case study in this volume.

[7] The stakes can, however, be significant for small or medium-sized enterprises. The EU cites one company's allegation that 15% of potential US sales were lost due to the multiplicity of standards and certification procedures it faced there. EU Trade Barriers Report, note 5 supra, at 20.

[8] US Trade Barriers Report, note 1 supra, at 110.

US officials also charge that the EU consistently sets standards that serve the interests of European companies, then devotes great effort to encouraging multilateral bodies to adopt the same standards.

The Trade Barriers Report notes an even more fundamental US concern: 'the European standardization and regulatory development processes lack adequate transparency and remain generally closed to U.S. stakeholders' direct participation at critical points...'.[9] Transparency and participation have been constant themes at least since the period of EU regulatory harmonization leading up to 1992.

The most important issue in this area is the adequacy of notification of proposed regulatory actions. The EU Commission generally notifies a proposed technical regulation under the TBT Agreement only after it has completed drafting a legislative proposal; until then it develops the proposal internally and consults with member states and private groups. The US argues that notice at this stage is too late for meaningful input, as proposals are already fully formed.[10] The Commission issues White and Green Papers in advance of some proposals, and these typically lead to intense consultations,[11] but they rarely include proposed texts. The Commission argues that notice at the proposal stage is timely because the legislative process only begins at that point.

The most important participation issue relates to opportunities for consultation prior to the adoption of regulations.[12] The US charges that the Commission's consultations are not generally open to all stakeholders; instead, the Commission invites particular organizations to present their views on proposals under development.[13] The US emphasizes the exclusion of foreign stakeholders from these consultations, but many European actors are left out as well. The US critique reflects its own regulatory process: the Administrative Procedure Act (APA) requires agencies to receive comments from anyone who wishes to submit them following public notice of proposed regulation. The EU responds that the APA is an inappropriate analogy, as the relevant EU procedures are *legislative*, not *administrative*. The President of the US is not required to consult with every stakeholder, domestic and foreign, before submitting a proposal to Congress.

Finally, the US criticizes certain substantive aspects of EU regulation. US officials complain that the EU does not provide satisfactory justifications for proposed technical regulations, as the TBT Agreement requires.[14] As in the

---

[9] US Trade Barriers Report, note 1 supra, at 110.

[10] See, eg, US Comments on European Commission's White Paper on Governance, 5 April 2002, at 2, available at http://www.useu.be/Categories/RegulatoryReform/Apr0502USCommissionWhitePaperGovernance.html, last visited 12 January 2003.

[11] See, eg, US Trade Barriers Report, note 1 supra, at 115 (discussing February 2000 Commission White Paper on chemicals policy).

[12] The US also argues that European organizations that adopt non-mandatory product standards, such as the Comité Européen de Normalisation, do not allow non-European companies to participate fully in their deliberations. See, eg, US Trade Barriers Report, note 1 supra, at 119.

[13] See US Comments on White Paper on Governance, note 10 supra, at 2.

[14] TBT Agreement, note 3 supra, Article 2.5 provides that, on request, a state adopting a technical regulation that may have significant trade effects shall explain the justification for the regulation in

Beef Hormones dispute, the US seeks justifications based on explicit risk assessments that incorporate relevant scientific information and demonstrate the need for the regulation in terms of health, safety or other legitimate goals.[15] Instead, the US perceives many EU regulations as responding to domestic political demands or broad interpretations of the precautionary principle.[16] In addition, the US complains that EU regulatory schemes are often structured in unnecessarily costly and intrusive ways.[17] These disagreements reflect deep differences in the philosophy of regulation, compounded by different political constellations.

For its part, the Commission raises a number of concerns with US standard-setting procedures. One issue is the complexity of the US regulatory system. Even if this is not intentionally discriminatory, it 'can represent an important structural impediment to market access'.[18] Two features of the US system are particularly important.

First, many US (voluntary) standards are privately established. Hundreds of private organizations set standards, creating an obvious transparency problem. Many of these bodies fail to distinguish standards that are essential to safety from those that address less significant quality issues. Private standards may require costly testing by different organizations, increasing the cost of compliance; may not lead to certification, limiting the ability to capitalize on compliance in the marketplace; and may overlap with requirements imposed by buyers. Even leading bodies like Underwriter's Laboratory make changes in their standards that appear abrupt and arbitrary to foreign suppliers.[19]

Second, under the US federal system, mandatory technical regulations are created at multiple levels, federal, state and local. The more than 2,700 state and local regulators rarely co-ordinate their actions, and there is no centralized source of information about them.[20] As the EU notes, 'it is not uncommon that equipment for use in the workplace is subject to US Department of Labor certification, a county authority's electrical equipment standards, specific regulations imposed by large municipalities, and other product safety requirements

---

terms of the substantive requirements of the Agreement. These include the principle that regulations shall not be more trade-restrictive than necessary to fulfil a legitimate objective, taking account of the risks of non-fulfilment. These risks are to be assessed, inter alia, on the basis of available scientific and technical information.

[15] The Transatlantic Business Dialogue (TABD) has also urged governments to base regulations on science-based risk assessments and to clarify the precautionary principle. See, eg, 2002 TABD Mid Year Report at 16, available at http://www.tabd.org/archive/reportsindex.html, last visited 12 January 2003.

[16] The US argues, for example, that EU restrictions on biotechnology products reflect politics rather than science, and that possible bans on certain chemicals reflect unacceptably broad applications of the precautionary principle. See US Trade Barriers Report, note 1 supra, at 111, 115.

[17] See, eg, ibid at 115 (chemicals proposal is costly, burdensome, complex and unworkable).

[18] EU Trade Barriers Report, note 5 supra, at 18.

[19] Ibid at 20.

[20] The EU also charges that the information on technical regulations and standards provided to foreign suppliers by US embassies, chambers of commerce and other sources is often incomplete. Ibid at 21.

as determined by insurance companies'.[21] Insurance requirements change rapidly with assessments of product liability risk. In many sectors, multiple standards fragment the market, eliminating potential economies of scale. Multiplicity also encourages foreign suppliers to use certified local components to reduce compliance costs, distorting trade patterns. In addition, many local (and some federal) procurement standards explicitly favour local suppliers.[22]

The EU also criticizes the US for its relatively limited use—or even awareness—of international standards set by organizations such as the International Organization for Standardization (ISO) and the International Electrotechnical Commission (IEC). The US claims that many of its standards are 'technically equivalent' to international standards, even if not identical. But the EU argues that the US adopts few international standards directly, and that in some important sectors US standards flatly contradict international standards, creating additional costs and barriers to trade. Private and local standards exhibit the greatest discrepancies, but some federal agencies also resist harmonization.[23]

As complaints on the subject suggest, the political economy of international standard setting is characterized by a transatlantic struggle for influence.[24] The US has long complained that Europeans have disproportionate influence on international standards bodies like IEC, because they are more active there and because each EU member state usually has a separate vote. In the US view, Europe sets regional standards (to favour local producers) in bodies like the Comité Européen de Normalisation, then votes as a bloc in an effort to transport those standards to the international level.[25] For its part, the EU charges not only that US regulators often ignore international standards, but that the US then 'actively seeks to deviate countries, with which it has particularly intense trade..., from the path of international standardization'.[26]

Finally, the EU charges that US standards bodies continue to rely unnecessarily on costly third-party conformity assessment procedures, even in areas like electrical equipment, computers and appliances, where quality control procedures and consumer awareness allow other national authorities to rely on self-certification by manufacturers.[27] This allegation represents an ironic role

---

[21] Ibid at 18.

[22] Ibid at 21.

[23] Ibid at 19, 20, 21. The multiplicity of standards bodies can exacerbate the problem. For example, while the American National Standards Institute follows the ISO standard on personnel certification for non-destructive testing, the American Society of Mechanical Engineers (ASME) does not. Ibid at 20–21.

[24] On the political economy of international standard setting, see generally (2001) 8 *Journal of European Public Policy* 3 (special issue).

[25] See, eg, WTO Committee on Technical Barriers to Trade, Minutes of the Meeting held on 21 July 2000, at 6, G/TBT/M/20 (29 August 2000), available at http://www.wto.org/english/tratop_e /tbt_e/ tbt_e.htm (allegation that preparation of IEC standard on low-frequency emissions from electronic equipment 'had been dominated by the European utilities' and hence might not reflect interests of all states).

[26] EU Trade Barriers Report, note 5 supra, at 21.

[27] Ibid at 19. The US has moved in the direction of self-certification in some electronics sectors.

reversal, as it is the US that usually argues for deregulation. The US, however, identifies other sectors in which the situation is reversed.

B. What roles do private actors and government departments play?

Business firms and associations have substantial influence on standards and technical regulations in both the US and the EU. Most product standards are adopted because firms demand them to enhance interconnectivity, avoid market segmentation and otherwise reduce costs. Firms have by far the best information on these matters, so standards bodies typically defer to their advice. Indeed, private associations often set product standards, especially in the US, with government agencies incorporating their output in legally binding regulations (eg, building codes). Private firms also influence regional and international standard setting in private bodies, mixed private-governmental organizations (notably ISO) and advisory committees. It would hardly be surprising in this context if firms sought standards that would give them an edge on competitors, or if regulators took protectionist effects into account, if only at the margins.[28]

Most technical regulations are designed not to create positive network effects for firms, but to control (perceived) negative external effects of products and processes on consumers, workers, the public at large or the environment.[29] In these settings regulatory agencies generally respond to demands from labour or other affected interests, issue activists or the public. Business firms may be unable to defeat such regulations, and may even find it politically costly to oppose them openly. However, firms still attempt to influence the form and content of regulations (typically on technical matters that non-specialists will overlook) in ways that advantage them. Since firms possess superior technical information and will bear many of the costs of regulation, legislators and regulators still look to them for advice.

Private firms are also the principal monitors of standard setting practices abroad. Because TBT issues are so technical, firms in the affected industries have the greatest capacity to identify inefficiencies in proposed foreign standards and estimate their likely economic effects. Governments therefore rely on exporters, foreign investors and other business interests to act as 'fire alarms', alerting legislators, trade and commerce officials and other agencies to proposed foreign standards that will affect them adversely.

Diverse government agencies respond to business complaints about foreign standards. It is common for firms to appeal to the agency with equivalent

---

[28] For a discussion of private and public standard setting as responses to different types of externalities, see K. W. Abbott & D. Snidal, 'International "Standards" and International Governance', (2001) 8 *Journal of European Public Policy* 345–70.

[29] The WTO TBT Agreement lists protection of life, health and safety, protection of the environment, prevention of deceptive practices and national security among the acceptable goals of technical regulations. TBT Agreement, note 3 supra, Article 2:2.

regulatory responsibility in their own country, with which they often have close working relationships. When officials in these agencies take up local complaints, they can easily initiate an expert 'transnational' dialogue—carried out below the level of 'the state'—with their opposite numbers in foreign agencies. Regulators on both sides are often part of a single 'epistemic community', professionally committed to regulation on the basis of sound scientific and technical principles.[30] The transnational approach is capable of resolving many disagreements, often through formal or informal harmonization on the basis of shared understandings, without escalation to political levels.

But the expert approach does not always succeed. Many standards are created by legislation, and politically sensitive legislators are often more resistant to harmonization and accommodation than regulators, especially when they are responding to the demands of influential interest groups or intense public preferences. Independent regulatory agencies sometimes share this reluctance to harmonize, even though they are prototypical expert bodies. For example, the EU has complained about several regulatory policies of the US Food and Drug Administration (FDA).[31] However, this appears to be a matter of zeal to fulfil a mandate defined in national terms, not political sensitivity.

The transnational approach also falters when regulatory disagreements are escalated to higher political levels. Trade authorities, foreign ministries and even heads of government may involve themselves in disagreements that have high stakes or affect particularly influential industries, such as disputes over hushkits, beef hormones and biotechnology. Relatively minor disagreements can also escalate when the affected interests frame them as reflecting general problems, like regulatory process, that have broader economic effects. Procedures like US section 301, and to a lesser extent the EU Trade Barriers Regulation, can facilitate escalation. So can the annual trade barriers reports issued by the US and EU, which cumulate disputes that are relatively minor in themselves and frame them as governance issues.

C. How do the parties manage disagreements over TBT issues?

TBT issues unfold in a dense institutional environment, with a number of mechanisms available for the management of disagreements.

First, the simplest mechanism is bilateral talks between technical and lower level policy officials in regulatory agencies, economic and trade agencies, and foreign ministries, including embassies and delegations. As already noted, such transnational dialogue can be highly effective. Officials will often modify proposals and regulations to reduce unforeseen trade effects or incorporate less costly or trade-restrictive measures not previously considered. Because private

---

[30] On the concept of epistemic community, see P. M. Haas, 'Knowledge, Power and International Policy Coordination' (1992) 46 *International Organization* 1.
[31] EU Trade Barriers Report, note 5 supra, at 22.

bodies set many standards, similar discussions take place between private associations, and between regulators and associations.[32]

Secondly, both sides also use the TEP institutions to manage standards and regulatory issues.[33] The 1999 'early warning' process has been used to place several TBT issues on the TEP agenda. Many of these items have been identified by the TABD, which regularly reviews and updates a list of early warning items.[34] Most government officials and business leaders view the early warning system and TABD's role as salutary: these institutions provide a rare opportunity to bring 'low politics' standards issues that resist expert resolution to the attention of policy-makers.

At the same time, however, there is an increasing sense that the TEP processes are excessively burdensome. Officials are constantly at work on issue papers and preparations for meetings. Even summits come every few months, losing some of their force as forums for high-level pressure and commitment. A recent EU review recommends dramatically streamlining the TEP process, including reducing the frequency of summits.[35] US officials generally share this goal. It remains to be seen whether a slimmed-down TEP will be as effective in managing low politics issues like standards, or whether disagreements of this kind will fall through the institutional cracks.

TABD has also pursued more ambitious policy goals, though without complete success. It has called on the US and the EU to adopt a policy of 'approved once, accepted everywhere'.[36] It has urged greater reliance on self-certification, through 'seller's declarations of conformity' backed up by monitoring schemes, product liability suits and other *ex post* mechanisms. It has proposed that governments use 'trade impact assessments' or similar procedures to ensure that regulators and legislators consider trade implications at all levels.[37] And it has long sought enhanced regulatory transparency and consultation, a campaign that bore fruit in the 2002 Guidelines for Regulatory Co-operation. TABD helped governments break a long-standing deadlock over transparency in the Guidelines, and is now working to further their implementation.[38]

---

[32] See ibid at 19–21 (describing complaint submitted by European Federation of Non-Destructive Testing to ASME).

[33] See, eg, Report of the Transatlantic Economic Partnership Steering Group, EU-US Summit, Goteburg, 14 June 2001, available at http://www.useu.be/summit/tepsummit0601.pdf, last visited 12 January 2003 (discussing use of early warning mechanism to resolve disputes, promote mutual recognition, draft guidelines for regulatory co-operation, and address other TBT issues).

[34] See, eg, TABD, Cincinnati Recommendations, 16–18 November 2000, Working Group I: Standards and Regulatory Policy, available at http://www.tabd.org/archive/confarchive.html, last visited 12 January 2003 (reviewing disputes nominated for early warning treatment and calling for improvements in early warning system).

[35] See 'New Impulse for EU-US Relations,' 20 March 2001, available at http://europa.eu.int/comm/trade/bilateral/usa/pr20032001.htm, last visited 12 January 2003.

[36] See, eg, TABD, Cincinnati Recommendations, note 34 supra. Such a policy would go well beyond the small number of sector-specific MRAs entered into by the US and EU, which TABD also supports.

[37] Ibid.

[38] See 2002 TABD Mid-Year Report, note 15 supra.

Thirdly, trade authorities in the US and the EU regularly raise standards issues in the WTO TBT Committee. For example, the US and other governments have voiced concern over various EU end-of-life proposals at virtually every recent meeting of the Committee; they also have criticized the Commission more generally for deferring notifications during the development of proposals.[39] Discussions in the TBT Committee are remarkably frank. Delegates criticizing foreign measures use terms such as 'discriminatory', 'lack of scientific basis', 'unnecessary' and 'no logical rationale'.[40]

D. Is the WTO TBT Agreement adequate?

Most standards disputes are handled outside the WTO, eg, between expert regulators or private associations. However, the TBT Agreement and its associated procedures are a significant part of the overall standards regime. The procedures and substantive rules of the Agreement should be separately assessed.

The procedural mechanisms of the Agreement are based on notification and justification. Member governments are required to notify the Secretariat (and give public notice) of proposed technical regulations and conformity assessment procedures not based on international standards, urgently adopted regulations, certain sub-national regulations, and so on. Notification is to be made at an 'early appropriate stage', in time for comments to be taken into account.[41] Other governments pass this information on to potentially affected local firms. Thereafter, typically at the request of such firms, governments may request justifications for regulations in terms of the substantive rules of the Agreement, and may submit comments to the regulating government.[42]

The notification/justification provisions of the Agreement are generally seen as its greatest strength. From the US perspective, these procedures help keep the EU regulatory system open to the outside world. Fears of a 'Fortress Europe' that uses standards as an adjunct to industrial policy have motivated US policy on TBT for many years. From the EU perspective, notification constitutes a key that can open to scrutiny at least some elements of the complex, multilayered US regulatory system.

In many respects, officials of the US and the EU see notification as working well. The TBT Committee has prescribed standard notification formats and otherwise streamlined the process. According to the Committee's annual reviews of operation, the US and the EU have notified about the same number of

[39] See, eg, WTO Committee on Technical Barriers to Trade, Minutes of the Meeting held on 30 March, 2001 at 8, G/TBT/M/23 (8 May 2001), available at http://www.wto.org/english/tratop_e/tbt_e /tbt_e.htm, last visited 12 January 2003.

[40] See, eg, WTO Committee on Technical Barriers to Trade, Minutes of the Meeting held on 9 October 2001, G/TBT/M/25 (21 November 2001).

[41] TBT Agreement, note 3 supra, Articles 2.9, 2.10, 3.2, 5.6–5.7. See also Article 10.

[42] Ibid, Articles 2.5, 2.9.4, 5.6. Similar principles apply to voluntary standards under Annex 3 of the Agreement, the Code of Good Practice for the Preparation, Adoption and Application of Standards.

regulations.[43] At the same time, however, there are persistent disagreements as to the adequacy and timeliness of notification and justification. In particular, US officials see the EU as being in almost constant violation of the letter or spirit of these provisions because of the practices discussed above, and other governments raise similar complaints.

The substantive rules of the Agreement—while viewed as appropriate and helpful—play a less significant role. This is largely because the rules are framed in quite general language, especially in comparison to the SPS Agreement, which was adopted in reaction to similarly imprecise language in the Tokyo Round TBT code.[44] Still, most trade officials do not believe that more precise TBT rules are needed at this time. The general attitude on both sides appears to be that the existing rules would be adequate if they were fully implemented in good faith.[45] There are, however, some significant differences over precisely what full implementation would mean.

One important area of controversy is the use of international standards. The Agreement provides that when international standards exist, members 'shall use them . . . as a basis for their technical regulations', except under specified conditions.[46] The EU views this provision as straightforwardly requiring wider US adoption of international standards. The US, however, emphasizes the Agreement's broad conception of 'international standards': unlike the SPS Agreement, which refers to specific institutions and bodies of standards,[47] the TBT Agreement contains virtually no definition of 'international standards' at all. This allows the US to rely on standards set in the marketplace, where US firms may have greater impact, and to avoid standards adopted by organizations like ISO and IEC, where the US fears European influence.

This disagreement also reflects a difference in regulatory philosophy. The US prefers standards that have proven themselves in the market, whether they were first generated by individual firms or by formal organizations. So long as market acceptance is contested, the US is willing to tolerate multiple standards, as it does domestically. The EU, in contrast, tends to favour standards established through formal processes with substantial government influence, and is more comfortable with unified standards. These differences are apparent in the very different

[43] See WTO Committee on Technical Barriers to Trade, Seventh Annual Review of the Implementation and Operation of the Agreement, at 4–7, G/TBT/11 /Rev.2, 13 March 2002, available at http:// www.wto.org/english/tratop_e/tbt_e /tbt_e.htm, last visited 12 January 2003.

[44] The US challenged early versions of EU restrictions on hormone-treated beef, ultimately found in violation of the SPS Agreement, under the Tokyo Round TBT agreement. The US believed that the generality of that earlier agreement would have allowed the EU to avoid a negative decision (the consensus rule of GATT also allowed it to block formation of a dispute settlement panel). As a result, the US pressed for the more specific rules of the SPS Agreement, especially its requirements for reliance on risk assessments and scientific evidence.

[45] See, eg, EU Trade Barriers Report, note 5 supra, at 19.

[46] TBT Agreement, note 3 supra, Article 2.4; see also Articles 2.6, 5.4–5.5, 9.

[47] For food safety standards, for example, the SPS Agreement specifies the standards promulgated by the Codex Alimentarius Commission. Agreement on Sanitary and Phytosanitary Measures, Annex A:3.

paths taken by the US and EU on the standardization of wireless telephony (GSM in Europe vs multiple inconsistent standards in the US) and more recently on third-generation (3-G) wireless services.[48]

The international system appears to be moving toward the US position. Recent OECD reports cite the need for international standards to be 'market-relevant' if national authorities are expected to rely on them.[49] The TBT Committee took a similar tack in its second triennial review of the Agreement, calling for international standards procedures to observe principles of effectiveness and relevance (including market relevance) as well as transparency, openness, impartiality and consensus, and coherence.[50]

E. Why have there been no formal TBT disputes?

With the diversity of products and sectors, regulations and institutions involved in TBT disagreements, there can be no definitive answer to this question. A number of explanatory factors appear relevant, although there is little available data with which to test alternate hypotheses. This section describes four general sets of factors; as discussed further below, these factors influence the resolution of different types of cases. Some of the relevant factors suggest lessons for the design and operation of the international standards regime; others operate largely independent of the institutional framework.

1. Low economic stakes

For the typical standards issue, international 'peace' has more to do with the nature of the underlying disagreement than with dispute management. As noted earlier, the economic stakes in many TBT cases are low, especially in comparison to high-profile trade disputes over anti-dumping procedures, subsidies, agricultural policy and the like. Policy-level officials are rarely even apprised of these low-stakes disagreements. Most are quietly resolved through expert discussions between commercial and regulatory officials or private associations. Even when they are not resolved, the machinery leading to formal dispute proceedings is simply not engaged.

When the affected firms are large or medium sized, they can usually adapt to new foreign standards at relatively low cost, and can often pass on some of that

---

[48] See M. T. Austin & H. V. Milner, 'Strategies of European Standardization' (2001) 8 *Journal of European Public Policy* 411–31; J. Pelkmans, 'The GSM Standard: Explaining a Success Story', (2001) 8 *Journal of European Public Policy* 432–53.

[49] See, eg, OECD, Working Party of the Trade Committee, Special Meeting on Technical Barriers to Trade: Summary Report by the Secretariat, TD/TC/WP/RD(2000)1/final (March 2000). Discussion also addressed the point that international standards bodies should include all significant stakeholders, private as well as public.

[50] WTO Committee on Technical Barriers to Trade, Second Triennial Review of the Operation and the Implementation of the Agreement on Technical Barriers to Trade, at 5, G/TBT/9, 13 November 2000, available at http://www.wto.org/english/tratop_e/tbt_e /tbt_e.htm, last visited 12 January 2003.

cost to customers. Once it becomes clear that high-level officials are unlikely to take up their complaints or resolve them expeditiously, firms simply adapt: changing product specifications or manufacturing processes, developing distinct models for sale in different markets, and the like. The costs of adaptation are more significant for small firms.[51] However, collective action problems make it difficult for small, dispersed firms to organize around standards issues, and such firms often lack the political influence to force issues onto the political agenda. Overall, adaptation undoubtedly means lost market opportunities and profits, but the impact on firms and national economies is modest.

2. The costs of formal dispute procedures

Especially in relation to the small stakes in most standards cases, the costs of formal dispute resolution in the WTO and other international forums—including executive and official time, monetary expense, political rancour and other considerations—are high. Government officials and business firms alike therefore avoid resort to formal dispute procedures except where a foreign regulation constitutes an egregious violation or affects a broad range of industries, or where constituent pressures are irresistible.

In US-EU relations the most persistent source of disagreements over standards is notification practice. Notification problems rarely constitute the type of egregious violation that justifies costly litigation: affected firms frequently have alternate sources of information, and trade effects are difficult to quantify. At the same time, some notification problems reflect fundamental disputes over governance, such as the question whether the proper analogy for Commission rule making is regulation (with public notice and comment) or legislation. In these situations, seemingly minor challenges to notification practice may in fact be 'hard cases' that can threaten the international regime itself, and are better kept out of litigation.

The imprecision of the substantive rules in the TBT Agreement also makes WTO litigation risky, as it is difficult for parties to predict the outcome. To be sure, many equally general provisions in GATT have been litigated repeatedly, but those disputes typically involve traditional trade policy measures. The application of international rules to standard setting remains considerably more uncertain.[52]

Another potential cost stems from concerns over reciprocity. The US and the EU both adopt technical regulations and standards on a daily basis; both engage in practices that could be construed as inconsistent with the TBT Agreement. In

---

[51] The vulnerability of smaller enterprises has been emphasized both by the EU, see EU Trade Barriers Report, note 5 supra, at 20, and the TABD, see 2002 TABD Mid-Year Report, note 15 supra, at 17.

[52] See TBT Agreement, note 3 supra, Articles 2.1–2.4. The national treatment and MFN provisions in Article 2.1 could presumably be applied to technical regulations without difficulty. Greater uncertainty exists with the other substantive provisions, such as the rule requiring members to ensure that technical regulations are not adopted or applied with the effect of creating unnecessary obstacles to international trade. Ibid, Article 2.2.

this setting, reciprocity exerts a strong restraining influence. In the US, at least, regulatory agencies counsel trade officials to think twice before challenging foreign actions under the TBT Agreement, lest equivalent US practices be called into question.

3. Dispute management

With modestly higher-stakes issues, officials have avoided litigation through less confrontational procedures to manage disagreements (and respond to constituent pressures). The several institutional tracks available for the management of TBT issues, including industry consultations, TABD, expert level bilateral consultations, TEP procedures, the OECD and the WTO TBT Committee, have proven very successful in heading off serious disputes. On issues like the EU end-of-life regulations, the use of multiple channels of consultation may have kept the regulatory process open for long periods of time, forestalling adoption of problematic regulations. In other cases contested standards have been adopted, but consultations have provided a procedural safety valve that maintains the possibility of compromise and makes litigation difficult to justify.

Even though persistent talk in multiple forums has been a successful dispute management strategy, however, it is not particularly cost-effective. The strategy may be threatened by moves to streamline TEP and other US-EU interactions. Even apart from those reforms, moreover, it seems inevitable that at some point an issue kept alive through consultations will escalate into a full-blown trade dispute.

4. International engagement

An issue underlying a number of US-EU standards disagreements is the (perceived) greater influence of European representatives in international standard setting bodies and their strategic use of those institutions. These concerns have to some extent been self-correcting: US firms have become more active in international and even European standards organizations. Increased engagement should translate into greater US influence on, and hence use of, international standards.

F. Addressing underlying causes

Throughout this paper, US-EU disagreements over specific standards issues have been shown to reflect more fundamental structural and philosophical differences on regulation and governance. Some characterizations of these positions come close to caricature, yet significant differences clearly exist. For example, on a wide variety of issues:

- The US is more atomistic, the EU more centralized. This is true both of voluntary standards (hundreds of private organizations in the US; a few regional organizations in Europe) and of technical regulations (2,700 municipalities in the US; predominantly regional or national standards in the EU).

- The US is more market-oriented, the EU more hierarchical. The US prefers standards that have proven their value in the marketplace, and is comfortable with conflicting standards until market approval is established; the EU is more willing to lead the market by selecting and mandating unitary standards.
- The US prefers to regulate on the basis of concrete evidence revealing identifiable risks and a clear balance of benefits over costs; the EU is more willing to regulate on a precautionary basis.
- The US adopts most mandatory standards through regulation, with procedures for public notice and comment from any concerned actor; the EU sets regulations through quasi-legislative processes, with Commission discretion to invite input from selected groups and deferred notification.

For several years the two sides engaged in talks designed to bridge these gaps. The effort was given impetus by the 1998 TEP Action Plan, which called on both governments to jointly define and implement principles or guidelines for regulatory co-operation, including improved dialogue among regulators and enhanced opportunities for public input. The 'principles or guidelines' terminology was meant to assure domestic interests that co-operation was not intended to threaten existing forms of government, but merely to state general norms and 'operational elements' that each side could implement voluntarily. TABD strongly supported the effort as a way to avoid disruptive disputes.[53]

Negotiations soon stalled, however, over differences like those discussed above. The November 2000 draft contained 'square brackets' in fully half its provisions, and neither side appeared willing to compromise on the open issues. The most significant disagreement involved transparency. The November 2000 draft article on the subject consisted only of alternative US and EU versions. The US text suggested nothing less than an APA-style 'notice and comment' procedure; the EU alternative suggested substantially less open procedures.

In April 2002, negotiators finally reached agreement on 'Guidelines on Regulatory Co-operation and Transparency'.[54] The Guidelines set forth agreed norms on a number of significant matters. They encourage regulators from the two polities to:

- consult and exchange information, formally and informally, in person and electronically, about ongoing and planned rulemaking and work programmes;
- examine the appropriateness and possibility of collecting similar (or complementary) data and using similar assumptions and methodologies to analyze the need for regulation; and to compare criteria and judgments about the need for and the form of regulation;

[53] See, eg, TABD, Cincinnati Recommendations, note 34 supra (urging governments to agree on long overdue guidelines).

[54] Guidelines on Regulatory Co-operation and Transparency, April 2002, available at http://www.ustr.gov/releases/2002/04/02–42.htm, last visited 8 November 2002. To complete the negotiations, both sides requested input from TABD, whose leaders suggested language that bridged the remaining gaps. See 2002 TABD Mid-Year Report, note 15 supra, at 14.

- exchange information on contemplated regulatory approaches and post-implementation reviews, with the aim of promoting greater convergence as well as the use of cost-effective approaches;
- examine opportunities to minimize unnecessary divergence in technical regulations, through harmonization, mutual recognition or other means.

In addition, provisions on the controversial issue of transparency are central to the Guidelines. The transparency provisions go well beyond providing information to other governments or affected foreign firms; they also focus squarely on increasing public awareness and involvement within the regulating polity. The Guidelines encourage officials to apply the following 'operational elements' of transparency as they develop technical regulations:

- provide the public with information about regulations development, consult with the public (including 'interested stakeholders, domestic and foreign') in an early and broad manner, and provide opportunities for public participation;
- more specifically, (1) provide announcements of proposed regulations at an 'early appropriate stage' in their development, while comments can be taken into account; (2) invite the public to submit comments; and (3) assist public commentators by providing explanations of proposed regulations (addressing the need for the regulation, its feasibility and likely impact, and possible alternatives) and disclosing the data and analysis relied on by regulators;
- respond to public questions and recommendations;
- take public comments into account and address the issues raised by them in an explanation accompanying final action.

While these provisions are less specific and detailed than the US APA, they certainly reflect its approach. EU acceptance of such procedures was facilitated by progress in the international discourse on regulation. For example, OECD discussions of regulatory reform while the Guidelines were being negotiated moved decisively in favour of enhancing public notice and input. Recent OECD reports characterize domestic and international transparency as hallmarks of efficient and legitimate regulatory practice.[55]

Even more important, the Commission itself engaged in a substantial exercise of rethinking EU governance in connection with discussions on enlargement. The Commission issued a White Paper on governance shortly before the Guidelines were adopted.[56] The White Paper identifies five principles of good governance: openness, participation, accountability, effectiveness, and coherence.[57] At

[55] See, eg, OECD, Working Party of the Trade Committee, Trade and Regulatory Reform: Insights from the OECD Country Reviews and Other Analyses, TD/TC /WP(2000)21/final, 3 November 2000, available at http: //www.olis.oecd.org/olis/2000doc.nsf /linkto/td-tc-wp(2000)21–final, last visited 12 January 2003.

[56] Commission of the European Communities, European Governance: A White Paper, Com(2001) 428 final, 25 July 2001, available at http://europa.eu.int/comm/governance/white_paper/index_en.htm, last visited 12 January 2003.

[57] Ibid at 10–11.

least the first three of these, if not all of them, involve transparency to the public.[58]

Implementation of the Guidelines, generally and through specific joint projects, is to be reviewed on an ongoing basis by the TEP Working Group on TBT. TABD has also initiated a private sector work programme on implementation. In the Guidelines, both governments agreed to identify areas for improvement and the expansion of regulatory co-operation, and to continue identifying means to enhance transparency and improve access to each other's institutions. At the May 2002 US-EU economic summit, the heads of government agreed to consider initial pilot projects in the motor vehicle sector.[59]

Although the Guidelines represent a significant step in addressing regulatory differences, their impact may be limited. For one thing, their field of application is narrowed in important ways. (1) They apply only to the US federal government and the services of the EU Commission; (2) they apply only to technical regulations,[60]—this includes legislative proposals, with the exception of processes relating to agricultural products; (3) they apply only to regulations affecting goods within the scope of the WTO TBT Agreement; (4) they call for co-operation only on regulations that either side believes may have significant trade impacts; (5) they are prospective, encompassing only regulations and amendments adopted after acceptance of the Guidelines.

Even within their field of operation, the Guidelines are voluntary undertakings, not legally binding commitments, although both sides represent that they will apply them 'as broadly as possible'. In addition, most of their provisions are cast in hortatory form that leaves regulators great flexibility. All of the 'operational elements' are phrased in terms of what regulators 'should' do, and many include additional hortatory elements. For example, regulators are encouraged only to 'examine the possibility and appropriateness' of using common assumptions and analytical methodologies.[61] Finally, because the Guidelines are to be implemented primarily through joint reform projects in specific sectors, much like the US-EU MRAs, their full benefits will be deferred for many years.

---

[58] The Commission has also proposed new principles for consultation with the public. See Commission of the European Communities, Consultation Document: Towards a Reinforced Culture of Consultation and Dialogue—Proposal—For General Principles and Minimum Standards for Consultation of Interested Parties by the Commission, 5 June 2002, available at http://europa.eu.int/comm/governance/whatsnew.htm, last visited 12 January 2003.

[59] See 'EU and US Agree on Positive Economic Agenda at Summit,' Brussels, 3 May 2002, available at http://europa.eu.int/comm/trade/bilateral/usa/pr030502.htm, last visited 12 January 2003.

[60] However, both sides agree to encourage standards and conformity assessment bodies to follow the Guidelines on transparency when 'interpreting' regulations. See Guidelines on Regulatory Co-operation and Transparency, note 54 supra, para 21.

[61] Both their voluntary character and their hortatory language weaken the legal obligation imposed by the Guidelines. Many provisions of the Guidelines are also phrased in imprecise terms, allowing flexibility in interpretation. In addition, the two governments retain all authority to interpret and apply the Guidelines, without any involvement by quasi-judicial or other third-party institutions. In sum, the Guidelines are weak on all three of the major elements of international 'legalization'. See K.W. Abbott *et al*, 'The Concept of Legalization' (2000) 54 *International Organization* 401–19.

II. The Hushkits dispute

This dispute concerned a 1999 EU Regulation (the 'Regulation')[62] that prohibited the registration and operation within the Community of certain older
aircraft that had been retrofitted to meet later-adopted multilateral noise standards. This was a technical regulation in the general sense of prescribing product
characteristics, but it differed from most TBT regulations in its focus on restricting services provided with the product rather than the sale of the product itself.[63]
The Community cited three interrelated factors as justifications for adopting the
Regulation: public complaints over noise near urban European airports,[64] proliferating local restrictions that threatened to disrupt the common aviation
market, and frustration at the failure of negotiations in ICAO to further update
multilateral noise standards.

The US challenged the Regulation in March 2000 under the dispute resolution
procedure of ICAO, alleging that it contravened several principles of the multilateral aviation regime.[65] Following a determination that ICAO had jurisdiction
to consider the dispute, the President of the ICAO Council, Dr Assad Kotaite,
initiated mediation proceedings at the parties' request. While mediation was
underway, the parties participated in substantive negotiations at ICAO. That
organization adopted a new noise standard and a broader set of noise management policies during 2001. The Community implemented these policies through
a directive that also repealed the Regulation as of April 2002.[66] In June 2002, the
US withdrew its complaint in ICAO.[67]

The hushkits case is unique among US-EU TBT disputes, not only because it
involved a regulation of services and was the subject of a formal dispute proceeding, but also because of its close connections with the specialized ICAO
regime: the negotiating stalemate at ICAO helped motivate the Regulation, US
industry and the US government framed their objections largely in terms of
ICAO principles, the US chose to utilize the ICAO dispute resolution procedure
(previously invoked on only three occasions), and agreement on new ICAO

[62] Council Regulation (EC) 925 /1999, 29 April 1999. The Council delayed implementation of the
Regulation for a year to allow bilateral negotiations with the US and multilateral negotiations in
ICAO to proceed. The Regulation entered into force on 4 May 2000. However, its most stringent
provisions, restricting the use of certain aircraft, were not to take effect until April 2002. As described
in this section, following the adoption of new multinational noise standards in ICAO, the Council
adopted a Directive on 26 March 2002 establishing new Community rules on aircraft noise and
repealing the Regulation.

[63] Of course, the Regulation had the effect of closing off the European market for the sale of
hushkits and retrofitted aircraft; it also limited those markets in third countries, to the extent that
prospective purchasers had intended to fly into the Community.

[64] Secondary environmental concerns included air pollution and fuel consumption by retrofitted
aircraft.

[65] Since the EC as such is not a member of ICAO, the complaint was filed against the 15 member
states individually.

[66] Directive (EC) 2002/30, 26 March 2002.

[67] See US Department of State Press Statement, 'US Withdrawal of Complaint at the ICAO,' 13
June 2002, available at http://www.state.gov/r/pa/prs/ps/2002/11096.htm, last visited 8 November

standards made it possible to resolve the dispute. While the case is unusually specialized, however, like other TBT disputes it involves broad questions of economic structure and regulatory policy.

A. Why did the dispute arise?

1. *Noise regulation by ICAO*

It is impossible to analyze the hushkits dispute without first filling in the regulatory background. The 1944 Chicago Convention on International Civil Aviation authorized ICAO to adopt standards and recommended procedures, as Annexes, in such areas as aircraft safety, economics and environmental protection. ICAO has been the principal source of noise standards for civil aviation since 1971, when it adopted Annex 16, 'Environmental Protection'. Volume 1, Chapter 2 of that Annex set maximum noise standards for types of jet aircraft first certificated as airworthy after its effective date (eg, the Boeing 727 and DC9).[68]

In 1977, ICAO adopted new, stricter noise standards, set out in Chapter 3 of Annex 16, Volume I. This rapid move to lower noise limits was made feasible by significant advances in technology, notably the development of high by-pass ratio engines.[69] Like the earlier ICAO standard, Chapter 3 applied only to aircraft types designed and certificated after its effective date (eg, the Boeing 777 and Airbus 340). Models certificated before 1977 remained subject to the less stringent Chapter 2 standards.

In spite of the new rules, public complaints about noise around airports continued to gather force. Aircraft fleets were becoming quieter as more Chapter 3 models were introduced, but growth in air traffic and development close to airports offset this effect. The continued operation of older, noisier Chapter 2 aircraft drew special attention from governments and in ICAO, but regulators had to balance competing economic concerns: protecting carriers' huge investments in Chapter 2 aircraft, many of which had decades of useful life remaining; creating certainty for planning; and considering the needs of developing countries, which disproportionately rely on older aircraft.

In 1990, the US Airport Noise and Capacity Act (ANCA)[70] unilaterally mandated the phase-out of Chapter 2 aircraft from US service, with a transition period for orderly adjustment lasting to the end of 1999. Shortly thereafter, the

---

2002. The US temporarily maintained its case against Belgium, challenging a Belgian decree that limited the hours of operation of certain aircraft.

[68] ICAO standards are designed to limit the negative effects of aircraft noise on humans. Since these occur almost exclusively when aircraft are flying near the ground, mainly around airports, ICAO sets maximum 'effective perceived' noise levels, measured in decibels, for particular aircraft types at three points: under the landing path, under the take-off path, and at the point to the side of the runway where downward noise is maximized. ICAO also specifies techniques for measuring effective perceived noise. See W. Franken, 'Experts Propose More Stringent Standards for Noise from Large Jets and Propeller-driven Aeroplanes' (2001) 56 *ICAO Journal* 8.

[69] Ibid.

[70] Pub L No 101–508, codified at 49 USC App sec 2151 et seq.

ICAO Assembly authorized (but did not require) all members to phase out the operation of Chapter 2 aircraft between 1995 and 2002, with limited exceptions, while urging members not to restrict Chapter 3 aircraft.[71] Most developed nations, including the EU, adopted Chapter 2 phase-out requirements on this schedule.[72]

The EU soon began pressing for a revision of Chapter 3, already 13 years old in 1990. While there had been no technical breakthroughs like those in the mid-1970s, a series of smaller developments made more stringent standards feasible.[73] The ICAO Committee on Aviation Environmental Protection (CAEP) engaged in technical work on the issue throughout the 1990s, but was unable to agree. From the EU perspective, the main problem was resistance by the US, which 'blocked all progress on the noise issue'.[74]

2. Hushkits

Facing a 1999 deadline for phasing out aircraft certificated only under Chapter 2, US operators—especially low-margin cargo and charter carriers—had a strong incentive to seek recertification of those aircraft as compliant with Chapter 3. Several approaches for doing so emerged. One was to impose operating restrictions, eg, lower maximum weights or speeds. A second was to 're-engine' the aircraft with quieter engines. The third and least costly was to fit existing engines with 'hushkits', sound-absorbing mufflers that were developed by US companies primarily to facilitate recertification.[75] Hundreds of older aircraft were tested and recertificated by the Federal Aviation Administration (FAA) after 1990 as complying with Chapter 3, primarily through the use of hushkits. European carriers used far fewer hushkits, in part because the EU phase-out period began later and extended longer than that in the US.[76]

Most hushkits were designed to enable an aircraft to meet Chapter 3 standards, but not to go beyond them. Further muffling would add cost and reduce performance. While the parties disputed all the data cited in the dispute, the EU argued that even the quietest recertificated aircraft exceeded the Chapter 3 standard by fewer than 5 decibels, whereas some newer models were 25 decibels quieter.[77]

---

[71] See J. Hupe, 'Experts Reformulating Strategy for Alleviating Aviation's Impact on the Environment' (2001) 56 *ICAO Journal* 5. The Assembly authorized special consideration for developing country carriers.

[72] Council Directive (EEC) 92/14, 2 March 1992.

[73] The technical problems were significant, however. See Franken, note 68 supra.

[74] See European Commission, Information Pack, 'Aircraft Noise: The Recertificated Aircraft Regulation'; telephone interview with official of Delegation of the European Commission, Washington, DC, 5 August 2002.

[75] See US Department of Transportation, Fact Sheet: European Union's Restriction of Hush Kitted and Re-Engined Aircraft, 26 June 2001, at 1; A. Depitre, 'Re-certification of Aircraft to New Noise Standards Remains an Important Issue' (2001) 56 *ICAO Journal* 14–15. ICAO standards did not explicitly authorize recertification.

[76] Other possible reasons for this difference are discussed below.

[77] See Aircraft Noise, note 74 supra, at 5–6; Regulation (EC) 925/1999, preambular para 5. The EC also criticized the recertification procedures of the FAA. See ibid at 4.

3. Political forces in the EU

Throughout the 1990s, member state governments and EU institutions faced strong political pressure from environmental groups, Green parties, local authorities and the general public to act on noise around airports. Community policies increasingly addressed the issue. For example, the fifth action programme on the environment, adopted in early 1993, set a goal of reducing all noise that endangers health and quality of life, including aircraft noise;[78] noise control was also part of the principle of 'sustainable mobility' implemented throughout the common transport policy.[79]

The specific political trigger for the Regulation was a series of unilateral operating restrictions imposed by individual European airport authorities on Chapter 2 aircraft. These included curfews, surcharges and even complete bans.[80] As the Commission put it, local restrictions were 'often different and sometimes conflicting, creating confusion for operators within the Community'.[81] (A similar profusion of local restrictions, with disruptive effects on interstate commerce, had led Congress to adopt ANCA in 1990.[82]) A Community-wide response was needed.

The Commission also asserted a more specific concern with recertificated aircraft that helped shape the Regulation: US owners of such aircraft might transfer them in large numbers to European operation around the 1999 US phase-out deadline rather than taking them out of service, significantly worsening the noise problem.[83] This rationale does not seem overly persuasive, as hushkits and re-engining represented significant investments made precisely to comply with the requirements of ANCA. Hushkit manufacturers characterized the transfer issue as 'a terrible misunderstanding', and cited data suggesting that few hushkitted aircraft were actually transferred near the deadline.[84] But the Commission argued that reputational considerations would still lead US carriers to rid themselves of these older aircraft.

[78] OJ 1993 C 138, cited in Regulation (EC) 925/1999, preambular para 3.

[79] Regulation (EC) 925/1999, preambular para 1.

[80] See M.W. Atwood, 'Noise Wars: The EU-US Dispute over Hushkits and Re-engined Aircraft', available at http://www.aea200.ea.faa.gov/aea60/noise/noise1a.htm, last visited 8 November 2002, at 2–3. Mr Atwood is counsel to the Noise Reduction Technology Coalition, makers of hushkits.

[81] Aircraft Noise, note 74 supra, at 1.

[82] See EU Hush Kits—Testimony by John Meenan, Senior Vice President for Industry Policy, Air Transport Association, before the House Committee on Transportation and Infrastructure, 9 September 1999, available at http://www.air-transport.org/public/testimony/display2.asp?nid=864, last visited 8 November 2002. Under FAA regulations implementing ANCA, US airports may not restrict aircraft federally certificated to Chapter 3 standards without FAA approval. See Atwood, note 80 supra, at 3.

[83] See Aircraft Noise, note 74 supra, at 3. With this problem in mind, the Community criticized the unilateral US decision to phase out Chapter 2 aircraft by 1999 and its failure to conform its deadline to that later set by ICAO. Ibid. The issue figures prominently in early discussions of the Regulation. See European Parliament, Legislative Observatory, legislative history of Regulation (EC) 925/ 1999, SYN/ 1998/0070.

[84] See Atwood, note 80 supra, at 8. The more serious concern might have been the transfer of non-hushkitted Chapter 2 aircraft for the period between the 1999 US deadline and the 2002 EC/ICAO deadline, but this was not the focus of the Regulation.

4. Adoption of the Hushkits Regulation

The EU began considering restrictions on recertificated aircraft as early as 1997. In that year Commission officials floated a proposal in the European Civil Aviation Conference (ECAC), comprising member state aviation officials. The FAA expressed concern, and the initiative was dropped. In March 1998, the Commission adopted a draft directive.[85] The European Parliament voted to strengthen the proposal in several ways, including transforming it into a regulation. The Commission accepted the change of legal form in an amended proposal; the 'common position' further strengthened the proposal's substantive provisions. The Council adopted the Regulation on 29 April 1999.[86] Some provisions were to take effect immediately, retroactive to 1 April, but the Council suspended application until 4 May 2000 to allow discussions with the US and in ICAO to proceed.

The Regulation addressed only 'civil subsonic jet aircraft' (CSJAs) that had been recertificated to Chapter 3 standards (RCSJAs). CSJAs included only aircraft above a stated weight or passenger capacity, and only those powered by engines with a by-pass ratio of less than three. RCSJAs included Chapter 2 CSJAs that had been recertificated after modification with hushkits, new engines or other technical changes, or after imposition of operational restrictions. Re-engined RCSJAs were only covered if the new engines had by-pass ratios of less than three.[87]

The Regulation imposed two major restrictions on RCSJAs.[88] First, under the 'non-addition' rule, RCSJAs could not be registered in a member state after the effective date (deferred to 4 May 2000)—unless they were already so registered on that date and continually thereafter. The 'unless' clause meant that RCSJAs previously registered in a member state could be transferred to a different member state after the Regulation, whereas they could not be transferred from a non-member to a member state. This variation was said to be necessary in a 'Community without internal frontiers'.[89]

Second, under the 'non-operation' rule, as of 1 April 2002 (the Chapter 2 phase-out date), RCSJAs registered in third countries could no longer operate at Community airports—unless they were registered in the same country on the effective date and had been operated in the EU between April 1995 and that date. This rule was necessary to 'minimize possible distortions of competition'

---

[85] See US Department of Transportation, Chronology: European Union's Restriction's [sic] against Hushkitted and Re-Engined Aircraft, 26 June 2001.

[86] Legislative history, note 83 supra.

[87] Regulation 925/1999, Article 2. The EU's reliance on by-pass ratio was controversial. As noted earlier, high by-pass engines were responsible for major advances in noise control during the 1970s. The Commission thus argued that the criterion was based on sound scientific evidence regarding noise production, and that the FAA had recognized a by-pass ratio of three as a useful cutoff point, see Aircraft Noise, note 74 supra at 5. US industry and the US government argued that reliance on by-pass ratio rather than direct measurements of noise output constituted an arbitrary design standard, see Atwood, note 80 supra; US Department of Transportation, Fact Sheet, note 75 supra.

[88] Regulation 925/1999, Article 3.

[89] Ibid, preambular para 7.

between EU and third country carriers. Even RCSJAs already registered in a member state could not operate at EU airports after 1 April 2002 unless they were operated there before the effective date. This restriction was designed to ensure equal treatment regardless of country of registration.[90]

US carriers,[91] hushkit makers,[92] policy observers,[93] and government agencies[94] were highly critical of the Regulation. They decried its economic effects,[95] its seemingly discriminatory character,[96] its reliance on design features like by-pass ratio rather than direct noise measurements,[97] its bypassing of the multilateral process,[98] and its impact as precedent.[99] They also suggested that political and economic motivations, not just environmental concerns, were behind its adoption. EU officials responded vigorously on all these points,[100] arguing that the Regulation was a 'reasonable and short-term answer to legitimate environmental concerns'.[101]

B. How was the dispute managed and resolved?

1. *Dispute management*

The hushkits dispute reached a high level of intensity around the adoption and deferred effective date of the Regulation, but earlier actions, including the

---

[90] Ibid, preambular paras 10–11. [91] See Meenan Testimony, note 82 supra.

[92] See Atwood, note 80 supra.

[93] See Economic Strategy Institute, 'What Is the EU Hush Kit Regulation?', available at http://www.econstrat.org/EUHushKit.htm, last visited 19 June 2001.

[94] See, eg, US Department of Transportation, Fact Sheet, note 75 supra.

[95] The US argued, even while application of the Regulation was deferred, that delayed and cancelled orders for hushkits and replacement engines amounted to $1.6 billion, and that the resale value of hushkitted US aircraft had been diminished by $500 million. See US Department of Transportation, Questions and Answers on Hushkits, 21 January 2000. The EU argued that these figures were overstated. See Aircraft Noise, note 74 supra.

[96] In addition to the discrimination inherent in the non-addition rule, US interests argued that the Regulation had been crafted so that certain equally noisy aircraft and engine types produced and used in Europe fell (sometimes by a small margin) on the acceptable side of the line. Further, all makers of hushkits were based in the US. See Meenan Testimony, note 82 supra. See also US Mission to the EU, Transcript: Press Briefing, David L. Aaron, Undersecretary of Commerce for International Trade, 14 March 2000, available at http://www.useu.be/ISSUES/hush0314.html, last visited 24 June 2001. ('You can not persuade us that this was anything other than a tricky way to exclude our companies.')

[97] See Economic Strategy Institute, note 93 supra.

[98] See US Department of Transportation, Questions and Answers, note 95 supra ('threatens the whole ICAO system for establishing global aviations standards'). The EU argued that ICAO standards only addressed certification of new aircraft types, not recertification of older types to more recent standards. See Aircraft Noise, note 74 supra.

[99] The concern of US industry was that the Regulation would undermine the viability of hushkitting, re-engining and similar techniques as strategies for dealing with the next generation of ICAO standards. See Atwood, note 80 supra, at 6–7. See also Aaron Press Briefing, note 96 supra ('our companies and many other countries are going to say... why should we work so hard to come up with a plan in ICAO, why should we start making investments based on ICAO rules, when suddenly the Europeans may just change the rules?').

[100] See Aircraft Noise, note 74 supra.

[101] Commissioner Loyola de Palacio, 'The EU Deeply Regrets the US Decision to File Article 84 Action with the International Civil Aviation Organization', 15 March 2000.

Commission's 1997 ECAC proposal and its 1998 draft directive, had already brought several dispute management techniques into play. One conclusion stands out clearly from the events of that period: failure to resolve the dispute can in no way be attributed to a lack of dispute management forums or procedures. As with TBT problems generally, officials utilized multiple channels throughout the dispute.

These techniques included:

- bilateral technical talks between aviation authorities, of the kind that have resolved many low-stakes TBT disagreements;
- political discussions between officials of member state governments and European institutions (eg, the Transport Commissioner, the President of the Council, the President of ECAC), on the one hand, and US agencies including the Commerce Department, the FAA and Transportation Department, and the State Department, on the other. Discussions took place at multiple levels, from technical to political to ministerial;[102]
- diplomatic contacts between US and member state embassies and the US and EU delegations in Brussels and Washington;
- talks at ICAO, including intensive technical discussions in CAEP;[103]
- discussions in the WTO Civil Aviation Committee;[104]
- consultations in the TEP institutions;
- talks in preparation for US-EU economic summits and at the December 1999 summit itself;
- discussions at the NATO summit in April 1999.

Congress held hearings on the subject, and each house adopted resolutions designed to pressure the EU.[105] In addition, according to the US, the President of the ICAO Council expressed concern over the proposed Regulation to the President of the EU Council.[106]

By March 2000, a deal to avert a formal dispute proceeding was nearly at hand. In essence, this would have involved: (1) a joint US-EU declaration to guide the ongoing CAEP negotiations; (2) US deferral or suspension of any ICAO filing; and (3) EU suspension of the Regulation pending completion of ICAO negotiations, or more accurately Commission efforts to obtain approval for such

---

[102] See, eg, US Department of Transportation, Chronology, note 85 supra.

[103] When the Regulation was adopted, the Council and Commission jointly issued a declaration committing themselves to work on a new ICAO standard as a high priority. The US and EU began active negotiations shortly thereafter. See Aircraft Noise, note 74 supra, at 1, footnote 1.

[104] See, eg, US Trade Representative, Assessment of the First Five Years of Operation of the GATT Agreement on Trade in Civil Aircraft, available at http://www.ustr.gov/wto/99ustrrpt/ustr99_aircraft.htm, last visited 26 June 2001.

[105] In March 1999, the House voted to rescind the waiver of US noise regulations that allowed Concorde to operate through New York if the Regulation were adopted; in September it called on the President to protest the Regulation in ICAO and use all reasonable means to persuade the EU to rescind it. In July 1999, the Senate voted to call for ICAO dispute resolution if the Regulation were adopted. See US Department of Transportation, Chronology, note 85 supra.

[106] This took place in March 1999. Ibid.

a suspension.[107] However, on 13 March this package fell through, for reasons that are not fully clear.[108] On 14 March, the US filed its complaint with ICAO.

2. *The ICAO dispute resolution proceeding*

US industry almost unanimously favoured ICAO as the venue for dispute resolution, framing the issue as one of unilateral EU action inconsistent with ICAO rules.[109] The US Department of Transportation was centrally involved in the dispute, and it too favoured resort to ICAO, an institution where it is bureaucratically active.[110] Even Congress favoured this approach: each house voted to pursue an ICAO proceeding if the EU did not rescind the Regulation.[111] The singular focus on an ICAO proceeding is striking, given that almost all the other disputes considered in this volume—involving a wide range of sectors and issues—were submitted to the WTO, which has a much stronger dispute resolution mechanism.[112]

Two considerations seem to have determined the strategy of US industry. First, ICAO is the lynchpin of a highly developed international aviation regime. ICAO administers a system of harmonized standards and legal principles that are crucial to the success of an international industry. For example, the Chicago Convention includes most-favoured-nation and national treatment principles that constrain national regulation, and it requires member states to accept airworthiness certifications issued by foreign governments. Especially for carriers, the most serious effect of the Regulation may have been its threat to harmonization and multilateralism. A WTO proceeding might have addressed the immediate problem,[113] but the broader benefits could be better protected in ICAO.

---

[107] See 'US Studying European Proposal to End Dispute over EU Hushkit Law, Officials Say', 17 *BNA Int'l Trade Rep*, 2 March 2000, 364.

[108] See 'EU Official Sacks US Hushkit Proposals: US Proceeds with Complaint Before ICAO', 17 *BNA Int'l Trade Rep*, 16 March 2000, 428. The Commission asserted that US industry had forced US negotiators to reject the compromise. See Commissioner Loyola de Palacio, note 101 supra. Former Undersecretary of Commerce Aaron essentially confirmed this view in comments at the initial Florence conference on this project, in July 2001. At the time, however, the US claimed that the deal had collapsed over a minor procedural point, EU unwillingness to allow the US to file an ICAO complaint before agreeing to suspend it. See Aaron Press Briefing, note 96 supra.

[109] See, eg, Meenan Testimony, note 82 supra. The Aerospace Industries Association asked the US Trade Representative if a section 301 filing against the Regulation were possible, but it too favoured action in ICAO. See 'USA Looks to ICAO to Settle European Hushkit Row', *Air Transport Intelligence*, 10 September 1999.

[110] See US Department of Transportation, Questions and Answers, note 95 supra. Undersecretary of Commerce Aaron indicated that a WTO complaint had been considered, but that the US preferred the ICAO route. See 'USA Looks to ICAO', note 109 supra.

[111] See US Department of Transportation, Chronology, note 85 supra.

[112] Some industry groups were willing to consider later resort to the WTO if ICAO did not produce a satisfactory outcome. See Atwood, note 80 supra, at 10.

[113] It is not clear, however, whether a WTO complaint would have been successful, especially because the Regulation formally restricted aviation services rather than the sale of a product. It does not appear that the US government performed a full workup of possible WTO arguments once attention focused on ICAO. Telephone interview with US Department of State official, June 2001.

Second, it was in the interest of US carriers to keep aircraft noise regulation firmly in the hands of ICAO, where they could exert their influence to defer adoption of more restrictive standards. (New standards would fall more heavily on the US industry, as European fleets were generally younger.)[114] ICAO environmental decision-making is complex and time-consuming: it begins with a CAEP recommendation, which must be adopted by consensus; the ICAO Council and the full membership must then endorse the recommendation. With developing countries generally opposing stricter regulation, the process is subject to extensive delays—as evidenced by the 20 year gap since the adoption of Chapter 3.[115]

The US filed its complaint under Article 84, the principal dispute resolution procedure of the Convention. This procedure contemplates a decision by the ICAO Council (with parties to the dispute not voting) on disagreements relating to the interpretation or application of the Convention and its Annexes that cannot be resolved by negotiation.[116] Parties may appeal from the Council to an ad hoc tribunal, if all agree, or to the International Court of Justice. If a state fails to comply with a Council decision, the Assembly can suspend its voting rights there and in the Council.

On 18 July 2000, the respondents filed preliminary objections challenging the jurisdiction of the ICAO Council to hear the US complaint. They argued that negotiations had not yet failed, that the US had not exhausted its remedies in European courts, and that the US was seeking excessive remedies that would create new obligations for ICAO members.[117] In December 2000, the Council found for the US on admissibility.[118]

The Council then asked the parties whether they wished it to hear the case at that time, or whether they preferred to continue negotiating with the mediation of the Council President. Both sides chose the latter option, as intense negotiations on a new noise standard were already underway. Dr Kotaite met separately with each side to clarify facts and positions, then met several times with the two sides together.[119] However, the substantive negotiations soon became the main locus of activity, with both sides looking to those talks to produce the conditions for resolution of the dispute.

---

[114] The US government was more willing than US carriers to accept new standards, as it also had to contend with public pressure over aircraft noise. But the industry undoubtedly had great influence on US policy.

[115] See Aircraft Noise, note 74 supra, at 2.

[116] None of the three earlier disputes reached the stage of Council decision.

[117] See Response of the United States of America to the Preliminary Objections Presented by the Member States of the European Union Before the Council of the International Civil Aviation Organization, 15 September 2000, available at http://www.state.gov/documents/organization/6840.doc, last visited 20 January 2003; Commissioner de Palacio, 'EU/US Aircraft Noise Dispute: EU United in Stance Before International Aviation Body,' 21 July 2000, available at http://www.eurunion.org/news/press/2000/2000038.htm, last visited 19 June 2001.

[118] See 'Contemporary Practice of the United States Relating to International Law, Admissibility of U.S.-EU "Hushkits" Dispute Before the ICAO' (2001) 95 *Am. J. In'tl L.* 410.

[119] Telephone interview with Dr L.J. Weber, Director of Legal Bureau, ICAO, 3 September 2002.

3. ICAO negotiations and Chapter 4

If the Regulation was intended to catalyze ICAO negotiations on new multilateral noise standards, it was quite successful. Even after the March 2000 collapse of a settlement that would have included a joint declaration on ICAO standards, US-EU and broader multilateral discussions in CAEP progressed rapidly.[120]

The EU sought new standards, to replace Chapter 3, that would limit aircraft noise 'at the source'. It also sought an ICAO decision authorizing or requiring all members to phase out marginally compliant Chapter 3 aircraft (eg, recertificated aircraft) or all Chapter 3 aircraft. Short of that, it sought authority for individual states or regions to impose Chapter 3 phase-outs. The US was willing to accept a technologically feasible noise standard, but sought to protect existing investments in recertificated aircraft and the ability to use recertification to comply with future standards. The US also opposed any broader Chapter 3 phase-out. More generally, the US favoured the kind of 'balanced approach' incorporated in ANCA, under which regulators must consider techniques like land use management and noise abatement procedures, depending on local conditions, rather than relying solely on source regulation.[121]

In January 2001, just weeks after the Council decision on admissibility, CAEP agreed to recommend a new standard limiting aircraft noise at the source, to be denominated Chapter 4.[122] The ICAO Council accepted this recommendation in June 2001.[123] The new standard would reduce maximum allowable noise by 10 decibels on a cumulative basis.[124] It would apply only to new aircraft types certificated after 1 January 2006, even though many recent production models already meet the standard. CAEP also recommended new procedures for recertificating Chapter 3 aircraft to Chapter 4; this action simultaneously preserved

---

[120] See Aircraft Noise, note 74 supra, at 2.

[121] See 'Global Noise and Emissions Standards for Civil Aircraft,' US Department of Commerce Aerospace News, available at http://www.ita.doc.gov/td/aerospace/ aerospace_noisenews1.html, last visited 8 November 2002; 'International Body Sets Noise Standards for Next-Generation Aircraft— No Forced Phase-out of Stage-3 Aircraft,' Noise Regulation Report, October 2001, available at http://www.netvista.net/~hpb/news/oct-22a.html, last visited 8 November 2002; Air Transport Association, 'International Agreement Reached on Aviation Environmental Matters', 11 October 2001, available at http://www.air-transport.org/public/news/pda.asp?nid=3363, last visited 8 November 2002; J. Garvey, 'Complex noise issue calls for environmentally and economically responsible solution' (2001) 56 *ICAO Journal* 20.

[122] See Hupe, note 71 supra; 'CAEP recommends further measures for reducing aircraft noise, engine exhaust emissions' (2001) 56 *ICAO Journal* 1.

[123] See ICAO, Aircraft Noise: Reduction of Noise at Source, available at http://www.icao.org/cgi/goto_atb.pl?icao/en/env/noise.htm;env, last visited 17 January 2003. For a discussion of the ICAO actions, see Commission of the European Communities, Explanatory Memorandum, in Proposal for a Directive of the European Parliament and of the Council on the Establishment of Rules and Procedures with Regard to the Introduction of Noise-Related Operating Restrictions at Community Airports, COM(2001)695 final, 28 November 2001, paras 2–3.

[124] Because newer aircraft designs reduce noise to different degrees at different points (eg, on take-off or on landing), the new standard requires a 10 decibel reduction in the sum of the perceived effective noise at the three standard measurement points, with no one point below its existing Chapter 3 maximum. See Franken, note 68 supra.

the option of recertification and regulated a process that the EU felt had been abused.[125]

CAEP could not reach consensus that a phase-out or other operating restrictions on Chapter 3 aircraft would be cost-effective; it left these issues to other ICAO organs. For its own future work, however, it agreed (consistent with its past deliberations) that noise management should be pursued through a balanced approach that allows environmental goals to be achieved in a cost-effective manner.[126]

At its 33rd meeting, 25 September to 5 October 2001, the ICAO Assembly adopted a 'Consolidated Statement of Continuing ICAO Policies and Practices Relating to Environmental Protection' to complement Chapter 4.[127] Under the new policy, members are to apply the balanced approach on an airport-by-airport basis. Each airport authority is to use a transparent decision process to consider alternative noise reduction strategies, including—as a last resort—operational restrictions like a phase-out of marginally compliant aircraft, and select the most cost-effective combination. Thus, while no member or group of members can restrict or phase out Chapter 3 aircraft on a blanket basis, individual airports can do so in the context of a balanced approach.

4. *New EU legislation and resolution of the dispute*

These actions by ICAO provided the substantive basis for settling the hushkits dispute. In November 2001, the Commission proposed new European legislation, in the form of a directive, to implement the new ICAO policies.[128] Directive (EC) 2002/30 (the 'Directive') was adopted on 26 March 2002.[129] In general, the Directive requires member states to adopt a balanced approach to noise on an airport by airport basis, considering the likely costs and benefits of alternative responses as well as individual airport characteristics, and imposing measures that are non-discriminatory and no more restrictive than necessary. It requires specific decision procedures, including public notice, consultation and appeal.

The Directive also makes special provision for restricting or even phasing out the operation of 'marginally compliant' Chapter 3 aircraft (now defined by noise production rather than the use of hushkits or similar devices), if an assessment demonstrates that such a restriction is necessary. In this sense the Directive is more restrictive than the Regulation, which only banned new registrations or service; however, the Regulation applied to the entire Community, while under the Directive only individual airports can impose operating restrictions. The

---

[125] See Depitre, note 75 supra.

[126] See Hupe, note 71 supra. In this connection CAEP adopted new guidelines for land use planning and noise abatement procedures.

[127] ICAO Resolution A33/7 (October 2001), available at http://www.icao.org/cgi/goto_atb.pl?icao/en/env/noise.htm;env, last visited 17 January 2003. This policy replaces an earlier consolidated statement of policies from 1998. The resolution includes annexes on the balanced approach, land use and similar issues.

[128] See Proposal for a Directive, 28 November 2001, note 123 supra.

[129] OJ 2002 L085/40–46.

Directive also provides for the review of operating restriction decisions by the Commission, with an appeal to the Council.

As part of the overall settlement, the Directive repealed the Regulation as of April 2002, when it was to come into effect for aircraft registered in third countries. Shortly thereafter, the US announced at ICAO that it was withdrawing its complaint.

C. The role of private interests and government departments

In the EU, an unusual coalition of private interests came together in support of the Regulation. This coalition included environmental advocates, the core *demandeurs* for such a measure. It also included groups concerned about aircraft noise in their communities, many of which were not active on other environmental issues. Crucial to the strength of the EU position, however, was the European aviation industry. As in the US before 1990, European carriers were increasingly hampered by proliferating local restrictions, and supported a uniform Community solution.

The Regulation was framed in a way that responded to the demands of environmental and community advocates while keeping the support of the European industry. Indeed, it was framed in one of the few ways that could have done so. First, the Regulation addressed many of the noisiest aircraft still flying,[130] although relatively few such aircraft were being operated in Europe. Second, it did not repeal, constrain or harmonize local noise restrictions, although it was presented as obviating the need for additional restrictions.[131] Third, the Regulation had little effect on European carriers. European fleets were much younger than US fleets: in particular, major European carriers[132] had upgraded to aircraft designed for Chapter 3 on a much larger scale than their US competitors. The Regulation fell more heavily on US carriers: although they could fly few recertificated aircraft on transatlantic routes, the Regulation limited the resale market for those aircraft.[133] Finally, all makers of hushkits were located in the US.

The Regulation was drafted by DG Energy and Transport.[134] Throughout the dispute, Commissioner Loyola de Palacio was the most visible figure on the Community side. This branch of the Commission was well placed to consider both the environmental aspects of the proposal—because of its experience in

---

[130] This would have been even more the case after the Chapter 2 phase-out in 2002. US interests noted, however, that some aircraft as noisy as those covered by the Regulation were not restricted. See, eg, US Department of Transportation, Fact Sheet, note 75 supra; Atwood, note 80 supra, at 5–6.

[131] See Aircraft Noise, note 74 supra, at 1.

[132] Some smaller, low-fare European startup carriers planned to rely more heavily on older aircraft. These firms were adversely affected by the Regulation, and opposed it.

[133] The most serious adverse effect was on carriers from developing and transitional countries that hoped to add recertificated aircraft to their fleets serving Europe. However, the Commission noted that even this effect was limited, as most recertificated aircraft could not be flown on any long-distance routes, eg, between Asia or South Africa and Europe. See Aircraft Noise, note 74 supra, at 6.

[134] See Legislative History, note 83 supra.

developing the Community's 'sustainable mobility' policy—and its impact on European industry. However, it was less well placed to consider the trade effects of the measure and the possible response of the US. The Regulation was adopted by the Industry and Transport Council. In the European Parliament, the responsible committee was concerned with environmental and consumer issues. While the legislative powers of Parliament are limited, the environment committee, and Parliament as a whole, acted aggressively to strengthen the Regulation and to oppose any settlement that would weaken it.[135]

In the US, the political situation was very different. There were no major beneficiaries of EU action, while three powerful industry groups were adversely affected:

- The manufacturers of hushkits, joined in the Noise Reduction Technology Coalition. These firms claimed to have lost from $150 million to $500 million in revenue even before the Regulation came into effect; they foresaw much larger losses if the Regulation set a precedent that hushkitting could not be used to comply with future noise standards.[136]
- US carriers, joined in the Air Transport Association. These firms had used hushkits and re-engining extensively to comply with the US Chapter 2 phase-out. While they flew few recertificated aircraft to Europe, they estimated the reduction in the market value of these older aircraft at well over $1 billion. They too were concerned with protecting these methods of complying with future standards.[137]
- US manufacturers of aircraft engines and parts, members of the Aerospace Industries Association. The Regulation might have cost these firms some sales related to older engines. More significantly, though, for these suppliers the Regulation set a worrisome precedent.

These groups had significant influence on the two US government departments most actively involved in the hushkits dispute: the Departments of Commerce and Transportation. It seems clear that the US industries had been largely responsible for delaying the adoption of new noise standards in ICAO, and were most responsible for the strong US government reaction to the Regulation. The unanimous position of US industry that ICAO was the most desirable forum in which to challenge the Regulation, for the strategic reasons discussed earlier, also went far to persuade Congress and the relevant Executive agencies to follow that route.

D. Impediments to resolution of the dispute

Several structural differences between the US and the EU impeded settlement of the hushkits dispute. These included differences in airport characteristics,

---

135 Ibid. See also 'EU Official Sacks US Hushkit Proposals', note 108 supra.
136 See Atwood, note 80 supra, at 6–7.
137 See Meenan Testimony, note 82 supra.

industry structure and regulatory policy, all deeply intertwined. The Regulation touched on these differences in ways that exacerbated the dispute. Even with numerous channels of dispute management, the structural problems were difficult to overcome. As the dispute unfolded, moreover, perceptions of inaccurate claims by each side led to a climate of mistrust.

In US cities, aircraft noise around airports has been a significant public concern for years. Inconsistent local responses led Congress to adopt uniform national standards and procedures as early as 1990. However, the situation in Europe is even more severe: many large and busy airports are located close to major urban areas, or even inside city limits (eg, Berlin-Tempelhof, London City). European authorities faced strong public demand for corrective action. Industry and agencies in the US may not have fully appreciated the constraints under which EU authorities were acting.

To a considerable extent, this was because the Regulation from the start seemed to single out US carriers and products. Community authorities argued that this was simply because older US fleets and US hushkit makers were responsible for more noise. But US interests saw the Regulation as a thinly disguised protectionist measure that had limited environmental benefits.[138]

This debate was intensified by disagreements as to the policies responsible for the differences in industry structure. In the US view, European carriers had been able to modernize their fleets because European aviation markets, dominated by publicly owned national carriers, were less competitive than the US market. European carriers were encouraged to upgrade to Chapter 3-designed aircraft, and regulated fare structures allowed them to pass on the costs of doing so.[139] The highly competitive, private US fleet was forced to rely more heavily on hushkits and other forms of retrofitting. In this context, the Regulation's exclusive focus on recertificated aircraft seemed not only economically damaging, but also unjust. In addition, to the US it was not irrelevant that during the 1990s Airbus emerged as a major aircraft supplier, with government support. Airbus benefited substantially from the replacement of older European aircraft.

In the EU view, it was the 1990 passage of ANCA, requiring a US phase-out of Chapter 2 aircraft by 1999, that forced US carriers to invest in hushkits rather than new, quieter aircraft models and to keep older aircraft flying longer than was otherwise economically feasible.[140] Eventually, however, US carriers would have to divest themselves of these ageing aircraft. If they were put in service in Europe the noise problem would be significantly worsened, so EU authorities had to prevent such transfers.

Deeper differences in regulatory philosophy also contributed to the tensions. Both governments faced public demands to reduce noise around airports, and

[138] EU authorities repeatedly argued that US estimates of the economic impact of the Regulation were overblown, but each such argument raised questions about the environmental benefits of the Regulation.
[139] See Economic Strategy Institute, note 93 supra.
[140] See Aircraft Noise, note 74 supra, at 3.

both were taking costly measures to control it. As with TBT issues more generally, though, the US took the position that once ICAO and governments had set noise standards, the market should be allowed to determine the most cost-effective means of complying with them, including technological innovations like hushkits. Furthermore, while hushkits may have allowed aircraft just barely to comply with ICAO standards, that is the nature of standards: regulated parties must meet them, but they need not go beyond them. The EU, in contrast, favoured a less market-oriented approach. The Commission argued that compliance with ICAO standards through the use of hushkits and similar techniques was not contemplated when Chapter 3 was adopted, and was less effective than the best available technologies, in this case upgrading to entirely new aircraft. The Regulation—and indeed the current Directive—was from the beginning aimed at restricting 'marginally compliant' aircraft—which the US saw simply as 'compliant'.

These differences in viewpoint led each side to reject data and arguments advanced by the other. Factual arguments over the noisiness of US- and European-made engines, the muffling effects of hushkits, the recertification techniques used by the FAA, the economic impact of the Regulation, and similar matters were almost totally unproductive. As the dispute continued, these arguments were increasingly taken as tactical distortions, leading to a climate of frustration and mistrust. Indeed, the hushkits dispute was never settled on its own terms; it was only resolved as part of a larger multilateral solution.

III. CONCLUSIONS

Although the hushkits dispute was unique, it reinforces several of the conclusions about dispute management that can be drawn from disagreements on ordinary TBT issues:

Economic stakes. Most TBT cases are resolved without formal dispute proceedings because of the low stakes involved. In contrast, the hushkits dispute was difficult to resolve because the stakes were substantially higher—at least as the issues were framed by the affected US industries. This is especially so when one considers the precedential concerns the US carriers and hushkit makers raised. One should not expect too much from low-key dispute management procedures in economically important disputes.

Industry influence. Industry demands many types of product regulation, especially harmonizing standards that facilitate co-ordination and multi-jurisdictional operations. This was also the case with the Regulation. While it did not in fact harmonize inconsistent local regulations (as the Directive does), European carriers sought and supported Community action to forestall further local regulation. They even supported new ICAO standards. Industry also functions as a 'fire alarm' for problematic regulation abroad; US carriers and hushkit makers clearly operated in this fashion. More controversially, industry often frames technical disagreements in expansive terms to persuade higher levels of government to take them up; such escalation can hamper settlement. The hushkits dispute lends some support to these conclusions as well.

Early transparency and consultation. The most significant debate between the US and the EU in the area of TBT regulation concerns the need for transparency and timely consultation on regulatory initiatives. Transparency and early consultation also facilitate the transnational dialogue that often leads to accommodation. The hushkits case confirms the importance of these factors. In particular, adoption of the Regulation seems to illustrate the US complaint that the Commission often fails to reveal its plans and engage in consultation until it completes a legislative proposal. US industry and the FAA were aware of earlier discussions in ECAC. Still, especially with a proposal tailored explicitly to address foreign interests, systematic efforts at early disclosure and consultation should be an essential dispute avoidance technique. By the time aviation authorities were fully engaged in the hushkits dispute, they were acting as advocates for national positions, not as members of an epistemic community seeking optimal regulation. The Guidelines on Regulatory Co-operation may have some beneficial effect in this regard, although they are limited to regulations involving goods subject to the TBT Agreement.

Trade impact assessment. Technical standard setting often creates adverse external effects that legislators and other non-specialist regulators do not fully recognize in advance. These are frequently incidental and unanticipated, but they can also constitute the hidden agenda of advocates for regulation. The WTO TBT agreement and its transparency and consultation requirements are intended to deal with just such problems. However, domestic procedures designed to reveal potential international effects at earlier stages of decision-making—such as a trade impact assessment—could do even more to prevent disputes. No such procedures appear to have been followed during consideration of the Regulation on hushkits. Indeed, in comments at the initial conference on this project in July 2001, Ambassador Hugo Paemen, head of the Delegation of the European Commission in Washington in 1999, suggested that Commission services other than Energy and Transport were unaware of the economic and foreign policy import of the hushkits proposal at the time the Commission approved it. The ensuing dispute makes a good case for the wider use of trade impact assessment procedures.

International negotiations. Disagreements over international standard setting are continuing features of US-EU TBT disputes. The usual arguments turn on the EU contention that the US does not follow international standards, and the US contention that the EU diverts international institutions to serve its narrow interests. International standards processes were even more central to the hushkits dispute, because of their importance to international aviation. The EU had long sought stricter ICAO noise standards, because of its environmental concerns and public demand, and probably also because its carriers were better positioned to comply than most of their competitors. The US, on the other hand, had for years resisted new standards, primarily because of the circumstances and the influence of its industry.

In this context, the Regulation can be seen primarily as a device to force the US and other governments to agree on new noise standards in ICAO. Such an agreement would have environmental and economic benefits for Europe, but these were longer-term goals; the immediate environmental and economic impacts of the Regulation were secondary. Such political techniques are difficult to avoid when powerful states are at odds in international forums; for example, the US has frequently used section 301 to pressure other states to negotiate in the WTO. When national regulations are adopted with this goal in mind, some earlier conclusions are no longer relevant. Trade impact assessment, transparency and early consultation, and technical discussion no longer constitute useful approaches, since foreign impact is precisely what is desired. Similarly, escalation to higher official levels may be desirable, since only there can national negotiating positions be changed.

Bilateral settlements. Finally, the hushkits case represents a class of disputes in which bilateral settlements—and forums devoted to bilateral settlements, such as the TEP institutions—are not necessarily desirable. Aircraft noise regulation may be an area where uniform international standards are essential, but there are undoubtedly many other areas where they are advantageous. Beyond uniformity as such, moreover, reliance on international procedures helps ensure that all concerned interests are represented in rule-making. The highly developed US and EU aviation industries, for example, are hardly representative of world aviation; ICAO negotiations make it possible for developing and transitional economy countries to help shape international rules.

9

International Competition Policy Co-operation

K. MEHTA*

I. INTRODUCTION

Competition policy has long histories in both the United States and the European Union and yet it was only in 1991 that a bilateral co-operation agreement in competition matters was concluded and entered into force. Prior to that, the framework for co-operation was provided by the OECD recommendation, compliance with which was voluntary.[1] The concept of a bilateral agreement can be traced to the then EC Commissioner for Competition, Sir Leon Brittan, who foresaw that the adoption of the EC's Merger Regulation could raise tensions over jurisdiction in relation to transborder mergers and risks of inconsistencies in regard to remedies. The need for a formal instrument of co-operation can, however, be explained by reference to the ongoing globalization process. While globalization of markets and internationalization of factor movements also has a long history it may be said that especially with the Single Market programme in the EU, the major motor force, from the mid-1980s, in transatlantic economic relations was the liberalization in the domestic EU economy, a process that inevitably reinforced the ongoing liberalization in international trade.

A particular feature of the international economic integration since the late 1980s has been the proliferation of transborder mergers and joint ventures with the emergence of a transatlantic market for corporate control and for corporate equity. Cross-border transactions, as compared with the coalescence of entities into national champions, have a number of redeeming qualities. They possibly contribute more to geographically widening and integrating markets, create greater potential for gains from trade and efficiencies as well as for competitive

* The views and opinions expressed are purely personal. I have greatly benefited from the helpful comments of my colleague Youri Devuyst. Comments made on the paper by Professor Merit Janow at the European University Institute Conference of 5–6 June 2001 are gratefully acknowledged and, where possible, referred to in the paper.

[1] See the successive Recommendations of the OECD Council of 5 October 1967, C(567)53(Final); 3 July 1973, C(73)99(Final); 25 September 1979, C(79)154(Final); 21 May 1986, C(86)44(Final); 27 July 1995, C(95)130(Final).

transfer of technology and innovation. Furthermore, the shift in focus away from national champions has brought to the fore a policy concern with international competition rather than international competitiveness. With these good reasons for concentrating on competition and enforcement of rules, competition policy in Europe has rightly assumed a central role in the policies to create and maintain an integrated and open internal market. It is against this background, of competition policy playing an increasingly important role on both sides of the Atlantic, that one has to see the development of a formal tool of EU-US bilateral co-operation and its development.

This paper begins with an outline of the framework of competition laws in the EU and the US. It proceeds in section III to describe the judicial developments that have confirmed in particular the extra-territorial scope of the laws. Section IV discusses the main elements of the EU-US bilateral agreements, while section V describes how the agreements have worked in practice. A consideration of the factors accounting for the relative success as well the unresolved sources of tension is attempted in section VI that ends with some comments on prospects for further developments in co-operation.

II. COMPETITION LAW IN THE EU AND THE US

In both the EU and the US the rules prohibiting anti-competitive conduct by undertakings have been in place for several decades. Their adoption was based on the recognition of the crucial role of competition between undertakings for assuring that economic activity is not deflected from attaining allocative efficiency through the creation and exercise of market power.

In the EU the basic competition rules already figure in the treaty establishing the European Coal and Steel Community. In the EEC Treaty of 1957 the objective of ensuring that competition in the common market is not distorted is amongst its fundamental principles. The Treaty articles that give substance to this principle can be summarized in three basic antitrust rules. The first prohibits all agreements or concerted practices between undertakings or associations of undertakings that may affect trade between member states and that have as their object or effect the prevention, restriction or distortion of competition within the common market. Such agreements are declared void. There is an exception for those agreements that are indispensable for improving the production or distribution of goods or for promoting technical or economic progress while allowing customers a fair share of the resulting benefits without eliminating competition in a substantial part of the products in question (Article 81). The second basic antitrust rule prohibits an undertaking singly or collectively abusing its dominant position in a substantial part of the common market in so far as intra-EU trade is affected (Article 82). In the third place, anti-competitive restrictions or dominant positions that are facilitated or created by public authorities are explicitly subject to antitrust scrutiny unless the application of such rules would obstruct the performance of tasks of general economic interest (Article 86 in combination with Article 81 or 82). In regard to mergers (or more precisely acquisition or change in corporate control of undertakings) Council Regulation 4064/89 sets out the procedures and exclusive competence for the Commission to prohibit operations of a Community dimension that create or strengthen a dominant position that would impede effective competition in a substantial part of the common market.

The reach of competition rules in the EU has grown apace with the completion of the Single Market in 1992 and as economic activity has permeated, with liberalization, privatization and deregulation to a number of sectors such as media, sport utilities, transport, and telecommunications that were either statutory monopolies or where integrated markets were underdeveloped.

In the US the adoption of comprehensive antitrust rules predated by several decades those adopted in the EU: their influence on and inspiration for EU rules is also readily apparent.[2] The Sherman Act of 1890 prohibits agreements restrictive of commerce; the prohibition extends to conduct amounting to monopolization, attempts to monopolize or combine or conspire to monopolize any part of interstate trade and commerce. The Clayton Act of 1914 prohibits such restrictive practices as price discrimination, exclusive and tying contracts, acquisitions of competitors and interlocking directorates—if 'the effect may be to substantially lessen competition or tend to create a monopoly'.[3] The section on price discrimination was further revised to protect the small firm, by complementing the oversight of the unfair tactics of the monopolistic supplier with that of the powerful buyer able to secure unjustifiable advantages vis-à-vis the small trader. The Clayton Act was revised and made more stringent in respect of horizontal mergers by the Celler Kefauver Act of 1950.

The prohibitions of the Sherman Act create criminal offences sanctionable by fines and even imprisonment: the Department of Justice (DOJ) has exclusive enforcement powers in relation to the Sherman Act. Clayton Act enforcement is a shared responsibility of two federal agencies—the Federal Trade Commission (FTC) and the antitrust division of the DOJ. In addition to federal enforcement several individual states have enacted their own antitrust laws that are enforced by state antitrust authorities. In the EU, while Article 81(1) and Article 82 can be and are applied by national competition authorities and national courts, the Commission alone can grant exemption decisions under Article 81(3).[4] The Commission

---

[2] E. Fox & R. Pitofsky, 'United States' in E.M. Graham & J.D. Richardson (eds), *Global Competition Policy* (1997), at 235.

[3] A.D. Neale & D.G. Goyder, *The Anti-Trust Laws of the United States of America. A Study of Competition Enforced by Law* (1980).

[4] The currently proposed revision of procedural Council Regulation 17/62, OJ 1962 P 013, foresees the removal of the Commission's monopoly of Article 81.3 and its replacement by a system of legal exception under which Article 81 in its entirety can be applied by national courts and national competition authorities. This revision would also mean that prior notification of restrictive agreements under Article 81.1 are no longer necessary. See Commission of the European Communities, *Proposal for a Council Regulation on the implementation of the rules on competition laid down in*

also has exclusive competence for mergers of a Community dimension while mergers, even if having cross-border effects but not satisfying the turnover thresholds set out in the EC Merger Regulation, fall to be assessed by national competition authorities. Parallel powers of enforcement of the prohibition rules contained in antitrust laws is thus a common feature in both the US and the EU.

III. Extra-territorial Enforcement of Antitrust Rules

The framework of competition law in the US and the EU, with their very comprehensive and general formulation of the laws, foresees the possibility and even the probability of extra-territorial enforcement. That the antitrust rules should apply without exception to all undertakings, whether domestic or foreign, active in a jurisdiction is without doubt essential to ensure effective enforcement against any anti-competitive conduct within a territory. Equally arguable, but perhaps more controversial, domestic markets and consumers may be significantly affected by anti-competitive conduct of undertakings situated outside the borders; furthermore national exporters may find that their access to certain third country markets is constrained by dominant market position or private restraints foreclosing the market in question. Thus it is that the US courts have developed since the Supreme Court's 1911 decision in *US v American Tobacco Co*, an expansive notion of US antitrust jurisdiction, elaborating what has come to be known as the 'effects' doctrine.[5]

Considerations of international comity developed by the courts during the 1970s have not in fact tempered the assertion of extra-territorial jurisdiction of US antitrust laws.[6] In fact the clarification provided by the Supreme Court in *Hartford Fire Insurance Co v California* (1993) would tend to suggest that comity would only be taken into account once jurisdiction has been established and could only have an impact on the outcome if the foreign undertaking was compelled to act in a way prohibited by US antitrust law. The effects doctrine can and has been used to challenge restrictive business practices exempt from foreign competition laws but not exempt from US antitrust law. Such exercise of extra-territorial jurisdiction is not surprisingly a source of tension in international antitrust, particularly as the US has its own exceptions to antitrust law such as exempting export cartels from US antitrust laws.

Articles 81 and 82 of the Treaty and amending Regulations (EEC) No 10117/68, (EEC) No 2988/74, (EEC) No 4056/86 and (EEC) No 3975/87, COM(2000) 582, 27 September 2000.

[5] J.P. Griffin, 'Extraterritoriality in US and EU Antitrust Enforcement' (1994) 67 *Antitrust Law Journal* 159.

[6] P. Torremans, 'Extraterritorial Application of EC and US Competition Law' (1996) 26 *European Law Review* 280. See also R.A. Brand, *Fundamentals of International Business Transactions* (2000), at 1105; E. Fox, 'National Law, Global Markets, and Hartford: Eyes Wide Shut' (2000) 68 *Antitrust Law Journal* 73.

The extra-territorial application of EU antitrust was clearly recognized by the *Wood Pulp*[7] judgment of the European Court of Justice (ECJ)[8] when it upheld the Commission's jurisdiction in applying Article 81[9] to an alleged price fixing agreement and concerted practice amongst non-EU producers of wood pulp. In upholding the applicability of EU competition rules to conduct occurring outside the EU, the ECJ did not endorse the Commission's advocacy of the effects doctrine. In the court's view it was not enough that the effects of the agreements and concerted practices in the common market were intended, direct and substantial: there was also a requirement that the agreement/concerted practice be *implemented* in the Community. Parties to an agreement/concerted practice that do not themselves or through subsidiaries or agents transact any business with customers in the Community cannot be said to have implemented the agreement/concerted practice in the EU.

In the field of merger control both in the US and the EU the pre-merger notification requirements and hence the substantive provisions apply to operations by undertakings situated completely outside national jurisdiction, to the extent that certain turnover thresholds are triggered (in the case of the EU) or if the operation meets minimum sales and asset acquisition requirements (US Hart-Scott-Rodino Act thresholds). Specifically the EC Merger Regulation establishes jurisdiction for the exclusive Commission competence to review operations satisfying certain global and EU turnover thresholds—the turnover could in effect be in products/services totally unrelated to the products/services which are the centre of the parties' transaction in question, on operations which themselves may involve no acquisition of assets in the EU.[10] Having an asset test in the notification trigger would certainly be one way to limit the requirement to notify operations having little conceivable impact in a jurisdiction and hence provide an obvious way to limit extra-territoriality.[11]

---

[7] OJ 1984 L27/85.

[8] Cases 89, 104, 114, 116, 117 and 125–129/85, *Ahlström v Commission* [1988] ECR 5193. See also D. Lange & J.B. Sandage, 'Wood Pulp Decision and its Implications for the Scope of EC Competition Law' (1989) 26 CMLR 136; W. Van Gerven, 'EC Jurisdiction in Antitrust Matters: The Wood Pulp Judgement' in B.E. Hawk (ed), *1989 Annual Proceedings of the Fordham Corporate Law Institute International Law and Policy Conference (1990)*, at 451.

[9] Article 81(1) states: 'The following shall be prohibited as incompatible with the Common market: all agreements between undertakings, decisions by association of undertakings and concerted practices which may affect trade between Member States and which have as their object or effect the prevention, restriction or distortion of competition within the Common market.'

[10] See F. Montag, 'Common Market Merger Control of Third-Country Enterprises' (1991) 13 *Comparative Law Yearbook of International Business* 47.

[11] In contrast to regulatory oversight applying to internationally traded products and coming under WTO rules, no jurisdiction to date has sought consultation with another on the way turnover triggers have been set to compel notification of merger and joint-venture operations and on defining notification rules that claim expansive jurisdiction over merger and joint-venture operations of foreign-based undertakings.

The Commission's jurisdiction over mergers involving non-EU undertakings whose activities are primarily located outside the EU was further clarified by the Court of First Instance's *Gencor* judgment of 1999.[12]

The case concerned a concentration of the mining and refining activities in platinum group metals (PGM)—the assets in question being located in South Africa although both the undertakings had the necessary turnover because of business interests (other than purely trading in PGM) in the EU. The conclusion of the court does not make any reference to where the concentration was implemented, a notion that was crucial in the *Wood Pulp* judgment. At least for mergers the court would appear to have embraced the 'effects' doctrine since the judgment asserts quite simply that, in the case of a concentration satisfying Community dimension criteria and leading to the creation or reinforcement of a collective dominant position (presumably where the relevant market is global), in the view of the court 'the applicability of the [merger] regulation to collective dominant position can not depend on its territorial scope'.[13] The judgment does not discuss issues of international comity. It does, however, include an 'international law' test: the Community has competence when it is *foreseeable* that a proposed concentration will have an *immediate* and *substantive* effect in the Community.

IV. EU-US BILATERAL CO-OPERATION AGREEMENTS COVERING APPLICATION OF COMPETITION POLICIES

As has been pointed out,[14] 'extraterritorial application of antitrust law, once seen as predominantly a characteristic of US law, is increasingly a practice followed around the world'. In consequence, the need for an agreement to provide a framework for enforcement *co-operation* and for avoidance of conflicting decisions and management of any consequent disputes has become increasingly compelling. All the more so as competition policy increasingly attained a central role in economic policy with the completion of the Single Market programme by 1992. Furthermore, the ongoing process of globalization has also had the effect of internationalizing the market for corporate control.[15] Significant transatlantic and global mergers and acquisitions could only be contemplated by business if there existed a predictable path to regulatory

---

[12] Case T-102/96 *Gencor v Commission* [1999] 4 CMLR 971. For an analysis see A.A. Bavasso, 'Gencor: A Judicial Review of the Commission's Policy and Practice: Many Lights and Some Shadows' (1999) 22(4) *World Competition* 45; F.E. Gonzalez-Diaz, 'Recent Developments in EC Merger Control Law: The Gencor Judgement' (1999) 22(3) *World Competition* 3.

[13] Para 153 of the judgment. The implication being that if at least two of the parties have an aggregate turnover of €250 million, not necessarily in the product in question in the EU, and even if the sales of the product represented a minor share of global sales in the product, territorial scope is established if the operation could lead to creation or reinforcement of a collusive dominant position.

[14] M. Janow, Comment on this paper (copy on file with author).

[15] Sir Leon Brittan, 'Jurisdictional Issues in EEC Competition Law', Hersch Lauterpacht Memorial Lecture, Cambridge, 8 February 1990 (copy on file with author).

clearance in the two main jurisdictions. Competition law could be applied extra-territorially but in reality this raised a number of practical problems for unilateral enforcement in terms of gathering vital information and evidence located outside national jurisdictions, in enforcing cease and desist orders, and in designing and enforcing compatible remedies in cross-border merger operations. Thus, if the competition authorities were determined on a policy of strict enforcement of antitrust rules in relation to cross-border anti-competitive conduct and to multi-jurisdictional mergers and joint ventures, then it came to be recognized by the relevant agencies that the instrument of *co-operation* was a necessity.

The bilateral co-operation agreement between the EC and the US was concluded and entered into force in September 1991.[16] The foreseen co-operation is limited to competition authorities, specifically the European Commission on one hand and the Antitrust Division of the DOJ and the FTC on the other. The US antitrust authorities had earlier concluded similar bilateral co-operation agreements with at least one member state's national competition authority. That agreement concerns the application of national competition laws rather than EC competition law.

A. Main provisions

The essential obligations under the agreement relate to (1) notifying the other party of enforcement actions that may affect its important interests; (2) exchange of non-confidential information; and (3) co-operation and co-ordination in enforcement activities within the limits of Articles VIII (confidentiality of information) and IX (existing law). The notification provisions as well as co-operation modalities cover both enforcement activities and review of multi-jurisdictional mergers or joint ventures. As a result of the notification requirements, competition authorities on both sides of the Atlantic are sufficiently informed from an early stage and at all the crucial steps of antitrust and merger procedures. The exchange of non-confidential information provisions supplement the information contained in the notification to permit discussions on enforcement priorities, policy developments and reviews through the organization of regular bilateral meetings at high level. In this way co-operation and co-ordination between the competition authorities has been sustained not only in regard to case-related matters but also in respect of the overall evolution of antitrust policy in the two regions in response to changes in the global economic environment. Largely due to the accumulated trust built up over the years, the

---

[16] Initially, the agreement had been concluded, on the EC side, by the Commission on its own. However, on 9 August 1994, the ECJ held that it was for the Council to conclude such an agreement. This defect was remedied by a joint decision by the Council and the Commission of 10 April 1995, approving the agreement and declaring it applicable from the date it had first been signed by the Commission (OJ 1995 L 131/38).

authorities have also found the framework of the agreement useful for the discussion of questions of international competition policy.

B. Positive comity

In its Article V the 1991 agreement also introduced the instrument of positive comity. Positive comity allows for the possibility that a competition authority would, at the request of another competition authority, initiate and prosecute an investigation into anti-competitive activities occurring within its jurisdiction that are harming the important interests of the requesting party. In the Council and Commission decision of May 1998[17] clarifying the notion of positive comity, 'adverse effects' are defined as meaning harm caused by anti-competitive activities to:

- the ability of firms in the territory of a party to export to, invest in, or otherwise compete in the territory of the other party; or
- competition in a party's domestic or import markets.

The situation that the mechanism is designed to address is nullification or impairment of market access opportunities whose principal cause is private anti-competitive conduct. The agreement specifically excludes mergers. The 1991 bilateral agreement (Article V), which remains fully in force, states explicitly that the requested party has full discretion whether or not to undertake enforcement with respect to the anti-competitive activities notified to it by the requesting party, just as the requesting party has full discretion in deferring or suspending its own enforcement activities. The 1998 agreement does not elaborate on the conditions under which the requested party may or may not accept the positive comity request. On the other hand it does spell out conditions under which the requesting authority would normally defer or suspend its pending or contemplated enforcement actions. Indeed, if the requested authority complies with some or all of the reasonable requirements enumerated in the 1998 accord—best efforts in enforcement, constant and due consultation—then it is incumbent on the requesting party to motivate its reasons for not deferring or suspending its own enforcement actions, given its discretion to initiate or subsequently reinstitute such actions fully intact. The agreement has thus to be seen as a mechanism alternative to extra-territorial exercise of antitrust law, in market access disputes where the cause is private market dominance.[18]

---

[17] OJ 1998 L 173/26.

[18] In her comment on this paper, Merit Janow draws particular attention to the policy decision of the US DOJ during the Reagan administration to remove so-called 'footnote 159', effectively exercising its prosecutorial discretion to enforce actions against those export restraints that harmed US consumers and not those that only harmed US exports. See also, Y. Devuyst, 'Transatlantic Competition Relations' in M.A. Pollack & G.C. Shaffer (eds), *Transatlantic Governance in the Global Economy* (2001), at 127.

V. CO-OPERATION IN PRACTICE

A. Co-operation under the bilateral agreements[19]

Co-operation and co-ordination in relation to cases has developed most pro-foundly as far as mergers are concerned since the parties to the operation invariably grant waivers to the exchange of confidential information. The result has been a model of co-operation between competition authorities that encom-passes appropriate and due notification, close contacts at appropriate points in the assessment and, most significantly, co-ordination on possible remedies and their evaluation in order to ensure that merger clearance resolves identified competition concerns in both jurisdictions.

In 2001 the EC notified 84 cases to the US authorities while it received in return a total of 37 notifications. Merger notifications were the most significant, accounting for 71 of EC notifications and 25 of those of the US authorities. If notifications are any guide to the intensification of co-operation then the period since 1997 has seen a major increase in contacts and consultation on case-related matters with the number of notifications more than doubling on the EC side and showing a substantial growth (from 36 in 1997 to 58 in 2000) on the part of the US authorities. The year 2000, in particular, marked a special peak in co-operation in view of mega-mergers in the 'new economy', media and telecoms, notably AOL/Time Warner, Time Warner/EMI, MCI WorldCom/Sprint, as well as Boeing/Hughes and Astra Zeneca/Novartis. In the MCI WorldCom/Sprint merger of two US-based companies, both authorities concluded that a prohib-ition was warranted. In the Alcoa/Reynolds operation, the two authorities concluded that the operation could only be permitted subject to divestment of one of the party's major production plants, which happened to be located neither in the US or EU but in Australia.

This high degree of inter-agency co-operation underlies the comment,[20] 'EU-US cooperation in competition/antitrust law enforcement has become something of a model for transatlantic cooperation generally'. Such collaboration also suggests that, where the EU and US authorities reach different conclusions about whether or not to allow a particular transaction, this is generally because the effects of the merger are assessed to be different in the two jurisdictions and not because of conflicting substantiate rules or their interpretation.

However, quantitative indicators of the number of consultations may provide one indicator of intensity of co-operation but it is clear that such a statistical measure does not measure the potential for conflict as posed by contradictory

---

[19] In addition to the bilateral accords, the Commission and the US agencies (DOJ and FTC) concluded on 31 March 1999 pursuant to Article IV of the 1991 agreement certain administrative arrangements concerning the mutual attendance of their staff, where appropriate, at hearings held in certain stages of their respective procedure in individual cases. Bulletin EU 3-1999 (18/43).

[20] M. Monti, 'EU-US Co-operation in the Control of International Mergers: Recent Examples and Trends', Speech at the Institute for International Economics, Washington, DC, 27 March 2001 (copy on file with author).

decisions. Transactions between EU and US firms could be considered to fall into one of the following three categories—those raising no competition issues in either jurisdiction; those raising different competition concerns in one or other or in both jurisdictions implying that the relevant geographic markets are not global; and finally there is the category of merger transactions where the relevant geographic market is indeed global and where competition concerns are raised in one or both jurisdictions. In the first two categories the potential for inter-agency conflict is relatively limited if not absent, each jurisdiction authorizing transactions subject, where necessary, to remedies relevant to the competition concerns in its jurisdiction. Co-operation focuses on ensuring that remedies are coherent and that divested assets in both jurisdictions are acquired by entities that would best sustain competitive constraints on the merging parties. Thus it is perhaps not surprising that quantitative measures of case co-operation would support the conclusion that EU-US competition relations are characterized by 'regulatory co-operation' aimed at achieving optimally a common enforcement goal.[21] However it is in the category of transactions where the relevant market is global that the issue of serious potential conflict can arise and reveal policy divergences that would test the conflict management provisions of the co-operation agreement. This aspect is considered further below.

B. Positive comity in practice

In the period since 1991 there has in fact been only one formal positive comity request under the agreement: this concerned the request by the US DOJ in 1997 to the EC to investigate the allegedly discriminating behaviour by Amadeus, a computer reservation system owned by Air France, and other European airlines vis-à-vis its competitor Sabre, owned by American Airlines.[22] The lack of formal requests suggests either that the problems of market access that the mechanism is supposed to address are uncommon or more likely that antitrust authorities in the EU and the US, when approached by their exporting undertakings with market access complaints, invite such firms to make use of the effective and more than adequate complaints procedures that are available in both the jurisdictions and which are open to all firms, domestic and foreign. The cases of informal positive comity requests referred to in the literature[23] are precisely those cases when the complaints procedure has been initiated by the foreign undertaking alleging discriminatory market access. To an important degree the value of the positive comity agreement has been to limit extra-territorial

[21] Devuyst, supra note 18, at 127.

[22] The Commission carried out an in-depth market enquiry that led to the opening of a formal procedure (1999) against Air France for alleged abuse of dominant position. The case was concluded in mid 2000 after Air France undertook to offer equivalent terms to those offered to Amadeus. Commission report to the Council and Parliament on the application of the Agreement between the European Communities and the Government of United States of America 2000.

[23] M.E. Janow, 'Transatlantic Cooperation on Competition Policy' in S.J. Evenett, A. Lehmann & B. Steil (eds), *Antitrust Goes Global. What Future for Transatlantic Cooperation?* (2000), at 29.

application of antitrust rules and hence also the tensions arising from such use. This development has no doubt been sustained by the recognition by undertakings that the appropriate instruments to redress problems of market accessibility already exist and are effective in both the EU and US jurisdictions. A credible enforcement authority faced with potential harm to consumer welfare in its territory has every incentive to act when market accessibility to foreign firms is limited through the exercise of market power.

VI. Evaluating EU-US Co-operation in Competition Policy

Analyzing the competition co-operation between the EU and US authorities brings to the fore a number of considerations that may be suggestive for other domains of transatlantic relations.

(1) Where there are, as here, significant interjurisdictional differences in procedures and substantive law, the principal channel of enforcement co-operation is, inevitably, case co-operation. As multijurisdictional operations, particularly mergers, have increased as a proportion of the authorities' caseload, such co-operation has also grown beyond simple consultation. Actual case co-operation as regards enforcement against transnational cartels is considerably less given the limitations on an exchange of confidential information. Notwithstanding that each jurisdiction thus separately pursues investigations into cartels having an impact on their territories, there has been a very substantial convergence in relation to leniency policy and provisions.

(2) Case-based co-operation has also given the impetus to early and closer collaboration in the development of competition policy. Examples include the review in both the EU and the US of policy in regard to competitor collaboration (horizontal agreements), the EU's vertical restraints review, and leniency notices. In addition, Commissioner Mario Monti and his US colleagues Charles James and Tim Muris agreed to expand and intensify the activities of the existing bilateral working group on mergers. The purpose is to identify areas where more convergence might be possible. To this effect several subgroups have been set up which look into various procedural and substantive aspects of merger control.[24] Needless to say intensive policy consultation does not always lead to common policies or to policy convergence. For instance, the EU has developed a distinctive policy to tackle public regulatory restraints, and there are evident differences in appreciating the role that a multilateral agreement on core competition principles under the WTO could have in addressing cross-border anti-competitive conduct and market accessibility.

---

[24] A. Schaub, 'Cooperation in Competition Policy Enforcement between EU and New Concepts Evolving at the World Trade Organization and the International Competition Network', Speech at the Mentor Group, Brussels, 4 April 2001, 11–12 (copy on file with author).

(3) The development of policy and case-related co-operation would also seem to depend on two other features that may easily be taken for granted. The first is the commonality in the sense of an activist enforcement policy stance in regard to antitrust violations and strict merger control. Second and related is that the common focus of competition policy has largely been governed by the objective of preserving an effective competitive process. The divergent assessments of the GE/Honeywell merger operation[25] thus dented the prevailing image of co-operation. Up to then the absence of any major multi-jurisdictional case that required balancing static versus dynamic efficiencies, or balancing short to medium-term consumer welfare gains against uncertain but possibly significant long-term losses had sustained a high level of co-operation despite different substantive criteria of competitive assessment. It is worth noting that the case coincided with a debate on how meaningfully, in an economic sense, each jurisdiction's substantive tests and law ensured the pursuit of allocative efficiency.[26]

(4) As already noted above in section V.A, a high level of case co-operation concerned transatlantic merger transactions where the relevant geographic markets and competitive concerns were distinct and the challenge was for the two authorities to arrive at coherent remedies. In a real sense the potential for policy divergence and its consequences may be considered more significant in the limited number of cases where the relevant geographic market was determined by both authorities as world-wide. The number of cases, where the principal markets affected by the transaction were world-wide amounts to at least 17,[27] overwhelmingly in the aircraft equipment, satellite and telephony sectors. Both jurisdictions prohibited the WorldCom/MCI/Sprint operation and all but two other transactions were cleared by both jurisdictions. The two examples of an exceptional situation where divergence in the substantive assessment did matter are Boeing/

---

[25] See point (iv) below for more details. GE is the world's largest producer of large and small jet engines and through GECAS is one of the largest aircraft leasing companies. Honeywell International is a leading firm in the production of avionics including navigating equipment, non-avionic products, corporate jet and engine starters. The operation was not opposed by US DOJ; it was prohibited by the EU Commission on 3 July 2001.

[26] See, eg, D.B. Andretsch *et al*, 'Competition policy in dynamic markets' (2001) 19 *International Journal of Industrial Organisation* 613–634; the prepared remarks of T.J. Muris, 'Merger enforcement in a world of multiple arbiters' before Brookings Institution Roundtable on Trade and Investment Policy, 21 December 2001 (copy on file with author); and OECD Committee on Competition Law and Policy's summary record of Roundtable on portfolio effects in conglomerate mergers, 6 December 2001.

[27] The cases are GE/Honeywell (aircraft engines, avionics), Allied Signal/Honeywell (avionics), Boeing/McDonnell Douglas (large commercial aircraft), Lockheed Martin/Loral (equipment for civil aircraft), DASA/FOKKER (aircraft), Metso/Svedala (rock crushing equipment), ABB/Elsag Bailey (spectometers, chromatographs), Boeing/Hughes (satellites and launch services), WorldCom/MCI (internet telephony), FT/DT/Sprint (telephony), MCI/WorldCom/Sprint (internet connectivity), Exxon/Mobil (oil and gas exploration), Shell/BASF joint-venture (PE technology), Astra/Zeneca, Astra Zeneca/Novartis, Ciba/Sandoz (pharmaceutical R&D), Shell/Montedison (PP technology). Several others such as Gencor/Lonrho were notifiable in the EU but not in the US as they did not meet the asset trigger for notification.

McDonnell Douglas and GE/Honeywell. In the former, the FTC's review of the merger concluded with the majority assessment that the low and falling market share of McDonnell Douglas would revert to the remaining two significant and effectively competing incumbents and so the acquisition by Boeing would not substantially lessen competition in the relevant market. For its part the EU Commission concluded that, as presented, the operation would risk reinforcing the dominant position of Boeing. In the GE/Honeywell transaction, which the US DOJ did not oppose (subject to remedies in a specific military market), the EU Commission concluded that the transaction would be incompatible with the common market given the dominant market position of GE in large aircraft engines and reinforcement of this position because of GE's strength in aircraft leasing and its financial strength combined with Honeywell's strong market position in the avionics business. These contradictory decisions pinpoint differences in the merger substantive test as a possible source of divergence; a small increment in market share could be interpreted as a reinforcement of a dominant position under the largely market-share based criterion of EU law, while leaving unaffected the market power of the parties as reflected by the Lerner index under a substantial lessening of competition criterion. The dominance test assesses the market position of the merged entity while the substantial lessening of competition considers the degree of competition in the market: to a large extent these may coincide, differences are not however excluded.[28]

(5) The co-operation agreement does not have provisions for resolving differences in substantive criteria; on the contrary the agreement explicitly upholds existing laws in the EU and the US. The private parties who are the addressees of the contested decision can then employ the judicial review process in place in the respective jurisdictions. It is not surprising then that neither the Boeing case nor the more recent GE/Honeywell case have led to suggestions for a dispute resolution mechanism. However, these policy divergences have given significant impetus to joint efforts under the Co-operation Agreement at seeking convergence in matters relating to questions of substance and procedure.

(6) In regard to managing the possible conflicts that may arise in the application of different substantive tests it has been suggested[29] that the expert antitrust community could have an important role to play. Professor Janow suggests that EU and US law differs on what constitutes dominance and abuse of

---

[28] The US criterion tests whether the post-merger oligopoly equilibrium is qualitatively and quantitatively consumer welfare reducing as compared with the pre-merger situation. EU law provides for a situation where a pre-merger dominant position is not impeding effective competition in the common market but whose reinforcement in the same or a connected market would impede effective competition in the common market. W. Kovacic, 'Transatlantic turbulence—the Boeing-McDonnell merger and international competition policy' (2001) 68 *Antitrust Law Journal* 805 argues similarly that the source of divergence was the EU's concern about entrenchment of dominance even though the EU had recognized that McDonnell was no longer a real force.

[29] M. Janow, supra note 14.

dominant position with the result that, in certain situations, preserving the 'competitive process' can have different meanings in application because the US antitrust law and policy tends to define its core mission in terms of consumer welfare rather than a notion of fairness. Expert economic and legal analysis have certainly in the past contributed to the sound development of antitrust enforcement aimed at assuring efficient allocation of resources whether within national boundaries or more globally. This avenue has the advantages of focusing on essentials, of objectivity, and encouragement of best practices that result from peer review.

The overall conclusion that is supported by this analysis of EU-US bilateral agreements in the field of competition policy is that co-operation has become an essential policy instrument in the assessment of multijurisdictional mergers and in combating cross border anti-competitive activity. There has also been some substantive cross-fertilization, mainly from US to EC practice, such as definition of the relevant market and the approach to assessment of mergers underlying the US mergers guidelines of 1992. However, given the underlying differences in substantial law between the US and EU, rare cases of conflict may and do arise. They do not put into question continued co-operation, which in the main concerns cases where the relevant markets are jurisdiction-specific. In view of that, proposals for further formally enhancing co-operation have focused on two areas: a second generation agreement to permit the authorities to exchange confidential information, and various steps towards some procedural harmonization of merger procedures. Furthermore, progress towards convergence is pursued through informal means such as joint working groups.

VII. BILATERAL CO-OPERATION — PERSPECTIVES

Co-operation in cartel enforcement would certainly be of substantial benefit if the authorities could exchange confidential information. However a number of difficult problems stand in the way: lack of harmonization of sanctions, differences in investigating powers, procedural differences, rules of disclosure and differences in substantive standards.[30] At the same time functioning leniency policy in each of the jurisdictions provides an effective way round the need to exchange confidential information. Leniency and, under certain circumstances, total immunity from sanctions enable each jurisdiction to acquire directly from the leniency beneficiary the information necessary to prosecute all the cartel members. While this latter alternative is a second best solution and not as expeditious in prosecuting and bringing to an end hardcore cartels, it is effective

---

[30] See a detailed discussion in G. Kiriazis, 'Obtaining and Sharing Evidence in International Cartel Investigations: Stocktaking and Perspectives in the EC', in *Advanced International Cartel Workshop* (New York: ABA Section of Antitrust Law, 15–16 February 2001), Vol 2, Table 33 (copy on file with author).

and has the advantage of not requiring substantial revision of the legislative framework.

The various suggestions[31] for simplifying, streamlining, harmonizing and worksharing between agencies in transnational mergers are directed at reducing transaction costs for firms and often require significant legislative changes: it being unclear which agency should make the requisite modifications in the absence of any agreed benchmarks. The most profound proposals imply an implicit multilateral accord on deferment of action by an agency, or a bilateral agreement that allocates jurisdiction for merger assessment to one authority. In fact the European Economic Area agreement falls precisely in this latter category where mergers creating or reinforcing a dominant position in the EEA fall to be assessed solely by the Commission, subject to the review of the ECJ. Thus the route of a far reaching bilateral agreement to allocate jurisdiction, eliminate conflictual decision making, and subject to a recognized review mechanism is not unknown although it is an exceptional structure.

As to future prospects, the various concrete suggestions for enhancing co-operation under the EU-US agreements in order to improve the efficacy of antitrust enforcement and additionally reduce transaction costs for firms and increase transparency, will no doubt meet with a favourable response from competition authorities. Credibility and efficacy of enforcement after all effectively remove the pressure to apply antitrust laws extraterritorially and thereby eliminates one major possible source of tension between jurisdictions. This perspective also seems to underlie the arguments advanced by those[32] who have put forward the need for a multilateral agreement on core competition principles, on capacity building, and on credible enforcement. The International Competition Network created in October 2001 has indeed been a catalyst in substantially advancing analysis in common and consensus building in order to focus on standards of best practice in relation to merger notification procedures.

A significantly different situation is presented when the source of potential conflict resides in different substantive standards between jurisdictions particularly in the competitive assessment of mergers. The European Commission's consultative Green Paper[33] on issues for consideration in the ongoing merger review exercise indeed invited comments on the substantive test of dominance versus substantial lessening of competition and on the role and scope of the

---

[31] See the report of International Competition Policy Advisory Committee (2000), submitted by advisory committee (J. Rill, P. Stern, M. Janov et al, February 2000) to Assistant Attorney-General Klein, US DOJ. In an interesting paper, Neven and Röller consider the problem of allocating jurisdiction in merger cases, coming to the conclusion that where the relevant market is global, conflict will only arise if antitrust agencies pursue objectives that are not purely related to competition criteria. Damien Neven and Lars-Henrik Röller, 'The Allocation of Jurisdiction in International Anti-Trust', University of Lausanne Research Papers No 9916.

[32] See E.M. Graham & J.D. Richardson, 'Issue Overview' in E.M. Graham and J.D. Richardson (eds), *Global Competition Policy* (1997), at 3.

[33] Green Paper on the Review of Council Regulation (EEC) 4064/89, COM (2001) 745/6, 11 December 2001.

efficiencies exception. There is thus an ongoing debate in the EU on possible changes to the applicable substantive test. The substantive standards that hold sway in any jurisdiction are a reflection of established case-law, legal precedents and evolutions in competition policy and so the rate of convergence of the substantive approach to competition problems is likely to be gradual. That there is some measurable progress towards convergence is undoubtedly due to what Larry Summers[34] has referred to in another context as globalization of economic thinking. Fortunately in the field of competition rules in contrast to other areas of regulatory oversight, the application of the rules to concrete cases is more dependent on guidelines, issued by the competition authority, and revision of guidelines is much more regular than revision of the substantive test. Furthermore, the guidelines have the further purpose to ensure a uniform enforcement practice within the jurisdiction given a particular test. The Commission's merger review resulted in a proposal to the Council at the end of 2002 that refines the substantive test as well as submits draft Commission guidelines for merger assessment.

In conclusion, in the absence of uniform antitrust laws the potential for conflicting decisions by competition authorities in multijurisdictional cases is a possibility and, given highly integrated transatlantic economic relations, the stricter authority[35] could *de facto* make decisions that have significant international spillovers. In other regulatory contexts, this type of problem is countered by adopting and requiring adherence to a common set of scientific principles; in the EU the consistency of decisions of the national authorities and of the Commission as regards individual cases and policy is assured in an effective way by a primacy rule and ultimate review of the ECJ. In contrast to other regulated domains, competition policy is not subject to current WTO rules: this distinction being justified on the grounds of maintaining prosecutorial discretion and independence of tribunals and courts which provide the necessary safeguards in terms of due process, adequate redress and possibility of private actions. The evident downside is an increasing multiplicity of jurisdictions that are involved in global transactions, each applying basically similar economic laws with a varying degree of sophistication. To the extent that convergence on common rules and their homogeneous application is not attained, an 'expanded toolbox for managing friction' such as exchange of information on best practices and joint analysis in the context of bilateral accords and discussions in other fora remains the most realistic way of avoiding conflict and friction.[36]

---

[34] L.H. Summers, 'Distinguished Lecture on Economics in Government: Reflections on Managing Global Integration' (1999) 13(2) *Journal of Economic Perspectives* 3.

[35] T.J. Muris, supra note 26, section II.

[36] M. Janow, supra note 14.

10

Managing US–EU Trade Relations through Mutual Recognition and Safe Harbor Agreements: 'New' and 'Global' Approaches to Transatlantic Economic Governance?

GREGORY SHAFFER*

I. Introduction

The US and European Community (EC)[1] increasingly face the difficult task of reconciling the objectives of protective social regulation, on the one hand, and free competition facilitated through open trade policies, on the other. Regulatory and trade policies may conflict for two primary reasons. First, domestic law-makers and regulators typically do not take account of the impact of domestic regulations on foreigners, primarily because foreigners do not have a voice in domestic political and regulatory processes. Second, regulatory divergence reflects genuine difference in constituent preferences, and there is no reason why these differences must be harmonized or made compatible.

Thus, the challenge confronting political leaders is to reduce redundant regulatory barriers to trade, where possible, without sacrificing democratic choice regarding the appropriate allocation of risks and the appropriate procedures for addressing them. The task is far from easy. To attempt to meet this challenge, US and EC political leaders, under the aegis of the New Transatlantic Agenda (NTA),[2] have devised some preliminary structures for transatlantic political

---

* The arguments set forth in this chapter are expanded in Gregory Shaffer, 'Reconciling Trade and Regulatory Goals: The Prospects and Limits of New Approaches to Transatlantic Governance through Mutual Recognition and Safe Harbor Agreements' (2002) 9 *The Columbia Journal of European Law* 29–77.

[1] The term EC is used in this chapter instead of EU (or European Union) because it is EC institutions that enter into bilateral agreements with the US under the 'first pillar' of the Treaty of European Union of 1992. The 1997 US-EC Mutual Recognition Agreement thus refers to the EC as a party, and not to the EU. Commentators, however, often use the term EU because it is broader in scope, covering all three pillars of activities.

[2] See M. Pollack & G. Shaffer, 'Transatlantic Governance in Historical and Theoretical Perspective' in M. Pollack & G. Shaffer (eds), *Transatlantic Governance in the Global Economy* (2001) 3, at 14–17.

and regulatory co-operation so that domestic regulatory processes are more likely to take account reflexively of the impact of domestic regulatory choices on non-constituents.

This chapter provides an overview of how the tension between the goals of domestic regulatory protection and liberalized trade have been addressed by the US and EC through transatlantic mutual recognition agreements and a hybrid form, the US-EC safe harbor principles on data privacy protection. The chapter assesses the prospects and limits, both politically and in the marketplace, of the US-EC Mutual Recognition Agreement (MRA) and its six sectoral annexes (of 1997), the US-EC Mutual Recognition Agreement on Marine Safety (initialled in June 2001), and the US-EC understanding on Safe Harbor Principles for data privacy protection (of 2000). The analysis is based on a review of relevant documentation coupled with interviews of dozens of US and EC regulatory and trade officials and private sector representatives.

The chapter advances four primary findings. First, transatlantic mutual recognition agreements need to be seen in the context of domestic and global business strategies to reduce regulatory compliance costs, to get new products quickly to market in a changing technological environment and thereby to enhance profits. Second, the agreements' implementation has been much more difficult than envisaged by business and government leaders on account of reactions in the marketplace and wariness of independent regulatory officials, particularly in the US. Third, the agreements and understandings have nonetheless spurred some domestic regulatory change, as well as some mutual recognition of product approvals. They also could spur some *de facto* harmonization of regulatory approval procedures and substantive standards, thereby reducing the potential for intergovernmental conflict in these sectors. Fourth, and perhaps most controversially, where there has been convergence, the convergence has tended toward EC—and not US—regulatory practices. As this chapter will show, the EC now has a sustained record under its single market programme of easing trade barriers among 15 EC member states working in 11 different languages, while retaining relatively high regulatory standards and considerable national diversity in implementation strategies. This practical experience, coupled with the EC's growing market power, has enabled EC regulators to put forward regulatory models that can be both attractive to firms and more pragmatic to adopt than their US counterparts.

II. HARMONIZATION AND MUTUAL RECOGNITION: THE EC'S 'NEW' AND 'GLOBAL' REGULATORY APPROACHES AND THE TRANSATLANTIC MARKETPLACE

A. Overview of the EC's co-ordination of national regulatory systems

Since 1985, the EC has adopted what it terms 'new' and 'global' approaches to European regulation, under which EC institutions only legislate 'essential requirements', delegate the determination of more detailed standards to quasi-public European standards organizations (the 'new approach'), and then co-ordinate quasi-public national certification bodies to certify products produced in any one member state for sale throughout the EC market (the 'global approach').[3]

In 1985, the European Commission issued a bulletin that set forth its 'new approach' to harmonization in response to the market-distorting and market-segregating impact of multiple national standards and the difficulty of appropri-ately overcoming them at the EC level, especially in light of rapidly changing technologies.[4] Under this 'new approach', the Council of Ministers (the Council) enacts framework directives for technical standards covering 'essential require-ments'. The Council then delegates the task of drawing up more-detailed stand-ards to industrial standardization bodies operating under the umbrella of three European standards organizations—CEN, CENELEC and ETSI.[5] These European standards organizations are comprised of national standards bodies that, in turn, include representatives from government, industry and other social groups. The European standards bodies vote on a simple majority basis,[6] facili-tating the adoption of 'non-essential' technical standards. These standards are not internally binding on the member states, so that member states retain some *de jure* autonomy. However, these standards have become *de facto* harmonized requirements for selling products within the EC on account of their importance in the marketplace.

Under what is termed the EC's 'global approach' to regulation, products may be tested and certified within any member state in order to receive a 'CE' marking (which indicates that they comply with '*Communite Europeen*' norms). All member states must recognize these certifications (ie, mandatory mutual recognition), such that certified products may circulate freely throughout the EC market. Each member state must approve and is responsible for oversee-ing the certification bodies (called 'notified bodies') within its jurisdiction and must notify the Commission's Enterprise Directorate-General (DG) of its ap-provals. Member state authorities periodically meet and exchange information about the operation of the process through working groups and committees created pursuant to the respective directives. They thereby attempt to build and retain confidence in the system.[7] This EC system can be characterized as governance by co-ordinated cross-border public-private networks.

---

[3] Guide to the Implementation of Directives Based on the New Approach and the Global Approach, http://europa.eu.int/comm/enterprise/newapproach/legislation/guide/document/1999_1282_en.pdf (visited 25 February 2002).

[4] Technical Harmonization and Standards: A New Approach: Bull. EC 1–1985.

[5] CEN is the acronym for the Comite Europeen de Normalisation (founded in 1961); CENELEC for the Comite Europeen de Normalisation Electrontechnique (founded in 1959); and ETSI for the European Telecommunications Standards Institute (founded in 1988).

[6] See M. Egan, *Constructing a European Market: Standards, Regulation and Governance* (2001) at 154–158 (noting two rounds of voting before decision by a majority vote, as well as other preliminary procedures).

[7] Firms and laboratories also remain subject to post-marketing member state regulatory controls, as well as market-reputational constraints.

B. Harmonization and mutual recognition in the transatlantic context: can the EC system be exported?

While there has been little effort to harmonize standards on a purely transatlantic basis, the US and European member states have negotiated through international fora. In turn, such international standards can facilitate the negotiation of bilateral mutual recognition agreements because, where parties operate under common standards and procedures, they more easily understand and develop trust in each other's regulatory practices. For example, the 1997 US-EC Mutual Recognition Agreement (MRA) is based largely on the mutual recognition of test results by 'Conformity Assessment Bodies',[8] which bodies, in turn, are evaluated pursuant to international standards set forth in ISO/IEC Guides. The international standard-setting bodies relevant to the sectors covered by transatlantic mutual recognition agreements include the International Standards Organization (ISO) (for a broad range of standards); the International Electrotechnical Commission (IEC) (for testing and certification standards); Codex Alimentarius (for food-related standards); the International Conference on Harmonization (for pharmaceutical standards); the Global Harmonization Task Force (for medical device standards); and the International Maritime Organization (for marine safety standards).

Mutual recognition agreements, in contrast, have been negotiated not internationally, but bilaterally or through regional fora. For example, the US and EC have or are in the process of negotiating mutual recognition agreements under the auspices of APEC and CITEL, as well as with individual countries, such as Canada, Australia, Japan, New Zealand and Israel.[9] The EC's experience in harmonizing and coordinating 15 national regulatory systems offers a model to be considered, and possibly exported, to these other contexts, including the transatlantic one. Yet, the EC's own experience also highlights the challenges that the US and EC face in governing the interface of their economies.

III. THE 1997 US-EC MUTUAL RECOGNITION AGREEMENT

A. What gave rise to the 1997 Mutual Recognition Agreement?

The issue of transatlantic standards became more important to firms engaged in transatlantic trade for two primary reasons. First, as transatlantic tariff barriers decreased, firms became more concerned with what they termed duplicative regulatory compliance costs. They pressed for their removal. This pressure increased with rising transatlantic investment, since divergent US and EC stand-

---

[8] 'Conformity Assessment Bodies' are the transatlantic analogue of 'notified bodies' operating within the EC market in the context of the EC's 'global approach'.

[9] See Mutual Recognition Agreements, http://europa.eu.int/comm/enterprise/international/indexb1.htm#intro (visited 26 February 2002).

ards and certification requirements most directly affect transatlantic corporate groups, and these groups more easily co-ordinate lobbying on both sides of the Atlantic.

Second, when the EC moved toward a single market, US firms challenged that the EC was erecting a 'fortress Europe' in which member states would use common 'single market' standards and certification procedures to prejudice US competition. US firms feared that they would be disadvantaged because, under the EC's 'global approach', only notified bodies located within the EC could test and certify products for marketing in the EC. Prior to the 'global approach', US-based laboratories acted as subcontractors for the testing of products under member state standards, and firms feared that this option might be foreclosed.

In response to these developments, US and EC authorities began to address seriously issues of regulatory co-ordination at the beginning of the 1990s.[10] In 1995, the US and EC signed the New Transatlantic Agenda (NTA) and its attached 'Joint Action Plan' which contained a detailed list of items to address. At the NTA's annual summits, negotiators were soon in search of 'deliverables' to show that the NTA was more than an empty symbol. Large businesses on each side of the Atlantic, working under the auspices of the Transatlantic Business Dialogue (TABD), promoted the concept of mutual recognition agreements, hoping to provide 'deliverables' that met business needs.[11] Although the TABD's formation was initiated by the US Department of Commerce and the European Commission in the fall of 1995, TABD rapidly became an independent voice, identifying areas of concern and co-ordinating pressure on officials to set timetables for the signature and implementation of mutual recognition agreements.

US and EC officials announced the 1997 MRA with a fanfare as a milestone in US-EC economic relations. Secretary Richard Daley of the US Department of Commerce proclaimed that the MRA could save businesses over $1 billion annually in unnecessary regulatory compliance costs.[12] The TABD estimated that about half of $110 billion of US exports to Europe require some form of EC certification, which now could be accomplished in the US. Officials announced plans for subsequent MRAs to cover an array of product and service sectors. Yet, as will be seen, both transatlantic businesses and government officials have become less enamoured with mutual recognition agreements in light of their experience with the 1997 agreement.

[10] See D. Vogel, *Barriers or Benefits: Regulation in Transatlantic Trade* (1997) at 9.
[11] The Transatlantic Business Dialogue was launched in 1995 at roughly the same time as the creation of the NTA. As documented by Cowles, the TABD consists of CEOs of over 200 of the largest firms on each side of the Atlantic. See M.G. Cowles, 'The Transatlantic Business Dialogue: Transforming the New Transatlantic Dialogue' in M. Pollack & G. Shaffer (eds), *Transatlantic Governance in the Global Economy* (2001).
[12] G. Yerkey, 'U.S., EU Conclude Standards Pact on Testing and Certification, Officials Say' (1997) 14 *Int'l Trade Rep* 1068 (citing Secretary of Commerce William Daley).

B. The 1997 MRA negotiations

US-EC negotiators initially discussed negotiating mutual recognition arrangements in 11 sectors, but ultimately whittled this down to six. As with all trade negotiations, the EC and US were concerned that the final results either favour their export industries or be 'balanced'. The US wished to conclude an agreement on telecommunications equipment first, but the EC refused because it felt that US firms would benefit more if the agreement covered only this sector. The EC used its political leverage by threatening not to sign any MRA involving telecommunications equipment without inclusion of MRAs covering medical devices and pharmaceutical good manufacturing practices.

The MRA negotiations required the involvement of multiple executive agencies since the negotiations comprised an overall framework agreement and six annexes covering the six separate sectors. The Office of the US Trade Representative and the Commission's Trade DG led the negotiations of the MRA framework agreement. Each of the annexes, however, was negotiated by the regulatory agency responsible for the sector concerned. On the European side, this was a simpler process on account of the centralization of the responsible agency officials within the Commission's DG Enterprise and these officials' long experience with co-ordinating the twin goals of regulatory protection and free trade within the single market. Because of this dual role, DG Enterprise officials are, in some ways, more analogous to the US Department of Commerce than to independent US regulatory agencies. On the US side, in contrast, separate independent federal agencies negotiated the annexes. The Federal Communications Commission (FCC) handled the telecommunications and electromagnetic compatibility annexes; the Occupational Health and Safety Administration (OSHA), a division of the Department of Labor, negotiated the electrical safety annex; the Food and Drug Administration (FDA) negotiated the annexes for medical devices and pharmaceutical good manufacturing practices; and the Coast Guard oversaw the recreational craft annex.

The involvement of both trade officials and regulatory officials resulted in *intra*-US agency conflicts, as well as transatlantic ones. Trade officials more aggressively pushed for an agreement, and US regulatory officials, in particular the FDA and OSHA, were reticent about accepting foreign certification of safety standards. Since these agencies are relatively independent compared to their EC counterparts, they obstructed agreement where they believed that their regulatory missions might be compromised. In the fall of 1996, negotiations almost broke down over inclusion of the medical device and pharmaceutical annexes.[13] Only intervention by Congress, following intensive lobbying efforts by private firms and the US Department of Commerce, overcame FDA opposition to their inclusion. In November 1997, Congress passed the FDA Modernization Act,

---

[13] See M. Egan, 'Mutual Recognition and Standard Setting: Public and Private Strategies for Governing Markets' in M. Pollack & G. Shaffer (eds), *Transatlantic Governance in the Global Economy* (2001) 179, at 191.

which specifically directed the FDA to 'support the Office of the United States Trade Representative, in consultation with the Secretary of Commerce, in efforts to move toward the acceptance of mutual recognition agreements'.[14] The Act specifically encouraged mutual recognition agreements 'between the European Union and the United States' in all product areas under FDA competence.[15] As the former EC Trade Commissioner Sir Leon Brittan states, 'governments proved to be more eager than their agencies to cooperate'.[16]

C. The 1997 Mutual Recognition Agreement

The 1997 MRA consists of a framework agreement and six annexes respectively covering telecommunications equipment, electromagnetic compatibility, electrical safety, recreational craft, medical devices, and pharmaceutical good manufacturing practices. Each of the annexes is, in fact, a separate agreement for a separate sector covering defined categories and lists of products.

The 1997 MRA does not cover recognition of the adequacy or equivalence of transatlantic standards, but is rather much less ambitious. These annexes only address mutual recognition of the results of conformity assessment procedures by 'Conformity Assessment Bodies' located in the exporting jurisdiction in accordance with the importing party's required standards and procedures. Since neither the US nor the EC relinquish sovereign control over the substance of their standards, transatlantic trading firms still must meet the separate requirements of the world's two largest markets. In addition, even these assessment evaluations are subject to varying pre-approval and post-approval conditions.

1. *Telecommunications and electromagnetic compatibility: relatively smooth regulatory co-operation*

The telecommunications and electromagnetic compatibility annexes should be viewed together because they both involve telecommunications equipment and their inclusion was sought by the telecommunications industry. These annexes' complementarity is reflected structurally, in that the parties have formed a 'Joint Sectoral Committee', consisting of members of the US FCC and the EC's DG Enterprise to monitor the annexes' implementation.[17] The responsible authority within each exporting jurisdiction (US or EC member state) is to designate the

---

[14] Food and Drug Administration Modernization Act of 1997, Pub L No 105–115, 111 Stat 2296 (codified as amended in sections of 21 USC § 301–394 (supp 1997)). See in particular FFDCA, section 383(c). See J. Chai, 'Medical Device Regulation in the United States and the European Union: A Comparative Study' (2000) 55 *Food & Drug LJ* 57, at 75.

[15] See FFDCA, section 383(c)(2).

[16] Sir Leon Brittan, 'Transatlantic Economic Partnership: Breaking Down the Hidden Barriers', in G. Bermann, M. Herdegen & P. Lindseth (eds), *Transatlantic Regulatory Cooperation* (2000), at 13.

[17] Different units of DG Enterprise are responsible for implementation of all internal 'single market' directives concerning industrial products, so that DG Enterprise is the European counterpart of US regulatory authorities in these domains.

conformity assessment bodies located within it.[18] These designations have been accomplished without controversy, unlike for other MRA annexes.

2. Electrical safety: regulatory tensions

EC negotiators insisted that the MRA include an annex covering electrical safety standards because the EC market has long been relatively deregulated and thus more open to US products. In contrast, the US system calls for regulatory reviews and product approvals by OSHA, a division of the US Department of Labor. EC authorities, acting on behalf of EC firms, desired to ease the regulatory burden for EC imports by having OSHA recognize product testing and certification, under OSHA standards, by conformity assessment bodies located in Europe. In addition, at least certain sectors of the telecommunications industry, and in particular from the EC, desired an MRA that covered not only all aspects of telecommunications product approvals, but also might lead to adoption within the US of a decentralized EC system. This annex has not been implemented, however, because of disputes with OSHA over the designation of European conformity assessment bodies.

3. Recreational craft: a simple annex

The recreational craft annex was the simplest to negotiate and implement. In the US, the applicable regulatory body, the US Coast Guard, already permitted firms to self-certify their products, so that there was no need for any European conformity assessment bodies. In contrast, products must be assessed by a 'notified body' within the EC, so that European recognition of US conformity assessment bodies could (at least in theory) reduce costs for US firms. However, US firms largely have continued to use pre-existing sub-contracting arrangements for European product assessment.

4. Medical devices: disappointment and delay

The US and EC agreed to include the annexes for medical devices and pharmaceutical good manufacturing practices in the MRA only after the EC, US trade officials, business lobbyists and Congress placed considerable pressure on a reticent FDA. Although the medical device annex was eventually included, the FDA insisted that the annex's coverage be more limited, even though the parties only agreed to mutually recognize testing reports and not each other's standards. First, the medical device annex only applies to less stringently regulated medical devices, subject to possible expansion based on an FDA 'pilot program'.[19] Second,

---

[18] Each EC member state has identified a ministry or delegated body which acts as the designating authority for conformity assessment bodies located within it. The US designating authority is the National Institute for Standards and Technology (NIST) of the US Department of Commerce, which works in conjunction with the FCC for these annexes. Telephone interview with Mary Sanders of NIST, 6 June 2001.

[19] See Chai, supra note 14 (providing an overview of FDA classification systems).

designated conformity assessment bodies are not selected by an authority of the exporting country, but rather by 'joint assessment'. Third, implementation of the Annex was made subject to a three-year transition period (to have ended in December 2001), during which the FDA organized a 'joint confidence building program'. In the fall of 2001, the parties agreed to extend this transition period for a further two years.[20] Fourth, designated conformity assessment bodies will not necessarily be permitted to perform all tests contemplated by the MRA, but only those in which the regulatory authority determines that they are competent. Fifth, while the annex uses the terminology of 'Conformity Assessment Bodies', domestic regulatory bodies retain ultimate authority to recognize the testing results.[21]

5. *Pharmaceutical good manufacturing practices: FDA reticence*

The least ambitious and furthest from implementation of the six annexes is that for pharmaceutical good manufacturing practices (GMPs). 'Good manufacturing practices' are those aspects 'of quality assurance which ensure that products are consistently produced and controlled to quality standards'.[22] The parties' intention in the pharmaceutical GMPs annex, the only annex not to rely on private conformity assessment bodies,[23] is to permit regulatory authorities on one side of the Atlantic to rely on regulatory authorities on the other to conduct on-site visits of manufacturing facilities. After the inspection, the foreign regulatory authority is to provide an inspection report regarding the manufacturers' compliance with good manufacturing practices. These inspection reports should 'normally be endorsed by the authority of the importing authority, except under specific and delineated circumstances' (Article 12).

The 'cornerstone' of the pharmaceutical GMP annex is each parties' determination of the equivalence of the regulatory system of the other party, which they 'aimed' to conclude by December 2001. The FDA, however, refused to recognize the equivalence of all but two member state systems, and thus the agreement was not implemented by the agreed date. The FDA faces a much more burdensome task to implement the MRA than do its European counterparts, who only need to work with one additional regulatory authority. The FDA claims that Congress has failed to allocate sufficient budgetary resources for the FDA to implement the 1997 MRA in a manner that ensures US public safety.[24]

---

[20] See G. Yerkey, 'Standards: U.S., Europe Near Agreement on Plan to Boost Trade in Marine Safety Equipment' (2002) 19 *Int'l Trade Rep* (BNA) 313.

[21] Articles 11 and 12 of the annex provide that 'reports prepared by the CABS listed as equivalent will normally be endorsed by the importing Party, except under specific and delineated circumstances' (listing a number of examples).

[22] This is the EC's definition, taken from Council Directive (EEC) 91/356 and included in Article 1.3 of the annex. The US definition is more verbose.

[23] The pharmaceutical GMP annex is not based on the use of private conformity assessment bodies, since public authorities alone certify pharmaceutical manufacturers' GMPs on each side of the Atlantic under relevant US and EC legislation.

[24] Telephone interview with FDA official, 7 June 2001.

6. *One-sided implementation of the annexes*

As of January 2002, only the three annexes of greatest initial interest to US negotiators were fully operational—those covering telecommunications equipment, electromagnetic compatibility and recreational craft.[25] In contrast, implementation of the annexes for electrical safety equipment, medical devices and pharmaceutical GMPs remain in dispute. The Commission, displeased that the unimplemented annexes are those that the EC initially imposed as conditions for the 1997 MRA, is reviewing its options.

D. New MRA for marine equipment: initialled June 2001: broadest in scope

On 12 June 2001, the US and EC initialled an Agreement on Mutual Recognition of Certificates of Conformity for Marine Equipment. Unlike the 1997 MRA and its six annexes, this new agreement provides for mutual recognition of each parties' standards and procedures as 'equivalent' for purposes of assessments conducted by conformity assessment bodies located in either parties' territory (Articles 3 and 4).[26] Pre-existing harmonization of standards in this sector, agreed under the auspices of the International Maritime Organization (IMO) in Geneva, made possible the parties' mutual recognition of the 'equivalence' of each other's standards. This new mutual recognition agreement should be much easier to implement because testing bodies will not be certifying under separate standards and procedures and thus less training and information exchange is required.

IV. THE 1997 MRA IN CONTEXT: MULTI-LEVEL BUSINESS AND REGU-LATORY STRATEGIES, DIVERGENT REGULATORY CULTURES, UNEXPECTED MARKET BARRIERS

A. The 1997 MRA in the context of domestic business strategies and regulatory challenges

Bilateral regulatory co-operation cannot be viewed outside of domestic and global business strategies and regulatory challenges. At the domestic level, trading firms hope that the MRA will promote domestic adoption of harmonized standards, on the one hand, and deregulated certification requirements, on the other. Firms' main target has been US independent regulatory authorities. They have had some success. Since 1998, the FCC has instituted a new programme pursuant to which private testing laboratories may certify new telecommuni-

---

[25] See http://europa.eu.int/comm/enterprise/enterprise_policy/index.htm (visited 23 February 2002).

[26] The relevant EC legislation is Council Directive (EC) 96/98 of 20 December 1996 on marine equipment, as amended by Commission Directive (EC) 98/85. The relevant regulatory authorities are the US Coast Guard and the relevant agencies in the 15 member states.

cations equipment, whereas formerly only the FCC could do so. With the encouragement of business, the EC has moved even further in some sectors, permitting manufacturer self-declarations of conformity for most telecommunications equipment since 1998, a much more important development for firms than the MRA itself. Also since 1998, the FDA has instituted a programme for private testing and certification of large categories of medical devices, starting with a pilot programme that it plans to expand. In response to primarily domestic demands, the FDA Modernization Act expressly authorized the FDA to rely on private testing bodies in its oversight of medical devices.[27]

Although the original goal of the MRA annexes may have been to facilitate transatlantic trade, firms simultaneously focused on the deregulation of domestic product approvals.[28] For example, deregulation of product marketing approvals is a core item on the TABD agenda. TABD, in its 2001 Mid Year Report, called for a model 'linked to a wider use of Supplier's Declaration of Conformity', and stressed the need for transatlantic adoption of the EC's global approach under the motto: 'Approved Once, Accepted Everywhere'.[29]

As for Europe, US firms hope to use transatlantic proposals for regulatory co-operation to change EC and member state legislative and regulatory procedures. In this case, firms would prefer that Europe adopt more of a US procedural model, as set forth in US administrative law.[30] As TABD argues, '[a] key element for further discussion between business and governments . . . is how to ensure transparency in the regulatory process . . . The rulemaking and implementation process must be open thereby permitting industry to participate meaningfully in the regulatory process.'[31] TABD urges, in particular, 'greater use of "impact assessment" on regulations . . . [which] should include estimating the costs and benefits of regulation as well as any regulatory alternatives'.[32] The US, in this case, has taken up TABD's proposals in the negotiation of a US-EC agreement on regulatory co-operation and transparency.[33]

Finally, the regulatory challenges confronted in the transatlantic context are also endogenous to US and European domestic contexts. Regulators have limited

---

[27] See 21 USCA 360(m). See also L. Horton, 'Mutual Recognition Agreements and Harmonization' (1998) 29 *Seton Hall L Rev* 692, at 707.

[28] Interview with FCC official, 8 June 2001. EC officials state that deregulation was likely not the initial goal with the MRA, but agree that this goal has become more central for firms. Interview with two officials from DG Enterprise, 15 June 2001, in Brussels.

[29] TABD, 2001 Mid Year Report, at 2 and 14, http://www.tabd.org/recommendations/MYM01.pdf (visited 10 March 2002).

[30] On differences between the US Administrative Procedure Act and EC administrative law, see, eg, M. Shapiro, 'Codification of Administrative Law: The US and the Union' (1996) 2 *European LJ* 26; and F. Bignami, 'The Democratic Deficit in European Community Rulemaking: A Call for Notice and Comment in Comitology' (1999) 40 *Harvard Int'l LJ* 451.

[31] TABD, 2001 Mid Year Report, supra note 29, at 14.

[32] Ibid at 16 (also adding '[b]usiness consultation and the consultation of other interested stakeholders should be part of the assessment process'). In addition, TABD proposes that all regulation be subject to a separate '"trade impact statement" at the cost-benefit analysis phase of regulatory activities and in the development of legislation'. 2001 Mid Year Report, at 8.

[33] Draft agreement on file with author.

resources. Top-down command and control regulation can be ineffective in an environment characterized by rapid technological change and high numbers and complexity. These traditional regulatory approaches can be ineffective in terms of the cost-effectiveness of regulators' use of limited public resources, business innovation, and the ultimate protection of citizens. Domestically, irrespective of international and transatlantic trade relations, there are pressures for regulatory change, and regulators are interested in developing new governance mechanisms to deploy their resources more effectively.

B. The 1997 MRA in the context of global business strategies

Businesses also view transatlantic MRAs in a global context. Firms, together with some government representatives, hope that transatlantic arrangements may be a stepping stone for reaching MRAs with third countries, thereby offering increased access to lucrative Asian and South American markets. The WTO Agreement on Technical Barriers to Trade and the General Agreement on Trade in Services explicitly encourage and lend legal support to the expansion of transatlantic MRAs.[34] Under WTO rules, countries that do not 'give mutual satisfaction' to third countries offering 'equivalent' procedures or standards are subject to WTO anti-discrimination claims under WTO most-favoured-nations clauses.[35]

Much more importantly than potential legal claims, each new MRA places pressure on third countries to enter into negotiations so that their firms are not disadvantaged—what Kalypso Nicolaidis refers to as a potential 'contagion effect'.[36] Transatlantic and third country negotiations thereby have reciprocal effects. Each MRA provides leverage to domestic firms to demand new MRAs (with transatlantic or third country counterparts, as the case may be) to equalize market access. The EC has signed MRAs with Australia, Canada, Israel, Japan and New Zealand, in addition to those signed with the US. The transatlantic MRA can, in this way, be seen as a step for the extension of MRAs globally, helping ensure that not only transatlantic markets, but also other foreign markets, will remain open to foreign competition.

C. The challenge of implementation: reconciling regulatory systems and cultures

The significant institutional asymmetries between the US and EC's respective regulatory systems and cultures creates a major challenge for transatlantic

---

[34] See K. Nicolaidis, 'Mutual Recognition of Regulatory Regimes: Some Lessons and Prospects' in *OECD Proceedings: Regulatory Reform and International Market Openness* (1996) 171, at 191.

[35] See D. Leebron, 'Mutual Recognition: Structure, Problems and Prospects', in *OECD Proceedings: Regulatory Reform and International Market Openness* (1996) 205, at 215.

[36] See K. Nicolaidis, 'Managed Mutual Recognition: The New Approach to Liberalization of Professional Services' at ¶ 97 http:// www.ksg.harvard.edu/prg/nicolaidis/managemr.htm#IV (visited 11 March 2001).

regulatory co-operation and the implementation of transatlantic mutual recognition agreements. Where regulators adopt similar regulatory structures and systems, and enact similar substantive standards, they more easily understand and accept each other's regulatory determinations. Regulatory symmetry facilitates regulatory trust and confidence, enabling regulatory co-operation to occur.

Although the US system is often characterized as fragmented and decentralized, its actual nature varies by sector. At times, the US system is relatively highly centralized, as when Congress delegates regulatory authority to an independent federal regulatory body, such as the FDA.[37] At other times, the US system is more fragmented, with regulation consisting of a patchwork of federal, state, and private voluntary standards with no overarching framework, as in the case of data privacy protection.[38] While some commentators maintain that the US grants private actors relatively more flexibility than in Europe,[39] this stereotype is belied in practice by a number of the sectors covered by the 1997 transatlantic MRA. For example, the FCC certified all telecommunications equipment until the negotiation of the transatlantic MRA, at which time it adopted a more decentralized EC model. The US OSHA requires OSHA-accredited laboratories to certify all electrical safety equipment used in the workplace, whereas the EC has permitted manufacturers to self-declare the equipment's conformity with EC requirements since 1973. The US Food and Drug Administration continues to certify most medical devices, whereas EC authorities have permitted testing by private notified bodies since 1994.

US and EC regulators work in different regulatory cultures, ones which (in the case of the MRA) make EC institutional adaptation easier. EC and European national regulators operate under the dual mission of ensuring free trade within the internal market, on the one hand, while ensuring public safety through high product and process standards, on the other. They thus are accustomed to interacting with foreign regulators and testing bodies on an on-going basis. The Commission's DG Enterprise and DG Trade units rarely tussled when negotiating and implementing the 1997 MRA. In contrast, the US FDA traditionally has defined its role solely as that of protecting US public health, and has not operated under a dual mission of also facilitating market exchange. Because the FDA is an independent regulatory authority anxious to protect its regulatory autonomy, US trade and commerce authorities encounter more difficulties in negotiating bilateral agreements concerning areas within the FDA's jurisdiction.

Implementation of transatlantic MRAs also has been much easier for the EC because EC regulatory authorities only have to adapt to one new regulatory

---

[37] See M. Pollack & G. Shaffer, 'The Challenge of Reconciling Regulatory Differences: Food Safety and GMOs in the Transatlantic Relationship' in M. Pollack & G. Shaffer (eds), *Transatlantic Governance in the Global Economy* (2001) 156.

[38] On data privacy protection, see *infra* notes 43 ff, and G. Shaffer, 'Globalization and Social Protection: The Impact of EU and International Rules in the Ratcheting Up of U.S. Privacy Standards' (2000) 25 *Yale J Int'l L* 1.

[39] See eg, M. Egan, *Constructing a European Market: Standards, Regulation and Governance* (2001) at 131 (calling the EC system more 'state-directed' and the US system more 'market-oriented').

system (the US') that is overseen in one language (English), whereas US authorities must adapt to 15 different regulatory structures operating in 11 different languages under the EC's umbrella. Simply as regards language, US conformity assessment bodies submit their applications and testing report in English, a language with which EC and member state regulators are familiar.[40] Expansion of an EC system that is well-adapted to accommodating regulatory diversity to include the US is a less significant change.

D. The unexpected challenge of market barriers to implementation

Transatlantic trade officials and businesses that first touted the benefits of US-EC MRAs now realize their underestimation of the difficulties of implementation. These constraints involve not just regulators and regulatory cultures, but market forces as well. From the perspective of manufacturers, they typically develop long-term working relationships with certifying laboratories, which constitute a form of cost-effective firm-laboratory partnership. Because manufacturers invest in educating these laboratories about their products and manufacturing processes, and the relationship of these products and processes to applicable regulatory requirements, the cost of changing laboratories may be significant. Moreover, a laboratory's mark itself may be important in some markets, so that firms may continue obtaining formal conformity assessment from EC notified bodies for the EC market and US laboratories for the US. As a result, most firms may continue using the same laboratories even though these laboratories cannot directly assess products as conformity assessment bodies, but must work through sub-contracting arrangements with accredited laboratories on the other side of the Atlantic.

As for laboratories, they will not invest in the accreditation procedures required to become a conformity assessment body if they fear that the benefits are limited or too uncertain. Accreditation costs can be substantial, involving seminars, workshops, training programmes, audits and joint inspections with authorities across the Atlantic. While 12 European notified bodies initially applied to be recognized as conformity assessment bodies under the medical device annex, two subsequently withdrew on account of costs.[41] As a result, both manufacturing firms and private laboratories have become, in the words of one Commission official 'a bit cool on the MRA'.[42]

Some domestic firms also benefit from domestic regulatory barriers to their transatlantic competitors. When there is no domestic constituency actively pressing for domestic regulatory change in a specific sector, implementation of the MRA faces greater hurdles. For example, there is no dominant US constitu-

---

[40] In contrast, even if European regulatory bodies submit documents to US regulatory authorities in English, the texts can be far from fluent.
[41] Interview with Commission official from DG Enterprise, 15 June 2001 in Brussels (concerning medical devices).
[42] Interview with official from DG Enterprise, 15 June 2001, in Brussels.

ency pressing for implementation of the electrical safety MRA. As a Commission official points out, this is not a 'balanced' MRA, since US-based firms do not require conformity assessment to sell electrical safety equipment in the EC market. In addition, most US producers allegedly encounter relatively less difficulty with OSHA's programme for their sales on the US market, and thus may gain an advantage against European competitors because of their experience with OSHA-certified laboratories. Finally, laboratories already certified by OSHA have a relatively protected market and do not desire competition from laboratories newly certified by European authorities. Thus, there is little US constituent pressure on OSHA to concede to the EC and recognize laboratories designated by EC member state authorities.

V. US-EC UNDERSTANDING ON PRINCIPLES FOR DATA PRIVACY PROTECTION: MANAGING CONFLICT AND MAINTAINING FREE TRADE THROUGH A HYBRID INSTITUTIONAL DEVELOPMENT

In July 2000, the US Department of Commerce and the European Commission formalized an agreement creating a set of 'Safe Harbor Principles' (the Principles) on data privacy protection, under which US-based firms may certify themselves in order to avoid European restrictions on data transfers to the US.[43] The Principles constitute a unique development in the governance of US-EC economic relations. To some, they represent the EC's exercise of coercive market power in an extraterritorial fashion in an attempt to leverage up privacy standards within the US.[44] To others, they represent a capitulation by EC trade bureaucrats to US trading concerns through a weak agreement filled with loopholes.[45] And finally, to some, including this author, they represent a compromise through new institutional development pursuant to which free transatlantic information flows may be preserved while satisfying legitimate EC concerns about the use of personal information concerning EC residents in a technology-intensive, interdependent globalizing economy.

Unlike the MRAs assessed above, the Safe Harbor Principles constitute a form of de facto *harmonization* of social standards. The Principles go beyond current regulatory requirements in the US, and thereby constitute a regulatory floor with which trading firms must comply if they wish to receive data from Europe without threat of challenge. This harmonization, however, is designed to affect only trading firms, and otherwise creates no legal obligations within the US. The US and EC may thereby claim that they formally retain autonomy to enact

---

[43] The agreement was formalized through an exchange of letters between Robert LaRussa, the Acting Secretary of the Department of Commerce and John Mogg, the Director of DG Internal Market (formerly DG XV) in the European Commission. See J.R. Reidenberg, 'E-Commerce and Trans-Atlantic Privacy' (2001) 38 *Houston L Rev* 717, at 739.

[44] See Shaffer, supra note 38, at 70–78 (citing US business reactions to the Directive).

[45] See, eg, Reidenberg, supra note 43, at 743–746.

whatever privacy legislation they deem appropriate. However, any firm which engages in cross-border exchange is subject to pressure to abide by the Principles. In this way, Europe's regulatory approach may have spillover effects within the US, leading to some convergence in data privacy practices, despite differing US and EC regulatory systems.

Although the extent of the Safe Harbor Principles' implementation remains an open question, the US-EC dispute and efforts at co-operation demonstrate the inherent interrelation between social regulation and open trade policies where regulation (or the lack thereof) has external effects. Alleged US under-regulation can jeopardize the privacy interests of EC residents. Alleged EC over-regulation can limit the commercial operations of US enterprises. In an interdependent transatlantic economy, US and EC authorities attempt to manage the ensuing conflicts of norms and mesh, where possible, their divergent regulatory systems.

A. Pooled sovereignty: the EC's market clout in an interdependent transatlantic economy

The US-EC agreement was spurred by the creation of the EC single market, on the one hand, and the interdependent nature of the US and European economies, on the other. The creation of the single market led to the EC's regulation of data privacy in the first place. Among the ironies inherent in the US-EC dispute is that the original purpose of the EC's Data Privacy Directive was not just to increase data privacy protection within the EC. It also was to ensure the uninhibited flow of data within the EC from the threat of unilateral restrictions by individual EC member states on account of their differing data privacy protection regimes.[46] The interlinked nature of social protection and liberalized trade in a single European market gave rise to the Directive.

Similarly, data privacy protection became a transatlantic issue because of the growing interdependence of the US and European economies and the rising importance of information technology. US affiliates in Europe produce over a trillion dollars of goods and services annually, constituting 'over half of all the foreign production of U.S. companies'.[47] These companies depend on information flows, not only with third party suppliers, customers, consultants, marketers and other service providers, but also internally, within their complex networks of affiliates, joint ventures and partnerships.

The US-EC dispute over the adequacy of US data privacy protection affects US privacy policies and practices because the EC exercises political and market

---

[46] The Directive was negotiated within the context of the threat of data transfer bans from certain member states with protective data privacy laws (such as France and Germany) to other member states with less stringent laws (such as Italy). See Shaffer, supra note 38.

[47] The above figures are from the prepared testimony of Assistant Secretary of Commerce Franklin Vargo before the House Committee on International Relations. See 'Issues in U.S.-European Union Trade: European Privacy Legislation and Biotechnology/Food Safety Policy,' *Federal News Service*, 7 May 1998.

power. In a globalizing marketplace, the EC's single market initiative has re-inforced the European Commission's position as a global actor.[48] The EC's huge internal market enables the Commission to exercise considerable political clout in the negotiation of international and transatlantic rules, including harmonized rules governing firm behaviour.

The shift of European regulation to the EC level has strengthened the EC's ability to represent the interests of its constituents in relations with the US. The EC member states have not simply 'lost' sovereignty in working through central-ized EC authorities. They have reallocated it in a manner which effectively enhances their negotiating authority (and in that way their autonomy) vis-à-vis the US.[49] In pooling their sovereignty, EC member states now speak with a more powerful voice transatlantically. The timing of the US' reaction to the threat of bans on data transfers from Europe reflects the EC's relative clout. It was not until the EC's Privacy Directive came into effect that US authorities drafted the Safe Harbor Principles and increased pressure on companies to raise their internal privacy standards. When the threat moved to the EC level, the US took the threat more seriously.

B. Overview of the EC Privacy Directive's internal requirements: ex ante and ex post controls

On 24 October 1998, Directive (EC) 95/46 on the Protection of Individuals with Regard to the Processing of Personal Data and the Free Movement of such Data[50] became effective. The EC, through its Directive, takes primarily a regu-latory approach to data privacy protection, as opposed to private ordering through market processes. The Directive is noteworthy for its broad scope of coverage. Except for public security, criminal law and related exceptions, it covers all processing of all personal data by whatever means, and is not limited to action by government, business sector or field of use (Articles 2–3). The Directive prohibits data controllers from processing information unless the individual 'unambiguously' consents to the processing and that consent is informed (Articles 7, 8, 10, 14). Information subject to the most stringent controls includes 'personal data revealing racial or ethnic origin, political opin-ions, religious or philosophical beliefs, trade-union membership, and the pro-cessing of data concerning health or sex life' (Article 8).

---

[48] The US increasingly negotiates with the EC as an independent political institution apart from its 15 member states. As Assistant Secretary of Commerce Franklin Vargo states, the NTA signed between the US and the EC in December 1995 'marks the first time that we are dealing with the EC as a political institution on a large scale'. Ibid.

[49] As Joel Trachtman states, '[s]overeignty, viewed as an allocation of power and responsibility, is never lost, but only reallocated'. A 'loss' of sovereignty 'may be viewed as a question of what is received, and by whom, in exchange for a reduction in the state's sovereignty, rather than simply a question of whether sovereignty is reduced'. Joel Trachtman, 'Reflections on the Nature of the State: Sovereignty, Power and Responsibility' (1994) 20 *Can-US L J* 399.

[50] See European Parliament and Council Directive 95/46, OJ 1995 L 281/1 [hereinafter Directive].

The Directive provides multiple means for enforcement. It requires member states to grant individuals a permanent right of access to obtain copies of the data about them and have it corrected or its use enjoined (Articles 12, 28). It obliges member states to provide a judicial remedy for infringements of data privacy rights, including the right to receive damages (Articles 22–24). To support effective enforcement, each member state must designate an independent public authority 'responsible for monitoring the application within its territory' of the Directive's provisions (Article 28). These supervisory authorities are to be granted significant powers, including the power to investigate processing operations, to deliver 'opinions before processing operations are carried out', to order 'the blocking, erasure or destruction of data', to impose 'a temporary or definitive ban on processing', and 'to engage in legal proceedings' against violators of the rights guaranteed by the Directive (Articles 18, 28).

C. Overview of US data privacy protection vis-à-vis the Directive's criteria

In contrast to the EC, the US has stressed 'self-regulation' by the private sector backed by regulation which tends to be sector-specific and less stringent. Congress' targeting of specific sectors and concerns is reflected in the following statutory titles: the Driver's Privacy Protection Act of 1994, the Video Privacy Protection Act of 1988, the Electronic Communications Privacy Act of 1986, the Cable Communications Policy Act of 1984, and the Fair Credit Reporting Act of 1971.[51] Overall, the US approach is fragmented, involving standard-setting and enforcement by a wide variety of actors, including federal and state legislatures, agencies and courts, industry associations, individual companies and market forces.[52] To a certain extent, the US' handling of data privacy issues reflects Americans' traditional distrust of a centralized government.[53] US legislation has provided citizens with significantly greater protection against the collection and use of personal information by government, in particular the federal government, than by the private sector.[54]

[51] In many cases, Congress has simply reacted to public scandals. In passing the Fair Credit Reporting Act, it responded 'to consumer horror stories of dealings with credit reporting agencies'. It enacted the Video Privacy Protection Act after the video rental records of Judge Robert Bork were published by a news reporter in the course of a campaign against his Supreme Court nomination.

[52] The fragmented, decentralized nature of the US regulatory process is described in S. Vogel, *Freer Markets, More Rules: Regulatory Reform in Advanced Industrialized Countries* (1996), at 217.

[53] See R. Kagan, 'How Much Do National Styles of Law Matter' in R. Kagan & L. Axelrod (eds), *Regulatory Encounters: Multinational Corporations and American Adversarial Legalism* (2000), at 11.

[54] The Privacy Act of 1974 is the only federal omnibus Act that protects informational privacy. Yet despite the legislation's broad title, the Privacy Act only applies to data processing conducted by the federal government, not by state governments or private entities. The vast majority of states lack omnibus privacy Acts, and rather offer scattered statutes applying to specific sectors or concerns.

D. The Directive's extraterritorial impact: ban on data transfers to countries lacking adequate privacy protection

Article 25 of the Directive provides that member states shall prohibit all data transfers to a third country if the Commission finds that the country does not ensure 'an adequate level of protection' of data privacy. Pursuant to Article 29 of the Directive, an EC Working Party prepared a series of documents that identified core principles under which the adequacy of a country's protections should be gauged.[55] These principles are in line with the EC's internal requirements.

Since it appeared that the US might not provide for 'adequate' data privacy protection under the Directive's criteria, US and EC authorities engaged in intensive negotiations to avoid a ban on data flows to the US, culminating in their agreement on Safe Harbor Principles. The Commission refrained from finding that the US, as a whole, inadequately ensures data privacy protection while the parties negotiated the content of the Principles. Once signed, the member states formally recognized that US firms' adherence to these Principles would be sufficient to protect them from member state challenge. Member state authorities, however, may still challenge transfers to firms that do not adopt the Principles. Privacy rights associations can trigger these proceedings by filing claims with supervisory authorities.[56] Even before implementation of the Directive, data transfers to the US were barred by British, French, German and Swedish courts and administrative authorities.[57]

E. The Safe Harbor Principles

The US Department of Commerce issued its first draft 'Safe Harbor Principles' in November 1998, within a month of the Directive becoming effective. These were opened for comments within the US and negotiated for almost 20 months with the Commission before they were finalized and approved by the EC.[58] The guidelines set forth seven core data privacy principles for industry to follow. Because the EC formally acknowledged the Principles as 'adequate' under the

---

[55] In July 1998, the Working Party incorporated earlier papers in a Working Document entitled *Transfers of personal data to third countries: Applying Articles 25 and 26 of the EU data protection directive.*

[56] Privacy International, a London-based privacy organization, has threatened to file claims against American Express and EDS for failing to provide adequate data privacy protection. See 'Will Amex and EDS Face Privacy Lawsuits in Europe?,' *Computergram Int'l*, 2 July 1998.

[57] See F. Cate, 'The EU Data Protection Directive, Information Privacy, and the Public Interest' (1995) 80 *Iowa L Rev* 431, at 438 (citing prohibitions on data transfers to the US from Britain (involving sales to a direct mail organization) and France (involving patient records)); C. Kuner, 'Beyond Safe Harbor: European Data Protection Law and Electronic Commerce' (2001) 35 *Int'l Lawyer* 79, at 84 (concerning Spain's fine levied on Microsoft Iberica SRL).

[58] The Safe Harbor Principles were approved by the Council of Ministers, but rejected by the European Parliament. However, under applicable EC law, Parliament's rejection did not affect the EC's acceptance of the Principles through the Commission's final decision.

Directive's criteria, the Principles provide US businesses with a 'safe harbor'. The seven Principles are:

(1) 'Notice': An organization must provide 'clear and conspicuous' notice to individuals 'about the purposes for which it collects and uses information about them, how to contact the organization with ... complaints, the types of third parties to which it discloses the information, and the ... means ... for limiting its use and disclosure'.

(2) 'Choice': An organization must provide individuals with a 'clear and conspicuous' choice to 'opt out' of how their personal information may be used and to whom it may be disclosed; 'for sensitive information (i.e., personal information specifying medical or health conditions, racial or ethnic origin, political opinions, religious or philosophical beliefs, trade union membership or information specifying the sex life of the individual), they must be given affirmative or explicit (opt in) choice if the information is to be disclosed to a third party or used for a purpose other than those for which it was originally collected or substantively authorized ... '.

(3) 'Onward Transfer': To disclose information to a third party, an organization must apply the 'Notice and Choice principles'.

(4) 'Security': Organizations must take reasonable measures to protect information from disclosure, misuse, alteration or loss.

(5) 'Data Integrity': Organizations 'may not process personal information in a way that is incompatible with the purposes for which it has been collected or subsequently authorized', and 'take reasonable steps to ensure that data is ... accurate, complete and current'.

(6) 'Access': An organization must grant individuals access to personal information held about them and the opportunity to have it corrected, except where the burden would be disproportionate to the privacy risks in the case in question.

(7) 'Enforcement': There must be 'mechanisms for assuring compliance' and 'consequences' for non-compliance, which must include 'readily available and affordable independent recourse mechanisms' and 'sanctions [that] must be sufficiently rigorous to ensure compliance'.

The US Department of Commerce and the Commission supplemented the Principles with a document entitled 'Frequently Asked Questions' (FAQs) designed to guide firms and authorities in the Principles' application. Many of the FAQs specify the scope of exceptions, thereby providing some leeway to US firms. Nonetheless, many firms find that the Principles require significant internal company adaptations.[59]

Companies join the Safe Harbor programme by annually certifying to the US Department of Commerce that they will comply with the Principles. The

Department of Commerce then places the company's name on its website list of certifying firms.[60] The firms' primary benefit from certifying is that EC member states may not challenge them under member state law or otherwise condition any data transfers to them. Moreover, US law applies to the Principles' interpretation, and US courts and administrative bodies hear all claims (although European courts and administrative bodies may still challenge the online collection of information from European residents by US-based firms).[61]

Self-regulatory organizations (such as BBB Online and TRUSTe, discussed below), backed by the US FTC, offer the primary means for the Principles' enforcement. In this way, the Principles' application resembles the EC's new and global approaches to internal market harmonization. As under the new approach, the Safe Harbor Principles set forth 'essential requirements' that firms must meet. As under the global approach, firms self-certify their adherence, which certification is backed first by audits from self-regulatory organizations, and then (ultimately) by the authority of the state. If a company adopts the Safe Harbor Principles and fails to comply with them, it subjects itself to challenge by the FTC for 'using unfair or deceptive acts or practices in or affecting commerce'.[62] In a letter to the Commission dated 14 July 2000, the FTC committed itself to 'give priority to referrals of non-compliance with self-regulatory guidelines . . . [and] safe harbor principles' respectively referred to it from certifying organizations and EC member state authorities. In this backhanded way, the Directive informally shapes US data privacy requirements, potentially becoming a baseline standard. Yet, it does so in a relatively flexible manner that respects US legal sovereignty and use of private oversight bodies.

F. Other means to comply with the Directive

The Safe Harbor Principles should not be viewed in isolation, since the Directive provides other ways to comply with it, in particular through obtaining 'unambiguous' consent from the 'data subject' in Europe (Article 7) and the signature of a 'model contract' with data privacy authorities in member states (Article 26). In January 2002, the Commission approved standard contract clauses covering privacy protection that can be applied to all data transfers from the EC,

---

[60] See http://www.ita.doc.gov/ecom.

[61] To the extent that US-based firms gather information online from web sites in Europe, they may be subject to enforcement in Europe under the Directive despite their signing up to the Safe Harbor Principles, an issue about which US and EC authorities have argued, but which remains unresolved. See Reidenberg, supra note 43, at 743 (citing inter alia EC Article 29 working group report maintaining that EC authorities have jurisdiction over such activities).

[62] See section 5 of the Federal Trade Commission Act, 15 USC § 45(a)(6). The Safe Harbor Principles provide that where 'an organization relies in whole or in part on self-regulation, its failure to comply with such self-regulation must also be actionable under Section 5 of the Federal Trade Commission Act'. Cf Reidenberg, ibid. at 740–741 (questioning whether FTC has jurisdiction to protect foreign consumers).

regardless of a firm's adherence to the Safe Harbor Principles.[63] US financial services firms were particularly interested in the content of this model contract since they currently are ineligible for certification under the Safe Harbor Principles because no federal authority (such as the FTC) has competence to enforce them.[64] When a draft model contract went beyond Safe Harbor requirements, the financial services industry reacted vehemently, pressuring the Treasury and Commerce Departments to send a joint letter to the Commission in protest, albeit to no avail.[65] Firms also can sign *ad hoc* contracts with individual member state data privacy authorities. In addition, firms can sign contracts with affiliates when transferring personal information, such as information contained in personnel files.

G. Implementation

The Safe Harbor Principles are still at an inchoate stage so that it remains too early to assess their impact. Some commentators questioned the effectiveness of the Principles given that only a few US companies initially signed them. However, as practitioners point out, companies will not certify their procedures until their operations are in compliance. Moreover, many companies waited to see the content of the Commission's 'model contract', which turned out to be more stringent than the Safe Harbor Principles themselves. Finally, US and EC officials had agreed on an implementation period during which firms would not be challenged, which period would be 'reviewed in mid 2001'.[66] As the review deadline approached, more companies certified themselves, or publicly announced their intention to do so.[67]

Regardless of whether they sign up for the Safe Harbor programme, companies engaged in transatlantic business operate in the shadow of the Directive's potential enforcement. Data privacy regulation in Europe has informed not only the tenor and context of debates in the US; it has shaped interest groups' appreciation of their options. Under the Directive, US businesses face potential litigation before European courts and administrative bodies unless they adhere

---

[63] See A. Mazumdar, 'European Commission Gives Final Approval to Model Clauses to Protect Personal Data' (2002) 19 *Int'l Trade Rep (BNA)* 187. The Commission will likely supplement this universal model contract with other models tailored for transfers of specific types of information. Interview with Fabrizia Benini, DG Internal Market, 13 June 2001, in Brussels.

[64] FTC jurisdiction does not cover the financial sector, so that other US federal agencies, such as the Office of the Comptroller of the Currency, would have to have the authority to make a similar commitment to the Commission to give priority attention to referrals.

[65] The content of the model contract ended up going beyond both the relevant US legislation (under the Gramm-Leach-Bliley Act) and the Safe Harbor Principles. See J. Kirwin, 'EC Dismisses U.S. Worry that "Model Contract" Will Hurt Safe Harbor Talks' (2001) 18 *Intl Trade Rep (BNA)* 537.

[66] See letter from Robert LaRussa of the US Department of Commerce to John Mogg, Director of DG Internal Market (formerly DG XV) of the European Commission, dated 17 July 2000 at http://www.export.gov/safeharbor (visited 5 March 2002).

[67] As of 13 June 2001, 52 companies had certified. As of 23 February 2002, the number of certifications had expanded to 156. As of 24 April 2003, the list had further expanded to 334. See Department of Commerce web site at http://www.export.gov/safeharbor (last visited 24 April 2003).

to the Safe Harbor Principles. Playing off the US-EC regulatory conflict and its media coverage, privacy advocates jacked up pressure on US federal and state politicians, regulatory authorities and businesses. Even though privacy advocates have criticized the Safe Harbor Principles, privacy advocates will use them as part of their larger strategies. The context in which US domestic debates over data privacy protection take place has been altered.

The Directive, in particular, has increased the demand for legal, consulting and other privacy services within the US. The Better Business Bureau OnLine created a privacy seal programme which incorporates the Safe Harbor Principles, and was revised to track 'safe harbor' negotiations.[68] The Electronic Frontier Foundation, a San Francisco-based public interest organization, has associated with information technology companies to launch a programme named TRUSTe to rate the privacy protection of Internet sites, which programme is certified under Safe Harbor.[69] As smaller companies find these certification programmes costly, trade associations such as the Direct Marketing Association designed their own enforcement programmes for their members to comply with Safe Harbor requirements.[70] Legislation, in this case foreign legislation, has helped raise the standards to be certified and spurred more companies to use seal programmes with oversight and sanctioning mechanisms.

The Directive has also spurred the creation of a new corporate position—the chief data privacy officer in companies' human resources divisions. These company employees attend conferences on the Directive and US privacy legislation,[71] write memoranda on privacy issues that they distribute within firms, and generally increase firms' awareness of privacy issues. In formulating and overseeing the implementation of company policies, they foster company compliance with applicable legal requirements. Finally, outside law firms increasingly provide advice to firms regarding the Directive and the Safe Harbor Principles, thereby again promoting adaptation of US business practice. This conjunction of lawyer, consultant and 'privacy officer' advice, rendered in the context of the Safe Harbor Principles, can lead to some convergence of privacy policies over time, reducing the chance of a major transatlantic trade dispute over data privacy.

Concomitantly, in negotiating and putting into operation the Safe Harbor Principles, European officials have become more comfortable with the potential of US governance approaches involving the use of private bodies, such as BBB OnLine, for the monitoring and certification of privacy practices. European

---

[68] Telephone interview with Gary Laden, Director BBB OnLine Privacy Program, 21 April 1999.

[69] The Electronic Frontier Foundation's website is located at http://www/eff.org. The TRUSTe website is at http://www.truste.org.

[70] Telephone interview with Charles Prescott, Direct Marketing Association, 6 June 2001 (noting that their survey showed that about half of their catalogue companies (representing 500 companies) worked with overseas orders, meaning that they would need to take account of the Directive and Safe Harbor Principles).

[71] To give just one example, at a symposium on data privacy organized by Westin's group, the Center for Social and Legal Research, in the fall of 1998, over 170 people, primarily from corporate human resource departments, attended. Interview with Peter Swire in Washington, DC, 26 March 1999.

officials have indicated that they are willing to entertain the adaptation to the European context of less-centralized US regulatory mechanisms for data protection. The President of the European Parliament even called the Safe Harbor approach a 'template for the future', serving as a potential model for regulation in other policy areas.[72]

H. The shadow of WTO rules

In an attempt to ward off EC action, US officials implicitly threatened to challenge any ban imposed by the EC before the WTO's Dispute Settlement Body.[73] However, provided that the EC does not apply the Directive in a manner that discriminates against the US, it is arguably in compliance with WTO rules.[74] First, on its face, the Directive applies equally to EC and foreign-owned goods and services providers, and thus should not violate national treatment or most-favoured-nation clauses.[75] Second, WTO jurisprudence supports the EC's position.[76] Thus, in the case of the EC data privacy enforcement, WTO rules should shield the EC from a US retaliatory threat. WTO rules thereby have reinforced pressure on the US to negotiate a set of more stringent, data privacy requirements in the form of the Safe Harbor Principles.

I. Conclusions on Safe Harbor

From a practical standpoint, the separate goals of protecting individual privacy, on the one hand, while ensuring trade liberalization, on the other, are insepar-able. Regulation in a jurisdiction with less stringent data privacy controls has significant externalities, thereby affecting residents in other jurisdictions. The Safe Harbor Principles are an example of an instrument for reconciling these regulatory concerns with the goals of liberalized trade. They represent a form of compromise that recognizes different institutional approaches and social values, yet nonetheless sets baseline rules where domestic values are affected by trade. To make them work, however, will require sustained, cross-border co-operation.

---

[72] Henry Farrell, 'Constructing the International Foundations of E-Commerce: The EU-U.S. Safe Harbor Agreement', *International Organization* (forthcoming, on file with author).

[73] For example, Ira Magaziner, formerly responsible for US discussions on electronic commerce issues, including privacy protection, stated that, '[i]n general, we in the U.S. don't recognize an extra-territorial attempt to shut down the electronic flow of data between countries. According to principles of international trade, I think that's a violation of WTO rules.' Kenneth Cukier, 'U.S. Under Fire over "Aggressive" Net Tax Stance,' *Comm Wk Int'l*, 2 March 1998.

[74] For a fuller analysis, see Shaffer, 'Globalization and Social Protection', supra note 38, at 46–55.

[75] For a brief assessment of whether the GATS or GATT would apply to this issue, see Shaffer ibid.

[76] See, eg, *Communication from The Appellate Body: United States—Import Prohibition of Certain Shrimp and Shrimp Products*, available in Westlaw, 1998 WL 716669 (WTO). Another relevant factor is that, under the Directive, individual companies meeting EC requirements may still transfer data to the US despite the imposition of a general ban. For an overview and analysis of the Appellate Body shrimp-turtle decision, see G. Shaffer, 'United States—Import Prohibition of Certain Shrimp and Shrimp Products' (1999) 93 *Am J Int'l L* 507.

These new experiments in governance are a much preferred way to proceed than through litigation before a supranational court, such as the WTO's Dispute Settlement Body. New institutional development requires creative problem-solving and political will. The Safe Harbor Principles are an example of what—potentially—can be accomplished.

VI. Conclusions: the prospects and limits of US-EC bilateral regulatory co-operation through mutual recognition agreements: moving toward an EC system?

Despite the significant difficulties of implementing the various US-EC bilateral agreements, they have also created frameworks for interaction among regulatory officials who are responsible for protecting the health and safety of residents in an array of areas. Even if these transatlantic regulatory interactions result in tensions, blockages and obstacles, the concerned regulatory authorities also become more educated about each other's systems and are simultaneously initiating and pursuing various informal parallel programmes which receive less attention than the conflicts, but may be more important in the long term. Sustained regulatory encounters promoted by the various bilateral agreements ultimately are much more important than abstract undertakings to engage in regulatory co-operation.[77] This regulatory interaction can lead to more protective social regulation *and* greater trade facilitation, both to consumers' benefit.

Harmonization, of course, is not an end in itself, and diversity is also a core value.[78] Regulatory diversity can reflect differences in constituent values, environmental conditions and other contexts. Nonetheless, in an increasingly interdependent transatlantic economy in which choices in one jurisdiction may have significant impacts on constituents in others, regulatory decisions are more informed—and more inclusive—when made in the context of sustained regulatory exchange. A central normative goal of transgovernmental regulatory co-operative efforts is to create frameworks that conduce national regulators to take into account reflexively the impact of their actions on affected, but otherwise unrepresented, foreign constituents, while remaining deferential to distinct national values and priorities.

A. Limits to transatlantic regulatory co-ordination

Nonetheless, irrespective of the potential benefits to firms and regulators, and irrespective of political pressure for regulatory adaptation, transatlantic

---

[77] Such abstract undertakings are reflected in the NTA, the TEP and their action plans, as well as the draft US-EU Guidelines/Principles on Co-operation and Transparency in Establishing Technical Resources which has been negotiated for years.

[78] See, eg, D. Leebron, 'Lying Down with Procrustes: An Analysis of Harmonization Claims' in J. Bhagwati & R. Hudec (eds), *Fair Trade and Harmonization: Economic Analysis* (1996) at 41; and D.C. Esty in D.C. Esty & D. Geradin (eds), *Regulatory Competition and Economic Integration* (2000); and D.C. Esty, 'Revitalizing Environmental Federalism' (1996) 95 *Mich L Rev* 595.

regulatory co-operation remains by no means a foregone conclusion. While the NTA and Transatlantic Economic Partnership create various frameworks for regulatory co-ordination, significant obstacles remain, whether on account of institutional asymmetries, market contexts, differences in culture and values, or concerns over legitimacy. The challenges of implementing the 1997 MRA demonstrate this. Where existing regulatory structures, cultures and standards mesh, then regulatory co-ordination becomes easier. However, where regulatory agencies such as the FDA and FCC experiment for the first time with delegating functions to private testing bodies, and, even more importantly, where regulatory agencies such as the FDA and OSHA are wary of new EC-like approaches, building and retaining the requisite trust and confidence requires considerable time and resources. Institutional learning curves are steep.

Cross-border regulatory interaction is not free, and thus the net benefits for regulators of the MRA remains an open question. Regulators on both sides of the Atlantic have had to dedicate considerable resources to implement the MRA, especially during the transition period. Just to start, the effort entails considerable up-front negotiation costs and the costs of regulators learning and becoming comfortable with each other's systems. For example, to implement the medical device annex, FDA has trained foreign private bodies in its methods, conducted joint inspections, and assessed detailed dossiers. A number of the European applicants submitted documents in a foreign language, which FDA returned for translation. Even after translation (at the Commission's expense), some applications were drafted in broken English, again complicating the FDA's task.[79] Similarly, the FDA maintains that it does not have the resources to verify the equivalence of all 15 member states' systems for implementation of the pharmaceutical GMP annex.[80]

B. Moving toward an EC model?

Overall, transatlantic institutional adaptation has been slow (and often creeping), but where it has occurred, it has been rather unidirectional, and will likely continue to be so.[81] Simply stated, the US has made most of the changes, whether through adoption of international standards that mirror EC ones, through delegation of testing and certification responsibilities to private laboratories (reflecting the EC's 'global approach'), or through co-ordination and oversight

---

[79] Telephone interview with FDA official, 7 June 2002.

[80] However, EC officials are unclear if the FDA is 'merely playing games' with its assertions about resource constraints. EC officials point out that the EC has also signed an MRA on pharmaceutical GMPs with Canada, and Canada has completed evaluation of all 15 member states' regulatory systems within a shorter transition period. Interview with Commission official, 18 June 2001, Brussels.

[81] There is, however, some move on the EC side to create independent regulatory authorities, such as the European Medical Evaluation Agency and a new European food authority, although these agencies typically will not have independent regulatory authority, at least to anywhere near the extent of their US counterparts. See, eg, M. Pollack & G. Shaffer, 'Food Safety and GMOs in the Transatlantic Relationship', in Pollack & Shaffer, supra note 2, at 159–160.

of these laboratories under a new US national programme analogous to those operating in the EC for over a decade.[82] Because the US lacked a co-ordinated system of accredited testing and certification laboratories, European officials were concerned about the ability of US regulators to guarantee the competence and quality of US conformity assessment bodies. In response, the US National Institute of Standards and Technology, a division of the Department of Commerce, created a new US programme named the National Voluntary Conformity Assessment Program. Taking from the EC model, the US programme aims to co-ordinate and oversee US conformity assessment bodies, and thereby provide greater confidence to regulatory officials, whether domestic or foreign.

The EC model is being exported in part because the model actually works in a manner that allows for regulatory diversity in a context of intensive economic exchange. The EC model works because it facilitates a great deal of interaction among political representatives, regulatory officials and affected constituencies through innovative procedures, such as the relatively decentralized 'new' and 'global' EC regulatory approaches that rely on sustained interaction among cross-border regulatory networks. Under this EC model, the vast majority of regulatory resources remain at the national, and not the EC supranational, level.

Yet, regardless of the EC model's appropriateness, the EC exercises significant market leverage in determining transatlantic standards and regulatory structures required to implement mutual recognition policies on account of the size of its single market, which is already larger than the US'. This leverage will only increase as the EC potentially expands its borders to encompass ten to 13 additional nations within a few years. Firms desiring access to the EC market place pressure on their national officials to adapt their own systems to accommodate reciprocal trading arrangements. As the EC enters into mutual recognition agreements with other OECD countries, such as Japan, Australia, New Zealand, Switzerland and Canada, and as these countries adapt their systems to interact with the EC model, the pressure on the US to adapt its own regulatory structures should augment. The same process occurs as the EC negotiates with other countries regarding the adequacy of their data privacy protection laws, and as these countries adapt by enacting new legislation affecting the export of data to the US. Consciously or unconsciously, the EC is steadily exporting its system globally. The 1997 MRA and the 2000 Safe Harbor Principles attest to this. In pooling their sovereignty at the EC level, European member states collectively exercise much more leverage in transatlantic and international negotiations over common regulatory standards and procedures.

---

[82] Similarly, the European Commission helped forge a 'European Organization for Testing and Certification' in 1990 in order to '(1) coordinate testing and certification practices to prevent firms from having to undergo multiple market entry and approval requirements, and (2) develop a common European framework to encourage mutual confidence and trust in member countries regulatory and self-regulatory testing and certification practices'. See, eg, M. Egan, *Constructing a European Market: Standards, Regulation and Governance* (2001) at 152.

C. Legitimacy: ensuring public health and safety while retaining open markets; the need for political will and resources to build transatlantic regulatory trust and confidence; the limits of unfunded mandates

Assessing the legitimacy of enhanced bilateral co-operation raises questions of both substance (outputs) and procedure (inputs). From a substantive perspective, bilateral co-operation cannot be accomplished on the cheap or it could result in deregulatory measures with little oversight. This result would lead to challenges that the system benefits only producer, and not consumer interests, and thus that regulatory outcomes are substantively illegitimate. From a procedural perspective, citizens justifiably fear that they will have less control and access to regulatory decision-making made outside of their own borders, raising issues of procedural legitimacy.

A number of consumer advocates, such as Public Citizen, distrust new transatlantic mutual recognition arrangements.[83] The transatlantic push for regulatory co-ordination and reform arguably has led to increased delegation of traditional public services to private testing bodies. US consumer advocates, in particular, distrust the adoption of the EC's decentralized approach based on manufacturer self-certifications and certifications by private laboratories. In part, this distrust could stem from the perception that, in the US context, private actors lack the tradition of co-operating with regulatory authorities that exists in more corporatist, state-directed European systems.[84] There is, however, no necessary link between private certification and increased risk to public health and safety, *provided* that these certification processes are based on high health and safety standards and are complemented by significant regulatory oversight and controls.[85] While there may well be a growing role for new governance mechanisms based on private monitoring and information exchange,[86] these mechanisms are unlikely to be successful unless backed by the prospect of state regulatory intervention.[87]

---

[83] See, eg, *U.S.-EU Mutual Recognition Agreement (MRA)—Congressional Hearing* http:// www.publiccitizen.org/trade/harmonization/MRA/articles.cfm?ID=6156 (visited 10 March 2002). M. Bottari, P. Lurie & S.M. Wolfe, *Public Citizen Comments on Pharmaceutical Annex to U.S.-EU Mutual Recognition Agreement*, http://www.publiccitizen.org/trade/harmonization/MRA/articles. cfm?ID=4302 (visited 10 March 2002).

[84] See, eg, Egan, supra note 81, at 131 (noting that, in the US, 'the public and private sector have remained much more distinct', and the policy style is less 'state-directed'); and Kagan, *Regulatory Encounters*, supra note 53, at 3 (noting the much more 'legalistic' and adversarial' regulatory style in the US).

[85] It is important to distinguish between deregulation of standards and deregulation of regulatory pre-market approvals. Arguably, the EC aims to raise substantive standards and deregulate procedural authorizations. Thus, a deregulation of product approvals does not necessarily mean that standards will be lowered. Rather, as with the experience of the EC's internal market, standards may be raised.

[86] See, eg, A.-M. Slaughter, 'Agencies on the Loose? Holding Government Networks Accountable' in G. Bermann *et al* (eds), *Transatlantic Regulatory Cooperation*, supra note 16, at 521–535 (providing proposals for enhancing the accountability and legitimacy of governance through transgovernmental networks); and A. Fung, D. O'Rourke & C. Sabel, *Can We Put an End to Sweatshops?* (2001).

[87] The need for back-up of state intervention is often referred to as the 'shadow of hierarchy'. See, eg, Egan, supra note 82; and Egan, supra note 13, at 205–206.

Building a transatlantic marketplace requires reconciliation of the twin goals of social protection and competition through open trade. These twin goals only can be reconciled through increased regulatory co-operation, which, in turn, will require sustained political will, institutional adaptation, and dedicated resources. EC member states have sustained such political will and dedicated such resources over decades in order to create the single market. And even so, they too have encountered significant setbacks and obstacles.[88] While it is far too early to pre-judge the 1997 MRA, it nonetheless is fair to question whether the requisite political will exists on each side of the Atlantic to ensure that regulatory resources are made available.

Regulators engaged in this process must gain and sustain trust and confidence in each other's decisions, in particular in areas affecting public health and safety where they are asked to rely on testing, assessments and accreditations by foreign laboratories and officials. Regulatory officials on both sides of the Atlantic complain that they simply do not have the resources to engage in the seminars, workshops, joint testing, inspections, and information exchange prescribed in the MRA, and necessary for its proper implementation. The Commission's DG Enterprise confirms that it has yet to locate the resources to implement properly the medical devices MRA. The FDA asserts that the MRA annexes under its responsibility constitute 'unfunded mandates', because Congress has instructed the FDA to co-operate with trade officials in the negotiation and implementation of mutual recognition agreements, but has not provided it with the requisite resources. FDA officials are frustrated by what they view as 'political pressure' from trade officials that 'complicates our regulatory mission'.[89]

This situation involves a curious reversal of arguments used by fiscal conservatives within the US. Whereas it was the Congress of the 'Gingrich Revolution' that decried 'unfunded mandates' without cost-benefit analysis and the provision of adequate federal funding to state authorities to implement Congressional dictates, now consumer advocates and federal regulators decry unfunded mandates for cross-border regulatory co-ordination. Some consumer advocacy groups go even further, arguing that businesses, not taxpayers, should pay these costs. Regardless of how the necessary regulatory resources are obtained, regulatory co-ordination and the MRA's proper implementation require them. Without such resources, MRAs could put consumer health and safety at greater risk, calling into question the substantive legitimacy of these arrangements. The prospects for transatlantic regulatory adaptation and co-ordination are neither self-effectuating nor foreclosed. Yet, there have been some successes, and they should be recognized.

---

[88] See Egan, *Constructing a European Market*, supra note 82, at 7 ('The task of market creation is extremely difficult given variations in the historical timing of regulatory development, in national institutional structures, and national legal traditions').

[89] Telephone interview with FDA official, 7 June 2001.

11

Lessons from the Dispute over the Massachusetts Act Regulating State Contracts with Companies doing Business with Burma (Myanmar)

M. SCHAEFER*

I. INTRODUCTION

The recent dispute between the United States and the European Union over a Massachusetts procurement statute that, in essence, imposed a 10 per cent negative preference against companies active in Burma involved a combination of two of the worst irritants in US-EU economic relations.[1] First, the Massachusetts law involves action by sub-federal governments in the US in possible contravention of international obligations. It was the EU that insisted during the Uruguay Round negotiations concluded in 1994 that GATT Article XXIV(12), the so-called federal state clause, and analogous clauses in other major WTO agreements, be clarified in a manner that makes crystal clear that

---

* The author would like to thank the commentator on this paper, Auke Haagsma, Advisor, EC Commission, for his commentary on the paper. Three central points that Mr Haagsma makes on procurement related disputes generally that could not be incorporated into the body of the paper but that are worth highlighting are the following: (1) violations of the Government Procurement Agreement by governments may be quite numerous because many violations may be hard to detect, eg, if they do not occur in the form of legislation or regulations but rather discretionary actions by officials on individual procurements; (2) the current review of the agreement should ensure that the GPA 'establishes a balance between the burden placed on purchasers and suppliers'; and (3) the EU would like to explore the possibility of establishing independent bodies in domestic systems that could be utilized to solve informally problems encountered in gaining access to contracts because it would de-politicize disputes, and suppliers are often reluctant to use more formal procedures (ie, 'bite the hand that (does not) feed them'). On the issue of state-level violations (which the author focuses on), Mr Haagsma was not enthusiastic at the prospects of relying on domestic litigation rather than WTO dispute settlement and confirmed EU frustration with the mechanisms in place or use of existing mechanisms by the US federal government to ensure state compliance. He noted that the EU is better able to ensure compliance of sub-national governments with the GPA because it has been 'incorporated into the EU legal order'.

[1] Mass Rev Stat, ch 7, sections 22G–22M.

federal states are fully responsible for the actions of their component units.[2] The EU's member states, most of which are unitary states, have long been concerned with the possible imbalance in trade agreement obligations that can be created if federal state clauses are drafted and interpreted to excuse federal states from responsibility for actions by their sub-federal governments.[3] Moreover, state procurement policies affecting market access by EU companies have historically concerned the EU as evidenced by their continual citation in the annual trade barrier reports issued by the EU Commission. However, the EU frustration with sub-federal behaviour in the US is not limited to the trade arena. For instance, Germany continued to pursue a case before the World Court against the US because Arizona did not notify a German national, charged with murder, of his right to meet with a consular official, even though the German national had already been executed.[4] Indeed, many European countries view the imposition of the death penalty by US states, irrespective of the nationality of the convict and consular notification issues, as a violation of international human rights norms.

Second, the Massachusetts statute had an extraterritorial regulatory effect. Similar to a secondary boycott, the Massachusetts statute sought to influence the dealings of foreign companies (as well as US companies) with Burma. Extraterritorial application of laws by the US has created friction with European countries at least since the 1960s.[5] These frictions are particularly notable in (but not exclusive to) the area of economic sanctions for foreign policy goals, such as the so-called Soviet Pipeline controversy in the mid-1980s, and the more recent example of the Helms-Burton Act seeking to penalize economic dealings with Cuba.[6]

The Massachusetts law was challenged in the WTO by the EU and in US domestic courts by the National Foreign Trade Council (NFTC), an association first created in 1914, and now including over 580 multinational corporations as members.[7] NFTC members include most of the largest US manufacturers and banks and account for 70 per cent of US non-agricultural exports.[8] The WTO case never reached an examination of the Massachusetts law by a dispute settlement panel. Instead, the law was held unconstitutional at all three levels

---

[2] It should be emphasized that this was just a clarification since GATT 1947's Article XXIV(12) was already interpreted as making federal states fully responsible for action by their sub-federal governments if it was within the federal government's constitutional powers to control the behaviour. See J. Jackson, *World Trade and the Law of GATT* (1969), at 110–117; M. Schaefer, 'Searching for Pareto Gains in the Relationship Between Free Trade and Federalism: Revisiting the NAFTA, Eyeing the FTAA' (1997) 23 *Canada-US LJ* 441, at 462–465.

[3] See M. Schaefer, supra note 2, at 465.

[4] *LaGrand Case (Germany v US)*, Judgment of 27 June 2001, available at http://www.icj-cij.org.

[5] See, eg, A. Lowenfeld, *Trade Controls for Political Ends* (1983) at 92–93.

[6] See Agora, 'The Cuban Liberty and Democratic Solidarity (Libertad) Act' (1996) 90 *Am J Int'l L* 419.

[7] See 'Supreme Court to Rule on Constitutionality of Massachusetts Burma Procurement Law' (1999) 16 *Int'l Trade Rep* 1958.

[8] NFTC Profile, available at http://www.usaengage.org/background/nftc.

of the US federal court system: the federal district court,[9] the federal appeals court,[10] and the US Supreme Court.[11] Yet, it is unclear what impact the Supreme Court's decision will have on future state and local sanctions efforts because many groups are reading the opinion quite narrowly. Thus, future disputes over similar measures can by no means be ruled out. This begs the question of what can be done to avoid similar disputes, or what is the best way to resolve similar disputes, if they cannot be avoided. Fortunately, the dispute over the Massachusetts Burma law points the way towards several methods for preventing and resolving future disputes between the EU and the US over not only state procurement sanctions laws enacted for foreign policy reasons but state and local laws more generally.

Part II of this paper briefly examines the human rights situation in Burma that prompted not only Massachusetts but also the US federal government and the EU to impose sanctions. Part III gives statistics regarding foreign investment in Burma as of 1998 when the EU-US dispute over the Massachusetts Burma law reached its peak. Part IV describes the process by which Massachusetts became bound to the Government Procurement Agreement (GPA). Part V explains the history and nature of sanctions imposed against Burma by the US federal government, the EU, and the state of Massachusetts. Part VI explains the rationale behind the diplomatic and procedural manoeuvres in the EU's WTO case and also analyzes the substantive claims of the EU under the GPA. Part VII analyzes the motivations and procedures regarding the NFTC's domestic court challenge to the Massachusetts Burma law. It proceeds to examine the constitutional claims upon which the NFTC based its suit and the results in US courts. Part VIII looks at the future of state procurement sanctions laws enacted for foreign policy reasons in light of the US court rulings. Part IX explores the implications of the Massachusetts Burma law dispute for EU-US dispute prevention and resolution and gives several recommendations regarding state foreign policy-related procurement sanctions laws. These recommendations for dispute prevention and settlement carry over to other forms (ie, non-procurement manifestations) of state foreign policy-related sanction laws. Finally, this part turns to look at protectionist motivated state legislation, finding that the recommendations for dispute prevention remain the same in this context, but the recommendations for dispute resolution change.

II. BURMA'S HUMAN RIGHTS RECORD

Burma, a country of nearly 42 million people, gained independence in 1948.[12] It was ruled by a democratically elected civilian government until a military coup

---

[9] *NFTC v Baker*, 26 F Supp 2d 287 (D Mass 1998).
[10] *NFTC v Natsios*, 181 F 3d 38 (1st Cir, 1999).   [11] *Crosby v NFTC*, 530 US 363 (2000).
[12] See US Dept of State: Report on Human Rights Practices (Burma), various years.

d'etat in 1962.[13] The military leadership has prevented the reinstitution of democracy through the intimidation, arrest, and killing of persons in the pro-democracy movement throughout the last four decades. In 1988, massive democracy demonstrations were held but this resulted in the arrest of the leaders of the movement and the killing of over 3,000 civilians by the military.[14] The military regime promised and held elections in May 1990.[15] However, the military regime feared losing the elections and placed soon-to-be Nobel Peace Prize winner Daw Aung San Suu Kyi, the leader of the National League for Democracy (NLD), under house arrest nine months prior to the elections.[16] The NLD won 392 out of 474 seats in the Parliament (with the military party winning only 11 seats) but the military regime rejected the results.[17] Throughout the 1990s, the military continued to detain NLD members to prevent them from organizing and attending party conventions, including several large scale detentions in 1996 and 1997. Burma also has grave problems relating to forced labour.[18] It is estimated that as many as 800,000 persons may be involved in coerced labour in Burma, producing as much as 10 per cent of its gross domestic product.[19]

III. FOREIGN INVESTMENT IN BURMA

In 1998, the year the EU asked for establishment of a WTO panel on the Massachusetts Burma law and the year the NFTC challenged the law in the US federal court system, the US was among the top five countries in terms of foreign investment in Burma.[20] Two EU member states, the United Kingdom and France, were the two largest foreign investors.[21] Oil and gas companies are the largest foreign investors in Burma, accounting for roughly two-thirds of all foreign investment in Burma since 1988.[22] Without any government action, pressure by stakeholders, including human rights organizations, led several major companies, including Pepsi, to withdraw from Burma prior to 1998.

---

[13] See US Dept of State: Report on Human Rights Practices (Burma), various years.
[14] See T. Guay, 'Local Government and Global Politics: The Implications of the Massachusetts Burma Law', 115 *Political Science Quarterly* (Fall 2000).
[15] See ibid.
[16] See L. Dhooge, 'The Wrong Way to Mandalay: The Massachusetts Selective Purchasing Act and the Constitution' (2001) 37 *Am Bus LJ* 387, 393–94.
[17] See ibid.
[18] See, generally, 'Business, Labor Pressure Administration over New Burma Sanctions', *Inside U.S. Trade*, 5 January 2001.
[19] See Dhooge, supra note 16, at 401 (citing report of the International Confederation of Free Trade Unions).
[20] See Guay, supra note 14.
[21] See Dhooge, supra note 16, at 395.
[22] See ibid.

IV. Binding Massachusetts and other States to the Government Procurement Agreement

The original GATT 1947 largely exempted government procurement practices from its major non-discrimination obligations of national treatment and most-favoured-nation treatment.[23] During the Tokyo Round negotiations of the 1970s that addressed non-tariff barriers (NTBs) for the first time in a significant manner in the GATT system, a Government Procurement Agreement (GPA) was negotiated in an effort to curb protectionist procurement policies. Like the other NTB 'codes' concluded during the Tokyo Round, ratification of the GPA was done on an à la carte basis.[24] Only a select group of industrialized countries elected to join the GPA in 1979. The agreement did not cover the procurement practices of sub-national governments.

When the EU and the US sought to expand coverage of the agreement during the time of the Uruguay Round negotiations, the EU made clear that coverage of US state-level procurement was a priority matter.[25] The US federal government originally contemplated binding all states to the renegotiated GPA. However, in response to political (not constitutional) limitations, the federal government chose a more flexible approach in which it would bind only those states whose governors submitted a voluntary 'letter of commitment' agreeing to be bound. The letters of commitment could limit the number of state agencies bound or carve out exceptions for certain goods or services and these were included in the annex to the GPA elaborating state coverage. The Governor of Massachusetts at the time, Bill Weld, was one of 37 state governors that submitted a letter of commitment to the US Trade Representative (USTR) agreeing to be bound to the GPA. The degree to which a particular state's legislature was involved in the process depended largely on inter-branch co-operation in the state. However, the National Conference of State Legislatures (NCSL), a DC-based organization, was informed of and apprised of the negotiations.

In order to determine whether a particular state-level procurement is covered under the GPA, a five-part analysis must be undertaken. First, the state must be listed in the US schedule annexed to the agreement. Second, the particular state agency undertaking the procurement must be listed under the state's name. Third, the contract must exceed the thresholds established by the agreement for state-level procurement, roughly $500,000 for goods and services, and $6.5 million for construction. Fourth, the particular good or service being procured must not be exempted from coverage. For instance, pre-existing preferences for domestic autos, steel and coal were exempted for all states covered. Additionally, individual states exempted other products of particular sensitivity, such as beef

---

[23] GATT, Article III:8.
[24] See J. Jackson, *The World Trading System* (2nd edn., 1997) at 76.
[25] The description that follows is drawn from Schaefer, supra note 2, at 472–73.

for South Dakota and boats for Washington. Fifth, other general exemptions must not apply, such as those for small and minority business set-asides. No state commitment forced a change in current state law, perhaps one reason why state legislatures were not involved to a significant degree by governors in the crafting of the letters of commitment. As a result, the GPA creates essentially a standstill obligation against new protectionist legislation by the states for covered procurements.[26] However, the coverage of 37 states to this degree under the agreement allowed the US to gain coverage of EU sub-national governments and EU heavy electrical and telecommunications procurements to a degree. The GPA entered into force on 1 January 1996. The agreement was an exception to the largely 'single package' approach to ratification of the Uruguay Round agreements.[27] The à la carte approach to ratification led to only 23 countries becoming party to the agreement.

There is no exception in the agreement for foreign policy-related procurement sanctions statutes at the state level. No state asked for such an exception (and the federal government almost certainly would not have negotiated one even if a state did make such a request). Indeed, at the time states were not focused on foreign policy sanctions laws in the procurement area because South Africa sanctions laws were eliminated several years earlier with the ending of apartheid and the transition to democracy in South Africa.

V. SANCTIONS AGAINST BURMA PRIOR TO THE EU-US DISPUTE

A. US federal government sanctions against Burma

The US government cut off direct financial assistance to Burma as early as 1988.[28] In July 1989, in response to the house arrest of Suu Kyi, the US government suspended tariff preferences under the Generalized System of Preferences.[29] The US government followed these measures with an arms embargo, downgrading its representation in Burma from an Ambassador to Chargés D'Affairs, and imposing visa restrictions on senior Burmese officials.[30]

In response to crackdowns against the pro-democracy movement, the US Congress imposed additional sanctions in September 1996. The 1996 federal law[31] continued the ban on bilateral assistance, directed the Secretary of the Treasury to instruct the US Executive Directors of the international financial institutions to oppose any loans to Burma, banned visas for Burmese government officials, and authorized the President to ban new investments in Burma if the Burmese government re-arrested Suu Kyi or committed large scale repression or violence against the democratic opposition. In April 1997, President Clinton

---

[26] See ibid.   [27] See Jackson, supra note 24, at 77–78; WTO Agreement, Annex 4.
[28] See Dhooge, supra note 16, at 404.   [29] See ibid.   [30] See ibid.
[31] Foreign Operations, Export Financing and Related Programs Appropriation Act, Public Law No 104–208, section 570 (30 September 1996).

announced his intention to impose a ban on new investment. Subsequently, on 20 May 1997, an Executive Order was issued instituting the ban on *new* investment.[32] The ban applied to all US persons. The Executive Order specifically exempted the sale of goods to Burma and non-profit activities. The Executive Order was issued not only pursuant to the federal Burma sanctions law but also the International Economic Emergency Powers Act (IEEPA).[33] IEEPA is a framework law delegating authority to the Executive to impose economic sanctions in response to 'any unusual and extraordinary threat...to the national security, foreign policy or economy of the United States'.[34] Several US multinational corporations voiced criticism of the sanctions, including United Technologies and Unocal.

Over the past few years, pressure has been brought to bear on both the Clinton Administration and subsequently the Bush Administration to impose additional sanctions on Burma. Much of this pressure arises from a November 2000 International Labour Organization (ILO) recommendation under Article 33 of the organization's charter, unprecedented in the 81 year history of the organization, calling on members of the ILO to review their relations with Burma and ensure that the Burmese government cannot take advantage of such relations to perpetuate or extend the system of forced or compulsory labour.[35]

B. EU sanctions against Burma

The EU also took action in 1996 to sanction Burma. Specifically, the EU expelled Burmese military personnel, banned the export of all armaments and military equipment to Burma, suspended financial assistance other than humanitarian, and banned visas for high ranking Burmese officials and their families.[36] In March 1997, the EU suspended tariff preferences for Burmese agricultural products and five months later extended the suspension to cover industrial products.[37]

C. Massachusetts sanctions against Burma

On 25 June 1996, three months prior to the passage of the federal Burma sanctions law and six months after entry into force of the GPA, Massachusetts Governor Weld, surrounded by Burmese activists, signed a law instituting procurement sanctions against companies active in Burma. Governor Weld, in the midst of a US Senate race at the time and originally against the legislation, was reportedly influenced somewhat by the fact that his opponent, John Kerrey, had

---

[32] Executive Order No 13047 (20 May 1997).
[33] 50 USCA, sections 1701–1706.   [34] See ibid.
[35] See 'Business, Labor Pressure Administration over New Burma Sanctions', *Inside U.S. Trade*, 5 January 2001.
[36] See Dhooge, supra note 16, at 403.
[37] See ibid.

been slow to endorse the idea of sanctions against Burma. Aggressive lobbying
by human rights activists and NGOs and the lack of any significant opposition
by the business community at the time also apparently helped change Governor
Weld's mind.

The principal sponsor in the Massachusetts legislature was Byron Rushing.
Representative Rushing was inspired in part by a 1993 talk by Desmond Tutu
indicating the effectiveness of sanctions in changing the policies of the South
African government. He was also lobbied by Simon Billenness, an analyst for an
asset management firm specializing in socially responsible investments and a
prominent figure in the Free Burma Coalition, a coalition of NGOs including the
Massachusetts Burma Roundtable, promoting action against Burma.[38] The Free
Burma Coalition used an internet and e-mail campaign very successfully to push
for boycott of products of companies active in Burma (such as campus boycotts
of Pepsi products) and to place pressure on governments to impose sanctions.[39]
Their website was established with the support of the Sorros Foundation and the
Open Society Institute.[40] Representatives Rushing and Billenness originally met
at a conference marking the end to the boycott of companies doing business in
South Africa.[41] It was there that Billenness first suggested to Rushing the possibility of a new target: Burma.[42] After familiarizing himself with the situation in
Burma, Rushing pulled the bill the Massachusetts' legislature drafted a decade
earlier regarding South Africa, struck the words South Africa from the
bill, replaced them with the word Burma, and introduced the bill.[43] The state
of Massachusetts does not have a large ethnic Burmese or Burmese-American
population, and indeed the groups pushing for sanctions did not have a
large Burmese-American contingent within their membership.[44] Thus, the
Massachusetts Burma law was not an instance in which a particular ethnic
group influenced foreign policy legislation.

Representative Rushing was not even aware at the time of drafting the bill that
Massachusetts was bound to the GPA. After learning of the GPA, Rushing was
quoted as referring to the agreement as the 'Government Procurement blah
blah'.[45] Rushing claimed the 'identifiable goal [of the law] is free democratic
elections in Burma'.[46] Upon signing the bill into law, Governor Weld called upon
other states and the US Congress to 'follow [Massachusetts'] example and make

[38] See P. Fitzgerald, 'Massachusetts, Burma and the World Trade Organization: A Commentary on
Blacklisting, Federalism, and Internet Advocacy in the Global Trading Era' (2001) 34 *Cornell Int'l LJ*
1, at 3.
[39] See ibid.
[40] See ibid.
[41] See ibid.
[42] See ibid.
[43] Comments by Representative Byron Rushing at the Annual Meeting of the American Society of
International Law, Panel on International Law and the Work of Federal and State Legislators, April
2001.
[44] See Guay, supra note 14.
[45] This quote appeared in *The Economist* magazine.
[46] See Statement of Representative Byron Rushing, 19 July 1995.

a stand for the cause of freedom'.[47] While the bill passed by a handy margin, some in the Massachusetts legislature did criticize the bill as an effort by the state to engage in 'its own little version of foreign policy' and suggested that the legislature should instead 'focus its efforts on creating jobs here at home and not try to dabble in foreign affairs'.[48]

The statute required the Secretary of the Massachusetts' Department of Finance and Purchasing to maintain a 'restricted list' of all companies 'doing business' in Burma.[49] Companies on the list were given the opportunity to rebut the information. In preparing the list, the Secretary was to rely on information from the United Nations and non-governmental human rights organizations. The statute prohibited the state from procuring from entities on the restricted list but made exceptions in cases in which the procurement was essential, for certain medical supplies, and when there was no 'comparable low bid or offer'.[50] The statute defined 'comparable bid' as an offer equal to or less than 10 per cent above the low bid from a company on the restricted purchase list.[51] Therefore, the statute did not act as an outright ban on all purchases from companies on the restricted list, but rather operated to impose a 10 per cent negative preference against companies on the restricted list.

VI. THE EU'S WTO CASE

A. Diplomacy and procedures

The EU first formally protested the Massachusetts measure in a démarche to the State Department in January 1997. A month later, the EU complained of the Massachusetts law at a WTO Government Procurement Committee meeting.[52] In June 1997, the EU formally requested consultations under the WTO Dispute Settlement Understanding.[53] However, Massachusetts found an ally in the form of the European Parliament. The EU Parliament condemned the Commission's decision to bring a WTO case and urged the EU to impose more stringent sanctions against Burma.[54]

Japan joined the WTO consultations a month later.[55] Several trilateral consultations were held over the course of the next year. The EU also sought to make

---

[47] See *Natsios*, 181 F 3d at 46 (1999).

[48] Statements of Representative Edward Teague and Representative Lucille Hicks, 19 July 1995.

[49] Mass Rev Stat, ch 7, sections 22H–22J.

[50] Ibid, sections 22H, 22I & 22J.

[51] Ibid, section 22G.

[52] See 'EU Complains Japan's Call for Bids on Satellite System Biased for U.S.' (1997) 14 *Int'l Trade Rep* 352.

[53] See 'European Union Seeks WTO Consultations Over Massachusetts Sanctions Law' (1997) 14 *Int'l Trade Rep* 1098.

[54] See European Parliament, Resolution of 17 September 1998.

[55] See 'Japan Weighs Making Appeal to WTO on Massachusetts Law on Burma Sanctions' (1997) 14 *Int'l Trade Rep* 1233.

an overture directly to Representative Rushing.[56] This was initially done through the UK consul in Boston. However, the EU sought and obtained approval from the State Department to consult directly with Rushing. EU officials together with the UK consul met with Rushing. At the meeting, the EU offered to drop their WTO complaint if Massachusetts amended their measure so as to exempt WTO-covered procurements, ie, procurements above the threshold of $500,000 for goods and services. However, Representative Rushing asked what additional measures the EU would take to place pressure on the Burmese regime. The EU took a pass on this conversation, seeking to avoid a situation in which it might have to negotiate state-by-state as states considered and adopted sanctions measures of this type. Moreover, Rushing ultimately became unwilling to consider amendment of the measure because of a domestic court challenge to the measure lodged by the NFTC. While amending the law to apply only to contracts below the GPA threshold would have eliminated the possibility of the WTO challenge, it would not have protected Massachusetts from challenge on domestic constitutional grounds.

The issue of extraterritorial sanctions was also a key issue of discussion at the May 1998 EU-US Summit. In addition to an agreement specifically relating to the Helms-Burton law, the EU and US arrived at a general agreement, albeit in a non-binding political commitment, on the extraterritorial application of foreign policy-related sanctions. Specifically, they agreed to 'not seek or propose, and [to] resist, the passage of new economic sanctions legislation based on foreign policy grounds which is designed to make economic operators of the other behave in a manner similar to that required of its own operators' and that sanctions would be targeted 'directly and specifically against those responsible for the problem'.[57] Given the EU's concern with the Massachusetts Burma law it is unsurprising that the declaration also included a statement regarding state and local sanctions. Specifically, the document stated that 'the policies of governmental bodies at other levels should be consonant with [the principles applicable to federal government sanctions] and avoid sending conflicting messages to countries engaged in unacceptable behavior'.[58]

In August 1998, Ambassador Barshefsky announced her intention to defend the Massachusetts law in any WTO panel proceeding.[59] A coalition of labour unions, religious groups and non-profit organisations had lobbied the Administration to defend the law. The potential challenge to the Massachusetts law also created a stir in Congress. Representative Dennis Kucinich (D-Ohio) introduced a bill in August that would have barred the US Department of Justice from using

---

[56] This story was relayed directly by Representative Rushing at the American Society of International Law Annual Meeting, Panel on International Law and the Work of Federal and State Legislators, April 2001.

[57] See Fitzgerald, supra note 38, at 42 (citing Brief for the European Communities and Their Member States as Amicus Curiae, available at 2000 Westlaw 177175).

[58] See ibid.

[59] See 'Coalition Praises USTR for Supporting Massachusetts Law' (1997) 14 *Int'l Trade Rep* 1403.

funds to challenge state laws inconsistent with trade agreements. The implementing law of the Uruguay Round, similar to many previous trade agreement implementing laws, prohibits private parties from suing states based on trade agreements but allows the federal Executive Branch to do so.[60] The implementing law also declares that any dispute settlement panel report shall not be considered as binding nor otherwise accorded deference in such a proceeding.[61] Instead, the court will consider the matter de novo. The Kucinich bill would have effectively eliminated the one avenue for ultimately forcing state compliance and thus undermined US Executive credibility at the negotiating table when dealing with state measures. The Kucinich bill was defeated by a margin of 228–200.[62]

In September 1998, the EU together with Japan requested establishment of a dispute settlement panel.[63] The motivation for elevating the dispute was not only Massachusetts' ultimate unwillingness to amend the measure, but at least equally important, the proliferation of measures at the local level, including some consideration by Massachusetts to extend its measure to companies active in Indonesia.[64] A Commission spokesperson described the request for a panel as a 'shot across the bow' but the EU's frustration with being on the defensive in the WTO as a result of the disputes with the US on beef hormones and bananas also played a role.[65] In recent decades, state and local sanction measures were enacted in surges. In the mid-1970s, 13 states enacted laws sanctioning companies trading with Arab countries that imposed a boycott on Israel. In the 1980s, more than 30 states enacted sanctions against companies active in South Africa. In fact, Massachusetts was the first state to impose sanctions against South Africa.

The city of Berkeley, California became the first sub-national government to sanction companies active in Burma.[66] While Massachusetts was the only state to follow suit, 22 other cities, including New York City and Los Angeles, also passed ordinances affecting procurement from companies active in Burma.[67] NGOs circulated the Massachusetts legislation to legislators in other states and cities and lobbied for its passage. At the time of the WTO challenge, state and city governments were considering or had already passed measures imposing sanctions seeking to punish other countries' behaviour, including not only

---

[60] Uruguay Round Agreements Act, section 102.   [61] ibid.

[62] See 'House Defeats Amendment Aimed at Protecting State Laws from Challenge' (1998) 15 *Int'l Trade Rep* 1387.

[63] See EU, 'Japan Will Initiate WTO Complaint Against U.S. Over State Law on Burma' (1998) 15 *Int'l Trade Rep* 1387.

[64] USA-Engage, State and Local Sanctions Watch List, March 2000, available at http://www.usaengage.org.

[65] See 'EU Suspends Suit on Massachusetts Law Penalizing Burma Links, Warns Other States' (1999) 16 *Int'l Trade Rep* 231. The point with respect to the EU's posture on beef hormones and bananas and its motivation in the Mass-Burma dispute was noted by the commentator to this paper, Auke Haagsma.

[66] See Sanctions Watch List, supra note 64.

[67] See ibid.

Indonesia but also Nigeria, Switzerland and China.[68] Ironically, this proliferation of state and local sanctions measures was occurring at the same time that the Congress and Executive Branch were engaged in serious discussions over reforming the use of sanctions.[69] Key elements in these discussions were the desirability of conducting cost-benefit analysis, including consideration of the effectiveness of sanctions, granting the president 'waiver' authority, automatic 'sunset' provisions, and strongly encouraging attempts to multilateralize sanctions prior to imposing unilateral sanctions.

The WTO approved establishment of the panel in November 1998.[70] However, in accordance with WTO dispute settlement rules, the EU and Japan suspended their WTO claim in February 1999 because a US district court invalidated the Massachusetts measure on US constitutional grounds in November 1998.[71] While the EU made clear it would re-open the WTO case if the district court ruling was reversed on appeal, invalidation of the Massachusetts law was upheld by the First Circuit Court of Appeals and ultimately by the Supreme Court. Accordingly, the parties to the WTO case never submitted formal briefs nor did a panel rule on the consistency of the Massachusetts measure with the GPA. It is nevertheless possible to examine, based on public statements and writings, some of the arguments that would have been made by the two sides in the case.

B. Substantive claims

1. Violation claims

The EU's first violation claim is based on GPA Article VIII(b) that deals with conditions for qualifying suppliers.[72] It states that 'qualification procedures shall be consistent with the following: . . . (b) any conditions for participation in tendering procedures shall be limited to those which are essential to ensure the firm's capability to fulfill the contract in question'. The EU argument must be that the activity in Burma has nothing to do with a firm's capability to fulfil a contract in Massachusetts. Massachusetts' rebuttal is that Article VIII only applies to pre-qualifying bidders for selective tender procedures and that a 10 per cent negative preference statute is not relevant to pre-qualifying bidders.[73] Additionally, the examples given of conditions that can be imposed, such as a

---

[68] See Sanctions Watch List, supra note 64.

[69] See, eg, 'Eizenstat Says Administration Plans to Submit Sanctions Reform Language' (1999) 16 *Int'l Trade Rep* 1118; 'Bicameral Sanctions Process Reform Act Introduced to Slow Unilateral U.S. Measures' (1999) 16 *Int'l Trade Rep* 535.

[70] See 'As High Court Reviews Case, EU, Japan Drop WTO Panel on State Law Burma Ban' (2000) 17 *Int'l Trade Rep* 308.

[71] See ibid.

[72] See ibid (also mentioning other Articles of the GPA upon which the EU based its violation claims).

[73] See 'Comments of Joel Trachtman, Symposium: States' Rights v. International Trade—The Massachusetts Burma Law' (2000) 19 *NYL School J Int'l & Comp L* 347.

bid bond requirement, only relate to the right to bid and not to the 'actual factors that [one] looks at to decide who gets' the contract.[74]

The second violation claim of the EU concerned Article XIII(4)(b). Article XIII(4) is titled 'Award of Contracts'. It requires the procuring entity to make 'the award to the tenderer who has been determined to be fully capable of undertaking the contract and whose tender, whether for domestic products or services, or products or services of other Parties, is either the lowest tender or the tender which *in terms of the specific evaluation criteria set forth in the notices or tender documentation is determined to be the most advantageous*'. The critical question is whether the evaluation criteria can only be related to cost and quality factors or can relate to non-economic political factors.[75]

The final violation claim is based on the national treatment obligation found in GPA Article III. It provides that with respect to procurement laws, each covered entity 'shall provide immediately and unconditionally to the products and services and suppliers of other Parties offering products or services of the Parties, treatment no less favorable than (a) that accorded to domestic products, services, and suppliers . . .'. The EU's argument under this article is hampered by the fact that, unlike GATT and GATS national treatment obligations, the GPA obligation does not contain the language of 'like' products, services and suppliers. The 'likeness' criteria has been interpreted by GATT panel's to preclude consideration of factors unrelated to the product itself in determining whether two products are like. For instance, if two products are similar in natural properties and qualities, end uses and consumer tastes, they will be found like even if they are made by dissimilar processes. With the language 'like' suppliers, the EU could argue by analogy that an EU supplier involved in Burma should not be discriminated against versus a US supplier not involved in Burma since a supplier's dealings with a third country do not make the suppliers unlike. Even without the language 'like', however, the EU could make the same argument. Massachusetts' response is that EU suppliers are treated equally with US suppliers.[76] If the supplier is active in Burma, a negative preference is imposed regardless of the nationality of the supplier. In other words, Massachusetts claims the relevant comparison is not between treatment afforded an EU company active in Burma and a US company not active in Burma but rather between an EU company active in Burma and a US company active in Burma.

The GPA Article III continues that each covered procuring entity 'shall not treat a locally-established supplier less favorably than another locally-established supplier on the basis of degree of foreign affiliation or ownership'. The EU might additionally argue that the Massachusetts law potentially discriminates against a US company, for example, on the basis that it is owned by a European company with investments in Burma.

---

[74] See ibid.   [75] See ibid.   [76] See ibid.

2. The realpolitik of WTO dispute settlement

While Massachusetts may have colourable textual arguments, at least with respect to some of the EU's claims, and the WTO Appellate Body and panels,
consistent with the WTO Dispute Settlement Understanding, place primary emphasis on the textual method of interpretation, it is undeniable that 'shared
community expectations' come into play behind the face of opinions.[77] WTO
panels have been traditionally and historically hostile to extraterritorial regulations (or those measures seeking to have extraterritorial effect).[78] While recent
interpretations of exceptions to GATT allow some leeway in extraterritorial
protection of the environment,[79] the realpolitik of WTO dispute settlement
probably means there is a good chance that a panel would find a Massachusetts-
type measure inconsistent with the GPA. Indeed, former USTR Ambassador
Yeuter predicted in strong terms that a WTO panel would rule against the
Massachusetts measure were they ever to examine its consistency with the GPA.[80]

3. Non-violation nullification and impairment claim

Just as the GATT does, the GPA allows for the possibility that a successful claim
can be brought against a measure, that while not a violation of the GPA, nullifies
and impairs benefits a party expected to accrue under the agreement.[81] These so-
called non-violation nullification and impairment cases have been very rare
under the GATT.[82] The test established by GATT panels is whether the party
could reasonably have anticipated such a measure being instituted subsequent to
the tariff concession. In this case, the question is whether the EU could reasonably have anticipated a measure that limits the access of EU suppliers to the
Massachusetts procurement market, subsequent to the binding of Massachusetts
to the GPA. Massachusetts might argue that it, along with many other states,
enacted such legislation less than a decade earlier with respect to South Africa.
Thus, the EU could reasonably have anticipated future human rights violations
and moral concerns of state citizens rising to such a level as to lead to the
enactment of such measures again. However, again, realpolitik suggests that a
WTO panel may be sympathetic to the plight of the EU.

---

[77] See, eg, R. Hudec, 'The Product-Process Doctrine in GATT/WTO Jurisprudence' in
M. Bronckers & R. Quick (eds), *New Directions in International Economic Law: Essays in Honour
of John H. Jackson* (2000) at 187, 200.
[78] See ibid.
[79] See *United States—Import Prohibition of Certain Shrimp and Shrimp Products*, WTO Doc WT/
DS58/AB/R (12 October 1998).
[80] See 'Former USTR Predicts U.S. Will Lose If WTO Challenge to Burma Law Proceeds' (1998) 15
Int'l Trade Rep 1642.
[81] See J. Jackson, supra note 24, at 115 (discussing non-violation complaints).
[82] See J. Jackson, W. Davey & A. Sykes, *Legal Problems of International Economic Relations*
(1995) at 195.

VII. US DOMESTIC COURT CASE

A. Motivations and procedures

In April 1998, the NFTC filed its complaint against the constitutional validity of the Massachusetts law in the US district court. Many other prior state foreign policy-related sanctions laws were not challenged by businesses for fear of a public backlash or consumer boycott of the company bringing such a suit.[83] With the NFTC filing suit, and the organization's name on the court papers, the risks of a backlash against an individual company were minimized.[84] Additionally, by acting in concert businesses were able to spread the costs of litigation.[85] As of April 1998, 44 US companies and over 300 foreign companies were listed on the restricted purchase list maintained by the Massachusetts Department of Administration and Finance.[86] Thirty-four members of the NFTC were on the restricted list, including Atlantic Richfield, Federal Express, Procter and Gamble, Unocal, and Halliburton.[87] The NFTC claimed that at least three companies severed ties with Burma in response to the Massachusetts law but many more did not and thus faced potential procurement sanctions.[88] Among the companies withdrawing from Burma, at least in part due to the Massachusetts law and consideration by other states of similar laws, were Apple Computer, Phillips Electronics, Hewlett-Packard, and Eastman Kodak.

The possibility of a WTO dispute settlement panel examining the measure under the GPA or the possibility of Massachusetts amending their law so as to only apply to non-GPA covered contracts did not dissuade the NFTC from bringing the challenge. First, even if the EU were successful in bringing a WTO case, the federal government may not have the political will to force a change in Massachusetts law. Thus, the EU could retaliate against US suppliers in its own procurement, further harming NFTC members. Second, even if Massachusetts amended its law, either voluntarily or in response to a suit by the federal government, the law would continue to apply to all procurements below the GPA threshold of $500,000 (or the bulk of all procurements). Third, the NFTC hoped for a broad constitutional ruling that would act as a deterrent to all states from engaging in foreign policy-related sanctions, whereas the WTO case could only act as a deterrent to GPA-covered states and only with respect to procurement manifestations of sanctions laws.

---

[83] See H. Fenton, 'The Fallacy of Federalism in Foreign Affairs: State and Local Foreign Policy Trade Restrictions' (1993) 13 *Northwestern J Int'l L & Bus* 563.

[84] See M. Schaefer, 'The Grey Areas and Yellow Zones of Split Sovereignty Exposed by Globalization: Choosing Among Strategies of Avoidance, Cooperation, and Intrusion to Escape an Era of Misguided "New Federalism"' (1998) 24 *Can-US LJ* 35, 65–66.

[85] See ibid.

[86] *Natsios*, 181 F 3d at 47.

[87] See ibid at 48.

[88] See ibid.

B. Claims

The NFTC challenge was based on three constitutional claims: pre-emption, the dormant foreign affairs doctrine, and the dormant foreign Commerce Clause. Prior to discussing the results of the court cases, some background and context on these three types of claims is necessary.

1. Pre-emption

Pre-emption claims are based on Article VI of the US Constitution, that make federal law supreme to state law, and an affirmative act by the US federal government. Pre-emption can occur in several different ways.[89] First, the federal government can expressly pre-empt state activity in a field (termed 'express' pre-emption).[90] Second, pre-emption can be implied, either because federal regulation in the field is so extensive (occupation of the field or simply field pre-emption)[91] or because the federal interest in the area is dominant (dominant federal interest pre-emption).[92] Third, pre-emption can arise because the state measure conflicts with the federal act, either because it is physically impossible to comply with both (direct conflict pre-emption) or because the state act stands as an obstacle to the achievement of the full purposes of the federal act (obstacles conflict pre-emption).[93]

The NFTC could not base its pre-emption claim directly on the GPA. Again, the Uruguay Round implementing law precludes private parties from bringing claims in US courts alleging the inconsistency of state laws with WTO agreements.[94] Instead, the NFTC based its pre-emption claim on the federal Burma sanctions law.

Additionally, there are strong arguments that the federal government has occupied the entire field of foreign policy-related sanctions. In addition to federal laws sanctioning individual countries, the Congress passed more generalized framework laws, most prominently the IEEPA,[95] delegating broad authority to the Executive to impose sanctions. Combined with the President's own powers in the foreign affairs field and the Executive Branch's constant monitoring of events and diplomacy around the world, one could easily find pre-emption of three kinds: field, dominant federal interest, and obstacles conflict (since the federal government must be presumed to have properly calibrated the degree of sanction, if any, taken against any given country).

---

[89] See generally, L. Tribe, *American Constitutional Law* (3rd edn., 2000) at 1172–1220.

[90] See, eg, *Shaw v Delta Airlines*, 463 US 85 (1983).

[91] See, eg, *Fidelity Savings and Loan Association v De la Cuesta*, 485 US 141 (1982).

[92] See, eg, *Hines v Davidowitz*, 312 US 52 (1941); *North Dakota v US*, 460 US 300 (1983).

[93] See, eg, *Florida Lime & Advocado Growers, Inc v Paul*, 373 US 132 (1963).

[94] See Uruguay Round Agreements Act, section 102; M. Schaefer, 'Are Private Remedies In Domestic Courts Essential for International Trade Agreements to Serve Constitutional Functions with Respect to Sub-Federal Governments?' (1996/97) 17 *Northwestern J Int'l L & Bus* 609.

[95] See 50 USCA, sections 1701–1706.

2. Dormant foreign affairs doctrine

The Constitution does not grant a general foreign affairs power to the federal government.[96] Instead, the Constitution allocates certain foreign affairs powers to the federal branches and denies other such powers to the states. No one questions that the federal government's foreign affairs powers are plenary and supreme. Further, the Supreme Court has declared on numerous occasions throughout history that foreign affairs powers are 'exclusive' to the federal government.[97] A dormant doctrine flows necessarily from an exclusive power.[98] In other words, even if the federal government does not act or utilize these powers, ie, the powers lie dormant, the states are prevented from taking actions in the area. It was not until the 1969 *Zschernig* case that the so-called dormant foreign affairs doctrine was utilized by the Supreme Court to strike down a state action (specifically, the application of an Oregon escheat statute that state judges utilized to criticize communist regimes).

In *Zschernig*, the Supreme Court appeared to establish a threshold effects test for determining the validity of state actions under the doctrine, specifically asking whether the state action has 'more than some incidental or indirect' effect on US foreign relations or a foreign country.[99] However, there is some evidence that the Court was concerned with the motive or purpose of the law as well.[100] Lower courts relied on the *Zschernig* doctrine on several occasions over the past several decades to invalidate state actions. Many of these lower courts, while according due respect to the threshold effects test, nonetheless placed considerable emphasis on the motive or purpose of the state action.[101] This is no surprise because motive or purpose review, that would ask whether the primary purpose of the state law is to change a foreign government's policy (or punish it for pursuing a particular policy), better suits the competence of the courts and better ensures their role as independent arbiters of constitutional questions. Courts recognize they have little ability to independently gauge the impact of a particular state action on foreign relations. Thus, under the threshold effects test, courts often turn to Executive Branch submissions and the views of foreign governments expressed in amicus briefs, diplomatic protests, and complaints within international organizations, all the while denying such views are dispositive.

More recently, revisionist scholars are questioning the continued viability of the *Zschernig* doctrine and believe that today's Supreme Court may be receptive to their arguments given the revival of states' rights by the Court in general.[102]

---

[96] See generally, H. Koh, *The National Security Constitution* (1991).

[97] See, eg, Chinese Exclusion Case, 130 US 581, 606 (1889).

[98] See M. Schaefer, 'Federal States in the Broader World' (2001) 27 *Canada-US LJ* 35, 36.

[99] See *Zschernig v Miller*, 389 US 432 (1969).

[100] See ibid at 429 and 434.

[101] See, eg, *Tayyari v New Mexico State University*, 495 F Supp 1365 (DNM 1980); *Springfield Rare Coin Galleries v Johnson*, 503 NE2d 300, 306 (Ill 1986).

[102] See, eg, J. Goldsmith, 'Federal Courts, Foreign Affairs, and Federalism' (1997) 83 *Va L Rev* 1617.

However, the two central foundations of this revisionist scholarship are dubious.[103] The first claim of the revisionist scholars is that the dormant foreign affairs doctrine is a relic of the Cold War.[104] In short, when our very existence was at stake, we could not afford any intrusions by states and localities into the foreign affairs field. However, the Cold War had a certain rationality (if one will forgive the use of that term). The mere fact that consequences would be draconian under 'mutually assured destruction' meant neither side was likely to overreact to a state or local measure. Today, foreign affairs are more complicated. The adversaries are not always as clear and these adversaries have many more quivers in their arrow, such as cyber war and rumours to destabilize financial markets, than the ultimate destructive act. The second claim of revisionist scholars is that one of the central policies behind the dormant foreign affairs doctrine, namely ensuring that the act of one state does not lead to retaliation against the nation as a whole, no longer holds since there are instances in which nations have targeted retaliation against a particular subnational entity.[105] However, this argument ignores the possible forms of retaliation, including hidden and subtle retaliation, the possibility of spill-over effects even from so-called targeted retaliation, and other functional arguments against state and local sanctions measures.[106] Moreover, other countries understand that the federal government has the ability to control state actions in the area and thus may direct retaliation against the state represented by the chair of an important Congressional committee or a state important to an upcoming Presidential election.[107]

3. Dormant foreign Commerce Clause

The Constitution allocates to the Congress the power to regulate interstate and foreign commerce.[108] However, for well over 150 years the Supreme Court has interpreted the Commerce Clause to act not only as a grant of power to the Congress, but also to act as a bar to state actions that discriminate against or unduly interfere with foreign commerce even when Congress has not acted to pre-empt the state measure, ie when the commerce power lies dormant. The Court appears to apply a balancing test under the dormant Commerce Clause, weighing the burden on commerce created by the state measure against its achievement of a legitimate, non-protectionist local purpose. However, some view this balancing that occurs on the face of opinions to be simply a way to tease out a protectionist purpose.[109] In cases involving foreign commerce, the Court applies the additional test of whether the state action 'prevents the federal government from speaking with one voice'.[110] This test as stated on one level

---

103 For a critique of the revisionist view, see M. Schaefer, supra note 98.
104 See, eg, P. Spiro, 'Foreign Affairs Federalism' (1999) 70 *Colo L Rev* 1223.
105 See ibid at 1261–1270.   106 See M. Schaefer, supra note 98, at 38–39.
107 See ibid.   108 US Constitution, Article I, section 8.
109 See, eg, D. Regan, 'The Supreme Court and State Protectionism: Making Sense of the Dormant Commerce Clause' (1986) 84 *Mich L Rev* 1091, 1148–49.
110 See, eg, *Japan Line*, 441 US 434 (1979).

makes little sense since a state measure can never really prevent the federal government from speaking with 'one voice' as the federal government could pre-empt all state activity in the field. Instead, state activity can prevent the federal government from speaking with a 'quiet voice' or exercising quiet diplomacy. The state action will force the federal government to be viewed as either allowing or curbing the state action and thus force it to send some kind of signal to the foreign government. In applying the test, the Court has stated the real risk it seeks to prevent is retaliation against the US as a whole for actions by a state.[111] This concern, at least in part, also underlies the threshold effects test of the dormant foreign affairs doctrine and thus the additional prong of analysis under the dormant foreign Commerce Clause (as courts often recognize) ends up looking quite similar to the dormant foreign affairs doctrine.[112]

The other question that arises is whether something less than explicit approval of the federal government can remove a state measure from scrutiny under the dormant Commerce Clause. The Court has held that strongly inferred toleration, eg, specific consideration by the Congress of the state measure and a rejection of pre-empting the state measure, can allow a state measure to clear the 'one voice' hurdle but not other portions of the dormant Commerce Clause analysis. The Court has reasoned in such cases that 'nothing requires the federal government to speak with any particular voice'.[113] However, what many misunderstand is that a simple failure to pre-empt does not constitute inferred toleration. The Congress must specifically (and perhaps on numerous occasions) turn its attention to and consider pre-emption of a particular state measure and ultimately decide against pre-emption for the inferred toleration to arise.[114] Massachusetts attempted to argue inferred toleration of their measure as a result of the ban on private causes of action based on the GPA and the failure of the federal Burma sanctions law to explicitly pre-empt the state sanctions law. However, with respect to the GPA, it does pre-empt state laws but only the federal government can bring such a case. The simple failure to explicitly pre-empt the Massachusetts Burma law in the federal Burma sanctions law cannot arise to inferred toleration because Congress did not turn sufficient attention and consideration to the possibility of pre-emption and must be assumed to know of the doctrines of implied and conflict pre-emption.

4. Market participant exception

One question that arises under both the dormant Commerce Clause and the dormant foreign affairs doctrine is whether these doctrines only apply to state

---

[111] See ibid.
[112] See *Trojan Technologies v Pennsylvania*, 916 F 2d 903 (3rd Cir, 1990) (keeping the two doctrines separate in its opinion but using a similar analysis for each); *Board of Trustees*, 562 A 2d at 752 ('[T]he concerns which underlie the foreign Commerce Clause are closely related to concerns underlying limits on a state's authority to affect foreign policy.').
[113] See *Wardair Canada v Florida Dept of Revenue*, 477 US 12 (1986).
[114] See *Barclays Bank*, 512 US 298 (1994).

regulatory conduct or also apply when the state acts as a market participant, ie, a buyer or seller of goods. It is well-settled law that there is a market participant doctrine to the dormant interstate Commerce Clause.[115] The market participant exception was created on several grounds. First, the text of the Commerce Clause refers to the power to 'regulate'.[116] Second, the state when acting as a market participant can be analogized to a private actor in the market.[117] Third, the budgetary expense of engaging in protectionist behaviour when acting as a buyer or seller reduces the risk to constitutional values protected by the dormant Commerce Clause.[118] The Supreme Court has strongly hinted that the market participant exception is available under the dormant foreign Commerce Clause and most lower courts have followed this strong hint.[119] Indeed, it would be hard to preserve the exception in the interstate context without allowing it in the foreign commerce context. In today's globalized economy a state action that affects interstate commerce will in most instances also affect foreign commerce. A state measure does not have to specifically target or discriminate against foreign commerce in order to be subject to the dormant foreign Commerce Clause constraints. Indeed, in the case in which the Supreme Court strongly hinted the exception would apply, only 10 per cent of the commerce affected by the state measure was foreign trade.[120]

Much less certain is whether the market participant exception applies to the dormant foreign affairs doctrine. While a Maryland state court examining that state's South Africa sanctions in the mid-1980s found the exception was available, the justifications for the exception appear not to apply in the context of the dormant foreign affairs doctrine. First, the textual basis disappears. The dormant foreign affairs doctrine is implied not from a particular clause granting the federal government power to 'regulate' a particular matter but rather an amalgam of clauses and the structure of the Constitution relating to foreign affairs. Second, the analogy to the private actor does not hold. The Supreme Court, in a discussion surrounding federal pre-emption of a state procurement law sanctioning federal labour law violators, found that 'government occupies a unique position of power in our international society, and its conduct, regardless of form, is rightly subject to special restraints' and 'in our system, states are simply different from private parties and have a different role to play'.[121] Third, procurement sanctions for foreign policy purposes are likely to be significantly less expensive in budgetary terms than procurement preferences for protectionist reasons.

[115] See generally, D. Coenen, 'Untangling the Market Participant Exemption to the Dormant Commerce Clause' (1989) 88 *Mich L Rev* (1989) at 395.
[116] See ibid at 436–37.
[117] See *Hughes v Alexandria Scrap Corp*, 426 US 794, 810 (1976).
[118] See Regan, supra note 109, at 1194; Coenen, supra note 115, at 434.
[119] See *South Central Timber Development Corp*, 467 US 82 (1983).
[120] See ibid.
[121] See *Wisconsin Dept of Industry v Gould*, 475 US 282, 290 (1986).

Finally, the market participant exception does not apply when a state's action has a regulatory effect on conduct in a downstream or upstream market in which it is not a direct participant. For example, the state of Alaska did not qualify for the market participant exception when it included in its contracts selling raw logs from state lands a condition that processing of the logs be done within the state.[122] Since the Massachusetts Burma law has a regulatory effect on its suppliers' relationships with Burma, the market participant exception, even if theoretically available, should not apply.

C. Results in federal court

1. Federal district court

The federal district court struck down the Massachusetts law on the basis of the dormant foreign affairs doctrine in November 1998,[123] leading to the EU and Japan suspending their WTO complaint a few months later. With respect to the other two claims by the NFTC, the district court found they had failed to carry the burden of proof with respect to pre-emption and that it was not necessary to rule on the dormant foreign Commerce Clause claim.[124]

In reaching its conclusion on the dormant foreign affairs doctrine claim, the court applied the threshold effects test most evident in the *Zschernig* opinion. Specifically, the court asked, quoting the *Zschernig* case, whether the law had 'more than some indirect or incidental effect, in foreign countries' or a 'great potential for disruption or embarrassment'.[125] Nonetheless, the federal district court first engaged in motive review, as most lower courts have done in applying the *Zschernig* test. The court highlighted that the only purpose of the Massachusetts Burma law was to sanction Burma for its human rights violations and to change these practices.[126] After engaging in motive review, the court returned to applying the threshold effects test. One of the factors the court looked to in determining whether the law violated the threshold effects test was the concerns the EU and Japan raised in the WTO.[127] Thus, the mere existence of the WTO dispute (irrespective of any finding of a WTO violation) had a minimal influence on the constitutional finding of a violation of the dormant foreign affairs doctrine. While the threshold effects test allows some minimal interplay in this regard, it should be kept in proper context. The holding of the federal district court would have been the same even if Massachusetts had never agreed to become bound to the GPA such that the EU and Japan could never have raised WTO compliance issues with the US with respect to the Massachusetts law. Nevertheless, a motive review test under the dormant foreign affairs doctrine better respects the nature of international agreements, such as the WTO, that cannot be directly invoked in a US court by a private party.

---

[122] See *South Central Timber Development Corp*, 467 US 82 (1984).
[123] See *Baker*, 26 F Supp. 287 (1998).   [124] See ibid at 293.
[125] See ibid at 291.   [126] See ibid.   [127] See ibid.

2. First Circuit Court of Appeals

The First Circuit Court of Appeals affirmed the district court's ruling but expanded the basis of the ruling to all three doctrines: pre-emption, dormant foreign affairs doctrine, and dormant foreign Commerce Clause.[128] The First Circuit began its dormant foreign affairs doctrine analysis by applying the *Zschernig* test. However, like the district court, the initial factor the First Circuit cited in drawing its conclusion that the law had more than some incidental effect on foreign relations was that the '*design and intent* of the law is to affect the affairs of a foreign country'.[129] As did the district court, the First Circuit proceeded to consider the protests of foreign countries to the law. Although it did not mention specifically the presence of the WTO dispute in this context, it is clear from the opinion that the court was aware of the proceedings. However, the First Circuit relied on the numerous other forms of protest to the law outside the WTO. For example, the EU lodged diplomatic protests with the State Department and filed an amicus brief in the case.[130] The grounds for the protest went beyond alleged WTO-inconsistency of the Massachusetts Burma law to include its extraterritorial regulatory effect. Thus, the WTO dispute played some role, but clearly a non-essential one, in the First Circuit's ruling on the dormant foreign affairs doctrine claim. The US Executive Branch, as it did before the district court, declined to file an amicus brief in opposition to the state law, to the chagrin of many in the business community.

The First Circuit also invalidated the law under the dormant foreign Commerce Clause for three reasons. First, it found that the statute facially discriminated against foreign commerce, even though it applied equally to foreign and domestic companies, because it attempted to regulate both sets of companies in their dealings with Burma.[131] Second, the court found that the law violated the additional prong of analysis in foreign Commerce Clause cases, the 'one voice' test, stating that this test was similar to, but distinct from the dormant foreign affairs doctrine.[132] Third, the court found that the state law essentially attempted to regulate conduct outside its territory, namely companies' dealings with Burma.[133] Previous Commerce Clause decisions found that states were precluded from regulating commerce that takes place wholly outside of the state's borders, regardless of whether the commerce has effects within the state, and that the critical inquiry was whether the practical effect of the regulation is to control conduct beyond the boundaries of the state.[134] The court refused to find 'inferred toleration' of the law by the failure to explicitly pre-empt the state law in the federal Burma sanctions law. The court found that a much higher degree of 'clarity and frequency of the refusal of Congress to act' to pre-empt is required to find inferred toleration.[135] In any event, inferred

---

[128] See *Natsios*, 181 F 3d 38 (1999).   [129] See ibid at 53 (emphasis added).
[130] See ibid.   [131] See ibid at 67.   [132] See ibid at 68.   [133] See ibid at 69.
[134] See ibid (citing, among other cases, *Healy v Beer Institute*, 491 US 324 (1989)).
[135] See ibid at 72.

toleration of Congress would only save the law under the 'one voice' portion of the dormant foreign Commerce Clause doctrine (ie, it does not save laws that have been found unconstitutional under that doctrine for other reasons, such as facial discrimination against foreign commerce or extraterritorial regulatory effect).[136]

Finally, the First Circuit found that the Massachusetts Burma law was preempted by the federal sanctions on Burma. It highlighted that pre-emption is more readily implied in the foreign affairs field and that the state law 'veered from the carefully balanced path that Congress constructed' by 'imposing distinct restrictions different in scope and kind from the federal law'.[137] For example, the federal law (combined with the Executive Order) only prohibited new investment by US companies whereas the Massachusetts law sought to terminate existing investment by both US and foreign companies through the leverage of the state's procurement market.

3. *US Supreme Court*

The Supreme Court unanimously (9-0) affirmed the First Circuit's decision but only on the grounds of pre-emption.[138] The Court found that the Massachusetts law stood as an obstacle to the achievement of the full purposes of the federal sanctions law, essentially basing its ruling on 'obstacles conflict' pre-emption. The Court held that the Massachusetts law 'undermines the intended purposes and natural effect of at least three provisions of the federal act, that is its delegation of effective discretion to the President to control economic sanctions against Burma, its limitation of sanctions solely to United States persons and new investment, and its directive to the President to proceed diplomatically in developing a comprehensive, multilateral strategy towards Burma'.[139] It explicitly declined to consider a broader sense of pre-emption, namely 'field preemption' (ie, that the entire field of economic sanctions against foreign countries was occupied by the federal government).[140] The Court also found it unnecessary to address the dormant foreign Commerce Clause and dormant foreign affairs doctrine claims.[141]

The WTO dispute settlement proceedings played a very small, non-dispositive role in the Court's analysis, even though pre-emption was not based on the WTO agreements and the Court did not even undertake dormant-type analysis. The Court only mentioned the WTO case in its obstacles conflict pre-emption analysis with respect to one of the three relevant provisions in the federal Act, namely the Congressional directive to the President to proceed diplomatically in developing a comprehensive, multilateral strategy towards Burma.[142] But the analysis regarding this provision of federal law also mentioned the formal diplomatic protests filed by the EU and Executive Branch statements indicating

---

[136] See ibid.   [137] See ibid at 73–76.   [138] See *Crosby*, 530 US 363 (2000).
[139] See ibid at 373–374.   [140] See ibid at 374, note 8.
[141] See ibid.   [142] See ibid at 382–83.

that the Massachusetts law was complicating efforts to build coalitions with allies with respect to Burma.[143] Moreover, the Court had already found as a matter of logic that the state law was a threat to the President's diplomatic efforts.[144]

As it did before the lower courts, Massachusetts argued that the Court should ignore the evidence of a WTO dispute because of the ban on private causes of action within the Uruguay Round legislation. Massachusetts argued that acknowledging evidence of the dispute effectively violated the ban on private causes of action. However, the Supreme Court rejected the argument because the claim in this case was pre-emption based on the federal Burma sanctions and not on the basis of the GPA.[145] The Court also rejected for the same reason Massachusetts' argument that the ban on private causes of action plus the federal government's decision to decline to bring its own suit on the basis of the GPA was evidence of inferred toleration.[146] Lastly, the Court rejected the argument that failure to expressly pre-empt the state law in the federal Burma sanctions law constituted implicit permission. The Court stated that a 'failure to provide for preemption expressly may reflect nothing more than the settled character of implied preemption doctrine that courts will dependably apply...'.[147]

Unlike the case before the lower courts, the US Executive Branch did submit an amicus brief to the Court asking that it declare the Massachusetts law unconstitutional on all three grounds.[148] Indeed, the list of amici in opposition to the law included six US Senators, 14 representatives, a host of business and agricultural groups such as the Chamber of Commerce and the American Farm Bureau, and a group of former government officials, featuring former President Gerry Ford and several former Secretaries of State, US Attorney-Generals, and USTRs. However, the number of amici supporting the Massachusetts law was also extremely large, including four US Senators, roughly 60 US representatives, 22 states, 16 municipalities, numerous state and municipal organizations, and numerous NGOs, such as Human Rights Watch and the Sierra Club.

D. The future of US sub-federal procurement sanctions laws

The proliferation of state sanction laws seems to have subsided somewhat with the Supreme Court's ruling against the Massachusetts Burma law. Indeed, proposals in numerous state legislatures, including California, Connecticut, New York, North Carolina, and Texas, to enact parallel laws died in committees or were otherwise abandoned even as the NFTC case worked its way through the lower courts.[149] However, any re-emergence of these laws or continued enforcement of laws similar to the Massachusetts Burma law will lead to further EU-US

[143] See *Crosby*, 382–83.   [144] See ibid at 382.   [145] See ibid at 386.
[146] See ibid at 386, note 24.   [147] See ibid at 386–388.
[148] Brief for the United States as Amicus Curiae Supporting Affirmance, 14 February 2000 (available at 2000 Westlaw 194805) [hereinafter 'US Government Amicus Brief'].
[149] See State and Local Sanctions Watch List, supra note 64.

tensions. Thus, it is critical how state legislators and officials read the Supreme Court's opinion.

Many proponents of state sanctions laws are referring to the Supreme Court's opinion as narrow and maintain they have considerable flexibility to adopt sanctions laws in the future.[150] For example, the deputy executive director of the NCSL has stated that the 'narrow decision leaves as many questions as answers on the appropriate role for states and localities in foreign affairs'.[151] The opinion has been referred to as narrow because the Supreme Court scaled back the grounds for invalidating the state law from those relied upon by the First Circuit. The First Circuit opinion was comprehensive, and it should be remembered by Massachusetts' officials and other state officials in the First Circuit, that its rulings on the dormant foreign affairs doctrine and the dormant foreign Commerce Clause, remain 'good law' in that Circuit. Additionally, it is not unusual for the Supreme Court to limit its opinions to the narrowest grounds and it was unanimous in ruling the Massachusetts law unconstitutional. More importantly, its opinion, properly read, leaves little to no room for state foreign policy-related sanctions measures.

Most federal sanctions laws, whether general or specific to a particular country or group of countries, contain features identical or similar to those found in the federal Burma sanctions law. First, most federal sanction statutes give the President discretion to control economic sanctions and, in fact, the sanctions reform effort of the past several years (that has not been wholly successful as of yet) highlighted the need to give the President 'waiver' authority with respect to sanctions. Even where an individual sanctions law does not include waiver authority, one can argue Congress has set the exact level of sanction it desires. Moreover, in nearly all instances, a more generalized statute (eg, IEEPA[152]) will be available to impose additional sanctions against the country and, in this sense, the President has discretion to control the level of sanctions. Second, in the case of any individual country, the Congress together with the President will have calibrated a particular level of sanction, the types of persons affected and the types of trade and investment covered, and so forth. State and local sanctions almost by necessity will change what must be assumed to be the careful calibration of sanctions. In the Burma case, federal sanctions were limited to US companies and to new investment. The Massachusetts law affected foreign companies and existing investment. Third, state and local sanctions will typically undermine the President's capacity to engage in effective diplomacy. While the federal Burma sanctions law gave a Congressional directive to the President to develop a 'comprehensive, multilateral strategy' with regard to Burma, the Court highlighted the President's own powers in the foreign affairs

[150] See, eg, 'Legal Experts Say Burma Law Opinion Leaves Sub-Federal Sanctions Options' (2000) 17 *Int'l Trade Rep* 1092.

[151] C. Tubbesing, 'Letter to the Editor: Rogue Nations Ruling Has Limited Effect', *Wall Street Journal*, 29 June 2000, at A27.

[152] 50 USCA, sections 1701–1706.

field as well. Thus, an express command by Congress in a particular instance is not essential to finding state sanctions laws an obstacle to Presidential diplomacy.

Finally, there is nothing in the Supreme Court opinion to suggest that state foreign policy-related procurement sanctions laws would survive scrutiny under the dormant foreign Commerce Clause or the dormant foreign affairs doctrine, even in cases in which the Court is unwilling or unable to find pre-emption. The dormant foreign Commerce Clause is well-established law and the market participant exception, while available for 'Buy American' or protectionist procurement laws, will not apply to foreign policy-related sanctions laws that mirror the Massachusetts Burma law, ie, that are similar to secondary boycotts. The dormant foreign affairs doctrine, while under increasing academic criticism,[153] has never been rejected by the Supreme Court. In fact, the Court did consider a claim under the dormant foreign affairs doctrine subsequent to *Zschernig*, and implicitly admitted the continuing vitality of the doctrine, although it ultimately rejected the claim because the state measure had 'insignificant international consequences'.[154]

VIII. IMPLICATIONS FOR EU-US DISPUTE PREVENTION
AND RESOLUTION

A. Dispute prevention

1. *Enhancing state legislators' and governors' fealty to their constitutional oath*

Conscientious state legislators and governors will apply constitutional constraints as they develop and vote on (or consider signing, in the case of governors) legislation.[155] Indeed, state legislators and governors are required to apply these constraints and not simply leave the application of such constraints to the courts should the measure be challenged after its enactment. The US Constitution requires that all state legislators take oaths or affirmations to uphold the federal Constitution.[156] When applying these constraints, a state legislator is not allowed to arrive at his or her own interpretation of the Constitution. Instead, a state legislator is bound to follow or, at the very least, give substantial deference to, US Supreme Court decisions. Thus, state legislators and governors should apply the doctrines of pre-emption, dormant foreign affairs doctrine, and dormant Commerce Clause prior to passing or signing legislation. The incorporation of these considerations into initiation programmes for new legislators, and

---

[153] See, eg, Goldsmith, supra note 102; Spiro, supra note 104.
[154] See *Ray v Atlantic Richfield Co*, 435 US 151, 180 (1978).
[155] See P. Brest, 'The Conscientious Legislator's Guide to Constitutional Interpretation' (1975) 27 *Stanford L Rev* 585 (discussing with respect to federal legislators); M. Schaefer, 'Conscientious State Legislators and the Cultures of Compliance and Liberalization Related to International Trade Agreements', *Proceedings of the American Society of International Law* (2001) at 52–57 (discussing with respect to state legislators).
[156] US Constitution, Article VI(3).

training programmes for counsel to the legislature and governor, may encourage legislators and governors to act in a conscientious fashion.

Importantly, state legislators and governors, as part of their pre-emption analysis, should be asking whether the laws they craft are in conformity with trade agreements, including the WTO. The fact that the implementing Acts for the WTO agreements only allow the federal Executive but not private parties to bring suits against the states based on non-compliance with the agreements, a mechanism described as 'weak preemption',[157] does not eliminate this duty. The conscientious legislator and governor must apply these constraints and not simply think in a tactical fashion by merely assessing the possibility of suit by the federal Executive, an act that may be politically difficult.[158] There is some recent anecdotal evidence that state officials are increasingly considering trade agreement constraints as they consider proposed legislation. For example, Ohio state senators introducing legislation to stiffen penalties for violation of state law requiring the use of domestically-produced steel in public works projects requested that the Ohio Legislative Service Commission prepare an analysis of the consistency of the bill with the GPA.

2. *Enhanced and regularized USTR/State Department outreach*

Since a significant number of state officials still lack awareness and familiarity with constitutional and international agreement constraints on their actions, or fail to give sufficient consideration to these constraints, it is important for the federal government to maintain a proactive outreach effort to both educate and cajole state officials.[159] Indeed, awareness needs to be raised not just with respect to legal constraints but also non-binding political constraints, such as the EU-US Summit agreement with respect to extraterritorial sanctions.

The outreach effort primarily should be the responsibility of the Office of the USTR and the US State Department. This outreach effort can begin through the national associations of state and local elected officials, such as the NCSL, the National Governors' Association, and the National Conference of Mayors. However, it should extend to the grassroots level with links to individual state legislatures and governors' offices. These outreach efforts should be regularized. The outreach efforts can extend not only to educating states on constraints on their activities but also elaborating on the federal efforts that are being made to resolve foreign policy problems that are of concern at the grassroots level. For instance, when asked why Massachusetts did not limit itself to simply passing a non-binding resolution on Burma, Representative Rushing responded that 'for years we passed resolutions on a lot of international issues, and we never even once got a letter back from the State Department. That's why we pass selective purchasing bills, because that gets [the federal government's] attention.'

---

[157] See C. Tiefer, 'Free Trade Agreements and the New Federalism' (1998) 7 *Minn J Global Trade* 45.
[158] See ibid.
[159] See M. Schaefer, 'U.S. States, Sub-Federal Rules, and the World Trading System' in Bronckers & Quick, *supra* note 77, at 525, 540–41.

Even on a limited, ad hoc basis, prior outreach efforts have shown positive results. For example, shortly after the EU raised concerns over the Massachusetts Burma law, USTR officials met with the National Governors' Association to urge states to consult with the USTR before considering sanctions legislation.[160] However, it appears that such consultations were only to focus on having state foreign policy-related sanctions proposals conform to the GPA, rather than the constitutionality and wisdom of such laws.[161] Nevertheless, federal government consultations with the states did prevent sanctions legislation from being passed in some states (eg, sanctions against Nigeria being considered by the Maryland legislature).[162]

3. *Experiment with the inclusion of state legislators and/or governors in meetings of the EU-US Summit and the Transatlantic Business Dialogue*

To further invest state officials in the process, and to further hammer home the complications of unilateral foreign policy-related sanctions by the states, the EU and US federal government could experiment with including a representative of the state legislators and a representative of the governors (eg, the lead legislator and lead governor on trade issues in their respective national associations) in meetings connected with the EU-US Summit. This would include meetings of EU-US trade officials as well as the Transatlantic Business Dialogue (and perhaps the other dialogues too). Presumably, the lead state legislator and governor will be better equipped and motivated to stem the tide of state foreign policy-related sanctions through their leadership positions in their national associations after attending the Summit meetings.

4. *Continuous and active monitoring and lobbying by businesses*

One of the reasons cited by commentators for Governor Weld's shift in position on the Burma sanctions law was the lack of strong, active business opposition to the law. Indeed, a group of businesses under the organizational heading USAEngage that has led the sanctions reform lobbying effort, admitted that the business community failed to realize in time the growing proliferation of state and local foreign policy-related sanctions laws.[163] It is clear that the internet increased the ability of NGOs and human rights activists to lobby multiple jurisdictions throughout the country and the world even with limited resources. The business community cannot cede the field to such groups and must highlight the limited effectiveness and costs of unilateral sanctions, particularly at the state and local level. However, the business community must not find itself simply in an antagonistic relationship with the NGOs, if for no other reason that consumer boycotts against particular companies can also be organized. Instead, the busi-

[160] See 'USA-Engage Announces Constitutional Challenge of State Law', *Inside U.S. Trade*, 13 February 1998 at 3–4.
[161] See ibid.
[162] See ibid.
[163] See Guay, supra note 14.

ness community must show some outreach and responsiveness to the concerns of these organizations without ceding principles of importance. Industry-wide and/ or individual corporate codes of conduct may be one means to address concerns of NGOs.

B. Dispute resolution

1. *Avoid use of WTO dispute settlement panels to challenge state foreign policy-related procurement sanctions laws*

The use of WTO dispute settlement is likely to be ineffective in stopping state foreign policy-related procurement sanctions laws. GPA obligations only apply to 37 states and only for contracts on goods and services above $500,000. Thus, even a successful WTO complaint would only partially cure the problem of state procurement sanctions legislation enacted for foreign policy reasons (and this assumes the state would amend its measure or the federal government would sue the state to come into compliance with the ruling). Given that future international trade negotiations need to further constrain state behaviour in areas such as procurement and trade-in-services, it is probably wise to avoid unnecessarily raising the ire of state officials with a WTO dispute settlement case. This is particularly true when a constitutional claim in domestic courts will be more effective at eliminating state procurement sanctions enacted for foreign policy reasons, as well as other manifestations of state foreign policy-related sanctions.[164] It is true, however, that the existence of a WTO dispute can minimally influence a domestic constitutional claim. But, at most, this supports proceeding with WTO consultations and does not require proceeding with a dispute settlement panel.

2. *Litigation in domestic courts provides a more effective and comprehensive constraint on state foreign policy-related procurement sanctions laws*

As seen in the case of the Massachusetts Burma law, domestic litigation is likely to be quite successful in challenging state procurement sanctions laws enacted for foreign policy purposes. The real problem is finding a plaintiff to bring the cases. Businesses had traditionally been hesitant to challenge such laws fearing they would create consumer backlashes or boycotts. Indeed, in the South Africa sanctions era the only case was brought against a divestment measure by the city of Baltimore, Maryland. Businesses were finally able to overcome this fear by acting collectively in the form of an organization, the NFTC, in the Massachusetts Burma case. However, if state officials misread the Supreme Court's decision, then a proliferation of state sanctions measures could occur again. Affected businesses will have to be ready and must continue to act collectively to bring future challenges in such instances.

---

[164] This conclusion is in accord with that of D. Price and J. Hannah, 'The Constitutionality of U.S. State and Local Sanctions' (1998) 39 *Harvard Int'l LJ* 443.

Amicus briefs by the Executive Branch opposing such laws will be taken into account by courts in such cases. Thus, it will be important for the Executive Branch to take the sometimes politically difficult position of opposing these state laws. Democratic administrations often share close links to human rights and environmental organizations that support such laws. However, they must make the honest case that these goals are damaged by divergent state and local measures that distract other countries' attention away from the problem country and towards the sanctions. Republican administrations are often strong protectors of states' rights. However, they must make the honest case that the field of foreign affairs is not like other fields in the constitutional division of powers.

Similarly, amicus briefs and diplomatic protests by foreign governments have some influence in these cases. As long as US courts continue to apply a threshold effects test under *Zschernig*, and even as courts engage in obstacles conflict pre-emption analysis, foreign governments can benefit their cause by submitting amicus briefs. Thus, business lobbying of, and co-ordination with, the Executive Branch and foreign governments in such cases can be helpful.

C. Looking beyond state procurement sanctions laws to other state foreign policy-related sanctions and protectionist behaviour potentially causing EU-US frictions

1. *Other sanctions measures*

Prior to the Massachusetts Burma case, procurement sanctions had become the preferred mode of foreign policy-related sanctions for state and local governments. Procurement sanctions are viewed by many state and local officials as the most effective mode given the tremendous buying power of state and local governments. The procurement mode of sanction was apparently first introduced in the era of South Africa sanctions in 1985 by the city of Pittsburgh, Pennsylvania. However, the predominant sanction in the era of South Africa sanctions was divestment measures, eg, prohibitions on the state pension funds being used for investments in companies active in South Africa. Some state officials are suggesting a return to divestment measures in light of the Supreme Court's decision concerning the Massachusetts Burma law. Other recent sanctions measures focus on the elimination of so-called 'sweatshops' and seeking reparations for past human rights violations. Domestic constitutional challenges to these types of sanctions measures are explored below.

(a) Divestment

State and local divestment measures concerning South Africa arose from state legislatures, governors' actions, pension-fund investment board actions, and even citizen initiatives. In its amicus brief to the Supreme Court in the Massachusetts Burma case, the US Executive Branch suggested that divestment measures might survive constitutional scrutiny without taking any formal position on the issue.[165] The brief argues that divestment statutes would not have as 'direct a regulatory effect' as the Massachusetts Burma law.[166] The discussion in the brief is certainly one factor state proponents of sanctions will take into account as they determine what, if any, measures to take in response to human rights concerns in foreign countries. Indeed, the discussion in the brief is regrettable because it was unnecessary to the case at hand and proponents of state sanctions legislation are likely to read it with 'rose coloured glasses'. Even the Executive Branch appears in its brief to be uncomfortable to some degree with leaving the door open with respect to divestment statutes. For example, the brief states that 'even if the Court were to hold that States have the latitude under the dormant Foreign Commerce Clause to adopt a policy of mandatory divestment from companies doing business in another country, it would not necessarily follow that states would have the same latitude to adopt a policy of mandatory divestment from companies doing business in another State'.[167] The brief makes this qualification even though the Supreme Court has indicated that measures affecting foreign commerce are to receive stricter scrutiny than those affecting interstate commerce.[168]

The constitutionality of a state divestment measure was only addressed in one case in the era of South Africa sanctions. In 1988, the Maryland Court of Appeals (the highest state court in Maryland) upheld the divestment ordinance of the City of Baltimore, rejecting challenges on the grounds of pre-emption, dormant foreign affairs doctrine and dormant Commerce Clause.[169] However, the court's analysis can be criticized on several grounds. First, the court did not give sufficient attention to all the possible bases of pre-emption, including obstacles conflict, dominant federal interest, and field. Second, the court found that the market participant exception applied to the dormant foreign affairs doctrine. As noted previously, the rationales for the exception have little force in the dormant foreign affairs doctrine context. It also found that the city measure had little impact on the South African government but it did not take sufficient account of the cumulative effect of state and local ordinances. It also failed to take account of the impact on relations between the US and other countries seeking change in South Africa. Moreover, in the Massachusetts Burma law case, the First Circuit hinted that it would have ruled differently than the Maryland Court of Appeals had it been called upon to review a divestment measure.[170]

(b) Anti-sweatshop

Another mode of sanction that states and localities are considering in response to the Supreme Court's decision, is to focus procurement sanctions against those companies 'benefiting' from human rights or labour rights violations. For example, the New York City Council considered a measure that would prohibit

---

[165] See US Government Amicus Brief, supra note 148.   [166] See ibid.
[167] See ibid.   [168] See, eg, *Japan Line*, 441 US 434 (1979).
[169] See *Board of Trustees v City of Baltimore*, 562 A 2d 720 (1989).
[170] See *Natsios*, 181 F 3d at 55–56.

the city from buying uniforms from apparel companies that pay wages below a 'non-poverty' level in foreign countries.[171] The ordinance was drafted and promoted by the Union of Needletrades, Industrial, and Textile Employees (UNITE).[172] Although the measure does not target a specific country (or companies operating in a specific country), the measure may still be subject to successful challenge on pre-emption, dormant foreign affairs and dormant foreign Commerce Clause grounds.

(c) Allowing claims/seeking reparations for prior human rights violations

California passed a law in 1999 allowing WWII prisoners of war to file suit in California courts against companies that used them as forced labour or that are affiliated with such companies.[173] While originally targeted at Germany, an agreement between the US and Germany led to the establishment of a settlement fund for claims against German companies. Instead, claims are being filed largely against Japanese companies and affiliates. A federal district judge has ruled that such suits are pre-empted by the allies' Peace Treaty with Japan, at least with respect to POWs from the 48 allied countries signing the treaty.[174] Subsequently, a federal district court judge ruled that claims by POWs from non-allied countries could not be allowed because the statute violated the dormant foreign affairs doctrine.[175]

In 1999, California also passed the Holocaust Victim Insurance Relief Act that requires insurers that do business in California and that sold policies in Europe during the Holocaust era to report information concerning those policies and the payment of benefits to the state insurance commissioner.[176] The reporting requirement also applies to insurance companies that do business in California and are 'related' to a company that sold Holocaust era policies.[177] Two foreign insurance companies challenged this reporting statute in federal court.[178] Two other related laws were also originally challenged but standing problems led to review of those laws being dropped. These laws allow California residents to bring claims for the payment of Holocaust era insurance policies (extending the statute of limitations to 2010) and require the state insurance commissioner to suspend the certificate of authority of any insurer who has failed to pay on valid Holocaust era policies.

The Ninth Circuit Court of Appeals overturned the federal district court ruling issuing a preliminary injunction against enforcement of the reporting law.[179] The Ninth Circuit found that the law did not have extraterritorial reach and thus it

---

171 See W. Greider, 272 *The Nation* (7 May 2001).   172 See ibid.
173 See Cal Code Civil Proc, section 354.6.
174 *In Re WWII Forced Labor Litigation*, 114 F Supp 2d 939 (ND Cal, 2000).
175 *In Re WWII Forced Labor Litigation*, 164 F Supp 1160 (ND Cal, 2001).
176 See Cal Insur Code, sections 13800–13807.
177 See ibid.
178 See *Gerling Global Reinsurance Corp of America v Quakenbush*, 2000 Westlaw 777978 (ED Cal, 2000).
179 See *Gerling Global Reinsurance Corp of America v Low*, 240 F 3d 739 (9th Cir, 2001).

fell within Congress' express delegation to the states to regulate the business of insurance.[180] The court also rejected the 'one voice' additional prong of the dormant foreign Commerce Clause challenge because Congressional approval of the state reporting measure could at the very least be inferred from the federal Holocaust Assets Commission Act of 1998.[181] In that statute, the Congress established a commission to 'conduct a thorough study and develop a historical record of' Holocaust era assets in the US, and directs the commission to take note of the work of the national association of (state) insurance commissioners with regard to Holocaust era insurance policies.[182] The court surmised that Congress must have expected that the insurance commissioners would be acting pursuant to state law, and that foreign affiliates of domestic insurance companies might be required to search records in order for the objectives of the federal law to be met.[183] The Ninth Circuit took a narrow view of the *Zschernig* doctrine, finding it inapplicable where a state law mainly involved foreign commerce and was not targeted at a particular country.[184] In spite of the ruling, it is important to keep in mind a different result may be reached in a case involving not just the reporting requirement but also the other laws dealing with claims for payments or suspension of a licence.

(d) Non-binding resolutions

One option that is being considered by advocates of state and local sanctions is simply to rely on non-binding resolutions to highlight issues and urge the US federal government to take stronger action on a particular foreign policy matter. It is important for state and local officials to be able to communicate their views on federal issues raising local concerns to federal government officials. Indeed, this is in part why state and local officials form national associations based in Washington, DC.

There seems little harm in most cases of state and local governments expressing their views on foreign policy issues in non-binding resolutions. Such resolutions can potentially survive either threshold effects or motive/purpose review under the dormant foreign affairs doctrine. There is also a longer historical practice of such resolutions by states and localities. Indeed, during oral argument in the Massachusetts Burma case, Justice Souter, the author of the Supreme Court opinion, suggested that 'perhaps the proper way to draw the line is to allow states to express themselves, to express their views ... so long as they do not go beyond the point of verbalizing ...'. The US Executive Branch amicus brief also stated that non-binding resolutions 'condemning the conduct of a repressive foreign regime' or 'petition[ing] Congress and the President to take

---

[180] See ibid at 744–746.
[181] See Pub L No 105–186, as amended by Pub L No 106–155, section 2, codified at 22 USC, section 1621 note.
[182] See ibid.
[183] See *Low*, 240 F 3d at 748–49.
[184] See ibid at 753.

action against the regime' would be constitutionally permitted.[185] In any event, in contrast to sanctions measures, non-binding or 'sense of' resolutions are unlikely to cause significant friction in EU-US relations.

2. Protectionist state legislation

Formal EU-US disputes over protectionist-motivated, as opposed to foreign policy-motivated, state and local legislation are likely to be rare for the foreseeable future. In the area of procurement, no state agreed to be bound in a manner that would require a change or liberalization of current procurement regimes. In essence, the EU achieved a standstill against new protectionism in state procurement done by certain entities within 37 states with respect to contracts above $500,000 for goods and services. The other 13 states maintain complete flexibility to enact new protectionist legislation. Indeed, at least two states, West Virginia and Ohio, have recently considered adopting preferences for domestically-produced steel (or strengthening penalties against the use of foreign-made steel) in public works projects.[186] The Massachusetts Burma case has raised awareness of the GPA among state officials. Thus, both West Virginia and Ohio made sure through research and contact with the office of the USTR that their proposed measures did not violate the GPA (neither state is bound to the GPA).[187] Thus, it is likely that disputes under the WTO for state violations of the GPA will remain rare. Additionally, complaints over 'buy-American' or 'buy-in-state' provisions in state procurement laws are unlikely to find their way into domestic courts. These protectionist procurement laws have survived, and are likely to continue to survive, any domestic constitutional challenges. Instead, state procurement preferences will continue to cause frictions mainly at the negotiating table as the EU seeks greater coverage of state and local procurement. However, should a state enact a protectionist procurement measure applicable to contracts above the GPA threshold, WTO dispute settlement will provide the best means to resolve the dispute since domestic litigation by private parties is unlikely to be successful.

States are also unlikely to violate other WTO agreements. For example, the GATS agreement creates only a 'standstill' obligation against new protectionist measures[188] and states seem not to be pursuing new protectionism in this area. Thus, in the near term, disputes over state measures affecting trade-in-services are likely to occur primarily within the confines of WTO negotiations for further services liberalization.

[185] See US Government Amicus Brief, supra note 148.
[186] See M. Schaefer, supra note 155, at 54.
[187] See ibid.
[188] See M. Schaefer, supra note 84, at 59.

12

Avoidance and Settlement of 'High Policy Disputes': Lessons from the Dispute over 'The Cuban Liberty and Democratic Solidarity Act'

H. PAEMEN

The US Cuban Liberty and Democratic Solidarity (LIBERTAD) Act of 1996,[1] better known as the Helms-Burton Act, was from its inception loaded with heavy political and emotional overtones. It certainly responded to the cravings of the Cuban-American community, which, since the establishment of the Castro regime, had been frustrated with the weak reactions of successive American governments and the inefficiency of the economic sanctions regime.

In the first years of the 1990s the anti-Castro forces in the US considered that the circumstances favoured a renewed effort to increase the pressure on the Cuban regime. A legislative initiative in that sense could benefit from the need for the Democratic Party to win the votes of the Cuban communities in the critical states of Florida and New Jersey. On the other hand, the association of such an initiative with similar proposals against some so-called 'rogue' states in the Middle East (the Iran and Libya Sanctions Act of 1996),[2] for which a wider support existed in the whole country, could enlarge the constituency for an anti-Cuba action. The downing of two planes, flown by Cuban-American activists, by the Cuban military was more than was needed to support a general outrage.

The Clinton administration was not very enthusiastic about new economic sanctions against Castro. They feared its interference with their electoral strategy and tactics. Also, some had serious doubts about the soundness of a policy of further isolation of the Castro regime, and had been thinking of some cautious steps in the direction of more engagement. But they were obliged to implement legislation that had been passed by large majorities in both houses of the Congress.

---

[1] 22 USC 6021–6091(Supp II) (1997).   [2] 50 USC 701 (1996).

I. Origin of the dispute

In the revolution following Fulgencio Batista's overthrow by Fidel Castro (1959), $1.8 billion in private property was seized from US citizens without compensation. In 1961, the US supported an attempt at a counter-revolutionary coup that failed (Bay of Pigs). In 1962, the Soviet leader Nikita Khrushchev tried to install strategic nuclear missiles on the island (Cuban missile crisis). At the end of the crisis (when the missiles were withdrawn in exchange for a US pledge not to invade Cuba), the US Congress decided on a trade embargo against Cuba (the Trading with the Enemy Act[3]). US citizens and companies were no longer allowed to do business in Cuba or to trade in any of the products or services of Cuba.

Cuba's economic problems, which were not primarily caused by the sanctions, became very severe after the collapse of the Soviet Union (1991), mainly because of the loss of annual aid of approximately $5 billion. As a reaction to the loss of aid, Mr Castro launched a programme to encourage foreign investment in Cuba.[4] This included trading in some of the property seized from US citizens. In the US the Government required American persons and companies who were US nationals before 1959, to register their possible claims with the US Foreign Claims Settlement Commission. There were 5,911 claimants in total.

The Cuban Democracy Act of 1992 (Toricelli Bill)[5] imposed an outright prohibition on the issuance of licences to foreign affiliates of US firms. They were prohibited by law from engaging in any transaction with Cuba. Amongst other restrictions, the law authorized the President to prohibit economic and military assistance, military sales, or debt forgiveness or reduction of debt owed to the US, to any country that provided assistance to Cuba. The Treasury Department also obtained the authority to impose civil fines and forfeitures of property for violators of US sanctions regulations.[6] This led to an outcry of criticism from US trading partners who claimed that this extension of extraterritorial jurisdiction by the US violated basic principles of international law. On 24 February 1996, Cuban MIGs shot down two US private airplanes. The heated public sentiment against the Castro regime encouraged Senators Helms and Burton to introduce legislation that allowed for further sanctions against Cuba. The new sanctions were aimed at companies using the property of US citizens expropriated by the Castro regime.

The first two parts of the law deal with US policy and sanctions against the Castro regime. Title I lays out how the existing international sanctions against the Castro government have to be strengthened, mainly through the enforcement and extension of the economic embargo of Cuba. Title II defines the forms of

[3] 50 USC App Sec (US Code Appendix Section, USA) 1 *et seq.*
[4] The International Legal Forum 3/1966, July/August 1996, p 170.
[5] 22 USC 6001 *et seq.*
[6] *The Economic Impact of U.S. Sanctions With Respect to Cuba*, US International Trade Commission, Investigation No 332–413, Publication 3398, pp 2–7, February 2001.

assistance that the US would give to a free and independent Cuba and to a transitional government that would prepare the foundations for a real democracy in Cuba. Parts III and IV have specific international implications. Part III ('Protection of Property Rights of United States Nationals') allows US citizens (who were US nationals before 1959 or had become US nationals after 1959) to file suit against companies that traffic in property seized from them without compensation. Part IV ('Exclusion of certain Aliens') requires the US State Department to deny US visas to the principals (and their families) of companies that traffic in expropriated property.

II. Reactions from foreign countries

Opposition to the Helms-Burton Act came from different countries. Most of them had already been critical of the US sanctions policy because of its ineffectiveness against the Castro regime and its economically negative impact on Cuban citizens. Moreover, countries that had companies doing business in Cuba, considered the new Act in violation of international law, because of its extra-territorial reach.[7] Their main objection to the law was that it sought to force foreign businesses to participate in the US economic embargo of Cuba by threatening to exclude them from exporting to or doing business in the US even if their products and activities had nothing to do with Cuba.[8] In a letter to Secretary of State Warren Christopher, dated 15 March 1995, Leon Brittan, European Commissioner for International Trade, wrote that the Helms-Burton Bill, if enacted, 'would revive our long-standing differences about the unilateral and extraterritorial aspects of various statutes implementing U.S. policy vis-à-vis Cuba'.[9]

Canada, which is Cuba's largest trading partner, amended existing legislation in order to allow Canadian companies to sue American companies in Canadian courts. New orders issued under the amended Foreign Extraterritorial Measures Act[10] require Canadian companies not to comply with US laws that prohibit US subsidiaries of Canadian companies from doing business in Cuba. The impact of the Helms-Burton legislation on the Canadian economy was immediately illustrated by letters sent by the State Department to officials and shareholders of the Canadian mining company Sherrit International: they were advised to disinvest themselves of their involvement in US properties in Cuba or have their US visas withdrawn after six weeks. The European Union asked for consultations in the

---

[7] The most interested countries were Canada and the EU. A vast legal literature on the different aspects of the Act exists already. See the *Index to Legal Periodicals and Books*.

[8] P. Morici, 'The United States, World Trade and the Helms-Burton Act', *Current History*, (February 1997), 87.

[9] Démarche by the European Union, Delegation of the European Commission, Washington, 5 March 1996, (1996) 35 ILM 398–399.

[10] Bill C-54, 45 Eliz II.

World Trade Organization (WTO) and announced the preparation of its own 'blocking statute' legislation.

It was in the light of this international outcry, that President Clinton, while not suspending the effective 1 August date of Title III (as he could have done), exercised a waiver provision in the same Title III that suspended for six months the possibility for US citizens and corporations to file suit. This means that liabilities and the right to assert a claim against anyone trafficking in confiscated property would not cease to exist. This waiver, based on section 306(c)(1)(B), requires a written determination by the President that 'such suspension is necessary to the national interests of the United States and will expedite a transition to democracy in Cuba'. It has been constantly renewed since then.

On 4 October 1996, the EU filed a complaint against the US in the WTO,[11] alleging that the law was not in compliance with the rules of the WTO and was inconsistent with its basic principles, because of its recourse to extra-territorial means as well as because of the threat and imposition of trade sanctions. On 22 November 1996, the EU adopted a regulation which made it impossible for an American judgment based on the Helms-Burton Act to be implemented in the Union (blocking statute).[12] The regulation also enabled EU companies to recover damages, including legal costs, resulting from the application of the Helms-Burton Act. It contains a requirement that, where a person's economic or financial interests are affected directly or indirectly, notification must be made to the European Commission within 30 days of obtaining information to that effect. The regulation prohibits explicitly compliance, whether it is active or by deliberative omission, with any requirement or prohibition based on or resulting from the specific laws, including the Helms-Burton Act (but also the Cuban Democracy Act and the Iran-Libya Act). There is, however, an exception for individuals and companies 'to the extent that non-compliance would seriously damage their interests or those of the Community'.

III. Efforts in view of a settlement

Although the European blocking legislation was the result of the strong stand requested by the member states of the EU against the US extraterritorial legislation, two other tracks were opened at the same time: challenging the US at the WTO and the negotiation of an agreement that would protect EU individuals and companies from the extraterritorial measures.

The EU complaint against the US in the WTO formally requested the establishment of a panel to consider the consistency of the US measures with the General Agreement on Tariffs and Trade (GATT 1994) and the General Agreement on Trade in Services (GATS).[13] The EU position relied on the prohibitions

---

[11] WT/DS38/1 and 2.   [12] Council Regulation (EC) 2271/96 OJ 1996 L 309.
[13] *United States: Cuban Liberty and Democratic Solidarity (LIBERTAD) Act of 1996*, Request for Consultations by the European Communities, WTO, WT/DS38/1 (13 May 1996).

by GATT 1994 against the use of import and export restrictions. It also referred to obligations spelled out in GATS including most-favoured-nation treatment (MFN), market access, national treatment, and transparency. The Title IV prohibition on entry into the US was challenged on the basis of the GATS Annex on the Movement of Natural Persons. The EU also argued that the US measures were contrary to the non-violation nullification and impairment provisions of GATT and GATS.

The US responded to the EU challenge by invoking the national security exception, which is part of both GATT and GATS. It allows any WTO member to take 'any action which it considers necessary for the protection of its essential security interests' on condition that they are 'taken in time of war or other emergency in international relations . . .'.[14] Relying on the self-judging nature of the exception the US claimed that Helms-Burton and the accompanying measures reflected important US national security and foreign policy concerns and that the WTO was not created to decide foreign policy and national security issues.

In an effort to de-politicize the conflict, the EU, in December 1996, adopted a 'common position' towards Cuba.[15] The document stressed the need for concrete advances in human rights and political freedoms in Cuba as a condition for improvement in the political and economic relations with the island. It had been prepared in close contact with some members of the US administration (State Department with EU Presidency and Commission). The 'common position' was quoted by President Clinton as the basis for announcing in January 1997 that he was suspending the right to bring suits under Title III for another six months.[16]

The informal contacts between the two sides continued and led to an agreement on 1 April 1997 by which they undertook to try to develop agreed disciplines and principles for the strengthening of investment protection which would deter the future acquisition of property expropriated in violation of international law. The US administration continued the suspension of Title III and undertook to seek from Congress a waiver of Title IV of the Helms-Burton Act. The EU agreed to suspend its action against Helms-Burton in the WTO.[17]

IV. THE UNDERSTANDING OF 17 MAY 1998

After a period of intensive negotiations, an 'Understanding with Respect to Disciplines for the Strengthening of Investment Protection' was agreed upon

[14] GATT 1947, Article XXI, GATS Article XIV bis.

[15] Common Position of 2 December 1996 defined by the Council on the basis of Article J.2 of the Treaty on European Union on Cuba, OJ 1996 L 322.

[16] 'Statement on Action on Title III of the Cuban Liberty and Democratic Solidarity (LIBERTAD) Act of 1996', 33 *Weekly Comp Pres Doc* (January 1997).

[17] *European Union–United States Memorandum of Understanding Concerning the U.S. Helms-Burton Act and the U.S. Iran and Libya Sanctions Act* (1997) 36 ILM 529.

on 17 May 1998 during the US–EU Summit in London (17–18 May).[18] The basic commitments would be: on the US side the Administration would ask Congress to make the waiver permanent against the respect by the EU of disciplines that would apply to expropriated properties. The objective of the Understanding was to inhibit and deter future investment in property illegally expropriated by a third state, through a set of disciplines, thereby strengthening the protection of investors. It would be made more difficult for new investors to take over the property that had been illegally expropriated.

As a general discipline, the Understanding foresees a registry permitting individuals to submit claims about property that they consider to have been expropriated illegally under international law. Putting a property on the registry will entail an obligation by EU and US authorities to assess and take appropriate account of that information when investors request government support or apply for commercial assistance to acquire the property. The Understanding also provides for specific disciplines that would apply where there is legal certainty about the illegality of expropriation—either through the ruling of an international court or following a conclusion between the parties that a claim is well founded and contrary to international law. Where the expropriation has already taken place, EU and US governments are obliged to make joint diplomatic representations to the expropriating state, deny government support and assistance for covered transactions in illegally expropriated properties, publish an enumeration of illegally expropriated properties and make public statements discouraging covered transactions in the properties enumerated.

In order to meet US concerns, the Understanding was complemented by a side-letter on Cuba where the Commission expresses its views that some elements of the expropriations in Cuba after 1959 appear to be in contravention of international law. The nature of the side-letter was not to condemn what happened in Cuba, but to ensure that EU national investment support agencies apply a heightened scrutiny when they are presented with future requests for investment support for projects in countries such as Cuba where there appears to be a record of expropriation. The Understanding does not mention the Iran-Libya Act, or the EU's WTO action. In a unilateral statement the EU said that it will not challenge either the Helms-Burton Act or the Iran-Libya Act provided that:

- the waiver of Title III remains in effect;
- the waiver authority for Title IV is exercised for EU individuals and companies;
- no action is taken against EU companies or individuals under the Iran-Libya Act; and
- by the expiration of the Clinton presidency a permanent Title III waiver has been granted.

---

[18] *US–EU Summit, Disciplines for Strengthening Investment Protection*, White House Fact Sheet (18 May 1998).

Both sides considered that these disciplines would become part of the Multilateral Agreement on Investment (MAI), which was being negotiated in the context of the OECD. The MAI negotiations, however, came to a halt in December 1998 without result and the Understanding suffered from substantially divergent interpretations by the two sides of different elements of the text.

The US Congress, rather than granting the legislative waiver, asked for a strict implementation of Title IV. New legislation in October 1998 affecting the trademark rights of a French company (Pernod-Ricard), relating to rum produced in Cuba, seemed an indication that there was no intention to restrict extraterritorial legislation. The EU for its part made public a 'EU Unilateral Statement' dated the same 18 May, in which it restated its 'strong opposition based both in law and in principle to the imposition of secondary boycotts and legislation with extraterritorial effect and retroactivity'.[19] In the same statement the EU declared that its commitment would not apply if one of the conditions on the US side was not fulfilled or 'by the time of the expiry of the President's term of office, no waiver without specific time limit in respect of Title III has been granted, as envisaged in II.5 of the same Understanding'.

V. WHY THE UNDERSTANDING FAILED

As was said before, the aim of this paper is not to rehash the arguments in favour of or against the substantial positions that have been taken by all sides on the Helms-Burton legislation. We were asked to concentrate on the settlement procedures that have been applied during the successive phases of the conflict.

On the EU side, which was confronted with the 'fait accompli' of the US legislation, three tracks can be distinguished:

(1) retaliation legislation aimed at neutralizing the effects of the Helms-Burton legislation on EU companies and citizens (blocking statute);
(2) challenge of the US legislation before the WTO, more particularly under the provisions of the 'Understanding on Rules and Procedures Governing the Settlement of Disputes';
(3) negotiation of a bilateral agreement aimed at the protection of the interests of EU citizens and companies through the establishment of a bilateral Investment Protection Understanding (officially: 'Understanding with Respect to Disciplines for the Strengthening of Investment Protection'). This Understanding was supposed to be open to other states and to be integrated, in a way to be defined later, into a MAI, which was being negotiated in the OECD.

---

[19] *EU Unilateral Statement*, 18 May 1998, http://europa.eu.int/comm./external_relations/us/extra-territoriality/index.htm.

The US was obliged to defend its legislation (the 'fait accompli') against the EU challenge in the WTO. It also accepted that it should actively explore the basis for a negotiated settlement of the dispute. From the (as yet) undecided, but also fairly defused situation of a formerly explosive conflict, one could conclude that diplomacy has gone to its limits in this case. This was only possible because of the strongest motivation on both sides of the conflict to look for a negotiated settlement. As was inferred before, the Clinton administration was not a strong believer in the virtues of unilaterally imposed economic sanctions in general, and was reluctant to apply them in a context where they had proved their ineffectiveness for 35 years.

On the EU side, the economic interests were rather minimal and the desire to please the Castro regime was limited. The political sensitivity against American unilateralism, however, was great, as was the belief in the inadequacy of the US policy vis-à-vis Cuba. But the safeguarding of the economic and political relationship was considered by the leadership as too precious a priority, especially in the post Cold War period, for a minor disagreement to put it in danger. There is no doubt that the talent, imagination and perseverance of the main negotiators on both sides contributed to the fact that every single course was explored repeatedly and in excruciating detail. As is the case in many negotiations, time was also challenged to work wonders. It certainly made it possible for the initial passions to calm down somewhat. A second way to defuse impetuous feelings was the enlargement of the issue beyond the specific Cuba context and the creation of a link with wider bilateral and/or multilateral undertakings.

It is very unlikely that the conflict will ever return to its initial intensity. Does this mean that the Understanding can still be the basis for the final solution? Wayne Smith called it 'an effort to reconcile mutually exclusive positions with smoke and mirrors'. He refers to some basic different interpretations of the text of the Understanding in relation to the 'internationalization'[20] of Helms-Burton, the significance of the Registry of Claims, the status of claims by Cuban Americans, the pattern of illegally expropriated properties, the reviews of Title IV waivers, future extraterritorial legislation, etc. He concluded that '[t]he EU-US Understanding of 18 May 1998 is in fact never likely to become operative'.

VI. Helms-Burton under the Bush Administration

In the meantime, no major incidents have occurred in the context of the Helms-Burton legislation. It seems that the Cuban government has translated the law into Spanish and made it widely available with the intention of reinforcing the Cuban citizens' distrust of the US. Foreign investment in Cuba has probably been somewhat deterred. European activity on the island has continued at its moderate pace. It is difficult to assess what the real impact of the Helms-Burton

[20] International Policy Report, March 1999.

legislation has been on foreign investment in Cuba. During a hearing at the House International Relations Subcommittee on Western Hemisphere Affairs on 24 March 1999, Michael Ranneberger, State Department Co-ordinator for Cuban Affairs, said that his Department had 'credible information that at least 19 firms have either pulled out or have altered their plans to invest in illegally confiscated property in Cuba'.[21] A study by the University of Florida found that although the US embargo against Cuba had hindered foreign investment, it had not deprived the island completely of foreign capital. One of the researchers, Paolo Spadoni, said that 'the Helms-Burton law had deterred, to some extent, new investors from doing business in Cuba', but added that the law 'had almost no effect on encouraging long standing investors to pull out of Cuba'. Cuban-American Congressman Lincoln Diaz Balart, a strong defender of the Helms-Burton law, dismissed the study and said 'that it did not chime with official Cuban figures'.[22] Third countries have been relatively quiet on the subject. At the 11th Ibero-American Summit in Lima on 23 November 2001 the 19 Latin American countries, Spain and Portugal 'call on the U.S. government to put an end to the application of the Helms-Burton Law, in accordance with the resolutions of the U.N. General Assembly...'.[23]

In the US a new administration has been in place since January 2000 and the US Senate has changed its majority with Senator Helms leaving the chair of the Foreign Relations Committee. Each semester President Bush has to decide on the extension of the Title III waiver. He has done so regularly, in a positive way, in letters sent in January and July, to the Chairmen and Ranking Members of the House and Senate Committees on Appropriations, the House Committee on International Relations, and the Senate Committee on Foreign Relations. The standard text is: 'Pursuant to section 306(c)(2) of the Cuban Liberty and Democratic Solidarity (LIBERTAD) Act of 1996 (Public Law 104–114), (the "Act"), I hereby determine and report to the Congress that suspension for 6 months beyond *(appropriate date February or July 1)*, of the right to bring an action under title III of the Act is necessary to the national interests of the United States and will expedite a transition to democracy in Cuba'.

Some members of the new administration have voiced their scepticism about the effectiveness of economic sanctions. Vice-President Cheney is one of them. Richard Haas, who is Director of the Planning Staff at the Department of State, has written extensively on International Relations and economic sanctions. In *Honey and Vinegar, Incentives, Sanctions, and Foreign Policy*, he writes:

Although the ultimate goal of the United States—the peaceful transition to a democratic, market-oriented Cuba—has not changed, the context in which this aim can be pursued has altered significantly. When stringent US sanctions were placed on Cuba in 1962, Cuba posed a threat to the United States as an outpost of communism in the Western

---

[21] *International Trade Reporter*, 31 March 1999.
[22] Factiva, Latin American Newsletters, 25 September 2001.
[23] Factiva, 24 November 2001, Copyright 2001 Xinhua News Agency.

Hemisphere and an ardent exporter of revolution to its neighbors. However, some forty years later and in the wake of the cold war, Cuba's importance has dwindled and its ability to promote radical politics among its democratizing neighbors has almost entirely collapsed. Arguably, the greatest threat that Cuba presents to the United States today is the tide of anxious and destitute refugees. Ironically, this situation is only worsened by the embargo, not mitigated by it. Not only has much of the rationale for isolating Cuba collapsed, but US policy toward the country—in particular the imposition of secondary sanctions—has created tensions with America's European allies that outweigh Cuba's importance. Finally, America's sanctions-dominated policy toward Cuba demands reevaluation...[24]

The WTO case has not be re-opened by the EU. Robert O. Keohane and Joseph S. Nye jr, both of Harvard University, wrote in that respect: 'The Helms-Burton legislation, for instance, did not lead to a formal case at the WTO, precisely because both the U.S. and the EU feared that any decision by the WTO against the United States could lead to an anti-WTO backlash in this country'.[25]

[24] R.N. Haas & M. L. O'Sullivan (eds), *Honey and Vinegar, Incentives, Sanctions, and Foreign Policy* (2000) at 183.
[25] R.O. Keohane & J. S. Nye jr, *Between Centralization and Fragmentation: The Club Model of Multilateral Cooperation and Problems of Democratic Legitimacy*, John F. Kennedy School of Government, Research Working Papers Series (2001), RWP01–004.

13

Strengthening the International Environmental Regime: A Transatlantic Perspective

DANIEL C. ESTY

Never have EU-US environmental relations seemed so strained. The list of differences in perspective, disagreements, and outright disputes is extensive: climate change, beef hormones, the risks and benefits of biotechnology in general and genetically modified organisms (GMOs) in particular, regulation and labelling of GMO food, the proper use of the 'precautionary principle', whether and how to create a Global Environmental Organization, 'trade and the environment' and building environmental sensitivity into the World Trade Organization (WTO), the proper role for environmental standards in export credit programmes, and the implementation of the Basel Convention on the Control of Hazardous Wastes and Their Disposal (unratified by the United States). The Bush Administration's decision to back away from the Kyoto Protocol brought long-simmering environmental tensions to full boil.

Not only are these environmental disputes a major source of irritation in EU-US relations in their own right, but they threaten to disrupt commercial relations between the two largest trading entities in the world as well. The resulting 'trade and environment' disputes cannot be dismissed lightly as transboundary pollution spillovers and the mishandling of shared natural resources can lead to serious economic consequences.[1] Indeed, as every economist knows, uninternalized externalities can lead to market failures that diminish the efficiency of international economic exchanges, reduce gains from trade, and lower social welfare, not to mention cause serious environmental degradation.

This chapter explores the transatlantic environmental relationship and tries to identify the underlying causes of the current strains. More broadly, it assesses the dispute settlement capacities of the international environmental regime, including both the UN Environment Programme (UNEP) and the numerous Multilateral Environmental Agreements (MEAs), and finds them severely wanting. Because a number of the EU-US environmental disputes have spilled

[1] D.C. Esty, 'Bridging the Trade-Environment Divide' (2001) 15 *Journal of Economic Perspectives* 113–130.

over or are threatening to spill over into the trade regime, this chapter also examines the WTO as an environmental dispute resolution mechanism—and finds it wanting as well. This analysis leads to the conclusion that a stronger system of international environmental governance is needed to accommodate the complexity of environmental challenges, to strengthen intergovernmental, trans-governmental, and transnational relationships, and to provide a more robust structure of checks and balances in support of systematic and effective inter-national environmental decision-making and action. The chapter closes with some thoughts on elements of a 'strengthening' agenda and what role the Transatlantic Partnership might play in bringing about the necessary reforms.

I. UNDERLYING CAUSES OF EU-US ENVIRONMENTAL TENSIONS

Europeans and Americans have had quite different domestic pollution control and natural resource management experiences over the past 40 years. These divergent histories translate into different attitudes about international environ-mental policy-making. As Vogel argues, from the 1960s until the 1980s, the US developed an elaborate environmental regime with major statutes and regula-tions covering air and water pollution, chemical exposures, solid and hazardous waste management, the cleanup of abandoned toxic waste sites, and a number of other issues.[2] Created in 1972, the US Environmental Protection Agency (EPA), the centrepiece of the US environmental regime, grew into a major institutional force in the ecological and public health risk reduction realm by the late 1980s, with a staff of 7,000 in Washington and 10,000 more employees in ten regional offices and various laboratories and research centres around the country.[3] Be-ginning in the 1980s and continuing with considerable vigour to the present day, there has also been a counter-pressure to 'lighten' the regulatory burden and to re-engineer the environmental regime for greater efficiency.[4] In any case (and to oversimplify somewhat), the American public has been left with a strong sense that the EPA (and other regulatory bodies acting in the environmental domain such as the Food and Drug Administration) are serious, tough-minded, and, if anything, likely to over-regulate.

This perception persists even though there is a long tradition of special interest efforts, especially from industry, to manipulate the law-making and regulatory processes through campaign contributions and lobbying.[5] Perhaps the presence of massive countervailing forces in the form of thousands of environmental

---

[2] D. Vogel, 'Ships Passing in the Night: GMOs and the Politics of Risk Regulation in Europe and the United States' (European University Institute Working Paper, No 2001/16).

[3] R.N.L. Andrews, *Managing the Environment, Managing Ourselves: A History of American Environmental Policy* (1999).

[4] Stewart, 'A New Generation of Environmental Regulation?' (2001) 29 *Capital University Law Review* 21–182.

[5] T. Lowi, *The End of Liberalism: Ideology, Policy and the Crisis of Public Authority* (1969); B.A. Ackerman & W.T. Hassler, *Clean Coal/Dirty Air* (1981); C. Lewis & the Center for Public

groups and other non-governmental organizations (NGOs) lessens the perceived threat of distorted outcomes and regulatory 'capture' leading to under-regulation. The transparency of the policy-making process also reinforces the credibility (perhaps unjustified) and legitimacy of the US domestic environmental regime. Indeed, the elaborate provisions of US administrative law—campaign finance disclosure requirements, lobbyist reporting rules, and especially the process requirements of the US Administrative Procedure Act (which provide for public 'notice and comment' and other carefully crafted opportunities for dialogue and debate on all proposed regulations)—make the regulatory process appear to be open, understandable, and reliable.

In the EU, a pattern of relatively low-key environmental regulation existed until the 1980s when it was replaced with a highly contentious, politicized, and increasingly aggressive regime of risk management and environmental controls within the EU (and within some member states as well).[6] But recent regulatory failures, including the dioxin scandal in Belgium and the mad cow scare, have left many Europeans underwhelmed by the performance of their regulatory bodies. A not-yet-fully-developed system of EU administrative law and, in particular, a lack of transparency as well as ongoing concerns about the EU's 'democratic deficit' has hurt European regulatory credibility. A number of observers note that the EU has still some distance to cover in creating a full-fledged regulatory system.[7]

Attitudes differ from one side of the Atlantic to the other on other issues that shape international environmental policy perceptions. As the widely divergent attitudes toward GMO food demonstrate, the US public generally sees promise in technological change while Europeans tend toward more scepticism. This translates into a tendency in Europe to favour a strong version of the 'precautionary principle', which argues that, in the face of uncertainty, errors should be skewed toward safety.[8] More generally, images of Nature vary. The European tradition of 'romanticism' imbues the natural world with a sense of balance and divinity that Americans do not broadly share. In fact, Americans, especially in the West, are inclined to see Nature as dynamic and even threatening—waiting to be tamed and transformed through human interaction into something more hospitable (and valuable).

Integrity, *The Buying of the Congress: How Special Interests Have Stolen Your Right to Life, Liberty, and Pursuit of Happiness* (1998).

[6] Vogel, supra note 2.

[7] B. Laffan *et al*, *Europe's Experimental Union: Rethinking Integration* (1999). Vogel, supra note 2.

[8] Cameron, 'The Precautionary Principle', in G. Sampson and B. Chambers (eds), *Trade, Environment and the Millennium* (1999), at 239–270; European Environment Agency, 'Late Lessons from Early Warnings: the Precautionary Principle 1896–2000' (2002) 22 *Environmental Issue Report* 11–194. But note that what constitutes 'safety' is highly contested. Many North Americans would argue that the European conception of the precautionary principle is actually a presumption in favour of the status quo (which may entail large risks) rather than a carefully constructed predisposition toward safety. Cross, 'Paradoxical Perils of the Precautionary Principle' (1996) 53 *Washington and Lee Law Review* 851–925; Adler, 'More Sorry than Safe: Assessing the Precautionary Principle and the Proposed International Safety Protocol' (2000) 25 *Texas International Law Review* 185.

Environmental politics also varies from one side of the Atlantic to the other. In Europe, green parties share power as part of the governing coalitions in France and Germany and play a major role in many other countries—leading politicians on both the left and right to pay obeisance to a range of pollution control and natural resource management issues.[9] The environment thus gets considerable attention on the European political agenda, and EU positions on international issues often have a distinctly green tint. From a US perspective, this green influence often gives the EU stance an air of unreality and sometimes leads to the EU position being written off as little more than posturing aimed at domestic European audiences. Such a dynamic seems to have sunk the compromise Kyoto implementation strategy that was on the table during the November 2000 negotiations in The Hague.

In fact, this breakdown in the climate change negotiations, engineered on the EU side by Dominique Voynet, France's Environment Minister and Green Party member (who chaired the EU delegation as the meeting occurred during France's EU Presidency), and Jürgen Trittin, Germany's Green Environment Minister, may show more about the immaturity of EU internal decision-making than it does about green party politics. In particular, a number of commentators have suggested that Europe's hard-line position was the result of a delegation dominated by Environment Ministers who had not carefully co-ordinated their position with other Ministries or EU Directorates General. A fuller vetting of the EU position with Finance Ministries, for example, might well have generated a more flexible negotiating stance.

In the US, the Green Party emerged as a 'spoiler' in the 2000 presidential election, angering many politicians (especially Democrats) who otherwise have environmental sympathies. More generally, Democrats in recent years have tended to promise much but deliver little on the environmental front, especially when it comes to international environmental challenges. The Republicans, in contrast, have promised little and delivered even less. Thus, the salience of environmental pressure in American politics remains in doubt.

In some cases, EU-US environmental differences reflect underlying ideological differences. The importance of divergent notions about justice, fairness, modern capitalism, and the proper role of the state cannot be underestimated.[10] One of the main issues in the EU-US divide over climate change, for instance, centres on which policy instruments are most appropriately deployed. The EU has pressed for a 'command and control' approach to the problem while the US has argued for the use of market mechanisms, most notably an allowance trading system.[11] The disagreement here emerges from rather deep differences of opinion over the appropriate governmental role in the issue and the appropriateness of using economic incentives to achieve results.

[9] E.E. Bomberg, *Green Parties and Politics in the European Union* (1998).

[10] Steffek, 'Free Trade as a Moral Choice', in *Resolving and Preventing US-EU Trade Disputes* (2001).

[11] D. Victor, *The Collapse of the Kyoto Protocol and the Struggle to Slow Global Warming* (2001).

II. INSTITUTIONAL WEAKNESS IN THE INTERNATIONAL ENVIRONMENTAL REGIME

While there are many underlying reasons for EU-US environmental tensions, the fact that these stresses have not been addressed and relieved must be seen in large measure as an institutional failure. The existing international environmental regime is seriously flawed, and the persistent EU-US fault lines are only one manifestation of its dysfunctional nature.[12] Indeed, it is striking that of all the sources of EU-US tension listed at the outset of this article, not one of them is being worked out through global-scale environmental institutions.

The international environmental architecture is poorly designed and sagging badly. UNEP, based in Nairobi, has a narrow mandate, a limited budget, and even more limited political support. Moreover, the structure of authority for international environmental action is highly fragmented and haphazard. UNEP competes for time, political attention, and resources with more than a dozen UN bodies including the UN Commission on Sustainable Development (CSD), the UN Development Programme (UNDP), the World Meteorological Organization (WMO), and the International Oceanographic Commission (IOC). The presence of several dozen independent treaty secretariats including the Montreal Protocol (ozone layer protection), the Basel Convention, the Convention on International Trade in Endangered Species (CITES), and the Climate Change Convention adds to the sense of fragmentation and confusion. The lack of organization and focus complicates the task of setting priorities, rationalizing budgets, and delivering efficient results—including functioning mechanisms for dispute resolution.

All of these bodies are underfunded and poorly staffed. They lack scientific and technical capacity. Data collection is spotty, and decisions are often made without much of an empirical foundation.[13] None of the various organizations have developed an authoritative environmental voice based on a reputation for analytic rigour. No one looks to UNEP for guidance in answering hard pollution control or natural resource management questions, and the MEAs do not have any better reputation for providing expert advice.

While several of the treaties include passing references to dispute resolution provisions, none of them have taken up this responsibility with any seriousness of purpose.[14] UNEP has no dispute settlement mechanism and has never even

---

[12] Esty, 'The Case for a Global Environmental Organization', in P. Kenen (ed), *Managing the World Economy: Fifty Years After Bretton Woods* (1994), at 287–309; 'The Value of Creating a Global Environmental Organization' (2000) 6 *Environment Matters* 12–14; 'Revitalizing Global Environmental Governance: A Function-Driven Approach' in D.C. Esty and M. Ivanova (eds), *Global Environmental Governance: Options and Opportunities* (2003) 181–203.

[13] Esty, 'Why Measurement Matters' in D.C. Esty and P. Cornelius (eds), *Measuring Environmental Performance: The Global Report 2000–2001* (2002), at 2–10.

[14] CITES (Article XVIII), for example, provides the following: 'RESOLUTION OF DISPUTES. 1. Any dispute which may arise between two or more Parties with respect to the interpretation or application of the provisions of the present Convention shall be subject to negotiation between the

played a role in providing 'good offices' or mediation to help resolve environmental problems between countries. There is an 'environmental chamber' at the International Court of Justice (ICJ), but it has never been used.[15]

With the exception of the Montreal Protocol, which does provide for trade restrictions with non-parties and non-complying parties,[16] the various MEAs do not have serious compliance monitoring and enforcement mechanisms. These structural gaps are understandable in the context of concerns about national sovereignty and the need for unanimity in treaty-making (leading to lowest common denominator outcomes). But the lack of capacity to highlight non-compliance, discipline 'free riders', and ensure that parties take their obligations seriously lowers the penalty for shirking responsibilities.[17] These limitations reflect the fundamental weakness of international law generally, but the existing structure of international obligations in the environmental realm is especially 'soft'.[18]

More generally, gaps in issue coverage plague the international environmental regime.[19] For many matters—eg, food safety—there are no clear lines of authority. Thus, on many of the issues that divide the EU and the US, no international environmental institution is readily available as a source of help. Nobody has stepped forward, for instance, to help resolve the EU-US 'beef hormones' case or to provide a scientific basis for managing GMOs. As a result, environmental problems often fester until a commercial dimension emerges, at which point they become trade disputes.

III. INADEQUACIES IN THE TRADE REGIME'S RESPONSE TO ENVIRONMENTAL CHALLENGES

Unlike the international environmental regime, the international trading system has a clear mission, a well-developed organizational structure in the WTO, a strong staff with true expertise, and a commitment to working with countries to

---

Parties involved in the dispute. 2. If the dispute cannot be resolved in accordance with paragraph 1 of this Article, the Parties may, by mutual consent, submit the dispute to arbitration, in particular that of the Permanent Court of Arbitration at The Hague, and the Parties submitting the dispute shall be bound by the arbitral decision.' Convention on International Trade in Endangered Species of Wild Flora and Fauna, Article XVIII (1973), as amended in 1979, and provisionally at Gaborone, 30 April 1983.

[15] Kalas, 'International Environmental Dispute Resolution and the Need for Access by Non-State Entities' (2001) 12 *Colorado Journal of International Law and Policy* 191.

[16] D. Brack, *International Trade and the Montreal Protocol* (1996).

[17] A. Chayes and A.H. Chayes, *The New Sovereignty: Compliance with International Regulatory Agreements* (1995); Jacobson and Brown Weiss, 'Strengthening Compliance with International Environmental Accords' (1995) 1 *Global Governance* 119–148.

[18] Sands, 'International Environmental Law: An Introductory Overview' in P. Sands (ed.), *Greening International Law* (1994); Bodansky, 'Customary (and Not So Customary) International Environmental Law' (1995) 3 *Indiana Journal of Global Legal Studies* 105–120.

[19] J.F. Rischard, *High Noon: Twenty Global Problems, Twenty Years to Solve Them* (2002); Speth, 'Recycling Environmentalism', 131 *Foreign Policy* (2002).

resolve disputes. But the trade regime lacks legitimacy as an environmental decision-maker and is thus not well placed to help nations overcome disagreements about pollution control or natural resource management.[20]

The legitimacy of modern governing bodies, whether domestic or international, derives from both the degree to which they reflect the political will of a community, normally demonstrated by majoritarian voting (in the spirit of Rousseau),[21] and the reason or rationality of the outcomes they generate (in the Kantian tradition).[22] Although suggestions have been made for broader WTO ties to national elected officials as a way to strengthen the trade regime's public acceptance,[23] the trading system suffers from a 'democratic deficit' in so far as its link to the public is indirect and mediated through national governments.[24] The WTO's capacity to make good environmental judgments is inevitably limited by its trade liberalization mission, which means that almost all decisions are viewed through a trade community lens. The WTO's credibility—and thus the organization's value as a forum for *environmental* dispute settlement—is limited furthermore by the closed nature of WTO procedures and the perceived trade bias of the substantive rules of the General Agreement on Tariffs and Trade (GATT).

It is perhaps unfair to judge the WTO from an environmental perspective in so far as the organization was not meant to be an environmental policy-making body. In fact, the WTO's efforts at environmental decision-making place great stress on the trading system, forcing it to operate in realms beyond its recognized competence. In light of this risk of over-reaching, a number of political leaders, trade officials, and other experts have called for the creation of a Global Environmental Organization to deal with pollution and natural resource management issues at the worldwide level.[25] Until this stronger international environmental regime emerges, the trade system cannot escape playing an environmental role.[26] In this regard, the WTO's legitimacy suffers from the organization's diplomatic tradition of closed-door discussions, lack of transparency, and limited access for

---

[20] Esty, 'The World Trade Organization's Legitimacy Crisis' (2002) 1 *World Trade Review* 7–22.

[21] J.-J. Rousseau and D.A. Cress, *On the Social Contract* (1988).

[22] Kahn, 'Reason and Will in the Origins of American Constitutionalism' (1989) 98 *Yale Law Journal* 449; T.M. Franck, *The Power of Legitimacy Among Nations* (1990); Bodansky, 'The Legitimacy of International Governance: A Coming Challenge for International Environmental Law' (1999) 93 *American Journal of International Law* 596.

[23] Esty, 'We the People: Civil Society and the World Trade Organization' in M. Bronckers and R. Quick (eds), *New Directions in International Economic Law: Essays in Honour of John H. Jackson* (2000), at 87–100; De Bievre, 'Re-designing the Virtuous Circle: Two Proposals for WTO Reform' in *Resolving and Preventing US-EU Trade Disputes* (2001).

[24] Keohane and Nye, 'The Club Model of Multilateral Cooperation and the World Trade Organization: Problems of Democratic Legitimacy' in P. Sauve *et al* (eds), *Efficiency, Equity and Legitimacy: The Multilateral Trading System at the Millennium* (2001), at 264–294.

[25] C.F. Runge, *Freer Trade, Protected Environment: Balancing Trade Liberalization and Environmental Interests* (1994); R. Ruggiero, 'Opening Remarks to the High Level Symposium on Trade and the Environment' (Geneva, Switzerland, 15 March 1999); L. Jospin, 'Development Thinking at the Millennium' (Speech to the Annual Bank Conference on Development Economics, Paris, France, 26 June 2000); Esty, supra note 12.

[26] Esty, supra note 1.

transnational actors, including environmental groups and other interested NGOs.

In the post-Seattle era, trade has become a high-profile international agenda item. Thus, the tradition of a small group of trade cognoscenti forming trade policy out of sight and under the public's radar is no longer viable. A more open and participatory process is needed in order to maintain the WTO's legitimacy in the trade domain, not to mention to build its authoritativeness in the environmental realm.

Furthermore, the existing trade system fails to generate the optimal degree of dialogue necessary for good policy-making and dispute resolution.[27] Effective decision-making, especially in areas where there is a high degree of uncertainty (unequivocally the case for environmental questions), requires debate that draws in arguments and positions from various perspectives to 'triangulate' on where the most durable and appropriate outcomes can be found. In this regard, the WTO's lack of both transparency and structured relationships with civil society crimps its governance potential and especially constrains the trade regime's performance on 'trade and' issues.[28]

A clearer role for NGOs at the WTO would help the trade regime build bridges to the global public on whose behalf actions are taken.[29] NGOs can serve as conduits for information flowing to the WTO on issues the public is thinking and worried about—and can explain to the public decisions being made within the trade regime. NGOs are also positioned to act as 'competitors' to governments—challenging the prevailing wisdom, advancing alternative perspectives and data, forcing officials to defend their positions and actions, presenting policy options and alternatives, and bringing fresh thinking to bear on hard problems.[30]

While a more open process can help to build understanding, soften disagreements, and ease disputes, if not properly structured, the benefits of a richer dialogue can be lost in a cacophony of voices and entangled interests that worsen policy gridlock.[31] What is required is 'politics' in the best sense of drawing out and comparatively assessing opinions, data, and policy options—supported by a clear picture of who is making what arguments and what interests these interlocutors represent.

[27] Wirth, 'Some Reflections on Turtles, Tuna, Dolphin, and Shrimp' (1998) 9 *Yearbook of International Environmental Law* 40–47; Howse, 'Democracy, Science, and Free Trade: Risk Regulation on Trial at the World Trade Organization' (2000) 98 *Michigan Law Review* 2329–2357.

[28] Dunoff, 'Trade And': Recent Developments in Trade Policy and Scholarship—and Their Surprising Political Implications', 17 *Northwestern Journal of International Law and Business* (Winter-Spring 1996–1997) 2/3, at 759–774.

[29] Esty, 'NGOs at the World Trade Organization: Co-operation, Competition, or Exclusion' (1998) 1 *Journal of International Economic Law* 123–148.

[30] Ibid; Esty and Geradin, 'Regulatory Co-opetition' in D.C. Esty and D. Geradin (eds), *Regulatory Competition and Economic Integration* (2001), at 30–48.

[31] Nichols, 'Extension of Standing in World Trade Organization Disputes to Nongovernmental Parties' (1996) 17 *University of Pennsylvania Journal of International Economic Law* 295.

Ensuring that the addition of new voices enriches the dialogue and adds legitimacy to the decision-making process requires clear rules governing participation.[32] Some sceptics of NGO participation in WTO processes raise questions about the accountability of NGOs. Such concerns are overblown.[33] Domestically, the views of an NGO receive as much weight as that group proves itself to deserve through the quality of its contributions to the issues under debate. The same principle applies internationally. There is, moreover, a reasonably vigorous 'marketplace' for public support and financial contributions that keeps NGOs on their guard. The one area where real progress could be made (both within the WTO and within various international environmental organizations) is in financial disclosure. Groups that want to play a role in global public policy debates should be asked to reveal the sources of their funding so others can judge how much credence to put into the arguments they advance.

While a more open trade regime could be vulnerable to special interest interventions that distort the policy-making process, the risk comes not from overt NGO participation in debates, but from behind-the-scenes lobbying, which more often involves producer interests than environmental ones.[34] The solution to this threat is, as noted earlier, better administrative law, *not* the exclusion of NGOs (and business interests) in the trade policy-making process.[35]

Beyond the general difficulty of using the WTO apparatus to make environmental decisions, the WTO dispute settlement mechanism has proven to be particularly ill-adapted to environmental problem-solving. Some of the complaints are procedural. Although the WTO procedures make provision for dispute settlement panels to draw on outside experts where technical issues are in question, the WTO itself is not well positioned to make decisions that involve scientific or environmental judgments.[36]

The basic functioning of the panel process falls short of modern standards of good governance. The taking of evidence behind closed doors, for example, violates the first principle of good justice in almost every society in the world. Indeed, 'secret tribunals' of any type garner little respect. Even if one accepts the limitations of the WTO (notably the fact that the structure of dispute resolution is country-to-country), the lack of access to the process by non-governmental entities creates unnecessary complications. The fact that NGOs cannot observe who is making what arguments and how decisions are reached irreparably

---

[32] Gemmill and Bamidele-Izu, 'The Role of NGOs and Civil Society in Global Environmental Governance' in D.C. Esty and M. Ivanova (eds), *Global Environmental Governance: Options and Opportunities* (2002).

[33] Esty, supra note 29; Charnovitz, 'Opening the WTO to Non-Governmental Interests' (2000) 24 *Fordham International Law Journal* 173–216.

[34] Esty, supra note 29.

[35] Esty, 'Toward Optimal Environmental Governance' (1999) 74 *New York University Law Review* 1495.

[36] Christoforou, 'Genetically Modified Organisms: Colloquium Article on Settlement of Science-Based Trade Disputes at the WTO: A Critical Review of the Developing Case Law in the Face of Scientific Uncertainty' (2000) 8 *New York University Environmental Law Journal* 622–648.

damages the legitimacy of the process. And the limitations placed on the filing of 'amicus' briefs by interested non-governmental parties hurt the WTO's reputation for procedural fairness and the sense that a full spectrum of issues and opinions are being considered.

On a purely functional basis, the WTO does not seem to have succeeded in finding ways to bring parties to settle disputes. Of the EU-US tensions listed earlier, only one, beef hormones, has been handled within the WTO context—and the record in this case is not very encouraging.[37] While some commentators have suggested that the WTO's consultation mechanism can be used more aggressively,[38] with regard to environmental disputes-in-the-making, there is little reason for optimism.

Perhaps more troublingly, the substantive rules applied by WTO panels do little to integrate environment and trade goals. Although the recent 'shrimp turtle' case seems to mark a watershed, traditional GATT jurisprudence,[39] especially interpretations of the requirements for invoking the environmental exceptions of Article XX, imposed a high burden on those seeking to advance pollution or natural resource standards or programmes with trade effects.[40] Until very recently, environmental policies were regularly held to be GATT-inconsistent because they could not be shown to be the 'least trade restrictive' policy option available.[41] This perceived imbalance has been a source of particular distress in the environmental community and has rendered the WTO unacceptable as a neutral forum for environmental dispute resolution in the minds of many.[42]

A more nuanced reading of the GATT has recently emerged, putting more emphasis on the Article XX chapeau requirements that turn on the issue of whether the policy in question represents arbitrary or unjustified discrimination. This new interpretation, which adheres more closely to the actual text of Article XX, first emerged in the Appellate Body decision in the 1996 'reformulated gasoline' case[43] and was reinforced in the 1998 Appellate Body 'shrimp turtle' ruling.[44] This more balanced jurisprudential approach appears to be a function

---

[37] Quick and Bluthner, 'Has the Appellate Body Erred?: An Appraisal and Criticism of the Ruling in the WTO Hormones Case' (1999) 2 *Journal of International Economic Law* 603–639; Neugebauer, 'Fine-Tuning WTO Jurisprudence and the SPS Agreement: Lessons from the Beef Hormone Case' (2000) 31 *Law and Policy in International Business* 1255–1284.

[38] Wethington, 'Commentary on the Consultation Mechanism Under the WTO Dispute Settlement Understanding During its First Five Years' (2000) 31 *Law and Policy in International Business* 583–590.

[39] Appleton, 'Shrimp/Turtle: Untangling the Nets' (1999) 2 *Journal of International Economic Law* 477–496; Wofford, 'A Greener Future at the WTO: The Refinement of WTO Jurisprudence on Environmental Exceptions to GATT' (2000) 24 *Harvard Environmental Law Review* 563–592.

[40] D.C. Esty, *Greening the GATT: Trade, Environment and the Future* (1994); Charnovitz, 'World Trade and the Environment: A Review of the New WTO Report' (2000) 12 *Georgetown International Environmental Law Review* 523–541.

[41] See, eg, *Tuna I Panel Report*, para 5.28 (30 ILM 1620); Wirth, supra note 27.

[42] Charnovitz, 'Environmentalism Confronts GATT Rules' (1993) 27 *Journal of World Trade* 37–52; *Tuna Report*, supra note 41.

[43] See *Gasoline Appellate Report*, at 25 (35 ILM 629).

[44] See *Shrimp Turtle Appellate Report*, at 151 (38 ILM 161–162); Wofford, supra note 39. But note that Trachtman argues that an arbitrary or unjustified discrimination inquiry can resemble a 'least

of the increasing professionalism of the WTO's dispute settlement procedures, most notably, the juridical sophistication of the Appellate Body.[45]

But while the potential exists for the WTO to play a more active role in EU-US environmental dispute resolution, it seems unlikely that the trade regime can really do much to narrow the transatlantic gap on critical issues. The WTO has not been able to bridge the EU-US divide on beef hormones despite a number of passes at the issue. The broader set of limitations enumerated above continue to limit the WTO's capacity as a forum for environmental dispute resolution. Fundamentally, the trade regime can address the trade dimensions of 'trade and environment' disputes, but it cannot substitute for a more dynamic international environmental regime.

IV. STRENGTHENING THE INTERNATIONAL ENVIRONMENTAL REGIME

Environmental disputes will persist between the EU and the US as well as more broadly until a deeper and more extensive international environmental regime takes shape. The current institutional structure remains too thin and weak to do the job.[46]

Environmental governance is a complex business. Problems arise on various geographic scales, requiring a multi-tier regulatory structure.[47] The questions that must be answered to resolve disputes and achieve successful shared decision-making require capacities in many areas including: ecological sciences, public health, risk assessment, cost-benefit analysis, economics, regulatory strategies and instrument design, data collection and analysis, performance measurement, and policy evaluation. Environmental questions therefore demand not only a multi-level but also a multidimensional governance structure.[48] Ensuring access to the full range of requisite skills and capacities will most likely require a regime that is multi-institutional and capable of drawing on a wide range of underlying disciplines.[49]

---

trade restrictive' rule. Trachtman, 'The Domain of WTO Dispute Resolution' (1999) 40 *Harvard International Law Journal* 333.

[45] Hudec, 'The New WTO Dispute Settlement Procedure: An Overview of the First Three Years' (1999) 8 *Minnesota Journal of Global Trade* 1–36; Wofford, supra note 39.

[46] L.C. Hempel, *Environmental Governance: The Global Challenge* (1996); Peterson, 'International Organizations and the Implementation of Environmental Regimes' in O.R. Young (ed), *Global Governance* (1997), at 115–151; H. French, *Vanishing Borders: Protecting the Planet in the Age of Globalization* (2000); Biermann, 'The Emerging Debate on the Need for a World Environment Organization: A Commentary', 1 *Global Environmental Politics* (February 2001) 1, at 45–55; P. Hein, *The End of Foreign Policy?: British Interests, Global Linkages and Natural Limits* (2001).

[47] A. Dua and D.C. Esty, *Sustaining the Asia Pacific Miracle: Environmental Protection and Economic Integration* (1997); Esty, 'The Case', supra note 12; Esty, 'The Value', supra note 12.

[48] Rosenau, 'Governance, Order, and Change in World Politics' in J. N. Rosenau and E.-O. Czempiel (eds), *Governance without Government: Order and Change in World Politics* (1992), at 1–29.

[49] Esty and Ivanova, 'Revitalizing Global Environmental Governance: A New Function-Driven Approach' in D.C. Esty and M. Ivanova (eds), *Global Environmental Governance: Options and Opportunities* (2002).

Putnam's model of 'two level games' centred on intergovernmental relations (often at the chief of government level)[50] thus presents too simple a picture for what is required in the international environmental domain. Slaughter's vision of a 'real new world order' that advances a disaggregated view of the state and sees decision-making as emerging from multidimensional transgovernmental connections and networks comes closer to a picture of environmental reality but may still be oversimplified.[51] The 'mixed networks' that Pollack and Shaffer describe seem most apt.[52] Such a structure, which blurs traditional boundaries and engages a broad array of actors—public and private—paints a more accurate picture and appears more normatively appropriate as well.

Decision-making and dispute resolution in the international environmental arena must thus be seen as a multi-level game where each level involves dozens of sub-games, each containing sub-sub-games. National governments not only negotiate with each other, but (in a healthy policy-making process) they have serious internal policy debates.[53] The battles between the US Environmental Protection Agency and the US Department of Energy over climate change policy, for example, are legendary. But this hard-fought process results in US government policies that are more analytically rigorous, systematically constructed, and durable.

Of course, the political decision-making process at both domestic and international levels involves interactions beyond the government domain, with the business world, NGOs, the scientific community, and other interested elements of civil society. Within each of these communities, further debates will be held. The environmental community will often, for instance, have long (and sometimes quite contentious) discussions among various groups before going to a meeting with government officials. Furthermore, many environmental groups will consult their memberships as they are defining their positions. Adding to the complexity, cross group alliances may also emerge with some business interests seeking allies in the NGO world or vice versa. Those who are unhappy with the outcome of the process at one decision-making level (eg, national) may also try to shift the 'action' forum to another level (eg, international or sub-national) adding further flux to the policy dynamic.[54]

As Breton notes, such governmental policy-making, involving a panoply of actors in a range of competitive and co-operative postures, strengthens decision-

[50] Putnam, 'Diplomacy and Domestic Politics: The Logic of the Two-Level Game' (1988) 42 *International Organization* 427–460.

[51] Slaughter, 'The Real New World Order' (1997) 76 *Foreign Affairs* 183.

[52] Pollack and Shaffer, 'Introduction: Transatlantic Governance in Historical and Theoretical Perspective' in M.A. Pollack and G.C. Shaffer (eds), *Transatlantic Governance in the Global Economy* (2001), at 3–44.

[53] Esty and Geradin, supra note 30.

[54] For example, those seeking to protect corporate interests from adverse regulatory changes broadened the circumstance in which compensation must be paid in NAFTA's Chapter 11 (Investment) far beyond what the US takings jurisprudence required. Mann and Araya, 'An Investment Regime for the Americas: Challenges and Opportunities for Environmental Sustainability' in D.C. Esty and C. Deere (eds), *Greening the Americas: NAFTA's Lessons for Hemispheric Trade* (2002).

making.[55] Esty and Geradin call this interplay 'regulatory co-opetition' and see value in both the horizontal and vertical dimensions of such a complex policy process, especially in the environmental domain where great uncertainties must be addressed.[56] In fact, it is the vitality of these multiple levels of interactions that determines the strength of the regime in question. The interweaving of institutions, actors, and overlapping decision processes generates the sort of vigorous policy debates and byplay that yields: (1) carefully considered and systematic decisions, (2) ongoing and serious policy review, oversight, and refinement, and (3) an appropriate structure of checks and balances that maximizes the chances that decisions will be fair, rational, acceptable, and durable. The existing international environmental regime does not even come close to providing the institutional support required for such decision-making and dispute resolution processes.

V. TRANSATLANTIC SUPPORT FOR A STRONGER INTERNATIONAL ENVIRONMENTAL REGIME

There is no substitute for functioning 'legislative' and 'judicial' functions, and it takes time to weave the dense fabric of relationships across actors and institutions that is required for successful international environmental governance. In the interim, there are steps that can be taken to strengthen the international environmental regime and to improve its performance. Some of these activities might be undertaken at the level of the Transatlantic Partnership.

One simple step would be to broaden the base of participation in the international environmental policy-making process, particularly with regard to troublesome issues. More perspectives and a broader set of options would help to illuminate opportunities for easing disputes if not to achieve full agreement.[57] In addition, some problems can be ameliorated by focusing attention on technical issues and thus narrowing the zone of dispute. As Haas has demonstrated, scientists can similarly close policy gaps by working on a problem across an international 'epistemic community'.[58] These strategies argue for concerted efforts to spin a stronger transatlantic policy web through more ongoing dialogue with a wider set of actors, covering not just government officials at various levels but also representatives of the business, environmental, scientific, and academic communities. The potential to build 'global public policy networks'—linking experts on key issues in ways that can shape governmental decision-making—should also be explored.[59]

---

[55] A. Breton, *Competitive Governments* (1996).   [56] Esty and Geradin, supra note 30.

[57] R. Fisher and W. Ury, *Getting to Yes: Negotiating Agreement Without Giving In* (2nd edn, 1992).

[58] Haas, 'Introduction: Epistemic Communities and International Policy Coordination' (1992) 46 *International Organization* 1–35.

[59] W. Reinecke and F. Deng, *Critical Choices: The United Nations, Networks, and the Future of Global Governance* (2000); Streck, 'Global Public Policy Networks as Coalitions for Change' in D.C. Esty and M. Ivanova (eds), *Global Environmental Governance: Options and Opportunities* (2002).

Efforts to create dispute resolution mechanisms aimed at environmental questions might also be considered. Special attention should be focused on various models of consultation, mediation, and alternative dispute resolution that could be invoked before the filing of a formal dispute. Such an option is already under consideration at the WTO.[60] To the extent that formal environmental dispute resolution mechanisms need to be enhanced, the EU and the US might agree to work together to invigorate the ICJ's Environmental Chamber, perhaps by agreeing to resolve a dispute utilizing this forum. A joint EU-US task force focusing on how to strengthen the existing portfolio of dispute resolution mechanisms within MEAs would also be beneficial.

Transparency is another agenda on which the EU and the US could work together. Such an initiative should begin with efforts to be more open (and to consult more intensively) on national environmental decision-making and regulation. Any EU-US effort in this regard could also extend to trying to make the WTO more transparent and thus more legitimate as a dispute resolution forum. More generally, a joint EU-US effort to build greater environmental sensitivity into the trade regime would help to build the credibility, authoritativeness, and perceived fairness of WTO decisions.

Fundamentally, any strengthening of the EU-US environmental relationship adds depth to the international environmental regime—and is therefore a constructive step. In fact, not only will EU-US co-operation reduce tensions along the critical transatlantic frontier, such efforts may facilitate broader international environmental collaboration and help to bridge the North-South divide that plagues the global environmental regime.

[60] See 19 *Inside US Trade* (8 June 2001) 23, at 1.

14

Dispute Prevention and Dispute Settlement in the Transatlantic Partnership—Telecoms, the WTO, and the Realization of the Global Information Society

LAWRENCE J. SPIWAK*

I. INTRODUCTION

Much has been said about the realization of the 'Information Society' on both sides of the Atlantic. As evidenced by the recent financial meltdown of the international telecoms industry, however, it is abundantly clear that—despite the plethora of rhetoric—public policies over the last several years have done little to promote entry and constrain dominant incumbents' ability to exercise market power (ie, raise prices and restrict output). While space constraints prevent a detailed exegesis of the complex and often subtle issues raised by telecoms restructuring, it is nonetheless important to understand how telecoms policies have affected trade relations in the transatlantic partnership.[1]

At first glance, telecoms restructuring should not have any effect on transatlantic trade relations, because trade and regulation seek to pursue fundamentally different goals. Economic regulation—just as its twin sister competition law enforcement—focuses upon *consumers* and the competitive process as a whole, rather than upon individual competitors. Trade policy, on the other hand, by its very definition, seeks to promote individual *competitors* (ie, competitors of the 'domestic' sort). Thus, while telecoms restructuring is certainly one of a number of policies that could affect international trade, the various national trade

---

* The author would like to thank Professor Mary Footer, University of Amsterdam, as well as the other participants of the Symposium, for their helpful comments on this paper.

[1] For a more complete exegesis of the issues raised in this paper, readers are referred to M. Naftel & L.J. Spiwak, *The Telecoms Trade War: The United States, the European Union and the WTO* (Hart Publishing, 2001), available at http://www.phoenix-center.org/telindex.html.

policies (which are very often not even in harmony with each other) may at times be in tension with overall telecoms restructuring efforts.[2]

Notwithstanding the above, trade concerns have increasingly but improperly crept into telecoms regulatory restructuring efforts on both sides of the Atlantic over the past several years, despite the presence of the landmark 1997 WTO Accord on Basic Telecoms Services. Thus, even though the first formal WTO complaint under the 1997 Accord was only recently filed, trade concerns at the regulatory level nonetheless created significant barriers to entry for new firms. As one would expect, the strain on the transatlantic partnership became impossible to ignore and did much to harm overall consumer welfare.

II. CULTURAL AND LEGAL ISSUES: DIFFERENCES AND SIMILARITIES

In order to have an informed discussion about dispute resolution in the transatlantic partnership, it is important for the stakeholders to appreciate the similarities and respect the differences between the parties. And, as discussed in this section, like all facets of the transatlantic partnership, understanding the respective histories, perspectives of, and expectations from, the telecoms industry is no exception.

A. State versus private monopolies

Unfortunately, given the legacy of the telecoms industry, local markets on both sides of the Atlantic are still dominated by incumbent operators who have both the incentive and ability to engage in strategic anti-competitive conduct. What is different about the two environments is that the United States has a legacy of *privately* owned monopolies that were subject to 'public utility' regulation (eg, price regulation via tariffs, reporting requirements, obligations to serve, etc), while Europe has a long history of *government* owned monopolies. Under any scenario, however, although the incentives motivating these monopolists were slightly different (the US monopolists were interested in maximizing monopoly rents to maximize shareholder value; the European monopolists—as branches of their respective governments—were more motivated to be a large source of civil service jobs and to provide subsidized service to select political constituencies), *their conduct was identical*—ie, they can and will (and do) raise prices and restrict output, not to mention have absolutely no incentive to innovate and bring advanced broadband services to market. As such, *all monopoly*, regardless of ownership structure, is fundamentally antithetical to consumer welfare.

With legitimate reasons, therefore, the issue of state-ownership has been a major issue of contention in the transatlantic partnership over the past few years. Although European law expressly permits government ownership of incumbent

---

[2] See *Antitrust Law Developments* (Fourth) 991 (1997).

monopolists,[3] from an economic perspective, government ownership of incumbent monopolists works at cross purposes towards government's core mandate to maximize consumer welfare.

Specifically, as noted above, all monopolists—regardless of ownership structure—can and will raise prices and restrict output. For this reason, an independent and transparent regulator is required to constrain such anti-competitive conduct in order to ensure that the rates charged by the monopolist are just, reasonable, and not unduly discriminatory. When government owns an equity share of the incumbent, however, then—by definition—any government regulator has a naked conflict of interest. While some European institutions have taken steps to highlight this important problem, far too many in Europe continue to believe that, notwithstanding the fundamental economics outlined briefly above, Europe should maintain the *status quo*.[4] Accordingly, if the debate is to move forward constructively, Europe must distinguish between the very different concepts of '*liberalization*' (ie, *privatization*) versus actually '*restructuring*' the underlying market from one characterized by one firm (ie, monopoly) to a market capable of sustaining many firms (ie, competition).

B. Pre-emption versus subsidiarity

The telecoms business is extremely multi-dimensional. At the micro-level, disputes over licensing, interconnection, collocation, rights of way, and universalization must all be resolved for even the most basic telephone call to be completed. Yet, because scale (and to a lesser degree scope) economies are so crucial in telecoms,[5] already high entry costs can multiply exponentially as firms re-litigate these difficult issues in each additional jurisdiction they seek to enter. Accordingly, when there are common economic markets that stretch over entire continents (ie, the EU and the US), a cohesive 'harmonized' analytical framework at the 'macro-geographic' level is nonetheless also required to facilitate new entry, even though these issues are 'local' in nature.[6] As such, a common theme on both sides of the Atlantic is the inherent tension between the 'local' level (state public service commissions in the US; member state national regulatory authorities

---

[3] See Consolidated Version of The Treaty Establishing the European Community OJ 1997 C340/173–308 (Treaty of Rome), Article 86 (http://europa.eu.int/eur-lex/en/treaties/dat/ec_cons_treaty_en.pdf). For a more complete discussion of this issue, see *Telecoms Trade War*, supra note 1, at 249–250.

[4] See, eg, 'eEurope Means Nothing Without eEntry: Regulatory Harmonisation, Subsidiarity and the Realisation of the Information Society', *Phoenix Center Policy Paper Series No 8* (October 2000) (http://www.phoenix-center.org/pcpp/PCPP8.pdf) and citations therein, reprinted in (2001) 7 *Telecommunications & Space Journal* 81.

[5] T.R. Beard, G.S. Ford & L.J. Spiwak, 'Why ADCo? Why Now? An Economic Exploration into the Future of Industry Structure for the "Last Mile" in Local Telecommunications Markets', *Phoenix Center Policy Paper Series No 12* (2001) (http://www.phoenix-center.org/pcpp/PCPP12.pdf); reprinted in (2002) 54 *Fed Com L J* 421 (http://www.law.indiana.edu/fclj/pubs/v54/no3/spiwak.pdf).

[6] See 'eEurope', supra note 4.

(NRAs) in the EU) and the national (Federal Communications Commission) or pan-European (European Commission) level.

In the US, the US Constitution sets forth the doctrine of 'pre-emption', which basically holds that when state law is inconsistent with Federal law, Federal law always wins. In fact, section 253 of the US Telecommunications Act of 1996 specifically empowers the US Federal Communications Commission (FCC) to pre-empt any State statute, regulation or legal requirement that has the 'effect of prohibiting the ability of any entity to provide any inter-state or intra-state telecommunications service.'[7] Moreover, the US Supreme Court has expressly held that the FCC has the authority to establish a standard national pricing methodology and interconnection rules under the 1996 Act.[8]

The European version, called 'subsidiarity', is not as strong. Basically, under the principle of subsidiarity,

In areas which do not fall within its exclusive competence [eg, telecoms], the Community shall take action, in accordance with the principle of subsidiarity, only if and in so far as the objectives of the proposed action cannot be sufficiently achieved by the Member States and can therefore, by reason of the scale or effects of the proposed action, be better achieved by the Community. [However, a]ny action by the Community shall not go beyond what is necessary to achieve the objectives of [the Treaty establishing the European Community][9]

Notwithstanding the above,

Subsidiarity is a dynamic concept and should be applied in the light of the objectives set out in the Treaty. It allows Community action within the limits of its powers to be expanded where circumstances so require, and conversely, to be restricted or discontinued where it is no longer justified.[10]

Thus, because individual EU member states continue to perceive that they have wide latitude to interpret EU Recommendations and to implement EU Directives and Regulations (ironically including the EU's recent package expressly designed to bring greater regulatory harmonization to telecoms), then by definition there will inevitably continue to be a sufficient amount of differ-

---

[7] 47 USC § 253.

[8] *Implementation of the Local Competition Provisions in the Telecommunications Act of 1996, First Report and Order*, CC Docket No 96–98, 11 FCC Rcd 15499, 15782–807, (1996) (Local Competition Order), aff'd in part and vacated in part sub nom *Competitive Telecommunications Ass'n v FCC*, 117 F 3d 1068 (8th Cir 1997) & *Iowa Util Bd v FCC*, 120 F 3d 753 (8th Cir 1997), aff'd in part, rev'd in part, and remanded sub nom *AT&T Corp v Iowa Util Bd*, 525 US 366 (1999) (*AT&T v Iowa Util Bd*), aff'd in part and vacated in part on remand, *Iowa Util Bd v FCC*, 219 F 3d 744 (8th Cir 2000), aff'd, *Verizon Tel Cos v FCC*, 122 S Ct 1646 (2002), *Order on Reconsideration*, 11 FCC Rcd 13042 (1996) (Local Competition First Reconsideration Order), *Second Order on Reconsideration*, 11 FCC Rcd 19738 (1996) (Local Competition Second Reconsideration Order), *Third Order on Reconsideration and Further Notice of Proposed Rulemaking*, 12 FCC Rcd 12460 (1997) (Local Competition Third Reconsideration Order), further reconsideration pending.

[9] Treaty of Rome, supra note 3, Article 5.

[10] Protocol annexed to the Treaty of the European Community—Protocol on the application of the principles of subsidiarity and proportionality, OJ 1997 C 340/105 at ¶ 3.

ences and disharmony among the various member states that can raise the entry costs of new firms.[11]

III. HOW THE INTERNATIONAL TELECOMS INDUSTRY WORKS — WHAT'S AT STAKE?

In order to understand how telecoms restructuring affects the transatlantic partnership, it is necessary to understand the international settlement-of-accounts regime. The international settlement-of-accounts regime was developed in 1865 by 20 European countries to provide for a standard, common method to divide the revenues for international service between originating and destination countries.[12] There are basically two components to this process.

On one hand, there is the 'accounting rate', which is the privately negotiated internal price between originating and terminating carriers. The accounting rate is related, sometimes very loosely, to the carriers' end-to-end facilities cost. The two carriers then agree to a 'settlement' rate—usually one-half of the accounting rate—to hand-off and terminate traffic to each other in the middle of the ocean (hence the phrase 'half circuit'). If there is an exact equal amount of traffic exchanged between the originating market and the destination market, then the originating and terminating carriers' 'settlement of accounts' will be zero.

Unfortunately, for those countries which generally have more outbound traffic than incoming traffic for nearly every international route (ie, the US), these settlement rates can create a substantial subsidy from the originating market's consumers to the destination market, particularly when there is no competition in the destination market and therefore the dominant incumbent can set these settlement rates far above cost. When this occurs, the carrier who has to 'settle-up' its account with its foreign correspondent effectively has to pay far more than necessary to terminate a call—which therefore means it must offer a higher price for service to potential end-customers (commonly referred to as the 'collection' rate). Thus, if a carrier can bypass having to pay a settlement rate to its foreign correspondent, then that carrier will have a significant cost advantage over its rivals.

The significance of this 'dual price' system for international telephony (ie, regulated collection rates and privately negotiated accounting rates) on market

[11] See, eg, Communication from the Commission to the European Parliament, the Council, the Economic and Social Committee and the Committee of the Regions, Fifth Report on the Implementation of the Telecommunications Regulatory Package (11 November 1999) (hereinafter '*Fifth Report*') (http://europa.eu.int/comm/information_society/policy/telecom/5threport/pdf/5threp99_en.pdf) at 10–11, where the European Commission presents a virtual laundry list of regulatory failures across the Community including, but certainly not limited to, the lack of regulatory independence due to a member state having an equity share in the indigenous dominant incumbent; NRAs that refuse to enforce aggressively the powers they have; NRAs who are more interested in social engineering rather than efficient economic outcomes; NRAs who lack sufficient powers; NRAs who are prone to regulatory delay; and an overall lack of resources and qualified staff.

[12] See Chapter 3, Box 3.1 of *Direction of Traffic, 1996*, ITU/Telegeography inc (1996).

conduct and performance cannot be underestimated because carriers' net revenue for international service is a function of *both* their accounting rates as well as their collection charges (ie, the rate charged to end consumers). Thus, if traffic is balanced on a particular route, the value of the accounting rate is essentially irrelevant since no settlement is necessary and each carrier's revenue will depend directly on its collection charge. On the other hand, however, where traffic is imbalanced, the accounting rate may have a significant effect on the commercial options of the two carriers.

For example, if a carrier has a significant incoming traffic deficit, then the settlement payments that it must make to its foreign correspondent limit its ability to reduce its collection charges. Conversely, a carrier with a net traffic surplus has little incentive to operate more efficiently or to reduce the accounting rate because of the net settlement benefits it receives under the *status quo*. For this reason, carriers that have relatively lower collection charges, often due to the competition from other carriers, and a net traffic deficit, are dissatisfied with the current accounting rate regime because the *status quo* tends to subsidize high cost monopoly carriers at the expense of lower cost carriers and end-users from competitive regimes. As one can imagine, because the US has a significant imbalance of traffic with the rest of the world, reducing these huge out-payments has been a centrepiece of US telecoms policies over the last few years.

IV. 1997 WTO ACCORD ON BASIC TELECOMS SERVICES

The 1997 WTO Accord on Basic Telecoms Services was supposed to address the international settlement rate problem *indirectly* by opening up local telecoms markets (ie, with more competition to terminate a call, the incumbent cannot raise price or restrict output, *ergo* settlement rates are brought in line with costs). Indeed, although settlement rate reform was a primary motivating factor behind the 1997 WTO Accord, the 1997 Accord deliberately avoided any mention of settlement rates throughout the entire document.

The unique key to the 1997 Accord was the Reference Paper, wherein member states agreed to implement and abide by certain regulatory principles. These principles include the adoption of competitive safeguards, interconnection, publicly available licensing criteria, independent regulators, the 'objective, timely, transparent and non-discriminatory' allocation and use of 'scarce resources' (eg, frequencies, numbers and rights-of-way) and, of course, universal service. If WTO member states fail to implement their WTO commitments, then other WTO member states may consider these failures as a breach of most-favoured-nation principles and seek redress from a WTO arbitration panel.

Significantly, this was the first major effort by the WTO community to use a 'best practices' approach to the issue. Yet, as highlighted above, (1) the complex economics of the local market; coupled with (2) the great discretion provided to individual member states to implement the Reference Paper, made the realization of the WTO's stated goal of increasing market access for basic telecoms services an extremely difficult task.

V. REGULATION, INCUMBENT SABOTAGE AND THE HIGH COST OF ENTRY INTO THE LOCAL MARKET

Although there is a WTO Accord on Basic Telecoms Services, it is nonetheless crucial to understand that telecoms is *not* like wheat, cars, wool, film or any other commodity that the WTO traditionally addresses. Rather, telecoms is *sui generis*.

First and foremost, entry into telecoms—particularly the local market—is an extremely expensive endeavour, forcing firms to commit huge fixed and sunk costs. The costs include both significant plant and, even more so, non-plant (eg, advertising, regulatory) costs.[13] Thus, new entrants typically 'bleed red ink'.

Second, telecoms is a business comprised of networks, and therefore the issue of 'network externalities'—ie, the value of a network to one customer increases as more people utilize the network—is a key economic factor.[14]

Third, given the presence of network effects and huge sunk and fixed costs, firms have to achieve scale economies quickly to pay back debt. What this means is that the local market for telecoms will be highly concentrated (ie, few firms). Thus, if the incumbent is one, then the market will probably only be able to sustain two more local access networks.[15]

Fourth, incumbents will *always* seek to sabotage the efforts of new entrants— ie, they will always seek to 'deny, delay, and degrade' new entrants' efforts to interconnect and hand-off telephone traffic.[16] After all, if a firm can make one dollar or euro more in deterrence than it can by competition, then it will *always* choose deterrence.

Finally, telecoms is a highly regulated industry, and therefore incumbents will play in the political arena to attempt to push for policies that will raise entry costs for new firms (eg, the implementation of asymmetrical build-out requirements and asymmetrical universal service contributions, the lack of meaningful enforcement and punishment of incumbent strategic anti-competitive conduct, and the like).[17] As such, even though the 1997 Accord calls for an independent regulator, regulatory capture by the incumbent remains a significant concern and barrier to entry for new firms.

---

[13] See Beard *et al*, supra note 5.
[14] Ibid.
[15] Ibid.
[16] Ibid.
[17] Ibid; see also G. Ford & T. Hazlett, *The Fallacy of Regulatory Symmetry: An Economic Analysis of the 'Level Playing Field' in Cable TV Franchising Statutes* (1999) (http://www.egroupassociates. com/Reports/fallacy.pdf).

VI. THE 'TELECOMS TRADE WAR' AND THE TRANSATLANTIC
PARTNERSHIP

As noted above, trade concerns have increasingly but improperly crept into telecoms regulatory restructuring efforts on both sides of the Atlantic over the past few years, despite the presence of the landmark 1997 WTO Accord on Basic Telecoms Services. Thus, even though the first formal WTO complaint under the 1997 Accord was only recently filed,[18] trade concerns at the regulatory level nonetheless created significant barriers to entry for new firms. As highlighted specifically in this section, the strain on the transatlantic partnership became impossible to ignore and did much to harm overall consumer welfare.

A. The European Union

Without question, there are numerous structural problems with telecoms markets worldwide. When it comes to many foreign countries (including EU member states), however, these structural problems are exacerbated because there often is very little culture that genuinely believes that market forces and economic theory can actually work. Instead, given Europe's history of socialism, if not outright communism, many people in Europe sincerely believe that state ownership for key sectors of the economy (eg, telecoms and electric utilities) are best left in the hands of the government. (After all, subsidized rates and plentiful civil service jobs are powerful political narcotics.) The biggest issue in international telecoms liberalization and restructuring, therefore, has been to convince European policy-makers and the European public at large that competition and good economic market performance—rather than state run monopolies (and the large amount of employment and subsidized services they provide)— is the best way to maximize consumer welfare in the long-run.

This lack of a competitive culture has placed a large strain on the transatlantic partnership, because, as noted above, the discretion provided to European WTO member states about how each country should adopt the pro-competitive principles contained in the Regulatory Reference Paper—coupled with the EU principle of 'subsidiarity'—is problematic in practice.[19] And, as further noted

---

[18] See infra.
[19] Several scholars predicted the potential lack of efficacy of the principles set forth in the Regulatory Reference Paper. For example, Drake and Noam argue that: 'Much is made over the acceptance of a regulatory reference model, making it seem like the adoption of some universal charter of telecommunications freedom. The reality is more modest. The "model" principles are mostly procedural, not substantive. They speak of "independence" of the regulator, but this merely refers to the independence from the monopolist, not from politics. As if formal independence prevents capture. The principles speak of openness, public licensing criteria, transparency, and objective allocation procedures. All this sounds good, but is worth little because of its vagueness, if a government drags its feet. For example, an openness of process can mean very little outside the public "sunshine" on the senior staff level before ceremoniously reaching the official decision event.' See W.J. Drake & E.M. Noam, 'The WTO Deal on Basic Telecommunications: Big Bang or Little Whimper?' (1997) 21 *Telecomm Pol'y* 799 at 816–17.

above, the significant amount of disharmony among the various EU member states has significantly raised the entry costs of new firms.[20] Thus, because even though many member states may meet the 'letter' of the Reference Paper, the reality is that many countries have imposed such egregiously high regulatory entry costs that any investment is economically untenable. As such, from an economic standpoint, a legitimate argument could be made that these markets are *de facto* closed.[21]

B. The United States

Yet, despite Europe's struggles with their liberalization and restructuring efforts, there are no 'white hats' in this business and the US has not had 'clean hands'. Indeed, for many years, the FCC—despite its pro-competitive rhetoric—engaged in a systematic pattern of behaviour to deter foreign entry into the US and to abrogate its commitments in the WTO. Such foreign entry-deterring policies ranged the full gamut—including, but certainly not limited to, the FCC's approach to universal service,[22] international cable landing certifications, international satellite spectrum allocation, and certainly last but not least, mergers and acquisitions.[23]

Yet, perhaps more egregiously, the FCC has done an extremely poor job of promoting competition in its own markets (terrestrial and wireless) at home, thus forcing the US telecoms sector into a financial meltdown.[24] And, unfortunately, it appears that conditions are not going to improve any time soon either.[25] While these policies are bad enough for American consumers, what makes matters even more distasteful is that the FCC hypocritically engaged in a

[20] See '*eEurope*', supra note 4.

[21] See, eg, *USTR Notes Progress on United Kingdom Telecommunications Issues, But Remains Concerned About Pace of Implementation*, Office of the USTR Press Release (21 December 2000) (http://www.ustr.gov/releases/2000/12/00–93.html).

[22] D. Molony, 'EC and US To Clash over Universal Service Funds', *Communications Week International*, 6 April 1998, at 1, 30.

[23] Naftel & Spiwak, supra note 1.

[24] For example, some of the major domestic US telecoms policies that have actually *increased*—rather than appropriately reduced—entry costs for new firms include, but a certainly are not limited to: (1) permitting the near total reconcentration (ie, state-sponsored horizontal market allocation) of the US incumbent telecoms, cable and radio industries; (2) failing to take unbundling and collocation efforts seriously (only a pathetic amount of all US access lines have been made available on an unbundled network element basis to date); (3) prematurely permitting dominant incumbents to re-vertically integrate in several states before local markets are competitive (ie, the incumbent is unable to engage in strategic, anti-competitive conduct, even if it tries); (4) politicizing universal service programmes to protect pet constituencies (thus making these programmes a self-defeating exercise); (5) engaging in numerous clandestine 'back room deals' among major industry players (eg, access charge reform via the so-called 'CALLS' proposal), thus depriving the public of procedural due process; and (6) acting as a 'frequency monopolist' and therefore choosing to sacrifice the efficient allocation of spectrum in favour of naked revenue raising—resulting in the delay of a significant chunk of radio spectrum deployed for use.

[25] L.J. Spiwak, 'Opinion: US Competition Policy—The Four Horsemen of the Broadband Apocalypse', *Communications Week International* (1 April 2002) (http://www.phoenix-center.org/commentaries/CWIHorsemen.pdf).

sustained pattern of forcing its dogmatic view of regulation upon the rest of the world in a mercantile game of 'Do as I Say, Not as I Do'. As explained in more detail in Section X below, however, fear of an official WTO finding that the US lacks 'clean hands' has contributed significantly to the US' hesitation to bring a formal WTO complaint until this year.

As a result, while we may be in the process of a 'telecoms revolution', US telecoms policies of the 1990s turned this revolution into a 'telecoms trade war' that came dangerously close to spinning out of hand.[26] Indeed, while we did not see any overt or direct retaliation against US firms, the FCC's hypocritical and mercantile conduct created a more subtle but nonetheless significant entry deterring result—ie, the US' actions over the last few years provided foreign NRAs with little incentive (actually, to be more accurate, a huge *disincentive*) to move restructuring forward constructively and aggressively in their home markets. Indeed, by failing to take the analytical 'high-ground' in favour of economically flawed power-politics, the US lost much of its credibility in the international telecoms community. In so doing, the FCC's ostensible 'pro-competition' policies over the past few years therefore became, in reality, a self-defeating exercise. Instead, a far more constructive measure would have been to co-operate with foreign regulatory bodies and help them approach the structural problems of telecoms restructuring *within the unique contexts of their respective home markets*—after all, economic first principles do not change with geographic borders.

VII. ILLUSTRATIVE CASE-STUDIES

A. Settlement rate benchmarks

As noted in the previous section, the 1997 WTO Accord very deliberately did not mention the thorny issue of settlement rate benchmarks. To fill this vacuum, almost immediately after the 1997 WTO Accord on Basic Telecoms Services was concluded, the FCC adopted a set of regulations that purported to limit the outflow of above-cost settlement rates by imposing a set of benchmark price caps on the amount US carriers could pay to their foreign correspondent to terminate a call. In order to mitigate the economic impact resulting from these benchmarks, the FCC established a sliding five-year compliance schedule depending on the level of economic development of the country. (Europe, as part of the developed world, had one year to bring itself into line with the FCC's benchmarks.[27]) Although the FCC tried to couch the issue by arguing that it was only exerting

[26] Naftel & Spiwak, supra note 1.

[27] In contrast, developing countries with low telephone penetration (teledensity) have five years to bring settlement rates in line with the FCC's benchmarks. Yet, what is so perverse about this policy is that the FCC is blatantly telling incumbent monopolists in these countries that if they keep teledensity low, the longer they can receive monopoly rents from settlement rates. In so doing, the FCC is actually hurting those countries that could benefit from competition the most.

jurisdiction for the US originating end of the call, the reality was that it was in effect seeking to extend its jurisdiction to the foreign destination market as well.

To justify this policy, the FCC essentially reasoned that these settlement rate benchmarks—even in a post-WTO world—were necessary to stop foreign monopolists from using these above-cost settlement out-payments, along with monopoly rents garnered from their home markets, to subsidize their service offerings in the US (ie, predate), thus driving US firms out of business. The big problem, however, is that the FCC's economics simply did not hold, much to the great consternation of the international community.

First, it is crucial to understand that any successful effort to predate must result in a firm's ability to drive out all of its competitors so that it can recoup its losses by charging supra-competitive prices. Thus, as a matter of common sense, if predation by foreign carriers is funded by above-cost settlement rates paid by US carriers to terminate traffic, then as US customers switch away from US carriers over to cheaper 'subsidized' foreign carriers, *the alleged subsidy comes to an end*. Moreover, given that US incumbent carriers (ie, the 'Baby Bells') are stronger than ever now six years after the passage of the 1996 Telecoms Act (both horizontally and vertically), it is highly unlikely that these firms are going anywhere any time soon, and therefore any possibility of recoupment is fleeting at best.

Second, in a post-WTO world, the vertical issues feared by the FCC are rapidly disappearing. For example, with the market opening commitments contained in the Accord, there are now competitive options in foreign destination markets to terminate an international call (although the significant 'last mile' problem remains largely unresolved on both sides of the Atlantic). Contributing to this improving situation is the presence of independent and transparent NRAs, combined with the implementation of cost-based interconnection rates in WTO member states, which further constrain (albeit far from completely) the incumbents' behaviour.

Accordingly, although the FCC likes to claim that its benchmark policy is the reason why international telecoms rates have fallen precipitously, the reality is that they very much had the proverbial 'wind at their backs'. In such a case, the settlement rate issue should have been resolved in a far more diplomatic tone instead of the rancour and ill-will the US engendered in the transatlantic partnership. Indeed, the US should be very glad that the EU—for whatever reason— chose not to impose a reciprocal measure in the face of the US' mercantile approach to international telecoms, as there was absolutely nothing to prevent any of the European member states from pulling the same shenanigans by passing a regulation that provided that their carriers could not pay more than 'x' amount to US carriers to terminate a call.

B. International spectrum

Wireless technology has blossomed over the last decade, producing a wide variety of fixed and mobile products and services. As demand continues to

increase and supply remains fixed, however, efficient spectrum allocation becomes particularly nasty if government needs to relocate incumbent users of
spectrum to another frequency band. In particular, because the cost of relocation—ie, new transmitters, receivers, etc—can be substantial, policy-makers
must decide the difficult (and incredibly political) question of who has to pay
for this relocation—incumbent users or new users?

One school of thought holds that because spectrum is a public asset and incumbent spectrum users enjoy the free use of that spectrum via licences, incumbent
spectrum users have no permanent right to use the spectrum in perpetuity and
must move, at their own cost, if government decides to reallocate that spectrum to
another use. On the other hand, because an auction gives the new users a 'faux'
property right in the spectrum, thus preventing the re-use of the spectrum for the
foreseeable future (a policy that is entirely necessary due to the huge sunk and
fixed costs associated with building a mobile network and the concurrent need to
have guaranteed access to a particular chunk of spectrum to warrant this investment), some argue that the new users should be forced to pay the relocation costs
for incumbent users as in the case of the FCC's PCS auctions of the mid-90s.[28]

In the case of the US allocation of spectrum for Mobile Satellite Services (MSS)
in the 2GHz band, due to the political clout of the US broadcasting industry, the
FCC adopted the latter approach and required new users of satellite spectrum to
pay relocation costs to incumbent users.[29] While this policy might have made
sense in the domestic context, such a policy made little sense in the international
context because if the US can impose spectrum relocation costs, then there is
absolutely nothing prohibiting every other country from imposing spectrum
relocation costs as well. As satellite systems are so dependent on economies of
scale and scope to be financially viable, however, such a domino effect would
raise entry costs exponentially so as to make the launch of a new satellite
constellation economically untenable.[30]

---

[28] The FCC used a slight variation of this mechanism to accelerate the opening up of spectrum for
mobile that would be created by the mandatory migration of broadcasters required to make way for
digital TV. There, although broadcasters were not obliged to move for many years, the FCC nonetheless held that auction winners could pay broadcasters to move in advance of the deadline to gain early
access to the spectrum.

[29] *In re Matter of Amendment of Section 2.106 of the Commission's Rules to Allocate Spectrum at
2 GHz for Use by the Mobile-Satellite Service*, Memorandum Opinion and Third Notice of Proposed
Rulemaking, FCC 98–309, 13 FCC Rcd 23,949 (1998) (hereinafter 'Third NPRM'), adopted in
relevant part, *Amendment of Section 2.106 of the Commission's Rules to Allocate Spectrum at
2 GHz for Use by the Mobile-Satellite Service*, ET Docket No 95–18, Second Report And Order
and Second Memorandum Opinion and Order, FCC 00–233 (rel July 3, 2000) (*2 GHz Second R&O
and Second MO&O*) at ¶¶ 106–112.

[30] See, eg, S. Nye, 'ICO Faces $2 Billion Bill as US Rejects EC Complaints', *Communications Week
International*, 2 December 1997 (reporting that Sir Leon Brittan, then-European Commission Vice
President and trade commissioner, warned the US that the FCC's policies of forcing new entrants to
pay spectrum relocation fees might provoke copy-cat actions in other countries in which case other
MSS operators, 'including the U.S.' own Iridium and Globalstar MSS operators, could find themselves
facing similar charges in other overseas markets'); see also 'Business and Regulatory: FCC on the
Defensive Over EU Satellite Concerns', *Communications Week International*, 25 August 2000.

Unsurprisingly, Europe—with its large satellite industry—was not pleased by the US' actions. In fact, the EU specifically warned the FCC that its approach could have significant impacts on the licensing of MSS and other global services in other countries and that the European Commission was 'particularly concerned' about the 'negative precedent' the FCC policies could set in other countries,[31] noting publicly that 'such a statement implies a tacit recognition that the FCC has not yet given proper consideration to the impact that the FCC spectrum management policies have at [the] international level'.[32] As such, the European Commission went on to note that it would:

remain attentive to the treatment given to European-based satellite systems in the U.S. The EC will be particularly attentive to any behaviour which is contrary to the spirit or letter of the commitments undertaken by the U.S. within the WTO agreement on basic telecommunications services.[33]

C. Mergers, acquisitions and joint ventures

The third major area where the 'telecoms trade war' created a major strain in the transatlantic partnership came in the form of mergers, acquisitions and joint ventures between US and European companies. These deals included British Telecom/MCI,[34] Deutsche Telekom/France Telecom/Sprint,[35] and British Telecom/AT&T.[36] While the FCC ultimately approved each of these transactions as in the 'public interest',[37] the FCC more often than not used these proceedings to raise trade concerns rather than to conduct any honest analysis of the competitive merits of each case—even to the point of throwing barbs and insults about their European NRA counterparts' failure to promote competition in the final orders.

Not surprisingly, the FCC's treatment of European carriers did not go unnoticed, and the opportunity for payback came when the European Commission could assert jurisdiction over two mergers of US firms who had significant European operations—MCI/WorldCom and MCI/Sprint. While the European

---

[31] EU Reply Comments to Third NPRM, supra note 24 at ¶ 8.   [32] Ibid.

[33] Ibid. at ¶ 10; see also European Commission Report on United States Barriers to Trade and Investment (July 2000) at 57–9 (http://europa.eu.int/comm/trade/pdf/US_bt2000.pdf).

[34] *MCI Comm Corp & British Telecomm PLC*, Declaratory Ruling and Order, 9 FCCR 3960, 75 Rad Reg 2d (P & F) 1024 (1994) [hereinafter BT/MCI I Order]; *MCI Comm Corp & British Telecomm PLC*, Declaratory Ruling, 10 FCCR 8697 (1995) [hereinafter BT/MCI II]; *The Merger of MCI Comm Corp and British Telecomm PLC*, Memorandum Opinion and Order, 12 FCCR 15,351, paras 298–303, 9 Comm Reg (P & F) 657 (1997) [hereinafter BT/MCI III Order].

[35] *Sprint Corp, Petition for Declaratory Ruling Concerning Section 310(b)(4) and (d) of the Communications Act*, Declaratory Ruling and Order, 11 FCCR 1850, 2 Comm Reg (P & F) 409 (1996).

[36] *In the Matter of AT&T Corp, British Telecommunications, plc, et al, For Grant of Section 214 Authority, Modification of Authorizations and Assignment of Licenses in Connection With the Proposed Joint Venture Between AT&T Corp. and British Telecommunications, plc*, Memorandum Opinion And Order, FCC 99–313, (rel 29 October 1999).

[37] Under section 310(b)(4) of the US Communications Act (47 USC § 310(b)(4)), no broadcast or common carrier licence may be controlled, directly or indirectly, by a foreign entity if the FCC finds that 'the public interest will be served by the refusal or revocation of such license'.

Commission eventually cleared the first case after requiring the merged company
to divest its Internet operations (particularly backbone facilities),[38] it rejected
the second merger outright.[39] More important, however, was that the European
Commission in both cases actually acted *before* the FCC had an opportunity to
rule on the case. Needless to say, the European Commission's actions—whether
motivated by retaliation, xenophobia, the merits, or procedure (or, as even some
suggested in MCI/Sprint in cahoots with the FCC who wanted political cover to
deny the merger)—further strained the transatlantic partnership.

VIII. THE FIRST SIGNS OF A *MEA CULPA*

By the end of the Clinton/Gore Administration, the effects of the 'telecoms trade
war' were becoming impossible to ignore, even by senior US policy officials. For
example, Federal Reserve Chairman Alan Greenspan took the unusual step of
criticizing these policies publicly, describing them as 'essentially adversarial' and
therefore antithetical to US consumer welfare. According to Chairman Greenspan,

[D]espite the remarkable success over a near half-century of GATT, the General Agreement on Trade and Tariffs, and its successor, the World Trade Organization, in reducing
trade barriers, *our trade laws and negotiating practices are essentially adversarial.* They
presume that a trade concession extracted from us by our trading partners is to their
advantage at our expense, and must be countered. Few economists see the world that way.
And I am rash enough to suggest we economists are correct, at least in this regard: *trade is
not a zero-sum game.* If trade barriers are lowered by both parties, each clearly benefits.
But if one lowers barriers and the other does not, the country that lowered barriers
unilaterally would still be better off having done so. Raising barriers to achieve protectionist equality with reluctant trading partners would be neither to our benefit, nor to theirs.
The best of all possible worlds for competition is for both parties to lower trade barriers.
The worst is for both to keep them up. *For these reasons, I am concerned about the recent
evident weakening of support for free trade in this country.* Should we endeavor to freeze
competitive progress in place, we will almost certainly slow economic growth overall, and
impart substantial harm to those workers who would otherwise seek more effective
longer-term job opportunities. Protecting markets from new technologies has never succeeded. Adjustments to newer technologies have been delayed, but only at significant cost.
*Even should our trading partners not retaliate in the face of increased American trade
barriers, an unlikely event, we do ourselves great harm by lessening the vigor of American
competitiveness.* The United States has been in the forefront of the post-war opening up of
international markets, much to our, and the rest of the world's, benefit. It would be a great
tragedy were that process reversed.[40]

[38] Case IV/M.1069 WorldCom/MCI OJ 1999 L116/1 (http://europa.eu.int/smartapi/cgi/
sga_doc?smartapi!celexplus!prod!CELEXnumdoc+lg=EN+numdoc=31999D0287).
[39] Case No COMP/M.1741–MCI WorldCom/Sprint [2000] (http://europa.eu.int/comm/competi-
tion/mergers/cases/decisions/m1741_en.pdf).
[40] Remarks by Chairman Alan Greenspan before the Dallas Ambassadors Forum, Dallas, Texas
(16 April 1999) (emphasis added).

IX. OLIVE BRANCH OR TROJAN HORSE?

The 2000 election brought in a new Administration, a new FCC Chairman (Michael Powell), and apparently a new approach to international telecoms. To illustrate how US international telecoms policy appeared to change, an excellent case-study can be found with the FCC's disposition of Deutsche Telekom's acquisition of US mobile operator VoiceStream Communications, which started under the Clinton Administration and was adjudicated under the Bush Administration.[41]

Once again, the FCC was forced to adjudicate a merger whereby a foreign monopolist sought to acquire a US firm (in this case, a mobile operator). Unlike the cases discussed in the previous section, however, Deutsche Telekom's (DT) acquisition of VoiceStream tested the mettle of the transatlantic partnership because the German Government still maintained a significant equity stake in DT. As such, any slap against DT by the FCC was *a fortiori* a slap against the German Government itself and, therefore, the case had to be approached with a good deal of diplomacy.

Although the case dragged on for over eight months due to political pressure from xenophobes on Capitol Hill who did not want a US carrier 100 per cent owned by a foreign company—much less a foreign company that has a significant equity interest held in it by its national government—when we examine the FCC's decision closely, however, it appears that Chairman Michael Powell's FCC appeared to seek a cessation of hostilities between the US and the international telecoms community.

For example, for the first time in recent memory, the FCC in the DT/Voice-Stream order was quick to point out that in balancing concerns about national security against the benefits of allowing foreign investment in the US, the FCC must be careful not to act too aggressively so as to 'avoid retaliation against U.S. investments in foreign markets'. While not an explicit *mea culpa*, perhaps one can infer a tacit recognition of, and apology from, Powell's FCC for the previous Administration's mercantile 'Pax Americana' approach of the last eight years.

Similarly, the FCC during the Clinton/Gore Administration never hesitated to criticize publicly any foreign regulatory agency for even the slightest perceived transgression against US firms. Yet, in the DT/VoiceStream order, the FCC refused repeatedly to comment on the effectiveness of RegTP, the German telecoms regulator (Die Regulierungsbehörde für Telekommunikation und Post), instead choosing to focus on the competitive effects of DT's entry into US markets. Thus, although the FCC legitimately found the record on RegTP 'mixed', it appropriately left the thorny issues of diplomacy to the US Trade Representative.

---

[41] *In re Applications of VoiceStream Wireless Corp et al and Deutsche Telekom AG, for Consent to Transfer Control of Licenses and Authorizations Pursuant to Sections 214 and 310(d) of the Communications Act and Petition for Declaratory Ruling Pursuant to Section 310 of the Communications Act,* Memorandum Opinion and Order, FCC 01–142, ___ FCC Rcd ___ (rel April 27, 2001).

But perhaps the most shocking act of reconciliation (either by design or, more likely, by accident) was the FCC's analytical evisceration of the ridiculous logic underpinning its efforts to impose settlement rate benchmarks. That is to say, as noted above in Section III, the FCC's benchmarks policies were motivated by the fear that somehow a foreign monopolist could use the monopoly rents derived from its home market, along with the 'above cost' settlement rates paid by US firms, to predate (ie, price below cost) in US origination markets, drive all of its competitors out, and then recoup its losses by charging US consumers supra-competitive prices. Yet, in the DT/VoiceStream order, the FCC specifically rejected this argument, reasoning that in a post-WTO world: (1) each termination market now has standard, cost-based interconnection rates; and (2) even assuming a foreign firm could slip one past its home regulators, given the maturity and competitiveness of the US international telecoms market, it is highly unlikely that a foreign monopolist could successfully predate, drive out incumbent operators and subsequently recoup.

X. THE INAUGURAL WTO CASE: UNITED STATES V MEXICO

A. Background

There is an old saying that bad facts make bad law. As noted above, because the US lacked 'clean hands' in its failed efforts to promote competition and reduce barriers to foreign entry within its own borders, the US was extremely reluctant to file a WTO claim under the 1997 Accord for fear of having a WTO Arbitration Panel (who may or may not understand the intricacies of the telecoms industry) make findings of fact or law that would hinder its own restructuring efforts. As such, if the US was going to complain to the WTO about other member states' failure to adhere to the 1997 Accord (of which, unfortunately, there are legion), then the US needed a potential target whose violations were so egregious and plentiful that no amount of retaliatory 'lack of clean hands' arguments in defence could detract from the merits of the case.

The US found its test case with Mexico, where Telmex—the incumbent Mexican monopolist with huge political power—rules telecoms with an iron fist. After the years of unsuccessful formal consultations with the Government of Mexico, on 18 February 2002, the US filed the first request for a WTO panel under the 1997 Accord.[42] The US levelled four basic claims against Mexico, namely:

(1) That the Mexican Government fails to ensure that Telmex provides inter-connection to US cross-border telecoms suppliers on reasonable rates, terms and conditions—in particular, that the rate charged by Telmex is neither

---

[42] WTO, *Mexico—Measures Affecting Telecommunications Services* (WT/DS204/3).

'cost based' nor 'sufficiently unbundled' as it includes charges unrelated to the service requested.

(2) That the Mexican Government fails to ensure that US basic telecoms suppliers have reasonable and non-discriminatory access to, and use of, public telecom networks and services—in particular, private leased lines and circuits.[43]

(3) For the same reasons set forth in the first two counts, that the Mexican Government fails to provide national treatment to US-owned commercial agencies—ie, Telmex provides itself with preferential treatment.[44]

(4) That the Mexican Government fails to prevent Telmex from engaging in strategic, anti-competitive conduct against rivals.

B. Implications of the case

While it is inappropriate to comment on the specific merits of this case, as this case is the first dispute under the 1997 Accord to be resolved by a WTO Arbitration Panel, it is nonetheless very important to highlight how this case could impact international telecoms restructuring efforts.

For example, the WTO will provide its first guidance as to what the definition of 'cost-based' rates should be. Incumbents globally have been pushing for historic embedded costs, which would raise entry costs for new firms. Both Europe and the US rejected this argument, and instead use a form of forward-looking, long-run incremental costs. (In fact, the US Supreme Court recently upheld the FCC's use of total element long-run incremental cost (TELRIC) pricing under the US Telecommunications Act of 1996.[45]) Yet, depending on the make-up of the WTO arbitration panel, the WTO could nonetheless accept the typical incumbent argument and reject LIRC pricing, thus throwing international restructuring efforts into a tailspin.

Similarly, it is unclear what a WTO panel would find to be adequate competitive safeguards to constrain strategic anti-competitive conduct by dominant incumbents. This issue has broad policy implications, as it calls directly into question member states' commitments for independent and strong regulators.

---

[43] Unfortunately, the FCC's complaints about the lack of competitive access to leased lines/special access services against Mexico are quite hypocritical, given that the current FCC refuses to take any action to curtail US dominant local incumbents from exercising their market power for the exact same services on the domestic front. See George Ford and Lawrence J. Spiwak, 'Set It and Forget It? Market Power and the Consequences of Premature Deregulation in Telecommunications Markets', *Phoenix Center Policy Paper No 18*, (July 2003) (http://www.phoenix-center.org/pcpp/PCPP18.pdf).

[44] As any competition from other Mexican carriers is so negligible, any generic preference for 'Mexican providers' has little practical effect on Telmex's strategic behaviour.

[45] *Verizon Tel Cos v FCC*, 122 SCt 1646 (2002); see also Lawrence J. Spiwak, 'The Telecoms Twilight Zone: Navigating the Legal Morass Among the Supreme Court, the D.C. Circuit, and the Federal Communications Commission', *Phoenix Center Policy Paper No 13* (August 2002) (http://www.phoenix.center.org/pcpp/PCPP13final.pdf).

XI. SUGGESTIONS FOR MOVING FORWARD

The Regulatory Reference Paper contained in the 1997 WTO Agreement on Basic Telecoms Services was billed as the breakthrough for international telecoms competition because it required member states to provide, *inter alia*, cost-based interconnection rates, an independent regulator with transparent procedures, universal service, etc. Yet, six years later, the global telecoms industry is in financial collapse, and competition is nascent at best.

Perhaps much of the blame can be traced back to the Reference Paper itself. Although the 1997 Accord attempted to use a 'best practices' approach, due to the nature of the WTO, member states are given great latitude on how they want to implement the Reference Paper. This discretion is problematic in practice, however, because even though many member states may meet the 'letter' of the Reference Paper, the reality is that many countries have imposed such egregiously high regulatory entry costs that any investment is economically untenable. As such, these markets are *de facto* closed, and there are few avenues of complaint and remedy under the current system.

In order to give the Reference Paper some 'teeth', perhaps consideration should be given to some sort of objective rational business test (RBT)—that is, given the current regulatory and legal environment, would a rational business enter and invest in a WTO member state as a competitor to the incumbent?

There are several advantages of such an approach:

First, private capital knows no geographic border and is the most objective (and universal) of standards—ie, is the entry/investment risk acceptable or too high? (After all, one of the primary motivations behind the WTO is to ensure the free flow of capital.)

Second, the RBT is a forward-looking standard and focuses on the current legal and regulatory environment rather than on the generic costs of entry. As such, the debate would not be about past entry, but whether a member state's current regulatory policies deter entry going forward.

Finally, such a standard would eliminate the animosity held by developing nations—ie, those member states with low GDP and therefore low demand for advanced broadband services—created by a 'one size fits all' or 'benchmarking/best practices' approach. Instead, the RBT would be able to account for specifically (and take off the table if necessary) the thorny socio-economic issues raised by the inevitable, yet politically-charged defiance that the complainant 'fails to account for the unique circumstances of the [insert Member State name here] market' argument.

Take the following two examples to illustrate the point:

First, while Brazil may have met its limited WTO commitments for basic telecoms services, Brazil's new build-out requirements require an entrant to invest nearly $1 billion over three years just to obtain a 1 per cent market share to gain access to the national numbering plan and guaranteed interconnection rights (which are essential for head-to-head competition with the incumbent). While these onerous asymmetrical entry barriers do not violate the current WTO regime, Brazil would violate the RBT test because Brazil's policies effectively make prospective entry so unprofitable as to render their market *de facto* closed.[46]

As a contrasting example, see the Global Crossing/US-Japan Cable Network Consortium cable landing petition dispute of two years ago. There, the now-bankrupt Global Crossing argued that US Government intervention in the WTO was required to deal with submarine cable landing disputes, not because of the ridiculously high interconnection rates in Japan, but because the costs of being in the telecoms business, such as construction costs and advertising, were too high.[47] This case would not trigger the RBT, however, because none of the factors alleged by Global Crossing had anything to do with National Treatment. As noted *passim*, telecoms is an extremely expensive business, and WTO remediation should not be triggered if a firm cannot afford the cost of doing business in the first instance.

XII. CONCLUSION

Over 200 years ago, Adam Smith, in his classic treatise *The Wealth of Nations*, powerfully demonstrated that whenever government attempts to co-ordinate the efforts of entrepreneurs, such policies almost invariably discourage economic growth and reduce economic well-being. Smith called this system 'mercantilism'.[48] According to Adam Smith, mercantilism 'retards, instead of accelerating, the progress of the society towards real wealth and greatness; and diminishes, instead of increasing, the real value of the annual produce of its land and labour' because of two basic reasons: a tendency of special interests to turn government programmes to their own narrow advantages, and a tendency of joint business efforts to result in collusion to reduce output and raise prices, especially when government willingly permits such collusion. As such, Smith explained that while 'the law cannot hinder people of the same trade from sometimes assembling together, it ought to do nothing to facilitate such assemblies; much less to render them necessary'.[49]

The 'telecoms trade war' of the last few years epitomizes precisely the type of conduct and harms Smith warned about. Indeed, while the original motivations for the aggressive international telecoms policies discussed herein were, at bottom, an ultimate desire to promote competition, the mercantile tact and tone used on both sides of the Atlantic simply distracted from the process. If

---

[46] Lawrence J. Spiwak, 'Perspective: There's not an Awful lot of Telecoms in Brazil', *Communications Week International*, 22 October 2001.

[47] For a full examination of this case, see Naftel & Spiwak, supra note 1, chapter 17.

[48] See J.C. Miller *et al, Industrial Policy: Reindustrialization Through Competition or Coordinated Action?* (1984) 2 *Yale J on Reg* 5.

[49] Ibid (citations omitted).

international telecoms policies are ever to realize the Information Economy and maximize consumer welfare, therefore, then both sides of the transatlantic partnership must first take more aggressive steps to create a 'constituency for competition' in their own respective domestic markets before they continue to throw more stones at each other.

15

North Atlantic Dispute Settlement for Air Transport

FREDERIK SØRENSEN*

The purpose of this paper is to look at case-studies concerning North Atlantic disputes in the air transport sector. Air transport as a sector has not created many conflicts, which in a European Union context have led to dispute settlement activity with the US. In order to explain why so little activity has taken place a short description of the development of the liberalized EU air transport policy is included and a separate section is included to look at the possible future for EU involvement. This policy to a large extent was inspired by the US deregulation in 1978, which resulted in a similar rule situation within the EU.

The paper will then try to look into the traditional situation based on bilateral agreements. It will subsequently go into the few cases which have occurred between the US and the EU. In addition the paper will look at the situation which might come about should the EU and the US enter into an air transport agreement to supersede the current bilateral agreements between the US and individual member states, either in a situation created by a potential ruling by the European Court of Justice (ECJ) or if EU competence is otherwise perfected.

It should be noted that air transport is only peripherally covered by the GATS system.[1] It therefore serves no purpose in general to go into details about the application of this system to air transport. However, this does not mean that the GATS has had no effects in the air transport sector. The US did make commitments concerning aircraft repair and maintenance, ie, repair stations in other countries working on US aircraft as well as the establishment in the US of foreign-owned repair stations. It should be noted that the US Congress at the initiative of trade unions was seized with the question of whether the US should apply restrictions to foreign repair stations. Diplomatic representations by the

---

* This paper has been improved in a number of places by contributions made by the commentator, Mr Richard Loughlin.

[1] Air transport market access has been exempted from the GATS together with all directly related services except three: aircraft repair and maintenance (including foreign repair stations), computerized reservation systems (CRS), and selling and marketing of air transportation. These have been specifically included by the GATS Annex on Air Transport Services.

EU pointed out that this would represent the introduction of more restrictions in this sector and therefore would be incompatible with the GATS. The issue was not further pursued by the US, which was confirmed in a letter by the then Secretary of Transportation. Since this situation did not really develop into a conflict it is only mentioned here and not discussed further in this paper.

I. DEVELOPMENT OF EU AIR TRANSPORT POLICY

The Treaty of Rome included Article 84, which stated that the Council could take any appropriate decision as to policy for air and sea transport. On that basis practically everybody in air transport thought that until such a decision was taken air transport was excluded from Treaty provisions. Consequently while policy was developed for other modes of transport nothing happened in air transport until 1974. In this year the ECJ took a decision concerning the application of social rules in the maritime sector. In this context the Court stated, contrary to general belief, that the general provisions of the Treaty did apply to sea and air transport and that the exclusion contained in Article 84 only applied to the provisions contained in the transport chapter. It took some time for the member states to get over the shock but in 1978 they had become convinced that an application of the general principles of the Treaty without attention being given to the specific characteristics of air transport would be too dangerous. They were also under the impression of the US deregulation, which came into effect in 1978. Therefore, the Council approved a priority list for air transport[2] in 1978. This was followed up in 1979 by a first memorandum on air transport (A Community Approach) issued by the Commission.

This was the start to a process where the EU in the course of a number of years developed an economic air transport policy for its internal market.[3] This policy introduced, step by step, not only a liberal system but also safeguards and harmonization measures with a view to permit time for adaptation and to achieve a level playing field. As a consequence, essential provisions included in the bilateral agreements between the 12 member states were therefore automatically replaced.

The final package, which was approved in 1992 and entered into effect on 1 January 1993, has created an economic regulatory framework for a common air transport market based on the freedom to provide air services. On the basis of the new provisions, a Community person (an individual or a company) irrespective of his Community nationality can create an air carrier anywhere within the Community and, with certain limitations until 1997, such an air carrier has the right to operate wherever opportunities might exist within the single market. The distinction between scheduled and non-scheduled air services has practically been eliminated in a regulatory sense, in particular for the

---

[2] See Annex 2.   [3] See Annex 1.

licensing of air carriers and access to the market. The discretionary powers of member states in respect of their own air carriers were eliminated.

This means that it is up to the air carriers themselves to decide in which mode they will operate. Air carriers are able to set prices freely and decide on the amount of capacity that they want to offer in the market. In other words this legislation has given Community air carriers commercial freedom. The competition rules also apply so that useful types of co-operation are permitted but cartels and other agreements of that nature as well as abuse of dominant positions are forbidden. The Community in particular pays close attention to the possibility of predatory behaviour and should be able to stop serious cases of that nature. State aids have been stopped except in a number of instances where they are considered to be in the common interest.

A number of safeguards and conditions were introduced or maintained. Operating licences cannot be granted unless the air carriers concerned demonstrate to their competent authorities that they are financially fit. These licences may also be revoked or suspended when the air carriers are unable to meet their actual and potential obligations. Insurance to cover liability in case of accidents is compulsory. Safety standards must be respected. When the market mechanisms do not result in needed services, for example to peripheral regions, possibilities exist to impose public service obligations. However, any exclusive concession which might result from this will have to be given on the basis of a competitive process, namely a tendering procedure, in which air carriers from the whole of the EU can participate. Where overcapacity has created serious economic difficulties for scheduled carriers of a given member state, the capacity to and from that state can be stabilized for a limited period. Fares decreases can be stopped when they have resulted in widespread losses among all carriers for the services concerned.

It was found necessary to take a number of supplementary actions to ensure a level playing field for the operators. Normally computerized reservation system (CRS) rules are mentioned as part of consumer protection but there are also quite a few concerns of air carriers in the context of CRSs. Air carriers need to be present in the CRSs and to have their products presented in a non-discriminatory way compared to their competitors. It is also useful to have competition between the systems so that fees are not unreasonable. Whether or not there is competition among air carriers the consumers are interested in having the services presented which are closest to their desiderata, be that in respect of schedules or price. The presentation must be as comprehensive as possible and truthful. For all these reasons a code of conduct for CRSs was developed in 1989 and revised in 1993 and 1999. The code ensures non-discrimination and equal rights of access to the services of the CRSs for air carriers and travel agents. For the consumers the code prescribes a neutral and comprehensive display.

In order to avoid congestion at airports and in their airspace becoming a bottleneck blocking the practical effects of the liberalization process, the EU has dealt with the issue of physical access to the infrastructure. Thus, a regulation on slot allocation was decided at the beginning of 1993, which acknowledges existing 'grandfather' rights and ensures that allocation is based on neutral, transparent and non-discriminatory rules. This means that today European and US policy objectives are fundamentally the same. Both favour competition. Both seek to protect consumer interests. Both believe in protecting the environment. The differences that have arisen have been matters of approach or timing. These kinds of disagreements will arise less frequently, and be resolved more readily, than disputes that spring from conflicting basic philosophies. Perhaps even more importantly, it suggests that there is great scope for co-operation to prevent future transatlantic disputes from arising in the first place. This will be looked into later in this paper.

While an internal market has been created for the Community in air transport it must be underlined that it only covers transport between and within member states. This has an unfortunate effect since externally the member states have continued to negotiate bilaterally according to the classical model without taking the Community into consideration. Unfortunately the classical model contains nationality clauses. It means that cross-border investments are not very attractive. For example Deutsche BA, in which British Airways has a controlling shareholding, finds it very difficult to get traffic rights to third countries since it is not owned and controlled by German nationals, which is required under the German bilateral agreements. Part of the difficulties for Swissair leading to its demise can also be accounted for by this phenomenon since Swissair acted too early by investing heavily in a number of EU air carriers before it could take control of them, ie, before an air transport agreement with the EU had been ratified which would eliminate nationality restrictions.[4] The Commission took legal action in 1998 before the ECJ in order to try to resolve this problem but it is not yet known whether this will be successful.[5]

II. The Bilateral Situation

Multilateral exchange of traffic rights was proposed at the end of World War II, at the Chicago Conference. The Conference succeeded in drafting the multilateral air navigation/air safety agreement known as the Chicago Convention, and it created the International Civil Aviation Organization (ICAO). However, the concurrent effort to multilateralize economic traffic rights through an international agreement stalled when only 12 states signed and none ratified the agreement.

Bilateral air services agreements soon flourished,[6] with each such partnership achieving the manner and degree of liberalization with which both parties were

---

[4] This agreement has now been ratified but unfortunately too late to help Swissair.
[5] For further discussion see later section on a Potential Air Transport Agreement.
[6] Today there are said to be some 3,000 such agreements in force worldwide.

comfortable. If dissatisfaction arose after the agreements were in effect, they could usually be amended. In the rare case that differences were irreconcilable, either party could renounce the agreement. This would result in a standstill for a few months or years until circumstances favoured a new agreement. Rarely has established air service been interrupted by an unresolved dispute, because in an aviation partnership, the parties have an especially strong interest in salvaging the relationship. Air transport services are not just a sector of trade. Air transport is an *instrument* of trade. In the transatlantic context, Canada and the US on the one side exchange some 55 million air passengers with Europe in a typical year. These citizens would not meekly accept a disruption in their transatlantic air service. Thus it is not surprising that there has been little recourse to the arbitration provisions in these bilateral agreements.

Bilateral agreements typically deal with market access, facilitation, non-discrimination, CRS and similar matters while competition rules (antitrust rules) and state aid are not covered. This has from time to time created uncertainties in situations where the US has applied its antitrust rules extraterritorially, or where the EU withheld approval of transatlantic airline alliances long after their approval by US authorities.

Bilateral agreements basically try to resolve conflicts on the basis of regular bilateral meetings and exchange of information when a problem comes up. If consultations cannot resolve the problem, which they normally can, sanctions may be invoked. Such sanctions typically would entail restrictions in market access. A conflict settlement mechanism from a bilateral agreement concluded by the US is shown in Annex 3. It is clear that it is trying to ensure a speedy process with a decision within a reasonable time period. However, if this is not possible it opens the way for interim measures.

The point here is that, decades before services generally were subject to trade disciplines under the GATS, air transport interests were analyzing and evaluating and reconciling their differences in a structured way. This approach was not structured in the sense of the nine steps laid out in the WTO Dispute Settlement Understanding (DSU), but air transport partners were continuously refining their understanding of one another's interests and sensitivities and coming to accommodations. Resolved disputes gave rise to clarifying amendments to the agreements, and these in turn prevented future disputes over the same issues. Thus, in the half-century from the Chicago Convention to the end of the Uruguay Round, the air transport sector had quite a large head start in resolving services disputes and in perfecting its agreements to reduce subsequent conflicts. Furthermore, while the operative terms of the bilateral agreements have become more detailed, the dispute settlement approach has retained its simplicity. In this context it is worthwhile pointing out that this dispute settlement procedure does contain a mandatory arbitration provision that can be invoked by either party without the agreement of the other. However, because solutions are usually improvised, arbitration is rare.

III. Actual cases of conflict[7]

A. Computerized reservation systems

It is important here to note that the WTO Dispute Settlement machinery cannot be used in US-EU disputes. While in principle CRS is a GATS covered sector, CRS also remains covered by all US bilateral air transport services agreements and by EU rules requiring reciprocity. Thus, neither the US nor the EU has made effective national treatment commitments for CRS, and both have taken out most-favoured-nation (MFN) exemptions.

Both the EU and the US have legislation in respect of CRS. The first US rules for CRS were issued in 1984. In the EU, a Regulation on a mandatory code of conduct was established in 1989 and revised several times subsequently. The two sets of rules are in general quite similar owing to the fact that the EU rules to a large extent were modelled on the US rules. It is generally acknowledged that in this area, if conflicts arise between the EU firms and third countries, the Commission will have to take the lead.

Despite all the above similarities, there have been two significant cases of conflict in this area. The first case concerns the sale of market information created by the CRS and sold on data tapes[8] to airlines. These tapes constitute a very important market analysis tool for the airlines since they permit the airlines to look at actual traffic flows on the basis of individual booking data. The

---

[7] Ten questions have been asked in general for the case-studies:

(1) Why did the dispute arise? What were the essential facts, incentives, conflicts of interests, and political pressures underlying the dispute?
(2) Which national and international, political and legal procedures were used for the settlement of the dispute? Were the applicable domestic procedures (eg, section 301 of the US Trade Act, the EC's Trade Barriers Regulation) and international dispute settlement procedures (eg, inside and outside the WTO) adequate? Which changes of the procedures would be desirable in order to reduce the risk of future similar disputes?
(3) What was the role of private interests in the emergence and settlement of the dispute before, during and after the invocation of WTO dispute settlement procedures?
(4) Which government departments were involved? How did they react to the private complaints? Have they been unduly subservient to industry pressures ('regulatory capture')?
(5) Which have been the main impediments to an amicable solution of the dispute? What was the role of third parties (states) intervening or involved in the dispute?
(6) Was the dispute due to the inadequacy of the applicable substantive rules (eg, inadequate guidance of 'result-oriented' trade rules stated in terms of trade effects)?
(7) Which changes in the applicable substantive rules could reduce the risk of future similar disputes? Is there a need for new additional bilateral or multilateral rules?
(8) Could the Transatlantic Partnership institutions contribute to the settlement of this kind of dispute? Who should initiate any such reforms (eg, for additional bilateral agreements and institutional co-operation among the EU and US)?
(9) How could the factors causing this kind of dispute be reduced? Should domestic policy-making processes be changed (eg, stronger involvement of domestic courts, parliaments, regulatory agencies)?
(10) Should the EU and US take joint initiatives in the Transatlantic Partnership and/or in the WTO for the better prevention or settlement of this kind of dispute?

Each case-study will attempt to cover these questions as appropriate.
[8] MIDT = Market Information Data Tapes.

airlines can therefore simulate what the effects would be of different operational and marketing strategies. The problem came up because there were differences between the EU and US rules that were perceived in Europe to give advantages to US air carriers. The EU rules impose strict non-discrimination concerning the sale of these tapes. If one airline can buy them then other airlines must also be able to do so. The US rules were basically the same, but contrary to the EU they reserved information on domestic air travel to US air carriers. Consequently the US air carriers could get a picture of the total market while the EU air carriers could only get a partial picture. The Association of European Air Carriers therefore lodged a complaint with the European Commission.

The EU rules contain a clause, which permits it to take retaliatory action if such discrepancies exist. However, going straight to a conflict immediately after a complaint had been lodged was not considered by the Commission and the Council to be a constructive approach. Negotiations were therefore taken up with the US. During the negotiations the EU claimed that the US should also make their data generally available since otherwise the EU might have to restrict access in a similar way as in the US. The negotiations came to a positive conclusion and the market data of US CRSs were made generally available on a reciprocal basis. One of the reasons for this outcome probably being that the US did not want to be seen as less liberal than the EU.

In the second case the US raised the issue based on a complaint from one of its CRSs. The CRS claimed that some European air carriers participated at a higher level in the CRS, which they controlled, while maintaining a low-level participation in the US system. This would be in conflict with the EU code of conduct. The EU CRS code prescribes that parent carriers[9] must be willing to provide the same data on pricing and available offers, which they provide to their own system, also to competing CRSs with the same speed and accuracy and that they would have to accept reservations through the competing systems as well.

Negotiations between the European Commission and the US Department of Transportation (DOT) and further investigation showed that there was indeed a deficiency. It was therefore decided that a more appropriate participation level should be established and contractual talks between the air carriers and the US CRS in question were arranged. At these meetings observers from both the Commission and, at their request, the DOT were present. The subsequent contractual negotiations between the air carriers and the US CRS were successful. Both of these cases show that regular contacts are useful since they establish trust that permitted a quick resolution of the problems. Furthermore, such regular contacts serve as a valuable means to prevent conflicts.

B. Competition co-operation agreement

In 1991 the EU and the US entered into a co-operation agreement on the application of their competition (antitrust) laws. The agreement involves the

---

[9] Parent carrier means an air carrier, which owns a CRS either wholly or partly.

Commission (EU) and the Department of Justice (US). It provides for consultation, co-operation (and co-ordination), exchange of certain information, the potential designation of one party as the lead party, and positive comity.[10] This agreement clearly has as its objective the avoidance of conflicts in enforcement cases as also stated in the agreement. The agreement does not apply to air transport, but in Europe, CRS activity is considered not to entail transport but to be a more general service activity and such activities are therefore considered to fall under the general application of the EU competition rules.

In this context the US raised a problem concerning provision of data to competing US systems. Under the positive comity clause the US asked the Commission to look into the matter. The problem concerned the provision of full information on air fares and their conditions. The US CRS claimed that without such information available in their system it was impossible to acquire the participation of travel agents in the countries concerned. The CRS in question was the same that had already been successful in the second case mentioned above. This complaint therefore showed that while, formally speaking, the problem had been resolved, in practice it did not work out. The CRS therefore preferred to submit their complaint under the competition rules this time around. A thorough investigation was carried out by the Commission. It was observed that there was a clear difference in the detail of data (pricing of airline products and development of new airline services, in particular, electronic ticketing), which were provided to the European system owned by the air carriers, as compared with the data provided to the competing US system. The problem could in fact be described as an abuse of dominant positions.

The Commission requested that the offending air carriers should open new contractual talks with the CRS, which resulted in clauses that ensured non-discriminatory treatment nearly to the extent that reverse discrimination would be prescribed, but this problem was corrected through consultation before the new contracts were signed. This chain of events showed that the co-operation agreement between the US and the EU on the application of competition and antitrust rules is a useful instrument and provides a means whereby a full-scale conflict can be avoided.

C. Alliances

The competition co-operation agreement does not apply to air transport as such. However, the Commission and the Department of Transportation have initiated an informal co-operation in respect of a number of alliance cases. This co-operation is more difficult than under the agreement since confidential information cannot be exchanged. Furthermore, the normal procedural competence has not been extended to the Commission for air transport to and from third countries. Any application of the competition rules therefore have to be done on

---

[10] Supplementary Agreement of 1998.

the basis of Articles 84 and 85 whereby any approval of an alliance is granted by the member state(s) in question while the Commission can direct the member states to take certain action[11] if they decide to approve the alliance.

This has created a time-consuming process in the EU and none of the major alliances between US and EU air carriers has yet been approved by the EU although the US has approved three: the STAR, Wings and the Skyteam alliances. This situation has not yet created any conflict but the longer this situation continues the more likely a conflict will become.[12] If a conflict develops I believe it would have to be handled by the Commission. However, it would be a very unusual situation because of the specific powers of the member states. This and the preceding case illustrate that a conflict settlement procedure for air transport as discussed below will be incomplete unless it also includes competition/anti-trust matters.

D. Hushkits

The EU adopted a Directive in 1999 on non-operation of hushkitted aircraft. The US objected formally to this Directive before its final adoption but (owing to claimed shortcomings in the transparency of the EU regulatory process) at a very late stage. Thus the objection came too late to stop its final adoption by the European Parliament and thereby leading to a compulsory adoption by the Council under the co-decision rules. This created a highly critical situation since certain US air carriers and manufacturing interests claimed that this would create serious economic hardship for them. They would be unable to use their aircraft within the EU and the resale value for these aircraft would be diminished since third country air carriers would also be barred from using these aircraft within the EU.

The problems were taken up in a number of meetings between the European Commission, the DOT and the Federal Aviation Administration, and the Departments of State and Commerce, which ended up at the highest level. Although numerous attempts were made to reach a compromise, this proved to be impossible in the short term. The US problems remained on the table since for the EU no other way seemed to exist to deal with serious environmental problems around its airports.

The US clearly contemplated sanctions of different kinds including a referral to the WTO but in the end decided to submit the case against EU member states to ICAO for decision by the ICAO Council. This procedure unfortunately (or perhaps fortunately) turned out to be rather lengthy. While the ICAO Council pondered the case, the work at ICAO to establish new standards for noise of aircraft continued. It is laudable that both sides participated in this work in a positive way. In fact, it turned out that new standards could be adopted at the

---

[11] Such action would normally be to prescribe conditions for the granting of the approval.
[12] The Star and the Wings alliances were accepted later in 2002.

ICAO assembly in the autumn of 2001. This was fortuitous since it allowed the EU to replace the offending Directive with a new one, which would create a better environmental situation without the offending elements. The conflict was therefore resolved without entering into a final confrontation and both sides must be commended on acting with a great sense of responsibility.

This whole chain of events led to a discussion of how best to avoid similar problems in the future. A principle of early warning was adopted in respect of the development of new legislation, sufficient for the US to analyze whether serious problems would be created and vice versa for the EU. While the role of transparency in the initial dispute became moot, enhanced transparency was embraced as a positive future measure. However, it should be mentioned that transparency was possibly not at issue but that the problem was perhaps more related to how one or the other side would handle the information received through this process of early warning. The US authorities were informed early on but at some levels the Directive was considered for quite some time as being solely a European affair.

It is perhaps ironic that it has recently come to my notice that this conflict was probably fought on the basis of wrong assumptions. The economic effects as claimed by the US side were probably more or less correct. However, the US air carriers were in fact much more afraid of the economic effect which would have been the consequence if the US authorities had decided to copy the EU action to stop the operation of hushkitted aircraft. Such an action became impossible the moment the US officially raised the issue with the EU.

IV. POTENTIAL AIR TRANSPORT AGREEMENT

A number of EU member states have negotiated 'Open Skies' agreements with the US. The Commission has taken these member states plus the UK (which concluded liberalizing amendments short of open skies) to the ECJ, claiming that the member states were not competent to conclude these agreements because of the existence of Community law. These cases were submitted in December 1998 but it is only now that they are nearing a final conclusion. This is not a legal action directed against the US but against the member states which have concluded these agreements. However, if the Commission is successful the present bilateral agreements with the US will have to be replaced by a single agreement. In fact the Advocate General gave as his opinion that the Member States indeed were incompetent to conclude these agreements as written, and that the agreements were therefore illegal.

It is clear that this outcome of the cases depends on the ECJ itself coming to the same conclusion. However, if it turns out that this is the outcome of the cases, it raises the question of how an air transport agreement with the US might look in respect of conflict settlement mechanisms. In other air transport agreements that the EU has concluded, the ECJ has been used as the final arbiter to clear up any case concerning the interpretation of the agreement. This solution quite clearly cannot be used in an agreement between the US and the EU.

Bilateral agreements as concluded by the US do contain a mandatory arbitration clause such as seen in Annex 3. However, the scope of an US/EU air transport agreement could be expected to be greater than the existing bilateral agreements and the US agreement with some APEC countries, and the appropriate wording of a conflict settlement mechanism therefore needs to be drafted very carefully. An interesting possibility might be if, in spite of the exemption of air transport from the GATS principles, it were possible to use the conflict settlement procedures of the WTO (DSU). They have turned out to be reasonably speedy and robust for trade in goods. The GATS agreement is in principle universally applicable to all service sectors. However, in reality air transport has been nearly completely exempted and among WTO members the real application depends on the extent of their respective commitments with respect to covered services. Nevertheless, an air transport agreement between the EU and the US should not be a closed one but could be open to participation by other countries. There might therefore exist a possibility that such an agreement could be taken up in the context of the air transport annex. However, there have only been three services disputes among the 200 or so submitted to the Dispute Settlement Body. It would be fair to say that this limited track record has not yet won the confidence of the air transport community in the possible application of the DSU to air transport.

ICAO is also involved in dispute settlement. First, disputes arising under the Chicago Convention, such as the hushkits dispute and other environmental, safety, and air navigation issues, can be presented to the ICAO Council if the efforts of the parties to negotiate a settlement have failed. This procedure has only been invoked five times, and all cases were resolved before a Council decision was rendered, negotiated through the good offices of the Council president and others. A Council decision may be appealed to the International Court of Justice. The relevant provisions of the Chicago Convention can be seen in Annex 5. The other relevant ICAO activity is its involvement in compiling guidance materials and model provisions for agreements exchanging economic rights. In this connection, ICAO is now preparing a draft template air services agreement to include dispute settlement provisions. These drafts can be seen in Annex 6.

So already there are several concepts for future settlement of aviation disputes. The framers of such agreements will have to consider the trade-off between simplicity, which seems to have worked fairly well so far, and refinement to deal with additional areas of disagreement. If a conflict settlement procedure needs to be incorporated in the US/EU agreement it is clear that it needs to be speedy and robust, since it is foreseen that matters concerning the application of competition (antitrust) rules and state aid rules might also need to be incorporated in the agreement, and the very survival of air carriers may depend on the resolution of such issues.

The elements of the existing co-operation agreement would be useful since they permit the exchange of information and the designation of one party as the lead party in the investigation of such matters. However, it would probably be necessary to go further and introduce the principle that when it is reasonably clear what one party will do then the other party should take that into account in deciding what it will do. The best possible outcome of such a procedure would naturally be if the second party were satisfied with the action of the first, but such an outcome would probably only be possible if considerable consultation took place. However, consultation can only constitute a first phase in any conflict settlement procedure. Seen as a whole the procedures must be speedy and cover: consultation, transparency, a forum to formally discuss the conflict and potential solutions, binding arbitration, and interim measures.

The EU, I believe, would be willing to go quite far. In the agreement which has been negotiated on a European Common Aviation Area, there are indeed clauses that open the way for binding arbitration. It is in this context that the GATS procedures might be useful. If this is not possible it is naturally feasible to use the ICAO Council in a similar manner, but ICAO does not have experience in dealing with economic issues such as mentioned above. Furthermore, until now ICAO has not really recognized the existence of the EU. Moreover, the EU member states still are individual members of ICAO.

A conflict settlement procedure, which is based on other air transport agreements negotiated by the EU but without the involvement of the ECJ, is shown in Annex 4. It is fairly close to a procedure accepted by the US in a bilateral agreement as seen in Annex 3. The difficulty with the US would probably lie in the fact that conflicts could also come up in the areas of application of the antitrust rules. On the other hand a procedure of this kind might be very welcome to deal with state aid problems, which are not covered in any of the existing bilateral agreements. At any rate, by comparing the two texts it would seem that the differences are not of such a nature that a bridge would be impossible. The main differences would seem to be that the bilateral procedure in Annex 3 does not include provisions on regular (periodic) consultation and nothing on interim measures. The procedure in Annex 4, on the other hand, is less specific on the presentation of the cases before the arbitration panel. However, both of these procedures would be speedier than the WTO DSU.

V. CONCLUSION

It is clear that in air transport there has so far been no need to develop any specific conflict settlement procedures between the US and the EU except for the early warning procedure. However, this situation is probably coming to an end, and it is time that serious thought is given to developing the most appropriate procedures in the context of an agreement between the US and the EU. Such procedures will have to be speedy, robust and cover: consultation, transparency, a forum to formally discuss the conflict and potential solutions, binding arbitration, and interim measures. It is high time that interested parties on both sides of the Atlantic begin to give it some thought. The ECJ should give its ruling in the Open Skies cases later this year and at that time it would be useful if some constructive thinking had taken place.

ANNEX 1: GRADUAL DEVELOPMENT OF EU AIR TRANSPORT POLICY

	Interregional 1983	1st pckge 1987	2 pckge 1990	cargo 1991	3 pckge 1992/93
Geographical scope					
Regional airports	x	x	x	x	x
Regional/main airports		x	x	x	x
Main airports			x	x	x
Domestic					x
Traffic Rights					
Multiple designation	x	x	x	x	
3/4 freedom	x	x	x	x	x
5 freedom		(x)	(x)	x	x
6 freedom	x	x	x	x	x
7 freedom				x	x
8 freedom					x
9 freedom					1997
Public service			(x)		x
Tariffs					
Cost relatedness	x	x	x		(x)
Flexibility zones		x	x		
Double disapproval			(x)		
Matching		x	x		
Free pricing				x	x
Capacity					
(60–40)		x			
60–40+			x		
Free	x			x	x
Air carrier licensing					
Economic fitness					x
Technical fitness					x
Ownership					x
Leasing rules					x
Carrier rights					
Against foreign state					
tariffs	x	x	x	x	x
capacity	x	x	x	x	x
access	x	x	x	x	x
licensing					x

(*Continued*)

ANNEX: (*Continued*)

	Interregional 1983	1st pckge 1987	2 pckge 1990	cargo 1991	3 pckge 1992/93
Against home state					
tariffs	x	x	x	x	x
capacity	x				x
access					x
licensing					x

ANNEX 2: PRIORITY LIST FOR AIR TRANSPORT APPROVED BY THE COUNCIL IN JUNE 1978

1. Common standards restricting the emission of nuisances due to aircraft;
2. Simplification of formalities (facilitation), particularly those relating to air freight;
3. Implementation of technical standards (JAR);
4. Provisions regarding aids and competition;
5. Mutual recognition of licences (aircrew and ground staff);
6. Working conditions (aircrew and ground staff);
7. Right of establishment;
8. Possible improvements to inter-regional services;
9. Search, rescue and recovery operations, and accident enquiries.

ANNEX 3: CONFLICT SETTLEMENT PROCEDURES IN A US BILATERAL AGREEMENT

Consultations

Either Party may, at any time, request consultations relating to this Agreement. Such consultations shall begin at the earliest possible date, but not later than 60 days from the date the other Party receives the request unless otherwise agreed.

Settlement of disputes

1. Any dispute arising under this Agreement, except those that may arise under paragraph x of Article y (Pricing) that is not resolved by a first round of formal consultations may be referred by agreement of the Parties for decision to some person or body. If the Parties do not so agree, the dispute shall, at the request of either Party, be submitted to arbitration in accordance with the procedures set forth below.

2. Arbitration shall be by a tribunal of three arbitrators to be constituted as follows:

   a. Within 30 days after the receipt of a request for arbitration, each Party shall name one arbitrator. Within 60 days after these two arbitrators have been named, they shall by agreement appoint a third arbitrator, who shall act as President of the arbitral tribunal;

b. If either Party fails to name an arbitrator, or if the third arbitrator is not appointed in accordance with subparagraph a of this paragraph, either Party may request the President of the Council of the International Civil Aviation Organization to appoint the necessary arbitrator or arbitrators within 30 days. If the President of the Council is of the same nationality as one of the Parties, the most senior Vice President who is not disqualified on that ground shall make the appointment.

3. Except as otherwise agreed, the arbitral tribunal shall determine the limits of its jurisdiction in accordance with this Agreement and shall establish its own procedural rules. The tribunal, once formed, may recommend interim relief measures pending its final determination. At the direction of the tribunal or at the request of either of the Parties, a conference to determine the precise issues to be arbitrated and the specific procedures to be followed shall be held not later than 15 days after the tribunal is fully constituted.

4. Except as otherwise agreed or as directed by the tribunal, each Party shall submit a memorandum within 45 days of the time the tribunal is fully constituted. Replies shall be due 60 days later. The tribunal shall hold a hearing at the request of either Party or on its own initiative within 15 days after replies are due.

5. The tribunal shall attempt to render a written decision within 30 days after completion of the hearing or, if no hearing is held, after the date both replies are submitted. The decision of the majority of the tribunal shall prevail.

6. The Parties may submit requests for clarification of the decision within 15 days after it is rendered and any clarification given shall be issued within IS days of such request.

7. Each Party shall, to the degree consistent with its national law, give full effect to any decision or award of the arbitral tribunal.

8. The expenses of the arbitral tribunal, including the fees and expenses of the arbitrators, shall be shared equally by the Parties. Any expenses incurred by the President of the Council of the International Civil Aviation Organization in connection with the procedures of paragraph 2b of this Article shall be considered to be part of the expenses of the arbitral tribunal.

ANNEX 4: AUTHOR'S SUGGESTED CONFLICT SETTLEMENT PROCEDURE FOR US/EU AIR TRANSPORT AGREEMENT

Joint Committee

Article x

1. A Joint Committee is hereby established which shall be responsible for the administration of this Agreement and shall ensure its proper implementation.

2. The Joint Committee shall also include the following Sub-Committees: Safety Sub-Committee, Environment Sub-Committee, Competition Sub-Committee and CRS Sub-Committee. The term 'Joint Committee' in this Agreement shall refer to the Joint Committee and/or the relevant Sub-Committee as appropriate.

3. The Joint Committee shall make recommendations and take decisions in the cases provided for in this Agreement including endorsement of SARPS. The decisions of the Joint Committee shall be put into effect by the Parties in accordance with their own rules.

4. The Joint Committee shall act by mutual agreement.

5. For the purpose of the proper implementation of this Agreement, the Parties shall exchange information and, at the request of any Party, shall hold consultations within the Joint Committee.

6. The Joint Committee shall adopt its own rules of procedure at the latest 21 days after the entry into force of this Agreement.

7. The Joint Committee shall consist of representatives of the Parties.

8. The Joint Committee shall meet at least once a year in order to review the general functioning of this Agreement, draw and update a list of arbitrators for the purposes of Article y, and whenever special circumstances so require, at the request of a Party.

9. The Joint Committee may decide to set up any working party that can assist it in carrying out its duties.

10. All activities of the Joint Committee shall be covered by professional secrecy.

Article xx

1. A decision of the Joint Committee shall be binding upon the Parties. Whenever a decision taken by the Joint Committee contains a request for action to be taken by a Party, the said Party shall take the necessary measures and inform the Joint Committee thereof.

2. The decisions of the Joint Committee shall be published in the Official Journals of the Parties. Each decision shall state the date of its implementation by the Parties and any other information likely to concern economic operators. The decisions shall be submitted if necessary for ratification or approval by the Parties in accordance with their own procedures.

Dispute settlement

Article y

1. A Party may bring a matter under dispute which concerns the interpretation or application of this Agreement before the Joint Committee.

2. A Party which deems that action by another Party is causing injustice or hardship to it, may request the Joint Committee to examine the situation. The

Joint Committee shall thereupon inquire into the matter, and shall call the Parties concerned into consultation. Should such consultation fail to resolve the difficulty, the Joint Committee may make appropriate findings and recommendations to the Parties concerned. If thereafter a Party shall in the opinion of the Joint Committee unreasonably fail to take suitable corrective action, the Joint Committee by a two-thirds vote may decide that such Party be suspended from its rights and privileges under this Agreement until such action has been taken.

3. The Joint Committee may resolve the dispute by means of a decision. It shall be provided with all information which might be of use in making possible an in-depth examination of the situation, with a view to finding an acceptable solution. To this end, the Joint Committee shall examine all possibilities to maintain the good functioning of the Agreement.

4. If the Joint Committee after three months from the date when the matter has been brought before it has not succeeded to resolve the dispute, any party to the dispute may refer the dispute to arbitration.

Each party to the dispute shall nominate an arbitrator within one month. The Joint Committee shall also nominate one, who shall act as President of the panel, within one month. If either Party or the Joint Committee fails to nominate an arbitrator, either Party may request the President of the Council of the International Civil Aviation Organisation to appoint the arbitrator or arbitrators.

The panel's decisions shall be taken by majority vote within three months from its constitution. Whenever a decision taken by the panel contains a request for action to be taken by a party to the dispute, the said party shall take the necessary measures and inform the panel thereof.

Emergency measures

Article z

A Party, in the case it considers that another Party has failed to fulfil an obligation under this Agreement, may take appropriate emergency measures, provided that the requirements of Articles **zz** and **zzz** are fulfilled.

Article zz

(Substantive requirements)
Emergency measures shall be restricted with regard to their scope and duration to what is strictly necessary in order to remedy the situation. Priority shall be given to such measures as will least disturb the functioning of this Agreement.

Article zzz

(Procedural requirements)

1. A Party which is considering taking emergency measures shall notify the other Party through the Joint Committee and shall provide all relevant information.
2. The Parties shall immediately enter into consultations in the Joint Committee with a view to finding a commonly acceptable solution.
3. The Party concerned may not take emergency measures until [one month] has elapsed after the date of notification under paragraph 1, unless the consultation procedure under paragraph 2 has been concluded before the expiration of the stated time limit. When exceptional circumstances [affecting vital safety or security interests] and requiring immediate action exclude prior examination, the Party concerned may apply forthwith the emergency measures strictly necessary to remedy the situation.
4. The Party concerned shall, without delay, notify the measures taken to the Joint Committee and shall provide all relevant information.

ANNEX 5: CHICAGO CONVENTION

Chapter XVIII—disputes and default

Articles 84: Settlement of disputes

If any disagreement between two or more contracting States relating to the interpretation or application of this Convention and its Annexes cannot be settled by negotiation, it shall, on the application of any State concerned in the disagreement, be decided by the Council. No member of the Council shall vote in the consideration by the Council of any dispute to which it is a party. Any contracting State may, subject to Article 85, appeal from the decision of the Council to an ad hoc arbitral tribunal agreed upon with the other parties to the dispute or to the Permanent Court of International Justice. Any such appeal shall be notified to the Council within sixty days of receipt of notification of the decision of the Council.

Article 85: Arbitration procedure

If any contracting State party to a dispute in which the decision of the Council is under appeal has not accepted the Statute of the Permanent Court of International Justice and the contracting States parties to the dispute cannot agree on the choice of the arbitral tribunal, each of the contracting State parties to the dispute shall name a single arbitrator who shall name an umpire. If either contracting State party to the dispute fails to name an arbitrator within a period of three months from the date of the appeal, an arbitrator shall be named on behalf of that State by the President of the Council from a list of qualified and available persons maintained by the Council. If, within thirty days, the arbitrators cannot agree on an umpire, the President of the Council shall designate an umpire from the list previously referred to. The arbitrators and the umpire shall then jointly constitute an arbitral tribunal. Any arbitral tribunal established under this or the preceding Article shall settle its own procedure and give its decisions by majority vote, provided that the Council may determine procedural questions in the event of any delay which in the opinion of the Council is excessive.

Article 86: Appeals

Unless the Council decides otherwise any decision by the Council on whether an international airline is operating in conformity with the provisions of this Convention shall remain in effect unless reversed on appeal. On any other matter, decisions of the Council shall, if appealed from, be suspended until the appeal is decided. The decisions of the Permanent Court of International Justice and of an arbitral tribunal shall be final and binding.

Article 87: Penalty for non-conformity of airline

Each contracting State undertakes not to allow the operation of an airline of a contracting State through the airspace above its territory if the Council has decided that the airline concerned is not conforming to a final decision rendered in accordance with the previous Article.

Article 88: Penalty for non-conformity by state

The Assembly shall suspend the voting power in the Assembly and in the Council of any contracting State that is found in default under the provisions of this Chapter.

ANNEX 6: SUGGESTED MODEL CLAUSES FROM DRAFT ICAO TEMPLATE AGREEMENT REGARDING DISPUTE SETTLEMENT AND CONSULTATION

Consultation

Alternative one

In the spirit of close co-operation, the aeronautical authorities of the Parties shall consult each other from time to time with a view to ensuring the implementation of and satisfactory compliance with the provisions of this Agreement.

(Latv-Denm #4027)

Alternative two

1. Either Party may, at any time, request consultations [relating to this Agreement] [on the interpretation, application, implementation or amendment of this Agreement or compliance with this Agreement].
2. Such consultations [which may be through discussion or by correspondence] shall begin within a period of 60 days from the date the other Party receives a [written or oral] request, unless otherwise agreed by the Parties.

(Icld-US #4369)

Note: The consultation process which may be seen as a regular process ('shall consult from time to time') or is triggered only when one Party requests it, is based on a relatively standardised formula although there are a number of different approaches in wording with regard to the purpose of the consultation, the format of the consultation and the form of the request. When the purposes of the consultation are spelled out one of the purposes may be amendment or modification of the agreement. A consultation provision may be found in this form in both traditional as well as liberalized or 'open skies' agreements, although the 'request' rather than the 'time to time' formulation is more likely to be used in liberalized or 'open skies' agreements, where the need for regular consultation may be considered to be less. The consultation provision is normally general in scope and some issues, such as aviation security and safety, but also capacity and tariffs, as well as amendment of the agreement, may be subject to separate and specific consultation processes as regards purpose, time-frames and so on.

A consultation provision would be necessary in a regional or plurilateral agreement but would require adaptation from the alternatives above to address, in particular, the extent to which, and basis on which, third parties from within that agreement could become parties to the consultation process. One criteria could be that they have a 'substantial interest in the subject matter of the consultations'. The possibility that one or more parties might initiate a consultation process would also need to be addressed.

Settlement of disputes

Alternative one

1. Any dispute arising between the Parties relating to the interpretation or application of this Agreement, [except those that arise under Article _ (Fair competition), Article - (Safety)] the Parties shall in the first place endeavour to settle it by [consultation and] negotiation.

2. If the Parties fail to reach a settlement by negotiation, the dispute may at the request of either Party, be submitted for decision to a Tribunal of three arbitrators, one to be named by each Party and the third to be agreed upon by the two arbitrators so chosen, provided that the third such arbitrator shall not be a national of either Party. Each Party shall designate an arbitrator within a period of sixty (60) days from the date of receipt by either Party from the other Party of a diplomatic note requesting arbitration of the dispute, and the third arbitrator shall be agreed upon within a further period of sixty (60) days. If either of the Parties fails to designate its own arbitrator within the period of sixty (60) days or if the third arbitrator is not agreed on within the period indicated, the President of the Council of ICAO may be requested by either Party to appoint an arbitrator or arbitrators. If the

President is of the same nationality as one of the Parties, the most senior Vice President who is not disqualified on that ground shall make the appointment.

3. The arbitration tribunal shall determine its own procedure.
4. The expenses of the tribunal shall be shared equally between the Parties.
5. The Parties undertake to comply with any decision given under paragraph 2 of this Article.
6. If and so long as either Party fails to comply with any decision given under paragraph 2, the other Party may limit, withhold or revoke any rights or privileges which it has granted by virtue of this agreement to the Party in default or to the designated airline or airlines in default.

(Latv-Denm #4027)

Alternative two

1. Any dispute arising between the Parties relating to the interpretation or application of this Agreement, [except those that arise under Article _ (Fair competition), Article - (Safety)] the Parties shall in the first place endeavour to settle it by [consultation and] negotiation.
2. If the Parties fail to reach a settlement by negotiation, the dispute may at the request of either Party, be submitted for decision to a Tribunal of three arbitrators, one to be named by each Party and the third to be agreed upon by the two arbitrators so chosen, provided that the third such arbitrator shall not be a national of either Party. Each Party shall designate an arbitrator within a period of sixty (60) days from the date of receipt by either Party from the other Party of a diplomatic note requesting arbitration of the dispute, and the third arbitrator shall be agreed upon within a further period of sixty (60) days. If either of the Parties fails to designate its own arbitrator within the period of sixty (60) days or if the third arbitrator is not agreed on within the period indicated, the President of the Council of ICAO may be requested by either Party to appoint an arbitrator or arbitrators. If the President is of the same nationality as one of the Parties, the most senior Vice President who is not disqualified on that ground shall make the appointment.
3. Except as otherwise agreed, the arbitration tribunal shall determine the limits of its jurisdiction in accordance with this Agreement and shall establish its own procedure. At the direction of the tribunal or at the request of either of the Parties, a conference to determine the precise issues to be arbitrated and the specific procedures to be followed shall be held no later than fifteen (15) days after the tribunal is fully constituted.
4. Except as otherwise agreed by the Parties or prescribed by the tribunal, each Party shall submit a memorandum within forty-five (45) days of the time the tribunal is fully constituted. Replies shall be due sixty (60) days later. The tribunal shall hold a hearing at the request of either Party or at its discretion within fifteen (15) days after replies are due.

5. The tribunal shall attempt to render a written decision within thirty (30) days after completion of the hearing or, if no hearing is held, after the date both replies are submitted. The decision of the majority of the tribunal shall prevail.
6. The Parties may submit requests for clarification of the decision within fifteen (15) days after it is rendered and any clarification given shall be issued within fifteen (15) days of such request.
7. Each Party shall [to the degree consistent with its national law] give full effect to any decision or award of the tribunal.

(OR)

The decision of the tribunal shall be binding on the Parties.

8. The expenses of the tribunal shall be shared equally between the Parties.

(OR)

Each Party shall bear the costs of the arbitrator appointed by it. The other costs of the tribunal shall be shared equally by the Parties, including any expenses incurred by the President of the Council of ICAO in implementing the procedures in paragraph 3 of this Article.

9. If and so long as either Party fails to comply with any decision given under paragraph 2, the other Party may limit, withhold or revoke any rights or privileges which it has granted by virtue of this agreement to the Party in default or to the designated airline or airlines in default.

(Mong-Sing # 3805)

Alternative three

Any dispute arising between the Parties relating to the interpretation or application of this Agreement, shall be settled by direct negotiations between the aeronautical authorities of the Parties. If the Parties fail to reach a settlement by negotiation the dispute shall be settled through diplomatic channels.

(Malb-Souf # 3774)

Note: There are three basic approaches to the settlement of disputes, although a fourth one regarding disputes on airline competitive practices arising in a liberalized agreement is set out in the following Article. Common to all of the three alternatives above is the referral of any dispute initially to the consultation process and/or direct negotiation between the Parties. Should that process fail to produce an agreement, or the Parties fail to reach a settlement of the dispute, then the approach is in the first two alternatives to either provide for the establishment of a three person arbitration tribunal but to leave it either to the tribunal to establish its own procedures (the first alternative above), or to set out not only the appointment process for the arbitrators but also the procedures, with time-frames, to be followed (the second alternative above).

The third approach is to refer an unsettled dispute to resolution through diplomatic channels. Within the first two approaches there are different approaches possible on the implementation of a tribunal decision and the division of the expenses. Furthermore, the nature of the matters that are to be addressed by the dispute settlement mechanism may differ. There may be a separate consultation process with regard to the article on fair competition (see below) or with regard to the article on safety and the first two alternatives above take this into account as optional wording. The arbitration process in bilateral air services agreements has rarely been used in practice, in part because of its costs and the time involved, though also because most disputes do not get beyond the stage of negotiation.

A settlement of disputes provision in a regional or plurilateral agreement could be one of the most difficult provisions to negotiate. Any of the three alternatives above could be the basis for such an article.

Dispute settlement for unfair competitive practices

1. Any dispute involving unfair competitive practices pursuant to Article _ which cannot be settled by consultations, may at the request of either Party be submitted to a dispute settlement panel. Such a panel may be used for mediation, determination of the substance of the dispute or to recommend a remedy or resolution of the dispute. The parties shall agree in advance on the terms of reference of the panel, the guiding principles or criteria, including the possibility of interim relief, and terms of access to the panel, bearing in mind the objective and need for a simple, responsive and expeditious process.

2. A panel may be constituted by an individual expert or experts drawn from a list of suitably qualified list of experts maintained by ICAO. The selection of the expert or experts shall be completed within fifteen (15) days of receipt of the request for submission to a panel. If the Parties fail to agree on the selection of expert or experts the selection may be referred to the President of the Council of ICAO. Any expert used for this mechanism should be adequately qualified in the general subject matter of the dispute.

3. A mediation should be completed within sixty (60) days of engagement of the mediator and any determination including, if applicable, any recommenda- tions, should be rendered within sixty (60) days of engagement of the expert or experts. The Parties may agree in advance that the panel may grant interim relief to the complainant, if requested, in which case a determination shall be made initially.

4. The Parties shall use their best efforts to implement the decision or deter- mination of the panel, unless they agree in advance to be bound such decision or determination. If the Parties agree in advance to request only a determin- ation of the facts, they shall use those facts for resolution of the dispute.

5. The costs of this mechanism shall be estimated upon initiation and appor- tioned equally, but with the possibility of re-apportionment under the final decision.

6. The mechanism is without prejudice to the continuing use of the consultation process or the subsequent use of arbitration under Article _ , or Termination under Article _.

Note: To address those commercial disputes, such as on pricing, capacity and other competitive practices that arise in a liberalized environment, and for which therefore an efficient and effective dispute settlement mechanism is needed, ICAO has developed guidance and a possible mechanism for use in the context of safeguards. The earlier article on safeguards gives effect to this ICAO guidance. The related article above provides for a specific mechanism for dispute settlement for unfair competitive practices. This dispute settlement mechanism is not intended as a substitute for the formal arbitration process, but rather as a means to resolve in a relatively simple, responsive and cost effective manner the kinds of disputes between the airlines over unfair competitive practices that are likely to arise when the Parties have agreed to move to a liberalized environment. The normal consultation process may resolve such disputes but could also have the effect of prolonging an unfair competitive practice to the commercial detriment of one or more airlines. Consequently, the above procedure, which is less formal and time consuming than arbitration, is designed, by means of a panel, to reach a resolution through mediation, fact finding or decision, using the services of an expert or experts in the subject matter of the dispute. The primary objective is to enable the Parties to restore a healthy competitive environment in the airline market place as expeditiously as possible. The mechanism requires the Parties to agree in advance on such matters as the purpose of the panel, viz its terms of reference and procedure, and in particular whether the panel is permitted to grant any interim or injunctive relief to the complainant. Such relief could take the form, for example, of a temporary freeze or reversion to the status quo ante. The two important time-frames built in to the mechanism are 15 days for selection of the experts to constitute the panel, and 60 days for the rendering of a decision or determination. Thus the emphasis is on minimising legal formalities and procedural time-frames, yet allowing adequate time for the panel to arrive at a decision or determination.

However, the use of the mechanism does not preclude the implementation of the arbitration process if that is also provided for in the agreement and if the above mechanism has failed to resolve the dispute to the satisfaction of one or more Parties. Nevertheless, it may be expected that the subsequent use of arbitration should be unnecessary if the Parties have committed to this complementary procedure for resolving certain kinds of commercial and time sensitive disputes.

With modifications, such as with regard to who would be the parties of standing in a dispute, this provision is suitable for adaptation as a specific dispute settlement mechanism when a safeguards provision is included in a regional or plurilateral agreement.

16

Dispute Prevention and Dispute Settlement in the Field of Intellectual Property Rights and Electronic Commerce: US—Section 211 Omnibus Appropriations Act 1998 ('Havana Club')

F.M. ABBOTT and T. COTTIER *

This case-study forms part of a collective work directed at examining whether WTO dispute settlement is functioning adequately in resolving disputes between the European Union (and its member states) and the United States, and to what extent there might be developed within the context of the Transatlantic Partnership useful alternative methods for resolving such disputes. While this case-study requires an elaboration of the factual background of the subject dispute and reference to the legal analysis and outcome at the WTO, the objective is neither to re-litigate nor to critically analyze the work product of the WTO dispute settlement system from a legal standpoint. The objective rather is to consider whether it might have been practicable to avoid WTO dispute settlement and whether such avoidance would have been preferable to the existing situation.

This case-study was initially prepared and presented by Professor Abbott at the Project participants' meeting in Florence. Professor Cottier acted as commentator, and subsequently prepared a written comment. The case-study author and commentator agreed that readers might benefit from having different perspectives on the implications of this case. We essentially agreed on legal analysis from the standpoint of interpretation of the TRIPS Agreement and Paris Convention. Our differences do not concern the decision of the panel and the Appellate Body, but rather what conclusions might reasonably be drawn from this 'legal event'. We have not tried to synthesize our contributions in the sense of producing a 'unified view', but instead set out a dialogue identifying our contributions.

* T. Cottier is indebted to Jianqiang Nie, research fellow at the WTI, for reviewing and amending his contribution.

Professor Abbott: As a general conclusion this case-study suggests that the dispute between Pernod Ricard, a France-based multinational distiller and distributor, and Bacardi-Martini, a US-based multinational distiller and distributor, should have been resolved as a private commercial dispute and not as a systemic test of world trade system rules. In this regard, third party arbitration or mediation under the auspices of an alternative dispute settlement forum may have proven quite helpful. Each private actor in the case entered into a commercial venture fully cognizant of ownership risks inherent in claims to intangible property that had been taken by the government of Cuba in the early 1960s. Both private parties sought the protection of their home government external commercial apparatus to ameliorate the consequences of the risks knowingly undertaken. Both the European Commission and the US Trade Representative (USTR) co-operated in converting the private commercial dispute into an international political dispute.

By politicizing the dispute, both the EU and US found themselves arguing legal positions that are most likely contrary to their longer term commercial interests. The major problem, however, is that a victory for the EU in WTO dispute settlement, which as a practical matter it did not achieve, would have entitled it to withdraw trade concessions from the US to enforce compliance. The withdrawal of such concessions would not directly benefit Pernod Ricard, and would likely harm US private operators other than Bacardi-Martini. In sum, the acts of the two private operators in knowingly taking risks in entering into legally tainted commercial relationships would result in harm to private operators that had not been a party to the risk-taking.

On the positive side in regard to WTO dispute settlement, the European Commission may have viewed this as the only practical way to diffuse internal political pressure being exerted by Pernod Ricard under the guise of 'Cuba policy'.[1] Either outcome at the WTO level would allow the Commission to take the position that the EU had exhausted avenues of recourse against the US in this matter, and thereby diffuse the dispute.

Similarly, if the WTO dispute settlement decision had been adverse to the US, this would have provided a means by which the USTR could have resisted further pressures to act on behalf of its private constituent. Because the decision of the Appellate Body requires only an insubstantial modification to US law, it is doubtful that it will have a significant impact on internal or external US policy.

It is difficult at this stage to say whether an alternative dispute settlement forum might have accomplished a similar end, or for that matter whether an end has been accomplished. The case remains open in terms of compliance by the US with the ruling of the Appellate Body.

Professor Cottier: Professor Abbott discusses *United States—section 211 Omnibus Appropriations Act of 1998* for his case-study on dispute prevention

---

[1] Bacardi has also invoked 'Cuba policy' from a US political standpoint, so this is not to paint either private operator in a more or less favourable light.

and dispute settlement relating to the third leg of the WTO legal order—the protection of intellectual property rights. The case is well chosen, given its complexity, its context of national security interests of the US, and its impact on transatlantic relations. The author ably analyzes the case and discusses it in perspective of the issues and questions raised by this project.[2] We should note at the outset that this is not a case primarily addressing intellectual property, let alone electronic commerce. The prime issue before the panel and the Appellate Body was whether section 211 of the Omnibus Appropriations Act of 1998 which bans protection and recognition of trademarks and trade names in connection with Cuban business relations, is compatible with the TRIPS agreement. It is a case more closely related to security and embargo policies affecting not only Cuban, but also European interests. It is not typical for transatlantic IPR related disputes. Before addressing the *problematique* of the case, it is therefore useful to recall briefly the overall record of transatlantic IPR disputes under the TRIPS Agreement. Here my point is that the WTO system has served transatlantic relations well and proves that WTO is a proper place to address IPR issues.

The overall record from 1995 to the end of April 2002 shows that 24 complaints were filed under the TRIPS Agreement. This amounts to nearly 10 per cent of all complaints.[3] The number of TRIPS cases that reached adjudicative dispute settlement panels and the Appellate Body and were adopted by the DSB, was seven (ie, 29.1 per cent of all TRIPS cases, much higher than the 23.5 per cent of the overall average).[4] Nine cases were settled by negotiations (ie, 37.5 per cent of all TRIPS cases), which is also significantly higher than the average of 13.7 per cent for all WTO cases.[5] This perhaps reflects the relatively clear nature of rights and obligations under the TRIPS Agreement, leaving governments little choice but to accept the need to adjust domestic legislation. Given the legislative history of the TRIPS Agreement, one might assume that most disputes relate to developing countries. It is, however, interesting to observe that the first years of the WTO show recourse predominantly in transatlantic relations. Of 15 complaints by the US and one by Canada, eight were addressed to the EC and its member states. The EC made seven complaints, four of them in a transatlantic context. Significantly, the EC was most assertive in bringing panel and Appellate Body proceedings. Out of seven cases adjudicated up to that point, five cases were brought by the EC. Two were directed against the US (including section 211 OAA) and two against Canada. The interpretation of fair use exceptions both in copyright and patent law brought about important clarification. Notably, both

[2] See the list of questions suggested for the case-studies in Ernst-Ulrich Petersmann's introduction to this volume, at pp. 4–5.
[3] The total number of complaints notified to the WTO since 1 January 1995 up to 30 April 2002 is 255, WT/DS/OV/6, p ii.
[4] The number of Panels and Appellate Body Reports adopted since 1 January 1995 to 30 April 2002 is 60 (23.5 per cent of all notified complaints).
[5] The total number of mutually agreed solutions in WTO since 1 January 1995 up to 30 April 2002 is 35 (13.7 per cent of all notified complaints).

reports were adopted at the panel stage and accepted for implementation. This record shows that dispute settlement in transatlantic relations on IPRs—key issues of leading technology and competitive edge—works well within WTO. While there was criticism in particular in relation to restrictive interpretation of fair use exemptions,[6] it is fair to say that WTO jurisprudence on TRIPS had a good start and laid a solid foundation in its first six years. From this point of view, there certainly is no general need for special third party mediation and transatlantic arbitration which Professor Abbott seems to endorse (Question 10), following proposals made by Professor Petersmann. We add that the same is true in the field of electronic commerce to the extent that domain names are concerned. The existing WIPO ICANN Domain Name Dispute Resolution System provides a forum that is fully operational for transatlantic domain name disputes and does not need further instruments.[7]

(1) Why did the dispute arise? What were the essential facts, incentives, conflicts of interests, and political pressures underlying the dispute?

Professor Abbott: The dispute arose against the backdrop of a long-standing political conflict between the US and Cuba, and a set of legal issues arising out of the takings by the Cuban revolutionary government in the early 1960s of property of Cuban and foreign nationals. Most of the legal conflicts between the US and Cuba regarding pre-revolution ownership of property involved claims of US nationals and were based on Cuba's alleged failure to follow international legal standards in the course of expropriations or nationalizations. There is extensive case-law in the US federal courts regarding this subject matter, and the legal issues arising out of the controversies have led to a number of legislative enactments by the US Congress.[8]

The Havana Club dispute concerns the nationalization by the Cuban revolutionary government of assets, including trademark interests, of Cuban nationals (members of the Arechabala family). The Cuban national owners of the assets were not compensated by the government. The US has taken the position that confiscations of this nature violate its strong public policy, and that the US government is entitled to reject claims of title to property arising out of such confiscations.

The EU and its member states have followed an approach to political relations with the post-revolutionary government of Cuba that is substantially different than that of the US. These differences have resulted in a number of foreign

---

6 See R. Howse, 'The Canadian Generic Medicines Panel: A Dangerous Precedent in Dangerous Times', (2000) 3(4) *JWIP* 493–507.

7 Cf A. Christie, 'The ICANN Domain-Name Dispute Resolution System as a Model for Resolving other Intellectual Property Disputes on the Internet', (2002) 5 *JWIP* 105.

8 See, eg, the seminal act of state doctrine decision of the Supreme Court, *Banco Nacional de Cuba v Sabbatino*, 376 US 398 (1964), as well as *First National City Bank v Banco Nacional de Cuba*, 406 US 759 (1972), and *Alfred Dunhill of London v Republic of Cuba*, 425 US 682 (1976), as evidence of this long-running saga.

political and economic disagreements. The most intense controversy arose following the adoption by the US of Helms-Burton legislation in 1996 that imposed a secondary boycott on transactions involving Cuban assets that in the view of the US were not properly obtained.[9] The US and EU tentatively resolved the Helms-Burton controversy in 1997 with the adoption of an understanding that avoided WTO dispute settlement.

The specific subject matter of the Havana Club dispute arose out of competing efforts by major multinational liquor distilleries and distributors to exploit a trademark that was initially held by the Arechabala family prior to the revolution.

Basic facts

The Arechabala family had owned a liquor producing and distribution business in pre-revolutionary Cuba (Jose Arechabala, SA or JASA). The business produced rum that was marketed under the trademark 'Havana Club'. The trademark was registered by the Arechabala family in Cuba and the US prior to its taking by the Cuban government. Following the taking, the Arechabala family did not renew the trademark registration in the US.

A Cuban government-owned enterprise registered the 'Havana Club' trademark in Cuba (in 1974) and on the Principal Register at the US Patent and Trademark Office (USPTO) (in 1976). That enterprise made and sold rum under the Havana Club trademark outside the US. US legislative restrictions on trade with Cuba prevented the Cuban state enterprise from marketing or selling Havana Club rum in the US.

In the early 1990s, the Cuban state enterprise entered into a joint venture, Havana Club Holding, SA or HCH, with the French Pernod Ricard with a view towards more actively promoting sales of Havana Club rum throughout the world.

In April 1997, Bacardi acquired from the Arechabala family such interests it might have in the trademark and associated rights of the Havana Club related business that it previously operated in Cuba.

Subsequent to purchasing the residual trademark rights in Havana Club from the Arechabala family, Bacardi orchestrated a successful legislative effort in the US Congress essentially aimed at nullifying with retroactive effect the registration by the Cuban state enterprise of the Havana Club mark at the USPTO. This was accomplished by retroactively denying effect to Cuba's assignment of the trademark to the Cuba-Pernod joint venture (HCH), by denying Cuba the right to renew the trademark (the trademark registration has not yet expired), and by instructing US federal courts not to recognize Cuba's claims to rights in the Havana Club mark.

(2) Which national and international, political and legal procedures were used for the settlement of the dispute? Were the applicable domestic procedures

---

[9] See generally A.F. Lowenfeld, 'Agora: The Cuban Liberty and Democratic Solidarity (Libertad) Act, Congress and Cuba: The Helms-Burton Act' (1996) 90 *AJIL* 419.

(eg, section 301 of the US Trade Act, the EC's Trade Barriers Regulation) and international dispute settlement procedures (eg, inside and outside the WTO) adequate? Which changes of the procedures would be desirable in order to reduce the risk of future similar disputes?

Professor Abbott: The Cuban-French joint venture (HCH) brought suit in the US federal district court seeking to enjoin Bacardi from using the trade name and trademark 'Havana Club' in connection with the marketing and sale of rum in the US. The petition was rejected by the federal district court primarily on grounds that legislation adopted by Congress during pendency of the proceeding required that it not recognize HCH's trademark claim, and that HCH's lack of access to the US market precluded it from succeeding on an unfair competition claim.[10] HCH appealed the decision to the US Court of Appeals for the Second Circuit, which upheld the decision of the district court.[11] HCH petitioned the US Supreme Court for a writ of certiorari, and the writ was denied.[12]

Although Pernod Ricard might have been expected to initiate a proceeding under the EU Trade Barriers Regulation seeking that the Commission pursue dispute settlement at the WTO,[13] I have not been able to find the record of such proceeding, nor were the EU officials present at the Florence meeting familiar with such an action in this case.

The claims of the EU against the US arise both under the Paris Convention on the Protection of Industrial Property (Paris Convention) and the WTO Agreement on Trade-Related Aspects of Intellectual Property Rights (TRIPS Agreement). The EU (or France) might have initiated a claim alleging breach of the Paris Convention before the International Court of Justice (see Article 28, Paris Convention). The EU did not pursue such a claim.

When the EU decided to pursue the claim at the WTO it was not challenging the operation of the US court process, but the authority of the legislative and executive branches. The federal courts had examined the claims of HCH exhaustively, and provided complete, well-reasoned and transparent decisions. Those decisions essentially confirmed that the US Congress and Executive Branch had operated within the recognized scope of their legislative authority by denying the Cuban-French joint venture validation of a trademark confiscated without compensation from Cuban nationals.[14]

---

[10] *Havana Club Holding, SA v Galleon, SA*, 62 F Supp 2d 1085 (SDNY 1999).

[11] *Havana Club Holding, SA v Galleon, SA*, 203 F 3d 116 (2d Cir 2000).

[12] *Havana Club Holding, SA v Bacardi*, 531 US 918 (2000).

[13] Council Regulation 3286/94, OJ 1994 L 349 laying down Community procedures in the field of the common commercial policy in order to ensure the exercise of the Community's rights under international trade rules, in particular those established under the auspices of the WTO ('Trade Barriers Regulation').

[14] At the request of a third WTO member, I had analyzed the legal claims involved in this case prior to the decision of the panel and the AB. I concluded that the EU, as a matter of intellectual property law and WTO law, was pursuing a very weak case. This conclusion was ultimately borne out by the decisions of the panel and AB.

In the *US—Havana Club* case,[15] the WTO Appellate Body (AB) applied the rules of the TRIPS Agreement and Paris Convention. The AB confirmed the panel's view that the Paris Convention Article 6 quinquies *telle quelle* ('as is') obligation is addressed to accepting trademarks for registration in the same form, and not to eliminating member discretion to apply rules concerning other rights in marks. It found that Articles 15 and 16 of the TRIPS Agreement do not prevent each member from making its own determination regarding the ownership of marks within the boundaries established by the Paris Convention. It decided that Article 42 regarding procedural rights does not obligate a member to permit adjudication of each substantive claim regarding trademark rights a party might assert, if that party is fairly determined *ab initio* not to be the holder of an interest in the subject mark. In sum, the AB confirmed the right of the US to refuse registration and enforcement of trademarks it determines to have been confiscated in violation of international law.

The AB observed that the national treatment obligation of the Paris Convention extended back to the 1880s, and that the parties to the case before it would be subject to the Paris Convention national treatment rule even were they not parties to the TRIPS Agreement. While the AB referenced both the TRIPS and Paris Convention rules, it did not refer to the different legal formulas used, instead highlighting that the decision to include a national treatment provision in the TRIPS Agreement indicated the 'fundamental significance of the obligation of national treatment to [the framers'] purposes in the *TRIPS Agreement*'.[16]

The panel in the *US—Havana Club* case decided that US legislation regulating trademarks that had been confiscated by the Cuban government was not inconsistent with Article 3, TRIPS Agreement. While there were in fact formal legal differences between the way US nationals and foreign nationals were addressed by the relevant legislation, the panel found that as a practical matter the possibility was extremely remote that a US national would receive preferential treatment. Certain favourable treatment of US nationals would require affirmative administrative action by US regulatory authorities (contrary to the longstanding practice of the authorities to refuse such action), and the US indicated that its regulatory authorities would not in fact act in a way that such preferential treatment would be provided.

The AB rejected the legal analysis of the panel, referring to the *US—Section 337* decision regarding Article III:4, GATT 1947.[17] In that earlier decision, the panel said that even though the possibility for a certain type of discrimination to take place under a legislative arrangement was small, the fact that the possibility

[15] WTO AB, *United States—Section 211 Omnibus Appropriations Act of 1998*, WT/DS176/AB/R, 2 January 2002 ('*US—Havana club*').

[16] Ibid, para 240.

[17] *United States—Section 337 of the Tariff Act of 1930*, Panel Report, adopted 7 November 1989, BISD 36S/345 ('*US—Section 337*').

was present constituted sufficient discrimination to present a national treatment inconsistency. In *US—Havana Club*, the AB said:

The United States may be right that the likelihood of having to overcome the hurdles of both Section 515.201 of Title 31 CFR and Section 211(a)(2) may, echoing the panel in *US—Section 337*, be *small*. But, again echoing that panel, even the *possibility* that non-United States successors-in-interest face two hurdles is *inherently less favourable* than the undisputed fact that United States successors-in-interest face only one. (AB Report, Havana Club, para 265.)

The AB's approach may strike those familiar with the *US—Section 337* decision as strained. In that case, the US had adopted a comprehensive administrative mechanism for patent (and other IP right) holders to seek remedies against infringing imports. That section 337 mechanism contained a number of features making it easier to obtain remedies against imports than to obtain remedies (in domestic infringement proceedings) against goods circulating in the US. One element of the section 337 arrangement (though not the most important one from a discrimination standpoint) was that an importer might in theory be subject to simultaneous proceedings at the US International Trade Commission (ITC) and in federal court regarding the same allegedly infringing conduct. (From a practical standpoint, the major discriminatory feature of the ITC procedure was its failure to allow for alleged infringers to assert patent counterclaims. Also, the ITC procedure was substantially more time-compressed than court proceedings.) From the standpoint of importers, the prospects for discriminatory application of US patent law were real and ever-present. It was not surprising in this context that the section 337 panel rejected US suggestions that the discriminatory features of the legislation were of no practical consequence.

The situation in *US—Havana Club* was significantly different. In *Havana Club* the AB was faced with a consistent US practice of refusing to grant licences of the type with which the EC expressed concern and a stated commitment by the US not to grant such licences in the future. Moreover, factual scenarios posited by the EC in which discrimination issues might arise were extremely unlikely. In this sense, the AB effectively decided that any formal differences in legal procedures would not withstand national treatment scrutiny, even if the practical consequences were extremely remote, and if the government adopting the procedures accepted not to use them.

The AB also applied Article 4, TRIPS Agreement in *US— Havana Club*.[18] The US legislation at issue provided formally different treatment on its face as

---

[18] It said: 'Like the national treatment obligation, the obligation to provide most-favoured-nation treatment has long been one of the cornerstones of the world trading system. For more than fifty years, the obligation to provide most-favoured-nation treatment in Article I of the GATT 1994 has been both central and essential to assuring the success of a global rules-based system for trade in goods. Unlike the national treatment principle, there is no provision in the Paris Convention (1967) that establishes a most-favoured-nation obligation with respect to rights in trademarks or other industrial property. However, the framers of the *TRIPS Agreement* decided to extend the most-favoured-nation obligation to the protection of intellectual property rights covered by that Agreement. As a cornerstone of the

respects nationals of Cuba and other foreign countries ('non-Cuban foreign nationals'). The AB noted again that this established a *prima facie* inconsistency. The US had attempted to rebut this inconsistency by demonstrating that as a practical matter there would be no discrimination among nationals of different foreign countries. The panel had accepted the US position. The AB rejected the panel's holding in reliance on a remote set of hypothetical circumstances suggested by the EC regarding differential treatment of non-US national trademark holders. The AB established an extremely rigorous standard for application of the most-favoured-nation principle which few formal differences in treatment of nationals from different foreign members are likely to survive.[19]

Although the WTO AB identified what it considered to be a minor procedural defect in the mechanism adopted by the US Congress to effectuate its decision

world trading system, the most-favoured-nation obligation must be accorded the same significance with respect to intellectual property rights under the *TRIPS Agreement* that it has long been accorded with respect to trade in goods under the GATT. It is, in a word, fundamental.' Ibid, para 297.

[19] The subject matter scope of the TRIPS Agreement, including its relationship to the WIPO conventions, was also considered in some detail by the AB. The panel in the *Havana Club* case decided that trade names were not 'intellectual property' within the meaning of Article 1.2, TRIPS Agreement, because they were not a 'category' of sections 1 through 7, Part II. The panel went on to consider whether Article 2.1, TRIPS Agreement, by incorporating Article 8, Paris Convention (obligating parties to provide trade name protection), brought trade names within the scope of intellectual property covered by the agreement. The panel reasoned that since Article 2.1, TRIPS Agreement, provided that the referenced Paris Convention articles were to be complied with 'in respect of' Parts II, III and IV of the TRIPS Agreement, and since those parts did not refer to trade names, Article 8, Paris Convention did not add obligations regarding trade names. The panel referred to negotiating history to confirm its conclusion, though the references are somewhat tangential to its reasoning.

The AB disagreed with the panel. It said: '335. ... To our mind, the Panel's interpretation ignores the plain words of Article 1.2, for it fails to take into account that the phrase "the subject of Sections 1 through 7 of Part II" deals not only with the categories of intellectual property indicated in each section *title*, but with other *subjects* as well. For example, in Section 5 of Part II, entitled "Patents", Article 27(3)(b) provides that Members have the option of protecting inventions of plant varieties by *sui generis* rights (such as breeder's rights) instead of through patents. Under the Panel's theory, such *sui generis* rights would not be covered by the *TRIPS Agreement*. The option provided by Article 27(3)(b) would be read out of the *TRIPS Agreement*. 336. Moreover, we do not believe that the Panel's interpretation of Article 1.2 can be reconciled with the plain words of Article 2.1. Article 2.1 explicitly incorporates Article 8 of the Paris Convention (1967) into the *TRIPS Agreement*. 337. The Panel was of the view that the words "in respect of" in Article 2.1 have the effect of "conditioning" Members' obligations under the Articles of the Paris Convention (1967) incorporated into the *TRIPS Agreement*, with the result that trade names are not covered. We disagree. 338. Article 8 of the Paris Convention (1967) covers only the protection of trade names; Article 8 has no other subject. If the intention of the negotiators had been to exclude trade names from protection, there would have been no purpose whatsoever in including Article 8 in the list of Paris Convention (1967) provisions that were specifically incorporated into the *TRIPS Agreement*. To adopt the Panel's approach would be to deprive Article 8 of the Paris Convention (1967), as incorporated into the *TRIPS Agreement* by virtue of Article 2.1 of that Agreement, of any and all meaning and effect.'

The AB's analysis confirms the view that the broad subject matter headings of sections 1 through 7, Part II, do not strictly limit the subject matter scope of 'intellectual property', and that subject matters addressed within the sections are included. This does not mean that the subject matter of 'intellectual property' is unlimited. In the case of trade names, they are covered subject matter because they are specifically incorporated by Article 8, Paris Convention. Nonetheless, to some extent the AB has adopted a broader rather than narrower view of the interpretation of 'intellectual property' in Article 1.2, TRIPS Agreement.

regarding the confiscated trademark, the AB affirmed in its entirety the authority of the Congress and Executive Branch to deny validity to the Cuban-French claim of trademark validity and ownership.

Since the EC's claim that the US lacked the power to deny ownership of the subject mark for the US was unsupported by the relevant international agreements—that is, the Paris Convention and WTO TRIPS Agreement—the EC's motives for initiating its complaint at the WTO were political rather than legal. That is, the EC sought to assure its local political constituency (ie, Pernod Ricard) that it would pursue its claim seriously.

Professor Cottier: I essentially agree with the legal assessment of *United States—Section 211 Appropriations Act of 1998* by Professor Abbott to the extent that it relates to the TRIPS Agreement. While it is possible to argue with the EC that the Act merely restricts the *exercise* of trademark rights and does not affect ownership in principle, it should be recalled that this is a matter of interpreting US domestic law, and thus a matter of fact. The US, under the standards of *India—Patent*[20] was obliged to establish a sound legal basis of its argumentation that the panel and the AB could not ignore. Moreover, the US refrained from invoking national security exceptions under Article 73 TRIPS Agreement which would have allowed even the removal of the procedural issues effectively challenging the Act. Finally, it was impossible to make a non-violation complaint under the present moratorium, and the EC was barred from making a potentially successful argument under the doctrine of protecting legitimate expectations. The case nevertheless contributed to the interpretation of the TRIPS Agreement in two ways: first, the AB clarified the relationship of the TRIPS Agreement and the Paris Convention by rendering WTO law applicable to trade names.[21] Secondly, the AB found that the US violated national treatment, and the most-favoured-nation treatment in procedural terms.[22]

(3) What was the role of private interests in the emergence and settlement of the dispute before, during and after the invocation of WTO dispute settlement procedures?

Professor Abbott: Private interests were responsible for the emergence and settlement of the dispute, and remain in that posture. On the US side, Bacardi sought commercial advantage by obtaining rights of the former Cuban owners of the 'Havana Club' trademark, and Pernod Ricard sought commercial advantage

[20] Paras 64–66 of AB Report, *India—Patent Protection for Pharmaceutical and Agricultural Chemical Products*, AB-1997–5, WT/DS50/AB/R, 19 December 1997.

[21] Para 341 of AB report: *United States—section 211 Omnibus Appropriations Act of 1998*, AB-2001–7, WT/DS176/AB/R, 2 January 2002.

[22] Ibid, para 296. The AB reversed the Panel's finding, and concluded that section 211(a)(2) and 211(b) OAA violated the national treatment obligations under the Paris Convention Article 2(1) and TRIPS Agreement Article 3.1, and the most-favoured-nation obligations under the TRIPS Agreement Article 4 (para 319), as they concerned 'original owners'. AB Report, *United States—section 211 Omnibus Appropriations Act of 1998*, WT/DS176/AB/R, 2 January 2002.

by entering into a joint venture with the Cuban government to exploit the mark. Neither the US nor EU private enterprise had an economic stake in this matter prior to 1990.

Pernod Ricard and Bacardi each successfully engaged the external commercial policy apparatus of its home government to pursue its private interest in this matter. In doing so, the respective governments have transformed a fairly ordinary commercial trademark dispute between two well-financed private enterprises into a matter of high politics, with attendant invocation of national (or regional) political interests.

(4) Which government departments were involved? How did they react to the private complaints? Have they been unduly subservient to industry pressures ('regulatory capture')?

Professor Abbott: The reported facts of the case indicate that on the US side:[23]

(1) Bacardi sought the assistance of members of the US Congress from its home State of Florida to introduce the legislation that would deny HCH rights in the trademark in the US.[24] Congress operated through its ordinary processes to accept the request from Bacardi that legislation be adopted to remedy what Bacardi portrayed as an injustice done to Cuban nationals and an American company providing an economic benefit to those nationals. Elected representatives from the State of Florida wish to appear 'anti-Castro', and the denial of rights in the Havana Club mark would be consistent with such appearance. It is difficult in this instance to draw a line between political interest and regulatory capture by industry since both factors are at work.

(2) The US Treasury Department operates to give effect to legislation affecting US trade with Cuba. In adopting implementing regulations based on the section 211 legislation, it is doubtful that Treasury Department officials maintained an interest in this matter beyond giving effect to the expressed will of the Congress.

(3) The USPTO is under the regulatory jurisdiction of the US Department of Commerce. In its maintenance of the Principal Trademark Register, it is doubtful that the USPTO had an interest in this matter beyond giving effect to the expressed will of Congress. As a former Patent Commissioner has indicated, the USPTO has maintained normal trademark registration relations with Cuba and its nationals.[25]

---

[23] The Reporter of this case has not interviewed the relevant actors to determine the internal course of the proceedings.

[24] See 'Prepared Testimony of Ignacio Sanchez on behalf of Bacardi-Martini before the House Judiciary Committee Subcommittee on Courts and Intellectual Property', *Federal News Service, Lexis-Nexis*, 21 May 1998.

[25] B. Lehman, 'A Victory of Law Over Politics', *NYLJ*, 29 March 2000, at 2, stating: '[t]he Cuban Assets Control Regulations, which create the legal framework for our embargo against Cuba, allow

(4) The US Department of State is responsible for managing foreign political relations with the EU and Cuba, and would defend the expressed congressional interest with representatives of the EU. The Department of State is receptive to pursuing the interests of the US business sector. It is also aware of EU sensitivities on the 'Cuba question', and would have an interest in avoiding disruption of US-EC relations.

(5) The Office of the USTR is principally responsible for conducting relations at the WTO, and would act to defend expressed Congressional will in threats and actions brought against it in WTO dispute settlement proceedings. The USTR is captured by US producer interests, and will only refrain from pursuing the interests of a particular US producer if there are more powerful US producers expressing competing interests.

As far as the EU side is concerned, the author has not conducted an investigation into the actions taken by Pernod Ricard to pursue this matter within the EU. One might assume that it first consulted the French government, including the Ministry of Foreign Affairs and the Ministry of the Economy, Finance and Industry. After overtures to the US Department of State and USTR were unsuccessful, the matter would be raised with the Trade Directorate at the European Commission, either directly or through pressure at the Council of Ministers level. As noted earlier, the author has so far not found reference to a Trade Barriers Regulation proceeding at the Commission.

(5) Which have been the main impediments to an amicable solution of the dispute? What was the role of third parties (states) intervening or involved in the dispute?

Professor Abbott: Each corporate side presumably views the dispute as a zero-sum game in which no compromise is possible. The USTR and the European Commission are acting on behalf of the private interests. The states that had reserved their third party rights in the WTO dispute each appeared to conclude that this was not a case about systemic WTO interests, and elected not to pursue the matter.

(6) Was the dispute due to the inadequacy of the applicable substantive rules (eg, inadequate guidance of 'result-oriented' trade rules stated in terms of trade effects)?

Professor Abbott: As a matter of US constitutional law, it is unarguable that Congress has the power to determine that the US will not recognize the validity

for reciprocal registrations between Cuban and American brands with the U.S. Patent and Trademark Office (PTO). As a former Commissioner of the PTO, I support this tenet, as is helps ensure our respective businesses are not at a competitive disadvantage once the embargo is lifted. Not clear, however, was whether or not these codified regulations applied to trademarks confiscated without compensation.'

of a claim to ownership of a trademark taken in violation of the strongly held public policy of the forum (which Congress also considered to be an action in violation of international law).[26] As a primary demandeur under the TRIPS Agreement, it is paradoxical that the US put itself in the position of advocate of the right of WTO members to determine trademark ownership autonomously; since this is a right that other countries are likely to invoke *vis-à-vis* the US in the future.

The EC made strained arguments concerning the meaning of the TRIPS Agreement trademark rules.

The decision of the WTO AB regarding a minor national treatment issue is the most that could be done to support the EC's position, but it is questionable whether the AB should have gone to such lengths in reliance on a precedent (the *US-Section 337* GATT panel decision) that involved a substantially more concrete national treatment deficiency.

It was not a defect in substantive legal rules that has produced the relevant result.

Professor Cottier: The present case is of prime interest and well chosen in the present context not for its specific IPR issues relating to trademarks and trade name. It is of interest as it raises the issue of lacking remedies and investment protection in EU-US relations. In the light of the assessment by the panel and the AB, section 211 OAA arguably amounts to a retroactive taking of a registered trademark. The legislation introduced by Congress seems to specifically aim at the operation of the European-Cuban joint venture (Havana Club Holding) and its future operations on the US market, all to the benefit of Bacardi-Martini. Constitutionally, it may be qualified as a bill of attainder which specifically seeks to penalize a particular company. Moreover, the legislation results in de facto protection of Bacardi-Martini's use of the trade name Havana Club, leaving competitors without efficient remedies to combat consumer deception and de facto appropriation of the trademark. Given the fact that the taking took place retroactively, many years after formal takings by the Cuban Government, it is difficult to argue that the legislation can be justified as an act of retaliation, in good faith. As a result, the legislation produces structural protectionism for US operators and significantly distorts conditions of competition. From this perspective, it is difficult to agree with Professor Abbott in responding to question 6 that 'it is unarguable that Congress has the power to determine that the US will not recognize the validity of a claim of ownership of a trademark taken in violation of the strongly held public policy of the forum'.[27]

---

[26] In an earlier draft, I had not qualified this statement with the phrase '[a]s a matter of US constitutional law', and Professor Cottier's comment in the following section refers to this unqualified assertion. While my own view is that, as a matter of customary international law, a forum state may refuse to recognize a taking by a foreign state of the property of its own nationals in certain circumstances, I accept that others may differ from this view, and so the proposition is not 'unarguable'.

[27] Supra note 26.

The case therefore may induce further examination as to whether US-EC relationship law needs to be amended in terms of investment protection. This is a matter also to be examined in the light of ongoing work on investment protection in WTO explorations under the mandate of the Doha Round. It would be interesting to explore whether or not and to what extent such interest could be protected under bilateral Investment Protection Agreements of the EU or its member states and the US in the future as no modern and recent agreements exist to this effect.[28] Procedurally, it would be interesting to explore whether the case could be brought before the International Court of Justice, invoking both the Paris Convention, any other agreement and customary international law on expropriation. Procedurally, it should also be explored to what extent the case could be brought before ICSID, the International Centre for the Settlement of Investment Disputes at the World Bank.[29] There is no room to discuss these options here in detail. What it shows, however, is the need to have a closer look at the interface and interaction of different instruments and procedural avenues available. WTO dispute settlement is generally efficient in the field of IPRs. This case suggests that alternative avenues and instruments may be more suitable to address the issue of takings. WTO law does not dispense and replace them, and a coherent overall system of existing or future remedies within and without the WTO is required. It is here, rather than for trade regulation, that perhaps the idea of creating special transatlantic arbitration for taking and regulatory taking of foreign investment could be contemplated.[30]

[28] Among 37 agreements concluded, no specific bilateral investment protection agreement between the US and members of the EU, or the EC itself exists at this time, cf http://www.worldbank.org/icsid/treaties/united-states.htm (visited 21 May 2002).

[29] Many EC members (including Austria, Denmark, France, Germany, Greece, Italy, Netherlands, Spain, Portugal, UK) and the US are parties to the Convention on the Settlement of Investment Disputes Between States and Nationals of Other States. The Convention came into force on 14 October 1966. Pursuant to the Convention, ICSID provides facilities for the conciliation and arbitration of disputes between member countries and investors who qualify as nationals of other member countries. Recourse to ICSID conciliation and arbitration is entirely voluntary, based on assent clause of investment treaty and arbitration clause in contract. However, once the parties have consented to arbitration under the ICSID Convention, neither can unilaterally withdraw its consent. Moreover, all ICSID contracting states, whether or not parties to the dispute, are required by the Convention to recognize and enforce ICSID arbitral awards. On 27 September 1978, the Administrative Council of the Centre authorized the Secretariat to administer at the request of the parties concerned certain proceedings between states and nationals of other states which fall outside the scope of the Convention on the Settlement of Investment Disputes between States and Nationals of Other States. They are (i) conciliation or arbitration proceedings for the settlement of investment disputes arising between parties one of which is not a contracting state or a national of a contracting state; (ii) conciliation or arbitration proceedings between parties at least one of which is a contracting state or a national of a contracting state for the settlement of disputes that do not directly arise out of an investment; and (iii) fact-finding proceedings. Source from the website of ICSID, http://www.worldbank.org/icsid, visited 23 May 2002.

[30] A look at NAFTA might be a source of inspiration, see A.Z. Hertz, 'Proceedings of the Canada-United States Law Institute Conference: NAFTA Revisited: Shaping the Trident: Intellectual Property under NAFTA Investment Protection Agreements and at the World Trade Organization' (1997) 23 *Can-US LJ* 261; D.M. Price 'Supplement: NAFTA Chapter 11 Investor-State Dispute Settlement: Frankenstein or Safety Valve?' (2001) 26 *Can-US LJ* 4.

(7) **Which changes in the applicable substantive rules could reduce the risk of future similar disputes? Is there a need for new additional bilateral or multilateral rules?**

Professor Abbott: This case might be used to raise the broad systemic question whether bringing intellectual property rights rules into the WTO was wise. However, that question might better be addressed in other contexts.

In a narrower context, the case is troubling because it has elevated a single dispute between two private operators into a WTO dispute. The TRIPS Agreement was presumably designed to address systemic IP enforcement issues, and not to serve as a court of appeals on individual cases or controversies. This case may demonstrate that virtually any private dispute can be given a systemic TRIPS character. A question that might be asked is whether there may be some threshold of systemic conduct that could be adopted as a filter within TRIPS rules.[31]

The dispute raises no demand for a change to substantive rules.

Professor Cottier: Professor Abbott argues that both parties co-operated in politicizing a commercial dispute into an international political dispute. They found themselves in a position to argue against long-term systemic interests. Had the EC won the case, it would have been entitled to withdraw concessions harming operators other than Bacardi-Martini in the US.[32] The latter statement assumes that the US would not adjust its legislation and, if this would be the case, reveals a general weakness of the WTO enforcement system. The withdrawal of concessions can be justified in terms of political economy, here in order to create pressure on Congress to repeal the legislation. According to Professor Abbott, it does not make sense in purely economic or commercial terms.

Yet, these constellations are not peculiar to this case. I would argue that most WTO cases emerge from commercial disputes. There are famous examples which are even termed colloquially according to private actors, such as *United States—section 337 of the Tariff Act of 1930* ('Akzo case');[33] *Japan—Photographic Films*

---

[31] See discussion of the issue of establishing a threshold of systemic conduct in F. M. Abbott, 'WTO Dispute Settlement and the Agreement on Trade-Related Aspects of Intellectual Property Rights' in E.-U. Petersmann, *International Trade Law and the GATT/WTO Dispute Settlement System* (1997) at 415.

[32] In particular, Professor Abbott argues that the private parties involved in the dispute might have benefited from a forceful suggestion of third party mediation in order to avoid prolongation of the commercial dispute. The most problematic part of WTO dispute settlement from his point of view is that a result favourable to the EU might have led to the withdrawal of trade concessions *vis-à-vis* the US. This would have had the consequence of injuring US private operators other than the party whose actions precipitated the dispute. This result would be inequitable from the standpoint of unrelated private parties. This argues, according to Professor Abbott, against the use of WTO dispute settlement, and in favour of another type of tribunal whose remedial powers are directed to the relevant private operators. F.M. Abbott, 'Case Study 14: Dispute Prevention and Dispute Settlement in the Field of Intellectual Property Rights and Electronic Commerce', Conference paper for Second Annual Conference, Florence, 3 and 4 May 2002—copy on file with the author.

[33] *United States—section 337 of the Tariff Act of 1930*, Panel Report, adopted on 7 November 1989, BISD 36S/345.

('Kodak-Fuji case').[34] In many more cases, of course, there are private entities who seek governments to instigate the review of national trade remedy measures directly affecting their operations (safeguards, subsidies, anti-dumping). It is therefore not possible to draw a line between systemic and commercial cases. Governments may take the nature of a dispute into account when agreeing to bring a case under section 301 of the US Trade Act,[35] or under the Trade Barriers Regulation,[36] and balance commercial and other foreign policy interests.

In this case, the EC would have been in a position to refrain from bringing a case given its arguably sensitive political and security nature. Perhaps it would have refrained from filing the complaint had there not been strong pressures following the rulings on *Bananas*[37] and *Hormones*.[38] I do not know to what extent the overall constellation is systematically discussed and taken into account between the EC Commission and the US Government in making procedural decisions on launching complaints. The overall economy and management of complaints might be a subject to discuss under a high level diplomatic Early Warning System, to be developed further (questions 8, 10). Even though WTO dispute settlement is explicitly defined not to amount to an unfriendly act and should be pursued as a matter of course, it is inevitable that an escalation of WTO transatlantic disputes may cause irritation and tensions which may spill over into other policy areas. Regular trade dispute monitoring should therefore be made part of a larger and higher level agenda in transatlantic relations.

(8) **Could the Transatlantic Partnership institutions contribute to the settlement of this kind of dispute? Who should initiate any such reforms (eg, for additional bilateral agreements and institutional co-operation between the EC and US)?**

Professor Abbott: Transatlantic Partnership institutions might have contributed to the settlement of this dispute by attempting to mediate the private interest claims. This is a case in which a shared positive outcome may well have been feasible (if not precluded by competition law concerns). For example, Pernod Ricard and Bacardi could have entered into an agreement under which Bacardi held the distribution rights in the US for Havana Club rum attendant on payment of a licensing fee to Pernod Ricard. There would thus be a sharing of the lucrative

---

[34] WT/DS 44/R, 31 March 1998.

[35] Title III, chapter 1, section 301 of the US Trade Act of 1974, as amended (19 USC, para 2411).

[36] Regulation (EC) 3286/94, OJ 1994 L 349.

[37] European Communities—Regime for the Importation, Sale and Distribution of Bananas, Complaint by the United States, WT/DS27/R/USA, 22 May 1997; European Communities—Regime for the Importation, Sale and Distribution of Bananas, Complaint by Mexico, WT/DS27/R/MEX, 22 May 1997; European Communities—Regime for the Importation, Sale and Distribution of Bananas, Complaint by Guatemala, Honduras, and Ecuador, WT/DS27/R/GTM, WT/DS/R/HND, WT/DS/R/ECU, 22 May 1997.

[38] AB, EC Measures Concerning Meat and Meat Products (Hormones), AB-1997-4, WT/DS26/AB/R, 16 January 1998; EC Measures Concerning Meat and Meat Products (Hormones), respectively, complaint by the US and Canada, WT/DS26/R/USA, WT/DS48/R/CAN, 18 August 1997.

US market. Alternatively, Pernod Ricard and Bacardi might have agreed to share access to the US market under the same trademark if and when the US lifts its embargo against imports from Cuba. There can of course be no assurance that the private parties would accept a mediated outcome to the dispute.

The key fact is that both Pernod Ricard and Bacardi understood as they developed their business plans that they were negotiating in a problematic political environment, and both elected to proceed in the face of well-known risks. When the risk factors turned into commercial reality, both sides sought the assistance of the political apparatus of their respective states. By turning their commercial dispute into a political dispute, each side deliberately aggravated US–EC political relations. The USTR and the European Commission in turn rewarded each private actor for its conduct.

Is it credible to suggest that Pernod Ricard is standing up for the right of a revolutionary government to confiscate property, or that Bacardi is standing up for the right of national private property holders to be protected against takings by revolutionary governments?

(9) **How could the factors causing this kind of dispute be reduced? Should domestic policy-making processes be changed (eg, stronger involvement of domestic courts, parliaments, regulatory agencies)?**

Professor Abbott: The trade policy apparatus of governments when asked to provide assistance to private enterprises might more carefully filter the interests they are requested to pursue. When private enterprises knowingly engage in transactions involving substantial risks, and those risks become reality, the enterprises might well be instructed to bear the consequences of their business decision-making. In the Havana Club case, a very substantial amount of public funds has been expended both in the EU and the US to represent private interests; not in the general public interest. It may well be queried whether this is the proper role of government entities.

(10) **Should the EU and US take joint initiatives in the Transatlantic Partnership and/or in the WTO for the better prevention or settlement of this kind of dispute?**

Professor Abbott: A strong argument could be made that the federal courts of the US properly handled the legal issues raised in this dispute, and that no adjustment in dispute settlement procedures is required.

The private parties involved in the dispute might have benefited from a forceful suggestion of third party mediation in order to avoid prolongation of the commercial dispute. It is not apparent that this would have resulted in a satisfactory solution since the parties presumably had ample opportunity to pursue a settlement, even with judicial suggestion of compromise, prior to the initiation of the WTO proceeding.

Although the author assumes that actions were undertaken in this regard, the European Commission and the USTR might have more forcefully attempted to persuade their respective private demandeurs that a compromise settlement should be reached, and that intergovernmental representation in the context of WTO dispute settlement was not an option available to them. However, the political influence of the parties in their domestic arenas may well have foreclosed such a result.

It is possible that a bilateral trade court might have rendered a decision that would have been more politically acceptable to the EU than the decisions of the US federal courts, and this would argue in favour of the establishment of such a tribunal along the lines suggested by Professor Petersmann. However, it is not clear that this would have presented major advantages over invocation of the WTO dispute settlement process once the prospects for settlement had been eliminated. The most problematic part of WTO dispute settlement from the standpoint of this case is that a result favourable to the EU might have led to the withdrawal of trade concessions *vis-à-vis* the US. This would have had the consequence of injuring US private operators other than the party whose actions precipitated the dispute. This result would be inequitable from the standpoint of unrelated private parties. This argues against the use of WTO dispute settlement, and in favour of another type of tribunal whose remedial powers are directed to the relevant private operators.

Professor Cottier: Finally, a word on direct effect of WTO law in this context. Assuming that US courts would have examined the implication of the Paris Convention (which they did before[39]), possible bilateral investment treaties or even WTO law (which they currently are barred from doing), what would be the implication for transatlantic dispute resolution? Under US constitutional law applying the latter in time rule, it is evident that under section 211 OAA of 1998, courts currently would not be in a position to overrule such legislation. In expounding international law, however, they might create enhanced awareness on both sides of the Atlantic of the legal complexities involved. Foremost, the analysis would strengthen the insight that direct effect and primacy of international law could assist in preventing such disputes from arising in the first place. The impact of special commercial interests on the legislative process would be counterbalanced by long-term principles and rules enshrined in treaties and the international legal order at large. Perhaps, the adage 'hard cases make bad law' would then be a less appropriate qualification of *United States—section 211 Omnibus Appropriations Act of 1998* than it currently deserves under a still fragmented legal regime.

---

[39] See *Cuno Incorporated v Pall Incorporation et al*, US District Court for the Eastern District of New York, 729 F Supp 234 (1989) where the rule of independence in the Paris Convention in practical terms is directly applied; reprinted in F. Abbott, T. Cottier & F. Gurry, *The International Intellectual Property System* (1999), Vol 1 at 663, 679.

Professor Abbott: Though I have previously advocated giving direct effect to the TRIPS Agreement,[40] recent experience of certain developing countries has given me reason to express a note of caution, at least as regards countries where legal resources are less well distributed than in the OECD countries. The problem is this: OECD-based enterprises with great financial resources and access to costly legal representation may attempt to use the TRIPS Agreement as a lever to influence government policy in developing countries through the local courts, despite the absence of reasonable or responsible legal claims under the Agreement. Until a systemic imbalance in capacity to utilize legal resources is addressed, direct effect for the TRIPS Agreement may result in legal battles taking place on uneven playing fields. I merely add this note of concern, while this may not be the appropriate forum for addressing this issue in the detail it deserves.

Professor Cottier: In conclusion, I concur with Professor Abbott's assessment of legal issues relating to the TRIPS Agreement and submit that the case demonstrates the need for high level dispute management and co-ordination before decisions to bring a complaint are made. Rather than for additional mediation of private interests, I would rather suggest assessing the political dimension of the case within an Early Warning System. It also shows that not all trade-related matters can be successfully addressed under current WTO law. Additional legal remedies beyond the current WTO and TRIPS Agreement need to be explored in response to takings and regulatory takings (investment protection), including sensitive issues where security and alleged national interests are touched upon. Existing legal remedies within and without the WTO need to be explored in order to assess the need for additional procedures. It is only in the light of a comprehensive analysis that the need for special transatlantic arbitration can be assessed. Direct effect of international law rules should be further examined in light of its potential to prevent transatlantic disputes.

---

[40] See, eg, F.M. Abbott, 'Intellectual Property Rights Treaties in the Law of the United States: The Direct Application Paradox', 2 *Translex* No 2:1 (June 1999).

PART III

ANALYTICAL CROSS-SECTORAL STUDIES

17

Legal Theories on International Dispute Prevention and Dispute Settlement: Lessons for the Transatlantic Partnership

F.D. BERMAN

INTRODUCTION

This chapter confines itself, as may be imagined, to the settlement of international disputes by *peaceful* means. Since the adoption of the UN Charter, the use of force to settle international disputes is prohibited to all members of the United Nations,[1] and this prohibition is now regarded as a rule of general international law.[2]

I. SOVEREIGN EQUALITY AND THE ROLE OF CONSENT

The classic international law theory on the peaceful settlement of disputes is based on the paradigm of disputes between States (ie, independent States) on issues which are regulated by international law. The disputing parties thus enjoy sovereign equality as a fundamental property. And the two characteristic principles on which the system is based derive from that sovereign equality, namely the 'free choice of means' and *consent* as the basis for compulsory jurisdiction, or indeed as the basis for any intervention by a third party in whatever capacity.[3] Whether that paradigm remains adequate is a question that has been much discussed; if not, there is a further question as to whether the theory on the peaceful settlement of disputes has sufficiently adapted itself. Both questions will

---

[1] UN Charter, Article 2(3); see also Article 1(1).

[2] I. Brownlie, *Principles of International Law* (1998), at 702.

[3] 'Declaration on Principles of International Law concerning Friendly Relations and Cooperation among States in accordance with the Charter of the United Nations' (annexed to UN General Assembly resolution 2625(XXV)); 'Manila Declaration on the Peaceful Settlement of International Disputes' (annexed to UN General Assembly resolution 37/10).

be touched on below. In the meanwhile, the implications of the classic theory need to be drawn out.

The principle of the 'free choice of means' entails that no one method of dispute settlement is legally privileged over any other. It means also that the parties to a dispute, even if they are bound by an existing obligation to refer it to a particular dispute settlement forum, remain free to choose another means of settlement by mutual agreement between them. Or rather, they remain free in that respect except to the extent that they may have entered into a commitment towards third parties *not* to resort to other means.[4] The principle further entails that, in the event of discordant preferences between the disputing parties, a measure of agreement is required between the parties over which means to apply. How far there can be said to be a general legal *duty* to agree on a choice of means is doubtful. Such a duty, if it existed, would have to be a derivative of a general legal duty to *settle* disputes, and it is far from certain that international law stretches that far. It remains an acceptable and lawful option for an individual State—or for a pair or group of disputing States in common—deliberately to allow a dispute to remain 'unsettled', in a form of legal limbo; the general obligation is rather not to resort to *other than peaceful means* when a solution to the dispute is being sought. If there were to exist a more stringent obligation to pursue a settlement, it would be confined to disputes of a kind 'the continuation of which' (in the repeated phraseology of Chapter VI of the UN Charter) 'is likely to endanger the maintenance of international peace and security'.[5] Even there, 'settlement' does not mean 'final legal solution', and there are several shining examples of *modus vivendi* designed specifically—with broad international support and approval—to draw the sting of a dispute while preserving intact the legal positions of the parties. A bilateral example is the series of understandings between the United Kingdom and Argentina which have allowed the development of relations after the Argentine invasion of and then expulsion from the Falkland Islands in 1982;[6] a semi-multilateral example is the Berlin Agreements of 1971/72 between the Four Powers, with the participation of the Federal Republic of Germany and the then German Democratic Republic;[7] a multilateral example is the Antarctic Treaty of 1959,[8] and the series of arrangements that have grown organically out of the fertile soil of that regime.[9]

The principle of 'consent', on the other hand, occupies a less fundamental position; it can be seen as a derivative of the 'free choice of means' principle, in the sense that the choice of a particular form of compulsory jurisdiction or third-party intervention represents the exercise of an option from amongst the

---

[4] Such undertakings are rare, but for a notable example see Article 292 of the Consolidated Version of the Treaty Establishing the European Union.

[5] Cf UN Charter, Articles 33(1), 34, 35(1), 36 and 37(2).

[6] Cf Joint Statement and Exchange of Letters dated 14 July 1999, at http://www.fco.gov.uk.

[7] (1971) 10 ILM 895.

[8] 402 UNTS, 71.

[9] eg 1080 UNTS, 175 (seals); (1980) 19 ILM 841 (marine living resources); (1991) 30 ILM 1455 (environmental protection).

available range of means of settlement. In a more fundamental sense, however, the consent represents the partial abrogation of sovereignty which is necessary in order to confer on a tribunal the power to impose an outcome on the States involved in the settlement process.[10] One primary point has, however, developed out of the extensive line of practice and jurisprudence since the earliest bilateral arbitration treaties and the adoption of the original 'Optional Clause' in the Statute of the Permanent Court of International Justice. It is that, although the required consent can be expressed at the moment at which a given dispute moves to settlement, this need not be so;[11] consent can equally validly be given in advance, in the form of the assumption of a binding obligation to accept a particular form of settlement, which can in turn be by way of a general treaty obligation, by way of a specific obligation related to the subject-matter of a particular treaty, or by way of an attenuated form of treaty-like obligation for a particular dispute, as in the early *Corfu Channel* case[12] or the recent *Bahrain v Qatar* case.[13]

The system just described is self-evidently one that developed out of a model which pitted against one another two disputants not merely of equal legal status, but of sovereign status as well. The continuing importance of 'sovereign equality' can be seen vividly at play in the recent decision of the International Court of Justice (ICJ) in the *Arrest Warrant Case (Congo v Belgium)*.[14] The system was shaped by—and suited itself to—a typology of dispute involving the application of 'pure' international law, or in other words a dispute that placed in opposition the direct interests of one State *as such* against the direct interests of another; the dispute over title to territory, or over boundaries, was the classic example. It required adaptation or extension to encompass the wider variety of cases in which the interest most *directly* affected (at least on one side of the dispute) was a private person, or commercial entity. This was achieved by the development of the procedural institution of 'diplomatic protection',[15] and in parallel the substantive rules for the 'minimum standard' for the treatment of foreigners: the State 'espoused' the claim of the private interest, but through the legal fiction that the injury was done to itself.[16] In more contemporary times, a good part of the function previously performed by these institutions has been taken over (or is capable of being taken over) by human rights regimes—to the extent that the latter are endowed with enforcement mechanisms. Alternatively, its function

---

[10] As the solution is, in a technical sense, 'imposed' on both (or all) parties, the winning party as well as the losing party, theory requires that the consent of all of them is given.

[11] See J.G. Merrills, *International Dispute Settlement* (1998), at 122–124 and the examples there given.

[12] ICJ Rep, 1949, 4: responses by the parties to a resolution of the Security Council.

[13] (Jurisdictional phase) ICJ Rep, 1994, 112: separate exchanges of letters between each of the parties and the King of Saudi Arabia.

[14] 14 February 2002; text at http://www.icj-cij.org/icjwww/idocket/iCOBE/iCOBE frame.htm.

[15] Currently under study by the International Law Commission; see the Reports at http://www.un.org/law/ilc/guide/gfra.htm, under 9.8 Diplomatic Protection.

[16] *Mavrommatis Palestine Concessions* Case, 1924 PCIJ Rep, Ser A, No 2, 12.

might be subsumed under the now widespread systems of bilateral and multilateral treaties for the protection of investment, which always have enforcement mechanisms of a kind. Sometimes the old and the new continue in existence side by side, as for example under the European Convention on Human Rights 1950 which offers both the possibility of State vs State proceedings and the possibility of direct vindication by the citizen of the private rights in issue. For present purposes, the interest of the old regime of diplomatic protection lies not so much in the question whether it continues to fulfil a necessary or viable function in the human rights or investment protection era, but rather in two further elements: first, the fact that the operation of the regime required a link between the State and the private interest sufficient to sustain the fiction of indirect injury to the State; and second, the fact that it made a connection between national judicial processes and those at the international level. The first—the link between the State and the private interest—remains firmly one of nationality, supplemented (but only to a very limited extent) by special rules about the protection of corporate interests or investments. The second—the connection with national judicial processes—is the inevitable consequence of the fact that the international process could only step in, through the fiction of the indirect injury to the State, once it had been demonstrated that the direct injury itself could not be properly remedied at source.[17]

II. Dispute settlement mechanisms

One further piece of general theoretical background needs to be touched in before proceeding to apply the analysis to the particular case of the Transatlantic Relationship. The range of dispute settlement mechanisms is potentially infinite. The classic listing is normally taken to be that contained in Article 33 of the UN Charter: 'negotiation, enquiry, mediation, conciliation, arbitration, judicial settlement, resort to regional agencies or arrangements', but this listing is immediately complemented by the *clausula*, 'or other peaceful means of [the parties'] choice'. So by definition the list does not claim to be exhaustive. Moreover, none of the procedures it refers to is subject to any form of rigid definition either in law or in practice; it would always be possible to add a variation or refinement to an existing procedure, or to create a hybrid between two or more of them.

This last factor raises a further question, namely whether the methods or mechanisms listed are quintessentially ones designed for dispute settlement properly so called, or whether, conversely, they have a potential application to the *prevention* of disputes.

---

[17] Usually referred to as the 'exhaustion of local remedies' rule. There is much current controversy over whether it continues to apply, and if so where; cf Crawford, *The International Law Commission's Articles on State Responsibility* (2002), at 22–23 and 264–265; Report of the International Law Commission on its 54th Session (Document A/57/10, paras 150–176).

A. What is meant by a 'dispute'?

Before proceeding to that examination, it is necessary to spend a while consider-ing the concept of a 'dispute' itself; what is meant by the term? Moreover, what is meant, for that matter, by the 'settlement' of a dispute?

The most frequently used definition (or at least description) of what goes to constitute a dispute is that put forward by the Permanent Court of International Justice (PCIJ) in 1924: 'a disagreement on a point of law or fact, a conflict of legal views or of interests between two persons'.[18] Although frequently referred to since in learned writings and by the ICJ, this old definition is not a particularly useful one. While refreshingly un-technical, it is too all-encompassing. Even if confined strictly to the public international field (by substituting 'States' for 'persons'), it would still bring in a myriad of cases in which governments would be surprised, not to say downright dismayed, to be told that they were 'in dispute' with other governments.[19] In short, the definition misses a necessary element of subjective recognition that an issue has crystallized to a point at which it needs to be solved and cannot be solved by the processes so far called into play. In context, that is to say within the formal context of the rules of jurisdiction of international tribunals, it is readily understandable why the PCIJ chose deliberately to exclude a subjective element of that kind, in favour of a purely objective and factual standard. Its choice does not however, on examin-ation, suit itself to the broader diplomatic and policy context of dispute settle-ment. It lacks some reference to a prior diplomatic process (or its equivalent) apt to turn the 'difference' or 'disagreement' into a 'dispute' in a meaningful sense of the term. Building in that kind of prerequisite would also serve the valuable purpose of providing a mechanism for defining what the dispute is, what (in other words) the issue actually in dispute amounts to—a question that has itself given rise to endless difficulty in the practice of international dispute settlement.[20]

A more useful definition of 'dispute' might thus be a somewhat more complex formula along these lines: *a disagreement on a defined issue of law or fact, or law and fact combined, which has brought the interests of two or more States into conflict and which they (or at least some amongst them) require to have settled.*

B. What is meant by 'settlement'?

That brings us immediately to the question of 'settlement'. The concept is an extraordinarily elusive one. In one sense it could be said that an international dispute can never be irrevocably 'settled'. A formal preclusion of the reopening

---

[18] *Mavrommatis Palestine Concessions* Case (note 15 above).

[19] Merrills, at note 11 above, offers a more careful formulation at 1, but even it (like the PCIJ formulation) would turn the current difference between the US Government and its allies over how to confront State-sponsored terrorism into a 'dispute'.

[20] See Merrills, ibid, at 17–20; Brownlie, at note 2 above, at 480–481, and the examples there cited.

of an issue could only happen within the equally formal framework of a system of compulsory jurisdiction (the doctrine of *res judicata*). But even the availability of a valid plea of *res judicata* could not prevent a State attempting to revert to a 'settled' issue in its bilateral dealings with the other party, or before some other forum. This is apt to lead at most to the emergence of a new 'dispute' in which the validity, or the continued validity, of the original settlement might be the prime issue. A sizeable proportion of 'classic' international disputes can be cast in the mould of the reopening of an earlier settlement of some kind which had been brought into being at some prior historical moment.[21]

C. 'Legal' disputes and 'political' disputes

This issue of 'settlement' can be further illuminated through an approximate division of the means of settlement between the 'legal' and the 'political'. With 'legal' means of settlement we think primarily of the binding decision of a court or tribunal, or some equivalent dispute settlement process leading to a binding outcome. The settlement is a 'legal' one both because of the process through which the binding decision has been arrived at, and because of the presumption that the substance of the decision will have been reached by applying law to the facts. By contrast, a purely 'political' settlement, whatever the means by which it is brought about, is one in which power relationships and a whole range of non-legal factors come into play to determine the terms of settlement. In between lies a varying spectrum of cases in which legal factors influence a 'political' settlement (almost invariably the case) or political factors a 'legal' settlement (unacceptable at the level of high principle, but perhaps not quite so unacceptable in practice). And there is of course an extremely important area of overlap between 'legal' and 'political' settlements, in that both of them depend (in equal measure?) on the *facts*, and therefore that methods have to be found in both instances to enable the facts to be established, and established with sufficient authority.

As between the two case-types, the 'legal' and the 'political', one would expect in the case of a 'legal' settlement that the necessary 'acceptance' of the settlement had been abstracted and secured in advance, whereas in the case of a 'political' settlement, its acceptance by a reluctant party, or even by both parties, might itself be the subject of political pressure brought to bear by third parties. But a further difference, which is of particular interest for this stage of the argument, resides in the fact that the degree of permanence instinctively associated with a 'legal' settlement does not necessarily attach to a 'political' settlement. The more purely 'political' the settlement, the more it is likely to be regarded, generically, as not lasting for all time, in much the same way as treaties of a highly political character, like treaties of alliance or mutual defence, are accepted as being

---

[21] Current examples are the UK/Spanish disagreements over Gibraltar or the Western Sahara situation. Much the same could be said of the cataclysm in the Balkans as the Yugoslav Federation disintegrated.

subject to an implied right of denunciation on notice.[22] This is not, of course, to pretend that it is only 'political' settlements which are prone to the phenomenon of re-opening. In recent times, we have the continuing dispute with Iraq over the implementation of the binding (and expressly accepted) terms of Security Council Resolution 687; or the double-arbitration between Chile and Argentina over the Beagle Channel,[23] not to mention the series of applications to the ICJ putting in issue awards under old arbitration treaties.[24]

There is another sense (not wholly removed from that just mentioned), in which the 'settlement' of an international dispute is intrinsically tied to the agreement of the parties, that is, to their mutual acceptance that a particular outcome does represent the solution or 'settlement' of the dispute. Even in the case of the binding decision of a third-party jurisdiction, the binding character of the original submission to the jurisdiction arises out of agreement. So also, if regional or global political organs begin to develop to a point at which the imposition of solutions on member States becomes a standing feature of their practice, and is recognized as 'settling' the underlying dispute, once again that recognition has its origin in the agreement of the participating States when becoming party to the regime. The role of agreement, perhaps after the event as well as beforehand, thus becomes inescapable, and opens in turn the way to the whole problematic of re-opening settled cases which is canvassed above.

D. How does a 'dispute' become 'settled'?

It follows also from what has been said above, however, that—except in the case of a judicial-type settlement—a dispute only becomes 'settled' when the parties *agree* that it is. This proposition applies just as well at the moment of settlement as it does for the continuing future. In other words, the parties must at some point move to an acceptance that a solution has been found to the issue that divides them. Such an acceptance need not be formal (or even written) but it must entail a commitment of some kind *vis-à-vis* the other party, a commitment endowed with a quality that in principle endures into the future.

Judicial settlement is an exception in that it leads to a *judgment*, a formal decision (*sentence*), to which the commitment of acceptance is already attached. Perhaps the same could be said of a solution imposed by a political organ, as indicated above, if and so far as the organ possesses compulsory powers. Such powers will have been conferred by the initial agreement between the parties.[25]

---

[22] Cf Vienna Convention on the Law of Treaties, Article 56.

[23] ILR, Vol 52, 93; and E. Lauterpacht, 'Whatever happened to the Beagle Channel Award?', in *Mélanges Michel Virally* (1991), at 359.

[24] eg *Case concerning the Arbitral Award by the King of Spain*, ICJ Rep 1960, 192.

[25] The classic case being the UN Security Council; note the formulation of Article 25 of the UN Charter: 'The Members of the United Nations agree to accept and carry out the decisions of the Security Council in accordance with the present Charter'.

A tentative definition of the *settlement of a dispute*[26] might therefore be along these lines: *that it refers to the completion of a process by which the dispute ceases to be an issue in the relationship between the parties, not necessarily permanently or with conclusive legal effect, but at least in such a way as to load the scales against the party subsequently seeking to reopen the issue.*

III. 'SETTLEMENT' vs 'PREVENTION'

Against that background, it can be seen that, in pure theory, there is nothing to distinguish the *settlement* of disputes from their *prevention*. From one point of view the settlement of a dispute (if it holds) is simply the prevention of future disputes on the same issue. From another point of view, the 'prevention of disputes' can be seen as a process which intervenes at an intermediate stage to stop a 'dispute' (as in the PCIJ's broad definition mentioned previously)[27] developing into a 'dispute' within the more complex definition proposed in this paper.

It is certainly true that (with the exception once again of the strictly judicial or arbitral forms) all of the methods in the traditional litany of dispute settlement processes are just as capable of use for dispute prevention. The point hardly needs demonstration for, say, negotiation, conciliation, mediation, fact-finding, etc. The same is valid *par excellence* for the handling of a dispute through some form of parliamentary process within the framework of an international organization. Very often such a parliamentary process will in any case be associated with the use of one of the settlement techniques just mentioned. Even in the case of judicial procedures strictly so called, however, it may not be entirely true that they are applicable only in the area of dispute settlement, rather than dispute prevention. For one thing, as Sir Robert Jennings has pointed out in the ICJ context, the issue brought by the parties before a court may not be identical or coterminous with the dispute between them. Nevertheless, its determination by the court may be the essential key that unlocks the way to success in dealing with the dispute as such by other means. A good example is the series of maritime delimitation cases submitted to the ICJ since the *North Sea Continental Shelf Cases* in the 1960s,[28] in which the parties explicitly reserve the resolution of the bilateral issue by negotiation in the light of the court's findings on the applicable law. A further example of the application of a similar technique would be the invocation of the ICJ's *advisory* jurisdiction to procure an authoritative opinion on a legal issue that underlies a dispute between two or more Member States which is being dealt with by an international organization to which they belong.[29] In all of these cases the boundary between 'settlement' and 'prevention'

---

[26] To be read in conjunction with the formula for a definition of 'dispute' put forward above.

[27] Text to note 17 above.

[28] ICJ Rep, 1969, 3; see also the *Libya/Tunisia* and *Libya/Malta* cases: ICJ Rep, 1982, 19 and ICJ Rep, 1985, 13.

[29] Cf *Western Sahara* case, ICJ Rep, 1975, 12.

is fluid and not always easy to discern; where it lies may depend as much on how the 'dispute' is defined as on anything else. Nor is it necessarily so that the movement between 'settlement' and 'prevention' must be all one way; the handling of a given case may shift from 'prevention' to 'settlement' and back again.

IV. SPECIAL REGIMES

One final word needs to be said about special regimes. What is envisaged here in particular is restricted to multilateral regimes involving both substantive rules of conduct and institutional machinery, notably those including machinery and/or processes for handling disputes between regime participants. The regime may be thematic, or geographically homogeneous, or both; and the dispute provisions may vary widely in their object and in their operation. Moreover, the parties may make use of the faculty allowed to them by general international law to disapply some of the normal rules that would otherwise apply within the dispute settlement field, or to create new rules for themselves. But the defining characteristic remains the combination of limited membership with substantive rules, institutional machinery, and special provision for handling *inter se* disputes. A general multilateral regime may see its overriding interest as lying in the simple fact of getting disputes settled (if they cannot be prevented). The greater the political content of the regime, the more likely this is to be the case. By contrast, a special regime of the kind in view here may set a much higher value on the *terms* on which individual disputes are settled (or conversely, on the price paid for dispute avoidance, or dispute prevention). This is for the simple reason that, within the closed walls of the regime, the terms on which individual disputes are dealt with are more likely to create precedents (that is to say, adverse precedents) for future cases than in a general, world-wide regime. Or, to put the same thought more positively, the parties to a special regime of this type are likely to feel a close interest in developing the regime and furthering its purposes. This is prone to lead to a collectivization of any dispute handling process, either by giving all parties a say in the terms of settlement (eg, through their voice in a deliberative body), or else (if the dispute is directed to a judicial process) by permitting or even encouraging a right of intervention in that process.[30] Even without a process of this kind, however, a more powerful form of collectivization can be brought about when the terms of settlement of particular disputes are remitted to a body representing the regime as a whole for endorsement before they become effective as between the parties.[31] Solutions of this kind are particularly prone to becoming absorbed into the bloodstream of the regime, to being relied upon and

[30] Cf Article 63 of the Statute of the ICJ, for the hearing by the court of cases involving an international convention, or Article 36 of the European Convention on Human Rights (as revised 1998), para 2 of which opens the way to third-party intervention in any case before the court, or (latterly) the third-party provision in Article 4(11) of the WTO Dispute Settlement Understanding.

[31] The classic GATT model, carried over, with significant modifications, into the WTO.

applied by other regime participants, so minimizing to a large extent the re-opening phenomenon discussed above.[32]

It has also to be remarked *en passant* that, however well-intentioned the creation of advanced special regimes may be, when they are brought together in the alchemist's crucible with the apparently adamantine principle of *consent* in respect of international jurisdiction, the transmutation can be less than edifying. It has recently led, for example in the maritime and environmental fields, to a displacement of the disputing ground from substance of the issue to a form of sterile jurisdictional competition.[33] Even where this distortion is avoided, however, advanced special regimes are liable to be infected by another unhealthy displacement: the tendency for the dispute 'solved' at the substantive level to re-emerge as an equally bitter dispute over the permitted response by the successful party to the substantive finding in its favour. This phenomenon is particularly evident now in the WTO.[34]

V. Is the traditional theory still adequate?

The question was posed at the beginning of this chapter whether the traditional theory is still adequate. It has nowadays become a commonplace amongst theorists of international law that an analysis which admits individuals and private entities as objects of the law, but retains States or governments as its sole subjects, is no longer remotely adequate to cater for the current complexities of the international legal system or for the ways in which international law and national legal systems interweave themselves into one another. States (governments) may indeed remain the principal subjects of international law; nevertheless the ways in which international law affects human lives and business interests transcends a subject/object dichotomy. A similar observation may be made for the impact on law-creation processes of non-traditional influences, of which disciplined non-governmental organizations (NGOs) are the most obvious example.[35] This does not, however, necessarily have an impact on international dispute settlement.[36] It is perfectly possible to conceive of a system in which non-State actors are beneficiaries of rights under international law, and even perhaps play a part of some kind in their creation, without by that token

---

[32] For a particularly interesting example see Hudec's discussion in this volume of the 1981 Understanding in the DISC case and the subsequent FSC dispute.

[33] See K. Boyle (1997) 46 *ICLQ* 37; see also Esty's chapter on the environment in this volume.

[34] Where an attempt is made to codify, and hence to control, it in Articles 22 and 23 of the DSU; see also E.-U. Petersmann, *The GATT/WTO Dispute Settlement System* (1997); Kohona (1994) 28(2) *Journal of World Trade* 23.

[35] Though not by any means the only one: another would be sub-State actors like national liberation movements or rebel groups.

[36] See the discussion in M. Brus, *Third Party Dispute Settlement in an Interdependent World* (1995), at 196–219.

acquiring a power to vindicate those rights directly on the international plane. Indeed, given the central place (described above) played by consent in the system for international dispute settlement, as it operates between States, it follows logically that specific consent, in an extended form, would be required to confer a jurisdictional right of action on private interests or individuals, if the purpose was to allow them to vindicate rights or claims directly against a State. The same conclusion follows, if the matter is looked at from the viewpoint of national legal systems; the general immunity enjoyed by a State from the jurisdiction of other States would bar an attempt to enforce an 'international' right in the courts of the individual's own State—unless of course the subject matter of the claim fell within the recognized exceptions to sovereign immunity.

The issue is complex. It lies at the frontier of the interaction between international and national law, and cannot be encapsulated in simple terms. It begs, moreover, the important underlying question whether 'dispute settlement' (in the global sense in which that term is used in the context of the present study, ie dispute settlement in the transatlantic relationship) is advanced or hindered by transferring control over dispute settlement processes downwards and outwards to a disaggregated collection of right holders whose approach is by definition bound to be determined by their private interests, and not by any conception of a public interest.[37] It would seem to be this notion, far more than any question of the standing of private interests in the diplomatic field, that legitimately conditions the policy approach of governments in deciding whether or not to construct dispute settlement procedures in such a way as to open them up to direct access by private interests.[38]

VI. THE EURO-ATLANTIC RELATIONSHIP

It is now time to try to apply some of the above analysis to the Euro-Atlantic relationship. In particular, how might a new dispute settlement mechanism for that relationship be evaluated on the theoretical plane?

The first point to make is surely to note the exceptionally close and densely-packed nature of the Euro-Atlantic relationship. This implies on the one hand the realistic possibility of creating institutional mechanisms to reflect and

---

[37] It goes without saying, of course, that the balance between dispute 'settlement' and dispute 'prevention' in the mind of a private right-holder would not necessarily coincide, either, with how that balance appears to the public policy-maker.

[38] The point illustrates itself graphically if the attempt is made to apply the definitions suggested in this paper for a 'dispute' and for 'settlement' to disputes to which a non-State entity is a party, or alternatively to find modifications to those suggested definitions so as to enable them to be applied to disputes of that class. It is evident, for example, that special considerations unique to the so-called 'International Sea-Bed Area' led to the Sea-Bed Disputes Chamber of the International Tribunal for the Law of the Sea being given jurisdiction over disputes involving parties of all descriptions, but not the principal Tribunal itself (Article 187 of the Third UN Convention on the Law of the Sea, Montego Bay, 1982).

embody the co-operative nature of the relationship from which they spring. On the other hand, the very denseness of the relationship implies also that it spans a whole range of fields, which may not be homogeneous in character, so that a different alignment of forces may apply in different areas of the same relationship. For example, the more political the area, the stronger the innate drive towards co-operativeness can be assumed to be. This could be expected to be especially marked in the political/security area. By contrast, economic and trading relationships, based as they are on a bias towards free trade and economic liberalism, will naturally and inevitably generate clashes of competition. In other words, what might be thought pathological in one area of the relationship would be thought natural and healthy in another area—*even though in both cases the potential for longer-term damage to the relationship itself is equally great*. This is due to the complexity of the *inter*-relationships between individual members within the broader overall relationship. This complexity will only increase with the accession of new members (formerly communist or formerly third world) to the European Union and to NATO.

The tentative conclusion would seem to be that, in the wide spectrum stretching from security relations for common defence, through political relations more generally, through economic relations, through to trading relations both worldwide and bilaterally, the premium at the security end lies in the *avoidance* or *prevention* of disputes, whereas at the trading end it lies in available and effective dispute *settlement procedures*, but in both cases the ultimate aim is the same, namely to ensure that no 'dispute' is allowed to build up to such a magnitude, or to persist for such a length of time, as to risk damaging the underlying relationship as such.

But a further aspect of this arrangement of forces needs also to be noted. It resides in the fact that, at the security/political end of the spectrum, the forces that need to be balanced out in managing a dispute are forces that lie in the hands of the governments. At the trading end of the spectrum, conversely, the forces directly in conflict are those of private enterprise. The role of the government is often an ambiguous and controversial one. It no longer corresponds to the classic model of diplomatic protection noted earlier, in which the fiction of indirect injury to the State through the person of its national was designed to allow the government the widest measure of discretion over how to pursue a claim generated by damage to private interests (indeed over whether to 'espouse' the claim at all), in short to facilitate the government's right to 'sacrifice' a private interest for wider international reasons. Whether or not that model ever existed in its pure form, it falls today in the majority of cases under the combined impact of various factors: the political difficulty governments have in resisting pressures from commercial interests; the *legal* difficulty of refusing to act, even in the broader public interest, in the face of modern constitutional notions of private entitlement; the creation of hybrid regimes which open the way to direct actions by private interests against governments *internationally* as well as nationally;[39] not to mention the virtual unworkability of the nationality link in the face of the sophistications of modern corporate ownership and in an era of mass migration. To put the question another way, is the very denseness of the Euro-Atlantic relationship such that the disputes it generates are liable to be so different from the classical paradigm of disputes between sovereign States that the methods for their resolution have to be so constructed that they also reflect a wider range of elements than normally goes into the settlement of inter-State disputes? For example, how could traditional methods be expected to cope with disputes that are essentially about competing claims to regulatory competence, or worse still about competing views about how joint or common regulatory competence ought to be exercised in substance? By the same token, legalized dispute settlement processes will inevitably be circumscribed by the 'terms of reference' phenomenon: the dispute settlement body will not be competent beyond the terms of the dispute submitted to it;[40] and, if it strays beyond those limits, its decision is unlikely to hold, or may even be legally challenged at the compliance phase.

The second point that emerges is that, whatever its other merits, a *general* dispute settlement mechanism for the Euro-Atlantic relationship would have an enormous burden to bear, a burden so great that it raises the question whether any single institution or mechanism could be robust and powerful enough to sustain it. From the theoretical point of view (as indicated earlier) a new mechanism could only become the exclusive vehicle for handling disputes in circumstances in which all parties had undertaken an irrevocable legal commitment not to resort to other means, in much the same way as the EU States have done (though even there the commitment is limited to Community disputes only). That would seem to suggest that exclusivity is an unattainable objective. Instead, the emphasis might be, firstly, on competitive attractiveness (*vis-à-vis* other available mechanisms), and, secondly, on a safety-net arrangement as in the UN Law of the Sea Convention[41] (or the Manila Declaration on the Peaceful Settlement of Disputes)[42] which ensures that there is a compulsory default option when the alternatives fail.

The final point is rooted less in theory than in practical engineering, though it does relate to the consideration noted earlier that none of the classic

---

[39] The creation of such rights, eg, in the investment protection field, necessarily entails that the contracting governments sacrifice an element of control over the management of disputes, including disputes which may affect the interests of a whole class of private parties; cf the as yet unresolved argument over whether the WTO dispute settlement processes should remain open to governments alone, and what role private interests should play in either case.

[40] Which could be determined either by the way in which the parties have chosen to define the issue in dispute, or else could have been determined more generally by the terms of the treaty framework within which the dispute settlement process operates; cf the discussion of the first Panel report in the chapter by Weiss on the Bananas dispute, at p 128 of this volume.

[41] See note 38 above.

[42] See note 3 above.

international procedures is subject to any form of rigid definition either in law or in practice. How particular dispute settlement institutions are constructed—and even more so how they are *operated* by those using them—is deeply influenced by national traditions and expectations about forms of government and forms of administration. The more that the different parties have in common, not just in shared values but also in shared practices, the greater the chance that the expectations of different participants will overlap sufficiently in the middle to allow a new consensual institution the prospect of working.[43] This will pose particular problems on the European side as it begins the process of integrating its new members. It will also pose severe problems on the US side as it comes to terms with the fact that the US system of government is of a very particular nature, and that the balance of governmental power as it has emerged at this particular moment in US history is not replicated anywhere else amongst its partners.[44] Without some such effort at comprehension, the scope for misunderstanding will remain, and may even grow, and with it will remain (or grow) the gulf that separates the theoretical possibilities of dispute settlement from their practical realization.[45]

---

[43] Cf the discussion of regulatory cultures in the chapter by Shaffer on Mutual Recognition and Safe Harbour Agreements at pp. 308–10 of this volume.

[44] The most striking element is undoubtedly the enormous autonomy possessed by the legislature under the US constitutional system as it has developed, reflected (or under present-day conditions exacerbated) by the rigid separation of powers which prevents representatives of government from being members of Congress. But there are sometimes striking differences also in the attitudes taken by national courts on either side of the Atlantic towards the extension, or alternatively the restraint, of national regulatory powers outside national boundaries. See also, at the more workaday level, the 'governance' (or 'Regulatory Philosophy') section of Abbott's chapter on Technical Barriers to Trade at pp. 249–53 of this volume.

[45] See in particular the telling chapter by Paemen in this volume on the dispute over the Helms-Burton Act.

18

Transatlantic Trade Conflicts and GATT/WTO Dispute Settlement

MARC L. BUSCH and ERIC REINHARDT*

I. Introduction

The story of dispute settlement at the World Trade Organization (WTO) is, in large part, the story of the transatlantic relationship between the United States (US) and European Community (EC).[1] *Primus inter pares* at the WTO, the US and EC together accounted for fully 38 per cent of global merchandise trade in 2000, more than the ten next largest trading economies combined (WTO 2001, 22).[2] Not surprisingly, US-EC disputes set the tone in the global economy more generally, notably on the eve of the Doha Round. Focusing on this salient dyad, observers on both sides of the Atlantic place a good deal of faith in the dispute settlement reforms ushered in by the Uruguay Round and embodied in the WTO's Dispute Settlement Understanding (DSU). Indeed, it is widely argued that these reforms have dramatically increased the WTO's capacity to resolve disputes, compared to the practices under the General Agreement on Tariffs and Trade (GATT). Have the reforms of the DSU, in fact, improved the outcomes of US-EC disputes?

With more than seven years of data available, we find that the WTO's dispute settlement data so far belie the conventional wisdom. At first blush, US-EC disputes appear to have ended with the defendant making the desired policy changes more frequently under the WTO than under GATT, although it is important to note that, overall, both systems have been highly efficacious overall, notwithstanding the limitations of international adjudication.[3] On closer

* We thank Roderick Abbott, Andrew Guzman, Bob Hudec, Valerie Hughes, Gabrielle Marceau, Petros C. Mavroidis, Volker Rittberger, Joel Trachtman, Boris Ulehla, seminar participants at Boalt Hall School of Law at Berkeley, and conference participants at the European University Institute for many helpful comments. For generous financial support, Busch thanks the Social Sciences and Humanities Research Council of Canada; Reinhardt thanks the University Research Committee of Emory University.

[1] The 15 members of the European Union (EU) identify their collective organization as the European Community (or Communities, to be precise) at the WTO.

[2] And this figure excludes intra-EC trade.

[3] L.R. Helfer & A.-M. Slaughter, 'Toward a Theory of Effective Supranational Adjudication' (1997) 107 *Yale Law Journal* 273–391.

inspection, however, the WTO's superior track record is not attributable to dispute settlement reforms *per se*. Rather, we find that the apparent success in resolving US-EC disputes since 1995 is due largely to the expansion of the WTO's scope in new areas, notably intellectual property (IP) and traded services. In fact, the new dispute settlement system has struggled to induce the defendant in US-EC disputes to liberalize where it counts most: namely, in the 'highest-stakes' cases. Likewise, when GATT-era cases pitting the US and EC against each other have recurred under the WTO, the institution, despite its greater clarity of law, has fared little better than its predecessor in resolving transatlantic disputes.

More interesting still, the pattern of transatlantic dispute outcomes across stages of escalation remains much the same as it did under GATT. That is, *early settlement* continues to be a pillar of the system, even though compliance with rulings is no more frequent. We thus argue that, in light of the track record to date, procedural legal reforms *per se* have not improved the outcomes of US-EC disputes. If, as we speculate below, the more legalistic WTO process may actually hinder pre-ruling bargaining, then the efficacy of US-EC dispute settlement may be at greater risk now than in the GATT era, since the institution appears to depend even more on early settlement for the vast majority of its successful outcomes.

The paper is in five sections. Section II surveys key dispute settlement reforms ushered in by the WTO, and elaborates how these are likely to influence US-EC disputes. Section III reports new data on all US-EC disputes at the WTO thus far, and offers a simple contrast with comparable GATT disputes. Section IV empirically tests our argument that the WTO's (nominally) better record in resolving US-EC disputes is due to factors other than the legal reforms embodied in the DSU *per se*. Section V interprets these results and discusses their implications.

II. The WTO dispute settlement mechanism

Observers have long marvelled that GATT dispute settlement worked at all, never mind that it worked quite well.[4] First codified in a small annex to the 1979 Understanding on Dispute Settlement on customary practices, and played out by different rules across the different covered agreements (notably the Tokyo Round codes), GATT dispute settlement lacked not only 'teeth', but a consistent set of rules more generally. Against this backdrop, the DSU has been heralded as a significant step forward in institutional design,[5] complementing the WTO's

---

[4] R.E. Hudec, *Enforcing International Trade Law: The Evolution of the Modern GATT Legal System* (1993).

[5] See, E.U. Petersmann, *International Trade Law and the GATT/WTO Dispute Settlement System* (1997); D.P. Steger & S.M. Hainsworth, 'World Trade Organization Dispute Settlement: The First Three Years' (1998) 1 *Journal of International Economic Law* 199–226; and H. Horn & P.C. Mavroidis, 'Economic and Legal Aspects of the Most-Favored-Nation Clause' (2001) 17(2) *European Journal of Political Economy* 233–279.

greater clarity of law. Indeed, Palmeter describes the DSU as 'perhaps the most significant achievement of the Uruguay Round negotiations, establishing what may be the most developed dispute settlement system in any existing treaty regime'.[6] By almost any metric, it would be difficult to argue otherwise: stricter timelines, the right to a panel (carried over from the 1989 Dispute Settlement Procedures Improvements), automatic adoption of reports (except by 'negative consensus'), and review by a permanently-constituted Appellate Body (AB) are among the most salient provisions of the integrated DSU which appear to fill in where GATT had seemed to fall so terribly short. The question, though, is how these reforms influence the litigation of disputes, particularly those involving the US and EC.

First, speedier procedures with stricter time limits are thought to boost confidence in the DSU by delivering 'justice' more promptly, and by beating various unilateral measures to the punch, notably US Section 301, which worked on a notoriously faster clock than did GATT. Second, the right to a panel removes the possibility that a defendant can block or considerably delay a case from being heard, a tactic that was widely viewed as the *sine qua non* of GATT power politics. Third, standard terms of reference, and the automatic adoption of reports, lend greater legal coherence to the system as a whole, and obviate the threat of a unilateral 'veto' by a recalcitrant defendant.[7] Fourth, the potential for review by the AB promises more consistency across rulings and a better-informed body of case-law with which to reason through the merits of a dispute *ex ante*.[8] Taken together, these reforms are expected to promote more liberalization by errant defendants in a timely manner, thereby restraining US resort to extra-legal enforcement through 'aggressive unilateralism'.[9]

The conventional wisdom is probably right about the benefits of many of the most salient of these reforms, including negative consensus and the formation of the standing AB. However, a more balanced assessment is necessary. To that end, we note that the legal reforms of the DSU may actually *raise* the transaction costs inherent in settling disputes by affording opportunities for longer delays, increasing incentives for foot-dragging in litigation, and motivating defendants to delay concessions.[10] Granted, each separate stage of the process now operates

---

[6] D. Palmeter, 'The WTO As a Legal System' (2000) 24 (1&2) *Fordham International Law Journal* 444–480.

[7] D. Palmeter & P.C. Mavroidis, 'The WTO Legal System: Sources of Law' (1998) 92 *American Journal of International Law* 398–413.

[8] R. Howse, 'Adjudicative Legitimacy and Treaty Interpretation in International Trade Law: The Early Years of WTO Jurisprudence' in J.H.H. Weiler (ed), *The EU, the WTO and the NAFTA: Towards a Common Law of International Trade* (2000).

[9] M.L. Busch, 'Accommodating Unilateralism? U.S. Section 301 and GATT/WTO Dispute Settlement', manuscript, Queen's School of Business, Kingston, Ontario (2000); and E. Reinhardt, 'Aggressive Multilateralism: The Determinants of GATT/WTO Dispute Initiation, 1948–1998', manuscript, Emory University, Atlanta, GA (2000).

[10] A.W. Shoyer, 'The First Three Years of WTO Dispute Settlement: Observations and Suggestions' (1998) 1 *Journal of International Economic Law* 277–302, and E. Reinhardt, 'Adjudication without Enforcement in GATT Disputes' (2001) 45(2) *Journal of Conflict Resolution* 174–195.

according to a tighter timeline, but this fact is overwhelmed by the new possibility, indeed, the inevitability[11] of successive rounds of litigation in the same dispute, culminating in up to 15 months' grace period for implementation,[12] the possibility of an Article 21.5 panel review (and possibly appeal), additional litigation or negotiations over 'sequencing' with respect to Article 22, and ultimately arbitration over the amount and form of retaliation. Put simply, a determined defendant can wring at least three years of delays from the system before facing definitive legal condemnation, enough time for 'temporary' measures—such as the March 2002 US steel safeguards—to wreak sustained havoc without possibility for retroactive compensation.[13] Further, the added stages of litigation, tight enforcement of terms of reference, the legal disincentives for disclosure, and the rules on standing, all serve to put the onus on disputants and third parties to legally mobilize as soon as possible in order to avoid losses on technicalities (ie, having the panel or AB deem a certain argument outside its terms of reference) later on.

From the outset of a dispute, concern for post-ruling delays, in particular, has the effect of undermining early settlement.[14] This is especially true if the rush to litigation draws in third parties or additional disputants, whose involvement has been shown to reduce the prospects for concessions by a defendant.[15] At the conclusion of a dispute, the DSU's superior enforcement power is also vastly overstated in relation to GATT; the hurdle in this regard has never been obtaining legal authorization *per se*,[16] but rather mustering the market power and political will to retaliate. In this sense, as Pauwelyn astutely observes, '[t]he "legalization" of disputes under the WTO stops, in effect, roughly where non-compliance starts'.[17] Taken together, these factors lead us to expect that transatlantic disputes under the WTO are *no more or less likely* to end with concessions (ie, policies aimed at market-liberalization on the part of the defendant) than

[11] Of the 11 initial panel reports in the dataset of completed US-EC WTO cases below, only *Section 301* and *US Copyright Act* were not appealed. And in the latter case, no fewer than three separate arbitrations were invoked, under Articles 23.1(c), 25, and 22.6, governing the 'reasonable period of time' for implementation, the level of nullification or impairment, and the level of retaliation.

[12] The grace period in *Australia—Salmon* was eight months, but generally it has been much longer.

[13] P.C. Mavroidis, 'Remedies in the WTO Legal System: Between a Rock and a Hard Place' (2000) 11(4) *European Journal of International Law* 763–813, and J. Pauwelyn, 'Enforcement and Countermeasures in the WTO: Rules are Rules—Toward a More Collective Approach' (2000) 94(2) *American Journal of International Law* 335–347.

[14] Eg, T.P. Stewart & M.M. Burr, 'The WTO's First Two and a Half Years of Dispute Resolution' (1998) 23 *North Carolina Journal of International Law and Commercial Regulation* 481–644 at 514.

[15] M.L. Busch, 'Democracy, Consultation, and the Paneling of Disputes Under GATT' (2000) 44(4) *Journal of Conflict Resolution* 425–446. See also below.

[16] R.E. Hudec, 'The New WTO Dispute Settlement Procedure: An Overview of the First Three Years' (1999) 8 *Minnesota Journal of Global Trade* 1–53 at 9–10; P.C. Mavroidis, 'Remedies in the WTO Legal System: Between a Rock and a Hard Place' (2000) 11(4) *European Journal of International Law* 763–813; C.M. Valles & B.P. McGivern (2000) 34(2) *Journal of World Trade* 63–84; and E. Reinhardt, 'Adjudication without Enforcement in GATT Disputes' (2001) 45(2) *Journal of Conflict Resolution* 174–195.

[17] J. Pauwelyn, 'Enforcement and Countermeasures in the WTO: Rules are Rules—Toward a More Collective Approach' (2000) 94(2) *American Journal of International Law* 335–347 at 338.

those brought under GATT. The one exception should be areas where explicit obligations did not previously exist—ie, IP and traded services—where we can expect WTO disputes to fare better than their counterparts under GATT, simply because of clearer disciplines.[18]

III. A FIRST CUT AT THE US-EC WTO DISPUTE RECORD

To assess empirically the DSU's track record, we assemble a dataset of 85 concluded transatlantic[19] trade disputes filed under GATT/WTO procedures from 1960 through 2001. Of these, 53 were brought under GATT, 32 under the WTO.[20] The first and most obvious question is simply, 'what is a dispute?'. Like Hudec,[21] we only count complaints in which formal GATT/WTO proceedings were explicitly invoked, ie, naming defendants and alleging the infringement of specific legal rights, most often in the form of an initial 'request for consultations'. We eliminate redundancy in the list of cases to avoid double-counting, following the approach of Horn, Nordström, and Mavroidis.[22] Specifically, in some cases, the US has filed on essentially identical issues several times against one or more EC members, plus the EC itself (eg, GATT's *Transfrontier Television* and *Income Tax Practices* cases; and, under the WTO, *Customs Classification*, DS62, 67, and 68; *Certain Income Tax Measures*, DS127-131; and *Flight Management Systems*, DS172, 173). We count each of these as just one dispute. Similarly, we drop *Bananas III* (DS16, late September 1995) because it was reworked and re-filed as *Bananas IV* (DS27, early February 1996) before any action could be taken.

In order to compare the efficacy of GATT and the WTO in inducing concessions by defendants, we need to control for the differing legal dispositions of each case. Hence we identify the stage reached and the direction of rulings for all disputes. Of the 85 US-EC disputes in our dataset, a panel was established in 43 cases (29 of 53 GATT complaints and 14 of 32 WTO complaints). Of those 43 panels, 36 issued substantive reports, which were appealed in 9 of the 11 WTO cases. Thus a large majority—58 per cent—of US-EC disputes have been resolved or dropped in consultations, or during panel deliberations. This

---

[18] Though less frequent, GATT disputes over IP or traded services did occur, resulting uniformly in negligible change from the status quo ante, eg, in the US-initiated 1989–1993 *Transfrontier Television* consultations and in the EC's 1987 *Aramid Fibres* complaint.

[19] 'Transatlantic' for these purposes denotes cases in which the disputants included the US, on one side, and the EC or an EC member state, on the other side.

[20] Our dataset does not include another 11 GATT disputes with missing outcome information as well as eight WTO disputes still underway. However, it *does* include tentative codings for four WTO disputes with manifest but still potentially reversible outcomes: *Foreign Sales Corporations* (DS108), *Anti-Dumping Act of 1916* (DS136), *US Copyright Act* (DS160), and *Section 211* (DS176).

[21] R.E. Hudec, *Enforcing International Trade Law: The Evolution of the Modern GATT Legal System* (1993).

[22] H. Horn, H. Nordström & P.C. Mavroidis, 'Is the Use of the WTO Dispute Settlement System Biased?' *CEPR Discussion Paper 2340* (1999).

percentage speaks to the importance of early settlement under the WTO, and is entirely in keeping with figures drawn from empirical work looking at all GATT-era disputes (Busch and Reinhardt 2000, 2002).[23]

In terms of the direction of any decisions rendered, we code the initial panel report, or the AB report, if appealed, according to whether it substantially favoured the complainant, was mixed, or favoured the defendant. Of the 36 rulings, 22 favoured the complainant, 7 were mixed, and 7 found for the defendant. This 'pro-plaintiff bias' also accords with previous studies of all cases brought under GATT, not just those between the US and EC.[24]

Finally, we follow Hudec[25] in defining outcomes as the policy result of a dispute, rather than the nature of a ruling *per se*.[26] In other words, the main question is whether the defendant liberalized the disputed trade policy prac-tice(s), conceding to some or all of the complainant's demands, and not simply whether a ruling (if there was one) favoured one side or the other. Using a measure that has meaning at each stage of dispute settlement, from consultations to an AB verdict, we code outcomes according to whether substantial, partial, or no concessions were made with regard to the contested trade measure(s). While such an approach has been used to study GATT disputes,[27] this paper is the first to systematically characterize WTO outcomes in the same way. By way of illustration, *Hormones* (DS26) scores as 'no concessions', and *Duties on Imports of Grains* (DS13) ended with 'full concessions'. *Bananas* (DS27) is perhaps the most difficult case to score; we give it a 'partial concessions' outcome due to the long delay before settlement, the multi-year time frame allowed for implemen-tation afterwards, and the incomplete relaxation of the discriminatory barriers in any case. Of the 85 US-EC GATT/WTO disputes, 49 per cent ended with substantial concessions, 20 per cent ended with partial concessions, and 31 per cent with no concessions.

With these data in hand, we can now contrast GATT and WTO dispute outcomes. As a first cut, consider Table 18.1, which provides a simple tabulation of the level of concessions achieved in US-EC disputes under the two regimes. Just 21 of 53 GATT-era conflicts (40 per cent) ended with substantial liberaliza-

[23] M.L. Busch & E. Reinhardt, 'Bargaining in the Shadow of the Law: Early Settlement in GATT/WTO Disputes' (2000) 24 (1&2) *Fordham International Law Journal* 158–172; and M.L. Busch & E. Reinhardt, 'Testing International Trade Law: Empirical Studies of GATT/WTO Dispute Settlement' in D.M. Kennedy & J.D. Southwick (eds), *The Political Economy of International Trade Law: Essays in Honor of Robert Hudec* (2002).

[24] E. Reinhardt, 'Adjudication without Enforcement in GATT Disputes' (2001) 45(2) *Journal of Conflict Resolution* 174–195.

[25] R.E. Hudec, *Enforcing International Trade Law: The Evolution of the Modern GATT Legal System* (1993).

[26] M.L. Busch & E. Reinhardt, 'Testing International Trade Law: Empirical Studies of GATT/WTO Dispute Settlement' in D.M. Kennedy & J.D. Southwick (eds), *The Political Economy of International Trade Law: Essays in Honor of Robert Hudec* (2002), at 470.

[27] R.E. Hudec, *Enforcing International Trade Law: The Evolution of the Modern GATT Legal System* (1993); M.L. Busch, 'Democracy, Consultation, and the Paneling of Disputes Under GATT' (2000) 44(4) *Journal of Conflict Resolution* 425–446; and E. Reinhardt, 'Adjudication without Enforcement in GATT Disputes' (2001) 45(2) *Journal of Conflict Resolution* 174–195.

TABLE 18.1. US-EC Dispute outcomes under GATT and the WTO

		Level of Concessions			
		None	Partial	Full	Total
Period	GATT (1960-1994)	18	14	21	53
	WTO (1995-)	8	3	21	32
	Total	26	17	42	85

χ^2 (2) $= 6.15$, $p = 0.046$

tion by the defendant, while fully 21 of 32 WTO cases (66 per cent) ended that way. This difference is statistically significant. Undeniably, the US and EC appear to have made more concessions to each other in disputes under the WTO than they did under GATT. But is this improvement in transatlantic trade tensions attributable to dispute settlement reform *per se*, or to something else?

IV. A SECOND CUT AT THE US-EC WTO DISPUTE RECORD

The better WTO dispute settlement record is even more impressive when we consider two differences in the kinds of cases filed under this institution, and its predecessor. As noted above, defendants are least likely to concede in multilateral disputes, perhaps because they have more trade at stake, or because co-ordination of deals is necessarily more complex. Interestingly, far more US-EC conflicts under the WTO have involved multiple parties (66 per cent) than under GATT (43 per cent). In addition, while the attachment of a 'non-violation nullification or impairment' claim at the end of a long list of violation arguments has often been the mark of either poor legal merits or poor strategy (the 'kitchen sink' approach),[28] it is more common in US-EC conflicts under the WTO (in 44 per cent of the complaints) than under GATT (30 per cent). For these reasons, we would expect WTO disputes to end with fewer, not more, concessions, and yet the opposite is true.

Nonetheless, we conjecture that the marked WTO improvement cannot be attributed to the increased legalism of the system *per se*. Most obviously, the WTO's expanded scope has made disputes successful where they were not before, especially in IP and traded services.[29] Better outcomes in these areas

---

[28] In the absence of a violation finding, a successful non-violation claim requires very strong and detailed evidence, which complainants are often unable to provide.

[29] B.M. Hoekman & M.M. Kostecki, *The Political Economy of the World Trading System* (2001), at 79.

would be expected even in the total absence of dispute settlement reforms. Rigorous statistical analysis bears out this contention. Furthermore, if the reforms have worked, they should yield successful outcomes even in the highest-stakes disputes. They have not. A related test of the efficacy of reform concerns GATT disputes that have recurred under the WTO. Looking case by case, we find that, on the whole, such disputes have fared no better than they did under GATT. Finally, if these dispute settlement reforms have accomplished anything, they should have improved the level of compliance with rulings. The data suggest otherwise. Accordingly, we submit that the frequency of early settlement in WTO disputes is probably driven not by any improved threat of enforcement *per se*, but by diplomacy and, perhaps, the normative weight of the institution, as it arguably was under GATT.[30]

A. Controlling for scope expansion

The WTO extended its reach into IP and services trade through the Agreement on Trade-Related Aspects of Intellectual Property Rights (TRIPs) and the General Agreement on Trade in Services (GATS), respectively. As a result, the WTO has rendered more disputes 'actionable' under the single integrated DSU. This is not to say that disputes in IP and traded services eluded GATT, for in fact GATT handled a small but highly contentious set of cases touching on these areas, with little effect on the status quo.[31] For its part, the WTO has adjudicated nine US-EC disputes in IP and traded services, as listed in Table 18.2.

A close look at these IP and traded services disputes is revealing. In particular, five of these nine cases are US complaints designed to speed up domestic legislation implementing TRIPs by individual EC member states (Portugal, Denmark, Sweden, Ireland, and Greece). It can be argued that these cases were far less acrimonious than most, because the TRIPs commitment was of recent vintage and the desire to comply was already manifest through proposed domestic legislation. Indeed, panel establishment and litigation never occurred in these five disputes. Not surprisingly, as Table 18.2 indicates, all five of these US-EC disputes ended with full concessions. The defendant fully, or at least partially, conceded in the other four IP and traded services disputes under the WTO as well, mostly prior to a panel ruling. This is not to suggest that IP and traded services disputes *per se* are easy to resolve. On the contrary, IP cases, in particular, are widely viewed as being among the most technical, and difficult, requiring

---

[30] R.E. Hudec, '"Transcending the Ostensible": Some Reflections on the Nature of Litigation Between Governments' (1987) 72 *Minnesota Law Review* 211–226; E. Reinhardt, 'Adjudication without Enforcement in GATT Disputes' (2001) 45(2) *Journal of Conflict Resolution* 174–195; and M.L. Busch & E. Reinhardt, 'Testing International Trade Law: Empirical Studies of GATT/WTO Dispute Settlement' in D.M. Kennedy & J.D. Southwick (eds), *The Political Economy of International Trade Law: Essays in Honor of Robert Hudec* (2002).

[31] eg, supra note 4. Neither did the US or EC budge as defendants in IP/services complaints brought by third parties under GATT, eg, Austria v Germany *Truck Traffic Restrictions* (1990) and Canada v US *Spring Assemblies* (1981).

TABLE 18.2. US-EC IP and services disputes under the WTO

DS	Start	Compl/ Def	Title	End	Level of Concessions
37	30-Apr-1996	US/PT	Patent Protection Under the Industrial Property Act	1996	Full
80	2-May-1997	US/BE	Measures Affecting Commercial Telephone Directory Services	1998	Full
83	14-May-1997	US/DK	Measures Affecting the Enforcement of Intellectual Property Rights	2001	Full
86	28-May-1997	US/SE	Measures Affecting the Enforcement of Intellectual Property Rights	1998	Full
82,115	14-May-1997	US/EC,IE	Measures Affecting the Grant of Copyright and of Neighbouring Rights	1998	Full
124,125	30-Apr-1998	US/EC,GR	Enforcement of Intellectual Property Rights For Motion Pictures and Television Programmes	2001	Full
160	26-Jan-1999	EC/US	Section 110(5) of the US Copyright Act ('Irish Music')	2002*	Partial*
174	1-Jun-1999	US/EC	Protection of Trademarks and Geographical Indications for Agricultural Products	2002*	Partial*
176	8-Jul-1999	EC/US	Section 211 Omnibus Appropriations Act ('Havana Club')	2002*	Full*

*denotes cases with apparent but still tentative policy outcomes.

a considerable outlay of resources on the part of the disputants and the WTO. Further, we are not arguing that the weaknesses on IP associated with US intransigence in the GATT-era *Aramid Fibres* and *Spring Assemblies* disputes (see notes 18 and 31) were fully corrected by TRIPs; the still-unfinished EC WTO complaint on the same US statute (*Section 337*, DS186) disconfirms this notion. Rather, the point is that TRIPs and GATS have induced, probably on a one-time basis, a special set of disputes distinguished by their direct relationship to these recent commitments, and are thus ready-made for full concessions. Put more simply, better dispute settlement procedures *per se* did not force the defendant's hand in these cases.

After controlling for the improved dispute outcomes achieved through this expansion of scope, does the more legalistic WTO dispute system still perform better than GATT? To find out, we use the technique of multivariate regression to model the probability that the defendant makes concessions in these US-EC disputes (see Table 18.3). This time-honoured method allows us to quantify the

TABLE 18.3. Ordered Probit Model of 85 US-EC GATT/WTO dispute outcomes, 1960–2001

Dependent Variable: Level of Concessions	Coefficient	Robust Standard Error
Intercept 1	0.179	0.351
Intercept 2	0.884**	0.351
Panel Established	2.048**	0.799
Ruling for Complainant	−1.306*	0.790
Mixed ruling	−1.719*	0.881
Ruling for Defendant	−2.351**	0.952
Complainant is US	−0.018	0.339
WTO Case	0.472	0.394
IP or Services WTO Case	1.419**	0.599
Agriculture	0.620*	0.332
Multilateral Case	−0.563*	0.296
Discriminatory Measure	0.873**	0.340
SPS or Cultural Case	−1.681*	0.848
Number of Observations	85 (53 GATT, 32 WTO)	
Model χ^2	32.34**, 11 d.o.f.	
Pseudo-R^2	0.195	
Percent Correctly Predicted	64.7	

*denotes one-tailed $p < 0.05$;** $p < 0.01$.

independent impact of one variable (the DSU reforms) while controlling for the effect of other variables (eg, scope expansion). The dependent, or outcome, variable is the level of concessions the defendant makes in each of the 85 cases: none, partial, or full concessions.[32] To explain the level of concessions, we include a dummy variable reflecting whether the case was brought under GATT versus WTO procedures (the shaded row in Table 18.3). A separate dummy variable identifies just those WTO-era cases on IP or traded services issues (ie, coded one for the nine cases in Table 18.2, and zero otherwise). If our explanation is right, the WTO variable should not be significantly different from zero (showing no difference between GATT and WTO overall), while the dummy for WTO-era IP or traded services disputes should be significant and positive. To make sure our estimates for these two variables are not driven by other important features of each dispute, the model also controls for whether a panel was established, the direction of a subsequent panel or AB report (if any), whether the US was the complainant, whether the dispute concerned an agricultural product, whether it was 'multilateral' (ie, with several disputants or third parties), and whether it centred on strictly discriminatory measures or covered

[32] Hence we use a particular form of multivariate regression known as *ordered probit*.

'sensitive' issues like health and safety (SPS) or cultural matters. The results in Table 18.3 indicate that the model fits the data adequately, correctly predicting about two-thirds of these dispute outcomes.

The main point to flag in Table 18.3 is that our hypotheses appear correct. Namely, while the variable for WTO disputes involving IP and traded services is positively signed and statistically significant, the WTO variable itself (shaded) is not significantly different from zero. The model indicates that, holding all other variables at their sample means, a dispute over IP or traded services is 43 per cent more likely to end with full concessions by the defendant under the WTO than it was under GATT. Yet the probability of concessions by defendants is *no more likely* now than under GATT, when one considers areas outside of IP and services trade.[33] Keep in mind that this result accounts for the differing legal dispositions of each case.

The regression provides a number of other interesting quantitative findings. Specifically, defendants are 22 per cent *less* likely to concede in multilateral as opposed to purely bilateral disputes; 43 per cent *less* likely to concede in SPS or cultural cases; yet 33 per cent *more* likely to concede in cases involving purely discriminatory measures; and 24 per cent *more* likely to concede in agricultural cases. Even more important for the argument in section D below, we find that in these 85 GATT/WTO US-EC cases, the defendant is much more likely to concede in advance of ruling, rather than after, regardless of the ruling's direction. In particular, a ruling for the defendant reduces the probability of full concessions by about 63 per cent; a mixed ruling by 43 per cent; and even a ruling for the *complainant* cuts the chances of concessions by roughly 25 per cent. Clearly, where the US and EC litigate to a verdict, concessions in transatlantic disputes are *less* likely.

B. The WTO's poor record in high stakes disputes

For many observers, the true measure of the success of a dispute settlement mechanism is how it handles the 'toughest' cases. Hence we categorize the WTO-era transatlantic disputes according to their approximate monetary and political stakes, either low/medium or high. A 'low' or 'medium' score applies when a dispute affects less than $50 million (or $150 million, respectively) of annual trade (eg, *Poultry Products*, DS100), or if the broader potential ramifications of the disputed policy are not in practice realized by virtue of the defendant's restraint from the start (eg, *Cuban Liberty and Solidarity Act*, DS38). Fully 25 of the 32 WTO-era US-EC conflicts fall into these two categories. A 'high' score indicates annual affected trade levels or authorized retaliation levels above $150 million and/or intense perceived significance for the future of WTO dispute settlement or the US-EC trading relationship. Table 18.4 lists these seven cases.

[33] The coefficient of *WTO Case* in Table 18.3 is positive but hardly larger than its standard error, so we cannot with statistical confidence reject the very likely possibility that the WTO has had no effect whatsoever.

TABLE 18.4. High Stakes US-EC WTO disputes

DS	Start	Compl/Def	Title	End	Level of Concessions
26	25-Apr-1996	US/EC	Measures Affecting Meat and Meat Products ('Hormones')	1999	None
27 (16) 62,67,68	5-Feb-1996	US/EC	Import Regime for Bananas	2001	Partial
	8-Nov-1996	US/EC,UK,IE	Customs Classification of Certain Computer Equipment	1998	Full
108	18-Nov-1997	EC/US	Tax Treatment For Foreign Sales Corporations	2002*	None*
136	9-Jun-1998	EC/US	Anti-Dumping Act of 1916	2002*	None*
152	25-Nov-1998	EC/US	Sections 301-310 of the Trade Act of 1974 ('Section 301')	2000	None
165	4-Mar-1999	EC/US	Import Measures on Certain Products from the European Communities	2001	Full

*denotes cases with apparent but still tentative policy outcomes.

If the DSU reforms have improved US-EC dispute outcomes, then we ought to find that the defendant has made substantial concessions in at least a few of these highest-stakes cases. After all, these cases matter most for the WTO dispute settlement regime by definition. The record in Table 18.4 is, however, rather poor, albeit somewhat tentative. The defendant fully conceded to the complainant's demands in just two of the seven cases so far, with a partial victory in one more. What is more, these three instances of concessions were largely driven by factors outside the dispute settlement system. For example, in the *Customs Classification* (DS62, 67, 68) case, the EC ultimately eliminated tariffs entirely on local area network (LAN) products, effectively reversing the reclassification which had prompted the US complaint. But this action resulted from the multilateral Information Technology Agreement (and was thereby compensated with additional US concessions), not from the US litigation, which in any case was rejected by the AB.[34]

The *Bananas* (DS16, 27) settlement, as announced in April 2001, delays true 'tariffication' of the quotas for five years and retains significant preferences for the ACP producers, to their great satisfaction.[35] Coming after nearly ten years of deadlock and bankruptcy for a leading US-owned exporting firm (Chiquita), this outcome can only be classified as a partial victory for the US. Insiders also frankly admit that the primary impetus for settlement was the EC's desire to remove obstacles to the imminent Doha Round, not from the WTO legal condemnation.

In the third case, *Import Measures on Certain Products* (DS165), premature US retaliation on the *Bananas* dispute was at issue. Though the preliminary

[34] General Accounting Office, *World Trade Organization: Issues in Dispute Settlement*, GAO/NSIAD-00–210 (August 2000), at 73–74.
[35] See remarks in *Financial Times*, 12 April 2001; *Business and Industry*, 13 April 2001.

sanctions were judged illegitimate, the AB approved the substitute measures in place by the time of its report. Hence, just as in *Customs Classification* above, the defendant's concessions once again were not motivated by WTO legal action. The US withdrew the retaliation only because of the nominal settlement by the EC on the *Bananas* case—no more than a technical success, if that, for the WTO.[36] The clear failure on *Hormones* (DS26) and the apparent (but perhaps still reversible) deadlocks on *Foreign Sales Corporations* (DS108) and *Anti-Dumping Act of 1916* (DS136) testify that defendants still do not concede where it counts most for the regime.

C. Déjà vu all over again

Another benchmark against which the DSU's mettle might be assessed concerns those GATT cases that have recurred under the WTO. If the DSU is truly an improvement over the GATT system, then it should have induced better outcomes in those disputes that repeated across these two regimes, providing for a 'second kick at the can'. What does the record show?

Consider the 1972-1984 *Domestic International Sales Corporation (DISC)* and the 1997-2002 *Foreign Sales Corporations (FSC)* complaints by the EC against US tax practices that subsidize exports, along with the accompanying counter-complaints by the US against alleged similar EC member state subsidies. The GATT-era *DISC* ruling, which the parties blocked from adoption for many years, is legendary for its 'faulty reasoning',[37] and the dozen years before settlement speak poorly for GATT's efficacy as well.[38] The relative rapidity, legal professionalism, and lack of veto of the WTO rulings on the EC's 1997 successor suit against the 1984 law implementing the *DISC* settlement, *FSC*, make the WTO shine in comparison.

But in other ways the WTO record in *FSC* is no better. WTO legalism has allowed the EC to force the issue, so that it now confronts the necessity to retaliate with a 'nuclear weapon'[39] (from $1–4 billion of sanctions per year), a desperately costly proposition for both disputants. The EC's recent appeasing statements contrast sharply with those on lower-stakes cases against the US, indicating a recognition that a settlement, even one that provides just a fiction of compliance, may be preferred.[40] (In this respect the EC faces the same situation

---

[36] To be fair, one could use the same reasoning to argue that the lack of US concessions in *Section 301* (DS152) should not count as a failure for the WTO dispute settlement system, since the ruling upheld the legality of the US statute.

[37] J.H. Jackson, 'The Jurisprudence of International Trade: The DISC Case in GATT' (1978) 72 *American Journal of International Law* 747–781, at 781.

[38] R.E. Hudec, *Enforcing International Trade Law: The Evolution of the Modern GATT Legal System* (1993), at 59–100.

[39] The term is US Trade Representative Robert Zoellick's (*International Trade Reporter*, 17 May 2001, 778).

[40] For instance, an anonymous European Commission official has suggested that compensation rather than strict compliance might be acceptable in the *FSC* case, saying, '[we want] to avoid this issue becoming a major dispute' (*Financial Times*, 15 January 2002).

as Canada did once retaliation against Brazilian aircraft subsidies was authorized in the *Export Financing Programme* case, DS46.) The WTO panel missed a
reasonable opportunity to forge an opening for a compromise, one more acceptable to the US Congress, by treating the case as linked to the earlier *DISC*
settlement. The *DISC* settlement may have achieved little, but at least it defused
a contentious issue that could have had negative effects for the regime. What
counts most, of course, is that the WTO dispute has not induced any more
change from the status quo US policy than the GATT complaint did, despite
the clearest legal rulings the institution could produce. Thus, here the WTO
exhibits little improvement.

Hormones, *Harbour Maintenance*, and *Bananas* offer comparable testimony.
The EC blocked a US panel request in the 1987 *Animal Hormones Directive*
complaint, and in reprisal the US blocked the EC's request for a panel to rule
against the subsequent unilateral US retaliation.[41] Under the WTO procedures,
unlike under GATT, the EC has been unable to block definitive legal condemnation of its policy, but the US has once again retaliated and the EC ban remains in
place, just as before. Similarly, the EC has twice disputed the US policy of taxing
shipping to pay for harbour maintenance (constituting an effective import tax),
once in 1992 (*Harbour Maintenance Fees*) and again in 1998 (*Harbour Maintenance Tax*, DS118). Neither case was brought before a panel. While the
Clinton administration proposed a change that may have satisfied the EC, the
necessary legislation was not passed. The best hope for change in the status quo
lies now in US domestic litigation, not in WTO action. Furthermore, in the two
GATT complaints against the banana import regimes of the EC and its member
states, the EC blocked adoption of not one but two adverse panel reports in 1993
and 1994. The DSB of course succeeded in adopting the WTO *Bananas* reports,
but as noted earlier, the ultimate concessions by the EC leave much to be desired
in extent and timeliness, and are probably attributable to other factors in any
case. Déjà vu, to be sure. Thus it would be hard to argue that the WTO is
succeeding where GATT once failed, in these recurrent cases.

D. The successes occur as early settlement, not compliance with rulings

One commonly held view in the literature is that the success of early settlement
under GATT is increasingly less evident under the WTO, especially in consultations.[42] While bargaining 'in the shadow of the law' proved efficacious under
GATT's more diplomatic system, the argument is that the DSU's reforms may
have made litigation attractive, motivating complainants to push for a definitive
verdict. As evidence, many observers point not only to the caseload at the panel

---

[41] R.E. Hudec, *Enforcing International Trade Law: The Evolution of the Modern GATT Legal System* (1993), at 574–575.

[42] O.L. Wethington, 'Commentary on the Consultation Mechanism Under the WTO Dispute Understanding During Its First Five Years' (2000) 31 *Law & Policy in International Business* 583–590 at 587.

stage, but the frequency of appeals to the AB. We show elsewhere[43] that the proportion of cases 'panelled' differs little across the GATT/WTO years, and that the WTO's greater caseload reflects growth in the institution's membership and volume of world trade. In terms of the transatlantic relationship in particular, early settlement is perhaps more important than ever, a point quite evident in Figure 18.1, which graphs the level of concessions achieved in WTO disputes ending at various stages of escalation.

The first point to make about US-EC disputes is that this dyad has tended to settle early at the GATT/WTO, with the defendant offering concessions in advance of a ruling 58 per cent of the time. In the WTO years, this stands at 66 per cent (21 of 32 disputes). The more telling question, of course, is whether

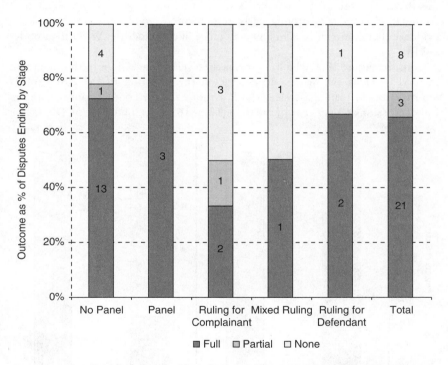

FIGURE 18.1. Early Settlement: The level of concessions in US-EC WTO disputes ending at different stages of escalation

Note: Darker area represents percentage of cases ending at the given stage (eg, prior to panel establishment) in which defendant fully concedes. Numbers in bars denote the actual number of cases in each subcategory; the total is 32. The listed ruling direction is that of the AB, not the panel, in appealed cases.

[43] M.L. Busch & E. Reinhardt, 'Bargaining in the Shadow of the Law: Early Settlement in GATT/WTO Disputes' (2000) 24 (1&2) *Fordham International Law Journal* 158–172.

early settlement produces positive results. Of this there can be no doubt. The data tell a remarkable story: of the 21 US-EC disputes ending in *full* concessions at the WTO, 16 were resolved in advance of a panel ruling. If we set a lower bar and examine disputes in which *any* concessions were offered, the data favour early settlement by a margin of 17 to 7. In short, it is only a slight exaggeration to suggest that all of the 'real action' in US-EC disputes is in early settlement.

The obvious retort to this would be that early settlement is, itself, a reflection of the reforms ushered in by the DSU. In other words, the propensity to settle early simply reflects the logic of bargaining in the shadow of 'strong' law, in that defendants plead good cases and complainants withdraw weak ones.[44] This would be convincing, were it not for the fact that the data are at odds with this logic. The key to this hypothesis would necessarily be that enforcement of compliance *ex post* is driving early settlement *ex ante*, and yet there is no evidence that compliance is in any way more likely under the WTO than under GATT.

Consider Figure 18.2, which compares the level of concessions by the defendant in GATT versus the WTO, depending on the direction of the panel (or, if appropriate, AB) ruling. Under GATT, a ruling for the complainant resulted in full concessions 63 per cent of the time (10 of 16 cases); under the WTO, facing

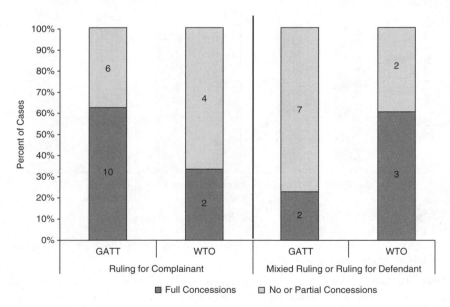

FIGURE 18.2.   Compliance: Level of concessions by ruling direction under GATT and WTO, for US-EC disputes

[44] J.H. Jackson, 'Dispute Settlement and the WTO: Emerging Problems' in *The Jurisprudence of GATT and the WTO: Insights on Treaty Law and Economic Relations* (2000), at 179.

an adverse ruling, the defendant has fully conceded just 33 per cent of the time (two of six disputes).[45] Granted, with only six WTO rulings unambiguously against the defendant, we cannot compare the regimes yet with statistical confidence, but so far the WTO is actually inducing *less* compliance with adverse rulings, in US-EC disputes. Hence, because compliance is still as significant a problem (if not more), the WTO's increased legalism is probably not responsible for the regime's continuing dependence on early settlement for most of its *successful* dispute outcomes.

However, could the WTO's greater legalism have improved upon GATT at least in the *easier* cases, if not in the most difficult transatlantic conflicts? If so, the infrequency of compliance does not necessarily mean dispute settlement efficacy has not increased, because higher-stakes cases may disproportionately go to panels and beyond. The fact that all seven of the highest-stakes conflicts in Table 18.4 witnessed rulings is certainly consistent with this explanation. Nonetheless, we argue this interpretation of the evidence misses the point, for three reasons. First, quite a few WTO disputes have ended with no or limited concessions by the defendant *without* being brought before a panel. For instance, in *Flight Management Systems* (DS172), the US objected to a one-time $25 million subsidy by France to Sextant Avionique, a supplier of avionics for Airbus, but the dispute died on the table. Just because a dispute involves small stakes, or does not continue through the litigation process, does not mean it will end with concessions by the defendant, as can be seen in Table 18.5.

Second, if procedural reforms have induced more early settlement because they darken the 'shadow of the law' in anticipation,[46] why do complainants sometimes fail to pressure defendants with the threat of a ruling, even in promising cases? The defendant failed to concede fully in *Harbour Maintenance Tax* (DS118) and *Trademarks and Geographical Indications* (DS174), but no panel

TABLE 18.5. US-EC WTO dispute outcomes by stakes

	Level of Concessions			
Stakes	*None*	*Partial*	*Full*	*Total*
Low/Medium	4	2	19	25
High	4	1	2	7
Total	8	3	21	32

Note: Fisher's exact test yields $p = 0.037$.

[45] *Bananas, Hormones, FSC, and Anti-Dumping Act of 1916* are the four WTO cases with no or partial compliance by this reckoning.
[46] J.H. Jackson, 'Dispute Settlement and the WTO: Emerging Problems' in *The Jurisprudence of GATT and the WTO: Insights on Treaty Law and Economic Relations* (2000), at 174.

request was made. Two ongoing disputes (thus not in our dataset) stand out in this regard. Of the 14 concluded US-EC WTO cases that went before a panel, the median delay between the request of consultations and panel establishment was just five months. But the EC has not made a panel request in *Section 337* (DS186) and *Section 306* ('Carousel Retaliation', DS200), even 27 and 22 months, respectively, since the complaints were filed. If improved legalism is indeed responsible for early settlement, the EC seems to have missed a golden opportunity to use the threat of a ruling to leverage concessions from the US.

Third, if the most vaunted procedural reforms—namely, removing the defendant's veto—have made early settlement more likely (at least in the easier cases), then we would expect much less early settlement under the GATT rules, where defendants could block the adoption of reports and even panel establishment. Yet early settlement was a hallmark of the GATT era.[47] Clearly the normative power of a GATT ruling, regardless of its legal adoption, was most important.[48] Successes in the form of early settlement in the WTO era are probably driven by the same dynamic.

V. IMPLICATIONS AND CONCLUSIONS

Long admired for its more legalistic design, the WTO's DSU has been heralded as a big step forward in dispute settlement. Indeed, many observers hold to the view that the DSU may well be the most significant outcome of the Uruguay Round, distinguishing the WTO from other international institutions more generally. We dissent from this view, arguing instead that the diplomacy of GATT is alive, but perhaps not well, at the WTO. Let us be clear on this point: we are encouraged by the pattern of concessions we observe in US-EC disputes, notably with regard to early settlement, but find that the DSU's reforms *per se* have not helped in this regard, and may ultimately hurt. We see these reforms leading to an overly litigious approach to dispute settlement, depriving the system of its greatest strength for managing transatlantic conflicts: namely, diplomacy. The fault lies not in the WTO itself, but in the membership's zealous drive to litigate, rather than confront the domestic politics of protectionism.

The empirical tests reported above are not exhaustive, but they are critical. We examined the implications of the DSU's greater scope, the stakes of the US-EC disputes under the WTO, and the institution's handling of cases that repeated from the GATT era. Our results suggest that the main contribution of the DSU is

---

[47] M.L. Busch & E. Reinhardt, 'Bargaining in the Shadow of the Law: Early Settlement in GATT/WTO Disputes' (2000) 24 (1&2) *Fordham International Law Journal* 158–172; and E. Reinhardt, 'Adjudication without Enforcement in GATT Disputes' (2001) 45(2) *Journal of Conflict Resolution* 174–195.

[48] R.E. Hudec, 'The New WTO Dispute Settlement Procedure: An Overview of the First Three Years' (1999) 8 *Minnesota Journal of Global Trade* 1–53.

that it has grown to include IP and traded services, but that even here, the data speak more to the kind of disputes arising under TRIPs and GATS than they do to the workings of these agreements *per se*. More to the point, the vast majority of US-EC disputes under TRIPs to date have centred on the phase-in of commitments that were already in progress. Thus, while we concur that the DSU's coverage of IP and traded services is, in fact, a significant improvement, the hardest test cases under TRIPs and GATS are likely still to come.

Our findings suggest, more provocatively, that the WTO has fared little better than GATT in its handling of high-stakes US-EC disputes, or GATT-era cases that have resurfaced since 1995. These strike us as obvious benchmarks against which to assess the workings of the DSU, and yet the data belie conventional wisdom: the DSU boasts a poor track record in resolving high stakes US-EC disputes, and has hardly proved effective when given a second 'kick at the can' in those disputes that have repeated from the GATT era.

The issue of early settlement under the WTO is more interesting still. The expectation is that we should see more early settlement under the WTO, since disputants have incentive to plead out a case in the shadow of strong law. If such a pattern was, in fact, evident, we could trace it to the DSU's legal reforms *per se* by looking for greater *ex post* compliance with panel and AB rulings. We find no such evidence. On the one hand, this leads us to marvel that early settlement, while not more evident under the WTO, remains a pillar of the system, much as it was under GATT. As US Trade Representative Robert Zoellick said in a speech to the European Parliament, '[w]e must be more creative in settling bilateral disputes. . . . Litigation is not always the solution for solving every problem.'[49] On the other hand, a statement like Zoellick's may be easy when one is the legal loser (*FSC* in this case), but restraint is difficult when the opportunity presents itself to begin a successful retaliatory lawsuit. We see reason to fear that early settlement—still the regime's main avenue for achieving successful dispute resolution—may be jeopardized by the DSU's enhanced legalism. Mike Moore is certainly correct in pointing out that 'settlement . . . is the key principle', without which 'it would be virtually impossible to maintain the delicate balance of international rights and obligations'.[50]

Unlike other observers, we do *not* recommend turning back the clock on the WTO in pursuit of more diplomatic times.[51] Rather, we propose three ways to enhance the DSU's efficacy: (1) resist the temptation to increase transparency in the consultation stage; (2) formalize the 21*bis* 'solution' to the sequencing problem; and (3) institute retroactive damages. First, calls to make the consultation stage more transparent, by giving the public more access or by bringing the

---

[49] *International Trade Reporter*, 17 May 2001, at 778.

[50] M. Moore, 'WTO's Unique System of Settling Disputes Nears 200 Cases in 2000' PRESS/180, WTO (2000).

[51] C.E. Barfield, *Free Trade, Sovereignty, Democracy: The Future of the World Trade Organization* (2001).

panel into the process,[52] are mistaken. Theory makes it clear that disputants will not 'deal' if offers made in pre-trial discovery can be introduced as evidence before a judge or a jury.[53] Greater transparency, by raising 'audience costs' in negotiations,[54] would have this effect. Along these lines, evidence from the GATT years[55] suggests that highly democratic pairs of states are more likely to settle early in consultations, likely because governments enjoy far more latitude in relation to their industrial constituents to strike deals at this stage of dispute settlement. The case-studies in this volume are instructive in examining how disputants approach consultations, and why, at times, they seem to be pro forma, whereas at other times, they facilitate concessions in the shadow of the law.

Second, disagreement over the sequencing of Articles 21.5 and 22 in the wake of a ruling has been a source of uncertainty and foot-dragging. And while the disputants in several cases to date have reached informal agreement on sequencing,[56] formalizing this is likely to build confidence in the dispute settlement system. Indeed, a number of countries are of the view that Article 21*bis*[57] would streamline litigation in the post-verdict phase of a dispute by requiring a compliance panel in advance of an arbitration panel, for example, and clarifying the appeals process with respect to 21.5 panels, in particular. Several of the case-studies in this volume offer a window on how disputants regard the post-verdict phase of dispute settlement, suggesting how this procedural reform might induce more settlement *ex ante*.

Third, it is well known that the DSU is about compliance with obligations, not retaliation, let alone retroactive damages. This means that there is ample room for a defendant to benefit from a protectionist measure for years while a case is heard, without fear that an arbitration panel would hold it accountable for its pre-ruling actions. We concur with a growing number of scholars who favour retroactive damages[58] as a way to curb the temptation for governments to act on domestic demands for protection, reaping electoral returns while awaiting a negative ruling at the WTO. The case-studies in this volume highlight how compensation may influence the calculus of disputants, and by extension how retroactive damages might shape the way cases are litigated, if at all.

[52] C.C. Parlin, 'Operation of Consultations, Deterrence, and Mediation' (2000) 31(3) *Law & Policy in International Business* 565–572.

[53] A.F. Daughety & J.F. Reinganum, 'Keeping Society in the Dark: On the Admissibility of Pretrial Negotiations as Evidence in Court' (1995) 26(2) *Rand Journal of Economics* 203–221.

[54] J. Fearon, 'Signaling Foreign Policy Interests: Tying Hands Versus Sinking Costs' (1997) 41(1) *Journal of Conflict Resolution* 68–90.

[55] M.L. Busch, 'Democracy, Consultation, and the Paneling of Disputes Under GATT' (2000) 44(4) *Journal of Conflict Resolution* 425–446.

[56] C.M. Valles & B.P. McGivern (2000) 34(2) *Journal of World Trade* 63–84.

[57] WT/MIN(99)/8; TN/DS/W/1.

[58] P.C. Mavroidis, 'Remedies in the WTO Legal System: Between a Rock and a Hard Place' (2000) 11(4) *European Journal of International Law* 763–813; and J. Pauwelyn, 'Enforcement and Counter-measures in the WTO: Rules are Rules—Toward a More Collective Approach' (2000) 94(2) *American Journal of International Law* 335–347.

   This paper offers some new empirical insights into the transatlantic relationship at the WTO, but its greatest service may be in raising questions not only
about these bilateral disputes, but the functioning of the dispute settlement
system more generally. Several questions stand out. Most obviously, are transatlantic disputes representative? Or is this bilateral relationship *sui generis*? Is the
WTO system more effective than GATT in deterring violations from arising?
And related to this, has the increasing legalism in dispute settlement procedures
affected states' propensity to file meritorious WTO suits? More generally, how
does the existence of other dispute resolution fora, notably under regional trade
agreements, influence the efficacy of the WTO system? And how are dispute
settlement outcomes related to the broader context of WTO negotiations?
These and other questions merit close scrutiny as the WTO turns a reflective
eye on the DSU on the eve of the Doha Round.

19

Renegotiation in Transatlantic Trade Disputes

HEINZ HAUSER and ALEXANDER ROITINGER*

I. INTRODUCTION

A great number of theoretical and empirical studies have examined the performance of the World Trade Organization (WTO) dispute settlement (DS) since its introduction in 1995.[1] Although the mechanism generally seems to be useful for settling disputes, a number of problems have been identified. To begin with, it is doubtful that developing countries have equal opportunities to enforce their rights. Secondly, some rulings have been criticized for their sole emphasis on promoting trade liberalization, ignoring in particular environmental concerns. Thirdly, the exact nature of settlement and its economic impact is unknown in most cases and is possibly not in accordance with WTO agreements. Yet, the most important problems—and we will focus on them—are apparently those related to disputed implementation of Dispute Settlement Body (DSB) rulings. Although the Dispute Settlement Understanding (DSU) sets a timeframe and urges the losing defendant to comply, there have been numerous delays, conflicts about interpretation of the text, severe threats, and high-profile cases of outright non-compliance.

Such implementation problems have been particularly relevant for the relationship between the United States (US) and the European Communities (EC). Some transatlantic disputes have received enormous publicity in this regard, and they are not expected to be the last. In fact, the situation seems to be so critical that two conclusions play a prominent role among observers. The first one claims that we are undergoing a series of 'trade wars'. This view is nurtured by aggressive speeches of politicians and the tendency to use the word 'sanction' when talking about the suspension of concessions authorized by the DSB. The

---

* We are grateful to Volker Rittberger, who made very helpful comments on an earlier version of this paper.

[1] See Leitner & Lester, 'WTO Dispute Settlement 1995–2002: A Statistical Analysis' (2003) 6 *JIEL* 251; Bütler & Hauser, 'The WTO Dispute Settlement System: A First Assessment from an Economic Perspective' (2000) 16 *JLEO* 503; Hudec, 'The New WTO Dispute Settlement Procedure: An Overview of the First Three Years' (1999) 8 *Minnesota Journal of Global Trade* 1, and the contribution by M.L. Busch & E. Reinhardt in this volume.

second one focuses on the specific role of the WTO in these conflicts and suggests that its credibility is severely at risk due to the alleged 'failure' of the DS in resolving them.

In what follows, we will question these conclusions. In our view, disputes are about renegotiation, not about war. Furthermore, even if there is no immediate compliance with a DSB ruling, the credibility of the WTO DS is not impaired, as long as its function is properly understood.

As reference point for our analysis, we offer in the following section a 'rule-oriented' perspective on disputes and non-compliance. The bottom line of this perspective is confronted in section III with an alternative view, which highlights the importance of flexibility through renegotiation in the face of incomplete contracting and 'local' lack of commitment. It will be shown that members of the WTO have had in mind to endow the agreements with a good portion of such flexibility when concluding them. Whereas section III is merely positive in nature, the fourth section adds some normative considerations about flexibility. Section V assesses three transatlantic disputes in light of the renegotiation perspective, and the last section concludes.

II. A RULE-ORIENTED PERSPECTIVE

Analysts who complain about alleged failures of the WTO DS implicitly argue that the level of 'rule orientation' among members is too low and that the best way to cope with such problems is to strengthen the bindingness of rulings.[2]

For the purpose of our paper, we emphasize two distinct facets of rule orientation in an international trade agreement. The first facet is relevant whenever a member alleges that a breach of contract has occurred. Then, someone has to determine whether this allegation is true. Such adjudication does not only give a clue of what is 'right' or 'wrong'. It also influences the distribution of contract value. In this context, rule orientation would have to be contrasted with power orientation.[3] The latter predicts that adjudication results in a solution which reflects the difference in power of the countries. The more powerful country is expected to attain a more favourable outcome *ceteris paribus*. In contrast, the rule-oriented determination makes reference to rules and procedures previously agreed upon, is based on equality of countries, and would include impartial third-party arbitration. It is argued that such rule orientation has continuously gained support since the establishment of the GATT, notably due to a more and more legalistic DS process.

The second facet of rule orientation takes the determination of breach as given and deals with the nature of remedial action. In the WTO context, it is about

---

[2] This might be achieved, for example, by raising the authorized retaliation level in case of non-compliance.

[3] See J.H. Jackson, *The World Trading System: Law and Policy of International Economic Relations* (1997), at 109.

implementation of a DSB ruling, and therefore about the legal effect of an adopted panel (or Appellate Body) report. Under the rule-oriented perspective, such ruling creates an international legal obligation upon disputing parties to carry out the decisions of the DSB.[4] A losing defendant is consequently obliged to 'specific performance' as regards the adopted recommendations. John H. Jackson examines the DSU and finds at least 11 clauses that support such rule orientation.[5] An opposite view would be that the losing defendant has free choice between compliance with the ruling, offering of concessions in other areas, or acceptance of retaliation in the form of suspension of concessions. The second facet of rule orientation is accordingly not contrasted with power orientation, but with flexibility of implementation.

It is this second facet that stands at the forefront of discussion today. There is indeed a debate about the question of to what extent members of the WTO must be guided by rule orientation when implementing a DSB ruling.[6] This debate is of utmost importance, and from now on, we will implicitly have in mind this second facet whenever we talk about 'rule orientation'.

There is no doubt that, from a static perspective, such rule orientation contributes decisively to the security and transparency of the world trading framework. However, taking into consideration that agreements are concluded and maintained by governments, which form expectations about their future usefulness, the rigidity incorporated in the bindingness of DSB rulings becomes an element of concern. Admittedly, rule orientation might eventually be the *preferred* way to settle a dispute, and the DSU says in Article 22:1 that '...neither compensation nor the suspension of concessions or other obligations is preferred to full implementation of a recommendation to bring a measure into conformity with the covered agreements'. However, a preference *per definitionem* leaves room for alternative solutions. And it cannot be interpreted as an obligation to go ahead in a particular way.

III. An alternative perspective: flexibility and renegotiation

Flexibility, which is understood as the provision of renegotiation opportunities between multilateral rounds of liberalization, is essential for the success of

---

[4] See Jackson, 'Designing and Implementing Effective Dispute Settlement Procedures: WTO Dispute Settlement, Appraisal and Prospects' in A.O. Krueger (ed), *The WTO as an International Organization* (1998) 161, at 169.

[5] See Jackson, 'The WTO Dispute Settlement Understanding—Misunderstanding on the Nature of Legal Obligation' (1997) 91 *AJIL* 60, at footnote 11.

[6] Schwartz & Sykes, 'The Economic Structure of Renegotiation and Dispute Resolution in the WTO/GATT System' (2002) 31 *JLS* S179; Sykes, 'The Remedy for Breach of Obligations under the WTO Dispute Settlement Understanding: Damages or Specific Performance?' in M. Bronckers & R. Quick (eds), *New Directions in International Economic Law* (2000), 347; and Bello, 'The WTO Dispute Settlement Understanding: Less is More' (1996) 90 *AJIL* 416, are prominent sources which tend to reject the claim that there is a legal obligation to comply.

international trade agreements. It allows adaptation to a changing environment, and it is necessary whenever governments should be induced to make far reaching long-term concessions.

In fact, rule orientation does not necessarily preclude renegotiation. After having demonstrated the need for renegotiation from a government perspective, we will describe a number of 'conventional' instruments that can be used for such a purpose. These are consistent with rule orientation, since they are based on explicit provisions of the WTO agreements. However, these tools unduly restrict flexibility. The deficiency is removed if violation and non-compliance are admitted as implicit instruments for renegotiation.

A. Motivations for renegotiation

There is an indefinite number of possible reasons why governments want to renegotiate an international trade agreement. We consider a broad concept of renegotiation here and use the term whenever a government deviates from a concession[7] between multilateral rounds of liberalization. This deviation provokes a response by affected trading partners, but it does not challenge the continuity of the agreement. Renegotiation is assumed to be about more protectionism, not about less. Using this definition, it should be stressed that such behaviour must entail costs for the initiating country. Otherwise, we would almost permanently be confronted with renegotiation. Benefits and costs of deviations have to be understood in terms of political economy. International trade agreements are concluded between governments, and each government chooses its trade policy by maximizing an individual objective function. The latter consists of a weighted sum of political contributions from lobby groups and some aggregate social welfare.[8] The structure of optimal protection is vulnerable to changes in different variables, such as the degree of political organization of lobby groups or the relative weight that the government attaches to political contributions compared to overall welfare. The general economic climate, the election cycle, or technological advance—to name just a few—can also have a substantial influence on the desired level of current protection. Such diversity of factors and the uncertainty characterizing their development make it impossible to write an international trade agreement that anticipates the future and makes all actions (or prohibitions) contingent on the evolvement of these variables. From a government perspective, any agreement is therefore characterized by too much 'rigidity': the concessions are not made sufficiently dependent on the future state of the world. Rigidity is one of two distinct forms of incomplete contracting, the other one being 'discretion'.[9] Discretion is given when a

[7] Such as a tariff binding, the abolition of quantitative restrictions, or the protection of an intellectual property right.
[8] This function is along the lines of Grossman & Helpman, 'Protection for Sale' (1994) 84 *AER* 833.
[9] See Battigalli & Maggi, 'Rigidity, Discretion and the Costs of Writing Contracts' (2002) 92 *AER* 798.

contract does not specify the concessions with precision. Expectations about the behaviour of contract partners might be disappointed after the conclusion of an agreement. In short, both rigidity and discretion can make governments *ex post* unhappy with their contract.

Though incomplete contracting can in many instances explain why governments want to renegotiate, this is not the only source. The WTO agreements represent a contract which covers an immense field of trade (and related) topics and which includes at present 146 member countries. Negotiations in the run-up to the conclusion of the Uruguay Round were highly complex, and delegations finally came under considerable pressure to achieve a successful result. It is highly probable that some elements of the agreements remained contentious until the very last day of negotiation, and that they remained so even after signing. The successful conclusion of the Round was then an expression of the political will to reach an agreement on essential points. The contentious elements found their way into the agreement and might even have been given an unambiguous wording.[10] Yet, at the same time they were implicitly left for future renegotiation. A 'local' lack of initial commitment therefore represents the second category causing the need for renegotiation. The term 'local' is used to make clear that all governments support the overall contract and that the lack of consensus is limited to minor aspects.

B. Explaining renegotiation provisions in international trade agreements

The previous paragraph identified why individual governments may want to renegotiate. However, this does not yet explain the inclusion of flexibility into an international trade agreement. Since renegotiation is about more protectionism, there are negative externalities on trading partners. Therefore, one might think that co-operation by means of an international agreement would have the task of avoiding just that.

In fact, there are two different reasons why governments co-operatively endow an international agreement with renegotiation provisions. The first one is identified by restating the economic concept of efficient breach of contract in political terms. Then, efficiency is reached when no government can be made better off without impairing the objective functions of other governments. For a given agreement, deviation by government G from a concession would be efficient in the above sense whenever the following condition is fulfilled: G's political benefits from deviation are higher than the political costs incurred by compensating foreign governments for their corresponding loss. In this case, G could compensate its trading partners and enjoy the surplus. Mere compensation

---

[10] Abbott & Snidal, 'Hard and Soft Law in International Governance' (2000) 54 *IO* 421, at 445, by contrast, describe the following solution in case that 'one sticky problem threatens to upset a larger *package deal*': 'Rather than hold up the overall agreement, states can incorporate hortatory or imprecise provisions to deal with the difficult issues, allowing them to proceed with the rest of the bargain.'

is of course only one option: additionally, part of the surplus might also go to the trading partners. We conclude that the political costs of compensation are the minimum costs c_{MIN} that G must bear in case of deviation in order for the criterion of political efficiency to be fulfilled.

The concept of efficient breach of contract is in fact a recipe to *raise* the mutual benefits of an existing international trade agreement. The concept provides no prediction on what happens if the breach (ie, deviation) is denied, except that additional benefits are foregone. However, there is a second explanation for renegotiation provisions in international agreements, which is more explicit on possible negative consequences of denial.[11] We assume once more that an agreement already exists and distinguish two different cases. In the first case, G would derive benefits from deviation, but these benefits are lower than the discounted value for G of future co-operation by means of the agreement. Although a renegotiation device might be efficient, it is not necessary in order to maintain the stability of the agreement: if there is no such device, deviation will not happen, since G does not want to risk termination of the agreement.[12] Yet, things change considerably in the second case, where, from G's perspective, today's benefits from deviation are assumed to exceed the discounted value of future co-operation. Now, G would resign from the agreement if the possibility for renegotiation were excluded, and co-operation would therefore be terminated. A renegotiation device could avoid such an outcome. Examining this stability argument for renegotiation further, we discover that the costs of the renegotiation device must not be higher than the discounted value of future co-operation: otherwise, the renegotiation device would be futile. We conclude that the discounted value of future co-operation defines the maximum costs c_{MAX}, and that the costs for using the renegotiation instrument must therefore be chosen from the efficiency interval $[c_{MIN}, c_{MAX}]$ at the time of designing an international trade agreement with a renegotiation device.[13]

There are two problems with our stability argument. One is the concept of renegotiation proofness.[14] It is difficult to believe that co-operation could break down *forever* absent a renegotiation device, even if a respective threat was

---

[11] Related insights and an extensive game-theoretic treatment can be found in Rosendorff & Milner, 'The Optimal Design of International Trade Institutions: Uncertainty and Escape' (2001) 55 IO 829.

[12] In the absence of a renegotiation device, a deviation *per definitionem* means the termination of agreement.

[13] Referring to our stability argument, one might ask if c_{MIN} still holds under long-term efficiency considerations. Assuming a hypothetical case where the costs of the renegotiation instrument are high enough to avoid deviation always but once, yet that the costs would have to be *below* c_{MIN} in order not to exceed the discounted value of future co-operation for G, one might tend to sacrifice short-term efficiency in this single instance of deviation in order to maintain the long-term stability of the agreement. However, such a constellation would require that the discounted value of future co-operation is lower than the costs of compensation for deviation, and this is not plausible since we have in mind a local renegotiation: the deviation from a concession is marginal in relation to the total amount of concessions included in the agreement, ie, the overwhelming part of co-operation remains untouched.

[14] See, eg, G.W. Downs & D.M. Rocke, *Optimal Imperfection? Domestic Uncertainty and Institutions in International Relations* (1995), at 83.

pronounced by potentially affected trading partners. Such a threat would be time-inconsistent, given that all future governments would have strong incentives to co-operate again, despite an earlier deviation. Yet, an appropriate consideration of renegotiation proofness must depend on a highly specified model, which cannot be envisaged here.

The second problem is the plausibility of the condition that, from G's perspective, the political benefits of deviation today exceed the political value of co-operation in all periods to come. We contend that politicians often have an extremely short time horizon. Due to the election cycle, future benefits are discounted heavily or might not be valued at all. Short-term political benefits from deviation, by contrast, can be the decisive factor for the survival of an incumbent government. Notwithstanding this argument, it is difficult to imagine a country resigning from the WTO. On the other hand, this difficulty might just be a consequence of the fact that the WTO *has* renegotiation devices.

So far, we have assumed that an agreement exists. Yet, the stability argument can be extended and even include the claim that no agreement would be concluded in the first place without renegotiation devices—or that it would be less comprehensive. Without flexibility provisions, governments might refrain from binding their hands if they expect that unforeseeable developments could make the deviation from a concession inevitable for political reasons. This reasoning seems plausible but has an important flaw. If we assume that resignation from an agreement re-establishes the pre-contract situation, a rational government would commit itself until this unfavourable situation occurs. It could thereby temporarily reap the benefits from co-operation, and return to the pre-contract world after deviation. However, such behaviour would almost certainly entail substantial costs, for example due to an expensive initial negotiation process or due to the loss of reputation at the moment of resignation. If these costs are higher than the expected benefits from temporary co-operation, no agreement will be signed.

C. A broad concept of renegotiation

It has already been mentioned that we use a broad concept of renegotiation, including all situations where a country wants to deviate from a concession. Looking at the WTO framework, such deviation might make use of 'conventional' means for renegotiation, such as invoking the safeguard clause, applying explicit provisions for the launch of renegotiations on previous concessions, or imposing anti-dumping and countervailing duties.[15] As explained further below,

---

[15] Anti-dumping and countervailing duties need not be seen as renegotiation devices when they are indeed directed against 'true' dumping or subsidization, however defined. In such cases, there is nothing to renegotiate, since there has never been an agreement on accepting such 'unfair' imports. Yet, looking at the practice of anti-dumping and countervailing duties and the attitude of panels and the Appellate Body in relevant cases, it seems that countries have substantial leeway in interpreting dumping or subsidization. They are obviously allowed to take measures beyond what is considered to be a re-establishment of 'fair trade'.

it makes perfect sense to add to this list the 'unconventional' act of simply violating the rules of an agreement and (possibly) refusing to comply with a subsequent DSB ruling.

Though the enumerated instruments for renegotiation seem to be very different in nature, they have important common properties. They all reflect the flexibility of the WTO agreements. When politically required by particular circumstances, members are enabled to deviate from a concession. The instruments allow the country to deviate locally without putting into question the overall adherence to the agreements, that is membership as such.[16] Nonetheless, each one is associated with distinct costs.

Is it really justified to talk about renegotiation when referring to measures such as invoking a safeguard clause or violating an agreement? Or are we just using a euphemistic expression for an inherently unilateral action that has not the least bargaining component? Consider the violation of an agreement: in fact, the (potential) defendant does nothing but adjust the level of concessions that he is ready to give in exchange for the current level of concessions provided by his trading partners. The latter then decide if they are ready to accept the new balance of concessions, or if they consider that the violation needs to be countered with an adjustment of their own. Taking a dynamic perspective, this mechanism of adjustment reflects a bargaining situation as long as members are ready to participate.

When using one of the renegotiation instruments, the initializing country intends to achieve an improved balance of mutual market access in a particular sector. This balance describes the country's sectoral access conditions on the respective foreign market in relation to the foreign access on the home market. As regards the downside of such an improvement, there is a trade-off between two kinds of cost: a compensatory reverse movement in the balance of market access (possibly in various sectors) on the one hand, and a worsening reputation balance[17] on the other hand. There is little reputation loss if the deviation is accompanied by (market access) concessions in other sectors, or by a bilaterally negotiated reciprocal withdrawal of concessions by the affected trading partner(s). In contrast, if a member uses renegotiation instruments that are not directly connected with a compensatory change of market access (eg, violations), it suffers higher reputation costs. Adding up compensatory market access costs and reputation loss, the total costs of each instrument are determined.

---

[16] Koremenos, Lipson & Snidal, 'The Rational Design of International Institutions' (2001) 55 IO 761, at 773, call this an 'adaptive institutional flexibility': 'The general goal is to isolate a special problem—such as a spike in steel imports from a few producing countries—and insulate the broader institution (in this case, the GATT/WTO) from its impact.'

[17] This balance is an expression for the relative reputation levels accredited to countries. It influences the relative positions of countries in future negotiations. Kovenock & Thursby, 'GATT, Dispute Settlement, and Co-operation', (1992) 4 *Economics and Politics* 151, at 160, acknowledge such costs and ascribe them to the breach of 'international obligation'. They argue that, '... we can think of this disutility as a loss of goodwill in the international arena or the political embarrassment that comes from being suspected of violation...'.

The instruments discussed do not only show different cost structures, they can also be distinguished by the prerequisites that have to be fulfilled before they can be used. The prerequisites describe the applicability of an instrument. For example, the safeguard clause requires imports in such increased quantities as to cause or threaten to cause serious injury to domestic producers. Furthermore, the increase in imports must be the result of both unforeseen developments and ongoing liberalization.[18] It is easy to see that the violation of an agreement has the broadest applicability: there are no prerequisites to fulfil. Once again, a trade-off can be observed: instruments with a high level of prerequisites tend to have low reputation effects. Actions that can be taken without any precondition generally induce more reputation loss.

D. Violation and non-compliance as renegotiation instrument

If there are conventional renegotiation instruments at our disposal, why do we still need an unconventional one? At the time of signing an agreement, the parties know that the future is full of uncertainty, and that some of their concessions were only made to secure the conclusion of the overall contract. Taking this into account, the stipulation that the use of renegotiation instruments is conditional on the fulfilment of predefined prerequisites neglects the motives for renegotiation. Future states of the world might force self-interested governments to take measures even if the revealed state does not correspond to one of those contractually described as prerequisite. And a local lack of commitment means that a government has never intended to comply with the respective rule, independently of a particular state of the world. In that sense, all conventional renegotiation instruments create flexibility—but their prerequisites cannot take account of all contingencies which would warrant a renegotiation of concessions.

The violation of an agreement is not based on the fulfilment of any prerequisites. Consequently, it has an unlimited applicability and can provide flexibility in all those states of the world where conventional renegotiation instruments are not available. For example, safeguards are inherently designed to protect domestic producer interests in times of rising imports. Yet, political pressure for renegotiation might come as well from other groups, such as consumers or environmentalists. Furthermore, political pressure from producers is not only correlated with import levels and their growth rate, as the current transatlantic steel conflict confirms.[19] In summary, there is good reason to believe that members occasionally search for a renegotiation instrument even if the legal safeguard measure is not at their disposal.

The rules of the WTO agreements are designed to allow a breach of contract, but at the same time to limit its extent and to compensate those who are

---

[18] See Article XIX:1 GATT and Article 2:1 of the Agreement on Safeguards.

[19] According to the European Commission, US steel imports have fallen by 33% since 1998, see *Neue Zürcher Zeitung*, 7 March 2002, p 23. Nonetheless, political pressure became so high that the Bush administration decided to take safeguard measures in March 2002.

negatively affected. The DS mechanism fits perfectly into this concept, and the critique of lacking credibility is probably caused by the fact that its primary function is not properly understood. The DSU states:

(1) The dispute settlement system of the WTO is a central element in providing security and predictability to the multilateral trading system. (2) The Members recognise that it serves to preserve the rights and obligations of Members under the covered agreements, and (3) to clarify the existing provisions of those agreements in accordance with customary rules of interpretation of public international law.[20]

Based on the theoretical considerations presented above, we argue that the DS cannot do justice to (1) if flexibility is unduly restricted. The task in (2) can be understood as assigning costs to the use of flexibility. Therefore, the function of the DS is: (a) confirming violation of an agreement, thereby affecting the reputation balance between complainant and defendant; and (b) defining the level of lawful retaliation and making it public. By exercising these functions, the DS process establishes the two cost components of potential non-compliance and sets the frame for a new bargaining situation between complainant and defendant. The description of the first function seems to ignore the role of clarification as requested in (3) by emphasizing confirmation of violation only. However, as a matter of fact, the DSB almost always supports the complainant,[21] making confirmation of violation the typical result of panel and Appellate Body activity.

The innovations of the DSU have reinforced the purported functions of the DS. First of all, their exercise will no longer be undermined by the defendant blocking a ruling: there is no possibility of avoiding the confirmation of violation and the determination of compulsory costs. On the other hand, it is now explicitly excluded that the two functions are undertaken by some self-designated national authority. As Article 23:2 DSU formulates, '[m]embers shall not make a determination to the effect that a violation has occurred, that benefits have been nullified or impaired . . . , except through recourse to dispute settlement'. As the past requests for authorization of suspension of concessions show, members negatively affected by non-compliance tend to exaggerate the incurred nullification or impairment.[22] If we understand the violation of an agreement as a renegotiation instrument, such distortion in the representation of costs would impair its usefulness. Hence, it is of utmost importance that there is an objective measurement of damage.

Secondly, there is now an almost unified process for disputes under all WTO agreements. This emphasizes that the activity of the DS should not depend on the

---

[20] Article 3:2. Numbers added.

[21] Reinhardt, 'Adjudication Without Enforcement in GATT Disputes' (2001) 45 *Journal of Conflict Resolution* 174, at 180, notes: 'the parties already know what their obligations are: the [DSB] ruling is just a formality whose likely content the disputants could often agree on in advance'. He observes a pro-plaintiff bias in those cases decided by a panel in the order of 4 to 1 for the GATT period.

[22] In the *Bananas* case, for example, the US calculated the level of nullification or impairment to be $520 million, compared with $191 million authorized by the DSB. In the *Hormones* case, the numbers were $202 and $117 million, respectively.

nature of violation. In fact, it would be an artificial restriction of flexibility without theoretical foundation if the possibility to renegotiate were made contingent on characteristics of goods or industry type. And indeed, it would crucially reduce the persuasiveness of our argument.

Thirdly, the complainant now has substantial agenda-setting power.[23] Together with a tight time frame for the work of both panels and Appellate Body, this ensures that the tasks of confirmation of violation and the determination of costs are not unduly delayed. Although an expeditious procedure cannot substitute for retroactive imposition of costs on violators, it contributes to limiting the time of free riding.

Last but not least, the possibility of an appellate review makes sure that the confirmation of violation is based on an accurate and perfectly reliable assessment of facts. This not only increases the predictability of rulings, but is especially important for a successful impact on the reputation balance as requested by the first function of the DS process. If rulings were based on an arbitrary determination, the reputation of the (losing) defendant would scarcely be affected.

Problems with implementation in general and cases of non-compliance in particular have apparently increased in recent years.[24] Three principal reasons for this development can be found. First of all, the broader coverage of the WTO agreements and the larger membership induce more disputes and thereby more cases in which non-compliance is an issue. Secondly, the surprisingly low number of non-compliance cases in the past is partly explained by the described possibility of a defendant blocking a negative outcome at various stages of the old DS process. It could be argued that such blocking was a form of early non-compliance with an expected unfavourable ruling. Thirdly, and most importantly, the often cited increasing confidence in the working of the new DS mechanism can also be interpreted as a growing recognition of its renegotiation aspects. Governments realize that the comprehensive agreements of the Uruguay Round have restricted their trade policy independence, yet that there is a DS process which allows them to 'buy' some flexibility and 'pay' a properly determined price for it.

E. Two casual observations regarding the WTO DS process

The discussion of violation and non-compliance will now be enriched by two casual observations as regards the WTO DS process. They are evidence that members of the WTO have actually had in mind to endow the agreements with a good portion of such flexibility when designing them. The first is that bilateral negotiations to find a mutually acceptable solution are de jure and de facto the preferred tool for the settlement of disputes. And the second is that when bilateral negotiations fail to prevent the DSB from issuing a ruling, and the defendant refuses to comply, there is de facto no enforcement effort.

---

[23] See Bütler & Hauser, supra note 1, at 509.
[24] See Pauwelyn, 'Enforcement and Countermeasures in the WTO: Rules are Rules—Toward a More Collective Approach' (2000) 94 *AJIL* 335.

As to the first observation, the DSU asks that bilateral negotiations take place before and during the formal DS process. This is generally seen to be a very desirable feature. We definitely agree, but suggest that the desirability of bilateral negotiations does not end at the moment of a DSB ruling. If a mutually acceptable solution 'is clearly to be preferred' (Article 3.7 DSU), there is no logical argument that invalidates this statement for the time after a DSB ruling. In fact, only the negotiation after a ruling can profit from a more equilibrated balance of bargaining positions due to the assignment of costs to the (losing) defendant by the DSB.

There is another crucial point that should be emphasized. The DSU requires that any solution found in bilateral negotiations shall be consistent with the WTO agreements and be notified to the DSB.[25] It is evident that the first request is almost useless without the second, but that notification is rarely taken as seriously as one might hope. However, even in cases where bilateral solutions are properly notified and in principle consistent with the agreements, caution is advisable in judging their economic success. There is a strong presumption that defendants are tempted to keep the substance of an initial violation, but to find an arrangement which circumvents WTO rules and is difficult to challenge therefore.[26] Although one might think that this is equally true for bilateral settlements before *and* after a DSB ruling, it is plausible to assume that the transparency of a solution is significantly higher in the second case. A DSB ruling does not only alter the bargaining positions, it also directs public attention to the dispute. The more 'problems' arise with the implementation of a ruling, the more certain it is that the media are carefully tracking any attempts of rapprochement between the parties and reporting the results. An eventual settlement that comes after a ruling might therefore be much closer to the rules than a more or less unnoticed deal in the run-up to a DSB ruling.

The second observation is the de facto absence of enforcement in the WTO. It is important to distinguish two aspects of this absence. One is that there has always been a *natural* limitation of enforcement efforts. Sovereign countries cannot be forced to behave in a particular way as long as drastic measures (such as military intervention) remain excluded. However, this does not mean that any enforcement effort is useless, and this brings us to the second aspect: countries can consciously create *artificial* limits of enforcement that are (far) below the natural limits.

What leads us to the conclusion that the natural potential for enforcement is not exploited in the WTO? A first indication is that panels and the Appellate Body generally refrain from suggesting specific implementation measures. Although they are allowed to formulate such suggestions,[27] they rarely go beyond

---

[25] Article 3:5 and 3:6 DSU, respectively.

[26] See Zimmermann, 'Gewährleisten umgesetzte WTO-Streitschlichtungsurteile offene Märkte? Eine Betrachtung am Beispiel des Zeitschriftenfalles' (2001) 56 *Aussenwirtschaft* 359.

[27] Article 19:1 DSU provides that: '[i]n addition to its recommendations, the panel or Appellate Body may suggest ways in which the Member concerned could implement the recommendations'.

'standard recommendations'. Three points follow immediately: defendants are not convincingly discouraged to maintain permanently at least part of the protective element of their initial violation;[28] secondly, due to the lack of guidance, any implementation is delayed; and last but not least, the final determination whether compliance has occurred needs greater scrutiny.

Enforcement is further weakened by the strictly limited market access costs that the DSB imposes in cases of non-compliance. The only function of such costs is restoring the balance of concessions. Due to the difficulties in calculating reputation costs, it cannot formally be proven here that total costs for non-compliance (ie, market access costs plus reputation costs) are actually lying in the efficiency interval $[c_{MIN}, c_{MAX}]$ defined above. However, it is contended that the signatories of the WTO at least had this interval in mind when designing the enforcement rules. The aim of restoring the balance of concessions is clearly inspired by c_{MIN}: even if reputation costs are low or almost absent, total costs will not fall short of the lower limit of the interval.[29] On the other hand, the total costs miss by far the maximum thinkable cost level of non-compliance: retaliation is strictly limited in its scope and duration. Only the complainant is allowed to retaliate, and there are restrictions as regards the choice of products for retaliation. In fact, the costs for non-compliance are not only below the maximum thinkable level, they are also below c_{MAX}. This can be seen if the discounted value of future co-operation for the government is approximated by today's political value of membership. Since non-compliance is not 'punished' with the denial of membership, the signatories wanted to keep total costs below c_{MAX}.

IV. SOME NORMATIVE CONSIDERATIONS

The argument so far has been merely *positive* in nature. We have identified the behaviour of self-interested governments in an international setting and described the flexibility of international trade agreements such as the WTO as an intended and politically desired feature of the world trading order. Now, four normative considerations are made.

The first consideration starts with the observation that the government objective function can differ from the maximization of social welfare. Although flexibility might be desirable from a global political perspective, it might not be in the interest of society. Obviously, in every period where flexibility is

[28] Horn & Mavroidis, 'Remedies in the WTO Dispute Settlement and Developing Countries Interests', *WTO 2000 Capacity Building Project Background Paper* (1999), argue that, '[w]hen limiting themselves to recommendations, WTO adjudicating bodies give ample discretion to the losing party. WTO Members are then, in principle, free to adopt any conduct they deem necessary in order to bring their measures in conformity with their international obligations.'
[29] This of course assumes that the restoration of the balance of concessions follows immediately after the violation. In reality, this is not given, but could be achieved by retroactive compensation.

applied, the ideal of free trade is compromised. Even if society has a strong preference for redistribution, trade intervention brings about greater allocative distortion than other redistributive instruments. Flexibility would therefore be a bad feature of the world trading system.

Valid as this argument is, it neglects two points. To begin with, redistribution is not the only aim of renegotiation, as the *Hormones* case exemplifies. Whereas border tariffs might primarily have been instruments for generating rents, domestic regulations are based on a variety of purposes. Condemning flexibility would therefore restrict trade policy even when it has no redistributive intention. Furthermore, if the lack of flexibility prevents governments from concluding new agreements, or impairs their enthusiasm towards existing ones, the negative social welfare consequences should by far outweigh those related with sporadically applied flexibility.

The second consideration relates to the predictability of world trade. Predictability is essential in order to reduce the risk premium for international transactions. It is argued that it could be strengthened further if international trade agreements created individual (private) rights, enforceable by national courts. Then of course, flexibility in trade policy would disappear.

Again, although the aim of predictability cannot be dissented, some objections to the argument as such must be brought up. Firstly, the costs of flexibility *also* contribute to the predictability of world trade by limiting the instances of applied flexibility. Secondly, little is won if predictability for trade covered under international agreements is increased, but the agreements are not comprehensive—this, of course, again relates to our stability argument. Thirdly, individual rights might be in conflict with social welfare, just as the government objective function is.[30] The *Hormones* case is again a good example: one might wonder what would happen if European beef importers attempted to impose their right for selling US hormone-treated meat.

Another important consideration relates to the fact that flexibility is obviously not distributed evenly among countries today. Small countries risk being denied any renegotiation instrument by the implicit threat of powerful nations to impose additional costs on them inside and outside the WTO sphere. As an example, both the US and the EC might credibly threaten to stop development assistance (eg, in the form of the *Generalized System of Preferences*) if a developing country does not comply with a DSB ruling. On the other hand, powerful countries might get flexibility too cheaply when applied against small nations because the latter could be unable to retaliate due to their foreign trade structure.

That said, we do not think that the argument can undermine the claim that flexibility is valuable and that a strict rule orientation is not desirable. In particular, one does not get rid of power imbalances by just strengthening rules. Instead of condemning flexibility, mechanisms should be designed that guarantee an equal distribution of flexibility and an appropriate cost level.

---

[30] See the contribution by Joel Trachtman in this volume.

Although this is not easy and out of reach for this paper, it merits at least as much attention as the debate about means for strengthening rule orientation.

The last consideration touches upon the consistency of our flexibility argument. One might claim that we implicitly fall back on the concept of rule orientation when describing the role of the DS process in face of violations. Otherwise, we would have to admit that the rules of the DSU are flexible, too, and then, all rules would be 'up for grabs'.[31]

In order to rebut this point, we argue that the DSU is different in nature from all those WTO agreements that consist of substantive norms on trade (de)regulation. Claiming that flexibility is a useful feature of the world trading order is neither suggesting that *any kind* of flexibility is desirable, nor that there is no need for provisions that prevent abuse. The DSU frames the use of flexibility and in particular defines its price. It stands above the other WTO agreements, since it is the only agreement that deals with violations of them. This special function allows us to exclude it from flexibility in application.

V. A NEW ASSESSMENT OF IMPORTANT DISPUTES: BANANAS, HORMONES AND FSC[32]

A. A short review

In 1993, the EC introduced a regulation establishing a harmonized regime on the importation of bananas. It consisted of a tariff quota system and continued historical privileges for African, Caribbean and Pacific (ACP) countries. These privileges had already been challenged before by a group of Latin American countries, but the EC and the ACP countries had blocked the panel report. The same happened with a second panel report in 1994. After the conclusion of a bilateral settlement with the original complainants and after the signing of the Uruguay Round agreements, a new group of countries (including the US and Ecuador) filed a complaint. For the third time, the EC lost the case in front of the panel and Appellate Body in 1997. The EC seemed to accept the ruling by requesting consultations as to the 'reasonable period of time' for implementation. An arbitrator decided that compliance with the ruling had to be reached by 1 January 1999. The EC made some amendments to the banana regime, yet these did not satisfy the complainants. A controversy started about the relationship between Articles 21.5 and 22 DSU, ie, about the question when the right to retaliate arises. Not surprisingly, the EC pushed for a renewed DS procedure, which should have to determine if the amended regime was consistent with the DSB ruling. The US on the other hand openly threatened to retaliate and indeed

---

[31] We owe the pronounced statement to Volker Rittberger, who made explicit this last consideration.

[32] See *EC—Regime for the Importation, Sale and Distribution of Bananas* (WT/DS27), *EC—Measures Affecting Meat and Meat Products (Hormones)* (WT/DS26), and *US—Tax Treatment for 'Foreign Sales Corporations'* (WT/DS108).

requested authorization to suspend concessions only two weeks after the end of the officially granted implementation period. This request was withdrawn in order to enable arbitration on the appropriate level of retaliation. After the arbitrators had requested further information on 2 March 1999 and thereby postponed a decision, the US nonetheless started to suspend customs clearance for a number of products on the next day. This step was subsequently challenged by the EC.[33] About one month later, the arbitrators finally determined the appropriate level of retaliation, which was set significantly lower than requested by the US. The US subsequently imposed retaliatory tariffs with an impact of $191 million. In May 2000, the US further increased pressure by adopting a so-called carousel provision, which brings about a periodical change of products affected by retaliatory tariffs. The EC requested consultations, but no additional steps in the DS process were taken. On 11 April 2001, a bilateral agreement was reached between the US and the EC.[34] The latter agreed to crucially modify the banana regime, leading to a tariff only system, due to start on 1 January 2006 at the latest. In return the US suspended its retaliatory tariffs on 1 July 2001, and they were permanently lifted after the EC adoption of the amendments.

There has been a long conflict across the Atlantic about the use of growth-promoting hormones. During the 1980s, the EC gradually reinforced their negative stance towards such additives. This development occurred despite a substantial amount of scientific work that found no indication of risk for human health. In 1989, the EC banned imports of red meat from animals treated with certain growth hormones. The US, an important exporter of hormone-treated beef, claimed that these measures represented a barrier to trade inconsistent with GATT rules. Similar to the *Bananas* case, all attempts to have this practice officially condemned by GATT authorities failed due to the blocking by the EC. Under the WTO, consultations about the disputed import regime started in 1996. A panel ruled against the EC in 1997, and so did the Appellate Body shortly after. Again, an arbitrator was needed to determine the reasonable period of time for implementation, and the respective period ended on 13 May 1999. Since the EC ignored the ruling, and further attempts to negotiate compensation on other issues failed, the US were authorized in July to impose retaliatory tariffs against imports of the EC up to the value of $117 million. These are still in place.

The origins of the *FSC* dispute can be traced back to 1971, when the US introduced the *Domestic International Sales Corporation* (DISC) provisions. These included a tax incentive to export and were challenged early by the EC. In 1984, the US introduced the FSC provisions, replacing the DISC system. The EC was not satisfied with these amendments, but further steps were postponed until 1997, when the EC requested consultations under the new DSU. A panel

---

[33] The step lost its significance after the arbitrators had made their decision, and was suspended.

[34] See Press Release of the European Commission, 11 April 2001, Document No IP/01/562. On 30 April 2001, an additional agreement could be reached between the EC and Ecuador. It is consistent with the US-EC agreement. See European Commission, Press Release from 30 April 2001. Ecuador in return gave up its right to suspend concessions as authorized by the DSB.

supported the claims of the EC in 1999, and the Appellate Body essentially upheld its conclusions. Just after the time for implementation had expired, the US amended the FSC provisions in November 2000. Again, the EC considered the reforms to be unsatisfactory and asked the WTO to authorize retaliation. However, this process was suspended, and the two parties agreed to ask a compliance panel whether the amended FSC provisions violate WTO agreements. Its report was circulated in August 2001 and emphasized a continued inconsistency. The Appellate Body confirmed the ruling of the compliance panel in all essential points in January 2002. In August 2002, the EU was entitled to impose more than $4 billion in trade retaliation.

B. Analysis

Looking for similarities among the three cases, one might start by noticing that all were lost by the defendant, who clearly violated one or various WTO agreement(s). The unwillingness to comply had two principal reasons:

(1) The disputed measures were of critical importance to the defendant. The import regime for bananas may make little economic sense for both the EC and ACP countries. However, it is probably the strongest *political* manifestation that the EC are still willing to assume responsibility for the destiny of their former colonies. The ban on hormones might not be justifiable by scientific research, but it seems to be the only possible answer to widespread fears among consumers in European countries. And the FSC regime is an essential part of a highly complex tax system, the abolition of which would cause considerable political and economic problems in the US.[35] Moreover, tax policy issues generally provoke high resistance among sovereign states when their autonomy seems to be at stake.

(2) The WTO agreements[36] did not provide an adequate instrument for renegotiation besides violation and subsequent non-compliance. In the *Bananas* case, the EC and the ACP countries were able to negotiate a waiver concerning the Lomé Convention in 1994, yet this waiver only provided an exemption from the most-favoured-nation clause and therefore was an unsuitable basis for the tariff quota system. Since the ban on hormone-treated beef was justified by consumer fears, the merely producer-oriented safeguard mechanisms were not at the EC's disposal. A general exception based on Article XX(b) GATT in order to protect human health could not be invoked, since the EC had agreed[37] to take respective measures only in accordance with an

---

[35] See Skeen, 'Knick-Knack Paddy Whack Leave the FSC Alone: An Analysis of the WTO Panel Ruling That the U.S. Foreign Sales Corporation Program is an Illegal Export Subsidy Under GATT' (2000) 35 *New England Law Review* 69, at 71 and 95. She discusses in particular the problems associated with replacing the FSC regime by a VAT system and concludes: '[s]olutions for the United States are limited and plagued with problems of feasibility and detrimental economic consequences'.

[36] And their predecessor, the GATT, respectively.

[37] As part of the Agreement on the Application of Sanitary and Phytosanitary Measures.

appropriate assessment of risk. As to the FSC case, both the complexities and interrelationships of tax regimes on the one hand, and the reluctance of the US to let others interfere with their sovereignty on the other hand, have been too strong so far to enable the parties to find a mutually acceptable solution by means of conventional renegotiation tools.

From a rule-oriented perspective, it is surprising to observe the readiness of the complainants at various stages to *renegotiate* an issue which had already been decided in their favour by the DSB. In the *Bananas* case, the EC did not only violate an agreement; they also blocked the initiation of a DS process as long as possible. They lost before the panel and the Appellate Body. They fought for an interpretation of the DSU which would simply have given them the right to maintain a deviation from contract without paying an appropriate price. They initiated a DS process themselves to challenge US retaliation measures. And, most noteworthy, they continued their non-compliance even after the arbitrators had authorized the imposition of US retaliatory tariffs and simultaneously rejected the EC claim that the amended regime would be inconsistent with WTO rules.[38] Despite such an intractable attitude, the US de facto never abandoned the policy of giving favourable consideration to striking a deal with the EC. The US were content with a level of authorized retaliation which was considerably lower than requested. And finally, they signed a bilateral agreement with the EC, which allows a temporary maintenance of the tariff quota system, and suspended (and later terminated) all retaliatory tariffs. The US obviously accepted the strong demand for renegotiation expressed by the EC. The US pressed for a DSB ruling in order to get a more favourable bargaining position, but they did not alter their readiness to negotiate after it had become obvious that the EC would not comply. On the condition that the latest bilateral agreement holds, a long standing dispute will have been successfully settled.

Obviously, such a positive conclusion is not yet justified as regards the *Hormones* case. A compromise seems to be even more difficult after the latest moves of the EC to ban permanently the growth hormone 17-beta oestradiol for any use with farm animals and to ban provisionally a group of other growth hormones used in beef production. In January 2002, a new regulation was passed which formulates the so-called 'precautionary principle' in EC food policy and which is refused by the US.[39] The authorized US retaliatory tariffs are still in place. However, the dispute has not escalated at all. As such, the above-mentioned carousel provision, which would also have affected retaliatory

[38] See Salas & Jackson, 'Procedural Overview of the WTO EC—Banana Dispute' (2000) 3 *JIEL* 145, at 149.
[39] See *Regulation (EC) 178/2002 of the European Parliament and of the Council of 28 January 2002 laying down the general principles and requirements of food law, establishing the European Food Safety Authority and laying down procedures in matters of food safety.* The US generally regards the principle as unscientific and arbitrary, see *Bridges Weekly Trade News*, Vol 6, No 7, 26 February 2002.

tariffs in the *Hormones* case, has not yet been implemented by the US. And though there are no signs that the EC are rethinking their position, a future bilateral agreement between the parties is not excluded.[40] Both sides have an interest in continuing bilateral talks: the US want to assure a more favourable market access for their beef products, and the EC is continuously confronted with the costs of retaliatory action and an impaired reputation balance. The violation of the agreement and the subsequent non-compliance by the EC had created a bargaining situation that was substantially altered by the DSB rulings. This bargaining is obviously not completed yet, and the structure of the final solution cannot be predicted so far. Nonetheless, it would be wrong to talk about failure of the DS process. Its contribution has been essential as it strengthened the interest of the EC to find a solution beyond simply refusing to act—the latter behaviour has become much more expensive.

The *FSC* case is undoubtedly the biggest challenged transatlantic trade distortion. It is therefore of paramount interest to the study of dispute settlement. Unfortunately, the latest ruling of the Appellate Body is still too recent to allow a complete assessment of the conflict. However, there are a number of indications that support the conclusion that a solution will be found on the bargaining table, and that no escalation is to be expected. There is no longer any doubt that the FSC provisions and their half-hearted amendments are in violation of WTO agreements. Their damaging effect on competing EC companies is huge, as the authorized level of retaliation confirms. Yet, just as the EC suspended requests for retaliatory measures and concluded an understanding[41] with the US in September 2000, Brussels now officially recognizes that the latest Appellate Body ruling will not lead to the simple abolishment of the FSC system.[42] Rather, new negotiations will take place. These will not be the same as before, since the balance of power between the two parties has considerably changed: it is now public knowledge that the FSC system is against multilaterally agreed rules. Furthermore, the EC is able rightfully to impose retaliatory measures. On the other hand, the EC do not possess unrestricted capabilities to impose a solution which is unacceptable for the US: any retaliation will be limited by binding arbitration, and it will have to be thoroughly designed in order to reduce harmful consequences for the EC (importers) themselves.

---

[40] EC Trade Commissioner Pascal Lamy criticized the adoption of the carousel provision as 'a step backwards in attempts to *negotiate* a settlement' (see *Bridges Weekly*, Vol 4, No 19, 16 May 2000; emphasis added). This statement came *after* the formal conclusion of the DS process and the introduction of authorized retaliation by the US.

[41] See *Understanding between the European Communities and the United States Regarding Procedures under Articles 21 and 22 of the DSU and Article 4 of the SCM Agreement*, published by the WTO as Document WT/DS108/12 on 5 October 2000.

[42] Pascal Lamy: 'Now it is up to the US to comply with the WTO's findings to settle this matter once and for all. *As to how, we look forward to rapid US proposals.*' Press release, Brussels, 14 January 2002. Emphasis added.

VI. Conclusion

Despite the fact that various analysts constantly predict the outbreak of notable 'trade wars', we do not observe such a development. The origins of the important disputes on bananas, hormones and FSC date back at least to the 80s. Nonetheless, they could not impede the two most powerful members of the WTO from successfully concluding the Uruguay Round. Nor did they deter them from launching a new round of liberalization in Doha in November 2001. More importantly, bilateral trade volumes grew rapidly during the years of alleged trade war: US merchandise exports to the EC more than doubled between 1990 and 2001, whereas US imports from the EC almost tripled.[43]

Non-compliance need not necessarily be analyzed under the perspective of an inadequate rule orientation. It can also be interpreted as part of renegotiation. Such renegotiation is unavoidable given the prevalence of incomplete contracting and local lack of consensus. Recognizing this, the WTO DS process primarily has the role of shaping a new bargaining environment by attributing costs to the continuing violation of contract.

Our argument suggests that non-compliance is much less a problem than many observers believe. This is not to say that the current DS is already perfect. Contentious and ambiguous issues such as the determination of a 'reasonable period of time' or the relationship between Articles 21.5 and 22 DSU must be tackled as soon as possible. Furthermore, free riding until the end of the implementation period could be made impossible by retroactive compensation. Yet, any reform would have to be directed towards reinforcing the renegotiation role of the WTO DS process, not towards banning non-compliance. Future research might test empirically to which extent the paradigms of rule orientation and flexibility contribute to a liberal trading regime. As we have demonstrated, there are strong indications which question the superiority of rule orientation.

[43] Based on data from the European Commission, DG Trade, November 2002.

20

'Early Warning System' for Dispute Prevention in the Transatlantic Partnership: Experiences and Prospects

W. MENG

I. THE 'EARLY WARNING SYSTEM' IN THE TRANSATLANTIC PARTNERSHIP

In March 2002, yet another severe trade conflict broke out between the EU and the US, when President Bush signed an order for safeguard measures in the steel sector. This raised harsh criticisms from the EU and other affected countries. There was an exchange of threats with trade sanctions from both sides. The notable tension between both political partners seemed to open a Pandora's Box of mutual retaliatory measures and of possible steps that might weaken the functioning and the reliability of the WTO Dispute Settlement system and possibly thwart the finding of constructive solutions in other disputed cases, particularly in the 'Foreign Sales Corporations' or the 'Hormones' cases.

Publicity creates a high profile for such disputes and a need for governments to act firmly in response. Sanctions and safeguards create economic victims and a challenge for governments to prove that they are able to defend national interests. They reduce the possibilities for a flexible and pragmatic response and—in any case—involve transaction costs to restore the previous mutual trust and the perception of being in the same boat when taking on the problems of globalization and development needs. The steel dispute could seriously affect the badly needed commonalities of both sides in the negotiations on the Doha agenda, although over the months both sides have now tried to lower the political stakes by reducing mutual damage and creating an atmosphere of mutual understanding. However there are now dispute settlement cases pending between the European Communities (EC) and seven other members and the United States (US) concerning the US definitive safeguard measures[1] and between the US and

[1] European Communities, Japan, Korea, China, Switzerland, Norway, New Zealand and Brazil v US WT/DS248, WT/DS249, WT/DS251, WT/DS252, WT/DS253, WT/DS254, WT/DS258 and WT/DS259: US—Definitive Safeguard Measures on Imports of Certain Steel Products.

the EC concerning the provisional safeguard measures applied by the EC as an answer.[2] It remains to be seen whether the outcome of these cases will reconcile the parties' differences by elucidating the unclear provisions of the Safeguards Agreement or whether these will be difficult cases like 'Hormones'[3] or FSC that might erode confidence in the dispute settlement system together with raising the criticism about 'judicial overreach' that can be heard, particularly in the US, after some of the latest decisions of the DSB.[4]

The WTO Dispute Settlement system is a remarkable achievement of the Uruguay Round—both in its design and its results so far. However it is an institution that is not yet immune from political doubts in the member states and it should not be overburdened by hard cases that might damage its standing in the world trade system. Non-compliance with recommendations of the DSB for political reasons would cause just such damage and must be avoided. The self-restraint of the EU and the US in the 'Helms Burton' case[5] has shown that the parties are—at least in cases involving national security questions— well aware of this delicate limit. So it is in their interest to avoid disputes if possible.

The steel dispute was already looming in the background when EU Commissioner Pascal Lamy, in 2001, commented favourably on an American wish to improve the 'Early Warning System' as one of the institutions of the Transatlantic Partnership, but with little hope for a resolution of the steel case—except prolonging the time until the outbreak of the public crisis:

No difficulty for improving our early-warning system. No problem at all. And we're looking at various ideas. The experience of steel, I think, is a case for not putting too many hopes in the fact that early-warning system—(laughter)—can do the trick. We will have to face these sort of things, for reasons we all know. And I'm fine, and I think I said it clearly publicly, and here again, that litigation is the last resort and we have to use many other things before. And I hope, for instance, that on this steel case, there still are a few months (?) before we go to litigation.[6]

This does not sound particularly enthusiastic about the 'Early Warning System', that was announced by the EU and the US during the summit meeting in Bonn 1999. In fact the dispute about steel safeguard measures that broke out

---

[2] EC—Provisional Safeguard Measures on Imports of Certain Steel Products (WT/DS260).

[3] EC—Measures concerning meat and meat products (hormones) (WT/DS26).

[4] See the critique of the decision of the Appellate Body on the 'Byrd amendment' (US—Continued Dumping & Subsidy Offset Act of 2000, WT/DS217,234) from Capitol Hill (*Inside US Trade*, 16 September 2002) and the proposal of Senator Baucus of 26 September to vitalize the 'Dole Commission' (Remarks To the Global Business Dialogue, *Inside US Trade*, 26 September 2002).

[5] US—The Cuban Liberty and Democratic Solidarity Act (WT/DS38). See J.H. Jackson & A.F. Lowenfeld, 'Helms-Burton, the U.S., and the WTO', *ASIL Insight*, March 1997 (http://www.asil.org/insights/insight7.htm); A. Lowenfeld, 'Congress and Cuba: The Helms-Burton Act' (1996) 90 *American Journal of International Law* 419 ff; W. Meng, 'Neuere Entwicklungen im Streit um die Jurisdiktionshoheit der Staaten im Bereich de Wettbewerbsbeschränkungen', *Zeitschrift für ausländisches öffentliches Recht und Völkerrecht* (1981), 469–513.

[6] Transcript of a press conference with European Trade Commissioner Pascal Lamy: preparations for Doha, bilateral issues, Washington, 7 June 2001.

publicly with the 'Steel Products Proclamation' of 5 March 2002[7] was only one prominent incident in a series of actual, upcoming or already resolved trade disputes between the two sides that heated the political atmosphere, used money and human resources and finally damaged the international trade order by reducing confidence on the side of the foreign traders as well as the consumers. *Bananas, Hormone treated Beef, Foreign Sales Corporations, Airbus A380, Carousel Retaliation* and the *Helms-Burton Sanctions Legislation* are just the most famous contentious cases between the EU and the US with many more disputes already broken out or at least foreseeable. And there were bitter discussions that are now only slowly becoming less acute on the purportedly unlawful extension of extraterritorial jurisdiction by the US in areas like competition, foreign trade and securities law and in other fields of law.[8]

In order to avoid the consequences of 'trade wars', both sides declared at their Bonn summit meeting in 1999 that they would institute an 'early warning' system,[9] a 'Doppler radar system for tracking trade storms', as the US Secretary of Commerce Daley once called it:

The relationship between the United States and the European Union is among the strongest in the world. We share a variety of common interests across a wide spectrum of economic, political, diplomatic, and global issues. In a relationship of this size and importance, it is inevitable that we have disagreements from time to time. If unresolved, these problems can quickly become high-profile and contentious. In an effort to minimize such disagreements, we are committed to an effective early warning system. We have agreed on general principles and mechanisms through which we will improve our ability to identify and facilitate resolution of differences at an early stage, before they create frictions. We will take further steps to improve the process as warranted.[10]

The Joint US-EU Statement on 'Early Warning' of 21 June 1999 remarks that such a system 'would meet the legitimate expectations of our citizens at a time of an increasingly interdependent economic relationship and closer political co-operation'. It does not only apply to economic and specifically to trade disputes, but encompasses general politics as well. Its general purpose is as follows:

Early warning is intended to improve the capacity of each side to take the other side's interests into account at an early stage when formulating policy, legislative, or regulatory

---

[7] Press release of the White House Press Secretary, 'To Facilitate Positive Adjustment to Competition From Imports of Certain Steel Products by the President of the United States of America a Proclamation', http://www.whitehouse.gov/news/releases/2002/03/20020305-7.html.

[8] Cf, W. Meng, *Extraterritoriale Jurisdiktion im öffentlichen Wirtschaftsrecht* (1994).

[9] Bonn Declaration released at the US-EU Summit, Bonn, Germany, 21 June 1999. One special area where the early warning problem was taken on even earlier was agriculture, 'to ensure that conflicts should not arise through lack of dialogue at an early enough stage in the legislative/regulatory process to permit each side to express its view on planned initiatives of the other, we envisage a system of early warning (Joint Statement of the 1998 London Summit on the Transatlantic Economic Partnership, §10 c) 9. See G.d. Jonquières, 'Dispute Settlement, Early Warning System, How can transatlantic trade disputes be avoided' (manuscript, 2001), http://www.iue.it/RSC/BP/Jonquieres.pdf.

[10] Remarks by Commerce Secretary William Daley to Transatlantic Business Dialogue Mid-year Meeting Dinner Washington, DC, 10 May 1999, http://www.useu.be/archive/daley512.html.

decisions, without thereby limiting each side's existing decision-making autonomy. Both sides re-affirm that the processes proposed hereafter are without prejudice to the parties' rights and obligations relating to international dispute settlement, notably under the rules of the World Trade Organization (WTO).[11]

While economic issues are to be treated in the Transatlantic Economic Partnership (TEP) Steering Group,[12] assisted as necessary by ad hoc or specialized working groups, the other issues will be covered by the New Transatlantic Agenda (NTA) Task Force. This does not exclude that specific cases might be dealt with by other channels. Between these bodies and the periodical Summit Meetings the Senior Level Group (SLG) will review early-warning items in order to filter them for the Ministerial Level or even the Heads of Government.

The Statement draws up a list of the methods to be used:

We will use the following means to identify, provide early warning of, and facilitate the resolution of problems:

a) The bedrock for early warning is transparency. This is provided for by information exchange as part of the existing foreign policy dialogue and by regulatory cooperation and mutual consultation being set up by different TEP working groups. This will not prevent any side from raising actively concerns as regards policy, legislative, or regulatory proposals under consideration by the other side.

b) Any issue which might have an impact on U.S.-EU relations may be raised. Each side will consult on issues raised by the other side.

c) Each side will seek to ensure that its internal procedures enable it to detect at an early stage trade, other economic, diplomatic, and global issues that have a transatlantic dimension, including policy, legislative, or rule-making initiatives. This should involve full communication between its own technical experts and policy officials, to ensure that its internal procedures enable it to fulfill this objective.

d) Potential trade and investment problems identified in the above process, both within and without the range of activities envisioned in the TEP Action Plan, should be brought to the attention of the TEP Steering Group. Diplomatic, global, and other problems should be brought to the attention of the NTA Task Force. This process includes the May 18, 1998 Transatlantic Partnership on Political Cooperation.

e) The TEP Steering Group and NTA Task Force will be tasked with ensuring appropriate follow-up procedures for items reported to them that have a potential for transatlantic policy frictions, notably by assigning contact points, facilitating consultations and agreeing on timelines for reporting back.

f) In its role in preparing for the U.S.-EU bilateral Summits, the SLG will identify problems which may need to be discussed by Leaders, primarily on the basis of inputs provided by the TEP Steering Group and the NTA Task Force.

g) We will invite the Transatlantic Legislators' (TLD), Business (TABD), Consumer (TACD), Environment (TAED), and Labor (TALD) Dialogues to contribute to this effort by identifying problems and offering proposals for resolution.

---

[11] Declaration of the EU-US Summit, http://europa.eu.int/comm/external_relations/us/intro/sum99.htm.

[12] Installed by the Transatlantic Economic Partnership, Action Plan, No. 4.

Since then the Groups have met twice a year, but there is very little specific information about their exact role in resolving emerging conflicts in an early stadium. The Reports for the TEP Steering Group, for example, deal in a rather detailed manner with its effort to bring about mutual recognition of standards and of legal requirements for services. However, concerning the 'Early Warning Mechanism', one merely finds the general sentences, that the Group 'discussed a number of items under the Early Warning mechanism established by the June 1999 EU-U.S. summit',[13] and that the representatives 'consulted closely, in accordance with the principles and mechanisms for early warning and problem prevention adopted at the U.S.-EU Summit in Bonn, on a number of specific issues that have the potential to adversely affect the broader transatlantic relationship'.[14] Neither these written statements nor the information given by persons who participated in the process of TEP and NAP give a clear picture about whether these discussions went beyond the common practice of negotiations in disputes about regulatory measures that were already finished, yet not in force pending consultations, as happened in the 'Hushkits case'[15] or in the dispute about envisaged European Data Protection rules.[16] There are off the record reports about a different readiness of states to use the mechanism: consultations in areas like technical requirements, sanitary and phytosanitary measures, and also environmental protection are said to be usually less successful than others, but there is little evidence of that in the official minutes. Therefore it will be necessary to refer later to private sources giving a more detailed insight

[13] Report of the TEP Steering Group to the Meeting of Trade and Economic Ministers, http://europa.eu.int/comm/external_relations/us/summit_05_00/report_tep_steering_grp.htm. Meetings on 15 March and 8 May 2000—the 2000 Queluz EU-US Summit.

[14] Report of TEP Steering Group to US-EU Summit in Washington (17 December 1999).

[15] Hushkits are mufflers for jet engines. The EC has prohibited by a Regulation the use of hushkits and mandated the use of planes that have been already built with noise reduced engines. Here the US objected saying that the new rule was unnecessarily burdensome to older planes of US origin. The EC Commission used a provision in the Regulation for suspending its entry into force for one year and meanwhile—unsuccessfully—negotiated possibilities to avoid a conflict with US interests. See Case 122/00, *Omega Air* [2002] 2 CMLR 9. The Regulation was adopted in the context of a dispute with the US. Since it was nevertheless desirable for the new aircraft noise and emission limitation measures to be taken at international level, the Council decided to delay application of the Regulation, as provided by Article 7, by one year in order to allow negotiations to be held. The dispute could not be resolved, and the Regulation came into force on 4 May 2000. The plaintiffs in the *Omega Air* case and the US in the negotiations contended that the new regulation might favour sales of new European aircraft. The court rejected this argument as it did not see any practical reason that would have buttressed this argument.

[16] In this respect the Report of the Senior Level Group to the 2000 Queluz EU-US Summit of 31 May 2000 states: '[o]n data privacy, subject to the review by the European Parliament, we aim to complete the remaining procedural steps for the Safe Harbour arrangement in July. We will continue our discussions in financial services in order to bring the benefits of safe harbour to this sector. Neither side anticipates problems with interruptions in data flows while they continue their good faith efforts to resolve these issues.' In this case there was a valuable attempt to bridge fundamental differences in regulatory philosophy (comprehensive regulation vs self regulation limited by targeted laws) by a 'safe harbor' solution, cf K.W.Grewlich, 'Telecommunications and "Cyberspace": transatlantic regulatory co-operation and the constitutionalization of international law' in G.A. Bermann, M. Herdegen & P.L. Lindseth, *Transatlantic Regulatory Cooperation—Legal Problems and Political Prospects* (2000), 273–299, at 289–291.

into some of the matters that were dealt with by the 'Early Warning Mechanism' (see Section IV below).

At the end of 2000 the Group discussed improvements of its procedure:[17]

The Steering Group discussed additional items under the Early Warning Mechanism established by the June 1999 U.S.-EU Summit and began an examination of how to refine the practical procedures that should govern the treatment of issues brought up under this mechanism. The Steering Group will aim to finalize concrete recommendations for procedures that could streamline and make more effective the process of identifying and addressing issues under the Early Warning Mechanism. It will also continue to encourage contributions by the various dialogues to early warning discussions.

The Report in summer 2001 stated that "early warning" discussions contributed to the satisfactory resolution of a number of cases'.[18] For the second half of that year further talks 'examining ways to ensure a more structured and consistent use of the Early Warning Mechanism' were provided for.

The Report of the Senior Level Group to the 2000 EU-US Summit in Queluz on 31 May 2000 shows how trade and economic policy and general foreign policy are being bundled in this group. In the latter area differences are being mentioned, for example the attitude towards the death penalty, but there is no hint in this report that there were 'problems that, if unresolved, could quickly become high-profile and contentious'. It seems that economic policy[19] is a particular field where an 'Early Warning System' might be needed more as an alternative to dispute resolution than in general foreign policy, where possible differences in evaluation and attitudes might be more obvious from the beginning and thus not unexpected.

However it should be remembered that the Early Warning System is just one facet of a broader array of methods designed to fill the principles of US-EC partnership as they are stated in the 1990 Transatlantic Declaration on EC-US Relations.[20] The main principle summing up the bottom line of this partnership shows that the aim is not only, in the negative sense, the avoidance of destructive conflicts, but positively an attempt to reach common solutions derived from common goals:

To achieve their common goals, the European Community and its Member States and the United States of America will inform and consult each other on important matters of common interest, both political and economic, with a view to bringing their positions as close as possible, without prejudice to their respective independence. In appropriate

---

[17] Report of the TEP Steering Group to the Meeting of Trade and Economic Ministers at the US-EU Summit, Washington, 18 December 2000.

[18] Report of the TEP Steering Group EU-US Summit, Göteborg, 14 June 2001.

[19] With its deep connections with technology, health care, environment and many other related areas.

[20] G.A. Bermann, 'Regulatory Co-operation between the European Commission and U.S. Administrative Agencies', [1996] *Administrative Law Journal of the American University* 933–983, at 955; H.G. Krenzler & G. Wiegand, 'EU-US Relations: More than Trade Disputes?' (1999) 4 *European Foreign Affairs Review* 153–180; S.E. Eizenstat, 'U.S. Relations with the European Union and the changing Europe' (1995) 9 *Emory International Law Review* 1–29.

international bodies, in particular, they will seek close co-operation. The EC-US partnership will, moreover, greatly benefit from the mutual knowledge and understanding acquired through regular consultations as described in this Declaration.

This applies to co-operation in the economic, educational, scientific, and cultural areas as well as to what the Transatlantic Declaration calls 'Transnational Challenge': combating terrorism, drug dealing and international crime, but also protection of the environment and prevention of the proliferation of weapons of mass destruction. The Declaration has been consolidated and enlarged in substantive as well as in institutional scope by the NTA of 3 December 1995. The attached 'Joint EU-US Action Plan' enumerates about 150 specific common actions the two sides have agreed upon covering all areas of politics and the interests of all layers of the societies. Here too the accent is far more on reaching common solutions rather than merely avoiding conflicts. In 1998 the EU and the US agreed during their summit meetings in Washington and Bonn on the 'Transatlantic Partnership for Political Co-operation' and the 'Transatlantic Economic Partnership'.[21]

Thus the Transatlantic Partnership has developed into a comprehensive co-operative effort of both administrations concerning the whole spectrum of political questions that affect them and need either co-ordination or even dispute prevention efforts. This article will deal primarily with the area of international trade policy, but this is, *mutatis mutandis*, a paradigm also for other areas of foreign policy. Here the whole spectrum of common interest from dispute avoidance to reaching common positions is at stake. However problems might be more acute in this field because of two particularities. Firstly, the mandatory WTO dispute settlement system and secondly the possibly immediate impact of policy decisions on everyday interests of people, which is the reason why today there is an increasing number of non-governmental organizations (NGOs) involved in observing and criticizing the developments in the WTO in the name of millions of 'stakeholders', workers, consumers and businesspeople.

II. DISPUTE PREVENTION AND DISPUTE SETTLEMENT

The Dispute Settlement System of the WTO is one of the most important achievements of the Uruguay Round and it is one of the most advanced patterns of its kind in public international law. It is designed to foster the rule of law and thus reduce the high, sometimes even prohibitive, costs of legal uncertainty in foreign trade. The Uruguay Round developed the old GATT Dispute Settlement System and in time gradually strengthened it in a remarkable way, making it a system close to adjudication. Since then an increasing number of disputes are referred to the new institutional system under the Dispute Settlement Understanding. In particular, smaller or developing states now have a better possibility

[21] Cf, Declaration of the Bonn Summit of 21 June 1999.

of getting their rights stated and preserved than in the former, more power oriented pre-WTO era.[22] However in this system there are still elements of diplomatic settlement present: consultations, good offices, conciliation, and mediation.[23] However Article 4, para 6 states that amicable solutions of disputes have to be notified to the institutions of the WTO in order to ensure transparency and discussion. Article 4, para 5 requires that such solutions be consistent with WTO law, a rule that seeks to guarantee that flexibility does not mean sacrificing the rule orientation of the system. Practice shows, like the development of the dispute about the Helms Burton legislation of the US mentioned above, that WTO members have often chosen their activities in dispute settlement according to the particular circumstances of the case and the problems at stake.[24]

The particular features of the compliance phase according to Articles 21 and 22 DSU may give way to a solution that affects the rule of law. Article 22, para 1 states that neither compensation nor the suspension of concessions or other obligations is preferred to full implementation of a recommendation to bring a measure into conformity with the covered agreements. Furthermore it says that compensation is voluntary and, if granted, shall be consistent with the covered agreements. However there are cases where return to compliance takes a considerable time, as was obvious in the bananas case and—still open with the EU refusing compliance—the hormones case. The authorized retaliation, according to Article 22, para 4, may not exceed the amount of compensation for nullification or impairment of rights under WTO law. This result may factually[25] lead to damage to producers and traders and—by the same token—to a transfer of benefits to the unlawfully protected economic actors for as long as the states do not comply with their duties.

Unlawful behaviour in international trade causes damage, which—under the present rules of WTO law—cannot be recovered from the violating state. Retaliation entails further—also non-recoverable—damage. The whole mechanism seems to be not quite appropriate to a system where the emerging rule of law is designed to yield predictability and to give incentives for more foreign trade that should improve the welfare of the trading nations. These are typical transaction costs of the present DSU system. There are further political costs inherent in the system. Trade disputes are sometimes inflated in the publicity to become 'trade wars', with a possibility of infecting the whole range of political relations between the conflicting nations. The dispute settlement system itself is costly to an extent that it may be barely affordable to the poorer states. This is acknowledged by Article 27, para 2 DSU and it is now subject to a range of activities

---

[22] Cf, J.H. Jackson, *The World Trading System. Law and Policy of International Economic Relations* (1997), at 102.

[23] Articles 4, 5 DSU.

[24] E.-U. Petersmann, 'Prevention and Settlement of International Trade Disputes between the European Union and the United States' (2000) 8 *Tulane Journal of International and Comparative Law* 233–258.

[25] But of course unlawfully. This shows that even in a highly sophisticated norm-driven system like the WTO, power politics are still particularly important to the outcome of disputes between states.

designed to ease this problem by granting help to these states in every respect. The Doha Declaration of the WTO ministerial conference 2001[26] particularly stressed the need for aid for technical co-operation and capacity building in WTO matters in general, including the dispute settlement field.

All these problems contributed to a renewed discussion about the increased use of diplomatic efforts to resolve trade disputes instead of complaints to the DSB. Another emerging argument is based on doubts about the appropriateness of panels and the Appellate Body to make decisions of sometimes immense political importance and their only very indirect democratic 'legitimacy'. There are domestic political situations, as in the Foreign Sales Corporations Case or the Hormones Case that cast doubt about the wisdom of using the dispute settlement mechanisms to resolve hard and politically sensitive cases. One might argue that the lack of integration of the international trading system as compared to the EU or NAFTA makes adjudication less robust to political requirements, so that the dispute settlement organs themselves have to strike a very delicate balance between being uncompromised by political influences and at the same time preserving their acceptance by the member states. On the other hand bilateral diplomatic dispute resolution between WTO member states may conflict with the rule orientation of WTO law despite the general requirement that all bilateral solutions shall be in conformity with the multilateral trade law.[27]

These problems of flexible dispute settlement can be avoided if states seek to prevent conflicts from the beginning. State activities—norms, licences, prohibitions, etc—are less likely to be challenged after they have been tested and approved in an early warning system. The transaction costs of the classical 'trial and error' of action, challenge, retaliation and compliance that changes the action can be avoided. Economic actors can trust that a statute or a regulation will not be subject to challenge by other WTO members. This strengthens confidence in the rule of law. Furthermore the possibly considerable political transaction costs of trade conflicts or even trade wars can be avoided. Certainly, an early warning system creates new costs itself, but it may be that they are a better investment than the costs of conflict resolution, for conflict avoidance contributes to the careful planning of a state's actions and to consideration of their economic implications—therefore also improving the functional efficiency of a norm.

However the cost benefit analysis has to be more careful in details, for situations of public choice are involved. Dispute prevention only seems to be a possible means if conflict is not the preferred option of the political decision makers. They may deliberately choose the conflict if this may bring them advantages in their domestic position, either because of a chance to successfully exercise political power relating to other states[28] or because they want to show

---

[26] WT/MIN(01)/DEC/1, 20 November 2001.
[27] Article 3.5 DSU and Article 11 of the Safeguards Agreement.
[28] This would imply an attempt to get an economic advantage by unlawfully exercising economic power.

to their constituents that their political possibilities of giving protectionist rents are fettered by international legal restraints.[29] If disputes are a strategic tool, initial prevention is probably not a valid alternative. The dispute between the EU and the US about the steel safeguards mentioned above is a perfect example of this case.[30]

Dispute resolution may also be deliberately chosen if the law is unclear and the parties want to clarify it for providing certainty in the future. If uncertainty is costly the resort to one model case to be decided under the DSU may be more appropriate than to act further in unmapped territories. The most obvious cases where dispute prevention might be helpful is if there is an asymmetry of information. The possibility of conflicts of state actions with the interests or actions of other states may not be known at all, or one state may not know about the importance of a conflicting position in another state under public choice criteria.[31] Transparency is necessary in order to avoid such conflicts and mechanisms of informing about the different national interests at stake. Since perfect and constant transparency seems to be impossible and not feasible given the parameters of state activities, special procedures may be created to raise possible differences in particular cases as early as possible.

Disputes between states may arise because of government activities, but also because of acts by the national parliaments. Governments will usually be more aware of and more sensitive to possible international disputes, while parliaments may either be not informed about and by time constraints not be able to pay due regard to possible international effects of their activities. They may also not be as sensitive to these implications. Furthermore governments may be more able to co-ordinate themselves with foreign governments than parliaments may do with their foreign counterparts. Therefore it seems to be more difficult to conceive of mechanisms of dispute prevention between parliaments than between governments.

Early warning systems are designed to provide conflict prevention.[32] This strategy is being applied to provide an early reconnaissance of areas of conflict that are not yet known and a 'time-out' for evaluating the stakes of a potential dispute and to negotiate about possible ways out of the crisis. The partners of the transatlantic co-operation have so many common interests and values that the basis for a rational dispute management should exist. The joint declar-

---

[29] This is a well known feature of using international law as an excuse for not yielding to domestic public pressures. These are external conflicts arising from internal disputes. Petersmann calls them 'secondary conflicts' as opposed to merely international 'primary conflicts'.

[30] However this case also involves legal uncertainty about the meaning of certain provisions in the Safeguards Agreement.

[31] For example the protection of environment in relation to other public goods (economic success, jobs, etc) may be seen differently in different states.

[32] K. Rupesinghe & M. Kuroda, *Early Warning and Conflict Resolution* (1992); A.P. Schmid, *Thesaurus and Glossary of Early Warning and Conflict Prevention Terms* (2000); K.v. Walraven, *Early Warning and Conflict Prevention: Limitations and Possibilities* (1998); International Peace Research Institute, *Early Warning and Conflict Resolution: A Conference Report*, 24–25 April, Oslo (1989).

ation of 1999 proves a desire to avoid unnecessary transaction costs and the institutional developments thereafter show that there is a chance of reaching that goal. But it is clear: early warning is a political procedure and it is certainly dependent on public choice perceptions as to whether it is able to prevent particular conflicts.

III. REGULATORY AND LEGISLATIVE CO-OPERATION

Disputes may often arise in the area of domestic legislation or regulation (exercised by the legislatures as well as the governments) about rules that are not particularly designed to regulate activities abroad, activities of foreign nationals or deliberately to influence the economy or other politically important values of foreign states. In a globalized economy many legal rules may affect in some way other countries although this influence was neither intended nor foreseen. Even if such influence may be obvious, foreign legislative or regulatory schemes might not be sufficiently known in order to spot a potential for conflicts from the beginning. Sometimes it might be better to explore the possibilities of harmonization, recognition, or other co-operation in the field of legislation or regulation, but this may be overlooked without some input of information to the governments as well as to the parliaments.

In the US as in the EU and its member countries, the administrations have manifold channels and influences on the legislative process. However, they might meet resistance to taking foreign concerns into consideration. The position of administrations as mediators between legislations may possibly be valuable, but not necessarily completely satisfactory. So it might be helpful to think about involving parliaments in the enterprise of co-ordination and dispute prevention as well. This could be done either by inviting parliaments to participate in early warning systems between governments or by institutions or meetings that are directly co-ordinating different national parliaments.

In both cases, the main thrust would be improving transparency, information on facts and backgrounds and providing for a discussion of concepts and caveats as well as basic conditions of the domestic legal order on either side. However the willingness to engage in such activities seems to be considerably more intensive in the governments than in the parliaments. This is clearly reflected in the development of the early warning system in the transatlantic relationship.

One focus of the Joint EU-US Action Plan attached to the NTA of 1995 is on regulatory co-operation:

We will strengthen regulatory cooperation, in particular by encouraging regulatory agencies to give a high priority to cooperation with their respective transatlantic counterparts, so as to address technical and other non-tariff barriers to trade resulting from divergent regulatory processes. We will especially encourage a collaborative approach between the EU and the U.S. in testing and certification procedures by promoting greater compatibility of standards and health and safety related measures. To this end, we will seek to develop pilot cooperative projects.[33]

The summits and SLG meetings since 1995 had regularly called for the elaboration of clearer guidelines to structure procedures and enhance their efficiency. In April 2002 the European Commission and the US Trade Representative finally issued the guidelines. They are shaped around the basic notions of transparency, predictability, mutual access to regulatory procedures, exchange of ideas and expertise, and the basic will to reach 'appropriate, harmonized, equivalent or compatible solutions'. They seek guarantees that high standards of protection of health or environment, full consideration of mandatory domestic legal requirements and of international obligations go along with transatlantic convergence and the objective not only of avoiding negative impacts, but also of creating positive gains of collaboration.

This concerns only the relation between the administrations concerning their regulatory activities. Parliamentary legislation, however, is equally a possible source of international conflicts. Governments may have influence on legislation either in preparing legislative acts or at least in informing parliaments about their views. This may be sufficient in many cases to make the legislators aware of possible conflicts with foreign states, but secondary information might not be as impressive and efficient as direct confrontation with foreign governments and parliaments.

The Bonn Declaration mentioned directly the 'Transatlantic Legislators Dialogue' (TLD) between members and committees of the US Congress and the European Parliament:

We will invite the Transatlantic Legislators' (TLD), Business (TABD), Consumer (TACD), Environment (TAED), and Labor (TALD) Dialogues to contribute to this effort by identifying problems and offering proposals for resolution.

This dialogue thus was initially not considered as independent, but linked to the government efforts of the NTA and the Early Warning System as a source for identifying problems and offering proposals on an equal level with the Transatlantic Business, Consumer, Environment, and Labour Dialogues. Legislators are here seen as a source of information and proposals for governments, like the other relevant actors mentioned. However, it seems clear that parliaments have a considerably different position in disputes between states and that their influence goes way beyond that of the other 'Dialogues'.

There already exist inter-parliamentary institutions like the Interparliamentary Union, the Arab Interparliamentary Union or the Conference of Speakers of European Parliaments. These are, however, not groups designed for 'early warning' activities. TLD is a new form of co-ordination apart from the regulatory co-operation between the administrations. It has originated out of the

---

[33] Cf, Part III of the Joint EU-US Action plan.

biannual meetings of the European Parliament and the US Congress.[34] The fiftieth meeting in January 1999 decided to launch TLD as a special institution. It uses video conferences for addressing questions of common interest ad hoc such as:[35]

- Internet and 3rd Generation telecommunications;
- Freedom of information and access to documents;
- Priority issues for the COP6 conference on Climate Change;
- US restrictions on steel imports.

The biannual meetings since then have dealt with topics that had the potential for dispute and were partly also the subject of the intergovernmental talks.[36] TLD has also now appointed permanent committee liaison persons. The internet appearance of TLD however does not indicate any particular successes of the interparliamentary activities.

The new format of the TLD may intensify the attempts to spot areas of potential conflicts and to take them on in ad hoc video conferences. It seems to develop activities—reaching beyond the concept of the Bonn Declaration and transcending the level of the other dialogues—that are not dependent on governmental co-operation and might prove a valuable addition. Given the external competence and experience of the governments and the particular powers of parliaments it may be favourable to interlink the regulative and the legislative dialogue—at least by co-opting members of parliament in order to improve and strengthen the 'early warning' capabilities of these procedures.

Consequently one should think about a participation of representatives of the parliaments in the negotiations of the Transatlantic Dialogue between the 'leaders' of the US and of the EU. This would be helpful in both directions: information from the parliamentary bodies on both sides on possible areas of necessary co-ordination or conflict prevention and information from the administrations on developments within the parliaments that might have the same importance. The second pillar could then be the dialogue between the US Congress and the European Parliament.

---

[34] This delegation consists only of members of the House of Representatives.

[35] http://www.europarl.eu.int/intcoop/tld/history_en.htm (28 October 2002).

[36] Examples of topics discussed at interparliamentary meetings include: 'Political issues: South East Europe and the Stability Pact; CFSP and the European Security and Defence Identity; NATO; Arms Control and National Missile Defence; Enlargement; CSCE; Changing role of UN; developments in Central and Eastern Europe; Russia and the CIS; Transatlantic Relations; Institutional Developments in the EU; Regional issues: Southern Africa, Middle East, South America, Central America, China, Asia-Pacific Rim, Panama, Gulf war, Yugoslavia, Somalia, Cuba, Bosnia; Economic and trade issues: EU/US trade relations; WTO; NAFTA; APEC; Information Society; Internet, Electronic Commerce and Data Protection; Telecommunication Issues; EU/US Perspectives on Multilateral Trade Issues (including TRIPs and TRIMs); Foreign Sales Corporations; ILSA/Helms-Burton and D'Amato Laws; EU Banana regime; Hormone-treated beef; Airbus/Boeing; Hushkits; Transatlantic Economic Partnership (TEP); Other issues: New Transatlantic Agenda (NTA); Transatlantic Legislators' Dialogue (TLD); Climate Change, Energy, Social Policies, Narcotics, Terrorism, Death penalty, Political and Legal Controls over Intelligence Activities' (see http://www.europarl.eu.int/intcoop/tld/welcome_en.htm).

Regulatory as well as legislative co-operation will certainly need some further tentative practice in order to develop techniques that may help to build a bridge between the common goal and the different national political, legal and administrative backgrounds. It will depend on the political gains and costs at stake—as outlined above—whether the cohesive forces and the expectation of gaining by stressing the commonalities will prevail over the antagonistic forces of competitive expectations. In any case it will be worthwhile to experience the potentially positive results of such efforts and to save the transaction costs of disputes. Regulatory and legislative co-operation is a most promising way to find out about potential reasons for conflict and avoid them before they have to be removed—at the planning stage.

IV. Input of private actors

The Bonn Declaration of 1999 invited the Transatlantic Business (TABD), Consumer (TACD), Environment (TAED), and Labour (TALD) Dialogues to contribute to the co-ordinative effort, comprising the Early Warning System, by identifying problems and offering proposals for resolution. In fact the TABD seems to be the most active factor in this process, while the other Dialogues either suffer from a lack of funds or are—like the Consumer Dialogue—still in the process of bundling widespread interests and developing around a hard core of active NGOs in order to be heard by the Commission and the Administration as a factor that has to be taken seriously.

The TABD took up the call from the 1995 summit in Madrid in the NTA[37] to make recommendations in order to boost transatlantic trade and investment. Since then it has held yearly CEO conferences adopting recommendations to the administrations by consensus. In 1999 at its Berlin Conference TABD answered the Bonn Declaration by nominating seven issues with a potential to harm transatlantic trade relations. Reports about these proposals and their treatment by the transatlantic partnership give more insight into the mechanism of early warning than the scarce public information. Looking at the particular features of these cases may also give a hint of arguments for and against the present procedure.

The first positive result apparently came in the case of a planned regulation of the Environmental Protection Agency (EPA) on recreational marine emissions that was not released by EPA after discussions with the business community in favour of the development of international standards. Another issue was the EU Directive mandating labelling of goods with metric units only. The industry and representatives of small business suggested a search for different solutions, so the EU Commission agreed—with the approval of the Parliament—to postpone the

---

[37] L. Schroeter, 'TABD brings together business, government to expand trade relationships', *Semiconductor Magazine*, May 2000, Vol 1, No 5.

entry into force of the Directive for ten years. Another case was the avoidance of the development of regional European standards on third generation wireless standards by a worldwide agreement between the concerned industrial actors.

The yearly conference of TABD is attended by the CEOs of the participating firms together with their staff, but also by high representatives of the administrations at a cabinet/Commission level. About 40 committees report to the CEOs Conference on five thematic groups of issues: Standards and Regulatory Policy, Business, Facilitation, WTO and Global issues, Small and Medium-Sized Enterprises, and Digital Economy. They have given important impetus, for example in the areas of standard setting and mutual recognition of standards.

There has been criticism by NGOs and the Transatlantic Consumers Dialogue about the influence of TABD on the administrations on both sides of the Atlantic. In an open letter of 26 September 2001,[38] the Representative of Corporate Europe Observatory, on behalf of 25 NGOs and six members of the European Parliament, urged Commissioner Lamy not to attend the TABD Conference in Stockholm in October 2001 because of the purported over-proportional influence of the business lobbies in the Transatlantic Dialogue. It claimed that the Transatlantic Dialogue gives to the business actors a powerful influence to press for deregulation because of the underlying ideology of liberalization at any price, whereby state regulation in itself is considered a potential barrier to transatlantic trade. This open letter discloses other subjects of the industry's nomination for the early warning procedure: the planned EU restrictions for genetically modified agricultural products (GMOs), the phasing out of the use of HFCs, greenhouse gasses harming the atmosphere, and a possible ban on animal testing for cosmetics. The Commissioner refused the criticism in a responding open letter stating the equal influence of all the private dialogues mentioned in the declaration of Bonn 1999 and stating at the same time the importance of private inputs in the dialogue.

Another public statement of concern to the press was made by the President of the 'Public Citizen'[39] NGO on behalf of the Transatlantic Consumers' Dialogue urging the administrations to equalize differences of power and efficiency between the dialogues and to provide immediate information about the initiatives of one Dialogue to the others and the opportunity to appear in hearings about the matters raised. This letter also mentions additional subjects of the early warning discussions: US auto safety regulations and EU legislation on transmissible spongiform encephalopathy (TSE).

These public discussions about the value and the problems of private participation in the Transatlantic Dialogue refer to important aspects: public participation must encompass all stakeholders; it must give them equal opportunities to explain their causes; and ensure that the input of the Dialogues is not transformed into an institutionalized international forum of competitive lobbying.

---

[38] http://www.corporateeurope.org/openletter.html.
[39] http://www.citizen.org/pressroom/release.cfm?ID=955.

However, the stakeholders must take care of the efficiency and representative character of their organizations. This shows an inherent weakness in the process, for it is natural that business interests are organized in national and international NGOs and usually well financed, while consumer interests are represented by NGOs without a mandate from the consumers themselves, thus without impressive infrastructure and without a truly democratic mandate for consumers who do not usually even know who is speaking in their name. This fact makes it even more necessary to consider the private inputs in the Transatlantic Dialogue truly and simply as information for the administrations that have to assess their interests from these and other sources.

But of course it may not be possible, in real life, to avoid the fact that administrations will consider contributions to the dialogue as lobbying interventions by groups that have to be pondered according to their influence and to the possible effect on the next elections. Alternatively, it is also inherent in the subject matter that these inputs will concern problems of personal interest to businesses and thus will always inherently be accompanied by lobbying. But it is likely to be an advantage if this may be subject to sufficient publicity if the administrations choose to make their consultations and all the inputs thereto as open and as transparent as possible. The public statements so far, however, do not meet this requirement. So it should be urged that transparency, one of the crucial elements of good governance in economic administration, should govern the whole process of dispute prevention. Diplomats may be more inclined to confidentiality, but even as the WTO itself is gradually opening up to more transparency in the conduct of its business, this should also be required from all the participants in the Transatlantic Dialogue.

The newest proposals of TABD for the improvement of the Early Warning Mechanism may lead in the same direction. On 29 October 2001, the CEOs expressed their strong support for such a system, for the 'inclusion of Trade Impact Statements in development of regulatory and legislative measures, and better communication between U.S. and EU regulators, legislators and government leaders, as a means to prevent domestic policy from impeding global trade'.[40] They stressed that dispute settlement should be the last resort for both sides and that they should rely rather on constructive dispute avoidance, by means of an Early Warning System as well as regulatory co-operation.

On 20 November 2001, a TABD Principals Meeting made more specific recommendations for streamlining the process.[41] In order to be eligible for identification as subject to the Early Warning Procedures certain criteria should be met to ensure that the items really may have a potentially negative impact on trade and have the potential to become a trade dispute. This seems to meet the criticism which warns that the system might become a mere complaint and lobbying enterprise that enhances the access of business circles to governments

[40] http://www.tabd.org/media/2001/102901.html.
[41] http://www.tabd.org/recommendations/oct2001.pdf.

and helps increase their influence in general politics. However, it will be the natural task of the administrations to draw a line between their interests and the one-sided interests of business. In the same 'Paper on the Early Warning System' TABD also requires certain specific automatic results of Early Warning notifications to the administrations: the right of stakeholders to be consulted and heard; and efficient dealing with complaints where members of the Transatlantic Legislators Dialogue should also be asked to participate.

These proposals may well improve the present situation if 'stakeholder' is not interpreted negatively as a synonym for complainant, but also comprises all the other parties affected by the measure that is attacked. Private involvement in dispute prevention seems to be vital, since economic actors are directly affected themselves and may more easily evaluate dangers and potential conflicts.

V. Prospects

Dispute prevention by means of the Early Warning System as well as by legislative and regulatory co-operation may be preferable in many cases to dispute settlement, even to the highly sophisticated WTO DS system. The events since the beginning of the 'Early Warning System' in 1999 have shown that many hard cases proved to be apparently resistant to early warnings. One could conclude from that, that transatlantic relations need further improvement in order to be more efficient, and that this applies particularly to the Early Warning System. This is also indicated by a Communication from the EU Commission to the Council in March 2001 on 'Reinforcing the Transatlantic Relationship':

7. The cornerstone of bilateral and multilateral trade and investment co-operation remains the Transatlantic Economic Partnership (TEP). Last year, the Commission together with the member states made an evaluation of the TEP. Despite setbacks in ensuring the timely implementation of the TEP Action Plan, the conclusion was that the TEP had proven a useful instrument for developing a co-operative agenda in the trade and investment fields and that it should be reinforced and given further impetus. Discussion with the US on how to achieve this could start soon with the new Administration.

8. On the bilateral side, the EU and the US have a dialogue on most issues covered by the TEP Action Plan. Despite the existence of some problems, work has been satisfactory and progress made, notably in areas such as technical barriers to trade, regulatory co-operation, consumer product safety, food safety, biotechnology and competition. For services, the outcome is mixed....

10. As far as trade disputes are concerned, there will always be some contentious issues given the deep inter-penetration of the world's two largest trading blocs. In practice, the number of disputes at any given time is limited. The key is managing these rifts and keeping them in perspective: at the most, 1–2% of the trade and investment flow is affected. Such questions, however, tend to attract media attention far beyond their economic importance. As a result, trade irritants are sometimes blamed for casting a shadow over other aspects of the relationship between the European Union and the

United States. In reality, there is little risk of a negative spill-over from individual disputes into the overall political relationship which is broader and deeper than ever before. In fact, both parties go to great lengths to contain disputes and avoid escalation.

11. The prevention of trade disputes remains a key goal in which respect and conformity with internationally agreed rules is crucial for solving potential conflicts. To this end, increased efforts should be made to find early solutions between the parties, and in this respect, the early warning mechanism for trade and investment matters is working satisfactorily within the TEP framework to identify contentious cases in the pipeline. Thought is being given to how the system can be improved, including a more structured follow-up. But in the end, even the best early warning system will not work in all cases and needs to be accompanied by improved co-operation and collective leadership.[42]

In a further Communication one month later the Commission made an attempt to draw conclusions for conflict prevention by activities on the European side:

29. It should no longer be necessary to argue the merits of an approach based on long-term preventive action. What is more, the essentially measured and co-operative nature of preventive action is bound to make it more acceptable to the recipient than a peacekeeping operation that may well involve the use of force. International co-operation and co-ordination will make it possible to ensure that preventive operations are undertaken on a complementary basis. The Commission is determined to mobilize Community instruments more effectively and in a co-ordinated fashion to support efforts deployed to prevent conflict, from far upstream to the last phases of a conflict developing into confrontation and crisis. This will include:

- building the objectives of peace, democracy and political and social stability more clearly into our assistance programmes. This should be reflected in our general approach as well as for example by placing greater emphasis on support to the building of stable institutions and the rule of law (including in policing and the administration of justice);
- ensuring also, in our assistance programmes, that account is taken of indicators of political exclusion, ethnic, social or regional marginalization, environmental degradation or other factors which, if unchecked, might lead to civil strife or violent confrontation;
- bringing added value to international initiatives on cross-cutting issues which may contribute to tension and conflict such as international crime, the spread of small arms, the diamond trade, drug trafficking, child soldiers;
- drawing on other means, e.g. trade policy instruments and trade and co-operation agreements, or tools derived from areas such as justice and home affairs, migration, social or environmental policy;
- developing new approaches and instruments to deal with conflict and crisis situations. The Rapid Reaction Mechanism for faster mobilisation of Community instruments is one example. The forthcoming Communication on linking relief

---

[42] Brussels, 20 March 2001, COM(2001)154 final, *Reinforcing the Transatlantic Relationship: Focusing on Strategy and Delivering Results.*

and rehabilitation to development will set out other means to exploit. Among available instruments, EC external assistance is certainly the most powerful one. It was used with some success, for example in Salvador and Guatemala, to re-establish a degree of structural stability. It is currently put to integrated use in the process of reconstruction and consolidation in the Western Balkans. Practical proposals made in this communication will help to further mainstream conflict prevention in external assistance.

Where the situation in a particular country suddenly deteriorates, long-term preventive work must give way to rapid reaction informed by a clear and coherent policy. Many ways exist to improve the quality of our response and in particular to make better use of Community or CSFP instruments, as discussed in this communication. Important recommendations have also been made in the Joint Report by the SG/HR and the Commission to the Nice European Council on conflict prevention. The Commission will closely work with the relevant Council bodies and in particular with the SG/HR and the Council Secretariat/Policy Unit on their implementation.

In the end, our capacity for action in response to conflicts is intrinsically dependent on three factors: a clear definition of Union objectives, the capacity to act and, most importantly, the political will to act. The effectiveness of the Union's action will depend, above all, on the extent to which it expresses a common political approach by the Member States of the EU. At the moment, conflicts of interest still tend too often to get in the way of rapid decision making. The forging of common values and interests into a set of clear common priorities and objectives on sensitive issues constitutes the real test of our ability to contribute to conflict prevention.[43]

VI. CONCLUSION

Dispute prevention by means of an early warning system seems to be preferable economically to dispute settlement because it would normally save transaction costs, with the exception of the cases where uncertainties in the legal texts have to be clarified determinatively.[44] But public choice considerations may trump economically rational solutions. Rent seeking lobbies may be more important to politicians in a given situation than economic rationality. In these cases, early warning would most probably not be successful. The opposite is true of cases where rent seeking may be refuted by governments by referring to obligations under public international law. Here early warning might successfully avoid the conflict and thus save transaction costs. The most conceivably successful case of early warning might concern cases of an initial asymmetry of information where only primary disputes (exclusively international disputes) about questions are concerned, that do not involve questions of basic national values,[45] but rather concern technical problems such as technical requirements, standards, etc.

---

[43] Brussels, 11 April 2001, COM(2001)211 final, *Communication from the Commission on Conflict Prevention.*

[44] This procedure creates transaction costs, but they remain calculable since damages have not to be paid—one of the obvious shortcomings of the DS system if it is analyzed economically.

[45] Such as, eg, basic concepts about public health or environment.

The Transatlantic Partnership began the valuable development of an 'Early Warning System' in 1999. The results so far have been mixed, but this seems the inevitable consequence of a tool that needs to be developed according to the particular needs and possibilities on both sides. Early Warning will not be able to avoid all conflicts since there are reasons in some cases, as stated above, to have resort to the dispute settlement mechanism provided by the WTO. The steel safeguards dispute mentioned above is a typical example of a 'secondary conflict'. Its development so far, however, also provides an example that a cooling off period of negotiations before the entry into force of disputed legal acts is always helpful to minimize damage to international trade relations. Where possible, the Early Warning System may provide for such a period in many cases of primary conflicts.

It is prudent to link the Early Warning System with a parallel co-operation between regulators and legislators. Since there is a mutual influence and control of the legislative and the administrative branch, although under different terms of constitutional law, it might also be favourable to provide for mutual participation in the respective co-operative institutions in order to maximize the prospects for conflict prevention at an early stage of law-making.

Procedures are apparently in prospective development. This gives hope that dispute prevention between two of the most important players in the world trading system will still improve. One important factor will be increased transparency and the input of all stakeholders in society. The final result should always be the same: economic efficiency and the preservation of the rule of law as a precious asset in the service of economic growth and prosperity, as well as for the preservation of fundamental rights safeguarding business activities. This is expressed in a nutshell by EU Trade Commissioner Pascal Lamy:[46]

> Consult before you legislate;
> Negotiate before you litigate;
> Compensate before you retaliate;
> And comply—at any rate.

---

[46] 'Has International Capitalism won the war and lost the peace?' Speech at the US Chamber of Commerce, 7 March 2001, p 6 of the paper, Speech 01/112 of the Chamber.

21

Private Parties in EC–US Dispute Settlement at the WTO: Toward Intermediated Domestic Effect

JOEL P. TRACHTMAN*

I. Introduction

This paper is intended to elaborate some considerations for use in evaluating the role of private parties in WTO dispute settlement between the US and EC. There is already a voluminous literature on transparency, *amicus* briefs and direct rights to sue, either in domestic courts or in international tribunals, with able scholars and policy-makers taking positions on every side. This paper draws on this literature, as well as on a US-based law and economics literature of standing and an EC-focused political science literature of the role of individual lawsuits in economic integration, to develop a matrix for analysis along two axes. The first axis seeks to analyze private participation into component parts, or 'modes of participation', including transparency, *amicus* briefs, espousal and various types of direct rights to sue. The second axis seeks to develop, in summary form in this context, a set of normative considerations by which to compare these modes of participation. By arraying the various modes of participation against the way in which they invoke these normative considerations, it is hoped to suggest an organized way to think about private participation.

Broader natural law or economic principles of free trade provide little basis for determining the scope and character of private participation. Rather, the scope and character of private participation in different fields of WTO law-based dispute settlement (either in domestic courts or in WTO tribunals) would be expected to vary depending on how the more specific normative considerations discussed in this paper are implicated in those fields. It is therefore necessary to engage in case-specific analysis of the utility of private rights to participate in the

* I would like to thank George Bermann, Claus-Dieter Ehlermann, Mary Footer, Robert Hudec, John Jackson, Gabrielle Marceau, Phil Moremen, Ernst-Ulrich Petersmann, Mark Pollack, Kal Raustiala, Eric White, and other participants in the European University Institute Conference on Dispute Prevention and Dispute Settlement in the Transatlantic Partnership, 3–4 May 2002, for their helpful comments on an earlier, and significantly longer, draft of this paper. Opinions and errors are mine. This paper is a companion to a paper co-authored with Philip Moremen and published as 'Costs and Benefits of Private Participation in WTO Dispute Settlement: Whose Right is it Anyway?', (2003) 44 *Harvard International Law Journal* 221.

context of particular legal rules, rather than a wholesale approach to private participation.

In Part II, I provide a brief taxonomy of the modes of private party participation that are conceivable in international dispute settlement, with special reference to how they presently operate or might operate in the WTO context. There are several main modes of participation, and infinite variations and combinations.

In Part III, I summarize a set of normative considerations (more fully developed in a companion work co-authored with Philip Moremen) by which to evaluate private party participation, and particular structures of private party participation. These normative considerations borrow significantly from two literatures that have developed in other contexts: (i) the political science literature analyzing the role of the European Court of Justice in European integration,[1] and (ii) the law and economics literature analyzing private rights of action and public enforcement within US domestic law.

II. WHAT ARE THE CHOICES? AN ANALYTICAL TYPOLOGY OF MECHANISMS FOR PRIVATE PARTICIPATION IN INTERNATIONAL DISPUTE SETTLEMENT

The WTO Dispute Settlement Understanding (DSU) provides states with significant rights to bring and otherwise participate in WTO dispute settlement cases.[2] Within the WTO system, private persons do not directly approve treaties or otherwise engage in legislation or administration. The question is, under what circumstances should they engage in litigation?

There are a number of different parameters by which to describe private participation in dispute settlement. The main components are the following: transparency, right of advocacy, rights of commencement, including espousal, exhaustion and standing, as well as other components such as indirect effect.

In the WTO at present, dispute settlement does not provide to private persons complete rights under any of the above categories. In this section, I will describe how these parameters are presented in general international law, in WTO law and in US and EC internal legal mechanisms allowing private parties to influence WTO dispute settlement, including Section 301 of the US Trade Act of 1974, the Trade Barriers Regulation and Article 133 of the Treaty of Rome.

It is important briefly to note that at traditional international law,[3] individuals had few rights at all, and even fewer rights to bring suit. In this generalization,

---

[1] See W. Mattli & A.-M. Slaughter, 'Revisiting the European Court of Justice' (1998) 52 *Int'l Org.* 177.

[2] See Articles 9 and 10 of the DSU. Also see EC—Regime for the Importation, Sale and Distribution of Bananas, Report of the Appellate Body, WT/DS27/AB/R (9 September 1997).

[3] I refer here to recent traditions. Under the early law of nations, both states and individuals had rights and duties. See M.W. Janis, *An Introduction to International Law* (1993) at 227–29.

both obligations and rights applied to states. This principle has been significantly eroded by the development of human rights law. However, especially in the area of international trade law, the traditional principle often applies.

Thus far, GATT and WTO law have followed the traditional international law model, and have (i) accorded few direct rights to individuals, and (ii) never permitted individuals direct access to bring claims at GATT or WTO dispute settlement. This traditional model in trade law is challenged by two kinds of regional integration developments, and by certain specialized developments in the WTO legal system.

Many examples can be drawn from regional integration. Since the 1963 *Van Gend en Loos* decision, the European Court of Justice (ECJ) has developed the rights of individuals to bring cases both in national courts and in the ECJ itself. Second, the Chapter 11 dispute settlement system in NAFTA (which itself is modelled on precedents in many bilateral investment agreements), provides an example of a specialized system for mixed arbitration, related to an international trade agreement. As the relationship between trade and investment becomes better understood, and as 'rights' to trade may be viewed as included in 'rights' to invest, it becomes less clear that such mixed arbitration is out of the question in the trade sphere.

With respect to specialized developments in the WTO legal system, we have also witnessed an expansion of individual rights. First, for example, the TRIPS and Government Procurement Agreement (GPA), in addition to requiring states to provide certain rights to individuals, require states to provide certain procedures for individuals to seek domestic review of certain determinations. While these are not rights to bring cases in the WTO dispute settlement system, they are private rights of access provided pursuant to WTO law.

In addition, in connection with the TRIPS and GPA, and wherever WTO law requires specific norms to be incorporated in domestic law, as in for example the Customs Valuation Agreement,[4] it effectively provides for 'intermediated domestic effect'.[5] I distinguish this from direct effect, where there is no need for an act of transposition, but the results may be the same: intermediated domestic effect may result in international norms becoming part of domestic law, even if the international instrument is not directly the source of the norm.

The traditional international law model includes the possibility of 'espousal': that a person's government would 'take on' his or her claim against another government, bringing that claim in international law. Section 301 of the Trade

---

[4] Agreement on Implementation of Article VII of the General Agreement on Tariffs and Trade 1994.

[5] Davey refers to this type of treaty mandate for private rights, as in TRIPS and the GPA, as 'intermediate direct effect'. See Panel Discussion: *Is the WTO Dispute Settlement Mechanism Responsive to the Needs of the Traders? Would a System of Direct Action by Private Parties Yield Better Results?* (1998) 32 *J World Trade* 148, 160 (remarks of William J. Davey). I use the slightly different term 'intermediated domestic effect' first, to use the word 'intermediated' to indicate that there is an act of transposition, and second, to refer to domestic effect, but not direct effect, because the effect is not direct, but requires an act of transposition.

Act of 1974 has achieved a degree of notoriety in connection with its use for 'aggressive unilateralism',[6] but is perhaps best understood in our context, and since the advent of the DSU is most often used, as a mechanism for espousal. The EC has its own cognate, in the 1994 Trade Barriers Regulation.[7] It is only used as a mechanism for espousal.

A. Transparency: rights of individuals to receive information

The WTO has already increased its transparency in terms of access of individuals to information about dispute settlement, although access is still incomplete. Many commentators agree that transparency would have few costs and substantial benefits in terms of accountability. However, many member states, including many developing states, resist greater transparency.

B. Advocacy: rights of individuals to provide information

The ability to advocate has both instrumental and intrinsic significance. This paper focuses on the instrumental aspect, viewing the right to submit an *amicus* brief as a lesser substitute for full private rights to litigate.

This paper cannot provide a full treatment of the *amicus curiae* issue. The WTO dispute settlement process could find a way to manage a system wherein *amicus* briefs were accepted, and perhaps has already done so. Panels have the authority, but not the obligation, to accept unsolicited (or solicited) briefs under Article 13 of the DSU.[8] The Appellate Body has similar authority. This authority is to be exercised on a case-by-case basis. However, under a regime of reasonably unrestricted access for *amicus* briefs, it would be highly impracticable for the dispute settlement system to undertake to recount and respond to each *amicus* brief in the way that it does for member state briefs. It appears that neither panels nor the Appellate Body are obligated to do so. Nevertheless, most member states of the WTO today seem to reject the possibility of *amicus* briefs.[9]

It is worth noting that aspiring *amici* have included not only NGOs, but also industry groups such as the American Iron and Steel Institute and the Specialty Steel Industry of North America. Thus, it is still too early to tell whether

---

[6] J. Bhagwati & H.T. Patrick (eds), *Aggressive Unilateralism: America's 301 Trade Policy and the World Trading System* (1990).

[7] Council Regulation 3286 of 22 December 1994 laying down Community procedures in the field of the common commercial policy in order to ensure the exercise of the Community's rights under international trade rules, in particular those established under the auspices of the World Trade Organization, OJ 1994 L349/71, amended by Council Regulation 356/95, OJ L41/3 of 23 February 1995 [hereinafter Trade Barriers Regulation].

[8] Understanding on Rules and Procedures Governing the Settlement of Disputes, 15 April 1994, Article 3.2, Marrakesh Agreement Establishing the World Trade Organization, Annex 2, in *Results of the Uruguay Round of Multilateral Trade Negotiations* 1 (1994) 404, 405 (1994) 33 ILM 1226, 1227 [hereinafter DSU]. Appellate Body Report: *EC—Measures Concerning Meat and Meat Products (Hormones)*, WT/ DS26/AB/R, WT/DS48/AB/R, adopted 13 February 1998.

[9] See WT/GC/M/60, 23 January 2001.

permission for *amicus* briefs would change the balance of power in WTO dispute settlement significantly. One possibility would be to appoint particular NGOs to represent particular viewpoints in advance, similarly to the appointment or certification of NGOs to attend certain intergovernmental conferences.[10]

C. Commencement: direct and derivative rights of action

At traditional international law, the private person with a grievance could petition his or her government, in the hopes the government would espouse the claim at international law.

1. *Espousal at general international law*

The traditional model of espousal involves a state taking up the claim of one of its nationals, 'by resorting to diplomatic action or international judicial proceedings on his behalf, a state is in reality asserting its own right, the right to ensure in the person of its nationals respect for the rule of international law'.[11] This statement by the Permanent Court of International Justice is interesting because it suggests that the right, in diplomatic protection cases, is not that of the individual that is being mediated through the state, but that of the state that arises as a consequence of treatment of the citizen. The authors of the US International Law Institute's Restatement (Third) of Foreign Relations Law are in accord: '[t]he claim derives from injury to an individual, but once espoused it is the state's claim, and can be waived by the state'.[12]

However, there is a conflicting, human rights-based, understanding of espousal and its role in society. David Bederman writes:

[T]he decentralization of initiative that is evident in human rights litigation marks a clear departure from the classic model of diplomatic protection by way of government espousal of claims. No longer should the pursuit of justice in such cases be the captive of political and diplomatic expediency. In this respect, human rights advocacy is a partial antidote to the strong U.S. foreign policy tradition of pragmatism and utilitarianism. Individual grievances have tended to be subordinated to the greater good of the nation in its pursuit of common foreign policy objectives.[13]

Bederman decries the sacrifice of the rights of the one to the good of the many, and applauds the role of direct rights to block such sacrifice in human rights

---

[10] Appellate Body Report: *US—Imposition of Countervailing Duties on Certain Hot-Rolled Lead and Bismouth Steel Products Originating in the United Kingdom*, WT/DS138/AB/R, adopted 7 June 2000 [hereinafter, 'Lead Bar']. For a critical analysis of the *Lead Bar* decision, see A.E. Appleton, 'Amicus Curiae Submissions in the Carbon Steel Case: Another Rabbit from the Appellate Body's Hat' (2000) 3 *J Int'l Econ L* 691.

[11] *Panevezys-Saldutiskis Railway (Est v Lat)*, 1939 P.C.I.J 16 (Ser A/B) No 76 (Judgment of 29 February). See E. Borchard, *The Diplomatic Protection of Citizens Abroad* (1915).

[12] *Restatement (Third) of Foreign Relations Law*, § 713, comment (a) (1987).

[13] D.J. Bederman, 'International Law Advocacy and its Discontents' (2001) 2 *Chi J Int'l L* 475, at 483–84.

cases. But we may back up a step and ask, does the individual right extend to include its assertion in international fora?

In at least some reductionist sense, all legal rights of individuals may be understood as human rights: if they are not rights associated with liberty, they are rights associated with property. Certain advocates of private rights of action in international trade law base their arguments on this foundation: that the right to trade is a human right of stature similar to more established political human rights. While a critical perspective might expand, and thereby possibly explode, the domain of human rights in this way, it may be worthwhile to consider whether different types of rights might be treated differently.

One way of understanding this is to recognize that, especially in the economic and social rights sphere, if not in the political rights and individual integrity rights sphere, few rights are fixed, unqualified and unconditional. For example, rights to ownership of property are qualified by obligations to avoid using the property to harm others. The degree of protection of any right is subject to analysis in terms of the availability and scope of a remedy. There is no particular reason to treat rights in the trade sphere differently—these rights are also not fixed, unqualified and unconditional, and may be qualified or conditioned with respect to the availability of remedies. The point is that, once we depart a natural law world, the very definition of the right depends on how its remedies are structured; that is, incomplete or 'inadequate' access to adjudication may be incorporated into a broader aggregate understanding of the scope and quality of a right.

2. Exhaustion of local remedies

Under general international law, a state is not ordinarily 'required to consider a claim by another state for an injury to its national until that person has exhausted domestic remedies, unless such remedies are clearly sham or inadequate, or their application is unreasonably prolonged'.[14] In any regime of private rights of action in connection with international trade law, the policies underlying this rule would merit consideration. In addition, the rationale behind the principle of exhaustion of local remedies may suggest some limits on private party access in connection with international dispute settlement. However, this circumstance is different, as without direct effect, there may be no local remedies to exhaust.

3. Special espousal

Under Section 301 and under the Trade Barriers Regulation, the US and EC[15] have established special statutory mechanisms for espousal within the trade sector.

(a) US Section 301

Section 301 has been the focus of much attention, so in this paper, I will simply discuss the salient elements. Section 301 is an internal conduit of US consti-

---

[14] *Restatement (Third) of Foreign Relations Law,* § 713, comment (f) (1987).
[15] I refer to the European Community, or EC, the economic entity within the European Union.

tutional authority to engage in certain types of trade relations: largely to complain about foreign trade barriers. The US Trade Representative (USTR) can
commence WTO proceedings pursuant to the operation of Section 301, or can
do so under other authority.

Super 301 and Section 301(a) provide for a certain degree of 'mandatory'
action, but, in truth, this action is not completely mandatory, and can be
forestalled, *inter alia*, by the President.[16]

Under Section 301, the government must follow a specified procedure and
provide reasons for its actions, in a more regulated manner than under traditional international law espousal. In response to a petition by an interested
person (which is broadly defined to include, *inter alia*, domestic firms and
workers, representatives of consumer interests and US product exporters), the
USTR is required to review the allegations and determine whether to initiate an
investigation. If the USTR determines not to open an investigation, it must
provide reasons. The USTR can also self-initiate an investigation. In any decision
to initiate an investigation, the USTR has discretion 'to determine whether
action under section 301 would be effective in addressing [the target] act, policy,
or practice'.[17]

Under Section 301, an investigation would include a request for consultations
with the foreign country concerned. If a 'mutually acceptable resolution' is not
reached by the end of the WTO consultation period, the USTR is required
promptly to request dispute settlement proceedings.[18]

In the 2002 Trade Policy Agenda and 2001 Annual Report of the President of
the United States on the Trade Agreements Program,[19] the USTR listed the
following open cases (those brought to WTO dispute settlement are in *italic*):
(i) Intellectual Property Laws and Practices of the Government of Ukraine
(Special 301), (ii) Wheat Trading Practices of the Canadian Wheat Board,
(iii) *EC—Importation, Sale, and Distribution of Bananas* (settled 11 April
2001), (iv) *EC—Measures Concerning Meat and Meat Products (Hormones)*,
(v) *Japan—Market Access Barriers to Agricultural Products*, (vi) *Canada—
Export Subsidies and Market Access for Dairy Products*. In its 2000 and 2001
National Trade Estimate Reports, the US did not identify any 'priority foreign
country practices', and therefore there were no investigations pursuant to
Super 301.

In its 2001 Annual Report, the US lists the following disputes brought to the
WTO, for which there was activity in 2001 (regardless of when they were

---

[16] Section 301(a)(1) of the Trade Act of 1974, 19 USC §2411(a)(1). The Section 301 Panel Report
considered earlier GATT jurisprudence finding that national acts that were still dependent on the
exercise of discretion, that were not mandatory, were not 'measures' suitable for adjudication. This
was the US argument in connection with the Section 301 Panel Report, see para 7.51. The Panel (at
least provisionally) accepted this jurisprudence, but found, in effect, that the threat posed by Section
301 was a 'measure' itself under the prohibition of Article 23 of the DSU.

[17] Trade Act of 1974 §302(c), 19 USC §2412(c).

[18] Trade Act of 1974 §303, 19 USC §2413.

[19] Available at http://www.ustr.gov/reports/2002.html [the 2001 Annual Report].

commenced) (disputes listed as brought pursuant to Section 301 in any of the USTR's 2001, 2000 or 1999 Annual Reports are in *italic*): (i) Argentina—Patent and Test Data Protection for Pharmaceuticals and Agricultural Chemicals (consultations continuing), (ii) Belgium—Customs Valuation of Rice Imports (settled without panel), (iii) Brazil—Customs Valuation (consultations continuing), (iv) Brazil—Patent Protection re HIV/AIDS (transferred from WTO litigation to new bilateral consultative mechanism), (v) *Canada—Export Subsidies and Tariff-Rate Quotas on Dairy Products (monitoring compliance with completed WTO dispute settlement)*, (vi) Canada—Patent Protection Term (compliance with completed WTO dispute settlement), (vii) Denmark—Measures Affecting the Enforcement of Intellectual Property Rights (settled after consultations), (viii) *EU—Regime for the Importation, Sale and Distribution of Bananas (settled after WTO dispute settlement)*, (ix) EU—Import Surcharge on Corn Gluten Feed (EU compensation for US wheat gluten safeguard, now expired), (x) EU—Protection of Trademarks and Geographical Indications for Agricultural Products and Foodstuffs (continuing consultations), (xi) India—Import Quotas on Agricultural, Textile and Industrial Products (compliance with completed WTO dispute settlement), (xii) India—Measures Affecting the Motor Vehicle Sector (appeal withdrawn), (xiii) Korea—Measures Affecting Imports of Fresh, Chilled, and Frozen Beef (compliance with completed WTO dispute settlement), (xiv) Mexico—Anti-dumping Investigation of High Fructose Corn Syrup from the US (completed dispute settlement), (xv) Mexico—Measures affecting Trade in Live Swine (consultations), (xvi) Mexico—Measures Affecting Telecommunications Services (consultations), (xvii) Philippines—Measures Affecting Trade and Investment in the Motor Vehicles Sector (settled before panel procedure begun), and (xviii) Romania—Minimum Import Prices (settled after consultations).

It is notable that while all of the WTO-eligible Section 301 cases in this sample used WTO dispute settlement,[20] only two of this group of US WTO cases were commenced pursuant to Section 301.

(b) EC Trade Barriers Regulation

The Trade Barriers Regulation was part of the EC Uruguay Round Legislation Package. It is intended to provide EC industries and individual enterprises with a formal facility to request the EC to espouse their complaints against foreign trade barriers as a result of a violation of international trade rules. Its predecessor, the 1984 'New Commercial Policy Instrument', was little used.[21] The Trade Barriers Regulation is limited to circumstances in which a third country practice gives rise to a right of action on the part of the EC under international trade agreements, including the WTO agreements. It provides for private persons,

---

[20] Ukraine is not a WTO member, and the Canadian Wheat Board case did not seem to involve WTO obligations.

[21] See J.C. van Eeckhaute, 'Private Complaints Against Foreign Unfair Trade Practices' (1999) 33 *J World Trade* 199, at 200.

including a single company, to bring a complaint in connection with impediments to EU exports. Representatives of entire industries can bring complaints about foreign trade practices that have adverse effects within the single market.

Once a complaint has been filed, the Commission has 45 days to decide whether it is admissible, followed by a five to seven-month investigation (depending on complexity).[22] Complaints are evaluated to determine the sufficiency of evidence to justify an investigation, and whether an investigation would be in the EC's interest. At the conclusion of the investigation, the Commission reports to an advisory Trade Barriers Regulation Committee, comprised of member state representatives, but chaired by a Commission official. Only the Council may take retaliatory measures, acting by qualified majority vote.

As of January 2002, the EC had 17 open cases under the Trade Barriers Regulation, including four against the US: (i) Measures Concerning Imports of Prepared Mustard (suspension of concessions relating to the Hormones case), (ii) Anti-dumping Act of 1916 (completed dispute settlement proceedings), (iii) Licensing for Musical Works (completed dispute settlement proceedings), and (iv) Rules of Origin for Textile Products (settled).

(c) EC Article 133 procedure

The EC brings more of its WTO cases pursuant to Article 133 of the Treaty of Rome. Article 133 (former Article 113) allows the Commission to submit proposals to the Council for implementation of the common commercial policy. As in other areas of EC law, there is some ambiguity whether the Commission may bring litigation on its own initiative, or whether it must obtain authorization under Article 133. 'Even though the [Article 133] Committee's opinion is not binding, the Commission would normally only proceed when there is a consensus among the Member States to support a Commission proposal.'[23] The Article 133 route is a mechanism for government espousal, and has no formal procedures for private party access.[24] However, most private parties seek espousal through this mechanism, rather than through the Trade Barriers Regulation.[25] Bronckers and McNelis note that the Article 133 route may involve reduced expenses for private persons, compared to a Trade Barriers Regulation case.[26] The existence of the Trade Barriers Regulation, with no formal need for Council action, may make it easier to reach consensus under Article 133.[27]

4. Standing in international courts

There is no requirement for 'direct effect' in international courts, such as WTO panels and the Appellate Body, with respect to law they are mandated to apply. However, in order for private persons to participate in international dispute

[22] Trade Barriers Regulation, Article 8.
[23] Eeckhaute, supra note 21, at 210–211.   [24] Ibid at 211.
[25] M. Bronckers & N. McNelis, 'The EU Trade Barriers Regulation Comes of Age' (2001) 35 *J World Trade* 427, at 428, 453–462 (providing a suggestive explanation of why this is the case).
[26] Ibid at 455.
[27] Eeckhaute, supra note 21, at 211.

settlement, they would be required to have standing—to be among the types of persons permitted to access the dispute settlement process. At this moment, private persons lack this type of standing.

It is worth noting that under EC law, since the founding of the Community, private persons have had standing to bring certain types of cases. Under Article 230 of the Treaty of Rome (former Article 173), as noted above, private persons have standing to bring cases against certain Community acts, where those acts are of 'direct and individual concern' to the person.

However, the provision that was responsible for greater access of individuals to the ECJ was Article 234 (former Article 177), providing for preliminary references to the ECJ in cases before certain domestic courts where a decision on a particular point of EC law is necessary to enable the domestic court to give judgment. The preliminary reference facility has been an engine of constitutionalization of the Treaty of Rome, but is itself dependent on the doctrines of direct effect and supremacy.

5. Remedies and individual rights

Of course, the world of private litigation is generally concerned with money damages, and occasionally injunctive relief. The WTO legal system has different currencies: (i) withdrawal of measures found to violate WTO law, (ii) temporary voluntary provision of compensation in the form of additional trade concessions by the member in violation, and (iii) temporary suspension of concessions by the complaining party.[28] Of course, these generally are not retrospective, and provide no remedy for injury caused by violations preceding the actual date of compensation or suspension of concessions.

On the other hand, to the extent that certain WTO law is incorporated within the domestic legal system, other remedies may apply. The most important example of this, and one that can interestingly be compared to other areas of trade law, is trade remedies litigation: dumping, subsidies and safeguards. In these areas, in which domestic legal rights and remedies are authorized and constrained, but not required, by WTO law, domestic law provides direct rights to private persons. In the area of dumping and subsidies, these rights are reasonably substantial and direct, and provide little discretion to the executive to constrain them. It is noteworthy that these rights relating to administered protectionism are enhanced by domestic rules permitting private parties to commence cases. The Byrd Amendment would go even farther, providing the possibility for monetary recovery by private persons.

D. Commencement: requirements for private rights of action

Every litigator knows that there are a number of hurdles to be crossed before a particular plaintiff can obtain a judgment in respect of a particular claim. At

---

[28] DSU, Article 22.

least under US domestic law, a private person could not bring a case under a treaty (itself) unless the relevant treaty right were self-executing, which means that the treaty has legal effect within the domestic legal system, and, in addition, the private person has standing.

1. *Applicability of law in domestic courts*

Treaties are said to be '*self-executing*' when they have a legal effect within a domestic legal system without a separate *act of transposition*.[29] Within the EC legal system, a similar concept is referred to as '*direct effect*'.[30] Neither self-executing nature nor direct effect necessarily means that any particular plaintiff would have a right to bring suit.[31] The question of particular individuals' rights to bring suit is referred to as *standing*. If a particular law has direct effect and a class of individuals has standing, we can say that there exist private rights of action. Where there is an act of transposition, we might say that the international obligation gives rise to '*intermediated domestic effect*'.

In any case involving a private plaintiff suing on the basis of international law, the first question to be asked is whether the law relied on by the plaintiff is available for his or her reliance. Is the law applicable by the relevant court in the relevant legal system?[32] Of course, in WTO litigation at the international level, where today only states may be parties, there is no question but that WTO law applies.

On the other hand, within the US and the EC, it appears that the direct effect of WTO law is sharply curtailed. In the US, the WTO agreements would seem to be applicable as law, but only a single plaintiff, the US Federal Government, has standing to invoke them in domestic courts.[33] Thus, we might say that WTO law itself has direct effect within the US legal system, but it has little actual effect because its availability to private plaintiffs is prevented by strict standing rules. Of course, it is important to recognize that certain parts of the WTO agreements were transposed into US law by separate legislation included in the Uruguay Round Agreements Act, and therefore are applicable by US courts in cases

---

[29] See J.H. Jackson, 'The Status of Treaties in Domestic Legal Systems: A Policy Analysis' (1992) 86 *Am J Int'l L* 310.

[30] 'Direct effect' and 'direct applicability' are argued by some to be different. See J.A. Winter, 'Direct Applicability and Direct Effect: Two Distinct and Different Concepts in Community Law' (1972) 9 *Comm Mkt L Rev* 425. But see C.D. Esposito, 'The Role of the European Court of Justice in the Direct Applicability and Direct Effect of WTO Law, with a Dantesque Metaphor' (1998) 16 *Berkeley J Int'l L* 138, at 141. This paper does not engage this discussion.

[31] *Restatement (Third) of Foreign Relations Law*, § 111, comment (h) (1987); J.H. Jackson, 'United States' in F.G. Jacobs & S. Roberts (eds), *The Effect of Treaties in Domestic Law* (1987).

[32] *Restatement (Third) of Foreign Relations Law*, § 111, comment (h) (1987).

[33] Uruguay Round Agreements Act § 102(c)(1), Pub L No 103–465, 108 Stat 4809, 4817 (1994), codified at 19 USC §§ 3512(b)(2)(B)(i)(1994). This provision states that only the US may have a cause of action or defence under any of the Uruguay Round Agreements by virtue of congressional approval thereof. The negative implication is that these agreements have domestic effect. But see S Rep No 103–412, at 21 (1994): '[t]he WTO Agreement and other Uruguay Round agreements ... are not self-executing and thus their legal effect in the United States is governed by implementing legislation'.

involving other plaintiffs. This is a regime of indirect, and selective, domestic effect: of intermediated domestic effect.

EC jurisprudence regarding the direct effect of WTO law is somewhat less settled, but also seems generally to conclude that individuals cannot invoke WTO law in EC courts.[34] It appears that the political bodies of the EC have control over the direct effect of international trade law:

> In conformity with the principles of public international law community institutions which have power to negotiate and conclude an agreement with a non-member country are free to agree with that country what effect the provisions of the agreement are to have in the internal legal order of the contracting parties. Only if that question has not been settled by the agreement does it fall for decision by the courts having jurisdiction in the matter, and in particular by the Court of Justice within the framework of its jurisdiction under the treaty.[35]

In its instrument adopting the WTO agreements, the Council declared its intention that they not be accorded direct effect.[36] Within the US also, the legislature or the executive can effectively indicate their preferences as to the self-executing nature of international agreements.[37] Where an agreement is not self-executing, 'it is the implementing legislation, rather than the agreement itself, that is given effect as law in the United States'.[38] This is 'intermediated domestic effect'.

Thus, it is reasonably clear and almost universally accepted that at least in these two legal systems, the ability of private persons to rely on WTO law in domestic courts is dependent on the exercise of discretion by the government, and is not automatic.[39]

2. *Standing in domestic courts*

Furthermore, as noted above, even given direct effect in domestic legal systems, generally only a certain group of persons would have standing to bring a case. It is not possible here to provide substantial detail on the issue of standing.

Under US law, the issue of standing to sue under particular federal statutes is a question first of the intent of Congress pursuant to the statute to provide a

---

[34] See, eg, Case C-149/96 *Portuguese Republic v Council* [1999] ECR I-8395; Case C-280/93 *Germany v Council (Bananas)* [1994] ECR I-4973. National courts are required to follow this jurisprudence, and are therefore not permitted to apply WTO law directly with respect to private persons. Case C-469/93 *Amministrazione delle finanze dello Stato v Chiquita Italia* [1995] ECR I-4533, paras 26–29. But see Joined Cases C-300/98 and C-392/98 *Parfums Christian Dior et al v Tuk Consultancy et al (Dior)* [2000] ECR I-11307, para 49 (member states may apply WTO law directly, where the particular WTO law issue remains within the competence of the member state).

[35] Case 104/81 *Hauptzollamt Mainz v C A Kupferberg & Cie KG* [1982] ECR 3641, para 17.

[36] Decision 94/800/EC, 22 December 1994, OJ 1994 L336/2, Concerning the Conclusion on Behalf of the European Community, as Regards Matters Within Its Competence, of the Agreements Reached in the Uruguay Round Multilateral Negotiations.

[37] *Restatement (Third) of Foreign Relations Law*, § 111, comment (h) (1987).

[38] Ibid.

[39] See J.H. Jackson & A.O. Sykes (eds), *Implementing the Uruguay Round* (1997).

private right of action.[40] The intent of Congress need not be explicit.[41] Second, the issue of standing is a question of the extent to which the lawsuit satisfies the constitutional requirement that there be a 'case or controversy' for determination by an Article III court.[42] In order to satisfy the 'case or controversy' requirement, a plaintiff must show 'injury in fact', causation, and redressability.[43] The 'injury in fact' must be '(a) concrete and particularized and (b) actual or imminent, not conjectural or hypothetical'.[44]

In EC law, there are similar doctrines of standing under Article 230 (former Article 173) of the Treaty of Rome. Article 230 requires that plaintiffs show that a Community act is of 'direct and individual concern' in order to bring annulment proceedings.[45] While 'direct and individual concern' is by no means equivalent to 'injury in fact', for the present purposes the analogy illustrates the common concern in these doctrines.

E. Other participation

There are several additional ways in which private parties may be enfranchised, incrementally, by virtue of WTO law. This section explores them briefly.

1. 'Interpretation conforme' and Charming Betsy

In *Von Colson*, the ECJ stated that 'it is for the national court to interpret and apply the legislation adopted for the implementation of the directive in conformity with the requirement of Community law, insofar as it is given discretion to do so under national law'.[46] Thus, in the context of EC directives, domestic law must be construed, so far as possible, in accordance with the relevant directive.

---

[40] For example, Congress authorized the federal district courts to entertain Clean Water Act suits initiated by 'a person or persons having an interest which is or may be adversely affected', 33 USC §§ 1365(a), (g).

[41] See R.B. Stewart & C.R. Sunstein, 'Public Programs and Private Rights' (1982) 95 *Harv L Rev* 1193 (arguing that judicial 'creation' of private rights of action is an important function).

[42] US Constitution Article III, § 2. For a recent case, see *Friends of the Earth, Inc v Laidlaw Environmental Services, Inc*, 528 US 167, 120 SCt 693, 145 LEd2d 610 (2000).

[43] *Lujan v Defenders of Wildlife*, 504 US 555, 560–561, 112 SCt 2130, 119 LEd2d 351 (1992). Between *Lujan* and *Laidlaw*, there is a substantial difference in the court's approach to suits based on the government's failure to regulate, or improper regulation.

[44] Ibid.

[45] See generally A. Peck, 'Standing for Protection of Collective Rights in the European Communities' (2000) 32 *Geo Wash J Int'l L & Econ* 367; A. Arnull, 'Challenging Community Acts—An Introduction' in H.-W. Micklitz & N. Reich (eds), *Public Interest Litigation Before European Courts* (1996) 39, at 43–46; N.A.E.M. Neuwahl, 'Article 173 Paragraph 4 EC: Past, Present and Possible Future' (1996) 21 *Eur L Rev* 17, at 19—23. For member states, the Commission and the Council, so-called 'privileged plaintiffs', Article 230 provides substantially broader rights of standing. Article 226 (former Article 169) permits the Commission to bring cases against member states for failing to fulfil obligations under the Treaty of Rome. See also Opinion of Advocate General Jacobs in Case 50/00 P *Unión de Pequeños Agricultores v Council* (21 March 2002) (proposing a new interpretation of the concept of 'individual concern').

[46] Case 14/83 *Von Colson v Land Nordrhein-Westfalen* [1984] ECR 1891, [1984] 2 CMLR 430.

540 *Joel P. Trachtman*

This applies even to pre-existing domestic legislation.[47] This principle is similar to the US law 'Charming Betsy'[48] canon of interpretation, to the effect that, so far as possible, domestic and international law should be construed so as to avoid conflict. This principle already applies to give WTO law some interpretive 'effect' within the US legal system[49] and the EC legal system.[50]

2. Francovich-*style responsibility*

In its 1991 *Francovich* decision,[51] and in subsequent jurisprudence, the ECJ has found member state liability for individual losses incurred as a result of certain breaches of Community law. This doctrine might be understood as an extension of the principle of direct effect, in so far as it provides rights to individuals based on unimplemented, or improperly implemented, directives. This provided a substantial new remedy for individuals in connection with member state violation of EC law.

3. Intermediated domestic effect: mandated private rights in domestic law, subject to international supervision

Perhaps the most interesting, and important, means of establishing rights of individuals in domestic courts in relation to international trade law is through intermediated domestic effect. This method is interesting, because it is selective and subject to negotiations. Its selectivity is important because it allows states to choose the areas in which the benefits (to states) of allowing private rights in domestic courts are sufficient to overcome the costs. On the other hand, it allows states to retain exclusive rights of action in other areas. Intermediated domestic effect applies in a number of areas, including the Agreement on Pre-Shipment Inspection, the Customs Valuation Agreement, TRIPS, the Government Procurement Agreement and certain areas of trade remedies.

The rights derived from intermediated domestic effect can be applied in domestic courts. It is also possible for a WTO member state to bring a WTO action where these rights are not sufficiently protected in the domestic system. In the specialized area of pre-shipment inspection, the WTO has established an 'Independent Entity' to serve to resolve disputes between national preshipment inspection entities and exporters.[52] These are different from a preliminary

---

[47] *Marleasing SA v La Comercial Internacionale de Alimentacion SA* [1990] ECR I-4135, [1992] 1 CMLR 305.

[48] *Murray v The Charming Betsy*, 6 US (2 Cranch) 64, 118, 2 LEd 208 (1804).

[49] See *George E. Warren Corp v US Environmental Protection Agency*, 159 F3d 616, 333 US App DC 26 (CADC 1998); *Federal-Mogul Corp v US*, 63 F3d 1572 (CAFC 1995).

[50] See Joined Cases C-300/98 and C-392/98 *Parfums Christian Dior et al v Tuk Consultancy et al (Dior)*, [2000] ECR I-11307, para 49; Case C-53/96 *Hermès International v FHT Marketing Choice BV (Hermès)*, [1998] ECR I-3603, para 35.

[51] Cases C-6/90 and C-9/90, *Francovich v Italy* [1991] ECR I-5357, [1993] 2 CMLR 66.

[52] See Decision of 13 December 1995, Operation of the Independent Entity Established under Article 4 of the Agreement on Preshipment Inspection, available at http://www.wto.org/english/news_e/pres96_e/psidoc.htm.

reference under Article 234 (former Article 177) of the Treaty of Rome, because they do not come from domestic courts, but depend on domestic executives.

4. *International supervision of domestic law: NAFTA Chapter 19, the North American Agreement on Environmental Co-operation and the North American Agreement on Labour Co-operation*

NAFTA developed three interesting mechanisms that do not impose significant *substantive* requirements, but add international legal supervision of the application of domestic law. Under Chapter 19, the North American Agreement on Environmental Co-operation and the North American Agreement on Labour Co-operation, member states of NAFTA agreed to allow international tribunals to review the quality of application and enforcement of domestic law. One might say that this is a case of 'international remedies without international rights'. It is contrasted with many other areas discussed in this paper, of international rights without international (private) remedies.

5. *Public attorneys general*

As we engage in comparative institutional analysis, and examine the types of institutions that may be available to enforce specified legal rules, it is necessary not only to consider the choice between state monopoly over litigation and various modes of private participation. It is also necessary to consider an international attorney general function. There could be a number of reasons why such a function could be useful. First, private enforcement may lack the specialization and economies of scale available to public enforcers. Public attorneys general may help to solve cost or collective action problems, and may protect parties that are too weak to assert their own rights. Public attorneys general also may be imbued with the public interest, so that their approach to litigation will be different from that of private attorneys general. On the other hand, public attorneys general would not be subject to the same kinds of pressures for diplomatic deference that individual states might suffer.

6. *Defensive rights to participate*

Some commentators have argued that it violates due process to allow particular private persons to be subjected to penalties pursuant to international law, without a right to participate. There are particular appealing circumstances, such as the WTO requirement that Australia recover subsidies paid in the *Australian Automotive Leather* Case.[53] However, there are no natural limits to this position: would it also apply to exporters equally hurt by illegal trade barriers? US constitutional understandings of compensable 'takings' under the

---

[53] Australia—Subsidies Provided to Producers and Exporters of Automotive Leather, Recourse to Article 21.5 of the DSU by the United States, Report of the Panel, 21 January 2000, WT/DS126/R/W, para 6.48. See S. Charnovitz, 'Economic and Social Actors in the World Trade Organization' (2001) 7 *ILSA J Int'l & Comp L* 259, at 269.

Fifth Amendment, and recent NAFTA Chapter 11 jurisprudence, suggest that it might be difficult to limit this basis for private defensive rights.

F. Section conclusion

This section has shown that there is already great diversity in international law with respect to private participation in dispute settlement. The following section seeks to provide some normative parameters by which to evaluate these alternatives.

III. A NORMATIVE PERSPECTIVE: COSTS AND BENEFITS OF PRIVATE PARTICIPATION

The normative perspective summarized in this section draws from prior work in this field, as well as from two literatures: (i) the law and economics of private participation in dispute settlement, and (ii) the political science literature of the role of private persons in litigation under EC law.[54] This normative perspective is developed at greater length in a forthcoming work. Due to space constraints, it can only be briefly summarized here, without specific application to the WTO dispute settlement context.

In the literature of law and economics, the overriding concern has been with the optimal structure of law enforcement.[55] Much of this literature, like much political science literature, assumes that law enforcement is like being thin and rich: you can never have too much. However, as suggested above, this perspective is derived from a particular type of, and concept of, law. If we consider trade law to be more like contract than like an array of *jus cogens* norms, we might accept a theory of 'efficient breach':[56] to the effect that there may be circumstances where compliance with the law is too costly. This concept may be anticipated by the parties and incorporated in their treaty or contract, as in GATT's escape clause, or it may be supplied by courts as an implicit term. Where the gain from breach exceeds the harm from breach, it is in society's interest to encourage breach, which in economic terms is a 'first-best' outcome.

Another useful analogy for our purposes relates to the possibility of derivative causes of action for shareholders of corporations. Under what circumstances should corporations have an exclusive right to represent the firm's interests, and under what circumstances should individual shareholders be permitted to bring

---

[54] See M.A. Pollack, M. Shapiro, K.J. Alter & L.R. Helfer, 'Do the Lessons of EU Legal Integration "Travel"' (2000) 13 *ECSA Rev* 2 (considering in a series of brief essays 'whether the study of EU legal integration has yielded generalizable hypotheses or lessons which might inform the study of other domestic or international legal systems').

[55] See A.M. Polinsky & S. Shavell, 'The Economic Theory of Public Enforcement of Law' (2000) 38 *J Econ Lit* 45.

[56] See A.O. Sykes, 'Protectionism as a "Safeguard": A Positive Analysis of the GATT "Escape Clause" with Normative Speculations' (1991) 58 *U Chi L Rev* 255.

derivative lawsuits in the 'right' of the corporation?[57] If we think of international trade law rights as the rights of the state, our question is when and to what extent individuals should have 'derivative' rights.

During the past ten years, political scientists, and some lawyers, have developed a fascinating cross-disciplinary social scientific debate regarding the role of the ECJ in European integration.[58] The ECJ has played a leading role in developing negative integration—legal interpretations of the Treaty of Rome that discipline member state regulation that impedes trade—as well as in 'constitutionalizing' the Treaty of Rome.[59] These scholars have included, for example, Karen Alter,[60] James Caporaso,[61] Geoffrey Garrett,[62] Walter Mattli, Anne-Marie Slaughter, Alec Stone Sweet, and others. One facet of this research examines the role of litigation by private individuals in economic integration in the EU. While the WTO is by no means the EU, it may be interesting to see what lines of inquiry may be drawn from this literature to shed light on the problem of private parties in WTO dispute settlement.

A. Externalities, incentives and accountability

Discretionary non-enforcement could be symptomatic of tit-for-tat deals between states,[63] leaving individual 'rights' unprotected. This proposition depends, of course, on whose right it is: that of the individual or that of the state. In turn, this question depends on whether, in the particular circumstance, the state is acting as intermediary for individuals. This, in turn, depends, in regulatory theory, on the scope and type of externalities, and the relative transaction cost profile. While this paper cannot add substantial detail on this particular issue, it submits that this is the core question in determining the role of private rights of participation: whose right is it anyway?

If these rights 'belong' to states, then it is appropriate to consider a model that examines interests of individual states in exchange between states. This model suggests that it is appropriate to facilitate exchange, and would therefore reject

---

[57] See J.C. Coffee, 'Understanding the Plaintiff's Attorney: the Implications of Economic Theory for Private Enforcement of Law Through Class and Derivative Actions' (1986) 86 *Colum L Rev* 669.

[58] For a review of this literature, see Slaughter & Mattli, supra note 1.

[59] E. Stein, 'Lawyers, Judges, and the Making of a Transnational Constitution' (1981) 75 *Am J Int'l L* 1; J.H.H. Weiler, 'The Transformation of Europe' (1991) 100 *Yale LJ* 2403; K. Lenaerts, 'Constitutionalism and the Many Faces of Federalism' (1990) 38 *Am J Comp L* 205.

[60] eg, K.J. Alter, 'The European Union's Legal System and Domestic Policy: Spillover or Backlash' (2000) 54 *Int'l Org* 489.

[61] eg, A. Stone Sweet & J.A. Caporaso, 'From Free Trade to Supranational Polity: The European Court and Integration' in W. Sandholtz & A. Stone Sweet (eds), *European Integration and Supranational Governance* (1998).

[62] eg, G. Garrett, D. Keleman & H. Schulz, 'The European Court of Justice, National Governments, and Legal Integration in the European Union' (1998) 52 *Int'l Org* 149.

[63] Research by Eric Reinhardt suggests that the US is more likely to bring a WTO case against another state that has brought a case against the US; E. Reinhardt, *To GATT or Not to GATT: Which Trade Disputes Does the U.S. Litigate, 1975–99?*, working paper dated November 2000, available at http://userwww.service.emory.edu/~erein/research/tg.pdf.

private participation in dispute settlement. If these rights belong to individuals, or are transferred by states for public interest reasons to an international organization, ie the WTO, then according to a public interest model, sole state control of these rights, by virtue of exclusion of private participation, would be inappropriate. Furthermore, if the public interest model applies, then it may be appropriate to establish an 'attorney general' function, similar to the role the Commission plays in the EC. The congruence between the individual private interests and this type of public interest model may hold, but there may well be circumstances where it does not. In any event, private rights would not necessarily *substitute* for an attorney-general function, because the interests of private persons may not be congruent with the broader public interest.

We should distinguish here between truly private plaintiffs suffering relatively direct harm, and NGO private plaintiffs seeking to address a general policy area. NGO private plaintiffs may have additional inefficient incentives to litigate cases. They may choose the cases that are easiest to win, or the cases that establish a particular point, instead of the cases that will satisfy their concerns the most.[64]

Where the right 'belongs' to the state, we might begin to develop a perspective that domestic ratification structures can suggest to us something about the types of private participation that may be appropriate. There may be too many individual cases to follow a domestic parliamentary or other procedure in each case, and Nichols suggests that 'the negotiation of trade regulations captures more attention than the adjudication of disputes under those regulations'.[65] However, given the role of dispute settlement in 'making' international trade law, the concerns are similar.

This normative concern would suggest that where substantial externalities exist, a regime of espousal would serve best to allow states to determine whether the social benefits exceed social costs. However, much depends on the magnitude of the externalities, and the social costs of internalizing them. Transparency would not seem to raise substantial problems in the case of externalities, assuming that the externalities are understood domestically and seen as meriting a regulatory response. Furthermore, where the right seems to belong to private persons, truly private rights would seem to raise fewer concerns here than NGO private rights, assuming that the truly private rights are carefully tailored to minimize externalities.

B. Toward an efficient quantity of WTO law litigation?

In international litigation, relating to international legal rights, where the rights exist 'for' states, states would be expected to have the level of incentives to

---

[64] See J.A. Rabkin, 'The Secret Life of the Private Attorney General' (1998) 61 *L & Contemp Probs* 179, at 190–92.

[65] P.M. Nichols, 'Extension of Standing in World Trade Organization Disputes to Nongovernment Parties' (1996) 17 *U Pa J Int'l Econ L* 295, at 316 (citations omitted).

litigate most close to optimal:[66] in order to enforce the rights for which they bargained. Private parties may have incentives to over-litigate.[67] Thus, Posner states that '[d]iscretionary nonenforcement is a technique by which the costs of overinclusion can be reduced without a corresponding increase in underinclusion (loopholes)'.[68] Of course, this analysis depends on an assumption that the government enforcement of WTO law is, on its own, approximately equal to an optimum level. Determination of the optimum level depends in the final analysis on a policy decision.

On the other hand, the political science literature suggests that it would often be beneficial to increase the level of litigation, especially litigation originating with private plaintiffs. This literature assumes a *telos* of integration, within the EC. For example, Stone Sweet and Brunell present a theory of European legal integration that relies on three causal factors: transnational exchange, triadic dispute resolution and the production of legal norms.[69] Their theory would suggest that policy-makers seeking greater integration, or seeking to facilitate transnational commerce, would promote increased transnational litigation. Alter and Conant question the causal relationship suggested by Stone Sweet and Brunell.[70]

Thus, quantity of litigation may be linked to (a) enforcement, and (b) integration.[71] To the extent that policy-makers find that greater enforcement and/or integration would be desirable, this vector would argue for an increase in rights of commencement in order to increase litigation.

[66] There might be a number of reasons why they would not be optimal. For example, the weak remedies in WTO litigation would serve as an artificial disincentive to litigation by states.

[67] See S. Shavell, 'The Fundamental Divergence between the Private and Social Motive to Use the Legal System' (1997) 26 *J Legal Stud* 1; S. Shavell, 'The Optimal Structure of Law Enforcement' (1993) 36 *J L & Econ* 255; Landes & Posner, 'The Private Enforcement of Law' (1975) 4 *J Legal Stud* 1; G.S. Becker, 'Crime and Punishment: An Economic Approach' (1968) 76 *J Pol Econ* 169; M.A. Cohen, 'Monitoring and Enforcement of Environmental Policy' in H. Folmer & T. Tietenberg (eds), *The International Yearbook of Environmental and Resource Economics* (1999) at 44.

[68] R.A. Posner, *Economic Analysis of Law* (5th edn, 1998) at 660.

[69] A. Stone Sweet & T.L. Brunell, 'Constructing a Supranational Constitution: Dispute Resolution and Governance in the European Community' (1998) 92 *Am Pol Sci Rev* 63. Stone Sweet and Brunell focus on dispute resolution that reduces the cost of exchange, thereby promoting commerce—they see these factors as interdependent. While increasingly, ECJ and WTO litigation may have this characteristic, the greater reduction in the transaction costs of commerce would be expected to derive from the availability of certainty in private law litigation, rather than from the quantity of public law litigation. Most preliminary reference cases (the type examined by Stone Sweet and Brunell) relate to challenges to member state law, asserting its incompatibility with EC law, or to EC secondary law, asserting its incompatibility with the Treaty of Rome. The ECJ and WTO do not participate significantly in traditional private law litigation.

[70] Alter, supra note 60; L. Conant, 'Europeanization and the Courts: Variable Patterns of Adaptation Among National Judiciaries' in M.G. Cowles, J. Caporaso & T. Risse (eds), *Transforming Europe: Europeanization and Domestic Change* (2001).

[71] See Mattli & Slaughter, supra note 1, at 202 ('without individual litigants, there would be no cases presented to national courts and thus no basis for legal integration').

C. One voice values, dispersed standing and diplomatic transactions

In the US, the idea that each individual or sub-state actor cannot 'control' US foreign policy through litigation is based on certain constitutional principles, and on a policy of speaking with 'one voice' in international relations.[72] These 'one voice' values have important limits, especially as international relations includes more and more topics traditionally included in domestic affairs. One way of determining the limits may be in trying to determine the extent of externalities that form a basis for governmental control.

Moreover, we must distinguish between one voice values where private litigants engage domestic courts which consequently become involved in international relations, and circumstances in which private litigants engage international courts. Where international courts are engaged, and domestic courts are not being requested to involve themselves in international relations issues, there seems less reason for 'one voice' concerns. In these circumstances, as US courts are not implicated, the US government is speaking with one voice, and the only discordant voice is that of an individual. Values of autonomy and free speech would suggest that this type of discord is not to be suppressed.

If multiple persons have rights to litigate regarding the same matter, then settlement or diplomatic compromise will be impeded.[73] If states share access to dispute settlement with private parties, states lose control over the enforcement of the right, and therefore lose the ability to negotiate a settlement with another state.

D. Dispersed standing as a commitment device: 'it's beyond my control'

Conversely, the inability to engage in future transactions may be accepted as a reciprocal commitment device, in order to assure compliance with a particular norm. Here, of course, the discretion being transferred is prosecutorial discretion. And it applies in cases where the bound state would act as plaintiff, rather than defendant. This kind of commitment might result in greater compliance by the potential respondent: if I precommit myself to punish you for violation, without any hope of forbearance, you are less likely to breach. This kind of commitment might alternatively provide reassurances to domestic constituencies, as an inducement to them to ratify a trade agreement.

---

[72] See NAFTA Statement of Administrative Action at 13 (private lawsuits could interfere with conduct of trade diplomacy). The one voice argument is important in a number of areas of US jurisprudence, including the Commerce Clause, the asserted exclusive foreign affairs power, the Act of State doctrine and the Alien Tort Claims Act. For a careful critique of the one voice arguments in this context, see E.-U. Petersmann, *Constitutional Functions and Constitutional Problems of International Economic Law* (1991) at 288–92.

[73] See C.G. Holderness, 'Standing' (1998) 3 *New Palgrave Dictionary of Economics and the Law* 505, 508; M.C. Jensen, W.H. Meckling & C.G. Holderness, 'Analysis of Alternative Standing Doctrines' (1986) 6 *Int'l Rev L & Econ* 205.

E. Informational advantages of private litigants

Some literature divides surveillance between centralized (government-effected) 'police patrols' and decentralized (private person-effected) 'fire alarms'.[74] A 'fire alarm' system allows the concrete concerns of private parties to be the basis for action. '[F]ire alarm oversight tends to be particularistic ... it arguably emphasizes the interests of individuals and interest groups more than the public at large.'[75] Sevilla finds that most GATT/WTO complaints from 1948–1996 were particularistic in nature—they arose from private parties' concerns, rather than from systemic issues.[76]

F. Protectionist and other bias

It may be that the public choice based bias of trade policy in favour of domestic producer interests would be accentuated by increased private access. That is, if it is expected that producer interests would be able to organize for litigation more effectively than consumer interests, we would expect a litigation bias in favour of producer interests. On the other hand, it might be argued that the executive has already been captured by producer interests, and any reduction of the monopoly enjoyed by the executive would diminish the producer bias. Within the US public law litigation system, as well as within the EC, it has been suggested that formal access to dispute resolution is disproportionately useful to wealthier interests.[77] This may help to explain developing country resistance to private party access.

It is worthy of note that domestic producers already have substantial private rights in important areas of 'administered protectionism': dumping and subsidies law. These private rights are not required by WTO law, but are permitted under WTO law. The US 'Byrd Amendment' provides increased incentives for this type of litigation, making this litigation more 'horizontal'. These private rights may be juxtaposed with the relative paucity of private rights for lawsuits to protect consumer interests, or foreign producer interests. Perhaps this is evidence that there is capacity for selection of areas in which to accord individuals private rights.

G. Choice of disputes for litigation

While governments may validly or inappropriately select disputes for diplomatic reasons, they may also select disputes for litigation for reasons of avoidance of

---

[74] See M.D. McCubbins & T. Schwartz, 'Congressional Oversight Overlooked: Police Patrols versus Fire Alarms' (1984) 28 *Am Pol Sci Rev* 165; C.R. Sevilla, *A Political Economy Model of GATT/WTO Trade Complaints* (Working Paper dated 1996). Sevilla considers WTO committees such as the Trade Policy Review Mechanism as the equivalent of 'police patrols', while dispute settlement complaints brought by private persons are the equivalent of 'fire alarms'.

[75] McCubbins & Schwartz, ibid at 172.

[76] Sevilla, supra note 74, at 16.

[77] L. Conant, *Justice Contained: Law and Politics in the European Union* (Cornell University Press, 2002).

'wrong' cases, or to avoid the possible development of undesirable (to them) legal rules. They may choose disputes in a way designed to develop a particular type of jurisprudence.[78] Private parties may not have these incentives, and may not forbear in the same way.

One of the reasons that especially NGO private plaintiffs have been eager to bring public interest litigation in other contexts is to force issues onto the agenda where legislatures declined to act. However, granting this power to NGO private plaintiffs, or to any private plaintiffs, might be seen as a usurpation of the legislative right of inertia,[79] raising issues of the proper relative roles of dispute settlement and legislation.

This problem is accentuated in the international sphere, as compared to the domestic arena. In the domestic arena, legislation is an everyday occurrence. However, in the WTO legal system, 'legislation'—treaty revision—is an unusual and difficult activity. This imbalance between adjudication and dispute resolution means that control of the adjudication agenda is even more important, as 'legislative reversal' is less available. On the other hand, it might be argued that given the difficulty of legislation, greater possibility for adjudication is needed.

H. Governmental control of arguments versus private control of arguments

We may separate the right to commence a lawsuit, allowing control of the agenda of litigation, with the right to make and have considered arguments, allowing control of the intellectual agenda of litigation (except to the extent that a panel or the Appellate Body may adopt reasoning that the parties have not argued). Both the Commission and the USTR have exercised care to assert certain types of arguments, and avoid certain other types of arguments, in an effort to foster a desirable set of precedents. Private persons, whether as litigants or as *amici*, might not have the same types of cross-sectoral or society-wide concerns, and might not have similar longer-term time horizons, and therefore might make different decisions about the arguments they would make. Governments that expect to be both complainants and respondents from time to time have a different perspective. There may be trade-offs between the current case and future cases.[80] This is another category of externality.

IV. CONCLUSION: CONSTRUCTING A SYSTEM, ONE PIECE AT A TIME

It is obvious that the normative considerations listed above cannot comprise anything approaching a formal model. However, it is hoped that they will

---

[78] See M.L. Stearns, 'Standing Back from the Forest: Justiciability and Social Choice' (1995) 83 *Cal L Rev* (1995) at 1309. Stearns suggests that preserving the governmental option to bring disputes in a particular order, with a particular type of outcome, is a rationale for standing doctrine.

[79] See M.L. Stearns, ibid at 1309.

[80] S. Charnovitz, 'Participation of Nongovernmental Organizations in the World Trade Organization' (1996) 17 *U Pa J Int'l Econ L* 331, at 353.

provide a checklist of considerations, with some degree of analytical detail, for use in considering proposals, like Professor Petersmann's for expanding private rights in WTO dispute settlement. These normative considerations exist at the level of cost-benefit analysis, rather than at the level of natural rights or natural law. Given this case-by-case cost-benefit analysis approach, a natural conclusion is that negotiated rules of intermediated domestic effect provide a good basis for beginning to approach private participation.

According to institutional economics theory, and subsidiarity, states have rights in international society because they may achieve more of what individuals desire than individuals acting separately. While this may not always be true in practice, and while it may not be operational as a positive theory, it seems attractive as a normative approach. It suggests that before transferring rights from states to individuals, we investigate the benefits that might flow from each institutional structure, and the costs, including transaction costs. The operational problem with this theory has important practical consequences: in this non-market context, our best preference revelation device for determining whether individuals are getting more or less of what they want, imperfect as it is, is the state.

So, arguments to the state about the types of private participation it should authorize are useful, but it is difficult for analysts to know when the state has it wrong and when it has it right. Analysts can help most by illuminating the different costs and benefits and ensuring their consideration.

We know that when states desire to provide private parties with rights in connection with litigation, they know how to do so. We have many instances of intermediated domestic effect. Why is it that private parties have substantial rights in connection with anti-dumping and anti-subsidies actions—with foreign mercantilist action—and such modest rights against domestic protectionist actions? Both in the US and in the EC, the question of domestic effect seems increasingly to be taken over by legislatures, as opposed to courts. This phenomenon is consistent with increasing intermediated domestic effect.

We also know that states seem to have developed acceptable, if not appropriate, ways to approve trade treaty commitments. Trade law litigation would seem to have similar, although perhaps attenuated, importance. After all, its role is the interpretation and application of treaty commitments. Therefore, it is worth comparing the role of private persons in formulating and approving the treaty commitments themselves, with their role in litigation.

It is worth recognizing the strategic perspective. NGO private plaintiffs and truly private plaintiffs are, first of all, strategic litigants. They seek the best forum for the outcome they desire. Where the NGO loses in the domestic legislative forum, and in the domestic judicial forum, it naturally seeks an international forum. It will continue to seek fora until it wins. From the institutional design standpoint, the question is whether it is a failure of subsidiarity to provide an external forum, where the matter is adequately addressed, procedurally, in domestic fora. Whether the matter is adequately addressed depends on consideration of the degree to which appropriate opportunities for voice are provided. This voice should exist at the appropriate decision-making level. If decisions about the US approach to a particular trade matter are best made at the US domestic level, it would seem inappropriate to provide an opportunity to negate those decisions at the international level. If the US voice is but one voice in the international trade community, it may be unfair to others to give those who participated in the formulation of the US voice an opportunity to speak in the international trade community.

Finally, if allocation of authority in litigation is concerned with allocation of authority in society more generally, then the institutional economics and subsidiarity perspective suggests that the real question is not about who or which values are to be empowered, but about who will decide. Litigation is a form of governance, related to legislation. Control over litigation is a form of governance, and should be informed by these analytical perspectives.

PART IV

PREVENTING AND SETTLING TRANSATLANTIC ECONOMIC DISPUTES: POLICY RECOMMENDATIONS

22

Strengthening the Sinews of Partnership: Resolving and Avoiding Transatlantic Economic Conflicts

DAVID L. AARON*

The economic relationship between the United States and the European Union is in the midst of a significant transition. Once predominantly about trade, it is increasingly affected by several new elements:

- the level of mutual transatlantic investment has doubled since the early 1990s;
- as the US and the EU move toward the 'new economy', they must cope with the implications of emerging technologies, such as bioengineering and the internet, in their markets;
- a new emphasis has emerged in transatlantic economic diplomacy on the importance of domestic regulations on such matters as food safety, the environment, and the treatment of personal data;
- as transatlantic economic issues increasingly revolve around matters previously regarded as 'domestic', representatives of domestic interests, including civil society groups, are increasingly interested in being more engaged in the transatlantic policy dialogue.

The Bush US administration and its European partners thus face a formidable challenge. Although each of these changes is important, when taken together they have fundamental implications for both the US-European relationship itself and the role of the transatlantic partners in the wider international arena. For the US and the EU, the prospect of economic gain is great, but so is the potential for conflict. Moreover, they must deal with the consequences of these changes while also addressing a number of persistent trade disputes and making progress in the World Trade Organization (WTO) on the 'Doha' multilateral trade Round. In the international arena, their success or failure in dealing with these issues will

* This paper is drawn from a revised summary and recommendations of two study group reports co-chaired by Ambassador Aaron and published by The Atlantic Council of the United States (rapporteur: Frances G. Burwell): *Changing Terms of Trade: Managing the New Transatlantic Economy* (April 2001); and *Risk and Reward: U.S. and EU Regulatory Cooperation on Food Safety and Environmental Protection* (November 2002) reproduced in revised form by kind permission of the Atlantic Council of the United States.

establish a pattern likely to be repeated elsewhere as the forces of globalization spread new technologies and industries around the world.

The Bush administration is responding to this challenge early in its tenure by obtaining 'fast track' negotiating authority and pursuing a resolution of US-EU disputes by quiet diplomacy. This has had success in the launch of a new trade round and ending the conflict over bananas. Nonetheless many stubborn issues remain and new problems loom.

A serious and extensive discussion of the transatlantic economic relationship with European leaders is needed at the summit level. It should be well prepared and take into account the broad scope of economic interaction, its importance within the global economy, and its growing impact on the domestic arena on both sides of the Atlantic. There should be a serious effort to identify areas of potential disagreement. But more important than predicting specific future disputes, US and European leaders should refocus their dialogue on the totality of their economic relationship and speak out in a way that will help their constituents better understand the importance of that interaction.

If such an effort is to succeed, however, it must be built on two strong foundation stones:

- A serious initiative to resolve the remaining outstanding transatlantic trade disputes. Although these persistent disagreements involve a relatively small portion of US-EU economic interaction, they have created much tension. For the transatlantic dialogue to move forward and address new issues, these stumbling blocks must first be removed.
- The effective integration of responsible civil society representatives into the policy dialogue. While business and labour have long been involved in the US-EU discussion, new constituencies, such as consumers and environmentalists, are now pushing to join the debate. Engaging these groups in a constructive manner will be essential both for the success of the transatlantic economy, but also for the success of the Doha Round.

The next few years will demonstrate whether the US and Europe can manage this transition constructively, or whether their economic relationship will continue to be troubled by disputes. To succeed, Washington, Brussels and the Member States must recognize the magnitude of the transition. They must then address persistent disputes and find ways to involve relevant constituencies in their dialogue. This will require that they each have a better regard for the policy processes and domestic pressures that guide the decision-making of the other.

But the US and the EU should also look beyond the immediate needs of their economic relationship. Given the many other shifts in the larger US-European political alliance, it is important that transatlantic economic interaction not be a continuing source of tension, but the basis of an effective partnership. Only then will the US and the EU be able to exercise real leadership in the multilateral trade talks, and, in the longer term, in the global economy as a whole.

Reaching this goal will first require a better understanding of the important elements shaping the transatlantic economy today. This calls for a focus on four issues: disputes and dispute resolution; new issues such as investment and competition policy; new technologies and industries; and new constituencies. In addition to reviewing these elements, this paper will specifically examine the need for regulatory co-operation in food safety and the environment.

I. DISPUTES AND DISPUTE RESOLUTION

Although they involve only a small portion of the US-EU economy, a series of persistent trade disputes—including bananas, Foreign Sales Corporations, GMOs—has caused much acrimony in the transatlantic relationship. Although the WTO has handled many cases effectively, its use in these politically sensitive cases has had serious limitations. Nor have retaliatory sanctions proven particularly effective as a means of enforcing WTO judgments in these instances. Some disputes could be avoided or ameliorated if a more robust 'early warning' system existed. But others, especially the politically sensitive ones, are likely to require a more focused, but flexible, effort if they are to be resolved.

First, the Bush administration and the EU should launch a high-level initiative to resolve the current outstanding disputes in a comprehensive framework. This will require bilateral negotiations across a range of issues and a focused leadership effort by each party to develop the necessary domestic consensus. Second, the US administration should work with the EU to construct a bilateral strategy for addressing future disputes. They should strengthen the early warning mechanism; prepare damage assessments prior to seeking redress; and develop a bilateral mediation process.

II. INVESTMENT AND COMPETITION POLICY

Investment is a rapidly growing part of the transatlantic economy and will become increasingly important in the US-EU relationship. Although the current situation is fairly benign, given the high stakes that would be affected by any serious disagreements, the US and the EU should work to create the appropriate mechanisms to help ameliorate or resolve such conflicts. Similarly, transatlantic co-operation on competition policy worked well, but is still ad hoc and has relied on compatible antitrust and merger policies which may well be changing under the Bush administration. A comprehensive multilateral investment or competition accord is unlikely to be negotiated in the near future, and may not be the best approach in any event. Instead, Washington and Brussels may find limited bilateral agreements on investment and competition to be more attainable and suitable.

The US and EU should give greater priority to bilateral discussions on investment issues, and closely examine the possibility of a bilateral investment accord. Such an accord would be limited in scope, and may ultimately be extended multilaterally. The new administration should also explore ways of reinforcing the current transatlantic co-operation on antitrust policy. This may involve a modest bilateral arrangement that would better harmonize the two review processes. As with an investment accord, an agreement on competition policy might also be introduced into an appropriate multilateral forum.

III. NEW TECHNOLOGIES AND INDUSTRIES

New technologies and industries, such as genetic engineering and e-commerce, will become a major part of the transatlantic economy during the next few years. The US and the EU often bring to these issues significantly different attitudes towards public risk and the role of the state, thus creating ample opportunities for misunderstanding and conflict. However, there are important mitigating factors, as public attitudes and regulatory frameworks evolve on both sides of the Atlantic. Because the WTO may not be effective or appropriate for addressing these issues, the creation of alternative mechanisms on either a bilateral or multilateral basis is necessary.

The US should press for greater clarity on the definition and use of the precautionary principle. Bilateral US-EU discussions may prove the best way to dampen transatlantic disputes on this issue. To advance both the public and governmental debates, it is time to establish non-governmental task forces to examine specific issues. Depending upon the particular topic, they should include representatives of relevant public policy groups, labour, and business, as well as legislators. Areas that may be especially ripe for this treatment are biotechnology, the environment and other regulatory issues.

IV. TRANSATLANTIC CONSTITUENCIES

Although the involvement of business and labour in the US-EU economic policy dialogue is well-established, other constituencies, including environmentalists and consumers, have been underrepresented. While governments will obviously remain the main parties in the policy process, without the increased participation of these groups in some manner, it will become even more difficult to resolve many of the most sensitive issues. The dialogues established under the New Transatlantic Agenda have had somewhat mixed success, and, where possible, they should be strengthened. But more effective participation of both existing and new constituencies might be better attained through discussions focused on specific issues. The selection of constructive participants will be key to the success of such fora; it is also important that they be linked to the legislative process on both sides of the Atlantic.

V. TRANSATLANTIC RELATIONS AND REGULATORY POLICY

As the foregoing suggests, US-EU trade disputes have focused increasingly on differences in regulation, rather than the traditional barriers of tariffs or subsidies. Regulatory requirements established primarily with domestic concerns and politics in mind can affect the free flow of international commerce. Such regulatory differences have contributed to US-EU disputes over a range of food and environmental issues, including beef hormones, genetically modified foods and feed, ozone depleting chemicals, and aircraft engines. As the US and European economies become ever more intimately linked, such regulation-based disputes are likely to increase in number and frequency, and because regulatory issues are intrinsically linked to domestic politics, these matters are likely to be sensitive and difficult to resolve. Their impact will go beyond trade policy, contributing to concerns about a rise in tensions in the transatlantic relationship overall.

In particular, environmental protection and food safety have been among the most volatile issues in the US-European relationship. While they are now overshadowed somewhat by the transatlantic debate over Iraq and other political and military matters, tensions over environment and food safety are just below the surface, and—if not addressed—will have enduring corrosive and divisive effects. Indeed, the recent acrimony over these issues has contributed to concern about erosion of shared transatlantic values and a deterioration in US-European relations generally.

Moreover, as recently demonstrated at the Johannesburg UN summit on sustainable development, the failure of the US and Europe to work together on these issues does not have only bilateral consequences. It represents a significant lost opportunity to provide leadership in addressing environment and food safety on a global level. The US and Europe have both been leaders in these areas—a fact that is too often overlooked in the current debate. Unless they now find a way to reconcile their different perspectives and approaches, the US and the EU will miss real opportunities to work together in addressing global environmental and public health issues.

The effect of these disputes reaches beyond the US and the EU, as standards established through US and EU regulations often become de facto international standards. The outcome of US and EU discussions will establish the pattern for how governments around the world deal with these new technologies and products, and will be key to the development of global regulations and markets.

A key element dividing the US and Europe has been their distinct views of precaution. Although both acknowledge the general need for precaution, especially when dealing with new technologies that might affect human health or environmental protection, they differ considerably over the desirability of a formal 'precautionary principle' and its application to broader policy areas. The EU has sought to expand the application of the precautionary principle. The US government has maintained that an internationally agreed precautionary principle is not appropriate for widespread application. The US also maintains that existing rules already acknowledge the right of governments to exercise precaution.

Efforts to resolve these regulatory disputes have so far met with mixed success. Use of the WTO dispute resolution procedure has been criticized by some who believe that the process ignores environmental considerations, but recent rulings indicate that the WTO will allow trade restrictions based on environmental concerns under certain circumstances. However, securing compliance on such politically sensitive issues can sometimes be problematic. As a result, the US and EU trade policy communities have recently given greater emphasis to bilateral negotiation and mediation as a more desirable way to reduce regulatory disputes, while reserving the right to pursue remedies through the WTO if consultations fail.

VI. GMOs AND FOOD SAFETY: A LESSON IN CONSUMER ATTITUDES AND REGULATORY POLICY

Developments in biotechnology in the areas of food and agriculture have presented the transatlantic relationship with one of its most difficult challenges, and future innovations in biotechnology are likely to test the relationship even more severely. In the US, agricultural biotechnology, including genetically modified foods and feed, has for the most part been accepted as part of the normal process of technological innovation in both farming and the food industry. In Europe, however, a string of food safety and other health scandals has damaged public confidence in regulatory institutions. Although none involved GMOs, these episodes made the public (and the politicians), extremely wary of such new technology. Thus, in seeking to bridge transatlantic differences, a key issue will be consumer confidence. Effective risk assessment and risk management will be essential, and ways must be developed to provide consumers with the information and choice they desire. US-EU differences over GMOs have also affected the international agricultural market as both Washington and Brussels have sought to convince other governments of the merit of their respective positions. This is not simply a matter of markets, however, as was demonstrated by the recent reluctance of some African governments to accept GM food aid, despite a looming famine.

Several conclusions can be drawn from the experience thus far with GM foods and feeds:

- Consumer confidence is the most important determinant of any future market for agricultural biotechnology. Central to this will be restoring the credibility of European food safety institutions.
- A credible scientific risk assessment process is essential as we proceed with the development of agricultural biotechnology products, including GMOs.

- Some form of labelling and 'traceability' may be useful in providing consumers with information and choice. But such mechanisms must not effectively close the market to safe products and must be implemented in a workable and verifiable way.
- The continuing US-EU dispute over GMOs threatens to evolve into a global rivalry over the use of agricultural biotechnology. How the US and the EU will resolve this dispute—or fail to resolve it—will have significant implications for future trade in biotechnology.

A. Recommendations

The US should encourage European efforts to restore public confidence in food safety institutions, and should thus be as supportive as possible of the new European Food Safety Authority (EFSA). Exchanges between the FDA and the EFSA should be established in order to facilitate sharing of perspectives and best practices, with the goal of enhancing the risk assessment capabilities of both institutions. The US should also continue to stress the central role of the Codex Alimentarius as the primary body for establishing food safety standards internationally.

Whenever possible, the US and the EU should move toward a more collaborative risk assessment process, especially in relation to GM products. The establishment of the EFSA may offer opportunities in this area, as may the current push for increased scientific co-operation under the New Transatlantic Agenda (NTA). It might be especially useful to consider whether a scientific risk assessment procedure that falls between the current GRAS ('generally regarded as safe') and food additives procedures would be useful. The end goal of this scientific collaboration should be to establish a foundation for a transatlantic mutual recognition agreement on agricultural biotechnology products.

Since some form of labelling and product tracing is probably inevitable in some countries, the US and the EU should focus their efforts on ensuring that such a scheme is workable and not misleading while providing consumers with sufficient choice. Labelling that allows the easy identification of GM-free products and the development of a market in those goods is most likely to provide consumers with the widest choice. Any such scheme must be enforceable through testing or certification. This may make it desirable for the US government to establish a certification regime for GMOs, after conducting a survey of existing certification practices to see which might serve as an appropriate model.

If the EU passes a labelling and traceability measure with requirements that are essentially unworkable, the US should give serious consideration to starting the process of pursuing a case through the WTO dispute resolution mechanism. That case should not challenge the EU's obligation to establish a certain level of safety for its citizens, but should be focused on the workability of any such scheme and ensuring that it is non-discriminatory.

VII. PROTECTING THE ENVIRONMENT: TRANSATLANTIC CONFLICT AND CO-OPERATION

Both the US and the EU (including the member states) have adopted many laws and regulations designed to protect their environments. Indeed, they have been in the forefront internationally in developing such rules. However, the different regulatory approaches behind these rules have led to disputes. Although disagreements to date have been limited in both number and scope, some have been especially persistent. Given the importance of environmental protection to both the European and US publics, the political sensitivity of these disagreements is likely to increase, leading to greater transatlantic tensions in the future. Moreover, these regulatory issues have a significant international dimension, as the standards and practices that develop out of the two dominant markets will inevitably affect those adopted by multilateral standard-setting bodies and international corporations.

The disagreement over the Kyoto Protocol on climate change is only the most visible example of transatlantic conflict over the environment. Other, lower profile cases—over hushkits for airplanes, electronic waste recycling, persistent organic pollutants, and ozone-depleting substances—have also generated serious tensions. These cases proved to be particularly complex because of the multitude of actors involved, most with primarily domestic orientations and agendas, and because of the impact of continually changing technologies. Finally, while the US and the EU often agree in their assessment of the risk, they sometimes use incompatible mechanisms to manage that risk and approach implementation and enforcement very differently.

Although both the US and the EU share the basic goal of environmental protection, they have pursued this objective through the development of distinct, and sometimes conflicting, regulations and standards. These regulatory differences have the potential to become another acrimonious area of transatlantic relations in the future. Efforts to reconcile US and EU regulatory regimes have been hampered by several factors, including: the involvement of multiple actors with multiple agendas; the impact of constant technological innovation; the divergent views of technical standards and of cost-benefit analysis; and differing emphases on implementation and enforcement.

Transatlantic differences over environmental matters should not be treated either as a mere technical question or a simple trade dispute. They reflect very divergent political choices, with the key differences being over risk management, rather than risk assessment. Avoiding an enhanced level of transatlantic tension over this issue will require greater US engagement in creating sound policy on environmental protection, and more willingness by both to seek out opportunities to share perspectives and develop a more collaborative approach.

A. Recommendations

The US and the EU should reaffirm their common commitment to environmental protection. On the US side, this will require greater engagement and leadership, especially from the White House and Congress. An interagency group on international aspects of environmental protection would help give this issue a higher profile across the government. The commitment of the US and the EU could also be demonstrated by a joint statement on environmental protection and its compatibility with international trade, to be issued at the next US-EU summit.

Although risk assessment has not been the major point of difference over environmental issues, encouraging more collaborative assessments, perhaps through the NTA scientific co-operation agreements, can help build a stronger foundation for US-EU understanding and co-operation in this area. Exchanges between appropriate US and EU agencies could be extremely useful in fostering the sharing of perspectives and development of co-operative activities and should be mandated and funded by Congress. Among the long-term aims might be the joint development of standards for environmental technologies that are compatible with international trading obligations and the design of appropriate mutual recognition agreements.

Collaboration in risk management will be essential in avoiding future tensions and could begin with a comparison of best practices, both in environmental protection and in regulatory policy—perhaps at the OECD. Such a comparison could be undertaken with the participation of industry and NGOs, as well as by US and EU agencies, and could be valuable in identifying specific mechanisms that contribute to environmental protection while not creating barriers to commerce.

US government and industry must re-engage on the issue of standards, particularly within the international standards setting bodies. This should not be treated as an area of mere technical discussion, but as an issue in which US leadership (from both the government and private sector) will be key in ensuring that the results are compatible with both protecting the environment and the obligations of international commerce. Establishing new congressional reporting requirements on the status of international standards and the actions of US agencies could provide the necessary stimulus. But this is not simply a government responsibility—US corporations should also be prepared to take on the necessary leadership roles in private-sector bodies.

VIII. Reconciling regulatory regimes

The US and the EU face the challenge of reconciling their regulatory regimes to attain two distinct—but not necessarily conflicting—goals: to protect the environment and consumers, and to fulfil the obligations of the international trading system. We are now at a fork in the road. If US and EU regulatory policy continues to be made without adequate regard for its international impact, future regulatory issues could easily erupt into yet another series of difficult and persistent transatlantic disputes. But if Washington and Brussels begin to exercise leadership on this issue, they could foster the development of new strategies for reconciling distinctive regulatory systems. A first step has been made with the agreement on Guidelines for Regulatory Co-operation and Transparency. Further steps, such as negotiating a 'time-out' provision that would require each government to stop the legislative process for consultations, could also be helpful. Over the long term, constructing a more collaborative approach could be much more effective in protecting citizens and the environment than continuing a pattern of rivalry and disputes.

Overcoming the current regulatory differences between the US and the EU will not be an easy task. There will not be one single step that by itself will make this endeavour a success; instead it will be a lengthy process involving changes in attitudes and procedures across many agencies and institutions. But neither the US nor the EU can afford any longer to write regulations on food safety and environmental protection in domestic isolation, only later to be forced to defend those rules in the international arena. As the transatlantic economies integrate, so must the regulatory processes that affect so much of the economic exchange across the Atlantic. By taking advantage of opportunities for greater consultation and eventually collaboration, the US and the EU will reduce the chance that regulatory policy will lead to a series of difficult confrontations. Instead they will be able to focus on working together in creating regulatory regimes that effectively protect consumers and the environment.

23

Preventing and Settling Transatlantic Disputes: The EU, the US, and the WTO

RODERICK ABBOTT

I. POLICY STATEMENT OF THE EU

It will be the general perception of observers, on the basis of frequent excitements in the media, that the years since 1995 when the WTO Agreement came into force have been filled with one trade war after another. Or at least that war was often threatened by one or the other party.

Legendary engagements, often over many months, even years, have fired the imagination: the lengthy dispute over imports of bananas in the European Union, the prohibition of imported beef when cattle have been treated with growth hormones, more recently the FSC export subsidy case which has finally led to an arbitration award of $4 billion to the EU—these are all important cases in terms of basic principles, different values on either side of the Atlantic, or simply entrenched tax law which is difficult to change.

The EU, having been at the losing end of some early WTO dispute cases which proved politically sensitive and difficult to solve, has always been in favour of settling cases bilaterally (in line with the WTO rules) wherever that is feasible. Witness the fact that we were ready to hold back on the WTO panels that had been established in 1996 and 1998 against the United States on the Helms Burton legislation and on the law in Massachusetts which prohibited imports from Burma (Myanmar) and from any countries that invested in or traded with that country.[1]

In the first case, we were able to negotiate a fragile cease fire, with waivers being granted to allow European service providers to continue activity in Cuba; and in the second, the panel examination was suspended and the US Supreme Court eventually struck down the State law. The desire to settle such disputes

---

[1] Another more recent example was the settlement of a complaint about the tariff treatment of imports of US origin rice into Belgium. Other examples include several cases involving the intellectual property legislation of EU member states (no panels were established), as well as one on US rules of origin on textile items. (In addition, there were other cases with non-transatlantic countries.)

bilaterally, and only to take matters to the WTO as a last resort, was encapsulated in a short verse which Mr Lamy had composed during the TABD meeting in November 2000:

> Consult before you legislate, negotiate before you litigate;
> Compensate before you retaliate, but comply at any rate.

Unfortunately it proved easier to find the right rhymes than it did to execute the philosophy behind the words. Let me suggest a number of reasons why this has been the case.

II. WHY DO SO MANY CASES GET REFERRED TO THE FORMAL WTO PROCESS (PANEL AND APPEAL)?

First is the fact that *Parliaments, Councils of Ministers and the Congress do not like having to modify the law unless there is a very good reason*. Administrations, on both sides of the Atlantic, even if they are persuaded that change is inevitable, find it difficult to obtain a change of attitude or of the law without a WTO ruling which says clearly that existing practice is illegal (a violation of WTO obligations). Examples of this phenomenon are legion: hormone beef or bananas on the EU side; Foreign Sales Corporations, Helms Burton, dumping issues and other trade remedy cases on the US side. Indeed our experience has been that in trade remedy cases, the US is unlikely to envisage any significant modification of their law or practice prior to a panel or Appellate Body (AB) ruling.

It is self-evident that, in the US system, where an individual Senator or Congressman has promoted a specific piece of legislation it will in principle be very difficult to modify that law unless it is clearly necessary to do so. Indeed, experience shows that even when legislation is found to be contrary to WTO obligations, this fact in itself is not enough to ensure a change in the legislation since domestic political factors intervene.[2] More generally, when the complaint concerns long standing policy and practice (as in the case of trade remedy legislation), similar domestic political factors are at work which make the resolution of problems without a WTO ruling very unlikely.

This is of course not uniquely a US situation, even if the details of the process are different. Cases such as the Hormone ban or the moratorium of approval of new GMO varieties have illustrated that it is difficult to respond to a WTO ruling (or in the GMO case, the likelihood that a complaint in WTO could be pursued) due to the weight of public opinion and consumer concerns.

Second is that *there are important clashes of basic values*, such as those that occur in the area of public health and consumer protection. Faced with the

---

[2] Current examples of such problems are the legislation on trademarks designed to protect US rum interests (the Havana Club trademark), or the so-called Byrd Amendment related to the revenue raised by anti-dumping duties. Other cases where a change of law has proved to be difficult include the FSC tax provisions, the Anti-Dumping Act 1916 or the US Copyright Act related to 'Irish country music'.

argument: 'sound science exists, analysis has shown no risk and let the market (consumer) decide' you find the counter-argument: 'science is not that clear, experts disagree, the public are not accepting that there is no risk, and a minimum level of consumer protection is needed'. In such an impasse, what to do next? The WTO is the only and best arbiter in such conflicts.

Third, you might have a clash between trade policy and more general development strategies. Behind the media froth over bananas, there are certain objective facts: small Caribbean islands depend on this trade, cannot easily diversify; the EU policy of giving preferential access to the African, Caribbean and Pacific (ACP) countries is of long standing, since 1975; bananas from central and Latin America already provide 80 per cent of EU imports; the US is not a banana producer. To quote from John Peterson: 'The US turned up the volume on bananas so high that any compromise.... became impossible ..... publication of a huge ($500 m) list of provisional retaliatory measures—blatant sabre rattling. Each side made the worst possible decision at every fork in the road.'

Lastly, we should perhaps look more carefully at the argument that WTO litigation is a second best route and that it carries a real cost for international economic relationships.

- *How do you measure the damage to the multilateral trading system, or to the WTO as an organization, or to Transatlantic relations*, from one additional dispute? or from 12?
- Does the damage depend on the subject matter, some being political/media rich, others being boring and technical?
- Is there not equally a cost in trying but failing to settle matters in the transatlantic context? The area of MRAs comes to mind.
- Does an implicit choice have to be made, between possibly damaging bilateral relations by using public, international fora, inter alia the WTO—and perhaps weakening its dispute settlement system over time by deliberately preferring another route, to one side?

III. OTHER POSSIBLE APPROACHES

Various ideas have been put forward for other ways to settle disputes before the panel stage, or to reduce the incidence of transatlantic disputes. In the light of the section above, there will always be certain types of dispute where a WTO ruling is felt to be necessary for progress to be made; but we should examine any suggestions which lead to improved dispute avoidance.

A. Mediation

This idea was proposed in the Atlantic Council policy paper, 'Changing the terms of Trade', of April 2001, but it was not spelled out in any great detail. One essential feature seemed to be the idea that mediation should go hand in hand with some type of *compliance commitment*; but it was not entirely clear whether this was an obligatory (or desirable) step to be taken before seeking a panel, or whether it was intended as a full alternative.

The WTO Director General had also at times encouraged parties to disputes to use more fully the 'good offices' and conciliation procedures contained in DSU Article 5, but without much visible response. Parties to disputes should also bear in mind perhaps the provisions of Article 3:7 which speaks of exercising judgment as to whether action under DSU procedures would be *fruitful*, and which states that a mutually acceptable solution is clearly to be preferred.

On the bilateral front, the change of US Administration brought in a new team to address these issues, and success in finding a solution to the long running banana problem in April 2001 perhaps encouraged thoughts of how other such problem areas could be tackled. At the Göteborg EU-US summit in June that year the question was supposed to be a major discussion item and even a 'deliverable'; but this aim was somewhat undermined by having a paper delivered to the European side too late for any reaction to be possible.

Elements in this were: a bilateral process of mediation, outside the WTO; a non-binding process; an 'independent' outsider would talk to each side and seek points of convergence and divergence, to prepare a more political negotiation; the mediator would not aim at an agreed factual analysis or at presenting the legal arguments, nor would he make any recommendations. While these ideas are worth considering it is not clear at what stage in the dispute mediation would occur (at the drafting stage of legislation of regulations? or after decisions have been taken?), nor how it would effectively improve the situation when there would be no recommendations to the parties and no binding outcome.

B. Moratorium

Gary Hufbauer, a former Department of Commerce official, has suggested a cooling-off period in current disputes with both sides forswearing any retaliatory measures until the end of 2003. The difficulty with this is that if one agrees not to act in ways which the DSU authorizes, it looks as if one is abandoning the legal rights that the DSU makes available and allowing the other party to escape its obligations. Politically speaking, it may make sense to exercise a degree of moderation in cases such as FSC and the steel measures; but to have a formal agreement never to use the means of pressure available is more problematic.

On the basis of past experience, eg in the Uruguay Round, some cooling off effect of this kind might be expected in any case as the Doha negotiations become more intensive through the next 18 months or more; and in addition, solutions to subsidy and other problems (how to apply the principle of sound science in SPS regulations; what trade measures to protect the environment and seek stronger disciplines from countries in that field would be acceptable) could increasingly be sought in the negotiating process rather than through the dispute settlement mechanisms. So, it seems unlikely that the specific suggestion would be acceptable (perhaps to both sides?) but in a pragmatic manner something not too different may emerge in the context of the negotiations.

IV. Do failures to resolve problems prior to the formal WTO litigation process matter so much?

One of the reasons behind the emphasis in this paper on transatlantic *dispute avoidance* is the perception that trade disputes between the EU and the US constitute a very large proportion of the total and form the bulk of the WTO's work on dispute settlement. This perception is fuelled by the media attention to such cases which is indeed high—EU-US disputes tend to be billed as 'another threat of a trade war'—and it is true that certain cases have been high profile in terms also of their substance.

But the statistics tell another story. While the EU and the US account for about 40 per cent of world trade, the ratio of their trade disputes to all disputes which have been reported out by panels and, in some cases, appealed, is only 18–21 per cent.[3] (A similar figure would be true for *complaints* by the EU and US against each other, in relation to all complaints notified to the WTO.) So there is not in fact anything out of proportion in the situation. Even this exaggerates the bilateral situation, *stricto sensu*, since some of the more notorious cases have placed the US *and others* against the EU (bananas and hormones) or the EU *and others* against the US (the so-called Byrd amendment in the anti-dumping area, and most recently the steel safeguard measures [4]).

This is not to suggest that we should take the matter lightly; even 16 transatlantic disputes laid out before the WTO is in some ways too many, and creates the perceptions of trade wars to which I have already referred. But at the same time we should remember that the Dispute Settlement Understanding and its mechanisms are still relatively new, and that the transfer of sovereignty which is implied (placing WTO members face to face with their violations and their obligations) is not an easy thing for all governments to accept. Consequently they often feel the need to defend themselves 'in court ' against a charge of WTO illegality rather than simply accepting that a law or practice has to be changed.

---

[3] Thus, 11 cases reported out of a total of 59 (September 2002) which is 18.6%; or if you add in cases in the pipeline (currently in panels) 16 cases out of a total of 78 which is 20.5%. Of the 11 cases, three were jointly taken with other parties, and of the 16 another three. So, if you take the strictly bilateral disputes, 10 out of a total of 78 represents only 12%.

[4] In the Byrd case there were ten plaintiffs altogether including the EU. In the steel case, eight plaintiffs. Moreover, many cases against US trade remedy measures have had a large third party participation supporting the complainant. In the latest FSC panel five countries intervened to support the EU case.

24

Policy Recommendations for Dispute Prevention and Dispute Settlement in Transatlantic Relations: Legal Perspectives

GEORGE A. BERMANN

The concrete case-studies and general policy analyses that were the subject of inquiry in the conferences culminating in the present volume have predictably generated a series of distinctly legal—as well as political—reflections on dispute prevention and dispute settlement in the transatlantic arena. One of the merits of the dual (concrete and abstract) approach that has been adopted for these conferences is its capacity to provide a check against the risks that would result either from divorcing this study from the realities of disputes or from relying exclusively on potentially idiosyncratic dispute scenarios.

It is in a sense reassuring to find, as I have, that the general policy analyses neither refute, nor are refuted by, the case-studies taken as a whole. The result is a more confident statement of reflections from a legal perspective than is often possible and, in turn, a more confident sketching of what appear to be the most relevant policy recommendations.

I think it useful, at the outset, however, to make a few assumptions, which may not—it must be said—be universally shared. The first such assumption is that categorization of disputes will continue to operate as a useful descriptive and prescriptive tool, in the sense that a meaningful typology of disputes should continue to inform the analyses and policy recommendations brought to bear on dispute prevention and settlement. The second is that we are not committed to the notion of establishing new formal structures specific to EU/US trade disputes. From a legal perspective, at least, there appears to be little to be gained, and possibly significant costs to be incurred, in establishing a Transatlantic Free Trade Agreement specifically for purposes of preventing or resolving EU/US trade disputes.

It seems to me that the recommendations to emerge that are most important from a legal perspective are the following:

I. Monitoring and improving transatlantic regulatory co-operation processes

Precisely because of the legal complexities inevitably associated with the WTO dispute resolution process in all its phases, it is important from a legal perspective that there be monitoring and improvement of existing government-to-government processes for identifying and resolving disputes at a pre-WTO stage.

A specific way that emerged from the discussions for making such improvement is early bilateral use of scientific advisory bodies. The case-studies, and common sense, suggest that empanelling such bodies, upon identification of a problem but prior to the crystallization of policy differences, would facilitate producing scientific or technical understandings that may be critical to the early settlement of differences.

II. 'Intermediate direct effect'

A recurring issue, both in the case-studies and the general policy analyses, has been the prospect of providing for an 'intermediate' form of direct effect of WTO obligations. For advocates of increased efficacy of international or supranational legal norms, direct effect has always had a strong appeal. (The contribution of direct effect to the efficacy of EC law is well established in the literature.)

But, it may ultimately be more advantageous to situate direct effect somewhat differently. Rather than posit direct access by private parties to domestic courts to enforce the disciplines of WTO law, consideration should be given to more 'mediated' forms of direct effect. This is recommended on account of the regulatory incoherence that may flow from having potentially countless numbers of private claimants asserting their claims before a multiplicity of generalist judges lacking expertise, or any form of primary responsibility, for fashioning a consistent and coherent response to WTO-based claims.

Thus, consideration should be given to shifting the centre of gravity in the giving of national direct effect of WTO law away from domestic courts in the first instance and toward the domestic administrative process.

III. A 'restatement' of wto law?

It rightly appeared idle to many participants in the conference deliberations to envision improvement in transatlantic dispute prevention and settlement in isolation from the evolution of substantive WTO law. This is especially the case, of course, because WTO law, from a practical point of view, is being more actively made in the course of dispute resolution than in international 'legislative' channels.

It is not too early for WTO case-law to be made subject to serious study and criticism, with a view not only to improving the application of WTO law principles, but also to clarifying them and rendering them more coherent. Indeed, from the point of view of favouring dispute prevention and settlement, it may be more important that the law be certain and coherent than that it be substantively 'ideal'.

That having been said, it may be premature, given the modest number of rulings on any single set of provisions in the WTO agreements, to initiate a 'Restatement' as such. But it is not too early to subject the body of rulings that have emerged to a rigorous collective substantive law review, with a view toward an eventual Restatement of sorts. This could prove a useful instrument in activating a 'political correction' mechanism whereby a pattern of misguided or inconsistent WTO rulings might be reversed.

IV. THE PROBLEM OF WTO 'INTERFACE' WITH OTHER INTERNATIONAL INSTITUTIONS

We have frequently observed the problem of 'interface' between the WTO and other international regulatory institutions. The problem commonly emerges in two contexts. One such context is that of 'linkages', that is to say, the question of whether and to what extent values other than facilitation of international trade should be taken into account in the elaboration of world trade law. The other context in which the problem arises is a more general one, namely that of legitimacy, democracy, and accountability.

The fact remains that the interface problem also has a more particular impact on WTO dispute prevention and settlement, if only due to the questions of 'proper forum' that inevitably arise. Not as much has been done as could be done by way of articulating the institutional relationship between the bodies primarily concerned with international trade and those primarily concerned with other values with which a trade imperative may from time to time conflict, or the substantive relationship between the norms and the rulings that these bodies produce. We are dealing with bodies, on the one hand, and norms and rulings, on the other hand, that are widely regarded as 'authoritative' within the realm they are authorized to regulate, but whose authoritativeness within the larger arena of international economic regulation is occasionally contested and in any event contestable.

Placing the interface problem in a dispute resolution context does not make addressing that problem any the easier. But it serves to make it all the more concrete and, in that sense, compelling.

25

Practical Recommendations for Policy Reforms in Order to Prevent and Settle US–EU Trade and Economic Disputes

H. PAEMEN

The trade and investment relationship between the United States and the European Union has led to a degree of integration of the two economies which is without equivalent in the world. Their exchanges have reached what economist Gary Clyde Hufbauer calls a 'mature stability', developing 'at about the same speed as the global tide of economic integration', but with still 'room for considerably more growth with further liberalization'.[1] It is not unreasonable to think that, as was the case in the past, intense competition will lead to occasional disputes, even if they concern a small number of the total exchanges.

Two opposite tendencies appear simultaneously in this respect. One pushes into the direction of progressive harmonization (with or without governmental guidance) of the market conditions on both sides; the other will regularly reveal new impediments as the integration extends into new sectors or as new legislation or regulatory measures are introduced on either side. Beyond these two factors, we should not neglect the recurring symptoms of more traditional syndromes like the ones of which the steel sector is an unfailing provider.

Following the proliferation of transatlantic disputes in the 1990s (bananas, hormones, GMOs, hushkits, steel, FSC, etc) a series of initiatives was taken in order to prevent or better handle these and future conflicts. These were:

- the creation of a 'New Transatlantic Marketplace' by progressively reducing or eliminating bilateral trade barriers;
- the establishment of a 'Transatlantic Economic Partnership' with an Action Plan intended to address trade issues before they become disputes;

---

[1] G.C. Hufbauer & F. Neumann, *US-EU Trade and Investment: An American Perspective*, conference paper presented at 'Transatlantic Perspectives on the US and European Economies: Convergence, Conflict and Cooperation' at the Kennedy School of Government, Harvard University, 11–12 April 2002.

- an effort to strengthen regulatory co-operation by encouraging the regulatory agencies on both sides to address technical and non-tariff barriers to trade and by promoting the conclusion of mutual recognition agreements;
- the creation of a horizontal forum for bilateral consultation and early warning with a view to preventing conflicts and resolving trade frictions.

The implementation of these initiatives would be monitored through the procedures set up in the context of the New Transatlantic Agenda (NTA) (1995): a Senior Level Group of high officials seconded by a Task Force.

One need not be a pessimist to conclude that the practical results of these initiatives were limited. Rather, it was thanks to some other factors that the heat was, at least temporarily, taken out of the bilateral trade disputes at the beginning of the new century:

- a more businesslike approach by new teams on both sides,
- the successful launching of new multilateral negotiations,
- a growing confidence in the WTO Dispute Settlement System, and
- probably also the sudden emergence of serious geopolitical and security concerns.

This does not mean, however, that on either side a solid framework to better manage future crises is now in place.

The reason for this unsatisfactory development was certainly not a lack of motivation at the level of the officials in charge of the implementation of the successive programmes. Nor can it be said that the political leaders were ambiguous in their statements when the initiatives were launched and their objectives solemnly proclaimed.

What has been lacking is foremost the capacity of the authorities on both sides to motivate and empower their bureaucracies and constituencies in such a way that the lofty objectives could be transformed into realities. The result was that the different programmes had no or very little direct impact on the pending disputes.

Much has already been written about what should or should not be done to prevent or to settle transatlantic disputes. In so far as the main goals pursued by the different programmes are still valid, some basic elements should be taken into consideration:

(1) It would be useful for the main objectives of the transatlantic economic partnership to be publicly reconfirmed at the highest level on both sides, especially in the light of some uncertainty about the overall priorities of the present US administration.

(2) Conflict prevention can only be successful through more intensive contacts and dialogues than those that took place in the framework of the NTA. They should occur directly between the legislative and regulatory authorities, the last ones being duly instructed and empowered by the political leaders. Efforts should be made to de-bureaucratize the monitoring and implementation of these processes.

(3) There is undoubtedly also room for more genuine and constructive dialogues between the representatives of the respective civil societies (consumers, environmental groupings, labour unions, Transatlantic Business Dialogue, etc), which were the most worthy innovation of the NTA.

(4) When disputes arise, as will inevitably be the case, they should be handled for what they are, ie disagreements concerning a very small part of the overall relationship, the solution of which can nearly always be found in the correct implementation of existing rules and procedures. It is probably, to some extent, their relative unimportance in relation to the overall partnership that has not discouraged the frequency of these disputes and their getting out of control in the past. The WTO Dispute Settlement System is a safe resort for trade disputes, but it should always be borne in mind that it envisages consultation and arbitration before recourse is taken to litigation.

(5) US-European relations suffer from being taken for granted and easy to mend when in jeopardy. It is well known that finding a date for the annual US-EU summits is a recurring nightmare for the scheduling officers. And the continuing personnel change on the European side, depending on the rotating presidency, does not foster a durable and systematic dialogue. The 'constituency' of the transatlantic relationship, as a consequence, is diffuse and latent. It cannot be mobilized without a special effort.

Each of these recommendations could be elaborated and refined at length on the basis of the experience gathered in the different chapters of this book. As would appear from such a review, transatlantic disputes have covered different policy areas in the past: trade policy measures (anti-dumping, subsidies, safeguard measures), sectoral policies (steel, agriculture), more general, societal issues (GMOs, hormone-fed beef, private data protection, politically founded economic sanctions). Their variety indicates that there is no single methodology to prevent or remedy conflicts.

More systematically, legislative and regulatory dialogues between the legislators and regulators of both sides would probably be the best way to avoid built-in conflicts. Apart from a judicious usage of the wide range of tools provided by the existing, official Dispute Settlement Systems (especially in the WTO), good offices, conciliation and mediation between interested parties and their organizations, as well as recourse to common transatlantic peer reviews and common (scientific) advisory boards should be explored as active contributions by the civil societies.

The regular consultations of the highest political authorities would then concentrate on the overall guidance of the partnership and the definition of policy objectives.

26

Preventing and Settling Transatlantic Economic Disputes: Legal and Policy Recommendations from a Citizen Perspective

ERNST-ULRICH PETERSMANN

During the 20th century, the United States has emerged as the most successful constitutional democracy and hegemonic military power whose national constitutional law and international postwar initiatives for the United Nations and Bretton-Woods systems continue to influence the laws and foreign policies of numerous states around the world. By the beginning of the 21st century, the European Union has become the first 'international constitutional democracy' whose integration law and international constitutional guarantees (eg, of human rights and parliamentary democracy) offer an alternative 'international integration paradigm' that has become accepted by almost all states in Europe and serves as a 'civilian power model' for other regional integration agreements, eg, in Africa and Latin America. Even though the EU and the US are built on similar basic principles of human rights and constitutional democracy, their constitutional experiences (eg, the high degree of 'constitutional failures' in European states), sources of legitimacy (eg, national law in the US, international law in the EU), institutions (eg, for EC legislation) and foreign policy-making processes differ fundamentally (eg, strong control by the US Congress, weak parliamentary control of foreign economic policies in the EU).

I. How to respond to the increasing transatlantic 'system frictions'?

The tensions between national constitutionalism in the US and international constitutionalism in Europe entail increasing 'system frictions' and foreign policy conflicts, for example over how the European Monetary Union can become a member of the state-centred International Monetary Fund (similar to EC membership in the WTO), and how the US focus on 'international unilateralism' (eg, non-participation in the UN Convention on Climate Change and its 'Kyoto Protocol', preventive war as declared policy option of the US security strategy) can be reconciled with the EU's focus on 'multilateralism' (eg, compliance with the UN's collective security system and with UN multilateral environmental agreements). Also, due to their different national and international approaches, the free trade agreements (FTAs) concluded by the US with less-developed countries in Africa, Asia and Latin America differ from the FTAs concluded by the EC, eg, with almost all third countries in Europe and Africa. In the WTO negotiations on 'Improvements and Clarifications of the WTO Dispute Settlement Understanding', the proposals submitted by the EU aim at further 'legalization' of WTO dispute settlement procedures (eg, by transforming *ad hoc* dispute settlement panels into a 'permanent panel').[1] By contrast, in response to 'concerns of the Congress regarding whether dispute settlement panels and the Appellate Body of the WTO have added to obligations, or diminished rights, of the United States' (as described in section 2101(b)(3) of the US Trade Act of 2002), the US has proposed in the Dispute Settlement Understanding (DSU) negotiations to enhance 'flexibility and control by WTO Members', and limit certain judicial elements in the dispute settlement process of the WTO.[2] The escalating number of transatlantic economic disputes is, to some extent, influenced by this broader context of 'system frictions' and calls for new transatlantic initiatives for more effective dispute prevention and dispute settlement methods. So far (June 2003), the 43 proposals submitted in the WTO negotiations on DSU reforms do not yet indicate an emerging consensus on how to prevent and settle WTO disputes more effectively.

Transatlantic policy co-ordination, dispute prevention and dispute settlement between the two most important economies which together account for almost half of world trade and international investments, are of decisive importance not only for *bilateral* EU-US relations but also for the future evolution of *worldwide* rules and institutions like the WTO, the IMF and the UN system. Interdisciplinary discussions on prevention and settlement of transatlantic disputes offer useful opportunities for re-examining traditional practices and perceived weaknesses in the prevention and settlement of transatlantic disputes. This is especially true if such discussions involve EU and US politicians, trade and foreign policy officials in Europe and the US, WTO dispute settlement panellists, WTO Appellate Body members, and other legal, economic and political experts from both sides of the Atlantic, as was the case at the two international conferences of the EUI project on Dispute Prevention and Dispute Settlement in Transatlantic

---

[1] Cf, E.U. Petersmann (ed), *Preparing the Doha Development Round: Improvements and Clarifications of the WTO Dispute Settlement Understanding* (EUI, 2002).

[2] Cf, Executive Branch Strategy Regarding WTO Dispute Settlement Panels and the Appellate Body—Report to the Congress Transmitted by the Secretary of Commerce, 30 December 2002, and, eg, the US proposal in WTO document TN/DS/W/28 of 23 December 2002 on 'Improving Flexibility and Member Control in WTO Dispute Settlement'.

Relations. This contribution draws seven policy conclusions from my introductory report in Part I of this book.

II. OPTIMAL DISPUTE PREVENTION STRATEGIES REQUIRE CLARIFICATION OF THE 'PUBLIC INTEREST': NEED FOR CITIZEN-ORIENTED RATHER THAN STATE-CENTRED OR POWER-ORIENTED APPROACHES

The classical international law paradigm of conflicts among 'state interests' does not adequately take into account the variety of transatlantic conflicts of interests. In order to identify 'optimal methods' for preventing and settling transatlantic disputes, we need a better understanding of their underlying conflicts of interests and a more precise definition of the 'public interest' to be pursued in transatlantic dispute settlement proceedings. Transatlantic relations are based on 'multi-level governance' and autonomous decisions by self-interested private economic actors (eg, investors, producers, traders, consumers), national governments, regional institutions (like the EC) and worldwide institutions (like the WTO Dispute Settlement Body). Transatlantic disputes reflect conflicts among these diverse private and public, national and international interests involved. Just as transatlantic rule-making and policy-making take place at different private, national and international levels, so must transatlantic dispute prevention and dispute settlement strategies intervene at the most appropriate level so as to prevent or settle conflicts of interests directly at their source without causing 'spill-over problems', such as additional rule-violations or unnecessary prolongation of costly dispute settlement procedures. For instance, the only 'prospective' rather than 'retroactive' nature of legal and judicial remedies at the WTO level (cf, Articles 3:7, 19:1 DSU) operates as an incentive for temporary violations of WTO rules at national levels because discriminatory trade restrictions enable governments to redistribute income in exchange for political support, and sanctions are unlikely for a period of up to three years until the WTO Dispute Settlement Body may authorize countermeasures (cf, Article 22).

What is the public interest to be protected in transatlantic disputes among the EU and the US? International legal theory suggests that compliance with international rules depends more on cost/benefit analyses,[3] the perceived legitimacy of the international rules,[4] and on 'internalization'[5] of the intergovernmental

---

[3] Cf, L. Henkin, *How Nations Behave* (1979) who asserts that, for reasons of cost/benefit analysis, 'almost all nations observe almost all principles of international law and almost all of their obligations almost all of the time' (at 47).

[4] Cf, T. Franck, *The Power of Legitimacy Amongst Nations* (1990) who identifies (at 24) the following four major factors for assessing a rule's legitimacy: its determinacy, rule-making process, conceptual coherence and conformity with the hierarchical rule system.

[5] Cf, H.H. Koh, 'Why do Nations Obey International Law?' 106 *Yale LJ* 2628, at 2646.

rules into domestic laws and policy-making processes than on intergovernmental adjudication and sanctions. The fact that transatlantic disputes affect less than 2 per cent of transatlantic trade and investment flows, and that the WTO Agreements have been approved by domestic parliaments on both sides of the Atlantic, confirms the awareness by the EU and US governments that compliance with their WTO obligations offers important mutual economic, legal and political advantages. Yet, the refusal by both the EU and US governments to allow individual citizens and private economic operators to invoke and enforce WTO rules in domestic courts also illustrates the prevailing mercantilist perception of WTO law and transatlantic relations: private complaints and petitions to enforce WTO rules are welcome (eg, pursuant to section 301 of the US Trade Act and the EC Trade Barriers Regulation) if they are directed against foreign governments; yet, domestic citizens are prevented from invoking WTO rules in their own domestic courts against violations of the rule of law by their own governments. Even though the US and EU constitutions commit governments to respect for international law (eg, in Article 300(7) EC Treaty), the US Congress and EU Council perceive compliance with the intergovernmental rules governing transatlantic economic relations as a matter of intergovernmental rights and obligations and government discretion.

Inside the EC, dispute settlement proceedings among EC member states have become very rare due to 'constitutional' dispute prevention mechanisms (like 'constitutional primacy' and 'direct effect' of EC common market rules, infringement proceedings initiated by the EU Commission, advisory opinions by the European Court of Justice (ECJ) and private enforcement of EC rules through national and EC courts). In transatlantic relations, however, the EU and US insist on 'state-centred' rather than 'citizen-oriented strategies' for defining the 'public interest' and for preventing, settling or escalating disputes. On both sides of the Atlantic, there are also 'power-oriented' calls to ignore legally binding international rules (eg the EC's WTO obligations for trade in hormone-fed beef and genetically modified organisms, the WTO obligations of the US vis-à-vis 'Foreign Sales Corporations'). Similar transatlantic disagreements also exist with regard to the law of other worldwide organizations (eg, Chapter VII of the UN Charter) and the need to adjust state-centred rules (eg, of the IMF Agreement) to the new reality of exclusive Community competencies (eg, for monetary and exchange rate policies involving the Euro).

The diversity of conference participants confirmed the diversity of transatlantic policy perspectives and of their underlying value premises. State-centred trade diplomats, government officials, international lawyers and 'realist' political scientists tend to identify the 'public interest' in transatlantic relations with alleged 'state interests' (or 'Community interests') and focus on rights and obligations of governments and the need for discretionary foreign policy powers, including the power to deviate from agreed international rules (eg, WTO law) ratified by domestic parliaments. This state-centred *external* policy approach differs fundamentally from the citizen-centred approach inside the EU: the *internal* customs union rules (eg, in Articles 25 and 28 of the EC Treaty) were legally and judicially protected as 'fundamental freedoms' of EC citizens. Whereas abolition and replacement of trade policy discretion by free movement of goods, services, persons and capital are celebrated as constitutional achievements inside the EU, trade policy discretion remains the prevailing paradigm in transatlantic relations.

From a normative constitutional perspective, it appears more convincing to define the 'public interest' in transatlantic relations in the same manner as among EU citizens and among US citizens, ie, in terms of 'constitutional principles of justice'[6] such as maximum equal freedom of citizens for mutually beneficial division of labour across frontiers, rule of law, individual access to courts, democratic governance, and social justice. From such a rational citizen-perspective, discriminatory market access barriers in violation of WTO rules, and related disputes in transatlantic relations, run counter to the general interest of EU and US citizens (eg, their common interest in maximizing consumer welfare and compliance with WTO rules ratified by domestic parliaments). Illegal trade barriers reveal 'government failures' and 'constitutional failures', such as the treatment of citizens as mere objects of international law and the lack of effective legal and judicial remedies enabling EU and US citizens to challenge the frequent abuses of discretionary trade policy powers by their own governments for the benefit of 'rent-seeking' interest groups (eg, agricultural, textiles or steel lobbies). Yet, such a 'constitutional definition' of the 'public interest' in terms of consumer welfare and equal citizen rights is currently not supported by the EU and US governments.

The diversity of value premises and policy perspectives entails divergent policy conclusions. For instance, trade negotiators claim that protectionist import restrictions, non-compliance with WTO dispute settlement rulings (eg, on the illegality of the EU's import restrictions on bananas and hormone-fed beef), the lack of co-decision powers of the European Parliament in the trade policy area (cf, Article 133 EC), and denial of judicial protection by EU and US courts against violations of WTO obligations by EU and US governments serve the 'public interest'. Citizens criticize such power-oriented trade policies as running counter to the general citizen interest in rule of law, consumer welfare, and judicial enforcement of treaties ratified by parliaments for the benefit of citizens. As long as 'trade policy rules' are construed and applied by governments in such open contrast to the 'constitutional principles of justice' inside the EU and inside the US, agreement on the 'public interest' and on optimal dispute prevention and

---

[6] As defined, eg, by the leading US legal philosopher, J. Rawls, *A Theory of Justice* (1971). In his book *The Law of Peoples* (1999), Rawls rejects the assumption of individual equal freedom as a normative basis for designing a worldwide 'constitutional contract among peoples' because, according to Rawls, the individualist values would show insufficient tolerance and respect for certain non-liberal societies. Yet, in transatlantic relations among constitutional democracies, there are no convincing reasons to depart from the rational self-interest of EU and US citizens in maximum equal freedom and equality of opportunity (normative individualism) for evaluating law and social institutions.

dispute settlement strategies will often remain elusive among trade politicians and rational citizens interested in maximum equal freedom, rule of law and consumer welfare. An interdisciplinary follow-up conference at Columbia University will analyze in more depth how WTO guarantees of freedom, non-discrimination, open markets and rule of law can be made more effective in transatlantic relations, focusing on legal and judicial remedies not only of governments but also of citizens vis-à-vis violations of WTO rules.

III. NEED FOR DISTINGUISHING TRANSATLANTIC DISPUTES ACCORDING TO THEIR UNDERLYING CONFLICTS OF INTERESTS

Dispute prevention and dispute settlement can be facilitated by distinguishing four different categories of transatlantic disputes according to their objects (ie, the policy measures challenged by the complaint), their underlying conflicts of interests, and the applicable rules.

A. Trade discrimination in violation of WTO rules: inadequate dispute prevention and judicial remedies

Most transatlantic disputes concern discriminatory market access restrictions or market distortions (eg, export subsidies) that have been introduced by EU and US governments in violation of WTO rules in order to accommodate 'rent-seeking' producer interests at home (eg, agricultural, textiles, steel producers) at the expense of domestic consumer welfare and of other general citizen interests (eg, in rule of law, low taxes). The EU and US governments negotiate and enforce reciprocal WTO guarantees of freedom and non-discriminatory conditions of competition at the intergovernmental level. But the same governments collude in preventing EU and US citizens from acquiring effective legal and judicial remedies against the violations of WTO rules by their own governments. Neither in the EU nor in the US can citizens hold their own governments legally and judicially accountable for violations of WTO rules. The European Parliament has no co-decision powers in the common commercial policy area (cf, Article 133). Trade policy-making in the US Congress and in the EU Council of Agricultural Ministers are often dominated by protectionist collusion among periodically elected politicians and powerful producer interests (eg, election campaign sponsors) without adequate regard to the general citizen interest in maximizing consumer welfare through non-discriminatory competition and rule of law.

Are there convincing reasons to define the transatlantic 'public interest' of EU and US citizens differently from the 'constitutional contract' that protects equal citizen rights, non-discriminatory competition, and rule of law inside the EU and inside the US? The economic, legal and political advantages of a transatlantic market do not depend on the nationality of the citizens, but on constitutional rules protecting the common citizen interest in rule of law and mutually benefi- cial division of labour across frontiers. If 'general citizen welfare' is defined in terms of rule of law, maximum equal freedom and consumer welfare, then the frequent transatlantic disputes about violations of WTO rules and welfare- reducing trade discrimination call for more effective legal and judicial remedies of EU and US citizens against protectionist abuses of foreign policy powers. Whereas the WTO prohibitions of *de facto* discrimination (eg, in GATT Article III:4, GATS Article XVII) may be more difficult to apply by domestic courts, many WTO prohibitions of *de jure* discrimination are sufficiently precise and unconditional for being applied by courts in the EC and US.

For political reasons, the 'governance failures' to protect the transatlantic citizen interest in open markets and rule of law (eg, compliance with WTO guarantees of freedom and non-discriminatory division of labour across the Atlantic) through legal and judicial safeguards similar to those inside the EU (where transnational market freedoms are legally and judicially protected as 'fundamental rights') or inside the US (where a common market is protected by the 'commerce clause' and other constitutional rules) could be overcome more easily through reciprocal EU-US agreements than through unilateral domestic reforms. The lack of effective legal and judicial remedies leads to 'secondary intergovernmental disputes' that reflect the same 'mercantilist bias' as trade policy-making in the EU and US: governments enforce WTO rules vis-à-vis other governments in response to domestic political pressures from export indus- tries through intergovernmental procedures (eg, WTO dispute settlement proceedings). Even though many of these intergovernmental disputes about violations of WTO rules could be prevented or 'decentralized' and 'de- politicized' by 'first best' legal and judicial remedies in domestic legal systems, the rulers collude in preventing effective national and international judicial enforcement mechanisms (eg, by excluding the general international law rules on reparation of injury from the scope of WTO law). Most Transatlantic Partnership institutions (eg, the various 'civil society dialogues') depend on the financing of EU and US governments; so far, they have hardly ever dared to call for citizen-oriented 'first best remedies', such as more effective parliamentary and judicial protection of citizen rights against abuses of trade policy powers.

B. 'Regulatory disputes' over legitimate internal regulations: need for 'competition among rules', regulatory co-operation, and transatlantic constituencies

As regards the increasing number of transatlantic disputes over conflicting internal regulations (eg, of transatlantic movements of goods, services, persons and capital), it was explained why disputes can be prevented most effectively through respect for legitimate domestic policy discretion and for the resultant competition among divergent domestic regulations in the EU and in the US— provided the regulations comply with relevant non-discrimination, necessity, and other legal requirements (eg, of WTO law). Transatlantic co-operation among legislators and among regulatory agencies based on respect for legitimate 'regulatory competition', 'negative comity', 'positive comity', mutual recognition of equivalent standards, joint risk assessments and co-ordinated rule-making were recommended as additional conflict prevention strategies (eg, for avoiding *de facto* discrimination). As law-makers and regulators inevitably focus on domestic interests and the WTO non-discrimination requirements (eg, in GATT Article III and GATS Article XVII) prohibit not only *de jure* discrimination but also *de facto* discrimination, transatlantic regulatory disputes are often more difficult to prevent and resolve than disputes over manifestly discriminatory border restrictions.

Intergovernmental regulatory disputes may involve 'primary conflicts of interests' caused by legitimate regulatory and democratic divergences (eg, more science-based health standards and more market-oriented social standards in the US than in Europe). Promotion of joint transatlantic constituencies, as in the case of initiatives by the Transatlantic Business Dialogue for mutual recognition of equivalent EU and US standards, can contribute to dispute prevention. Intergovernmental dispute settlement procedures (eg, in the ICJ, WTO, ICAO) and transgovernmental dispute prevention (eg, among competition, trade, environmental and health authorities) may be more appropriate than private recourse to national or international courts, especially if the balancing procedures and applicable law applied by such courts disregard relevant international rules (eg, WTO law). The legal and political authority of WTO dispute settlement rulings adopted by all 144 WTO members may have a greater influence on domestic policy-making processes than domestic court judgments that decide on individual private complaints and exercise judicial deference vis-à-vis national legislation in violation of international law.

C. 'Wrong disputes': transatlantic dispute prevention 'in the shadow of the law'

The case-studies have identified a few 'high policy disputes' and 'wrong complaints' whose political dimensions may render them inappropriate for judicial proceedings. Such disputes (eg, over the application of US sanctions vis-à-vis Cuba to EU companies) may be settled more effectively through political rather than legal procedures. Examination of their 'BATNA' (= Best Alternative to a Negotiated Agreement) may prompt parties to conduct the negotiations 'in the shadow of the law' (eg, after the establishment of a WTO Panel on the EC's complaint in the 'Helms-Burton dispute') in order to improve their negotiation positions. 'Alternative dispute resolution techniques' were shown to have been used successfully in elaborating mutually beneficial 'compromise deals' (eg, for the settlement of the dispute over the Helms-Burton legislation). The institutionalized 'Transatlantic Early Warning System' focuses so far on intergovernmental and transgovernmental dispute prevention. Transatlantic regulatory co-operation (eg, among EU and US competition authorities) could be used more actively for dispute prevention and dispute settlement procedures involving private interests (eg, in merger control proceedings, health, environmental and trade impact assessments).

D. Disputes over private rights: scope for decentralizing and de-politicizing intergovernmental disputes

The case-studies of transatlantic disputes over private intellectual property and investors' rights suggest that some of these intergovernmental disputes may be successfully decentralized and de-politicized by empowering citizens to defend their private rights in domestic courts, or through 'mixed investor-state arbitration' (eg, pursuant to WIPO arbitration procedures), provided domestic courts or international arbitral tribunals are not prevented from applying all relevant applicable rules (eg, WTO rules). The secretive and incoherent arbitral jurisprudence under Chapter 11 of NAFTA, especially on the balancing of private and public interests in the case of alleged 'regulatory takings' of investor rights, illustrates the need for transparent judicial procedures and for more coherent 'balancing principles'. The refusal by the EU and US governments to allow private citizens and domestic courts to challenge WTO violations by their own governments remains the main obstacle to decentralization of transatlantic disputes.

IV. POLICY RECOMMENDATIONS FOR DE-CENTRALIZING AND DE-POLITICIZING 'SECONDARY INTERGOVERNMENTAL DISPUTES'

Intergovernmental disputes over discriminatory market access restrictions and over private rights were described as 'secondary international disputes' if they can be decentralized and 'de-politicized' by enabling domestic courts and EU and US citizens to protect private rights, non-discriminatory competition and rule of law in transatlantic relations (including precise and unconditional WTO prohibitions of trade discrimination). Two policy recommendations were made in order to prevent such secondary intergovernmental disputes:

First, just as legal and judicial challenges of most interstate trade barriers *inside* Europe and *inside* the US are left to private complainants and domestic courts, EU and US citizens should be enabled to challenge discriminatory transatlantic market access restrictions in domestic courts (or in a joint *Transatlantic Market Court*) based on reciprocally agreed rules, including precise and unconditional WTO prohibitions of trade discrimination (eg, GATT Article III:2 and 4). EU and US participants in the transatlantic division of labour should no longer be treated as mere objects of power politics in the trade policy arena. Human dignity and human rights call for protecting citizen rights, rule of law and non-discriminatory competition of EU and US citizens in transatlantic relations more effectively than is possible under intergovernmental WTO dispute settlement proceedings and related trade wars.

Second, a Transatlantic Free Trade Area (TAFTA) remains the most effective legal and political strategy for protecting general citizen interests in free transatlantic movements of goods, services and investments, and in more effective citizen rights and judicial remedies vis-à-vis protectionist abuses of trade policy powers. A TAFTA could enable political and legal reforms (eg, of anti-dumping laws) that appear politically impossible at the worldwide level of the WTO, including promotion of transatlantic judicial co-operation and private access to a Transatlantic Market Court composed of respected EU and US judges. Such a transatlantic 'regime change' could support and complement joint EU/US leadership for worldwide trade liberalization, market regulation and institutional reforms in the WTO focusing on consumer interests, citizen rights and democratic international governance. Even though worldwide liberalization in the WTO offers more economic gains than bilateral liberalization, regional integration enables more far-reaching legal and political reforms and can complement worldwide market integration (cf, Article XXIV GATT, Article V GATS). There are no convincing reasons why the EC and the US are concluding free trade area agreements with an ever increasing number of third countries around the world, yet not among themselves.

V. Policy recommendations for preventing 'primary intergovernmental conflicts'

Transatlantic disputes over non-discriminatory internal regulations and 'high policy disputes' were described as 'primary intergovernmental disputes' that often involve conflicts of legitimate national and/or international interests.

A. Prevention of 'primary conflicts' through the 'early warning system'

The transatlantic 'Early Warning System' for mutual information and dispute prevention relies on a network of periodically meeting working groups at different policy levels (eg, the Steering Group for the Transatlantic Economic Partnership, the Task Force for the New Transatlantic Agenda, the Senior Level Group preparing the biannual Summit Meetings, the Transatlantic Legislators' Dialogue). The Transatlantic Business Dialogue (TABD), Consumer, Environment and Labour Dialogues offer additional in-put from civil society representatives for identifying problems and proposals for their resolution. Apart from exchanging information and discussing possible solutions, the various groups have promoted 'regulatory co-operation', eg, in the area of health and safety standards.[7] The agreed 'guidelines on regulatory co-operation' aim at extending

---

[7] See the contribution by Meng in this book.

transparency and mutual dialogue among regulators outside the agricultural sector.[8] The recent proposal from the TABD for 'inclusion of Trade Impact Statements in development of regulatory and legislative measures, and better communication between US and EU regulators, legislators and government leaders, as a means to prevent domestic policy from impeding global trade' makes use of techniques which have been used also in some European states so as to prevent inconsistencies of national legislative projects with EC law. [9]

Dispute prevention through the Transatlantic Partnership institutions has been characterized by 'considerable complicity' among the highest levels of EU and US governments.[10] The compromise over the Helms-Burton legislation, reached at the 1998 Transatlantic Summit Meeting, suggests that US politicians are more conscious today that unilateral application of US sanctions to enterprises in Europe risks triggering transatlantic disputes and 'blocking legislation' in Europe. The early warning notifications and discussions have contributed to prevention of 'primary conflicts' over non-discriminatory technical regulations (eg, for the sale of pleasure boats in the US, the application of noise muffler devices to aircraft in Europe). The early warning system was *not* capable of resolving major 'legislative conflicts' over 'public interest legislation' (eg, on the health risks of beef hormones, US copyright legislation balancing the rights of copyright holders with the interests of small restaurants and bar owners). The vested interests and discriminatory rules underlying 'contingency protection measures' (eg, US anti-dumping and countervailing duties on imports of steel) likewise appear too strong to be influenced by early warning notifications and discussions. Apart from the TABD's initiatives for dispute prevention and regulatory co-operation (eg, in the context of the EU-US agreements on mutual recognition of regulatory standards), there is little empirical evidence of the contribution of the transatlantic 'civil society dialogues' to dispute prevention and dispute settlement.

B. Prevention of 'primary conflicts' through transatlantic co-operation among legislators, regulators and administrations

The Transatlantic Legislators' Dialogue has not yet led to systematic early notifications of potentially conflicting legislative proposals in the EU and the US. Various case-studies (eg, by Mehta and Shaffer) confirm that transatlantic 'regulatory co-operation' (eg, in the field of competition policy and mutual recognition of technical standards) can effectively prevent 'primary disputes' in

---

[8] See *Financial Times*, 13 April 2002.

[9] On 'trade impact assessments' of proposed EC regulations and directives so as to avoid EC measures being adopted without awareness of their conflict-potential for transatlantic trade, see also G. de Jonquières, 'How Can Transatlantic Trade Disputes be Avoided?' in *Resolving and Preventing US-EU Trade Disputes*, Six Prize-Winning Essays (EUI, 2001), 33, at 40.

[10] See J. Peterson, 'Get Away from Me Closer, You're Near Me Too Far: Europe and America after the Uruguay Round' in M. Pollack & G. Shaffer (eds), *Transatlantic Governance in the Global Economy* (2001), 45–72.

transatlantic relations. The transgovernmental network of competition authorities, and their decentralized enforcement of non-discriminatory competition
rules focusing on consumer welfare and on judicial protection of individual
rights, offers the most successful model for transatlantic dispute prevention.

Experience with mutual recognition and harmonization of technical standards
inside the EC suggests that there is scope for additional transatlantic regulatory
co-operation. The unilateral US safeguard measures on steel in 2002 illustrate,
however, the limited contribution of 'regulatory co-operation' to the prevention
and settlement of 'secondary disputes' (eg, over discriminatory 'contingency
protection measures'). Due to the WTO's discriminatory anti-dumping and
other safeguards provisions and their protectionist abuses on both sides of the
Atlantic, transatlantic co-operation among trade bureaucracies risks remaining
less successful than transatlantic co-operation among competition authorities
which share a much stronger commitment to non-discriminatory competition
rules. Legal and judicial protection of citizen rights against market restrictions
and distortions by their own governments has been the driving force for liberalizing and transforming Europe. It corresponds best to the constitutional ideal of
the American and French revolution, ie, because all rights of democratic governments are derived from citizen rights, they must be constitutionally restrained so
as to protect maximum equal freedom for mutually beneficial co-operation
across frontiers. Such 'constitutional reforms' of transatlantic trade protectionism are, however, unlikely to come about 'top down' because of the self-interests
of trade politicians and trade bureaucrats in trade policy discretion (eg, for
redistributing 'protection rents' to their constituencies) and in avoiding judicial
review of their violations of WTO rules by independent judges at the request of
adversely affected citizens.

VI. Need to promote 'positive disputes' by enabling citizens to protect themselves against abuses of foreign policy powers

In and among constitutional democracies, conflicts of interests among individuals, legal disputes, and their judicial settlement are inevitable elements of open
societies. Also many transatlantic disputes can be viewed positively as engines of
peaceful change through legal and judicial clarification and enforcement of
agreed rules—provided citizen rights and individual access to courts are effectively protected. This is also true for intergovernmental disputes in the WTO
which often have 'external effects' on trade relations with third countries (eg,
regarding the interpretation and application of the relevant WTO rules by third
states) that may be better taken into account through negotiations and dispute
settlement proceedings at the multilateral WTO level than through dispute
settlement proceedings at bilateral or national levels. The greater international
legal and political authority of WTO dispute settlement rulings may enable the

overcoming of 'government failures' (eg, WTO-inconsistent legislation) that could not be corrected through domestic politics.

From the point of view of domestic citizen welfare, trade policy powers are among the most dangerous policy powers because they enable governments to impose taxes and redistribute income among domestic citizens without effective parliamentary control (notably in the EU) and often without effective judicial remedies. In the absence of adequate constitutional and judicial restraints, discretionary trade policy powers can easily undermine rule of law and trigger unnecessary 'secondary intergovernmental disputes' that could be resolved more efficiently through 'first best policy instruments' at home. The focus of domestic regulators on powerful domestic interests ('protection bias') will continue to give rise to regular trade and investment disputes in transatlantic relations among the largest trade and investment partners on earth. Various legal and political criteria for defining and distinguishing 'positive' and 'negative conflicts' were discussed.

Inside the EU and inside the US, discretionary trade policy powers have been replaced by constitutional guarantees of non-discriminatory division of labour among free citizens subject to democratic legislation and judicial safeguards. EC law has overcome the 'introverted constitutionalism' of nation states by 'multi-level constitutionalism' based on national and international judicial protection of *international* guarantees of freedom and non-discrimination as fundamental citizen rights. In the US, by contrast, the US Congress insists on its power to overrule all international agreements ('later in time rule'), and 'international constitutional law' (as inside the EC) is rejected as being incompatible with the US conception of national sovereignty and democracy.

The long-standing efforts by EU and US trade politicians at limiting citizen rights and judicial review in transatlantic disputes over violations of WTO rules reflect bureaucratic self-interests (eg, in avoiding judicial control). In transatlantic relations no less than in European integration, such power politics can be 'disarmed' most effectively through reciprocal international commitments to freedom, non-discrimination, rule of law and effective judicial remedies of citizens across frontiers, for example in the context of a TAFTA between the EU and the US. Yet, notwithstanding the proposals for a TAFTA between the EU and Canada similar to the TAFTA between the EU and Mexico, a TAFTA between the EU and the US is no longer on the agenda of politicians on either side of the Atlantic. Nor is there political support for other 'transatlantic constitutional restraints' similar to those in European integration law (eg, establishment of a Transatlantic Market Court with direct access for EU and US citizens).

The historical emergence of common markets in the EU and US illustrates the central role of courts for liberalizing market access barriers, protecting individual rights and realizing common markets. A non-discriminatory transatlantic market will remain utopian without constitutional and judicial safeguards and stronger legislative and judicial co-operation between the EU and US. Neither the traditional methods of intergovernmental diplomacy and dispute resolution (eg, in the WTO), nor the modern transgovernmental networks of lower-level government experts (eg, among EC and US competition bureaucracies), are substitutes for legal and judicial protection of individual freedom of trade among EU and US citizens as the most democratic strategy for preventing intergovernmental disputes in transatlantic relations.

VII. A CITIZEN-ORIENTED TRANSATLANTIC MARKET COURT COULD REINFORCE THE LEGAL AND JUDICIAL PROTECTION OF EU AND US CITIZEN INTERESTS

This contribution proceeds from the premise that the 'principles of justice' recognized in EU and US constitutional law also call for constitutional safeguards of maximum equal freedom of citizens in transatlantic relations so as to enable EU and US citizens to enhance their mutually beneficial co-operation through non-discriminatory division of labour and rule of law across the Atlantic. Even though worldwide liberalization through GATT/WTO rules offers more income gains than bilateral liberalization, a transatlantic market could go beyond what is politically possible in the WTO and promote joint EU-US leadership for citizen-oriented reforms of the state-centred WTO system. The lack of political support for a transatlantic market (see below A) and for a Transatlantic Market Court (below B) makes it, however, necessary to examine alternative ways of protecting EU and US citizen rights in transatlantic relations more effectively (below VIII).

A. Obstacles for a transatlantic market: European 'multi-level constitutionalism' vs hegemonic US foreign policy discretion

American and European constitutionalism rely on 'in-put oriented legitimacy' (eg, inalienable human rights) as well as on 'out-put oriented' procedures (such as parliamentary and 'deliberative democracy'). Their foreign policy approaches differ, however, in important ways that impede the realization of a transatlantic market:

The current negotiations in the 'European convention' on a new 'European Constitution' reflect a political consensus that democratic peace and economic welfare in Europe depend on 'multi-level constitutionalism' (such as constitutional and judicial protection of human rights and 'market freedoms' at national and international levels, eg, by the ECJ, the EEA Court and the European Convention on Human Rights). The US Congress has never accepted equivalent 'international constitutional restraints' (see, eg, the non-ratification of the Inter-American Charter of Human Rights); the North American Free Trade Agreement (NAFTA) has none of the 'supranational' characteristics of EC law. The US National Security Strategy of 2002 insists on hegemonic foreign policy options (such as pre-emptive military attacks) that, from the perspective of the EU as an international civilian power, appear inconsistent with respect for international law (eg, chapter VII of the UN Charter).

European constitutional law (eg, Article 6 EU Treaty, Articles 81 *et seq* EC, the EU Charter of Fundamental Rights) protects human rights and fundamental citizen rights in the economy (eg, the common market) no less than in the polity through an 'international limiting constitution' (eg, abolishing national trade policy discretion) and an 'international enabling constitution' (eg, prescribing common competition rules and policies). This European concept of an 'international economic constitution'—which emerged as a reaction to 'constitutional failures' in Europe that the US never experienced (such as periodic wars, cartelization of national economies by political dictators)—remains alien to the US (see, eg, the US reluctance vis-à-vis the EC proposals for WTO competition rules). Due to effective protection of a common market inside the US through US constitutional law and US competition law, the US Congress and, since the 1930s, also the US Supreme Court, see no need for protecting 'common market freedoms' as fundamental citizen rights. Hence, the policy recommendation in the contribution by Trachtman to leave the design of economic markets to legislative discretion; and the fatalistic policy conclusion in the contribution of Palmeter that the 'protectionist capture' of the US Congress by rent-seeking producer lobbies leaves little hope for legislative reforms of the welfare-reducing 'contingency protection laws'.

European integration confirms that protectionist government failures can be overcome by reciprocal free trade agreements enabling citizens to invoke and enforce equal freedoms across frontiers in domestic courts. The 'European model' of free trade agreements with a few basic provisions differs, however, fundamentally from the 'NAFTA model' of more than 1,000 pages of treaty text riddled by protectionist exceptions. Even if initiatives for a TAFTA should succeed in overcoming protectionist pressures at home (eg, from agricultural, textiles, steel producers, defence and aviation industries) and could serve as a 'pace setter' for multilateral liberalization in the WTO,[11] it remains doubtful whether a TAFTA could succeed in limiting 'government failures' that even the EC Treaty failed to discipline. For instance:

- The more than 100 successive EC banana market regulations, adopted in manifest violation of GATT/WTO law, illustrate the weakness of the EC institutions to resist protectionist pressures and to comply with the EC Treaty requirement of acting in conformity with international law (Article 300(7)).
- The 'hormone beef dispute' showed how the EU Commission, after having mishandled the 'mad-cow disease', acted unduly subservient to popular pressures and failed to respect the WTO requirements for science-based health regulations based on prior 'risk assessment procedures'. The current EC

---

[11] On the potential disadvantages of a TAFTA for worldwide liberalization see R.J. Langhammer, D. Piazolo & H. Siebert, 'Assessing Proposals for a Transatlantic Free Trade Area' (2002) 57 *Aussenwirtschaft* 161–185.

warnings that a WTO dispute settlement ruling against the EC restrictions on genetically modified organisms might not be implemented by the EC, have triggered questions in the US Congress of why the US should not follow the example of the EC and ignore WTO dispute settlement rulings.
• Transatlantic disputes have revealed so many other inconsistencies in EC policies (such as the non-invocation by the EC, in the 'hormone-beef dispute', of the precautionary principle in Article 5:7 of the WTO Agreement on Sanitary Measures) that public confidence in the EU Commission and in the EU's foreign policy proposals (eg, for incorporating additional 'precautionary principles' into WTO law) remains very limited.[12]

B. A Transatlantic Market Court protecting citizen rights across frontiers?

There is no shortage of intergovernmental procedures for the settlement of transatlantic disputes. EU and US citizens lack, however, effective legal and judicial remedies to protect themselves against the frequent violations of WTO rules by their own governments. Many recent EU-US disputes in the WTO (eg, over EC import restrictions on bananas, Belgium's administration of customs duties for rice, the US Anti-dumping Act of 1916, the 'Burma sanctions' by Massachusetts) were accompanied by simultaneous recourse to domestic courts in the EU and the US. Such domestic court proceedings often remain less effective than WTO dispute settlement proceedings, for example in view of the comparatively shorter deadlines for terminating WTO panel proceedings within six to nine months and the reciprocal tendency of judges in the EU and US to ignore WTO law and its legally binding effects on all government organs.

The WTO guarantees of *transnational* freedom and non-discrimination go far beyond the autonomous legal guarantees in EU and US foreign trade laws. From a citizen perspective, *international* agreements protecting liberal trade and rule of law across frontiers are no less important for maximizing consumer welfare and citizen welfare than *national* rules on liberal trade and rule of law inside national borders. Since EU and US citizens have no direct access to the WTO dispute settlement system, and EU and US judges hardly ever apply WTO law, the EU and US should strengthen the 'domestic law effects' of international law (notably WTO rules) on a reciprocal basis. Such legal and judicial remedies could be co-ordinated and reinforced by a Transatlantic Market Court with jurisdiction to decide on private complaints of EU and US citizens against violations of transatlantic prohibitions of trade discrimination (including certain precise and unconditional WTO prohibitions). The private judicial remedies at

---

[12] The public distrust vis-à-vis the EC Commission reached unprecedented heights in the *First report on allegations regarding fraud, mismanagement and nepotism in the European Commission*, published by the Committee of Independent Experts at the request of the European Parliament on 15 March 1999 prior to the resignation of the Commissioners in 1999 (see, eg, para 9.4.25 of the report at http://wwweuroparl.ep.ec/experts/en/9.htm: 'It is difficult to find anyone who has even the slightest sense of responsibility').

national and transatlantic levels could obviate intergovernmental disputes. Divergent domestic jurisprudence could be co-ordinated through 'preliminary rulings' by the Transatlantic Market Court (eg, on the interpretation of WTO rules and Transatlantic Partnership agreements) at the request of domestic courts or through recourse to WTO dispute settlement mechanisms.

NAFTA provides (eg, in chapters 11 and 19) for direct citizen access to international dispute settlement proceedings as a remedy for perceived deficiencies in domestic administrative and judicial proceedings (such as excessive judicial deference and disregard to WTO law in US anti-dumping proceedings). A Transatlantic Market Court could serve similar functions by offering EU and US citizens—on a reciprocal and therefore politically more acceptable basis, beginning in a few agreed areas (such as the WTO Agreements on Safeguards and on Government Procurement)—effective legal and judicial remedies against illegal abuses of trade policy powers by their own governments. Rather than undermining the WTO dispute settlement system, 'competition' and co-operation between such a Transatlantic Court and WTO dispute settlement bodies could promote 'dialogue among judges' and a higher legal quality of judgments.

A Transatlantic Market Court could also help to reduce the 'producer bias' of many WTO rules by protecting general citizen interests and citizen rights across frontiers. The court should be supplemented by a reciprocal EU-US agreement enabling their citizens to invoke certain precise and unconditional WTO guarantees of freedom, non-discrimination and rule of law in domestic courts so as to overcome the 'introverted focus' of domestic courts on their respective domestic legal system and the reciprocal refusal of law-makers in the EU and US to make WTO rules 'self-executing'. European integration law demonstrates that domestic courts are capable of interpreting, applying and enforcing liberal international trade rules on a reciprocal basis. The 'empowerment' of EU and US citizens and judges to defend the rule of law, including respect for international agreements ratified by parliaments, would offer the most democratic means of preventing intergovernmental transatlantic disputes through strengthened citizen rights and transatlantic co-operation among judges.[13]

VIII. THE TRANSATLANTIC PARTNERSHIP SHOULD INITIATE WORLDWIDE GOVERNANCE REFORMS

The Transatlantic Partnership should be used more creatively as 'a laboratory for new forms of governance among the world's two largest economies'.[14] It so far

---

[13] On the relevant European experience see A.M. Slaughter, A. Stone Sweet & J.H.H. Weiler (eds), *The European Courts and National Courts* (1997).

[14] Cf, Pollack & Shaffer, supra note 10, at 291, who emphasize the dominant influence of 'high-level Clinton administration and European Commission officials' as architects and central actors of the NTA (293): 'the New Transatlantic Agenda can be interpreted as a case of "COG collusion" between a Clinton administration and a European Commission, each of which has been arguably more sympathetic to the goal of market liberalization than their respective domestic constituencies' (295).

lacks 'constitutional checks and balances' that effectively constrain the protectionist domestic pressures which trigger so many transatlantic disputes. The multiple levels of transatlantic co-operation have strengthened co-operation between EU and US government executives and their domestic key constituencies (notably through the TABD) in one-sided 'producer-driven' ways. Transatlantic co-operation between EU and US legislators, and judicial protection of citizen rights across frontiers by EU and US judges, remain neglected. There is currently no political support for the proposed Transatlantic Market Court and TAFTA; and the state-centred 'NAFTA model' of international integration promoted by the US differs fundamentally from the citizen-centred 'EU model' and 'multi-level constitutionalism' advocated by the EU. Joint EU-US leadership for worldwide liberalization, market regulation and democratic reforms in the WTO could be facilitated by new forms of transatlantic co-operation and constitutional limitations on state-centred unilateralism. Transatlantic co-operation—like the numerous other free trade area agreements concluded by the EU and US—offers only *regional* 'first best policies'. From a *global perspective*, regional trade liberalization remains sub-optimal. Yet, if the consensus-based WTO negotiations should fail, transatlantic initiatives can—and should—serve as pace-maker and path-finder for consensus-building in the WTO on more effective global integration law protecting mutually beneficial trade, rule of law, and democratic peace worldwide.

27

Managing System Friction: Regulatory Conflicts in Transatlantic Relations and the WTO

MARK A. POLLACK

One of the core themes of this volume has been the increasingly integrated nature of the transatlantic marketplace, and the corresponding rise of transatlantic disputes about non-tariff—and especially regulatory—barriers to trade. Chapter 2 of the book examined the growing number of transatlantic regulatory disputes arising from domestic US and EU regulations in areas such as environmental or consumer protection and data privacy, and suggested that these disputes represent 'system friction' between the respective regulatory systems of the US and the EU. Such regulatory disputes, it was noted, present particular difficulties for the Dispute Settlement Understanding (DSU) of the WTO, as well as for bilateral attempts at regulatory co-operation, and call for distinct solutions.

In this policy statement, I review some of the policy implications of these findings with regard to the adoption of future multilateral, bilateral, and domestic reforms. First, I discuss the particular challenges posed by regulatory disputes for WTO dispute settlement, and point to possible reforms that might alleviate (or exacerbate) those challenges. Second, I review three particularly prominent proposals for reform of the transatlantic partnership—a transatlantic free trade area, a more elaborate early warning system, and greater regulatory co-operation—underlining the promise, as well as the limits, of each. Finally, I discuss possible unilateral reforms that the EU and the US might undertake in their respective regulatory systems, noting that such reforms, while unlikely to prevent all future disputes, may at least provide national regulators and legislators with an incentive to consider the trade-distorting effects of future regulations.

Running throughout the statement are two basic arguments. First, I suggest that transatlantic regulatory disputes create specific challenges that call for policy responses distinct from those best suited to the prevention and settlement of traditional trade disputes (eg, those over tariffs, quotas, subsidies, and contingent protection). Secondly, however, I suggest that there is no magic bullet, no simple reform or set of reforms that will definitively solve the ongoing problem of system friction between the US and the EU. Useful reforms are possible,

I argue, at the domestic, bilateral, and multilateral levels, but even taken together these reforms will at best serve to manage—and not to eliminate—regulatory differences that are likely to persist, and to irritate transatlantic trade relations, for the foreseeable future.

I. MULTILATERAL REFORMS: REGULATORY DISPUTES AT THE WTO

One of the primary themes of Chapter 2, and of subsequent case-study chapters, is the difficulty of litigating regulatory disputes at the WTO, where panels and the Appellate Body must weigh the aims and provisions of national regulations against the disciplines of WTO trade law, and where non-compliance with disputed decisions may lead in time to a decline in support for the WTO among governments and citizens in the affected countries. However, as Petros Mavroidis points out in his trenchant analysis of food-safety disputes, even a dispute like the beef-hormones case—often pointed to as an example of a 'bad case' or 'wrong dispute' because of strong European public opposition and subsequent EU non-compliance following the WTO decision—can have significant advantages for both the litigants and the WTO system as a whole. In the beef hormones case, Mavroidis argues, the WTO decision served the dual purpose of increasing the transparency of the dispute (which might otherwise have taken place behind closed doors in bilateral negotiations) and clarifying the meaning of the Sanitary and Phytosanitary Standards (SPS) Agreement (most notably regarding the importance of scientific risk assessment underlying domestic regulations).

We should not, therefore, assume that all regulatory disputes are 'bad cases' in which WTO dispute settlement is to be eschewed in favour of bilateral dispute prevention. Indeed, there exist no clear criteria whereby we might designate whole categories of disputes—including regulatory disputes—as 'bad cases'. Ultimately, the identification of 'bad cases' represents a case-specific and highly uncertain balancing of the benefits of litigation emphasized by Mavroidis and the potential dangers of public anger at, and government non-compliance with, the rulings of the Dispute Settlement Body (DSB).

Nevertheless, it can be argued that many of the most controversial WTO cases, in terms of public outcry and subsequent non-compliance, have centred around the trade-distorting effects of domestic environmental, food-safety, and consumer-protection regulations. Furthermore, as we have seen in Chapter 2, both the EU and the US have historically been reluctant to bring such disputes formally before the WTO, with genetically modified foods as the most obvious—but far from the only—example.

In this context, the findings of this volume suggest, future reforms of substantive WTO law and of the DSU should aim to make the multilateral trade regime more effective in settling both traditional and regulatory disputes, while minimizing the prospects of 'bad cases' that would undermine the legitimacy of the system. In recent years, a number of authors have put forward proposals for reforms of the DSU that hold the promise of increasing the efficiency of WTO dispute settlement for *both* regulatory and traditional trade disputes. Numerous authors, for example, have proposed reforms of the WTO system of remedies, including proposals to allow the DSB to award retroactive damages (so as to reduce the current incentive for member states to drag out legal proceedings for up to three years with impunity) and the award of punitive damages (to increase the incentive for losing parties to comply with the decisions of the DSB). A complete review of these proposed reforms is beyond the scope of this brief contribution,[1] but the primary point here is that many proposed reforms would be beneficial in the settlement of regulatory as well as traditional disputes, but do not target the specific problems of regulatory disputes.

A much smaller number of proposed WTO reforms would focus specifically on the clarification of WTO provisions regarding the compatibility of national regulations with WTO legal obligations. Foremost among these proposals has been the EU campaign to clarify the meaning of the 'precautionary principle' within the SPS Agreement, and to insert comparable provisions into the Technical Barriers to Trade (TBT) Agreement. The precautionary principle, according to the European Commission, is explicitly recognized in the SPS Agreement and implicitly recognized in the TBT Agreement and GATT 1994, but the Commission argues that these provisions are vague, and hence that 'leaving these matters to dispute settlement is not a workable option because there is no precedent in WTO dispute settlement'.[2] Other WTO members, however, including the US, have argued that the EU seeks an excessively broad definition of the precautionary principle, which could be used as a means of arbitrary protectionism, and have opposed reopening the question of the precautionary principle within the Doha round of WTO trade negotiations. Even in the unlikely event that the EU should succeed in its efforts to secure new language on the precautionary principle in the next trade round, however, our expectations for genuine clarification should be modest. In previous negotiations—including the SPS Agreement and the 2001 Cartagena Protocol regarding the transborder shipment of genetically modified organisms—negotiators have papered over substantive differences with vague or equivocal language about the use of the precautionary principle and about the relationship between the Cartagena Protocol (which

---

[1] The literature on potential reforms of the DSU is burgeoning, particularly in recent years with the approach of the review of the DSU in 2003–2004. For good discussions of potential reforms, including a wide range of proposals, see, eg, F. Weiss, *Improving WTO Dispute Settlement Procedures* (2000); BP Chair in Transatlantic Relations, *Resolving and Presenting US-EU Trade Disputes: Six Prize-Winning Essays*, with an introduction by Peter Sutherland (Florence: European University Institute, Robert Schuman Centre for Advanced Studies, 9 May 2001); S. Charnovitz, 'Rethinking WTO Trade Sanctions,' *American Journal of International Law*, Vol. 95 (2001); C.E. Barfield, *Free Trade, Sovereignty, Democracy: The Future of the World Trade Organization* (2001); the chapter by Marc Busch and Eric Reinhardt in Part III, and other chapters in this volume.

[2] Commission of the European Communities, 'Trade and the Environment: What Europe Really Wants and Why,' RAPID Memo 01/365 of 12 November 2001, accessed via Lexis-Nexis Academic Universe on 9 February 2003.

explicitly endorses the precautionary principle) and WTO law. Given the starkly differing views of the EU, the US and other WTO parties, future negotiations are likely to adopt similar compromises. For this reason, while clarifications about the scope and procedure of the precautionary principle are worth seeking, the most likely outcome of such negotiations is likely to be continued ambiguity, and a continuing (and no doubt controversial) role for the DSB as the authoritative interpreter of that ambiguous language.

Finally, there is a third category of proposed reforms, namely reforms aimed primarily at the enforcement of WTO law in traditional trade disputes, but which might pose additional problems for the prevention and settlement of regulatory disputes. Most prominent here are proposals to increase individual access to justice—either by providing legal standing for individuals at the WTO, or through the direct effect of WTO law in domestic legal orders—in the enforcement of WTO legal disciplines. Such direct effect of WTO law, Petersmann argues in this volume, would have the advantage of allowing individuals in the EU and the US to claim their rights under international trade law, and provide a corrective to the producer bias in domestic policymaking and in governmental litigation strategies. Indeed, as Petersmann points out, there is ample precedent for such an approach in the EU, where national regulations have been subjected to the disciplines of EU law, allowing individual European citizens to challenge the actions of their own governments that violate the fundamental freedoms of trade in goods, services, labour and capital. Yet, thus far, neither the US nor the EU has demonstrated a willingness to allow similar direct effect of WTO trade law in domestic legal orders.

Such unwillingness, Petersmann suggests, is due largely to the producer bias of governments on both sides of the Atlantic, where consumers are unable to challenge protectionist measures adopted by their own governments. In addition to such protectionist impulses, however, the case-studies of transatlantic regulatory disputes in this volume suggest an additional reason for caution in moving to direct effect of WTO law. In many cases[3] the US government and the European Commission have resisted challenging each other's domestic regulations through WTO litigation, not primarily for protectionist reasons, but rather for fear of bringing 'bad cases' and inciting a public backlash or prolonged non-compliance with WTO decisions. By contrast, direct effect of WTO law would limit governments' ability to weigh the costs and benefits of bringing particularly sensitive cases, and could potentially open the floodgates of legal challenges to widely supported environmental, consumer-protection and other regulations on both sides of the Atlantic. Furthermore, as Petersmann notes, domestic courts in the various polities are unlikely to apply WTO law consistently across jurisdictions, raising the potential for additional conflicts about inconsistent national judicial interpretations of WTO legal obligations. Indeed, it is largely for this reason that Joel Trachtman, in his contribution to this volume, proposes a more

---

[3] See Appendix I of Chapter 2 in this volume.

limited 'intermediated domestic effect' designed to secure some of the benefits of direct effect without such an opening of the floodgates.

In sum, there is no reason to suggest that the US or the EU should eschew entirely the litigation of regulatory disputes before the WTO, which has substantial advantages over strictly bilateral deals in terms of transparency, clarity, and protection of third-party rights. These advantages could be extended further, moreover, through the types of reforms discussed above. Nevertheless, given the very large number of potential regulatory disputes between the US and the EU, and the political sensitivity of some of those disputes, both sides have shown a strong preference to avoid any potential 'overloading' of the DSU, opting instead for extensive bilateral co-operation.

II. BILATERAL REFORMS: REGULATORY CO-OPERATION AND EARLY WARNING

Thus far, the US and the EU have chosen to prevent and/or settle regulatory disputes overwhelmingly through bilateral co-operation and negotiation, with mixed results. As we have seen in this book, bilateral co-operation among regulators has prevented and/or managed regulatory disputes in a wide range of issue-areas, with competition policy standing out as a particularly successful case, although in other areas such as food safety the practical benefits of regulatory co-operation have been slow to appear. Similarly, bilateral negotiations (often in the shadow of WTO litigation) have yielded successful resolutions to conflicts such as the long-standing bananas dispute, while in other areas (eg, beef hormones, Foreign Sales Corporations) final settlement of the disputes remains elusive. For this reason, analysts have proposed a number of bilateral initiatives, with three potential reforms receiving the greatest attention.[4]

First, as Petersmann points out in this volume, a number of analysts and policymakers have proposed that the US and the EU pursue the establishment of a Transatlantic Free Trade Area (TAFTA). The potential costs and benefits of such a proposal have been well analyzed elsewhere, and require only a brief summary here.[5] The potential benefits, according to Petersmann, would include the substantial welfare benefits from transatlantic trade liberalization, as well as a potential spur to stalled WTO negotiations (or alternatively as a back-up in the event that such negotiations end in deadlock). On the other hand, critics of the proposal point out that a TAFTA would be extraordinarily difficult to negotiate,

---

[4] BP Chair in Transatlantic Relations, *Resolving and Presenting US-EU Trade Disputes: Six Prize-Winning Essays*, includes a number of proposals for bilateral as well as WTO dispute-settlement reforms.

[5] For a strong statement of the benefits of a TAFTA, see Petersmann's contributions in Parts I and IV of this volume. For critical views, see P.A. Messerlin, *Measuring the Cost of Protection in Europe* (2001); and R.J. Langhammer, D. Piazolo & H. Siebert, 'Assessing Proposals for a Transatlantic Free Trade Area' (2002) 57 *Aussenwirtschaft* 161–185.

since it would require the two sides to address precisely those issues—such as agriculture, audiovisuals, and anti-dumping—that have divided the US and the EU and stalled agreement in previous WTO talks; yet, such an agreement would deliver only a fraction of the welfare benefits of a successful WTO trade round. Most important for our purposes here, however, is the fact that only an extraordinarily ambitious TAFTA, characterized by systems for regulatory harmonization or mutual recognition, and with a Transatlantic Court to interpret the provisions of such an agreement, would effectively address regulatory conflicts between the two sides, which would otherwise continue to be dealt with through trade diplomacy and WTO litigation (as within the current NAFTA).

In light of the substantial difficulties in the way of an ambitious TAFTA, Petersmann acknowledges, it makes sense to focus our attention on less ambitious but potentially productive reforms of the bilateral US/EU relationship, and of the machinery of the New Transatlantic Agenda (NTA) and the Transatlantic Economic Partnership. In this context, it has become common to call for the further development of the transatlantic early warning system, described in detail by Meng in his contribution to this volume. The transatlantic early warning system, according to Meng and other participants, has proven useful to US and EU officials in identifying the trade-distorting potential of proposed domestic regulations, and there is some evidence that such a system could have prevented the hushkits dispute examined by Kenneth Abbott in this volume. Nevertheless, we should resist the temptation to put too much faith in the current, or even in a reformed, early warning system. In most of the cases in this book, the origins of disputes lay not in a lack of warning—since public officials as well as private actors such as the TABD were nearly always aware of potential disputes well in advance—but rather in the fact that national regulators or legislators opted to adopt trade-distorting regulations despite the predictably adverse effects on international trade and investment. In that context, the most productive reforms of the early warning system would be ones that either (a) required a legislative 'stand-still' if and when the system identified potentially trade-distorting impacts of proposed legislation, or (b) more effectively integrated national legislators alongside the executive-branch officials that currently dominate the system. The former reform, however, would compromise the regulatory sovereignty of each side, and is therefore unlikely to garner support from either side; while the latter would confront the difficulty, already familiar from the Transatlantic Legislators' Dialogue, of encouraging participation from legislators (especially in the US Congress) for whom transatlantic relations represent a relatively low priority.

Perhaps the most promising reform of the bilateral US/EU relationship, therefore, is the further development of transatlantic regulatory co-operation, which can contribute to the prevention and settlement of regulatory disputes through the exchange of information and best practice, the provision of early warning of potential disputes, the avoidance or management of conflicting regulatory decisions, and the gradual building of mutual trust among regulators. Such regulatory co-operation is now widespread across a range of issue-areas, and its potential is most apparent in the area of competition policy, where merger control authorities on both sides of the Atlantic have co-operated in investigating cases and in co-ordinating their respective merger decisions.[6] In other areas such as food safety, where regulatory approaches remain distinct between the US and EU, regulatory co-operation has not yet yielded resolution of difficult disputes in areas such as hormone-treated beef and genetically modified foods; yet even in these areas, regulators have remained in regular contact, increasing mutual understanding and helping to manage—if not prevent or settle—simmering disputes over the trade-distorting effects of national regulations.

The further development of regulatory co-operation between US and EU authorities should therefore be a priority within the NTA. Yet, as Gregory Shaffer demonstrates clearly in his analyses of the Safe Harbour Agreement and the US/EU Mutual Recognition Agreements, regulatory co-operation is neither cheap nor easy, and successful co-operation faces multiple obstacles, including: persistent differences in regulatory procedures and administrative law in the two polities, which may result in different and incompatible regulations; the independence of US regulatory agencies, which may resist compromising domestic mandates 'at the altar of international trade'; the difficulty of committing sub-federal states with considerable independence on each side; and the insistence on both sides that any co-operation respect the regulatory sovereignty of each polity.

These difficulties do not mean that regulatory co-operation is not worth pursuing, but they do suggest that both sides need to devote considerable resources—including financial resources and personnel earmarked specifically for international co-operation—to transatlantic efforts. Furthermore, while short-term goals can and should be set for such co-operation, in practice the immediate payoffs of transatlantic co-operation may be modest in areas such as food safety, where regulatory styles differ substantially between the EU and the US. Indeed, many of the benefits of regulatory co-operation may accrue in the long term, as regulators in the US and Europe become increasingly familiar with the regulations and regulatory styles, and as mutual trust develops among European and American regulators. Finally, and at the risk of complicating already difficult and complex arrangements, transatlantic regulatory co-operation should be conducted with as much transparency as possible vis-à-vis third parties, and within the framework of existing standards bodies such as the Codex Alimentarius. Put simply, any regulatory agreement between the US and the EU is quite likely to become the global standard in that area, and third parties therefore have an intense interest in ensuring that such agreements are reached openly and do not produce fresh discrimination vis-à-vis the rest of the world.

---

[6] See the contribution by K. Mehta in Part II of this volume.

III. Unilateral reforms: internalizing the trade externalities of national regulations

The basic weakness of the US/EU Early Warning System discussed above is that it fails to alter the incentives of regulators and legislators inclined to ignore the trade-related externalities of proposed domestic regulations that might act in practice as non-tariff barriers to trade. As a result, various authors have suggested that the US and the EU move to adopt (either independently or concurrently) administrative-law reforms designed to focus the attention of domestic regulators and legislators on the potential trade-distorting features of proposed regulations. The TABD, for example, has proposed that the US and the EU both undertake 'Trade Impact Assessments' of draft regulations, so that legislators are made aware of the potential trade implications of proposed regulations *before* they are adopted. Such a procedural change could be undertaken within the respective domestic systems of the US and the EU, and without compromising the regulatory sovereignty of either side, and would have the advantage of implicating legislators who thus far have been largely absent from the NTA process.[7]

Finally, both the US and the EU would do well to implement the non-binding 'EU/US Guidelines on Regulatory Co-operation and Transparency' endorsed by the two sides in April 2002. In addition to encouraging bilateral regulatory co-operation, these joint guidelines call for both sides to apply potentially far-reaching principles of transparency in rule-making, including public notification of, and comment on, proposed regulations. These principles, which are consistent with the provisions of the US Administrative Procedure Act and with the recent (but not legally binding) Commission White Paper on Governance, would *not* ensure against the adoption of trade-distorting domestic regulations, which would remain within the prerogative of domestic legislators. Together with the use of Trade Impact Assessments, however, they would ensure that the international-trade implications of domestic regulations would be analyzed and debated by regulators, legislators, and the general public prior to the adoption of those regulations. Like the other reforms discussed above, these domestic reforms would not eliminate transatlantic regulatory disputes, but they would contribute to the management of the system friction that is likely to characterize the transatlantic partnership for the foreseeable future.

---

[7] Some countries, such as the United Kingdom, have established guidelines for policymakers to take trade implications of proposed regulations into account, but neither the US nor the EU currently employs any statutory requirement to undertake such an impact assessment.

Index